The Translator and Editor

LAURENCE SENELICK is Fletcher Professor of Drama and Oratory at Tufts University and a recipient of the St. George medal of the Russian Ministry for Culture for his service to Russian art and theater. His many books include *Russian Dramatic Theory from Pushkin to the Symbolists*, *Anton Chekhov* (Macmillan Modern Dramatists), and *The Chekhov Theatre: A Century of the Plays in Performance*, which won the Barnard Hewitt Prize of the American Society for Theatre Research. His translations of Russian drama are collected in *Russian Satiric Comedy* and *Russian Comedy of the Nikolaian Era*.

A NORTON CRITICAL EDITION

ANTON CHEKHOV'S SELECTED PLAYS

Authoritative Texts of

THE BEAR

IVANOV

THE WEDDING

THE CELEBRATION

THE SEAGULL

UNCLE VANYA

THREE SISTERS

THE CHERRY ORCHARD

VARIANTS AND LETTERS

CRITICISM

DIRECTORS ON CHEKHOV

Translated and Edited by

LAURENCE SENELICK

TUFTS UNIVERSITY

W. W. NORTON & COMPANY

New York • London

W. W. Norton & Company has been independent since its founding in 1923, when William Warder Norton and Mary D. Herter Norton first published lectures delivered at the People's Institute, the adult education division of New York City's Cooper Union. The Nortons soon expanded their program beyond the Institute, publishing books by celebrated academics from America and abroad. By mid-century, the two major pillars of Norton's publishing program—trade books and college texts—were firmly established. In the 1950s, the Norton family transferred control of the company to its employees, and today—with a staff of four hundred and a comparable number of trade, college, and professional titles published each year—W. W. Norton & Company stands as the largest and oldest publishing house owned wholly by its employees.

The text of this book is composed in Fairfield Medium with the display set in Bernhard Modern.
Composition by Binghamton Valley Composition.
Manufacturing by the Courier Companies—Westford Division.
Production manager: Benjamin Reynolds.

Library of Congress Cataloging-in-Publication Data

Chekhov, Anton Pavlovich, 1860–1904.
[Plays. English. Selections]
Anton Chekhov's selected plays / translated and edited by Laurence Senelick.
p. cm.—(Norton critical edition)
Includes bibliographical references.
Contents: Ivanov—The bear—The seagull—The wedding—The celebration—Uncle Vanya—Three sisters—The cherry orchard.

ISBN 0-393-92465-3 (pbk.)

1. Chekhov, Anton Pavlovich, 1860–1904—Translations into English.
I. Senelick, Laurence. II. Title. III. Series
PG3456.A13S46 2004
891.72'3—dc22   2004058324

W. W. Norton & Company, Inc., 500 Fifth Avenue, New York, N.Y.
10110–0017
www.wwnorton.com

W. W. Norton & Company Ltd., Castle House,
75/76 Wells Street, London W1T 3QT

1 2 3 4 5 6 7 8 9 0

For Virginia Scott and Dick Trousdell,
Uncle Vanya's foster parents

Contents

Preface

Chekhov's dramatic reputation is based largely on his last four plays. They are included here, accompanied by the last version of his first produced play, *Ivanov*, as well as by three "vaudevilles," farces that account for his celebrity as a comic author. This edition is meant for those students, theater people, and lovers of Chekhov who do not read Russian but who wish to have as much information as they can get about the plays. It is therefore heavily annotated, not merely to provide explanations of obscure names and terms, but also to point out jokes and subtleties in the originals and to explain the translator's choices.

A number of features included herein intend to improve readers' understanding of Chekhov and his plays. First, I have included a choice of variants. Plays in pre-Revolutionary Russia had to undergo two censorships, one for publication and one for performance. Occasionally, the censorship required deletions or rewrites of lines that, in the case of speeches about Arkadina's liaison with Trigorin in *The Seagull* or Trofimov's remarks about social conditions in *The Cherry Orchard*, were never restored in Chekhov's lifetime. In other cases, such as *Ivanov*, Chekhov kept tinkering with the play for years, the final published version being quite distinct from the two different stage versions of 1887 and 1888. Often a Chekhov play was published in a magazine before it was produced, and, in rehearsal, the director required or suggested changes. For example, Stanislavsky insisted that Act II of *The Cherry Orchard* end with a love scene between Anya and Trofimov. Here the variants may coincide more exactly with Chekhov's ideas than do the final versions. The fewest variants appear in *Uncle Vanya*, since it was a thorough revision of a pre-existing play, *The Wood Goblin*.

I have seen no reason to include variant inversions of words or minor changes that would be of interest chiefly to Slavic specialists who can consult the Russian originals, but I have left in anything that can provide more information about a character or insight into Chekhov's working methods. Except when the changes were made at the instigation of third parties, I do not recommend pasting these remnants from Chekhov's wastepaper back into the plays. He was a shrewd editor of his own work, regularly deleting lines that were too explicit, repetitive, or caricatural. In his case, less is definitely more.

Next, I have provided every mention of a play in this collection that Chekhov made in a letter. Although some of his juicy letters and pungent remarks have already been translated, this is the first time many of his comments, particularly those dealing with finances or specific performances, have appeared in English. I hope the plenitude will help in gauging Chekhov's fluctuating attitudes toward his dramatic works.

In selecting critical essays, I have tried to avoid the "usual suspects"—the essays and articles regularly reprinted in anthologies. I also avoided work by critics who cannot read Chekhov in the original, because they tend to overlook details. This edition therefore includes a number of essays that are either new to the English-speaking reader or have been relegated to obscurity despite their perspicacity (for example, George Calderon's introduction to his translation of Chekhov's plays, one of the earliest accounts in English, is also one of the best).

It is my firm conviction that directors who have staged Chekhov usually provide valuable insight. I have therefore added a final section, "Directors on Chekhov," that draws primarily on Russians and Europeans who have a resumé of powerful and influential productions.

Over the years, my translations of Chekhov have benefited greatly from the directors and companies that have staged them. My thanks go to all of them for enhancing my understanding. Among the many individuals, scholars, and theater people who deserve my gratitude are John Emigh, Donald Fanger, Spencer Golub, André Gregory, John Hellweg, Simon Karlinsky, Nils Åke Nilsson, Emma Polotskaya, Herta Schmid, Virginia Scott, Julie de Sherbinin, Anatoly Smeliansky, Jurij Striedter, Richard Trousdell, and the late Irene Worth.

LAURENCE SENELICK

A Note on the Translations

The texts of Chekhov's plays on which these translations are based are of those in Volumes 11, 12, and 13 of A. P. Chekhov, *Polnoe sobranie sochineniy i pisem v tridtsati tomakh* (*Complete Works and Letters in Thirty Volumes* [Moscow: Nauka, 1978]). They were drawn from the latest versions published in Chekhov's lifetime and subject to his revision: *The Seagull* and *Three Sisters* as published in the magazine *Russian Thought* (*Russkaya Mysl*); *Uncle Vanya* in the collected *Plays* (*Pyesy*, 1897); *The Cherry Orchard* in an anthology of contributors to the magazine *Knowledge* (*Znanie*) and simultaneously in Chekhov's collected works published by Adolph Marks (1901), which, in its second edition (1902), also included *Ivanov, The Bear, The Wedding*, and *The Celebration*.

Anatoly Smeliansky, dean of the Moscow Art Theater school, recently taught a class of American acting students. He described how Ivanov, at the end of the play of that name, shoots himself on stage, and how he, Smeliansky, had seen dozens of actors trying to expire before the audience's eyes. "But in our translation," a student protested, "he runs offstage to commit suicide." Smeliansky was nonplussed. Could it be that all the performances he had seen had been a travesty of Chekhov's intent? Only after he consulted the original Russian and saw that Chekhov had indeed written that Ivanov "runs to one side and shoots himself" (*otbegaet v storonu i zastrelitsya*) was he reassured. Meanwhile, the translation—one that was well reviewed, frequently acted, and is still readily available—continues to mislead readers.

Chekhov himself had his doubts about the efficacy of translation, and after reading some Russian prose translated into French, concluded that transmission of Russian literature into another language was pointless. Later, when his own plays began to be translated, he lamented that purely Russian phenomena would have no meaning for foreign audiences. To offset these misgivings, the translator of Chekhov must be as sedulous in making choices as the author was in composing the original work.

From his earliest farces, Chekhov wrote plays with an eye to their

being performed. He often had specific actors in mind, and, despite
his discomfort with histrionic convention, he expected his dialogue
to be recited from the stage. Therefore, translating his plays entails
problems different from those encountered in translating his prose
fiction. At first sight, the vocabulary and sentence structure seem
straightforward; under scrutiny, however, the seeming simplicity
turns out to be illusory.

The literary psychoanalyst Gregory Zilboorg, initiating American
readers to Russian drama in 1920, stated point-blank that Chekhov
was fundamentally untranslatable, more so even than Aleksandr
Ostrovsky and Maksim Gorky. "Chekhov's plays lose their chief element in translation into whatever other language: the particular harmony and rhythm of the original. The student must bear in mind
that studying Chekhov's drama in English he actually studies only
some elements of them, the rest being lost in a foreign language."[1]

The "harmony and rhythm" so lost derive from a number of
sources. First, Chekhov uses language to consolidate his major plays:
recurrent phrases echo off one another, often for ironic effect.
George Bernard Shaw was another playwright well aware that it was
precisely this adhesive repetition of key words that knit a play
together. He scolded his German translator,

> The way in which you translate every word just as it comes and
> then forget it and translate it some other way when it begins (or
> should begin) to make the audience laugh, is enough to whiten
> the hair on an author's head. Have you ever read Shakespear's
> *Much Ado About Nothing*? In it a man calls a constable an ass,
> and throughout the rest of the play the constable can think of
> nothing but this insult and keeps on saying, "But forget not,
> masters, that I am an ass." Now if you translated *Much Ado*,
> you would make the man call the constable a Schaffkopf. On
> the next page he would be a Narr, then a Maul, then a Thier,
> and perhaps the very last time an Esel.[2]

In Chekhov, a commonplace uttered in the first act may return to
resonate with fresh significance. For example, in *Uncle Vanya*, Astrov
complains that when people cannot understand him, they call him
"weird" (*stranny*); later, Yelena uses that very word to describe him,
thereby revealing that she does not understand him. To translate it
as "weird" in its first occurrence and "odd" in its second would be to
lose Chekhov's thematic irony, the cement he employs to bind the
play together. The same holds true for *chudak* (crackpot) and its
derivatives. Similarly, in *Three Sisters*, the phrases *vsyo ravno* (it

1. Gregory Zilboorg, "A Course in Russian Drama," *The Drama* (Nov. 1920), 69.
2. *Bernard Shaw's Letters to Siegfried Trebitsch*, ed. Samuel A. Weiss (Stanford: Stanford,
   1986), 30 (December 26, 1902). The words translate as "sheep's head," "fool," "muzzle,"
   "beast," and "ass."

doesn't matter, it's all the same) and *nadoelo* (fed up, sick and tired) recur regularly, and in *The Cherry Orchard*, changes are rung on *neschastye* (unhappiness, misfortune, trouble). It is the translator's obligation to preserve these verbal leitmotifs as much as possible.

Lexical and etymological elements subliminally affect the atmosphere. In *Uncle Vanya*, words based on *dush*—(implying psyche and soul) and *dukh*—(implying breath and spirit) help create a sense of stifling and suffocation. In *The Cherry Orchard*, earthy terms such as *nedotyopa* (half-chopped) contribute to the theme of hewing down the cherry trees. Literary allusions to the Russian classics (Pushkin, Lermontov, Gogol, Krylov, Ostrovsky) enrich the cultural context; for the educated Russian of Chekhov's time, they would have been immediately familiar.

Second, Chekhov is extremely careful in choosing which words to use at any given moment. A French translator has pointed out that in *The Seagull*, Chekhov employed three separate words for *why*: *otchego, zachem,* and *pochemu.* I have been very careful to observe those choices, translating them as "how come," "what for," and "why." Hence, in this translation the famous opening line is not "Why do you always wear black?" but instead "How come you always wear black?", which distinguishes Medvedenko's way of asking a question from that of others.

Every character in Chekhov speaks in a particular cadence. Compare Pishchik's short asthmatic phrases with the run-on grandiloquence of Trofimov or with Anya's iambic meters. Although both Vershinin and Tusenbach spout speeches about the future, one can tell merely by the tone and phrasing which one is speaking. When Nina Zarechnaya starts picking up Arkadina's phrases, Chekhov gives us insight into her character.

Third—and this is difficult to pin down—the specific gravity of a statement may reside in its structure. Since Russian can reassemble the elements of a sentence to make a particular emphasis, English has to find a way of reproducing this. Mere phrasebook translation, offering a direct statement, can betray the subtle emphases of the original. To render Charlotta Ivanovna's *"Uzhasno poyut éti lyudi"* as "These people sing horribly" is to miss her idiosyncratic syntax and the course of her thought (which implies, "It's awful the way these people break into song at the drop of a hat"—although to spell that out explicitly would be to over-translate).

Finally, certain words and phrases that held a special meaning in Chekhov's time may require that an explanation be imbedded in the translation, particularly if it is meant to be performed. *"Nado delo delat"* should not be rendered literally as "It is necessary to do something," or even as the customary "We must work," because it has to convey the idea that it is an outdated and platitudinous slogan of liberalism. The quotations from Nekrasov's poems have to reflect the pseudo-progressivism of the person doing the quoting. Just what sort of foods are the *raznye kabuli* that the Professor imposes on the Voinitsky household? (They are in fact spicy Central Asian stews, which accounts for his dyspepsia and offers a vivid contrast to the nanny's homely noodles.)

The same applies to jokes. Chekhov often imbeds *jeux de mots* and facetious phrasing as depth charges; the translator's first task is to be aware of them, and then to find a way of making them detonate properly. At the beginning of *Ivanov*, Count Shabelsky complains that Anna has no more musical ear than a *farshirovannaya ryba*. Earlier translations have rendered this as "stuffed pike" or "stuffed trout," both of which miss the point. Shabelsky is always teasing Anna about her Jewish origins (in an early version of the play, he even calls her a *rebbitzin*, or rabbi's wife); the fish in question is therefore not a piece of taxidermy but gefilte fish instead.

These particularities of Chekhov come in addition to the usual problems experienced in translating from Russian: the passive constructions, such as *Tyazhelo mne* (literally, "it is heavy to me"); the distinction between verbs of imperfect and perfect action (the difference between *strelilsya* and *zastrelilsya*, Konstantin's having shot himself and having shot himself for good); and onomatopoeic sounds that are overlooked or scanted. The last lines of *Uncle Vanya*—the repeated *my otdokhnyom*—consist of soft, aspirated sounds, easily drawn out and wafted into the air. "We shall rest" (or worse, "We will rest"), with its terminal dental sound, cannot be manipulated by an actress in the same way.

Reviewers who rarely if ever read a work in the original are fond of praising a translator for making the dialogue sound "smooth." Imagine a French translator of David Mamet or a German translator of Eugene O'Neill, playwrights noted for erratic dialogue, being praised for their smoothness! I have not attempted to "smooth out" Chekhov where he is rough or to second-guess his choices. In *Ivanov*, for example, there is stilted dialogue over which Chekhov himself fussed for years; it alternates with some of the most saltily colloquial dialogue in any Chekhov play. The contrast between Ivanov's fustian soliloquies and Avdotya Nazarovna's pungently folksy idioms ought not to be elided in translation. In this regard, I bear in mind Prince Mirsky's remark that "no one in real life ever spoke as Chekhov's people do."[3]

I have not pretended that Chekhov is anything other than Russian. Although I have converted weights and measures into Western

3. D. S. Mirsky, *Contemporary Russian Literature 1881–1925* (London: George Routledge & Sons, 1926), 94.

equivalents so that an audience can more easily gauge distances and density, I have left currency, beverages, and, in particular, names in their Russian forms. Modern readers and audiences rapidly adjust to patronymics, diminutives, and nicknames. What is the point of turning Pavel into Paul and Yelena into Helen unless one refers to *Uncle Jack* instead of *Uncle Vanya* and *Ivanov* as *Johnson*?

Guide to Transliteration and Pronunciation

When a Russian name is a Cyrillic transliteration of a European name, I have used the European form; for example, Mühlbach, Tusenbach, Charlotta, Maupassant, and Buckle.

Cyrillic	System Used in this Book	Pronunciation
Аа	a	*f*a*ther*
Бб	b	*b*ank; (at the end of words) to*p*
Вв	v	*v*et; to*w*el; (at the end of words) dea*f*
Гг	g	*g*et; (at the end of words) brea*k*
Дд	d	*d*addy; (at the end of words) ve*t*
Ее	e, ye (when it begins a name)	m*e*t; m*i*tt; *y*eah
Ёё	yo	b*o*rder; *y*ore
Жж	zh	vi*s*ion; pu*sh*
Зз	z (except when it indicates a German *s*)	*z*eal
Ии	i	ch*ee*se; *i*f
Йй	i; y (at the end of names)	unstressed vowel
Кк	k	*k*ept
Лл	l	*l*og
Мм	m	*m*ama
Нн	n	*n*o
Оо	o	(stressed) *o*rder; (unstressed) *a*rtistic
Пп	p	*p*age
Рр	r	*r*ake
Сс	s	mi*ss*
Тт	t	*t*en

Уу	u	sp*oo*n
Фф	f	*f*orm
Хх	kh (except when it indi- cates a German *ch*)	*h*ah; a*ch*
Цц	ts	i*ts*
Чч	ch	*ch*ief
Шш	sh	*sh*oe
Щщ	shch	fish *ch*owder
Ъъ	*omitted*	No sound value
Ыы	y	ph*oo*ey
Ьь	*omitted*	No sound value
Ээ	é	v*e*t; d*ay*
Юю	yu	*you*; s*ue*
Яя	ya	*ya*hoo

Combinations of vowels

-ай	ay	*eye*
-ый	y	i*ts*
-ий	y	*e*ven
-ия	iya	tri*age*
-ье	ye	*yeah*
-ьи	yi	*yip*

Phonetic Pronunciation of the Names in the Plays

'H indicates an aspirated h, usually represented in Roman letters by *kh*, as in *Chekhov*—which should be sounded more like *Chehoff* than *Chek-off*.

The Bear

Yelena Ivanovna Popova	yeh-LYEH-nah ee-VAH-nahf-nah pah-PAW-vah
Grigory Stepanovich Smirnov	gree-GAW-ree stih-PAH-nah-veech SMEER-nahf
Luka	Loo-KAH
Nikolay Mikhailovich	nee-kah-LYE mi-'HAY-lah-veech
Korchagin	kahr-CHAH-gheen
Vlasov	VLAH-sahf
Gruzdyov	grooz-DYAWF
Yaroshevich	yah-rah-SHAY-veech
Kuritsyn	koo-REET-sin
Mazutov	mah-ZOO-tahf
Tamara	tah-MAH-rah
Dasha	DAH-shah
Pelageya	pih-lah-GAY-ah

Ivanov

Nikolay Alekseevich Ivanov	nee-kah-LYE ah-lik-SAY-eh-veech ee-VAH-nahf
Kolya	KAWL-yah
Nikolasha	nee-kah-LAH-shah
Anna Petrovna	AH-nah pit-RAWF-nah
Anya	AHN-yah
Anyuta	AHN-yoo-tah

xix

Sarra	SAH-rah
Matvey Semyonovich Shabelsky	maht-VAY sim-YAWN-ah-veech sha-BYEHL-skee
Matyusha	maht-YOO-shah
Pavel Kirillych Lebedev	PAH-wel kee-REE-litch leh-beh-DYEHF
Pasha	PAH-sha
Pashenka	PAH-shehn-kah
Zinaida Savishna	zee-nah-EE-dah SAH-veesh-nah
Zyuzyushka	ZYOO-zyoosh-kah
Sasha	SAH-sha
Aleksandra Pavlovna	ah-lik-SAHN-drah PAHV-lahv-nah
Sanichka	SAHN-eech-kah
Sashenka	SAH-shyehn-kah
Shura	SHOO-rah
Shurka	SHOOR-kah
Shurochka	SHOO-rahch-kah
Yevgeny Konstantinovich Lvov	yehv-GAYN-ee kahn-stahn-TEE-nah-veech lVAWF
Marfa Yegorovna Babakina	MAHR-fah yeh-GAWR-ahf-nah ba-BA-kee-nah
Marfusha	MAHR-foosh-ah
Marfutka	MAHR-foot-kah
Dmitry Nikitich Kosykh	DMEE-tree nee-KEE-teech KAW-see'h
Mikhail Mikhailovich Borkin	mee-'hye-EEL mee-'HYE-lah-veech BAWR-keen
Misha	MEE-sha
Michel Michelich	mee-SHEHL mee-SHEHL-eech
Avdotya Nazarovna	ahf-DAWT-yah nah-ZAH-rahf-na
Yegorushka	yeh-GAW-roosh-kah
Pyotr	PYAWTr
Gavrila	gav-REE-lah
Gavryusha	gav-RYOOSH-ah
Plesniki	PLEHS-nee-kee
Ovsyanov	ahf-SYAH-nahf
Zarev	ZAHR-yehff
Korolkov	kah-rahl-KAWF
Angot	ahn-GO
Balabalkina	bah-lah-BAHL-kee-nah
Babakalkina	bah-bah-KAHL-kee-nah
Mushkino	MOOSH-keen-ah
Zaimishche	ZYE-meesh-cheh

Dudkin	DOOD-keen
Budkin	BOOD-keen
Dobrolyubov	dah-rah-LYOO-bahf
Chatsky	CHAHT-skee
Gerasim Nilych	gheh-RAH-seem NEEL-ich
Barabanov	bah-rah-BAH-nahf

The Wedding

Yevdokim Zakharovich Zhigalov	yehv-dah-KEEM zah-'HAHR-ah-veech zhee-GAH-lahf
Nastasya Timofeevna	nahs-TAHS-yah tee-mah-FAY-ehf-nah
Darya Yevdokimovna	DAHR-yah yehv-dah-KEEM-ahf-nah
Dashenka	DAH-shehn-kah
Epaminond Maksimovich Aplombov	ay-PAH-mee-nahnd mahk-SEE-mah-veech ah-PLAWM-bahf
Fyodor Yakovlevich Revunov-Karaulov	FYAW-dahr yah-KAWF-lyeh-veech reh-VOO-nahf-kah-rah-OO-lahf
Andrey Andreevich Nyunin	ahn-DRAY ahn-DRAY-eh-veech NYOO-neen
Andryusha	ahn-DRYOO-sha
Anna Martynovna Zmeyukina	AHN-nah mahr-TEE-nahf-na zmay-OO-kee-nah
Ivan Mikhailovich Yat	ee-VAHN mee-'HEY-lah-veech YAHT
Kharlampi Spiridonovich Dymba	'hahr-LAHM-peespee-ree-DAWN-ah-veech DEEM-bah
Dmitry Stepanovich Mozgovoy	DMEE-tree stih-PAH-nah-veech mahz-gah-VOY
Osip Lukich Babelmandebsky	AW-seep LOO-keech bah-byehl-mahn-DIHB-skee

The Celebration

Andrey Andreevich Shipuchin	ahn-DRAY ahn-DRAY-eh-veech shee-POO-cheen
Tatyana Alekseevna	taht-YAH-nah ah-lik-SAY-ehf-nah
Kuzma Nikolaevich Khirin	kooz-MAH nee-kah-LYE-eh-veech 'HEE-reen
Nastasya Fyodorovna Merchutkina	nahs-TAHS-yah FYAW-dah-rahf-nah mir-CHOOT-kee-nah
Katya	KAH-chah
Onegin	ah-NYEH-gheen
Seryozha	sir-YAW-zhah
Grendilevsky	gryehn-dee-LYEHF-skee
Boris Matveich	bah-REES maht-VAY-eech
Berezhnitsky	byeh-ryehzh-NEET-skee

The Seagull

Irina Nikolaevna Arkadina	ee-REE-nah nee-kah-LYE-eff-nah
Konstantin Gavrilovich Treplyov	kahn-stahn-TEEN gahv-REEL-ah-veech Trip-LYAWF
Kostya	KAWST-yah
Gavrilych	gahv-REEL-ihch
Pyotr Nikolaevich Sorin	PYAW-tr nee-kah-LYE-yeh-veech
Petrushka	pit-ROO-shash
Nina Mikhailovna Zarechnaya	NEE-nah mee-'HEIL-ahf-nah zah-RYECH-nye-ah
Ilya Afanasevich Shamraev	eel-YAH ah-fah-NAHSS-yeh-veech shahm-RY-ef
Polina Andreevna	pah-LEE-nah ahn-DRAY-ef-nah
Marya Ilyinishna	MAHR-ya eel-YEEN-eesh-nah
Masha	MAH-shah
Mashenka	MAH-shin-kah
Boris Alekseevich Trigorin	bah-REESS ah-lik-SAY-eh-veech tree-GAWR-een

Evgeny Sergeevich Dorn — yihv-GHEHN-ee sehr-GAY-eh-veech DAWRN

Semyon Semyonovich Medvedenko — sim-YAWN sim-YAWN-ah-veech myehd-VYEHD-in-kah

Yasha — YAH-shah

Odessa — ah-DYEHSS-ah

Nekrasov — nik-RAHSS-ahff

Duse — DOO-zah

Pavel Semyonych Chadin — PAH-wehl sim-YAWN-eech CHAH-deen

Rasplyuev — rahss-PLYOO-yehf

Sadovsky — sah-DAWF-skee

Tolstoy — tahl-STOY

Turgenev — toor-GHEHN-yehf

Suzdaltsev — sooz-DAHL-tsehf

Elizavetgrad — ill-EEZ-ah-vyeht-grahd

Izmailov — eez-MY-lahf

Matryona — maht-RYAW-nah

Pushkin — POOSH-keen

Kharkov — 'HAHR-kahf

Yelets — yell-YEHTS

Uncle Vanya

Aleksandr Vladimirovich Serebryakov — ah-lik-SAHND'r vlah-DEE-mir-ah-veech syeh-ryehb-yah-KAWFF

Yelena Andreevna — yehl-YAY-nah an-DRAY-ehf-nah

Lenochka — LYEHN-ahch-kah

Sofya (Sonya) — SAWF-yah (SAWN-yah)

Sonechka — SAWN-itch-kah

Mariya Vasilyevna — mah-REE-ah vah-SEEL-yeff-nah

Ivan (Vanya) Petrovich Voinitsky — ee-VAHN (VAHN-yah) pit-RAW-veech voy-NEET-skee

Mikhail Lvovich Astrov — mee-'high-EEL LVAW-veech AHS-trahf

Ilya Ilyich Telegin — eel-YAH eel-EECH tel-YAY-gheen

Marina Timofeevna — mah-REE-nah tee-mah-FAY-ehf-nah

Batyushkov	BAHT-yoosh-kahf
Grigory Ilyich	gree-GAW-ree eel-EECH
Ivan Ivanych	ee-VAHN ee-VAHN-eech
Kharkov	'HAHR-kahf
Konstantin	kah-stahn-TEEN
Trofimovich	trah-FEEM-ah-veech
Malitskoe	MAH-leet-skah-yeh
Pavel Alekseevich	PAH-well ah-lick-SAY-eh-veech
Rozhdestvennoe	rahzh-DIST-vehn-nah-yeh
Tula	TOO-lah
Vera Petrovna	VIH-rah pit-RAWFF-nah
Yefim	YEH-feem

Three Sisters

Andrey Sergeevich (Sergeich)	ahn-DRAY sir-GAY-yeh-veech (sir-GAY-eech) PRAW-zah-raff (ahn-DRYOO-sha, an-DRYOO-shahn-cheek)
Prozorov (Andryusha, Andryushanchik)	
Natalya Ivanovna (Natasha)	nah-TAHL-yah ee-VAHN-ahf-nah (na-TAH-sha)
Olga Sergeevna (Olyushka, Olya)	AWL-gah sir-GAY-ehf-nah (AWL-yoosh-kah, AWL-yah)
Masha (Mariya Sergeevna, Mashka, Mashenka)	MAH-sha (mah-REE-yah sir-GAY-ehf-nah, MAHSH-kah, MAH-shehn-kah)
Irina (Arinushka, Arisha)	ee-REE-nah (ah-REE-noosh-kah, ah-REE-shah)
Fyodor (Fedya) Ilyich Kulygin	FYAW-dahr (FYEHD-yah) eel-EECH koo-LEE-gheen
Aleksandr Ignatyevich Vershinin	ah-lick-SAHND'r eeg-NAHT-yeh-veech vir-SHEE-neen
Nikolay Lvovich Tusenbach	nee-kah-LIE l'VAW-veech TOO-zehn-BA'H
Vasily Vasilyevich Solyony	vah-SEE-lee vah-SEEL-yeh-veech sahl-YAWN-ee
Ivan Romanovich (Romanych) Chebutykin	ee-VAHN rah-MAHN-ah-veech (rah-MAHN-eech) cheh-boo-TEE-keen
Aleksey Petrovich Fedotik	ah-lick-SAY pit-RAW-veech fyeh-DAW-teek
Vladimir Karlovich Rodé	vlah-DEE-meer KAHR-lah-veech rah-DAY

Ferapont	fir-ah-PAWNT
Anfisa	ahn-FEE-sah
Basmanny	bahs-MAHN-nee
Berdichev	bir-DEE-chehf
Bobik	BAW-beek
Bolshoy	bahl-SHOY
Chekhartma	cheh-'hahrt-MAH
Cheremsha	cheh-rehm-SHAH
Chita	chee-TAH
Dobrolyubov	dah-brah-LYOO-bahf
Kirsanovsky	keer-SAHN-ahf-skee
Kochane	kah-'HAHN-eh
Kolotilin	kah-lah-TEE-leen
Kozyrev	KAW-zee-ryehf
Krasny	KRAHS-nee
Lermontov	LYEHR-mahn-taff
Marfa	MAHR-fah
Moskovsky	mahs-KAWFF-skee
Nemetskaya	nyeh-MYEHT-sky-ah
Novo-Devichy	NAW-vah-DYEH-vee-chee
Potapych	pah-TAH-peech
Protopopov, Mikhail Ivanych	prah-tah-PAW-pahff, mee-'high-EEL ee-VAH-neech
Pyzhikhov	PEE-zhee-kahff
Saratov	sah-RAH-tahff
Skvortsov	skvahr-TSAWF
Spiridonych	spee-ree-DAWN-eech
Stanislav	STAHN-ee-slahv
Testov	TYEHS-tahf
Tsytsykar	tsee-tsee-KAHR
Zasyp	zah-SEEP

The Cherry Orchard

Lyubov Andreevna Ranevskaya	lyoo-BAWF ahn-DRAY-ehf-nah rahn-YEHF-sky-ah
Lyuba	LYOO-bah
Anya	AHN-yah
Anichka	AHN-eech-kah
Varya	VAHR-yah
Varvara Mikhailovna	vahr-VAHR-ah mee-'HEIL-ahf-nah
Leonid Andreich Gaev	lyaw-NEED ahn-DRAY-eech GUY-ehf

Lyonya	LYAWN-yah
Pyotr Trofimov	PYAWTr trah-FEE-mahf
Petya	PIT-yah
Semeonov-Pishchik	seem-YAWN-ahf PEESH-cheek
Charlotta Ivanova	shahr-LAW-tah ee-VAHN-ahf-nah
Semyon Panteleich Yepikhodov	sim-YAWN pahn-til-YAY-eech ippy-'HAW-dahf
Avdotya Fydorovna	ahv-DAWT-yah FYAW-dahr-ahf-nah
Dunyasha	doon-YA-sha
Firs Nikolaevich	FEERSS nee-kaw-LYE-yeh-veech
Yasha	YAH-shah
Dashenka	DAH-shin-kah
Fyodor Kozoedov	FYAW-dahr kah-zah-YAY-dahf
Mentone	mawn-TONE
Kharkov	'HAHR-kawf
Petrusha	pit-ROO-shah
Anastasy	ah-nah-STAHSS-ee
Grisha	GREE-shah
Yaroslavl	yah-rah-SLAHV-l
Yefimushka	YEH-feem-oosh-kah
Karp	KAHRP
Polya	PAWL-yah
Yevstigney	iv-steeg-NAY
Deriganov	dir-ee-GAHN-ahf
Yegor	ye-GAWR
Znoikov	ZNOY-kahf
Kardamonov	kahr-dah-MAWN-ahf
Yashnevo	YAHSH-ni-vah
Ragulins	rah-GOO-leenz
Volga	VAWL-gah

General Introduction

A popular attitude towards Chekhov nowadays is summed up in a newspaper cartoon, "Influences," by Sid Harris. The three boxes depict an author at his desk, a mechanic in his garage, and a baseball player leaning on his bat. The bespectacled writer is speaking to an invisible interviewer, saying, "Mainly the short-story writers—Hemingway, Eudora Welty, and, of course, Chekhov." Then comes the mechanic: "There was a teacher in high school, and the owner of the first garage I worked in. Then, of course, Chekhov." And, finally, the ball player: "I had a great batting coach in the minors, and I try to emulate the great outfielders, like DiMaggio and Mays. And, of course, there's Chekhov."

This is the inevitable Chekhov: the Chekhov who pervades any discussion of modernism in fiction or theater, the Chekhov who has become a graven image on the Mount Rushmore of contemporary aesthetic sensibilities. It is as a dramatist, however, that Chekhov has persisted most indelibly in the collective consciousness. Although his fiction still exercises a powerful influence on writers and still nourishes academic discussion, he is thought of first and foremost as a playwright.

Chekhov's plays occupy a unique place in the history of drama. They derived from no obvious forerunners and produced no successful imitators. Despite his obvious influence on any number of important playwrights, there is no school of Chekhovian playwriting. Somehow, within the space of a few years, Chekhov managed to bring together elements that created, to paraphrase Gorky, a new kind of drama, which heightened reality to the point at which it turned into a profoundly inspired symbol.

Chekhov himself approached the theater and playwriting with a deep distrust, a fear that the demands of the stage would coarsen or distort his carefully wrought perceptions. As a boy in Taganrog, he delighted in the melodramas and operettas performed at the local playhouse, but as a young journalist in Moscow in the 1880s he poured vials of scorn on what he saw to be the ingrained mediocrity of professional theater practitioners. According to his friend Ivan Bunin, he regarded most actors as "vulgarians, thoroughly steeped in vanity."[1] Still, his attraction to the theater persisted. The backstage world appeared in many of his stories, and, significantly, his first published collection, *Fairy Tales of Melpomene* (1884), was of comic anecdotes dedicated to the Muse of Tragedy.

Chekhov's early plays, written with an eye to stage production, clearly display his sense of the conflict between the pedestrian demands of the theater and the need to express his own concerns dramatically. His farces are extremely stageworthy, but differ from most curtain raisers only in their shrewd observation of human foibles. Chekhov's discomfort with having to use traditional dramatic conventions is apparent in the disjointed and contrived nature of *Ivanov* (1887; revised 1888) and *The Wood Goblin* (1889). They emerge from a period in his life when he was striving to perfect his skill as a short-story writer, to increase the subtlety of the techniques available to him, and to depict states of unfulfilled desires, misconstrued ambitions, and futile endeavor. Transferring these concerns to writing for the stage, aware as he was of its fondness for platitudes and cheap effects, drove him to agonies of frustration.

Yet, when he gave advice to would-be playwrights, he limited himself to matters of technique. For instance, in 1889, he offered these adages to a young novice:

> "If you have hung a pistol on the wall in the first act, then it has to be shot in the last act. Otherwise, don't hang it up."
>
> "It is unconscionable of authors to bring on stage messengers, bystanders, policemen. Why force the poor actor to get into costume, make himself up, while away hours on end in a nasty draft backstage?"
>
> "In drama you mustn't be afraid of farce, but philosophizing in it is disgusting. Everything goes dead."
>
> "Nothing is more difficult than writing a good vaudeville. And how pleasant it is to write one."[2]

Essentially, there were two prevalent traditions of nineteenth-century playwriting from which Chekhov could draw. One was the mode of the "well-made play," which dominated European and American stages. Based on strict rules of construction, the well-made play involved a central intrigue, intricate manipulation of the hero's fortunes, contrived episodes of eavesdropping, revealing soliloquies, misdelivered letters, and a denouement in which good triumphs and evil receives its just deserts. Its leading exponent, Eugène Scribe,

---

1. From Ivan Bunin's posthumously published, *O Chekhov* (*About Chekhov*) (New York: Chekhov Publishing House, 1955). Translations from the Russian are mine unless otherwise stated.
2. Ars. G. in *Teatr i iskusstvo* (*Theater and Art*) 28 (1904). The author, real name Ilya Yakovlevich Gurlyand (b. ca. 1863), was a student at the time he met Chekhov in Yalta in 1889, and was later a journalist and professor.

declared that the function of such a play was solely to entertain, not by mirroring real life, but instead by providing an improved surrogate for life. Many of the greatest "box-office hits" of all time have been enacted within the constraints of the well-made play.

Later on, the well-made play attempted to encompass social problems, setting forth in its neat five-act structure a "burning question of the day" such as women's rights, divorce, or unemployment, and just as neatly resolving it by the fall of the curtain. As the Russian critic Vasily Sleptsov pointed out, the social question and the mechanical plot seldom bore an organic relationship to one another. The question was usually embodied in the *raisonneur*, a character such as a doctor or lawyer who, in Sleptsov's image, is a bottle brought on, uncorked, its message poured out, and then packed away until needed again.

The other dramatic tradition available to Chekhov was purely Russian. From Gogol onward, Russian playwrights had composed open-ended dramas, loose in structure and combining elements of comedy and pathos. The most prolific dramatist of Chekhov's youth, Aleksandr Ostrovsky, used such plays to depict *byt*, the everyday life of merchants and civil servants, and to capture the rhythms and idioms of vernacular speech. Many of Ostrovsky's types recur in a modified shape in Chekhov: the dispossessed and victimized young girl seeking to make a life for herself reappears as Nina; the boorish peasant who buys the estate in *The Forest* is refined into Lopakhin. However, Ostrovsky and his imitators took a definite moral stance. The apportionment of good and evil in their plays is as strict as in melodrama. Chekhov's view of life was too complex to allow such a simplistic viewpoint, and his sense of form too sophisticated for him to adopt Ostrovsky's lax principles of construction.

In practice, Chekhov repudiates his predecessors in radical ways. Chekhovian drama has been defined as imitation of stasis, with action so gradual and nonprogressive as sometimes to be imperceptible. Nevertheless, even though central actions such as Treplyov's attempted suicide or the sale of the cherry orchard take place offstage, Chekhov produces a sense of development through the sequential placement of characters and their concerns. He creates an illusion of life in motion by juxtaposing apparently static elements, implying relationships in objects by aligning them in a kind of montage.

Given the uniqueness of Chekhov's plays, the rise of his reputation is something of an anomaly. Shortly before his death in 1904, anyone would say the greatest living Russian writer was Tolstoy. Tolstoy's imposing position as a moralist and reformer; his eminence at the panoramic novel, the genre most honored by the nineteenth century,

which preferred monumentality; his political stance as the unassail-
able opponent of autocracy—these and other features made the sage
of Yasnaya Polyana the voice of humanitarian culture to the world
at large.

Chekhov, on the other hand, was regarded as a purely local phenomenon. Within the Russian Empire, his reputation was fragmented among various publics. The common reader remembered
him chiefly as the author of a number of funny stories. The intelligentsia saw him as a chronicler of its own malaise, particularly in
the plays staged by the Moscow Art Theater. Political factions on
the right and left dismissed him as a fence-sitter, too cowardly to
take sides in ideological battles. The literary avant-garde deplored
his lack of religious uplift and "sublimity."

Outside Russia, Chekhov was viewed at best as an exotic petit-
maître, trading in doom and gloom. The Poles patriotically neglected
him, the Germans interpreted him as another exponent of the tragedy of fate, and the Georgians noted sarcastically that only ethnic
Russians would fritter away their time as trivially as his characters
do. In France, standard works on Russian literature around 1900
shrugged off Chekhov: Waliszewski described his drama as "completely devoid of action and psychological differentiation of characters," while Melchior de Vogüé declared the full-length plays too
pessimistic for the French, full of impotent heroes with "enigmatic
Slavic souls."[3] In the first two English-language reference books to
include Chekhov, both published the year before his death, those
same dramatic characters were cited as "fit subjects for the psychi-
atrist" and "a strange assemblage of neurotics, lunatics and semi-
lunatics," obsessed with solving the riddle of life.[4]

In Russia, too, the respect and affection Chekhov's memory had
accrued began to evaporate. At the jubilee celebrations in 1910,
some dissenting voices could be heard above the chorus of praise.
At a meeting of the St. Petersburg Literary Society, the prominent
feminist author Olga Shapir renewed the charge that he was a poet
of gray, humdrum depressives, adding the complaint that his women
especially lacked clear outlines or strong emotion—despite the fact
that since the 1880s Chekhov had been sympathetic with political
reform movements.[5] In a period of activism and engagement, Chekhov's deliberately peripheral stance grew increasingly distasteful. It

3. K. Waliszewski, *Littérature russe* (Paris, 1900), 426; de Vogüé, quoted in Yu. Felichkin,
   "Rol teatra v vospriyati tvorchestva Chekhova vo Frantsii," in *Literaturny Muzey A. P.
   Chekhova: sbornik statey i materialov (The Chekhov Literary Museum: A Collection of Articles and Documents)* V (Rostov, 1969), 155.
4. Leo Weiner, *Anthology of Russian Literature*, Volume II (New York, 1903); A. Bates, *The
   Drama* (London, 1903), 73.
5. "V Peterburge," *Chekhovsky yubileiny sbornik (Chekhov Jubilee Anthology)* (Moscow,
   1910), 530.

culminated in the Bolshevik rejection of Chekhov after the October Revolution.

That rejection was due in part to Chekhov's inextricable association with the Moscow Art Theater, a symbiosis rich in ironies. It was ironic that Chekhov, who deeply admired skilled acting technique, should have been imposed on the cultural consciousness of his times by a troupe of amateurs and semi-professionals. It was ironic that Kanstantin Stanislavsky (1863–1938), who had cut his teeth as an actor and director on Shakespeare, Schiller, and operetta, and whose dearest ambition was to stage historically veristic productions of the classics, should find his most important challenge and success in re-creating the dreary world of his contemporaries, inevitably ennobling Chekhov's characters along the way. It was ironic that a theater whose founders intended to be a school for the mass public should find itself explicating the intelligentsia to the intelligentsia. It is perhaps the irony of ironies that the Art Theater, having discovered its most successful modus operandi in its staging of Chekhov, tried to apply it to all sorts of unlikely authors with to-be-expected failure, while Chekhov himself chafed at what he felt were willful departures from his meaning and intention.

He complained, "at the Art Theater, all those prop-room details distract the spectator, keep him from listening. . . . Let's take *Cherry Orchard* . . . Is this really my *Cherry Orchard*? Are these really my types?. . . . With the exception of a couple of performers, none of it's mine . . . I write life . . . This gray, everyday life . . . But that does mean annoying moaning and groaning . . . They make me lachrymose, a really boring writer . . . It's starting to get on my nerves. . . ."[6]

Whatever the discrepancy between Chekhov's vision and that of the Art Theater, what struck the spectators of the original productions most forcefully was that company and author seemed to be totally and intimately amalgamated; the plays seemed to be written and staged by the same person. When the actors at provincial theaters simplemindedly played Chekhov in a dismal monotone, the result was boredom; whereas the Art Theater revealed the covert, repressed feelings underlying the bad jokes and banal conversation. What distinguished Chekhov's drama from all other plays at that time was what Stanislavsky called the "submarine" course of the through action, which renders the dialogue nearly allegorical. Every individual scenic moment was carefully worked out in terms of the integrity of the entire production, to create an effect of seamlessness. Everyday or material reality went beyond mere naturalism to achieve

6. Yevtikhy Karpov, "Dve poslednie vstrechi s A. P. Chekhovym" (My last two encounters with Chekhov), *Ezhegodnik imperatorskikh teatrov* (*Yearbook of the Imperial Theaters*), V. (1909). It should be noted that Bunin considered Karpov's reminiscences to be a tissue of lies.

the famous *nastroenie* (mood). Stanislavsky's layering of "mood" or "atmosphere" is essentially a symbolist technique. Just as the words "Balzac was married in Berdichev" in *Three Sisters* overlay another, more profound emotional significance, so the tableaux of ordinary life, abetted by sound and lighting effects, opened into a "beyond" of more intense reality.

Those who saw Chekhov as a realist were deceived by Stanislavsky's veristic productions and the seeming looseness of the plays' dialogue and structure. Like all great artists, however, Chekhov was highly selective in what he chose to take from reality. The director Vsevolod Meyerhold recalled an occasion in 1898 when *The Seagull* was in rehearsal at the Moscow Art Theater, and an actor boasted of how backstage "frogs were to croak, dragonflies were to buzz, dogs to bark."

"What for?" Anton Pavlovich asks in a surly voice.

"Realism," replies the actor.

"Realism," repeats A. P., with a grin, and, after a brief pause, says: "The stage is art. There's a genre painting by Kramskoy, with the faces magnificently painted. What if the nose were to be cut out of one of the faces and a real one stuck in? The nose is 'realistic,' but the painting is spoiled."

One of the actors tells him proudly that at the end of the third act of *Seagull*, the director wants to bring on stage the whole domestic staff, some woman with a crying child.

Anton Pavlovich says:

"It isn't necessary. It's the same as if you're playing a piano *pianissimo*, and meanwhile the lid of the piano collapses."

"In life it often happens that a *forte* breaks into a *pianissimo* quite unexpectedly," one of the acting company tries to object.

"Yes, but the stage," says A. P., "demands a certain conventional quality. We have no fourth wall. Nevertheless, the stage is art, the stage reflects the quintessence of life, you don't have to put anything extraneous on stage."[7]

Perhaps the symbolist writer Andrey Bely put it best when he described *The Cherry Orchard* as "loops from the lace of life," realistic details scrutinized so closely that the dimension beyond them is revealed. He suggested that Chekhov became an unwitting symbolist as his surface layer of reality turned transparent and disclosed the hidden profundities beneath. A similar analogy might be made with pointillist painting: up close, the individual specks of color make no sense and create no discernible pattern; but at the proper dis-

---

7. V. E. Meyerhold, "The Naturalistic Theatre and the Theatre of Mood." For the full text, see this volume, pp. 598–607.

tance, the shapes reveal themselves in new and often striking ways, their relationships fall into place. In this respect, his plays fit Goethe's prescription for a stageworthy drama: "each incident must be significant by itself, and yet lead naturally to something more important."[8]

This scenic extension of the Russian tradition of literary realism enabled the intelligentsia to behold its hopes and fears on stage in terms it readily adopted. As the poet Osip Mandelshtam wrote in 1923,

> For the intelligentsia to go to the Moscow Art Theater was almost equal to taking communion or going to church. . . .
> Literature, not theater, characterized that entire generation. . . . They understood theater exclusively as an interpretation of literature . . . into another, more comprehensible and completely natural language.
> . . . The emotional zeal of that generation and of the Moscow Art Theater was the emotional zeal of Doubting Thomas. They had Chekhov, but Thomas the intellectual did not trust him. He wanted to touch Chekhov, to feel him, to be convinced of his reality.[9]

The illusion of life created by Stanislavsky, his emphasis on subtext and context, provided that reality, and gave Chekhov a novel-like amplitude that satisfied the intelligentsia's need for theme and tendentiousness.

The Bolsheviks had extra-literary uses for the theater. No less tendentious, they fomented performance that was stark, immediate, and viscerally compelling. The new demands made on art in the aftermath of the October Revolution had a Medusa-like effect on the Art Theater, freezing it in place. Locked into its aging repertory, the Art Theater found itself and Chekhov both repudiated as irrelevant excrescences of an obsolete bourgeois culture. Sailors at special matinees for workers shouted, "You bore me, Uncle Vanya!", while ideologues and journalists called for his suppression in favor of a vital, swashbuckling, romantic drama. Émigrés reported Lenin complaining about *Uncle Vanya*, "Is it really necessary to stir up such feelings? One needs to appeal to cheerfulness, work and joy."[1] Such vital creators of Bolshevik theater as Meyerhold and Yevgeny Vakhtangov turned to the vaudevilles when they sought to stage Chekhov, and

8. J. P. Eckermann, *Conversations with Goethe in the Last Years of His Life*, trans. S. M. Fuller (Boston: Hilliard, Gray, 1839), 168 (July 26, 1826).
9. Osip Mandelshtam, in *Teatr i muzyka* (*Theater and Music*) 36 (November 6, 1923).
1. *Moskovsky Khudozhestvenny teatr v sovetskuyu épokhu. Materialy, dokumenty* (*The Moscow Art Theater in the Soviet Era: Materials, Documents*) 2nd ed. (Moscow, 1974), 124; V. A. Nelidov, *Teatralnaya Moskva (sorok let moskovskikh teatrov)* (*Theatrical Moscow—Forty Years of Moscow Theatres*) (Berlin-Riga, 1931), 436.

the only full-length play of his to be regularly performed in this period was *The Cherry Orchard*, treated as a satiric farce mocking the estate owners and their parasites.

While Chekhov languished at home, abroad he was promulgated by a diaspora. The 1920s and '30s are the decades of the émigré's Chekhov; fugitives from the Revolution saw themselves as Ranevskayas and Gaevs, expelled from a tsarist Eden. The tours of the Moscow Art Theater and its offshoot the Prague Group disseminated the style and look of the original, now aging, productions, while defectors perpetuated a Stanislavskian approach in Europe and America. Even those refugees who had never practiced the Art Theater approach carried on under its banner—Theodore Komisarjevsky in England and Georges Pitoëff in France. Their Chekhov was lyrical, enigmatic, moonstruck, and, above all, steeped in romantic nostalgia. European and American audiences accepted this without demur. After all, if Chekhov was a particularly Russian author, then who better to interpret him than a Russian—any Russian? Chekhov, a man of sorrows acquainted with grief, came to be seen as elegiac, wistful, and, like Noël Coward's white elephants, "terribly, terribly sweet."

After the Second World War, in countries under Soviet hegemony, Chekhov and the Art Theater interpretation, now heavily adulterated by Socialist Realism, were thrust down the throats of Czech, Polish, East German, and Hungarian audiences. Little wonder that, left to their own devices, they spewed him out again and sought to discredit and supplant the Stanislavsky legacy.

The revival of Chekhov's drama in Europe is due to a Czech and an Italian: Otomar Krejča and Giorgio Strehler, both leftists, but of quite different stripe. At his theater near Prague, Krejča worked in collaboration with his actors to realize what Gorky had once called the cold, cruel Chekhov—an impassive creator who flung his characters into an absurd world. There they beat their wings futilely against the meaninglessness of existence. Without being either a programmatic existentialist or a doctrinaire absurdist, Krejča distilled his own experience as a victim of postwar Soviet domination into an interpretation of Chekhov that administered the shock of recognition to audiences throughout Europe.

Strehler employed elegance and metaphor in his 1956 *Cherry Orchard*, arguably the most influential Chekhov production of modern times. His white-on-white decor, with its overhead membrane of petals in a diaphanous veil, was copied from Bucharest to Indiana. Strehler sought to conflate all the levels of meaning in the play: the narrative, the sociohistorical and the universally metaphoric. The toys in the nursery, for instance, went beyond realistic props to become emblems of the characters' lost innocence and retarded emotions. Strehler universalized the nostalgia of Komisarjevsky and Pitoëff by enlarging it beyond the private sphere, while Krejča's productions grew ever more schematic, insisting on the collective grotesque of the Chekhovian world.

In Soviet Russia during the 1960s, Chekhov was co-opted by a generation of idealists opposed to one of cynics. *Ivanov* became the play for the times, repeatedly revived. Anti-domesticity was proclaimed by scenery that lacked walls and doors: manor houses were made to look like skeletal prisons, and the branches of the cherry orchard became sterile and gnarled.

The English-speaking world has been the most resistant to extreme reforms in the performance of Chekhov. Psychological realism remains the preferred format, and the Chekhovian estate has become as familiar as the old homestead or the derelict country house. "Chekhov has been ennobled by age," says Spencer Golub. ". . . He is as soothing and reassuring as the useless valerian drops dispensed by the doctors in all his plays . . . an article of faith, like all stereotypes . . . the Santa Claus of dramatic literature."[2] This may account for the large number of plays about Chekhov's life, in which he turns into Drs. Dorn, Astrov, or Chebutykin, depending on the playwright's bent. It is also the case that the English-speaking theater has, until very recently, been dominated by playwrights rather than directors. A Chekhovian resonance can be found more in the plays of leading dramatists from Rodney Ackland to Tennessee Williams than in extraordinary staging.

Anywhere else in the world, the reinterpretation of Chekhov, defying the conventional homilies and exploding the traditional conventions, was the work of directors. At least until the end of the nineteenth century, one could trace the stage history of Shakespeare or Molière through actors and their treatment of individual roles. Chekhov's career as a dramatist, however, coincided with the rise of the director as prime mover in the modern theater, and the nature of his last plays derives in part from his awareness—if not his full approval—of what a director's theater was capable of. Following the Wagnerian notion of *Gesamtkunstwerk*, it required the integration of every component: the actors had to become an ensemble led by a virtuoso conductor. We can compare the Hamlets of great actors to some advantage and insight, but to compare the Ranevskayas of individual actresses makes no sense outside the context of the directorial visions for the productions in which they appeared.

Writing in 1960, Harry Levin pointed out that the opening of a New York apartment building called The Picasso signaled the domesti-

---

2. In *Newsnotes on Soviet and East European Drama and Theatre* III: 3 (November, 1983): 2–3.

cation, and hence the end, of modernism.[3] When the enfant terrible
becomes the elder statesman and once-new coinages turn into commonplaces, efforts must be made the recapture the original effect.
The acceptance of Chekhov as a readily recognizable cultural totem
makes him available for all kinds of co-optation. In the 1970s, the
process of dismantling the Soviet icon of Chekhov continued. Anatoly Efros converted *The Cherry Orchard* to a graveyard. Yury Lyu-
bimov flung open the wall of the Taganka Theater during his *Three
Sisters* to reveal the Moscow streets outside: "You yearn for Moscow?" he seemed to be saying. "Well, here it is, in all its noise, grubbiness, and squalor!" Fifty years of false aspiration were debunked
in a moment.

Later, Yury Pogrebnichko recreated *The Three Sisters* as a museum
exhibit behind a velvet rope, cluttered with the detritus of the past,
forcing the post-Soviet spectator to come to terms with a regime that
left him washed up on the shoals of the present. Henrietta Yanov-
skaya put her *Ivanov* on roller-skates, to show him attempting to
evade the responsibilities of his sordid situation. In the United
States, the experimental Wooster Group dismantled *Three Sisters* by
means of video screens and improvization, to evoke the modern
world of mass media and to create a hybrid theatrical language. The
seamless web of the Stanislavskian simulacrum is fragmented into
jagged shards of interrupted meaning and faulty recollection. Dramatists remote from Chekhov's sensibility, language, and concerns,
such as Pam Gems, Edward Bond, David Mamet, Trevor Griffiths,
Lanford Wilson, David Hare, Brian Friel, and Richard Nelson, trans-
mogrify his works in new versions, refracting their own preoccupa-
tions. This need of the English-speaking playwright to wrestle with
Chekhov has become a rite of passage: there is something compul-
sively Oedipal in this recurrent grappling with the one universally
admitted patriarch of the modern stage.

Chekhov as patriarch may be a jarring image. Let us return to
Chekhov's replacement of Tolstoy as the Russian man of letters par
excellence. Even as late as the 1940s, the Communist critic György
Lukács could point to Tolstoy as the paradigm of universal genius
who transcended his otherwise crippling bourgeois milieu through
the power of his demiurgic creativity. In our less heroic age, however,
Tolstoy seems unsympathetic; like Blake's Old Nobodaddy, he glow-
ers at us disapprovingly from beneath his beetling brows. Tolstoy's
creative achievements and his moral demands on us seem the titanic
labors of some mythic era, impossible to us puny mortals. They also
exude a confidence and self-righteousness that are luxuries too costly

3. Harry Levin, "What was Modernism?" (1960), in *Varieties of Literary Experiences*, ed. S.
Burnshaw (New York, 1962), 307.

for the spiritually impecunious survivors of the twentieth century. Even Tolstoy's death was exemplary: his solitary demise in the railway station at Astapovo is the stuff of tragedy—Lear succumbing on the heath, this time unreconciled with Cordelia.

Chekhov's death, which has been often retold and reworked as fiction, is, in contrast, a comedy of errors. It too is exemplary, but as farce; from his alleged last words, "It's a long time, bless my soul, since I've had champagne" (which echoes *Uncle Vanya*'s Nanny: "a long time since I've had noodles"), to the transport of his corpse in a freight car marked OYSTERS, to a military band straying from a general's funeral to double in brass at his graveside. Compared to Tolstoy, Chekhov is the more accessible and familiar figure. His irony has greater appeal than does Tolstoy's moral absolutism. His vaunted objectivity, not all that objective under scrutiny, is more welcome because it is less judgmental than Tolstoy's. His inability to write a novel—his preference for small forms, open endings, and ethical ambiguities—appeals to our post-modern fondness for the marginal and our wary distrust of the grand gesture. Tolstoy the schoolmaster stands over his text, ferule in hand, to make sure we have learned the lesson; Chekhov endears himself by modestly bowing himself out, protesting that it is all in the words.

Yet for all this modesty over the course of a mere century Chekhov has reached the rank of Shakespeare. They are bracketed together as the greatest playwrights of all time. To cite only one such statement, the Polish director Andrzej Wajda has remarked, "Theater in our European tradition derives from the word, from literature, the Greeks, Shakespeare, Chekhov."[4] Note the absence of Ibsen from this statement; he might deserve better, with his endeavors to raise everyday experience to an epic level. Ibsen's grandiosity takes risks: when he succeeds, the effect is breathtaking; when he fails, it is involuntarily ludicrous. Chekhov sedulously avoided the grandiose, the overtly poetic, and the tragic pose—or, he undercut them when they arose inadvertently.

Despite what Wajda says about the word, part of Chekhov's special appeal comes from what he leaves out—another legacy from the symbolists, the pregnant pause. Often what is left unsaid—the awkward gaps in conversation, the sentences that trail off in the air, the interstices of pauses—matters most in Chekhov's plays. Of course, Stanislavsky, who distrusted understatement, amplified and multiplied the Chekhovian pause, turning it into a pretext for veristic stage effects. An actor who worked at the Art Theater in 1908 and 1909 recalled that the pauses "were held precisely by the numbers and the

---

4. Quoted in Maciej Karpinski, *The Theatre of Andrej Wajda*, trans. C. Paul (Cambridge: Cambridge UP, 1989), 124.

actors were recommended to count the seconds mentally during the duration of the pauses."[5] This mechanical rendition loses touch with the essence of the Chekhovian pause, itself a precursor of what Beckett referred to as the transitional zone in which being makes itself heard.

What justifies the coupling of Shakespeare and Chekhov? I would suggest that John Keats, in a famous letter of 1818, put his finger on it. Reacting to a performance of Edmund Kean as Richard III, Keats mused on Shakespeare's protean brilliance:

> . . . at once it struck me, what quality went to form a Man of Achievement especially in Literature & which Shakespeare possessed so enormously—I mean *Negative Capability*, that is when a man is capable of being in uncertainties, Mysteries, doubts, without any irritable reaching after fact & reason . . . [6]

Walter J. Bate paraphrases this to mean that "in our life of uncertainties, where no one system or formula can explain everything . . . what is needed is an imaginative openness of mind and heightened receptivity to reality in its full and diverse concreteness."[7] To put it another way, Shakespearean mastery requires a negation of the writer's own ego, a sympathetic absorption into the essential significance of the writer's object. Chekhov seems to have attained that state of authorial absence.

For Keats, as for the other English Romantics, Shakespeare's brilliance at negative capability was exhibited by his extensive gallery of characters, all equally vivid, multifaceted, and imbued with idiosyncratic opinions, idioms, and behavior. Chekhov can hardly exhibit such variety or plenitude in his plays; the narrow, seemingly repetitive nature of his dramatic world was a ready target for satire and parody even in his lifetime. But another, earlier letter of Keats comes to our aid. In it, he divides ethereal things into three categories:

> Things real—things semireal—and no things—Things real—such as existences of Sun Moon & Stars and passages of Shakspeare—Things semireal such as Love, the Clouds &c which require a greeting of the Spirit to make them wholly exist—and Nothings which are made Great and dignified by an ardent pursuit . . . [8]

Chekhov admits the existence of real things in his writings and endows them with significance beyond their material status; how-

5. A. A. Mgebrov, *Zhizn v teatre* (*A Life in the Theater*), ed. E. Kuznetsov (Leningrad, 1920), Volume I, 224–25.
6. *The Letters of John Keats, 1814–1821*, ed. H. E. Rollins (Cambridge, Mass.: Harvard UP, 1958), I: 184.
7. W. J. Bate, *John Keats* (New York: Oxford UP, 1966), 249.
8. Letter to Benjamin Bailey (March 13, 1818).

ever, the existence of semireal things such as love remains problematic and nebulous for his characters. Still, the confines of the Chekhovian world teem with Keats's "Nothings" to be made great and dignified by ardent pursuit. As Stanislavsky intuited, a samovar in Chekhov was not the same as a samovar in Ostrovsky; it, along with the pauses and sound effects and changeable weather, bespoke the overall tone and reflected the inner life of the characters. Leonid Andreev, who introduced this concept into the Russian language, referred to this interrelationship of everything in Chekhov as an example of "panpsychism," the theory that all matter has consciousness. The same soul animates whatever appears on stage:

> On the stage Chekhov must be performed not only by human beings, but by drinking glasses and chairs and crickets and military overcoats and engagement rings . . . it all comes across not as items from reality or true-to-life sound and its utterances, but as the protagonists' thoughts and sensations disseminated throughout space.[9]

This goes beyond the sympathetic fallacy; it creates a distinctive microcosm, instantly recognizable whatever the vagaries of directors. This unifying factor ties together even the most seemingly non-communicative dialogue and solipsistic yearnings.

When Mariya Knebel, Stanislavsky's last pupil, came to the Abbey Theatre in Dublin in 1968 to direct *The Cherry Orchard*, the actors were surprised that she did not require a samovar onstage.[1] The samovar had always been the indispensable token of Chekhov's foreignness. In recent decades, however, in production after production, the samovar has been supplanted as an emblematic prop by an old Victrola with a morning-glory horn. Chekhov is still associated with the past, but not a specifically Russian or historic past. His "pastness," like that of any great dramatist, is part of a continuum with the present. The suggestion of this change is that somehow the screechy recorded voices played back on a turntable return the past to us in a distorted, nostalgic form, which we interpret as our needs require.[2]

In his book *The Theatrical Event*, David Cole refers to *illud tempus*, an archetypal realm that the theater must depict, "not so much

9. Leonid Andreev, *Pisma o teatre* (1912), trans. as "Letters on Theatre," in *Russian Dramatic Theory from Pushkin to the Symbolists*, ed. and trans. L. Senelick (Austin: University of Texas Press, 1981), 240–41.
1. Mariya Knebel, " 'Vishnyovy sad' v Irlandii," *Teatr* 5 (1969): 158–66.
2. Even the first production of *Three Sisters* in 1901 gave the critic Innokenty Annensky the sense of a phonograph reproducing his own world: "The phonograph presents me with *my* voice, *my* words, which, however, I had been quick to forget, and as I listen, I naively ask: 'Who is that talking through his nose and lisping?' " I. F. Annensky, "Drama nastroeniya. Tri sestry," in *Knigi otrazhenii* I (St. Petersburg: Trud, 1906), 147.

when it first occurred as where it is always happening."[3] Beyond the reality the estates and garrison towns of Chekhov's plays held for their original audiences, they have now taken on a polysemic existence. They transcend a specific society to become archetypal realms. The spellbinding lake of *The Seagull* has more in common with the island of *The Tempest* than with a landscape in Turgenev. The rooms in the Prozorov home can expand to the dimensions of Agamemnon's palace or dwindle to the claustrophobic cells of Beckett. The early critics of Chekhov could not have been more wrong when they condemned him as the poet of an obsolescent set, circumscribed by its own eccentricity. Just as the Shakespearean *illud tempus* shines through modern dress and radical transpositions, the Chekhovian *illud tempus* gains in eloquent meaning from its disguises, even when Thomas Kilroy transfers *The Seagull* to the Ireland of the Celtic Twilight or Tadashi Suzuki plunges the officers of *Three Sisters* into Absurdist baskets or the Irondale Ensemble Project turns *Uncle Vanya* into a 1940s radio announcer in Charlevoix, Michigan. Without shedding its specificity, the world of the Chekhovian intellectual has become as remote as Camelot and as familiar as Grover's Corners, as exotic as Shangri-La and as homely as Kasrilevka. It instantly conjures up a long-vanished way of life that nevertheless compels us to adduce current counterparts. The persistence of the identifiable and idiosyncratic world suggests that he never stopped being Chekhov our contemporary.

---

3. David Cole, *The Theatrical Event: A Mythos, a Vocabulary, a Perspective* (Middletown, Conn.: Wesleyan UP, 1975), 8.

THE TEXTS OF THE PLAYS

The Bear

As usual, Chekhov's earliest reference to his work in progress was off-handedly negative: "Having nothing better to do, I wrote a vapid little French-style vaudevillette (*vodevilchik*) entitled *The Bear*" (letter to I. L. Leontyev-Shcheglov, February 22, 1888). No sooner had it appeared in print than Chekhov's friends insisted that he submit it to the dramatic censor and recommended the perfect actors to play it. The censor was not amused, disturbed by the "more than strange plot" and the "coarseness and indecency of the tone of the whole play," and he forbade its production. He was overruled, however, by a superior in the bureaucracy who, by suppressing a few lines, rendered it suitable for the public. The play had its premiere at Korsh's Theater in Moscow on October 28, 1888, with the clever ingénue Nataliya Rybchinskaya as Popova and Chekhov's boyhood friend Nikolay Solovtsov as Smirnov. Solovtsov, a tall, ungainly fellow with a stentorian voice, had probably been in Chekhov's mind for the role of the bear as he wrote it.

The Bear was a runaway success; the audience for the first performance roared with laughter and interrupted the dialogue with applause, and the newspapers praised it to the skies. Theaters all over Russia added it to their repertories and the best Russian actors clamored to play in it. In Chekhov's lifetime, it brought him regular royalties, and the play has been regularly revived on professional and amateur stages all over the world ever since.

The plot updates Petronius' ancient Roman tale of the Widow of Ephesus, which Christopher Fry later turned into the one-act play, *A Phoenix Too Frequent*. That ribald fable tells of a widow whose grief for a dead husband melts under the ardor of the soldier guarding the corpse of a crucified criminal. She eventually colludes with him to replace the body stolen during their lovemaking with her own deceased spouse. Chekhov substitutes for the corpse the carriage-horse Toby, a token of the widow's transference of affection.

The Bear's comedy derives from the characters' lack of self-knowledge. The widow Popova fancies herself inconsolably bereaved, a fugitive from the world, while Smirnov takes himself to be a misogynist to the core. They both are *alazons* in the classic sense: figures made ludicrous by pretending to be more than they actually are. If the languishing Popova is based on the Petronian source, Smirnov is a descendant of Molière's Alceste, professing a hatred of society's hypocrisy but succumbing to a woman who exemplifies that society. The two poseurs come in conflict, and the roles reverse: the inconsolable relic snatches up a pistol and,

3

like any case-hardened bully, insists on a duel, while the gruff woman-hater finds himself incapable of facing down his female opponent. (The improbable duel most outraged the censors.) It is destined that the dimpled widow and the brute in muddy boots will fall into one another's arms by the final curtain.

Nevertheless, the comedy is also grounded in the economic hardships of Russian rural life. Like *Ivanov*, the play begins with a landowner having to pay an installment on a loan and not having the money to do so. Smirnov's boorishness is prompted as much by his desperate fear of losing his estate by defaulting on his mortgage as is Ivanov's funk by his inability to pay his workmen or his creditors. This financial stress remains a constant in Chekhov's plays, motivating the basic action of *Uncle Vanya*, and culminating in the overriding themes of lending and loss in *The Cherry Orchard*.

The Bear

A Joke in One Act

Dedicated to N. N. Solovtsov[1]

Characters

YELENA IVANOVNA POPOVA, a young widow with dimples in her cheeks, a landowner
GRIGORY STEPANOVICH SMIRNOV,[2] a middle-aged landowner
LUKA, Popova's man-servant, an old fellow

A drawing-room in Popova's manor house.

I

POPOVA (*in deep mourning, her eyes fixed on a portrait photograph*) *and* LUKA.

LUKA   This won't do, mistress. . . . You're running yourself down is all. . . . The housemaid and the cook are out picking berries, every living thing rejoices, even the tabby cat, she knows how to have fun, running around outside, tracking dicky birds, while you sit inside the livelong day, like in a nunnery, and don't have no fun.

1. Nikolay Nikolaevich Solovtsov (born Fyodorov, 1857–1902), a schoolmate of Chekhov's in Taganrog, who became an actor at the Alexandra Theater in St. Petersburg from 1882 to 1883, and who was actor and director at Korsh's Theater in Moscow from 1887 to 1889. He staged Chekhov's play *The Wood Goblin* at Abramova's Theater in 1889–90.
2. An ironic name, from *smirny* (peaceful, serene).

Honest to goodness! Just figure, a year's gone by now, and you ain't set foot outside the house!

POPOVA   And I never shall . . . What for? My life is already over. He lies in the grave, I've buried myself within these four walls . . . We're both dead.

LUKA   There you go again! And I shouldn't listen, honestly. Nikolay Mikhailovich is dead, that's how it is with him, it's God's will, rest in peace . . . You done your bit of grieving—and that's that, time to get on with your life. Can't go on weeping and wearing black for the next hundred years. In my time my old woman died on me too . . . So what? I grieved a bit, I cried off and on for a month, and then I was over her, but if I was to weep and wail a whole lifetime, it'd be more than the old girl was worth. (*Sighs.*) You've neglected all the neighbors . . . You don't go visiting yourself, and you don't invite nobody here. We're living, if you don't mind my saying so, like spiders,—we never see the light of day. The foot-men's liveries have been et up by mice . . . It'd be a different matter if there wasn't no decent people, but after all the county's packed with ladies and gents . . . In Ryblovo there's a regiment posted, officers like sugarplums, you can't get your fill of looking at 'em! And in camp not a Friday goes by without a ball and, just figure, every day the brass band plays music. . . . Eh, mistress dearie! Young, beautiful, the picture of health—all you need is to live and enjoy yourself . . . Beauty's not a gift that lasts forever, y'know! Ten years from now or so, you'll be in the mood for preening and dazzling the officer gents, but it'll be too late.

POPOVA (*Resolutely.*)   I beg you never to talk to me about that sort of thing! You know, from the day Nikolay Mikhailovich died, life has lost all meaning for me. It may look to you as if I'm alive, but looks are deceiving! I have taken an oath not to remove my mourning until I'm laid in my grave, nor to see the light of day . . . Do you hear me? Let his spirit see how much I love him . . . Yes, I know, you're well aware that he was nothing but unjust to me, cruel and . . . and even unfaithful, but I shall be faithful to the day I die and show him that I know how to love. There, from the other side of the grave, he will see that I am just as I was before he died . . .

LUKA   Better'n this kind o' talk, you should take a turn in the garden, or else have 'em hitch up Toby or Paladin and pay a call on the neighbors . . .

POPOVA   Oh! (*Weeps.*)

LUKA   Mistress! Dear lady! What's wrong? God bless you!

POPOVA   He was so fond of Toby! He always rode him over to the Korchagins and the Vlasovs. He sat a horse so wonderfully well!

Such a graceful expression when he tugged at the reins with all his might! Remember? Toby, Toby! Tell them to give him an extra portion of oats.

LUKA   Yes, ma'am!

(*The doorbell rings insistently.*)

POPOVA (*Startled.*)   Who's that? Tell them I am in to nobody!

LUKA   Yes indeed, ma'am! (*Exits.*)

II

POPOVA (*alone*).

POPOVA (*Looking at the photograph.*)   You see, *Nicolas*, how I know how to love and forgive . . . My love will flicker out when I do, when my poor heart ceases to beat. (*Laughs through tears.*) And aren't you ashamed? I'm a good girl, a faithful little wife, I've locked myself up in a fortress and will be true to you to the day I die, while you . . . aren't you ashamed, you chubby thing? You cheated on me, made scenes, left me on my own for whole weeks at a time . . .

III

POPOVA *and* LUKA.

LUKA (*Enters, anxiously.*)   Mistress, there's somebody asking for you. Wants to see you . . .

POPOVA   But didn't you tell him that I am in to nobody since the death of my husband?

LUKA   I told 'im, but he don't want to listen, he says it's very urgent business.

POPOVA   I am *in — to — no — bo — dy*!

LUKA   I told him, but . . . some kind o' maniac . . . he cusses and shoves right into the room . . . he's there in the dining room right now . . .

POPOVA (*Irritated.*)   All right, show him in . . . How uncouth!

LUKA (*exits.*)

How tiresome these people are! What do they want from me? Why do they have to disturb my serenity? (*Sighs.*) No, it's obvious, I really shall have to get me to a nunnery . . . (*Musing.*) Yes, a nunnery . . .

IV

POPOVA, LUKA, *and* SMIRNOV.

SMIRNOV (*Entering, to* LUKA).   Numbskull, you're too fond of hearing yourself talk. . . . Jackass! (*On seeing* POPOVA, *with dignity.*)

Madam, may I introduce myself: retired lieutenant of artillery, landowner Grigory Stepanovich Smirnov! Forced to disturb you on the most urgent business. . . .

POPOVA (*Not offering her hand.*)   What can I do for you?

SMIRNOV   Your late husband, whom I had the honor to know, left two I.O.U.s owing me twelve hundred rubles. Because tomorrow my interest payment to the bank[3] falls due, I would ask you, madam, to repay me the money today.

POPOVA   Twelve hundred! But what was my husband in debt to you for?

SMIRNOV   He bought oats from me.

POPOVA (*Sighing, to* LUKA.)   Now don't you forget, Luka, to tell them to give Toby an extra portion of oats.

(LUKA *exits.*)

(*To* SMIRNOV.) If Nikolay Mikhailovich still owes you money, why, it stands to reason, I shall pay; but, please forgive me, I have no cash on hand today. The day after tomorrow my foreman will be back from town, and I'll ask him to pay you what's owing, but in the meantime I cannot comply with your request . . . Besides, today is exactly seven months since my husband died, and the way I'm feeling now I am completely indisposed to deal with financial matters.

SMIRNOV   And the way I'm feeling now, if I don't pay the interest tomorrow, I'll be up the creek good and proper. They'll foreclose on my estate!

POPOVA   The day after tomorrow you'll get your money.

SMIRNOV   I don't need the money the day after tomorrow, I need it now.

POPOVA   Excuse me, I cannot pay you today.

SMIRNOV   And I cannot wait until the day after tomorrow.

POPOVA   What's to be done, if I don't have it at the moment?

SMIRNOV   In other words, you can't pay up?

POPOVA   I cannot . . .

SMIRNOV   Hmm! . . . Is that your last word?

POPOVA   Yes, my very last.

SMIRNOV   Your last! Positively?

POPOVA   Positively.

SMIRNOV   Thank you very much indeed. We'll just make a memo of that, shall we? (*Shrugs his shoulders.*) And people expect me to be cool, calm, and collected! Just now on the road I ran into the tax collector and he asks, "Why are you always losing your temper, Grigory Stepanovich?" Well, for pity's sake, how can I keep from losing my temper? I need money like crazy. . . . I rode out yester-

3. The Gentry Land Bank, established by the government in the 1880s to offer financial assistance to impecunious landowners.

day morning almost at dawn, dropped in on everyone who owes me money, and not a single one of them paid me! I'm dog-tired, spent the night in some godforsaken hole—in a kike pothouse[4] next to a keg of vodka . . . Finally I show up here, forty miles from home; I hope to get something, and they greet me with "the way I'm feeling now!" How can I keep from losing my temper?

POPOVA   I believe my words were clear: when the foreman returns from town, you'll get it.

SMIRNOV   I didn't come to the foreman, but to *you*! What the blue blazes—pardon the expression—do I need with your foreman!

POPOVA   Forgive me, my dear sir, I am not accustomed to that peculiar expression and that tone of voice. I will not listen to you any more. (*Exits quickly.*)

V

SMIRNOV (*alone*).

SMIRNOV   Say pretty please! "The way I'm feeling now . . ." Seven months ago her husband died! But do I have to pay the interest or don't I? I ask you: do I have pay the interest or don't I? So, you had a husband die on you, there's some way you're feeling now, and the rest of the double-talk . . . the foreman's gone off somewhere, damn him to hell, but what do you expect me to do? Fly away from my creditors in a hot-air balloon or what? Or run off and bash my skull against the wall? I ride over to Gruzdyov's—he's not at home. Yaroshevich is in hiding; I have a fatal falling-out with Kuritsyn and almost throw him out a window; Mazutov[5] has got the trots; and this one has a way she's feeling. Not one of the lousy deadbeats will pay up! And all because I've been too indulgent to them—I'm a soft touch, a pushover, a sissy! I'm too delicate with them! Well, just you wait! You'll learn who I am! I won't let you pull anything over on me, damn it! I'll stay here, I'll stick around until she pays up! Brr! . . . I'm really angry today, really angry! Anger is making the thews in my thighs quiver. I have to catch my breath . . . Phooey, my God, I'm even coming over faint! (*Shouts.*) You there!

---

4. In Western Russia, many rural inns were run by Jews, and a standard anti-Semitic joke was that the inns were flea-infested clip joints.
5. Joke names: Gruzdyov, from *gruzd*, a kind of mushroom; Kuritsyn, from *kuritsa*, hen; Mazutov, from *mazut*, fuel oil.

VI

SMIRNOV *and* LUKA.

LUKA (*Enters.*)   What's wrong?
SMIRNOV   Get me some kvas[6] or water!
         (LUKA *exits.*)
No, what kind of logic is that! A man needs money like crazy, he's
on the verge of hanging himself, and she won't pay because, don't
you see, she's indisposed to deal with financial matters! . . .
Honest-to-God weaker-sex logic, all her brains are in her bustle!
That's why I never liked, still do not like, to talk to women. For
me, it's easier to sit on a keg of gunpowder than talk to a woman.
Brr! . . . I've got goosebumps crawling up and down my skin—
that's how much that petticoat has enraged me! All I need is to
see in the distance some "weaker vessel" and my calves start to
cramp with anger. It makes you want to call for help.

VII

SMIRNOV *and* LUKA.

LUKA (*Enters and serves water.*)   The mistress is sick and won't see
anyone.
SMIRNOV   Get out!
         (LUKA *exits.*)
Sick and won't see anyone! Then don't, don't see me. . . . I'll sit in
this spot here until you hand over the money. You can be sick for
a week, and I'll sit here for a week. . . . You can be sick for a year—
and I'll stay a year. . . . I'll have what's due me, my fair lady! You
don't get to me with your mourning weeds and dimples on your
cheeks. . . . We know the meaning of those dimples! (*Shouts out
the window.*) Semyon, unhitch the horses! We'll be here for a
while! I'm sticking around! Tell 'em in the stable to give the horses
oats! Again, you swine, you've got the left trace-horse tangled up
in the reins! (*Mimicks him.*) "It makes no never mind . . ." I'll give
you no never mind! (*Walks away from the window.*) Disgusting . . .
the heat's unbearable, nobody pays what they owe, I got no sleep
last night, and now this petticoat in mourning with *the way she's
feeling now.* . . . My head aches. . . . Should I have some vodka or
what? I suppose a drink'll be all right . . . (*Shouts.*) You there!
LUKA (*Enters.*)   What d'you want?
SMIRNOV   Get me a glass of vodka!

6. A refreshing drink of low alcohol content, made from fermented black bread and malt,
much preferred to beer by the peasantry. Lopakhin orders it in Act One of *The Cherry
Orchard.*

(LUKA *exits*.)

Oof ! (*Sits and looks around*.) Got to admit, I'm a pretty picture!
Covered with dust, boots muddy, haven't washed or combed my
hair, straw on my vest. . . . I'll bet the little lady took me for a
highway robber. (*Yawns*.) It is a bit uncouth to show up in a drawing room looking like this. Well, never mind . . . I'm not here as a
guest, but as a bill collector. There's no rules of etiquette for bill
collectors . . .

LUKA (*Enters and serves vodka*.)   You're taking a lot of liberties,
    sir . . .
SMIRNOV (*Angrily*.)   What?
LUKA   I . . . I didn't mean . . . I strictly . . .
SMIRNOV   Who do you think you're talking to? Hold your tongue!
LUKA (*Aside*.)   Jumped right down my throat, the monster . . . Why
    the hell did he have to show up?
        (LUKA *exits*.)
SMIRNOV   Oh, I really am angry. So angry that I think I could grind
    the whole world into dust . . . I'm even feeling faint . . . (*Shouts*.)
    You there!

                                VIII

POPOVA *and* SMIRNOV.

POPOVA (*Enters, averting her eyes*.)   Dear sir, during my lengthy iso-
    lation I have grown unaccustomed to the human voice and I can-
    not bear shouting. I earnestly beg you not to disturb my peace!
SMIRNOV   Pay me my money and I'll go.
POPOVA   I told you in plain Russian: I don't have any loose cash at
    the moment. Wait until the day after tomorrow.
SMIRNOV   I also had the honor of telling you in plain Russian: I don't
    need the money the day after tomorrow, but today. If you don't
    pay me today, then tomorrow I shall have to hang myself.
POPOVA   But what am I supposed to do if I haven't got any money?
    How very peculiar!
SMIRNOV   So you won't pay me right this minute? No?
POPOVA   I can't . . .
SMIRNOV   In that case, I shall stay sitting here until I get it . . . (*Sits*.)
    The day after tomorrow you'll pay up? Wonderful! I shall sit until
    the day after tomorrow just like this. Look, see how I'm sitting.
    . . . (*Jumps up*.) I ask you: do I have to pay the interest tomorrow
    or not? . . . Or do you think I'm joking?
POPOVA   Dear sir, I ask you not to shout! This isn't a stable!
SMIRNOV   My question was not is this a stable, but do I need to pay
    the interest tomorrow or not?

POPOVA   You don't know how to behave in the presence of a lady!

SMIRNOV   Yes, ma'am, I do know how to behave in the presence of a lady!

POPOVA   No, you don't! You are an ill-mannered, boorish fellow! Respectable people don't talk to ladies this way!

SMIRNOV   Ah, this is wonderful! How would you like me to talk to you? In French or something? (*Maliciously, lisping.*) *Madame,* shay voo pree[7] . . . I'm absolutely delighted that you won't pay me my money. . . . Ah, *pardon,* that I'm disturbing you! Isn't the weather lovely today! And how that mourning becomes you! (*Bowing and scraping.*)

POPOVA   That's not witty, it's rude.

SMIRNOV (*Mimicks her.*)   *That's not witty, it's rude!* I don't know how to behave in the presence of a lady! Madam, in my lifetime I've seen more women than you've had hot dinners! Three times I fought a duel with firearms over a woman! I've walked out on a dozen women and ten have walked out on me! Yes, ma'am! There was a time when I played the fool, got all sticky-sentimental, talked the sweet talk, laid on the soft soap, clicked my heels . . . I loved, suffered, bayed at the moon, went spineless, melted, turned hot and cold . . . I loved passionately, madly, you-name-it-ly, damn it; squawked like a parrot about women's rights; spent half my fortune on hearts and flowers; but now—thanks but no thanks! You won't lead me down the garden path again! Enough is enough! Dark eyes, flashing eyes,[8] crimson lips, dimpled cheeks, the moon, low whispers, heavy breathing—for all this, madam, I now don't give a tinker's dam! Present company excepted, but all women, great and small, are phonies, showoffs, gossips, troublemakers, liars to the marrow of their bones; vain, fussy, ruthless, their reasoning is a disgrace; and as for what's in *here* (*slaps his forehead*), forgive my frankness, a sparrow could give ten points to any thinker in petticoats! You gaze at some romantic creature: muslin, moonshine, a demigoddess, a million raptures, but take a peep into her soul—a common- or garden-variety crocodile! (*Grabs the back of a chair; the chair creaks and breaks.*) But the most outrageous thing of all is that this crocodile for some reason imagines that its masterpiece, its prerogative and monopoly, is the tender passion! Damn it all to hell, hang me upside-down on this nail— does a woman really know how to love anyone other than a lapdog? In love she only knows how to whimper and snivel! While a man suffers and sacrifices, all of her love is expressed only in swishing the train on her dress and trying to lead him more firmly by the nose. You have the misfortune to be a woman; you probably know

7. Mispronunciation of French: *je vous prie,* I beg you.
8. *Dark eyes, flashing eyes:* the first words of "Ochi chyornye," a well-known Russian folksong.

what a woman's like from your own nature. Tell me on your honor: have you ever in your life seen a woman be sincere, faithful, and constant? You have not! Faithfulness, constancy—that's only for old bags and freaks! You'll sooner run into a cat with horns or a white blackbird than a constant woman!

POPOVA   I beg your pardon, but, in your opinion, just who is faithful and constant in love? Not the man?

SMIRNOV   Yes, ma'am, the man!

POPOVA   The man! (*Malicious laugh.*) The man is faithful and constant in love! Do tell, now there's news! (*Heatedly.*) What right have you to say that? Men faithful and constant! If it comes to that, let me tell you that of all the men I've known and still know, the very best was my late husband. . . . I loved him passionately, with every fiber of my being, as only a young, intelligent woman can love; I gave him my youth, happiness, life, my fortune, breathed through him, worshipped him like an idolater, and . . . and—then what? This best of men cheated me in the most shameless manner on every occasion! After his death I found in his desk a whole drawer full of love letters, and during his lifetime—horrible to remember!—he would leave me alone for weeks at a time, make advances to other women before my very eyes, and betrayed me, squandered my money, ridiculed my feelings. . . . And, despite all that, I loved him and was faithful to him. . . . What's more, now that he's dead, I am still faithful and constant to him. I have buried myself forever within these four walls, and until my dying day I shall not remove this mourning. . . .

SMIRNOV   (*A spiteful laugh.*)   Mourning! . . . I don't understand who you take me for? Don't I know perfectly well why you wear that black masquerade outfit and have buried yourself within these four walls? Of course I do! It's so mysterious, so romantic! Some young cadet or bobtailed poet will be walking by the estate, he'll peer into the window and think: "Here lives the mysterious Tamara,[9] who for love of her husband has buried herself within four walls." We know these tricks!

POPOVA   (*Flaring up.*)   What? How dare you say such things to me!

SMIRNOV   You've buried yourself alive, but look, you haven't forgot to powder your face!

POPOVA   How dare you talk to me that way?

SMIRNOV   Please don't raise your voice to me, I'm not your foreman! Allow me to call things by their rightful names. I'm not a woman

---

9. Russian literature knows several Tamaras: a famous queen of Georgia (1184–1213), a Georgian Lorelei a wandering spirit in Lermontov's poem "Tamara," and the Georgian maiden who flees to a nunnery to avoid the Demon's love in Anton Rubinstein's opera from Lermontov, *The Demon* (1871).

and I'm used to expressing opinions straight out! So be so kind as not to raise your voice!

POPOVA   I'm not raising my voice, you're raising your voice! Be so kind as to leave me in peace!

SMIRNOV   Pay me the money and I'll go.

POPOVA   I haven't got any money!

SMIRNOV   No, ma'am, hand it over!

POPOVA   Just out of spite, you won't get a kopek! You can leave me in peace!

SMIRNOV   I don't have the pleasure of being either your spouse or your fiancé, so please don't make scenes for my benefit (*Sits.*) I don't care for it.

POPOVA (*Panting with anger.*)   You sat down!

SMIRNOV   I sat down.

POPOVA   I insist that you leave!

SMIRNOV   Hand over the money . . . (*Aside.*) Ah, I am really angry! Really angry!

POPOVA   I do not choose to have a conversation with smart alecks! Please clear out of here! (*Pause.*) You aren't going? No?

SMIRNOV   No.

POPOVA   No?

SMIRNOV   No!

POPOVA   Very well then! (*Rings.*)

IX

The same and LUKA.

POPOVA   Luka, escort this gentleman out!

LUKA (*Walks over to Smirnov.*)   Sir, please leave when you're asked! There's nothing doing here. . . .

SMIRNOV (*Leaping up.*)   Shut up! Who do you think you're talking to? I'll toss you like a salad!

LUKA (*Grabs his heart.*)   Heavenly fathers! . . . Saints alive! . . . (*Falls into an armchair.*) Oh, I feel faint, faint! I can't catch my breath!

POPOVA   Where's Dasha? Dasha! (*Shouts.*) Dasha! Pelageya! Dasha! (*Rings.*)

LUKA   Ugh! They've all gone out to pick berries . . . There's no one in the house . . . Faint! Water!

POPOVA   Will you please clear out of here!

SMIROV   Would you care to be a little more polite?

POPOVA (*Clenching her fists and stamping her feet.*)   You peasant! You unlicked bear! Upstart! Monster!

SMIRNOV   What? What did you say?

POPOVA   I said that you're a bear! A monster!

SMIRNOV   (*Taking a step.*)   Excuse me, what right have you got to insult me?

POPOVA   Yes, I am insulting you . . . well, so what? You think I'm afraid of you?

SMIRNOV   And do you think because you're a member of the weaker sex, you have the right to insult people with impunity? Really? I challenge you to a duel!

LUKA   Saints in heaven! . . . Holy saints! . . . Water!

SMIRNOV   We'll settle this with firearms!

POPOVA   Just because you've got fists like hams and a bull's throat, you think I'm afraid of you? Huh? You're such an upstart!

SMIRNOV   I challenge you to a duel! I brook no insults and therefore I'll overlook the fact that you are a woman, a frail creature!

POPOVA   (*Trying to shout over him.*)   You bear! You bear! You bear!

SMIRNOV   It's high time we rid ourselves of the prejudice that only men have to pay for insults! Equal rights are equal rights, damn it all! I challenge you to a duel!

POPOVA   You want to settle it with firearms? As you like!

SMIRNOV   This very minute!

POPOVA   This very minute! My husband left some pistols behind . . . I'll bring them here at once . . . (*Hurriedly goes and returns.*) I shall take great pleasure in pumping a bullet into your thick skull! You can go to hell! (*Exits.*)

SMIRNOV   I'll smoke her like a side of bacon! I'm no snot-nose kid, no sentimental puppy! Female frailty has no effect on me!

LUKA   Dear, kind master! . . . (*Gets on his knees.*) Do me the favor—pity me, an old man, clear out of here! You've skeered me to death, and now you're fixing to shoot up the place!

SMIRNOV   (*Not listening to him.*)   Shooting at one's fellow human—that's what I call equality, women's rights! That puts both sexes on an equal footing! I will plug her on principle! But can you call her a woman? (*Mimicks.*) "Damn you to hell . . . I'll pump a bullet into your thick skull!" What's that all about? She got flushed, her eyes blazed . . . She accepted my challenge! Honest to God, it's the first time in my life I've ever seen . . .

LUKA   For heaven's sake, go away! I'll have prayers said for you forever!

SMIRNOV   Now *that's* a woman! *That's* something I can understand! An honest-to-God woman! Not a sourpuss, not a limp rag, but flames, gunpowder, a rocket! I'm almost sorry I'll have to kill her!

LUKA   (*Weeps.*)   Master . . . my dear sir, go away!

SMIRNOV   I actually like her! I really do. Even if she didn't have dimples in her cheeks, I'd like her! Even willing to forgive her the debt . . . and my anger's gone . . . Wonderful woman!

X

The same and POPOVA.

POPOVA (*Enters with pistols.*) Here they are, the pistols. . . . But, before we fight, you will be so kind as to show me how to shoot . . . Never in my life have I held a pistol in my hands.

LUKA Save us, Lord, and be merciful. . . . I'll go see if I can find the gardener and the coachman. . . . How did this disaster land on our head? (*Exits.*)

SMIRNOV (*Glancing at the pistols.*) You see, there are different types of pistols. . . . There are special dueling pistols, the Mortimer, with percussion caps. What you've got here are revolvers of the Smith and Wesson make, triple action with an extractor, battlefield accuracy. . . . Splendid pistols. . . . Cost at least ninety rubles the brace. . . . You have to hold a pistol like this . . . (*Aside.*) Her eyes, her eyes! An incendiary woman!

POPOVA This way?

SMIRNOV Yes, that way. . . . Whereupon you raise the cocking-piece . . . then take aim like so. . . . Head back a bit ! Extend your arm, in the appropriate manner. . . . That's it. . . . Then with this finger squeeze this doodad here—and that's all there is to it . . . Only rule number one is: keep a cool head and take your time aiming. Try not to let your hand shake.

POPOVA Fine . . . It's not convenient to shoot inside, let's go into the garden.

SMIRNOV Let's go. Only I warn you that I shall fire into the air.

POPOVA Of all the nerve! Why?

SMIRNOV Because . . . because . . . It's my business, that's why!

POPOVA You're chickening out? Are you? Ah-ah-ah-ah! No, sir, no worming out of it! Please follow me! I won't rest until I've blown a hole in your head . . . that very head I hate so much! Are you chickening out?

SMIRNOV Yes, I am.

POPOVA That's a lie! Why don't you want to fight?

SMIRNOV Because . . . because I . . . like you.

POPOVA (*Malicious laugh.*) He likes me! He dares to say that he likes me! (*Points to the door.*) You may go.

SMIRNOV (*Silently puts down the revolver, takes his cape, and goes. Near the door he stops. For half a minute both look silently at one another; then he says, irresolutely crossing to* POPOVA). Listen here

. . . Are you still angry? I'm damnably infuriated as well, but, don't you understand? . . . How can I put this? . . . The fact is, you see, the way the story goes, speaking for myself. . . . (*Shouts.*) Well, is it really my fault that I like you? (*Grabs the back of a chair, the chair creaks and breaks.*) What the hell sort of breakaway furniture have you got? . . . I like you! Understand? I—I am practically in love!

POPOVA Get away from me—I hate you!

SMIRNOV God, what a woman! Never in my life have I seen anything like her! I'm done for! I'm destroyed! I'm caught in the mousetrap like a mouse!

POPOVA Get out of here, or I'll shoot!

SMIRNOV Go ahead and shoot! You cannot understand what bliss it would be to die beneath the gaze of those wonderful eyes, to die from a gunshot fired by that small, velvety, dainty hand. . . . I've gone out of my mind! Think it over, come to a decision right now, because once I leave this place, we shall never meet again! Come to a decision. . . . I'm a gentleman, a respectable fellow, I have an income of ten thousand a year . . . if you toss a coin in the air, I can shoot a bullet through it. . . . My horses are superb. . . . Will you be my wife?

POPOVA (*Outraged, brandishes the revolver.*) Shoot! Twenty paces!

SMIRNOV I've gone out of my mind . . . I don't understand a thing . . . (*Shouts.*) You there, water!

POPOVA (*Shouts.*) Twenty paces!

SMIRNOV I've gone out of my mind! I've fallen in love like a little kid—like a fool! (*Grasps her by the arm, she shrieks in pain.*) I love you! (*Gets on his knees.*) I love as I have never loved before! Twenty women I've walked out on, ten have walked out on me, but not one of them did I love the way I love you. . . . I've gone all touchy-feely, I've turned to sugar, I'm limp as a dishrag. . . . I'm kneeling like a fool and offering you my hand. . . . It's a shame, a disgrace! It's five years since I've been in love, I swore never again, and all of a sudden I'm head over heels, out of character like a long peg in a short hole![1] I offer you my hand. Yes or no? You don't want to? You don't have to! (*Gets up and quickly goes to the door.*)

POPOVA Hold on. . . .

SMIRNOV (*Stops.*) Well?

POPOVA Never mind, you can go. . . . Although, hold on. . . . No, go, go away! I hate you! Or no . . . Don't go! Ah, if you'd had any idea how really angry I am, really angry! (*Throws the revolver on the table.*) My fingers are swollen from that awful thing. . . . (*Tears her*

---

1. Chekhov uses the phallic image, *ogloblya v chuzhoy kuzov*, a long shaft in someone else's wagon.

handkerchief in rage.) Why are you standing there? Clear out of here!

SMIRNOV Good-bye.

POPOVA Yes, yes, go away! . . . (*Shouts.*) Where are you off to? Hold on . . . Go on, though. Oh, I'm really angry! Don't come over here, don't come over here!

SMIRNOV (*Crossing to her.*) I'm really angry at myself! I fell in love like a schoolboy, got on my knees. . . . Goosebumps are creeping up and down my skin. . . . (*Rudely.*) I love you! I need to fall in love with you like I need a hole in the head! Tomorrow I've got to pay the interest; hay-making's begun, while you're here. . . . (*Takes her round the waist.*) I'll never forgive myself . . .

POPOVA Get away! Hands off! I . . . hate you! Twenty pa-paces!
  (*A protracted kiss.*)

XI

The same, LUKA *with an axe, the* GARDENER *with a rake, the* COACHMAN *with a pitchfork and* WORKMEN *with staves.*

LUKA (*On seeing the kissing couple.*) Saints in heaven!
  (*Pause.*)

POPOVA (*With downcast eyes.*) Luka, tell the stableboys that Toby gets no oats today.

CURTAIN

Variants to *The Bear*

Lines come from publication in the newspaper *New Times* (*Novoe Vremya*) (NT), the censor's copy (Cens.), the lithographed publication (Lith.), the periodicals *Performer* (*Artist*) (P) and *Alarm Clock* (*Budilnik*) (AC).

After as a guest . . . — for God's sake . . . (NT, Cens., Lith., AC) (Page 10)

After really am angry — devil take me quite! How can I not get angry? (NT) (Page 10)

After have walked out on me — and now I know perfectly well how to behave with them. (NT, Cens, Lith, P, AC) (Page 11)

After fussy — mischievous as kittens, cowardly as rabbits (NT) (Page 11)

After you won't get a kopek! — you'll get it a year from now! (NT, Cens., Lith, P, AC) (Page 13)

After (*Rings.* — *Enter* LUKA.) (NT, Cens., Lith, AC) (Page 13)

After An upstart! — A crude dullard! (NT) (Page 13)

After like a side of bacon! — There won't be a wet patch left on her! (NT) (Page 14)

After A shame, a disgrace! — I feel myself now in such a nasty situation you can't imagine! (NkT, Cens., Lit, P, AB)(Page 16)

Ivanov

Chekhov wrote *Ivanov,* his first work to be staged, at the prompting of the theatrical impresario Korsh and in the wake of the creative gust that produced the important transitional story "The Steppe." Chekhov dashed off the play in a couple of weeks in October 1887, pleased with its "unhackneyed subject" and its lack of longueurs. He defined his own originality this way in a letter to his brother Aleksandr, dated October 24, 1887:

> Modern dramatists pack their plays with angels, cads, and buffoons exclusively—well, go find those elements anywhere in Russia! If you look, you'll find them, but not in such extreme types as playwrights need. . . . I wanted to create something original: I did not portray a single villain or angel (though I could not refrain when it came to buffoons), I did not indict anyone or acquit anyone.

Ivanov was first played at Korsh's Theatre in Moscow on November 19, 1887, for the benefit of Nikolay Svetlov, who created the role of Borkin; it enjoyed a mixed success. The actors' praise and the audience's plaudits made Chekhov euphoric, and he wrote to Aleksandr, "You can't imagine what's happened! From that insignificant turd that is my playlet . . . the devil knows what has occurred . . . in his thirty-two years in the theater, the prompter had never seen anything like it." He triumphantly signed himself, "Schiller, Shakespearovich Goethe" (to Aleksandr, November 24, 1887). But his younger brother Mikhail recalled the event differently: "The success of the performance was uneven; some hissed; others, the majority, noisily applauded and called for the author; but in general *Ivanov* was misunderstood, and for a long time afterwards the newspapers were explicating the personality and character of its leading hero." The impressionable playwright gradually came to the conclusion that the audience had welcomed Ivanov himself as a distillation of the zeitgeist. His mooning and moaning and his fits of self-castigation summed up for the generation of the 1880s its own pusillanimous torpor during the "dark decade," a period of political repression and social inaction. Ivanov's death provided a vicarious expiation.

That was not what Chekhov had had in mind. Superficially, Ivanov—his name the Russian equivalent of "Jones"—seemed another common- or garden-variety "superfluous man"; Chekhov described him as "a university graduate, in no way remarkable; a somewhat excitable, ardent nature, strongly inclined to honorable and straight-forward enthusiasm, like most educated gentry." His past was nobler than his present: his projects for serving the people, rational farming, and higher education have evaporated. Chekhov, however, wanted to avoid idealizing this disillusionment, by then a stale treatment, focusing instead on an examination by the character himself of the reasons for his empty life and contemptible behavior. Ivanov was to suffer through his own awareness of wasted potential and vestigial honor. A basic dramatic problem was keeping the audience from romanticizing Ivanov's pessimism and, at the same time, keeping Ivanov from looking like the immoralist that Doctor Lvov makes him out to be.

The stage portrayal of this complex inner turmoil was tricky for an inexperienced playwright, trying to employ age-old strategies of dramatic carpentry to contain a rich psychological subject. Basically, the "plot" might have come from a typical society melodrama: A scoundrel abandons his exploited wife in hopes of repairing his fortunes by wedding a young heiress. This sensational storyline is how Ivanov's actions look to outsiders such as Lvov. Ibsen had already managed to sublimate such a triangle into the internalized conflicts of *Rosmersholm* (1886), with the bedeviled intellectual Rosmer torn between coequal calls to duty. Chekhov, however, was constrained to write long expository speeches, endless explanations, confessions, and acts of contrition to counter his audience's preconceptions of heroism and villainy.

The earliest revision was for the Alexandra Theater in St. Petersburg. Chekhov wrote, "Now my Mr. Ivanov will be much better understood. The finale doesn't satisfy me exactly (except for the shooting, everything is weak), but I am comforted that its form is still not finished" (December 19, 1888). Originally, Ivanov had died on stage of a heart attack; Chekhov realized that this posed a problem for an actor while it undermined the real causes of Ivanov's destruction.

The play's lifeblood is gossip. In the first act, we hear of slanderous rumors about Ivanov, but no one takes them too seriously. In the second act, the school for scandal is in session at Lebedev's home, but the gossipmongers are so caricatured that again their power to harm is discounted. Ivanov is now associated with Borkin's shady machinations, however. In Act Three, Lebedev still refuses to believe the tattle, though he warns Ivanov about it. Aided by Lvov, the rumors reach Anna's ears, provoking her confrontation with her husband and her collapse. In the play's first version, this theme continued into Act Four, with even Lebedev succumbing to doubts about

Anna's death. Ivanov, definitively charged with villainy by the Doctor, dies of a heart attack "because", said Chekhov, "he can't endure the outrageous insult" (letter to Aleksandr, November 20, 1887).

This turned the play into a tract about provincial narrowmindedness, and, indeed, many contemporary critics described Ivanov as the honorable but vacillating victim of scandalmongers. So Chekhov added Sasha to the attackers in Act Four, and had Ivanov taking active measures in his own defense. He gave him a long monologue about dreams of becoming the young Ivanov once more. "If Ivanov turns out looking like a cad or a superfluous man, and the doctor is a great man . . . then, obviously, my play won't come off, and there can be no talk of a production" (to Suvorin, December 30, 1888).

Doctor Lvov therefore needed touching up. In traditional drama, doctors were *raisonneurs*, whose sagacious moralizing clued the audience into the way to think about the characters. Lvov, however, does not heal breaches; he creates them through his purblind and self-righteous assumptions. In this respect, he much resembles Gregers Werle in Ibsen's *The Wild Duck*, who, in his quixotic attempt to strip away illusions, destroys the lives of those around him. Chekhov's task was to make sure that Lvov did not come across either as an objective spokesman or as a fatuous prig. "Such persons are necessary, and for the most part sympathetic. To draw them as caricatures, even in the interests of the stage, is dishonorable and serves no purpose" (to Suvorin, December 30, 1888).

Rehearsals for the Petersburg production went badly, despite a strong cast, and Chekhov quarreled with the comic actor Vladimir Davydov, who played the lead in a monotonous style to indicate seriousness. The opening night was a huge success, but Chekhov sneaked away, regarding the ovation as a binge that would later give him a severe hangover. He continued to revise *Ivanov*, dropping one comic character, Dudkin, and generally toning down the farcical elements. A third version appeared in 1889, with more explanations between Lvov and Anna and the removal of Ivanov's dream monologue in the last act. He intended to "sum up everything that's been written so far about whining and languishing people, and in my *Ivanov* put an end to such writing" (to Suvorin, January 7, 1889). This determination shows the revised *Ivanov* to be not a reconstruction of his earlier play, but instead a counterblast to it and its ilk. Even then, Chekhov was not content; he kept touching it up until 1901.

Chekhov never managed to eliminate the mannerisms of boulevard drama that vitiated the subtlety of his concept. The Act Two curtain, with a consumptive wife intruding on her husband in the arms of another woman, is effective claptrap; at least we are spared the fainting described in the next act. Scenes of vituperation rise, in the best melodrama manner, to one consummate insult: "Kike bitch," Ivanov screams at Anna in his ugliest moment; "Bastard" (or "Cad", "Villain"—*podlets* is too dated to be translated easily) is the summation of Lvov's contempt for Ivanov. Chekhov was to handle the slanging match between Arkadina and Treplyov in *The Seagull* more dexterously. Even the final suicide is, as the critic Kugel opined, "a sacrifice made by Chekhov's soul to the god of theatrical gimmickry," literally ending the play with a bang. It may have been copied directly from Luka Antropov's popular comedy-melodrama *Will-o'-the-Wisps* (1873).

For a modern audience, the play anti-Semitic slurs in *Ivanov* are a problem. The Jews were the largest and most persecuted minority in the Russian Empire, officially segregated into an area of Western and Southern Russia known as the Pale of Settlement. Seen as aliens, they were severely limited as to education and profession as well as residence, heavily taxed, and often subjected to the periodic massacres known as pogroms. Although Chekhov privately used the slighting term *zhid* ("yid," "kike") without thinking twice, at a time when anti-Semitism was public policy his tolerance and lack of prejudice were exceptional. His fiction is filled with admirable or sympathetic Jewish characters. Two years before he wrote *Ivanov*, he may have proposed to the Jewish Yevdokiya Éfros. Later, her husband, the lawyer Yefim Konovitser, became one of many Jews on friendly terms with Chekhov; another was the painter Isaak Levitan. In 1898, Chekhov broke with his close friend and associate, the publisher Suvorin, because Suvorin's newspapers supported the anti-Semitic faction in the Dreyfus affair.

Ivanov is shown married to a Jew as a token of his quixotic social idealism. It is akin to a white South African marrying a Zulu woman in protest against apartheid. Ivanov's revulsion from Anna is indicative of his general loss of ideals. The comedown from his once noble if unrealistic stance to his present moral torpor is revealed at the end of Act Three, when he insults her. In contrast, Count Shabelsky's Jewish jokes are awkward displays of affection; there were more of them in the play's earlier version, wherein Anna is referred to as a "*rebbitzin*" or "rabbi's wife."

Even toned down, the comic characters in the revised version were little more than a series of tics; they hardly seem to exist on the same plane as the leads. Kosykh is nothing more than his obsession with card playing; Zinaida becomes the epitome of her stinginess, "Gooseberry Preserves." Gradually, Chekhov learned how to make farcical elements more revelatory of his plays' inner meanings. On the other hand, Shabelsky's reluctant wooing of a rich widow sardonically comments on Ivanov's own conscience-stricken interest in Sasha. Here the comedy has the Shakespearean function of a reflective subplot, with the result that "two weddings are spoiled."

Within the conventional framework, however, a Chekhovian sense of atmospherics begins to emerge. He knew well the resonance that derived from a properly chosen setting, and structured the play to alternate private and public life. We first see Ivanov *solus*, seated in a natural surrounding against the background of his house. He is outside the house because it represents to him a suffocating prison to be escaped. The primal image of isolated Ivanov is almost immediately shattered by Borkin with his gun. The unused firearm of the opening will be recalled in the gunshot that ends the play.

As if to exacerbate the incursions into his privacy, Ivanov flees to a more peopled spot, the party at the Lebedevs', but there the guests are already yawning at the very boredom he hoped to avoid. Act Two begins in a crowd of persons, some so anonymous as to be designated merely as FIRST GUEST and SECOND GUEST. This chorus makes common knowledge deeds performed in private. Even before Ivanov and Shabelsky appear, their lives are trotted forth as slander and conjecture; Ivanov's innermost motives are distorted and his most intimate action here, the embrace of Sasha, is intruded upon by the worst possible witness, his wife.

Act Three returns to Ivanov's study, which ought to be his sanctum, but is, as the stage direction makes clear, a jumble—a visual metaphor for the disorder of his existence. His papers, presumably the products of his brain and the instruments of his labor, lie cheek by jowl with food and drink, consumed by others who expatiate on gastronomy. Coming as it does after Anna's melodramatic discovery, this interlude strikes the note of triviality and neutralizes what might otherwise be overly theatrical. It is Chekhov's way of cooling overheated actions by pairing them with the banal. Ivanov himself seems aware of this, for he resents the impinging of his workaday fellows on his moping. Their commentary reduces his soul-searching to cheap and obvious motives.

"It's like living in Australia!" says Kosykh, evoking the provincial barbarity where vast expanses stretch between estates, and yet privacy is impossible. The last act interweaves public and private worlds as the wedding party prepares for benediction before going to church. The event could not be more gregarious, despite the personal nature of the conjugal bond, and the characters have difficulty finding a quiet corner in which to unburden their minds. Ivanov's entrance is regarded as a tactless invasion, a bridegroom seeing the bride before the ceremony, and his self-destruction is enacted before a crowd of horrified onlookers.

Suicide as a public act is the logical climax of Ivanov's continual self-dramatization. The leading male characters put a literary construction on life. The Count and Lebedev tend to compare persons to characters in Gogol, and life to events in French plays and novels;

they quote tags from well-known poems and songs. Ivanov points the comparisons inward: "I am dying of shame at the thought that I, a strong, healthy man, have turned into Hamlet or Manfred, or a superfluous person." Dr. Lvov labels Ivanov a Tartuffe, Molière's classic hypocrite. During the wedding preparations, Ivanov is told not to be a Chatsky, the comic hero of Griboedov's *Woe from Wit* (1823) who regarded his society with scorn and was taken by it to be a madman. Ivanov's problem often seems to be an overabundance of role models, none of which adequately expresses his complexity. Despite the conspectus of opinion that runs from Sasha's hero worship to the malign slanders of the party guests, Ivanov's character does not get beyond his own verbose self-scrutiny. "How can a man see into another man's soul?" he asks Lvov. Chekhov did his best to present the evidence fairly, but he had yet to achieve the proper form.

Ivanov

A Drama in Four Acts

Characters

IVANOV, NIKOLAY ALEKSEEVICH, Permanent member of the Council for Peasant Affairs[1]

ANNA PETROVNA, his wife, born Sarra Abramson[2]

SHABELSKY, MATVEY SEMYONOVICH, Count, his maternal uncle

LEBEDEV, PAVEL KIRILLYCH, Chairman of the Rural Board[3]

ZINAIDA SAVISHNA, his wife

SASHA, the Lebedevs' daughter, twenty years old

LVOV, YEVGENY KONSTANTINOVICH, a young country doctor[4]

BABAKINA, MARFA YEGOROVNA, a young widow, landowner, daughter of a rich merchant

KOSYKH, DMITRY NIKITICH, a tax collector

1. A district committee to supervise self-governing peasant communes; its members might include the district police chief, a justice of the peace, and a "permanent member," a salaried official appointed by the government on the nomination of the Rural Board. The "permanent member" was highly responsible for the control of rural institutions.
2. As a converted Jew, Sarra had to take a Christian saint's name and patronymic.
3. *Zemstvo*, an elective council created in 1864 to administer minor regional economic, educational and sanitary matters; its elected members included both landowners and peasants. Throughout the 1880s, a period of political repression, the *zemstvos* worked sluggishly.
4. "Good grief, all one had to do was pronounce these words for a Russian intellectual, a university student, a coed to make a respectful face. Once a country doctor came onstage, the audience's sympathy was enlisted, he was the 'luminous personality,' the 'social idealist,' he has the right to be the 'positive' character in the play.
   "And suddenly this hero . . . is left alone and says: 'What the hell! It's bad enough *they don't pay me for my visits* . . . etc.' So: one stroke, just one lie, and the mask is off." (V. I. Nemirovich-Danchenko, *Out of the Past* [1938].)

BORKIN, MIKHAIL MIKHAILOVICH, a distant relative of Ivanov and manager of his estate
AVDOTYA NAZAROVNA, an old woman of no fixed profession
YEGORUSHKA, a poor relation of the Lebedevs'
FIRST GUEST
SECOND GUEST
THIRD GUEST
FOURTH GUEST
PYOTR, Ivanov's manservant
GAVRILA, the Lebedevs' manservant
GUESTS of both sexes
MANSERVANTS

The action takes place in a district[5] of Central Russia.

Act One

A garden on IVANOV's *estate. Left, the façade of a house with a veranda. One of the windows is open. In front of the veranda is a broad, semicircular expanse with paths leading straight ahead and to the left, to the garden. At the right, little garden settees and tables. A lamp is lit on one of the latter. Evening is drawing on. At the rise of the curtain one can hear a duet for piano and cello being practiced in the house.*

I

IVANOV *and* BORKIN.
IVANOV *is sitting at a table, reading a book.* BORKIN, *wearing heavy boots and carrying a rifle, appears at the bottom of the garden; he is tipsy; after he spots* IVANOV, *he tiptoes up to him and, when he has come alongside him, aims the gun in his face.*

IVANOV (*On seeing* BORKIN, *shudders and jumps up.*) Misha, God knows what . . . you scared me . . . I'm jittery enough as it is, but you keep playing these stupid jokes . . . (*Sits.*) He scared me, so he's pleased with himself . . .
BORKIN (*Roars with laughter.*) Right, right . . . sorry, sorry. (*Sits beside him.*) I won't do it any more, no more . . . (*Takes off his visored cap.*) It's hot. Would you believe, sweetheart, I've covered over ten miles in something like three hours . . . I've knocked myself out . . . Just feel my heart, the way it's pounding . . .
IVANOV (*Reading.*) Fine, later . . .
BORKIN No, feel it right now. (*Takes his hand and puts it on his*

5. *Guberniya*, a provincial region administered by a governor and divided into counties (*uyezdy*).

chest.) You hear it? Boom-boom-boom-boom-boom-boom-boom. That means I've got heart trouble. Any minute I could keel over and die. Say, would you be sorry if I died?

IVANOV   I'm reading . . . later . . .

BORKIN   No, seriously, would you be sorry if I suddenly up and died? Nikolay Alekseevich, would you be sorry if I died?

IVANOV   Stop pestering me!

BORKIN   Dear boy, tell me, would you be sorry?

IVANOV   I'm sorry that you reek of vodka. It's disgusting, Misha.

BORKIN (*Laughs.*)   I really reek? I can't believe it . . . Actually, I can believe it. At Plesniki I ran into the coroner, and the two of us, I must admit, knocked back about eight drinks apiece. Fundamentally, drinking is very bad for your health. Tell me, is it really bad for a person's health? Is it bad for you?

IVANOV   This is unbearable, for the last time . . . Get it through your head, Misha, that this teasing . . .

BORKIN   Right, right . . . sorry, sorry! . . . Take it easy, sit down . . . (*Gets up and walks away.*) Incredible people, you're not even allowed to talk. (*Comes back.*) Oh, yes! I almost forgot . . . Let's have it, eighty-two rubles! . . .

IVANOV   What eighty-two rubles?

BORKIN   To pay the workmen tomorrow.

IVANOV   I haven't got it.

BORKIN   Thank you very kindly! (*Mimicks him.*) I haven't got it . . . After all, don't the workmen have to be paid? Don't they?

IVANOV   I don't know. I haven't got anything today. Wait 'til the first of the month when I get my salary.[6]

BORKIN   Just try and have a conversation with characters like this! The workmen aren't coming for their money on the first of the month, but tomorrow morning!

IVANOV   What am I supposed to do about it now? Go on, saw me in half, nag at me . . . And where you did you pick up this revolting habit of pestering me whenever I'm reading, writing or . . . ?

BORKIN   What I'm asking you is: do the workmen get paid or not? Eh, what's the use of talking to you! . . . (*Waves his hand in dismissal.*) Landowners too, the hell with 'em, lords of creation . . . Experimental farming methods . . . Nearly three hundred acres of land and not a penny in their pocket . . . It's like a wine cellar without a corkscrew. I'll go and sell the carriage-horses tomorrow! Yes sir! . . . I sold the oats while they were still standing in the field, tomorrow I'll go and sell the rye. (*Strides up and down the stage.*) You think I'll wait for an invitation? Do you? Well, no sir, you're not dealing with that sort of person . . .

6. His government salary as Permanent Member of the Council for Peasant Affairs.

II

The same, SHABELSKY (*offstage*), *and* ANNA PETROVNA.

SHABELSKY'S VOICE (*From the window.*)   It's impossible to play with you . . . You've no more ear than a gefilte fish, and your touch is a disgrace.

ANNA PETROVNA (*Appears in the open window.*)   Who was talking out here just now? Was it you, Misha? Why are you stamping around like that?

BORKIN   Talk to your *Nicolas-voilà*[7] and it'd get you stamping too.

ANNA PETROVNA   Listen, Misha, have them bring some hay to the croquet lawn.

BORKIN (*Waves his hand in dismissal.*)   Leave me alone, please . . .

ANNA PETROVNA   Really, what a tone to take . . . That tone of voice doesn't suit you at all. If you want women to love you, never get angry with them and don't act self-important . . . (*To her husband.*) Nikolay, let's turn somersaults in the hay!

IVANOV   Anyuta, it's bad for your health to stand in an open window. Go in, please . . . (*Shouts.*) Uncle, shut the window!
     (*The window is shut.*)

BORKIN   Don't forget, day after tomorrow, the interest has to be paid to Lebedev.

IVANOV   I remember. I'll be at Lebedev's today and I'll ask them to postpone it . . . (*Looks at his watch.*)

BORKIN   When are you going over there?

IVANOV   Right now.

BORKIN (*Quickly.*)   Hold on, hold on! isn't today, I think, Shu-rochka's birthday? . . . Well, well, well, well . . . And me forgetting all about it . . . What a memory, eh? (*Skips.*) I'll go, I'll go . . . (*Sings.*) I'll go . . . I'll go for a swim, chew some paper, take three drops of ammonia[8] and it's off to a fresh start. . . . Darling, Nikolay Alekseevich, sweetie pie, love of my life, you're always a nervous wreck, no kidding, you're whining, constantly melancholeric,[9] and yet you and I, no kidding, could get a hell of a lot of things done together! I'm ready to do anything for you . . . You want me to marry Marfusha Babakina for your sake? Half the dowry is yours . . . I mean, not half, but all of it, take all of it!

IVANOV   If you're going to talk rot . . .

BORKIN   No, seriously, no kidding, you want me to marry Marfusha?

7. An in-joke for the play's first audiences. *Nicolas-voilà* (French, "It's Nick in the nick o'time!") was a tagline from a song in a musical farce popularized by the actor Davydov, who created the role of Ivanov.
8. Chewing perfumed paper was to sweeten the breath, and taking ammonia was to cure a hangover.
9. Russian, *merlekhlyundiya*, Chekhov's joking version of *melancholy*, which he picked up from medical school slang. Masha repeats it in *Three Sisters*.

Go fifty-fifty in the dowry . . . But why am I talking to you? As if you understood me? (*Mimics him.*) "If you're going to talk rot." You're a good man, an intelligent man, but you haven't got an ounce of, what d'y'call it, you know, get up and go. If only you'd do things in a big way, raise a little hell . . . You're a neurotic, a crybaby, but if you were a normal man, you could make a million in a year's time. For instance, if I had two thousand three hundred rubles right now, in two weeks I'd have twenty thousand. You don't believe me? You think I'm talking nonsense? No, it's not nonsense. Just give me two thousand three hundred rubles, and in a week I'll show you twenty thousand. On the other side of the river Ovsyanov is selling a strip of land, just across from us, for two thousand three hundred rubles. If we buy that strip, we'll own both sides of the riverbank. And if we own both sides, you understand, we have the right to dam the river. Get it? We could put up a mill, and as soon as we announce that we want to build a dam, everyone who lives down river will kick up a fuss, and right away we go *kommen Sie hier*,[1] if you don't want a dam, pay up. Get it? Zarev's factory will pay us five thousand, Korolkov three thousand, the monastery will pay five thousand . . .

IVANOV It's all hocus-pocus, Misha . . . If you want us to stay friends, keep it to yourself.

BORKIN (*Sits at the table.*) Of course! . . . I knew it! You won't do anything yourself, and you tie my hands . . .

III

The same, SHABELSKY, *and* LVOV.

SHABELSKY (*Coming out of the house with Lvov.*) Doctors are just like lawyers, the sole difference being, lawyers only rob you, while doctors rob you *and* kill you . . . Present company excepted. (*Sits on a little settee.*) Quacks, charlatans . . . Perhaps in some Utopia you can come across an exception to the general rule, but . . . over the course of a lifetime I've squandered about twenty thousand and never met a single doctor who didn't strike me as a barefaced imposter.

BORKIN (*To Ivanov.*) Yes, you won't do anything yourself and you tie my hands. That's why we don't have any money . . .

SHABELSKY I repeat, present company excepted . . . There may be exceptions, although, even so . . . (*Yawns.*)

IVANOV (*Closing the book.*) Doctor, what have you got to say?

LVOV (*With a glance at the window.*) The same thing I said this

1. German: "Come here."

morning: She has to go to the Crimea at once. (*Walks up and down the stage.*)

SHABELSKY (*Bursts out laughing.*)   The Crimea! Why don't you and I, Misha, hang out a shingle as medicos? It's so easy . . . A woman sneezes or coughs because she's bored, some Madame Angot or Ophelia.[2] Quick, take a scrap of paper and prescribe along scientific principles: first, a young doctor, then, a trip to the Crimea; in the Crimea, a strapping Tatar . . .

IVANOV (*To the Count.*)   Ah, stop pestering, you pest! (*To* LVOV.) To go to the Crimea, you need money. Suppose I find it, she definitely refuses to take the trip . . .

LVOV   Yes, she does.

(*Pause.*)

BORKIN   Say, Doctor, is Anna Petrovna really so seriously ill that she has to go to the Crimea?

LVOV (*With a glance at the window.*)   Yes, tuberculosis.

BORKIN   Psss! That's no good . . . For some time now I've noticed from her face that she wasn't long for this world.

LVOV   But . . . don't talk so loudly . . . you can be heard in the house . . .

(*Pause.*)

BORKIN (*Sighing.*)   This life of ours . . . Human life is like a posy, growing gloriously in a meadow; a goat comes along, eats it, end of posy . . .

SHABELSKY   Nonsense, nonsense, and more nonsense! (*Yawns.*) Nonsense and monkeyshines.

(*Pause.*)

BORKIN   Well, gentlemen, I keep trying to teach Nikolay Alekseevich how to make money. I've let him in on one wonderful idea, but my pollen, as usual, has fallen on barren ground. You can't hammer anything into him . . . Look at him: melancholy, spleen, tedium, depression, heartache . . .

SHABELSKY (*Rises and stretches.*)   You're a brilliant thinker, you come up with something for everyone, you teach everyone how to live, but you've never taught me a single thing . . . Teach me, Mr. Know-it-all, show me the way to get ahead . . .

BORKIN (*Rises.*)   I'm going for a swim . . . Good-bye, gentlemen . . . (*To the Count.*) You've got twenty ways to get ahead . . . If I were in your shoes, I'd make about twenty thousand in a week. (*Going.*)

SHABELSKY (*Goes after him.*)   What's the gimmick? Come on, teach me.

2. Shabelsky cites literary heroines at random. Madame Angot, a French market-woman of the French Directoire period, renowned for her salty speech, is a character in Charles Lecocq's comic opera *La Fille de Madame Angot* (1872), which Chekhov may have seen in Moscow in 1878. Ophelia is Polonius' daughter, once loved by Hamlet.

BORKIN   There's nothing to teach. It's very easy . . . (*Returns.*) Nikolay Alekseevich, give me a ruble! (IVANOV *silently gives him the
money.*) *Merci!* (*To the Count.*) You've still got a handful of aces.

SHABELSKY (*Going after him.*)   Well, what are they?

BORKIN   In your shoes, in a week I'd make about thirty thousand, if
not more. (*Exits with the Count.*)

IVANOV (*After a pause.*)   Redundant people,[3] redundant talk, the
pressing need to answer stupid questions; Doctor, it's all wearied
me to the point of illness. I've become irritable, touchy, impatient,
so petty that I don't know what I am any more. Whole days at a
time my head aches, I can't sleep, ringing in my ears . . . And
there's   absolutely   nowhere   to   escape   to . . . Absolutely
nowhere . . .

LVOV   Nikolay Alekseevich, I have to have a serious talk with you.

IVANOV   Talk away.

LVOV   It's concerning Anna Petrovna. (*Sits.*) She won't consent to
go to the Crimea, but she might if you went with her.

IVANOV (*After thinking about it.*)   If we were to go together, we'd
need money. Besides, they certainly wouldn't give me a leave of
absence. I've already taken one leave this year . . .

LVOV   Let's assume that's true. Now, moving on. The most important treatment for tuberculosis is absolute peace and quiet, and
your wife doesn't have a moment's peace. She's constantly upset
by the way you treat her. Excuse me, I'm concerned and I'll speak
bluntly. Your behavior is killing her.

(*Pause.*)

Nikolay Alekseevich, give me some cause to think better of you!

IVANOV   It's all true, true . . . I'm probably terribly to blame, but my
mind's messed up, my soul is tied down by a kind of indolence,
and I can't seem to understand myself. I don't understand other
people or myself. (*With a glance at the window.*) They can hear
us. Let's go, let's take a walk.

(*Gets up.*)

My dear friend, I should tell you the story from the very beginning.
But it's long and so complicated that I wouldn't finish before
morning.

(*They walk.*)

Anyuta is a remarkable, an exceptional woman . . . For my sake
she converted to my religion, cast off her father and mother,
turned her back on wealth, and if I'd demanded another hundred
sacrifices, she would have made them without blinking an eye.
Well, sir, there nothing at all remarkable about me and I made no

3. *Lishnye lyudi*, literally, superfluous people, a technical term in Russian culture, popularized by Ivan Turgenev: well-born, well-educated members of society who fail to contribute
anything to it. Ivanov applies the term to himself in Act Two.

sacrifices at all. Though it's a long story . . . the whole gist of it, dear Doctor (*hesitates*), is . . . to make a long story short, I married when I was passionately in love and swore love everlasting, but . . . five years have gone by, she's still in love with me, while I . . . (*Splays his hands in a gesture of futility.*) Now you're going to tell me that she'll die soon, but I don't feel any love or pity, just a sort of void, weariness. Anyone looking at me from the outside would probably think this is awful; I don't understand myself what's going on inside me . . . (*They go off down a garden path.*)

IV

SHABELSKY, *then* ANNA PETROVNA.

SHABELSKY (*Enters, roaring with laughter.*)   Honest to God, he's not a crook, he's a visionary, a virtuoso! Ought to put up a monument to him. He's a thorough blend of modern pus in all its variety: lawyer, doctor, speculator, accountant. (*Sits on a low step of the veranda.*) And yet he seems never to have gone to school anywhere, that's what's amazing . . . What a brilliant criminal he probably would have been, if he'd picked up a bit of culture, the liberal arts! "In a week," he says, "you could have twenty thousand. You've got a hand full of aces," he says, "your title as Count." (*Roars with laughter.*) "Any girl with a dowry would marry you" . . .

(ANNA PETROVNA *opens the window and looks down.*)

"Want me to make a match between you and Marfusha?" he says. *Qui est ce que c'est* Marfusha?[4] Ah, that Balabalkina creature . . . Babakalkina . . . the one that looks like a washerwoman.

ANNA PETROVNA   Is that you, Count?

SHABELSKY   What's that?

(ANNA PETROVNA *laughs.*)

SHABELSKY (*In a Jewish accent.*)   Vot you should leffing at?

ANNA PETROVNA   I was remembering a certain saying of yours. Remember, you said it at dinner? A thief unchastised, a horse . . . How did it go?

SHABELSKY   A kike baptized, a thief unchastised, a horse hospitalized are not to be prized.

ANNA PETROVNA (*Laughs.*)   You can't even make a simple play on words without malice. You're a malicious person. (*Seriously.*) Joking aside, Count, you are very malicious. Living with you is depressing and terrifying. You're always grumbling, grousing, you think everyone's a scoundrel and a villain. Tell me, Count, frankly: have you ever said anything nice about anyone?

SHABELSKY   What sort of cross-examination is this!

4. Broken French, "Who on earth is this Marfusha?"

ANNA PETROVNA   You and I have been living together under the same roof for five years now, and never once have I heard you speak of people neutrally, without sarcasm or sneering. What harm have people done you? Do you think you're better than everyone else?

SHABELSKY   I certainly don't think that. I'm the same blackguard and swine in man's clothing[5] as everyone else. *Mauvais ton*, an old has-been. I always have a bad word for myself too. Who am I? What am I? I was rich, independent, somewhat happy, and now . . . a parasite, a freeloader, a dislocated buffoon. If I get indignant, if I express disdain, people laugh in my face; if I laugh, they shake their heads at me sadly and say: "the old man's off his rocker" . . . Most of the time, though, they don't listen to me, take no notice of me . . .

ANNA PETROVNA (*Calmly.*)   Screeching again . . .

SHABELSKY   Who's screeching?

ANNA PETROVNA   The owl. It screeches every evening.

SHABELSKY   Let it screech. Things can't get worse than they already are. (*Stretches.*) Ah, my dearest Sarra, just let me win one or two hundred thousand, and then watch me kick up my heels! . . . You wouldn't see me for dust. I'd run away from this dump, from free-loading, and I wouldn't set foot here 'til Doomsday . . .

ANNA PETROVNA   And just what would you do if you won?

SHABELSKY (*After a moment's thought.*)   First of all I'd go to Moscow and listen to gypsy music. Then . . . then I'd scamper off to Paris. I'd rent an apartment, attend the Russian church . . .

ANNA PETROVNA   What else?

SHABELSKY   I'd spend whole days sitting by my wife's grave, lost in thought. I would sit at her grave like that 'til I kicked the bucket. (*Pause.*)

ANNA PETROVNA   That's awfully depressing. Shall we play another duet or something?

SHABELSKY   All right. Get out the music.

(ANNA PETROVNA *exits.*)

V

SHABELSKY, IVANOV, *and* LVOV.

IVANOV (*Appearing on the path with* LVOV.)   Dear friend, you got your degree only last year, you're still young and vigorous, but I'm thirty-five. I have the right to give you advice. Don't marry Jewish girls or neurotics or intellectuals, but pick out something ordinary, drab, without flashy colors or extraneous sounds. Generally speak-

5. Literally, swine in a skullcap. Both this phrase and *mauvais ton* (bad form) are from the last act of Gogol's comedy *The Inspector General* (1836), in a letter defaming town officials.

ing, match your life to a standard pattern. The grayer and more monotonous the background, the better. My dear man, don't wage war singlehanded against thousands, don't tilt at windmills, don't run headfirst into walls . . . God forbid you go in for any experimental farming methods, alternative schools, impassioned speeches . . . Shut yourself up in your shell and go about your petty, God-given business. That's more comfortable, more authentic, more healthy. Whereas the life I've led, what a bore! Ah, what a bore! . . . So many mistakes, injustices, so much absurdity . . . (*On seeing the Count, annoyed.*) You're always spinning around in front of us, Uncle. You never let me have a moment's privacy!

SHABELSKY (*In a tearful voice.*)   Damn it all, there's no place for me anywhere. (*Jumps up and goes into the house.*)

IVANOV (*Shouts after him.*)   There, I'm sorry, I'm sorry. (*To LVOV.*) Why did I have to insult him? No, I'm definitely going to pieces. Got to get a grip on myself. Got to . . .

LVOV (*Overwrought.*)   Nikolay Alekseevich, I've been listening to you and . . . and, excuse me, I'll speak frankly, no beating about the bush. Your voice, your intonations, let alone your words, are so full of heartless egotism, such cold cruelty . . . A person near and dear to you is perishing *because* she is near to you, her days are numbered, while you . . . you cannot love, you take walks, hand out advice, strike poses . . . I cannot find a way to express it, I haven't got the gift of gab, but . . . but I find you deeply repugnant!

IVANOV   Could be, could be . . . A third party might have a clearer picture . . . It's quite possible that you do understand me . . . I'm probably very, very much at fault . . . (*Lends an ear.*) I think the horses have been brought round. I have to go and change . . . (*He walks to the house and stops.*) Doctor, you don't like me and you don't conceal the fact. It does your heart credit. (*Exits into the house.*)

LVOV (*Alone.*)   This damned temper of mine . . . Again I missed my chance and didn't talk to him the way I should . . . I can't talk to him coolly and calmly! No sooner do I open my mouth and say a single word, when something here (*points to his chest*) starts to choke up, goes in reverse, and my tongue cleaves to the roof of my mouth. I hate this Tartuffe,[6] this puffed-up swindler, most heartily . . . Now he's going out . . . His unhappy wife's one pleasure is in his being near her; she breathes through him, pleads with him to spend at least one night with her, and he . . . he cannot . . . For him, you see, the house is stifling and claustrophobic. If he spent even one night at home, he'd put a bullet through his brain from sheer ennui! Poor fellow . . . he needs wide open

---

6. The religious hypocrite in Molière's comedy *Tartuffe; or The Imposter* (1664–67).

spaces, so he can perpetrate some more underhanded acts . . . Oh, I know why you ride over to those Lebedevs every night! I know!

VI

LVOV, IVANOV (*in a hat and overcoat*), SHABELSKY, *and* ANNA PETROVNA.

SHABELSKY (*Coming out of the house with* IVANOV *and* ANNA PETROVNA). Really, *Nicolas*, this is inhuman! You go out every night by yourself and leave us all on our own. Bored stiff, we go to bed at eight o'clock. This is an abomination, not life! How come you can go out and we can't? How come?

ANNA PETROVNA   Count, leave him alone! Let him go, let him . . .

IVANOV (*To his wife.*)   Well, where would you, a sick woman, go? You're sick and you mustn't go out of doors after sundown . . . Ask the doctor here. You're not a child, Anyuta, you have to be sensible . . . (*To the Count.*) And why should *you* go out?

SHABELSKY   I'd go to blue blazes, I'd crawl down a crocodile's gullet rather than stay here. I'm bored! I'm petrified with boredom! Everybody's sick and tired of me. You leave me at home so she won't be bored on her own, and I've nagged her to death, chewed her to pieces!

ANNA PETROVNA   Leave him alone, Count, leave him! Let him go if it gives him pleasure.

IVANOV   Anya, why take that tone? You know I don't go there for pleasure! I have to discuss the terms of the loan.

ANNA PETROVNA   I don't understand why you feel the need to make excuses. Go ahead! Who's keeping you here?

IVANOV   Friends, let's not devour one another! Is this absolutely necessary?

SHABELSKY (*In a tearful voice.*)   *Nicolas*, dear boy, do please take me with you! I'll get an eyeful of those crooks and idiots and, maybe, have some fun. Honestly, I haven't been anywhere since Easter!

IVANOV (*Annoyed.*)   All right, let's go! I'm sick and tired of the lot of you!

SHABELSKY   Really? Well, *merci, merci* . . . (*Merrily takes him by the arm and leads him aside.*) May I wear your straw hat?

IVANOV   You may. Only hurry up, for pity's sake!
(*The Count runs into the house.*)
How sick and tired I am of the lot of you! But what am I saying, my friends? Anya, I'm speaking to you in an impossible tone. This is something new for me. Well, good-bye, Anya, I'll be back by one.

ANNA PETROVNA   Kolya, darling, do stay home!

IVANOV (*Excited.*)   My sweetest, my dearest, unhappy woman, for pity's sake don't keep me from going out at night. It's cruel, unfair on my part, but let me commit this injustice! The house weighs on me like lead! As soon as the sun goes down my mind starts to be poisoned by tedium. Such tedium! Don't ask why it's like that. I don't know myself. I swear to the God we believe in, I don't know! I'm gloomy here, and when you go to the Lebedevs, it's even worse there; you come back from there, it's still gloomy here, and so it goes all night long . . . It's totally hopeless! . . .

ANNA PETROVNA   Kolya . . . then you should stay here! We'll talk about things, the way we used to . . . We'll have some supper together, we'll read . . . The grouch and I practiced lots of duets for you . . . (*Embraces him.*) Do stay!

    (*Pause.*)

I don't understand you. This has been going on all year long. Why have you changed?

IVANOV   I don't know, I don't know . . .

ANNA PETROVNA   And why don't you want me to go out with you in the evenings?

IVANOV   If you must know, then, I suppose I can tell you. It's rather cruel to talk this way, but it's best to get it out . . . When I'm tormented by tedium, I . . . I start to stop loving you. At times like that I run away from you. In short, I have to get out of the house.

ANNA PETROVNA   Tedium? I understand, I understand . . . You know what, Kolya? You should try, as you used to, to sing, laugh, lose your temper . . . Stay here, we'll laugh, have some homemade cordial, and we'll chase away your tedium in a minute. Would you like me to sing something? Or we'll go, sit in your study, in the shadows, the way we used to, and you can tell me about your tedium . . . Your eyes are filled with such pain! I'll gaze into them and cry, and we'll both feel better. . . . (*Laughs and cries.*) Or, Kolya, what? The flowers return every spring, but joy never does?[7] Am I right? Well, go on, go on . . .

IVANOV   Pray to God for me, Anya! (*He goes, stops and thinks.*) No, I can't. (*He exits.*)

ANNA PETROVNA   Go on . . . (*Sits at the table.*)

LVOV (*Paces up and down the stage.*)   Anna Petrovna, make yourself a rule: as soon as the clock strikes six, you have to go to your room and not come out until morning. The evening damp is bad for your health.

ANNA PETROVNA   Your wish is my command, sir.

LVOV   What's "your wish is my command, sir" supposed to mean? I'm talking seriously!

7. A quotation from a folksong.

ANNA PETROVNA   But I don't want to be serious. (*Coughs.*)

LVOV   There, you see, you're coughing already . . .

VII

LVOV, ANNA PETROVNA, *and* SHABELSKY.

SHABELSKY (*Comes out of the house in hat and overcoat.*)   Where's
    Nikolay? Have the horses been brought 'round? (*Goes quickly and
    kisses* ANNA PETROVNA's *hand.*) Good night, lovely lady! (*Makes a
    face.*) Gevalt![8] Excusink me, pliss! (*Rapid exit.*)

LVOV   Buffoon!
        (*Pause; the distant strains of a concertina are heard.*)

ANNA PETROVNA   How boring! . . . Over there the coachmen and the
    cooks are having a dance, while I . . . I'm like a thing that's been
    discarded . . . Yevgeny Konstantinovich, why are you pacing back
    and forth? Come over here, sit down!

LVOV   I can't sit down.
        (*Pause.*)

ANNA PETROVNA   They're playing "The Goldfinch" in the kitchen.
    (*Sings.*) "Goldfinch, goldfinch, where have you been? Drinking
    vodka on the hills so green?" (*Pause.*) Doctor, are your father and
    mother still alive?

LVOV   My father's dead, my mother's alive.

ANNA PETROVNA   Does it bore you when your mother's around?

LVOV   I've no time to be bored.

ANNA PETROVNA (*Laughs.*)   "The flowers return every spring, but joy
    never does." Who quoted that line to me? God help my memory
    . . . I think Nikolay quoted it. (*Lends an ear.*) The owl is screeching
    again!

LVOV   Then let it screech.

ANNA PETROVNA   Doctor, I'm beginning to think that Fate has dealt
    me a losing hand. Most people, who may be no better than I am, lead
    happy lives and never pay for their happiness. But I have paid for
    everything, absolutely everything! . . . And at such a cost! Why am I
    being charged such high interest? . . . My dear man, you're always
    so solicitous of me; you're so tactful, you're afraid to tell me the
    truth, but you think I don't know what sort of illness I have? I know
    all too well. Still, it's boring to talk about . . . (*In a Jewish accent.*)
    Excusink me, pliss! Do you know how to tell funny stories?

LVOV   I don't.

ANNA PETROVNA   Nikolay knows how. And I'm starting to wonder so
    much at the unfairness of people: why don't they reciprocate love
    for love, why do they pay back truth with lies? Tell me: how long

8. Yiddish, "Alas!"

will my father and mother go on hating me? They live nearly forty miles from here, but I can feel their hatred, night and day, even in my dreams. And what can you prescribe to make sense of Nikolay's tedium? He says he stops loving me only in the evenings, when he's gnawed by tedium. I can understand that and put up with it, but imagine if he's fallen out of love with me completely! Of course, that's impossible, but what if all of a sudden? No, no, I mustn't even think about it. (*Sings.*) "Goldfinch, goldfinch, where have you been?" (*Shudders.*) The horrible thoughts I have! . . . Doctor, you're not a family man, so you can't understand a lot of this . . .

LVOV   You wonder . . . (*He sits beside her.*) No, I wonder, wonder at you! Now, explain, spell it out for me, how could you, an intelligent, honorable, almost saintly woman, have let yourself be so brazenly tricked and dragged into this nest of screech owls? Why are you here? What do you have in common with this cold, heartless . . . but let's leave your husband out of it!—what do you have in common with this vacuous, vulgar milieu? Oh, good God in heaven! . . . this constantly grumbling, decrepit, insane count, this creepy super-swindler, Misha, making his vile faces . . . Explain to me, what are you doing here? How did you end up here?

ANNA PETROVNA (*Laughs.*)   That's exactly the way he used to talk . . . Word for word . . . But his eyes are bigger, and when he used to talk about something with enthusiasm, they'd be like glowing coals . . . Keep talking, keep talking!

LVOV (*Rises and waves his hand in dismissal.*)   What am I supposed to talk about? Please go inside . . .

ANNA PETROVNA   You say that Nikolay's this and that, six of one, half of a dozen of the other. How do you know this? Can you really analyze a person in six months' time? Doctor, he's a remarkable man, and I'm sorry that you didn't get to know him two or three years ago. Now he's depressed, taciturn, doesn't do anything, but in the past . . . Such splendor! . . . I fell in love with him at first sight. (*Laughs.*) One glimpse of him and I was caught in the mousetrap, *snap!* He said: let's go . . . I cut myself off from everything, you know, the way people snip off withered leaves with a scissors, and I went . . . (*Pause.*) And now it's different . . . Now he goes to the Lebedevs', to be entertained by other women, while I . . . sit in the garden and listen to the owl screeching. . . .

(THE WATCHMAN *taps.*)[9]

Doctor, don't you have any brothers?

LVOV   No.

(ANNA PETROVNA *sobs.*)

---

9. On Russian country estates, watchmen made rounds tapping on a board to warn intruders of their presence. Also see *Uncle Vanya*, Act Two, and *The Seagull*, Act Four.

Well, what is it now? What's wrong with you?

ANNA PETROVNA (*Rises.*)   I can't help it, Doctor, I'm going to go over there . . .

LVOV   Over where?

ANNA PETROVNA   Where he is . . . I'll drive over there . . . Have them harness the horses . . . (*Runs into the house.*)

LVOV   No, I definitely refuse to practice under such conditions! It's not bad enough that they don't pay me a penny, but they also turn my feelings inside-out! . . . No, I refuse! Enough is enough! . . . (*Goes into the house.*)

CURTAIN

Act Two

A reception room in the Lebedevs' house. There is an entry directly into the garden; doors right and left. Antique, expensive furniture. A chandelier, candelabra, and pictures, all under dustcovers.[1]

I

ZINAIDA SAVISHNA, FIRST GUEST, SECOND GUEST, THIRD GUEST, KOSYKH, AVDOTYA NAZAROVNA, YEGORUSHKA, GAVRILA, MAIDSERVANT, OLD LADY GUESTS, YOUNG LADIES *and* BABAKINA.

ZINAIDA SAVISHNA *is sitting on a sofa. On both sides of her in armchairs are old-lady guests; on straight chairs, young people. In the distance, near the entry to the garden, people are playing cards;*[2] *among the players:* KOSYKH, AVDOTYA NAZAROVNA, *and* YEGORUSHKA. GAVRILA *is standing by the door at right;* THE MAIDSERVANT *is handing round a tray of sweetmeats. Throughout the Act, guests circulate from the garden to the door at right and back again.* BABAKINA *enters through the door at right and heads for* ZINAIDA SAVISHNA.

ZINAIDA SAVISHNA (*Delighted.*)   Sweetheart, Marfa Yegorovna . . .

BABAKINA   How are you, Zinaida Savishna? I'm honored to congratulate you on your birthday girl . . . (*They exchange kisses.*) God bless . . .

ZINAIDA SAVISHNA   Thank you, sweetheart, I'm pleased to see you . . . Well, how are you feeling?

---

1. Furniture in manor houses was kept under dustcovers when a room was unused or the family was away. It is a sign of Zinaida Savishna's niggardliness that it should remain covered during a party.
2. The game being played is whist (Russian, *vint*), closely related to bridge. Each player holds thirteen cards.

BABAKINA Thanks ever so for asking. (*Sits next to the sofa.*) How are you, young people?

(*The guests rise and bow.*)

FIRST GUEST (*Laughs.*) Young people . . . Are you so old?

BABAKINA (*Sighing.*) What place do we have among the youngsters?

FIRST GUEST (*Laughs respectfully.*) For heaven's sake, how can you? You may be what's called a widow, but you could give a nine-point handicap to any young woman.

(GAVRILA *serves* BABAKINA *from a tea tray.*)

ZINAIDA SAVISHNA (*To Gavrila.*) Why are you serving it like that? You should bring some preserves. Gooseberry or something . . .

BABAKINA Don't go to the trouble, thanks ever so . . .

(*Pause.*)

FIRST GUEST Did you come by way of Mushkino, Marfa Yegorovna?

BABAKINA No, Zamishche. The road's better there.

FIRST GUEST True enough, ma'am.

KOSYKH Two spades.

YEGORUSHKA Pass.

AVDOTYA NAZAROVNA Pass.

SECOND GUEST Pass.

BABAKINA Lottery tickets, Zinaida Savishna sweetheart, have gone right through the roof again.[3] Have you ever heard of such a thing? The first drawing already costs two hundred and seventy, and the second well-nigh two hundred and fifty . . . Never heard of any-thing like it . . .

ZINAIDA SAVISHNA (*Sighs.*) It's all very well for those who've got a lot of them . . .

BABAKINA Don't you think so, sweetheart; they may cost a lot, but they make an unprofitable investment for your capital. The insur-ance alone will be the death of you.

ZINAIDA SAVISHNA That's so, but all the same, my dear, you go on hoping . . . (*Sighs.*) God is merciful . . .

THIRD GUEST The way I see it, *Mesdames*, I consider that at the present time it's very unprofitable to have capital at all. Gilt-edged securities may earn very small dividends, but putting money in circulation is extremely risky. As I understand it, *Mesdames*, the man who has capital at the present time is more precarious situation than the man who, *Mesdames* . .

BABAKINA (*Sighs.*) That's so true! (*The* FIRST *yawns.*) How can a person yawn in the presence of ladies!

FIRST GUEST Pardon, mesdames, it was an accident.

3. Russians of limited means made a run on the five-p... interest-bearing lottery tickets issued by the stock exchange in 1864 and 1866; in 1... ...ice was raised and stabilized at a hundred rubles a ticket.

(ZINAIDA SAVISHNA *gets up and exits through the door at right; a prolonged silence.*)

YEGORUSHKA Two diamonds.

AVDOTYA NAZAROVNA Pass.

SECOND GUEST Pass.

KOSYKH Pass.

BABAKINA (*Aside.*) Good Lord, it's so boring, you could drop dead!

II

The same, ZINAIDA SAVISHNA, *and* LEBEDEV.

ZINAIDA SAVISHNA (*Entering from the door right with* LEBEDEV, *quietly*). Why are you planted out there? What a prima donna! Sit with the guests. (*Sits in her former place.*)

LEBEDEV (*Yawns.*) Ugh, forgive us sinners! (*On seeing* BABAKINA.) Good Lord, our pot of jam is sitting here! Our Turkish delight! (*Greets her.*) How is your most precious little self?

BABAKINA Thanks ever so.

LEBEDEV Well, hallelujah! . . . Hallelujah! (*Sits in an armchair.*) Well, well . . . Gavrila!

(GAVRILA *serves him a shot of vodka and a glass of water. He drinks the vodka and chases it down with water.*)

FIRST GUEST Your very good health!

LEBEDEV What do you mean, good health? I have croaked yet, and I'm thankful for that. (*To his wife.*) Zyuzyushi, where's our birthday girl?

KOSYKH (*Tearfully.*) Tell me, for heaven's sake: how come we didn't take a single trick? (*Leaps up.*) Well, why did we lose, damn it all to hell!

AVDOTYA NAZAROVNA (*Leaps up, angrily.*) Because, my good man, if you don't know how to play, don't sit in. Since when are you entitled to lead somebody else's suit? That's how you got stuck with that pickly ace of yours!

(*They both come out from behind the table.*)

KOSYKH (*In a tearful voice.*) If I may, my friends . . . I was holding diamonds: ace, king, queen, jack and eight low cards, ace of spades and one, you understand, one lousy little heart, and she, for some damn reason, couldn't call a little slam! . . . I bid no trumps . . .

AVDOTYA NAZARONA (*Interrupting.*) I'm the one who bid no trumps! You bid: two no trumps . . .

KOSYKH This is a disg . . . If I may . . . you had . . . I had . . .

4. To lead is to play the first card of one's suit. A trick is the four cards played in each round. A slam is obtaining all tricks in one hand. A trump is the last card dealt out—the turn-up. To call for a . . . signal one's partner to lead trumps.

you had . . . (*To* LEBEDEV.) Now you be the judge, Pavel Kirillych
. . . I was holding diamonds: ace, king, queen, jack and eight low
cards . . .

LEBEDEV (*Covers up his ears.*)   Stop, do me a favor . . . stop . . .

AVDOTYA NAZAROVNA (*Shouts.*)   I was the one who bid: no trumps!

KOSYKH (*Fiercely.*)   Call me a villain and an outcast if I ever sit down
to play with that old stickleback again! (*Quickly exits into the garden.*)

> (*The* SECOND GUEST *follows him out.* YEGORUSHKA *remains at
> the table.*)

AVDOTYA NAZAROVNA   Oof! . . . He's got me all overheated. . . . Stickleback! . . . Stickleback yourself!

BABAKINA   Well, now you've gone and lost your temper, granny!

AVDOTYA NAZAROVNA (*On seeing* BABAKINA, *throws up her hands.*)   My
honeybun, my beauty! . . . She's here, and, blind as a biddy, I
didn't see her . . . Sweetie-pie . . . (*Kisses her on the shoulder and
sits beside her.*) What a treat! Let me take a good look at you, my
snow-white swan! Poo, poo, poo . . . evil eye begone![5]

LEBEDEV   Well, now she's wound up . . . You'd better find her a
bridegroom . . .

AVDOTYA NAZAROVNA   And I will! I won't go quiet to my grave, with
all my sins on my head, until I get her married and your Sanichka
too! I won't go quiet . . . (*Deep sigh.*) Only there now, where are
you to find bridegrooms nowadays? There they sit, these bridegrooms of ours, as crestfallen as drenched roosters! . . .

THIRD GUEST   An extremely feeble simile. The way I look at it, *Mesdames*, if young people nowadays prefer a celibate life, the guilty
party is, so to speak, social conditions . . .

LEBEDEV   Now, now! No philosophizing! I don't care for it!

III

The same and SASHA.

SASHA (*Enters and goes up to her father.*)   Such splendid weather,
and you're sitting in here, ladies and gentlemen, in this stuffy air.

ZINAIDA SAVISHNA   Sashenka, don't you see that Marfa Yegorovna is
here?

SASHA   Sorry. (*Goes to* BABAKINA *and greets her.*)

BABAKINA   You're getting to be quite standoffish, Sanichka, quite
standoffish, haven't paid me a single visit. (*Exchanges kisses.*) Congratulations, sweetheart . . .

SASHA   Thank you. (*Sits next to her father.*)

---

5. Since compliments might attract envy and, hence, the evil eye, bad luck was averted by
spitting three times over one's shoulder.

LEBEDEV Yes, Avdotya Nazarovna, it's hard to find bridegrooms nowadays. Not just bridegrooms—you can't get a passable best man. The young people these days, no offense meant, have, God bless them, an off taste, like leftovers reheated . . . Can't dance or talk or have a serious drink with 'em . . .

AVDOTYA NAZAROVNA Well, drinking's one thing they know all about, just let 'em at it . . .

LEBEDEV There's no great trick to drinking. Even a horse knows how to drink . . . No, I'm talking serious drinking! In our time, used to be, you'd get worn out at lectures all day long, and as soon as it was dark, you'd go straight to wherever a fire was blazing and spin like a top 'til dawn came up . . . And you'd dance, and flirt with the young ladies, and that took know-how. (*Flicks himself on the throat.*[6]) Used to be, you'd blather and philosophize 'til your jaw came unhinged . . . But nowadays . . . (*Waves his hand in dismissal.*) I don't understand . . . They're wishy-washy, neither this nor that. In the whole district there's only one decent fellow, and he's married (*sighs*) and it looks like he's starting to go crazy too . . .

BABAKINA Who's that?

LEBEDEV Nikolasha Ivanov.

BABAKINA Yes, he's a good man (*makes a face*), only so unhappy! . . .

ZINAIDA SAVISHNA You said it, sweetheart. How can he be happy? (*Sighs.*) What a mistake he made, poor thing! He married his kike bitch[7] and figured, poor thing, that her father and mother would heap mountains of gold on her, but it came out quite the opposite . . . From the time she converted, her father and mother wouldn't have anything to do with her, cursed her . . . Not a penny did he get out of them. He's sorry for it now, but it's too late . . .

SASHA Mama, that's not true.

BABAKINA (*Heatedly.*) Shurochka, why isn't it true? After all, everybody knows it. If it weren't for gain, why else would he marry a Jew girl? Aren't there plenty of Russians? He miscalculated, sweetheart, miscalculated . . . (*Vigorously.*) Lord, and now doesn't he make it hot for her! Simply laughable. He'll come home from somewhere and right away he goes: "Your father and mother cheated me! Get out of my house!" And where can she go? Father and mother won't take her in, she could become a housemaid, but she wasn't brought up to work . . . So he rags on her and rags on her, until the Count stands up for her. If it weren't for the Count, he would have done her in long ago . . .

AVDOTYA NAZAROVNA Besides that, sometimes he locks her up in the

6. A gesture meaning "Let's get drunk."
7. Zinaida Savishna uses the abusive term *zhidovka* (female kike or yid), whereas Babakina uses the slightly more respectful *yevreika* (Jewess).

cellar with "Eat your garlic, you so-and-so!"[8] . . . She eats it and
eats it, 'til she starts to stink from the inside out.

> (*Laughter.*)

SASHA   Papa, that's got to be another lie!

LEBEDEV   Well, so what? Let 'em gossip if it keeps 'em healthy . . .
(*Shouts.*) Gavrila!

> (GAVRILA *serves him vodka and water.*)

ZINAIDA SAVISHNA   So that's why he's ruined, poor thing. His business, sweetheart, has quite fallen off . . . If Borkin weren't looking
after the estate, there wouldn't be anything for him and his kike
bitch to eat. (*Sighs.*) As for us, sweetheart, the way we've suffered
on account of him! . . . Suffered so much that only God can tell!
Would you believe, my dear, for three years now, he's owed us
nine thousand?

BABAKINA (*Horrified.*)   Nine thousand!

ZINAIDA SAVISHNA   Yes . . . It was that hubby dear of mine who
arranged to lend it to him. He can't tell the difference between
someone you can lend to and someone you can't. The principal
I've given up on already, may it rest in peace, but I wish he'd pay
the interest on time.

SASHA (*Heatedly.*)   Mama, you've told us about this a thousand times
already!

ZINAIDA SAVISHNA   What's got into you? Why are you standing up
for him?

SASHA (*Rises.*)   But how can you have the heart to say such things
about a man who never did you any harm? Why, what has he done
to you?

THIRD GUEST   Aleksandra Pavlovna, if I may put in a word or two! I
respect Nikolay Alekseich and always considered it an honor to
know him, but, entre nous, he strikes me as a confidence trickster.

SASHA   Well, bully for you, if that's how he strikes you.

THIRD GUEST   In evidence I proffer the following item, which was
related to me by his attaché or, so to speak, cicerone[9] Borkin. Two
years ago, during the cattle epidemic, he bought livestock, insured
them . . .

ZINAIDA SAVISHNA   Yes, yes, yes! I remember that incident. I've heard
about it too.

THIRD GUEST   Insured them, mind you, then infected them with
cowpox and collected the insurance money.

SASHA   Ah, that's all nonsense! Nonsense! Nobody bought cattle and

---

8. Anti-Semitic prejudice held that garlic was a favorite food of Jews and that they stank of
it.
9. Italian, a guide who shows antiquities. The pretentious Third Guest is misusing foreign
words.

infected them! Borkin himself concocted that scheme and bragged
about it all over the place. When Ivanov found out about it, Borkin
had to beg his forgiveness for two weeks running. Ivanov's only
fault is that he's a soft touch and doesn't have the heart to kick
Borkin out. His fault is that he trusts people too much! Everything
he had has been filched and pilfered from him; because of his
generous projects anyone who wanted could make a fortune out
of him.

LEBEDEV   Shura's a hothead! That'll do!

SASHA   Why do they talk such nonsense about him? Ah, all this is
boring, so boring! Ivanov, Ivanov, Ivanov—there's no other topic
of conversation. (*Goes to the door and returns.*) I'm amazed. (*To
the young people.*) I am truly amazed at your patience, gentlemen!
Aren't you bored just sitting here this way? The very air is con-
densing with ennui! Say something, entertain the young ladies,
show signs of life! Well, if all you can talk about is Ivanov, then
laugh, sing, dance, something . . .

LEBEDEV (*Laughs.*)   Tell 'em off, tell 'em off good and proper.

SASHA   Well, listen, just do me this favor! If you don't want to talk,
laugh, sing, if that's all a bore, I beg you, I implore you, at least
once in your life, out of curiosity, just as a surprise or a practical
joke, gather your strength and suddenly think up something witty,
brilliant—at least say something outrageous or obscene—so long
as it's funny and original! Or suddenly come up with something
infinitesmal, barely perceptible, but the tiniest bit like an achievement, so that the ladies, at least once in their lives, might look at
you and go, "Aah!" Listen, you want to please the ladies, don't
you? Then why don't you make an effort to please them? Ah, gentlemen! You're all wrong, wrong, wrong! . . . One look at you and
the flies drop dead and the lamps go black with soot. Wrong,
wrong! . . . I've told you a thousand times and I'll go on telling you,
that you're all wrong, wrong, wrong!

IV

The same, IVANOV, *and* SHABELSKY.

SHABELSKY (*Entering with* IVANOV *from the door at right.*)   Who's
speechifying around here? You, Shurochka! (*Roars with laughter
and shakes her hand.*) Congratulations, my angel, may God postpone your death and make sure you're not reincarnated . . .

ZINAIDA SAVISHNA (*Gleefully.*)   Nikolay Alekseevich, Count! . . . .

LEBEDEV   Bah! Who do I see? . . . Count! (*Goes to meet him.*)

SHABELSKY (*On seeing* ZINAIDA SAVISHNA *and* BABAKINA, *extends his
arms in their direction.*)   Two goldmines on one sofa! A sight for

sore eyes! (*Greets them; to* ZINAIDA SAVISHNA.) How are you, Zyu-zyushka? (*To* BABAKINA.) How are you, my little puff-ball?

ZINAIDA SAVISHNA I'm so pleased. You're such an infrequent guest here, Count! (*Shouts.*) Gavrila, tea! Please, take a seat! (*Gets up, exits through the door right, and immediately returns with an extremely preoccupied look.*)

  (SASHA *sits in her former seat.* IVANOV *silently exchanges greet-ings with everyone.*)

LEBEDEV (*to* SHABELSKY.) Where've you turned up from out of the blue? What wild horses have dragged you here? This is a surprise, or I'll be damned . . . (*Kisses him.*) Count, you're a real cutthroat! Respectable people don't behave this way! (*Takes him by the arm down to the footlights.*) Why haven't you visited us? Angry or some-thing?

SHABELSKY How am I supposed to visit you? Flying on a broomstick? I haven't got horses of my own, and Nikolay won't take me with him, makes me stay with Sarra so she won't get bored. Send your own horses for me, and then I'll pay you a visit . . .

LEBEDEV (*Waves his hand in dismissal.*) Oh, sure! . . . Zyuzyushka would rather drop dead than use the horses. Old pal, dear man, you really are dearer and sweeter to me than the lot of them! Of all the old-timers, you and I are the only ones left! "In you I love my bygone suff'rings, In you I love my wasted youth."[1] Joking aside, I could almost weep. (*Kisses the Count.*)

SHABELSKY Cut it out, cut it out! You smell like a wine cellar . . .

LEBEDEV Dear heart, you can't imagine how bored I am without my friends! Ready to hang myself from tedium . . . (*Quietly.*) Zyu-zyushka and her moneylending have driven away all the respect-able people, there's only Zulus left . . . these Dudkins,[2] Budkins . . . Here, have some tea.

  (GAVRILA *serves the Count tea.*)

ZINAIDA SAVISHNA (*Worried, to* GAVRILA.) Well, how are you serving it? You should bring some preserves . . . Gooseberry or some-thing . . .

SHABELSKY (*Roars with laughter; to* IVANOV.) There, didn't I tell you? (*To* LEBEDEV.) I made a bet with him on the way that, as soon as we got here, Zyuzyushka would immediately offer us gooseberry preserves . . .

ZINAIDA SAVISHNA Count, you're still the same scoffer . . . (*Sits.*)

LEBEDEV Twenty kegs they made of it, how else can you get rid of the stuff ?

1. Lines from Lermontov's poem "No, 'tis not thee I love so warmly" (1841), which was set to music by at least three contemporary composers.
2. Dudkin (Mr. Bagpipe), "son of a rich factory owner," was a character in the first version of *Ivanov*. Chekhov cut Dudkin from the script in the interests of a more serious play, and divided his lines between First and Third Guests.

SHABELSKY (*Sitting beside the table.*)   Still saving up, Zyuzyushka? Well now, are you a millionaire yet, eh?

ZINAIDA SAVISHNA (*With a sigh.*)   Yes, if you judge by appearances, nobody's richer than we are, but where's the money coming from? Nothing but talk . . .

SHABELSKY   Well, yes, yes! . . . We know! . . . "We know how badly you play chess"[3] . . . (*To* LEBEDEV.) Pasha, tell me on your honor, have you saved up a million?

LEBEDEV   For heaven's sake, I don't know. You'd better ask Zyuzyushka . . .

SHABELSKY (*to* BABAKINA.)   And my chubby little puffball is soon going to have a little million! Good grief, she's getting prettier and plumper not by the day, but by the hour! That's what it means to have lots of dough . . .

BABAKINA   Thanks ever so, your highness, only I don't like being made fun of.

SHABELSKY   My dearest goldmine, how am I making fun of you? It's simply a cry from the heart, a spontaneous overflow of feelings that finds issue at my lips . . . I love you and Zyuzyushka infinitely . . . (*Merrily.*) Excitement! . . . Ecstasy! I can't gaze on either one of you indifferently . . .

ZINAIDA SAVISHNA   You're just the same as ever. (*To* YEGORUSHKA.) Yegorushka, put out the candles! Why do you let them burn for no reason, if you're not playing?

    (YEGORUSHKA *is startled; puts out the candles and sits down.*)
(*To* IVANOV.)   Nikolay Alekseevich, how is your lady wife getting on?

IVANOV   Badly. Today the doctor definitely confirmed that she has tuberculosis . . .

ZINAIDA SAVISHNA   You don't say so? What a pity! (*Sighs.*) We're all so fond of her.

SHABELSKY   Hogwash! . . . It's not tuberculosis, just medical quackery, hocus-pocus. Æsculapius[4] wants to hang around, so he comes up with tuberculosis. Luckily the husband's not the jealous type. (IVANOV *makes a gesture of impatience.*) As for Sarra herself, I don't trust a single one of her words or movements. In my whole life I've never trusted doctor or lawyers or women. Hogwash, quackery, and hocus-pocus!

LEBEDEV (*To* SHABELSKY.)   You're an incredible character, Matvey! . . . You put on this misanthrope act and show it off like a retarded kid with a new toy. You're as human as anyone else, but once

---

3. A line from Gogol's *Dead Souls*: the blustering Nozdryov says it to Chichikov when they are playing chess for a stake of the former's dead serfs.
4. Ancient Greek god of medicine; in this Latin form, a fanciful term for a physician.

you start talking, it's as if your tongue were spewing poison or you had a hacking cough . . . Yes, honest to God!

SHABELSKY   What am I supposed to do? Be lovey-dovey with swindlers and scoundrels, I suppose?

LEBEDEV   Just where do you see swindlers and scoundrels?

SHABELSKY   Present company excepted, of course, but . . .

LEBEDEV   There's that "but" of yours . . . This is all an act.

SHABELSKY   An act . . . You're lucky you don't have any sort of worldview.

LEBEDEV   Why should I have a worldview? I sit, expecting to drop dead any minute. That's my worldview. You and I, my boy, haven't got time to concoct worldviews. That's how it goes . . . (*Shouts.*) Gavrila!

SHABELSKY   You've Gavrila-ed it up enough already . . . Look how red your nose has got! . . .

LEBEDEV (*Drinks.*)   Never mind, dear heart . . . I'm not going to get married today.

ZINAIDA SAVISHNA   It's been a long time since Dr. Lvov paid us a call. He's quite forgotten us.

SASHA   My pet peeve. A sense of decency on two legs. He can't ask for some water or smoke a cigarette without showing off his exceptional decency. Walking or talking, it's tattooed on his forehead: *I am a decent person!* It's boring to have him around.

SHABELSKY   Narrowminded, strait-laced sawbones! (*Mocks him.*) "Clear the way for precious honest toil!" He squawks at every step like a parrot, and thinks he's actually a second Dobrolyubov.[5] Anyone who doesn't squawk is a lowlife. His views are wonderful in their profundity. If a peasant is well off and lives like a human being, that means he's a lowlife, money-grubbing exploiter.[6] I wear a velvet jacket, and a valet helps me dress—I'm a lowlife too, and a slave-owner.[7] So decent, so decent that decency is oozing from every pore! He can't find a place good enough for him. He's got me scared. . . . Honest to God! . . . Look at him sideways, out of a sense of duty he'll punch you in the snoot or call you a lowlife.

IVANOV   He has been awfully hard to take, but all the same I like him. There's something sincere about him.

SHABELSKY   A pretty sort of sincerity! Last night he walks up to me and out of the blue: "Count, I find you deeply repugnant!" Thank

5. Nikolay Aleksandrovich Dobrolyubov (1836–1861), liberal critic and journalist, who had a great influence over Russian youth in the 1860s. His article on Ostrovsky's plays, "The Kingdom of Darkness," suggested that Russia was in thrall to conservative, domestic tyranny. The term "kingdom of darkness" crops up in Borkin's compliments in the next scene.
6. *Kulak*, literally, fist; applied to sharp-dealing, tight-fisted tradesmen and rich peasants.
7. Since the serfs were not emancipated until 1861, Shabelsky probably owned serfs in his youth.

you very kindly! And it's not done simply, but tendentiously: his voice quavers, and his eyes blaze, and his knees knock together . . . To hell with his stilted sincerity! So he thinks I'm repulsive, nasty, that's natural enough . . . So do I, but why say it to my face? I may be a trashy person, but, after all, be that as it may, I've got gray hairs . . . Untalented, insensitive decency!

LEBEDEV Well, well, well! . . . I guess you've been young once your-self and can understand.

SHABELSKY Yes, I was young and foolish, in my time I played Chat-sky,[8] unmasking villains and swindlers, but never in my life did I call a thief a thief to his face or mention the rope in the hanged man's house. I was well-bred. But this dimwitted sawbones of ours would feel he had reached the pinnacle of his mission, seventh heaven, if fate gave him the chance, in the name of principles and humane ideals, to bash me in the snoot in public or hit me below the belt.

LEBEDEV All young people have their quirks. I had an uncle who was a follower of Hegel[9] . . . he used to invite a houseful of guests, get drunk, stand on a chair and go: "You're ignoramuses! You're going to Hell! A new dawn awaits!" Blah-blah, blah-blah, blah-blah . . . He'd keep telling them off . . .

SASHA What did the guests do?

LEBEDEV Nothing. . . . They'd listen and go on drinking. Once, though, I challenged him to a duel . . . My own uncle. All on account of Francis Bacon.[1] I remember I was sitting, God help my memory, just the way Matvey is, and my uncle and the late Ger-asim Nilych were standing over there, roughly where Nikolasha is . . . Well, sir, Gerasim Nilych asks me, dear friend, a question. . . .

v

The same and BORKIN *(dressed foppishly, holding a package, skipping and humming, enters from the door at right. A murmur of approval.)*

Together { YOUNG LADIES Mikhail Mikhailovich!
LEBEDEV Michel Michelich! Do my ears deceive me? . . .
SHABELSKY The life of the party!

BORKIN Here I am again! *(Runs over to* SASHA.*)* Noble signorina, I

8. Chatsky is the leading character in Griboedov's comedy *Woe from Wit* (1821–1823), a young man returned from abroad who is disgusted by the hypocrisy of Moscow society. The society, in turn, decides on the basis of his antisocial behavior that he is mad.
9. German philosopher G.W.F. Hegel (1770–1831), whose systematic dialectics rejected irrationality.
1. Francis Bacon (1561–1626), empirical philosopher and natural scientist, who insisted on facts. Bacon's experiential approach is at the furthest pole from Hegel's abstractions.

make so bold as to congratulate the universe on the birth of such a marvelous blossom as yourself . . . As a token of my delight, I venture to present you (*hands over the package*) with fireworks and Bengal lights[2] of my own making. May they light up the night just as you brighten the shadows of this kingdom of darkness. (*Theatrical bow.*)

SASHA Thank you.

LEBEDEV (*Roars with laughter, to* IVANOV.) Why don't you fire this Judas?

BORKIN (*to* LEBEDEV.) Pavel Kirillich! (*To* IVANOV.) My patron . . . (*Sings.*) *Nicolas-voilà*, ho-hi-ho! (*Goes 'round to everyone.*) The most respected Zinaida Savishna . . . The most divine Marfa Yegorovna . . . The most venerable Avdotya Nazarovna. The most highnessy Count . . .

SHABELSKY (*Roars with laughter.*) The life of the party . . . Hardly in the door and the mood's brightened. Have you noticed?

BORKIN Oof, I'm worn out . . . I think I've greeted everyone. Well, what's new, ladies and gentlemen? Nothing special that hits you over the head? (*Vigorously to* ZINAIDA SAVISHNA.) Ah, listen, mamma dear . . . As I'm riding over here just now . . . (*To* GAVRILA.) Let me have some tea, Gavrusha, only no gooseberry preserves! (*To* ZINAIDA SAVISHNA.) As I'm riding over here just now, peasants on the riverbank were stripping bark from your willow bushes. Why don't you lease out your willow bushes?

LEBEDEV (*to* IVANOV.) Why don't you fire this Judas?

ZINAIDA SAVISHNA (*Alarmed.*) Why, that's perfectly true, it never crossed my mind!

BORKIN (*Does gymnastics with his arms.*) I can't sit still . . . Mamma dear, anything special we can turn our hand to? Marfa Yegorovna, I'm in good form . . . I'm in tiptop shape. (*Sings.*) "Once again I stand before you . . ."[3]

ZINAIDA SAVISHNA Organize something, otherwise we'll die of boredom.

BORKIN Ladies and gentlemen, why these long faces? They're sitting around like jurymen in a box! . . . Let's come up with something. What would you enjoy? Truth or dare, jump-rope, tag, dancing, fireworks? . . .

YOUNG LADIES (*Clap their hands.*) Fireworks, fireworks! (*They run into the garden.*)

SASHA (*To* IVANOV.) Why are you so boring today?

IVANOV My head aches, Shurochka, and I'm bored . . .

2. Fireworks used for signaling.
3. The opening line of a gypsy ballad based on a poem by V. I. Krasov. Chekhov also puts this song into the mouth of Dr. Dorn in *The Seagull*.

SASHA   Let's go into the drawing-room.

> (*They go out the door at right; everyone goes into the garden,
> except* ZINAIDA SAVISHNA *and* LEBEDEV.)

ZINAIDA SAVISHNA   That's my idea of a young man: the minute he
arrives, everyone cheers up. (*Turns down the big lamp.*) Since
they're all in the garden, there's no need to leave lights burning.
(*Puts out the candles.*)

LEBEDEV (*Following her.*)   Zyuzyushka, we have to give the guests
something to eat . . .

ZINAIDA SAVISHNA   Look at all these candles . . . no wonder people
think we're rich. (*Puts them out.*)

LEBEDEV (*Following her.*)   Zyuzyushka, for heaven's sake, you
should give people something to eat. . . . They're young, they must
be starving by now, poor things . . . Zyuzyushka . . .

ZINAIDA SAVISHNA   The Count didn't finish his tea. A waste of perfectly good sugar.

LEBEDEV   Drat! . . . (*They go into the garden.*)

VI

IVANOV *and* SASHA.

SASHA (*Entering with* IVANOV *from the door at right.*)   Everyone's
gone into the garden.

IVANOV   That's the way things are, Shurochka. I used to work a lot
and think a lot, and never get tired; now I don't do a thing or think
about anything, and I'm exhausted body and soul. Day and night
my conscience bothers me; I feel that I'm deeply at fault, but
where that fault lies, I can't figure out. And then there's my wife's
illness, lack of money, the constant grumbling, gossip, pointless
talk, that stupid Borkin . . . My home has become loathsome to
me. Living in it is worse than torture. I tell you frankly, Shurochka,
something else that's become unbearable for me is the company
of my wife, who loves me. You are an old friend and you won't
mind if I'm frank. I came to your place to have some fun, but I'm
bored here too, and my home pulls me back again. Forgive me, I'll
leave right away, nice and quietly.

SASHA   Nikolay Alekseevich, I understand you. You're unhappy
because you're lonely. You need someone close to you to love you
and understand you. Only love can reinvigorate you.

IVANOV   Well, is that so, Shurochka? All we need is for an old dead
duck like me to embark on a new love affair! God keep me from
such a disaster! No, Miss Know-it-all, it's got nothing to do with
love affairs. I tell you, as God is my judge, I'll put up with all of it:
the tedium and neurosis and pennilessness and loss of my wife

and premature old age and loneliness, but what I will not put up
with, will not endure, is to make a mockery of myself. I am dying
of shame to think that I, a strong, healthy man, have turned into
a Hamlet or a Manfred, or a redundant person[4] . . . what the hell
is going on! Some pathetic types are flattered when you call them
Hamlets, or redundant, but for me it's a disgrace. It wounds my
pride, shame overwhelms me, and I suffer . . .

SASHA (*Joking, through tears.*)   Nikolay Alekseevich, run away with
me to America.

IVANOV   I feel too listless to walk to that doorway, and you come up
with America . . . (*They walk to the entry to the garden.*) Actually,
Shura, it must be hard for you to go on living here! When I look
at the people around you, it terrifies me: which of them will you
marry? The only hope is for some passing lieutenant or university
student to abduct you and elope . . .

VII

The same and ZINAIDA SAVISHNA.

(ZINAIDA SAVISHNA *comes out of the door at left with a jar of
preserves.*)

IVANOV   Sorry, Shurochka, I'll catch up with you . . .

(SASHA *exits into the garden.*)

Zinaida Savishna, forgive me, I've come here with a request . . .

ZINAIDA SAVISHNA   What's the matter, Nikolay Alekseevich?

IVANOV (*Hesitates.*)   The fact is, you see, the day after tomorrow is
the date my note falls due. I'd be very much obliged if you could
offer an extension or let me add the interest to the principal. At
the moment I have absolutely no money . . .

ZINAIDA SAVISHNA (*Alarmed.*)   Nikolay Alekseevich, how can this be?
What kind of a system is this? No, don't even think of such a thing,
for heaven's sake, don't torment an unhappy woman like me . . .

IVANOV   Sorry, sorry . . . (*Goes into the garden.*)

ZINAIDA SAVISHNA   Pooh, good heavens, how he upset me! . . . I'm
trembling all over . . . trembling . . . (*Goes out the door at right.*)

VIII

KOSYKH.

KOSYKH (*Enters at the door left and crosses the stage.*)   I was holding
spades: ace, king, queen, jack, eight low spades, ace and one . . .

---

4. Manfred, the hero of Lord Byron's eponymous poem; a romantic outlaw who, with the
help of magic, controls the spirits of nature. The poem greatly influenced Pushkin and
Lermontov. Redundant person, see note 6, page 30.

one teensy little heart and she, damn her to hell, can't call one little slam! (*Exits through door at right.*)

IX

AVDOTYA NAZAROVNA *and* FIRST GUEST.

AVDOTYA NAZAROVNA (*Enters from the garden with* FIRST GUEST.) How I'd like to tear her to shreds, the tightwad . . . how I'd like to tear her to shreds! Is this a joke? I'm sitting here from five o'clock, she could at least offer me a little rusty herring . . . What a house! . . . What entertainment! . . .

FIRST GUEST   It's so boring, you could simply bang your head against the wall! What people, God have mercy! . . . The boredom and hunger could make you howl like a wolf and start gnawing on people . . .

AVDOTYA NAZAROVNA   How I could tear her to shreds, sinner that I am!

FIRST GUEST   I'll have a drink, old girl, and then—off home! And I don't need any of your brides. How the hell can a man think of love if he hasn't had a nip since lunch?

AVDOTYA NAZAROVNA   We'll go, have a look around, or something . . .

FIRST GUEST   Ssh! . . . Nice and quiet! I think there's some schnapps in the dining room, in the sideboard. We'll worm it out of Yegorushka . . . Ssh!

(*They go out through the door at left.*)

X

ANNA PETROVNA *and* LVOV (*entering through the door at right.*)

ANNA PETROVNA   Never mind, they'll be delighted. Nobody here. They must be in the garden.

LVOV   Now, why, I ask you, did you bring me here to these vultures? It's no place for you and me. Decent people shouldn't have anything to do with such surroundings!

ANNA PETROVNA   Listen, Mr. Decent Person! It isn't nice to escort a lady and the whole way talk about nothing but your decency! It may be decent but, to put it mildly, it's boring. Never talk to women about your own virtues. Let them find them out for themselves. My Nikolay, when he was your age, did nothing but sing songs and tell shaggy-dog stories when women were around, and yet they all knew what sort of a man he was.

LVOV   Oh, don't talk to me about your Nikolay. I understand him only too well!

ANNA PETROVNA   You're a good man, but you don't understand a thing. Let's go into the garden. Nikolay never made comments like "I'm a decent person! I'm stifling in these surroundings! Vultures! An owl's nest! Crocodiles!" He left the menagerie alone, and when he did occasionally get upset, the only thing I'd hear from him would be, "Ah, how unjust I was today!" or "Anyuta, I feel sorry for that fellow!" That's how he used to be, but you . . .

(*They go out.*)

XI

AVDOTYA NAZAROVNA *and* FIRST GUEST.

FIRST GUEST (*Entering from the door at left.*)   It's not in the dining room, so I bet it's somewhere in the pantry. We've got to worm it out of Yegorushka. Let's go through the drawing room.

AVDOTYA NAZAROVNA   How I'd like to tear her to shreds! . . .

(*They go out through the door at right.*)

XII

BABAKINA, BORKIN *and* SHABELSKY.

(BABAKINA *and* BORKIN *run in from the garden, laughing; behind them, laughing and rubbing his hands, minces* SHABEL-SKY.)

BABAKINA   Such boredom! (*Roars with laughter.*) Such boredom! They all walk and sit around as if they'd swallowed a poker! All my bones are numb with boredom. (*Skips about.*) Have to limber up!

(BORKIN *takes her 'round the waist and kisses her on the cheek.*)

SHABELSKY (*Roars with laughter and snaps his fingers.*)   I'll be damned! (*Wheezes.*) In a manner of speaking . . .

BABAKINA   Let go, take your hands away, you shameless creature, or else God knows what the Count will think! Leave me alone!

BORKIN   Love of my life, red carbuncle of my heart! . . . (*Kisses her.*) Lend me two thousand three hundred rubles! . . .

BABAKINA   N-O—no. Anything else, but when it comes to money— thanks ever so . . . No, no, no! . . . Ah, take your hands off me!

SHABELSKY (*Minces near them.*)   Little puffball . . . She has her charms . . .

BORKIN (*Seriously.*)   That's enough. Let's talk business. Let's consider things objectively, in a businesslike way. Answer me straight, without equivocation or hocus-pocus: yes or no? Listen to me! (*Points to the Count.*) He needs money, a minimal income of three thousand a year. You need a husband. Want to be a countess?

SHABELSKY (*Roars with laughter.*)   A wonderful cynic!

BORKIN   Want to be a countess? Yes or no?

BABAKINA (*Upset.*)   You're making this up, Misha, honestly . . . And people don't do business this way, off the cuff like this . . . If the Count cares to, he can himself or . . . or I don't know how this suddenly, all at once . . .

BORKIN   Now, now, don't confuse the issue! It's a business deal . . . Yes or no?

SHABELSKY (*Laughing and rubbing his hands.*)   Actually, how about it? Damn it, should I really commit this dirty deed myself? Eh? Little puffball. . . . (*Kisses* BABAKINA *on the cheek.*) Superb! . . . A tasty little pickle! . . .

BABAKINA   Leave off, leave off, you've quite upset me . . . Go away, go away! . . . No, don't go away!

BORKIN   Quickly! Yes or no! We've got no time . . .

BABAKINA   You know what, Count? You drive over to my place on a visit for two or three days . . . We'll have fun there, not like here . . . Drive over tomorrow . . . (*To* BORKIN.) No, you were joking, weren't you?

BORKIN (*Angrily.*)   Now who'd start joking about serious business?

BABAKINA   Leave off, leave off . . . Ah, I feel faint! I feel faint! A countess . . . I feel faint! . . . I'm falling . . .

(BORKIN *and the Count, laughing, take her by the arms and, kissing her on the cheeks, lead her out the door at right.*)

XIII

IVANOV, SASHA, *then* ANNA PETROVNA.

(IVANOV *and* SASHA *run in from the garden.*)

IVANOV (*Clutching his head in despair.*)   It can't be! Don't, don't, Shurochka! . . . Ah, don't!

SASHA (*Passionately.*)   I love you madly . . . Without you, there's no meaning to my life, no happiness and joy! For me, you're every-thing . . .

IVANOV   What for, what for? My God, I don't understand a thing . . . Shurochka, don't do this!

SASHA   In my childhood you were my only joy; I loved you and your soul, like myself, and now . . . I love you, Nikolay Alekseevich . . . With you anywhere to the ends of the earth, wherever you want, even the grave, only, for God's sake, soon, otherwise I'll suffo-cate . . .

IVANOV (*Bursts into peals of happy laughter.*)   What is this? Does this mean starting life over from the beginning? Shurochka, does it? . . . Happiness is mine for the taking! (*Draws her to him.*) My youth, my prime . . .

(ANNA PETROVNA *enters from the garden and, on seeing her husband and* SASHA, *stops as if rooted to the spot.*)

IVANOV Does it mean coming to life? Does it? Back to an active role again?

(*Kiss. After they kiss,* IVANOV *and* SASHA *look around and see* ANNA PETROVNA.)

IVANOV (*In horror.*) Sarra!

CURTAIN

Act Three

IVANOV'S *study. Desk, covered with an unruly sprawl of papers, books, official letters, knickknacks, revolvers; alongside the papers, a lamp, a carafe of vodka, a plate of herring, pieces of bread and pickled gherkins. On the wall, regional maps, pictures, shotguns, pistols, sickles, riding crops and so on. It is midday.*

I

SHABELSKY, LEBEDEV, BORKIN, *and* PYOTR.

SHABELSKY *and* LEBEDEV *sit beside the desk.* BORKIN *is center stage astride a chair.* PYOTR *stands by the door.*

LEBEDEV France has a clear and well-defined policy . . . The French know what they want. They need to give the Krauts a good thrashing and that'll be that, while Germany, my boy, is singing a very different tune. Germany has plenty of other irons in the fire besides France . . .

SHABELSKY Hogwash! In my opinion, the Germans are cowards and so are the French . . . They give each other the finger behind their backs. Believe me, it won't go beyond giving each other the finger. They won't fight.[5]

BORKIN The way I see it, why fight? What's the point of all these arms buildups, conferences, defense budgets? You know what I'd do? I'd get together all the dogs in the whole nation, infect them with a good dose of Pasteur's rabies,[6] and let 'em loose behind enemy lines. All the combatants would be raving mad within a month.

LEBEDEV (*Laughs.*) That head may not look all that large, but it

---

5. In 1887, Germany's militarism provoked a strain in its relations with France, and war nearly broke out three times in the course of that year.
6. Louis Pasteur, the French bacteriologist (1822–1895) was in the news; his Institut Pasteur, whose aim was to treat hydrophobia by inoculation, opened in Paris in 1888.

swarms with big ideas, countless multitudes of 'em, like fishes in the sea.

SHABELSKY   A virtuoso!

LEBEDEV   God bless you, you're good for a laugh, Michel Michelich! (*Stops laughing.*) Well, gentlemen, "only warlike talk is heard, but as for vodka, not a word."[7] *Repetatur!*[8] (*Fills three shot-glasses.*) Our good health! (*They drink and take a snack.*) A little bit of herring, the appetizer of all appetizers.

SHABELSKY   Well, no, gherkin's better . . . Learned men have been pondering from the dawn of time and never come up with anything cleverer than a pickled gherkin. (*To* PYOTR.) Pyotr, go and get more gherkins and tell 'em in the kitchen to bake four onion tarts. And see that they're hot.

   (PYOTR *exits.*)

LEBEDEV   Another good thing to eat with vodka is caviar. Only how? Got to use your head . . . Take a quarter pound of pressed caviar, two bulbs of green onion, olive oil, mix it all up and, you know, like this . . . a little lemon juice on top . . . To die for! You could go crazy from the smell alone.

BORKIN   Another nice thing to chase down vodka is fried smelts. Only you've got to know how to fry them. You've got to gut them, then roll them in fine breadcrumbs and fry them crisp, so they crunch between your teeth . . . cru-cru-cru . . .

SHABELSKY   Yesterday at Babakina's there was a good appetizer— button mushrooms.

LEBEDEV   No kidding . . .

SHABELSKY   Only prepared some special way. You know, with onion, bay leaf, all sorts of spices. As soon as they took the lid off the saucepan, it gave off a vapor, an aroma . . . sheer rapture.

LEBEDEV   How about it? *Repetatur,* gentlemen! (*They drink.*) Our health. (*Looks at his watch.*) I don't think I can wait 'til Nikolasha shows up. It's time for me to go. At Babakina's, you say, they served mushrooms, but you have yet to see a mushroom at our place. Would you like to tell me, Count, why the hell you spend so much time at Marfutka's?

SHABELSKY   (*Nods at* BORKIN.)   That one, he wants to marry me off to her . . .

LEBEDEV   Marry? . . . How old are you?

SHABELSKY   Sixty-two.

LEBEDEV   Just the age for getting married. And Marfutka's the ideal mate for you.

---

7. A line from Denis Davydov's *Songs of an Old Hussar* (1817), the poetic diary of a versifying army officer.
8. Latin: Do it again!

BORKIN   It's got nothing to do with Marfutka, but with Marfutka's coin of the realm.

LEBEDEV   Which is what you're after: Marfutka's coin of the realm . . . You want some green cheese from the moon as well?

BORKIN   As soon as the man's married, he'll line his *poches*,[9] then you'll see green cheese. You'll be drooling for it.

SHABELSKY   Bless my soul, he's really serious. This genius is convinced that I'm obeying his orders and getting married . . .

BORKIN   How else? Didn't you already agree to it?

SHABELSKY   You're out of your mind . . . When did I agree to it? Pss . . .

BORKIN   Thank you . . . Thank you very much! So this means you're going to let me down? One minute he's getting married, the next he's not . . . who the hell can tell the difference, and I've already given my word of honor! So you're not getting married?

SHABELSKY (*Shrugs his shoulders.*)   He's serious . . . A wonderful fellow!

BORKIN (*Exasperated.*)   In that case, what was the point of getting a respectable woman all hot and bothered? She's frantic to be a countess, can't sleep, can't eat. . . . Is that a laughing matter? . . . Is that the decent thing to do?

SHABELSKY (*Snaps his fingers.*)   What then, what if I actually do commit this dirty deed all by myself? Eh? For spite? I'll go and commit the dirty deed. Word of honor . . . Might be fun!

(*Enter* LVOV.)

II

The same and LVOV.

LEBEDEV   Our regards to Æsculapius . . . (*Gives* LVOV *his hand and sings.*) "Doctor, save me, my dear fellow, thoughts of death turn me quite yellow . . ."[1]

LVOV   Nikolay Alekseevich still isn't here?

LEBEDEV   Well, no, I've been waiting for him for over an hour. (LVOV *impatiently paces up and down the stage.*) Dear boy, how is Anna Petrovna?

LVOV   In a bad way.

LEBEDEV (*Sighs.*)   May I go and convey my respects?

LVOV   No, please, don't. I think she's sleeping . . .
(*Pause.*)

9. French: pockets.
1. Paraphrase of a line from "The Doctor Serenade" by W. Ch. Dawinhof (words by A. M. Ushakova).

LEBEDEV   An attractive woman, a splendid woman . . . (*Sighs.*) On Shurochka's birthday, when she fainted at our place, I stared into her face, and that's when I realized that she hasn't long to live, poor thing. I can't understand why she took a turn for the worse just then. I run in, lo and behold: she's white as a sheet, lying on the floor; Nikolasha is kneeling beside her, white as well; Shurochka's all in tears. The whole of the next week, Shurochka and I went around in a daze.

SHABELSKY   (*To* LVOV.)   Tell me, my respected apostle of science, which scientist discovered that the most salutary thing for chest ailments is private visits from a young physician? It's a great discovery! Truly great! How would you classify it: as allopathy or homeopathy?[2] (LVOV *is about to reply, but makes a scornful gesture and exits.*) If looks could kill. . . .

LEBEDEV   You're giving your tongue a workout! Why did you insult him?

SHABELSKY   (*Irritated.*)   And why does he lie to me? Tuberculosis, no hope, she's dying . . . He's lying! I can't stand it!

LEBEDEV   What makes you think he's lying?

SHABELSKY   (*Rises and walks around.*)   I cannot abide the thought that a living human being suddenly, for no reason at all, can up and die. Let's change the subject!

III

LEBEDEV, SHABELSKY, BORKIN, *and* KOSYKH.

KOSYKH   (*Runs in, panting.*)   Is Nikolay Alekseevich at home? Good afternoon! (*Quickly shakes everyone's hand.*) At home?

BORKIN   He is not.

KOSYKH   (*Sits and jumps up.*)   In that case, goodbye! (*Drinks a glass of vodka and has a quick bite.*) I'll move on . . . Business . . . I'm exhausted . . . I can barely stand on my feet . . .

LEBEDEV   What wind has blown you here?

KOSYKH   I've been at Barabanov's. We were playing whist all night long and only just finished . . . I lost every last thing . . . That Barabanov plays like a shoemaker! (*In a tearful voice.*) Just you listen: I was holding hearts the whole time . . . (*Turns to* BORKIN, *who jumps away from him.*) He leads diamonds, I go hearts again, he goes diamonds. . . . Well, not one trick. (*To* LEBEDEV.) We try to take four clubs. I've got an ace, queen and four more clubs, ace, ten and three more spades . . .

---

2. Allopathy is curing a disease by inducing a different kind of disease; homeopathy is treating a disease by minute doses of drugs that would induce disease-like symptoms in a healthy person.

LEBEDEV (*Covers his ears.*)   Spare me, spare me, for Christ's sake, spare me!

KOSYKH (*To the Count.*)   You know what I mean: ace, queen, and four more clubs, ace, ten, three more spades . . .

SHABELSKY (*Pushing him away with his hands.*)   Go away, I don't want to hear it!

KOSYKH   And suddenly, of all the bad luck: the ace of spades was trumped first round.

SHABELSKY (*Grabs a revolver off the desk.*)   Get out of here or I'll shoot!

KOSYKH (*Waves his hand in dismissal.*)   What the hell . . . Can't a man even talk to people? It's like living in Australia: no common interests, no solidarity . . . Every man lives on his own . . . Anyway, I've got to go . . . it's time. (*Takes his cap.*) Time is money . . . (*Gives* LEBEDEV *his hand.*) Pass! . . .

(*Laughter.*)

(KOSYKH *leaves and bumps into* AVDOTYA NAZAROVNA *in the doorway.*)

IV

SHABELSKY, LEBEDEV, BORKIN *and* AVDOTYA NAZAROVNA.

AVDOTYA NAZAROVNA (*Cries out.*)   Blast you, you've knocked me off my feet!

EVERYONE   Ah-ah-ah! . . . The unavoidable! . . .

AVDOTYA NAZAROVNA   Here they are. I've been looking for them all over the house. Good afternoon, my fine feathered friends, greetings, greetings . . . (*Greets them.*)

LEBEDEV   What's she doing here?

AVDOTYA NAZAROVNA   Business, my good sir! (*To the Count.*) Business on your behalf, your grace. (*Bows.*) I was told to give you my regards and ask after your health . . . And she, my baby-doll, told me to say that if you don't come this evening, she will cry her little eyes out. "So," she says, "my dear, take him aside and whisper secretly in his ear." But why secretly? We're all friends here. And in a case like this, we're not robbing the henhouse, it's by law and by love, by mutual agreement. Never, for all my sins, do I touch a drop, but in a case like this I'll have a drink!

LEBEDEV   And so will I. (*Pours.*) And you, you old crow, you're still going strong. I've known you for well-nigh thirty years and you've always been old . . .

AVDOTYA NAZAROVNA   I've lost count of the years . . . Two husbands I've buried. I would have taken a third, but nobody'll have you without a dowry. Eight or so children I've had . . . (*Takes a glass.*) Well, God grant we've embarked on a successful venture, God grant it ends in success! May they live long and prosper, and may we behold them and rejoice! May they abide in harmony and love . . . (*Drinks.*) Pretty strong vodka!

SHABELSKY (*Roaring with laughter, to* LEBEDEV).   But, do you realize, the strangest thing of all is that they take it seriously, as if I . . . Wonderful! (*Rises.*) Or else, actually, Pasha, should I commit this dirty deed on my own? For spite . . . new tricks for an old dog, as they say! Eh, Pasha? No kidding . . .

LEBEDEV   You're talking drivel, Count. Our concern, yours and mine, my boy, is to be mindful of our deaths, for Marfutka and her coin of the realm have passed you by long ago . . . Our time is over.

SHABELSKY   No, I will do the deed! Word of honor, I'll do the deed!
        (*Enter* IVANOV *and* LVOV.)

V

The same, IVANOV, *and* LVOV.

LVOV   Please grant me just five minutes.

LEBEDEV   Nikolasha! (*Goes to meet* IVANOV *and kisses him.*) Good afternoon, my dear friend . . . I've been waiting for you a whole hour.

AVDOTYA NAZAROVNA (*Bows.*)   Good afternoon, my dear sir!

IVANOV (*Bitterly.*)   Gentlemen, once again you've turned my study into a barroom! . . . I've asked each and every one of you a thousand times not to do it . . . (*Walks over to the desk.*) There, look, you've spilled vodka on the papers . . . crumbs . . . pickles . . . it's really disgusting!

LEBEDEV   Sorry, Nikolasha, sorry . . . Forgive us. You and I, dear friend, have some very important business to talk over. . . .

BORKIN   So do I.

LVOV   Nikolay Alekseevich, may I have a word with you?

IVANOV (*Points to* LEBEDEV.)   He's the one who needs me. Wait, you're next . . . (*To* LEBEDEV.) What's on your mind?

LEBEDEV   Gentlemen, I'd like to speak in private. Please . . .
        (*The Count exits with* AVDOTYA NAZAROVNA, *followed by* BORKIN, *then* LVOV.)

IVANOV   Pasha, you can drink as much as you like; it's your funeral; but please don't let my uncle drink.[3] He never drank at my house before. It's bad for him.

LEBEDEV (*Alarmed.*)   My dear boy, I didn't know . . . I didn't even notice . . .

---

3. Sonya repeats this line to Astrov in *Uncle Vanya*, Act Two.

IVANOV   God forbid, but if that old baby should die, you're not the
one who'll feel bad, I am . . . What do you want? . . .

LEBEDEV   You see, my dear friend. I don't know how to begin, so
that it doesn't sound so heartless . . . Nikolasha, I'm embarrassed,
I'm blushing, my tongue's twisted, but, dear boy, put yourself in
my place, bear in mind that I'm a man under orders, a flunky, a
doormat . . . Do forgive me . . .

IVANOV   What do you mean?

LEBEDEV   The wife sent me . . . Do me a favor, be a friend, pay her
the interest! You wouldn't believe how she's nagged, worn me
down, tortured the life out of me! Get her off your back, for
heaven's sake! . . .

IVANOV   Pasha, you know I haven't got any money right now.

LEBEDEV   I know, I know, but what am I to do? She won't wait. If
she sues you for defaulting, how can Shurochka and I look you in
the face again?

IVANOV   I'm embarrassed myself. Pasha, I'd be glad if the earth swallowed me up, but . . . but where am I to get it? Teach me, where?
The only thing left is to wait for autumn when I can sell the wheat.

LEBEDEV (*Shouts.*)   She won't wait!

   (*Pause.*)

IVANOV   Your position is an unpleasant one, a delicate one, but
mine's even worse. (*Walks and thinks.*) And one can't come up
with anything . . . There's nothing left to sell . . .

LEBEDEV   You should ride over to Mühlbach, ask him; after all, he
owes you sixteen thousand. (IVANOV *waves his hand in hopeless
dismissal.*) Here's how it is, Nikolasha. . . . I know you'll start
swearing, but . . . respect an old boozehound! Between friends . . .
Regard me as a friend. . . . You and I are both students, liberals
. . . Mutual ideas and interests . . . Both alumni of Moscow U. . . .
Alma mater . . . (*Takes out his wallet.*) I've got some money stashed
away, not a soul at home knows about it. Take a loan . . . (*Takes
out money and puts it on the desk.*) Pocket your pride, and take it
for friendship's sake . . . I'd take it from you, word of honor . . .

   (*Pause.*)

There it is on the desk: one thousand one hundred. You ride over
there today and hand it to her in person. "There you are," say,
"Zinaida Savishna, I hope it chokes you!" Only don't give any clue
that you borrowed it from me, God forbid! Otherwise I'll never
hear the end of it from Gooseberry Preserves! (*Stares into* IVANOV's
face.) There, there, don't be like that! (*Quickly takes the money off
the desk and puts it in his pocket.*) Don't! I was joking . . . Forgive
me, for Christ's sake!

   (*Pause.*)

Your heart is aching?

> (IVANOV *waves his hand in dismissal.*)

Yes, business. . . . (*Sighs.*) A time of grief and sorrow has come to you. A man, my good friend, is like a samovar. It doesn't always stand in a shady spot on the shelf, but sometimes it's heated with burning coals: psh . . . psh! That simile isn't worth a damn, well, let someone smarter come up with a better one . . . (*Sighs.*) Misery hardens the heart. I don't feel sorry for you, Nikolasha, you'll land on your feet, the pain will lessen but I'm offended, my boy, and annoyed by other people . . . Do me a favor. Tell me, what's the reason for all this gossip? There's so much gossip circulating about you in the district, my boy; watch out, our friend the district attorney might pay you a visit . . . You're a murderer and a bloodsucker and a thief and a traitor . . .

IVANOV   It's all rubbish, now I've got a headache.

LEBEDEV   All because you think too much.

IVANOV   I don't think at all.

LEBEDEV   Well, Nikolasha, don't you give a damn about all that and come and see us. Shurochka's fond of you, she understands and appreciates you. She's a decent, good person, Nikolasha. Nothing like her mother and father, but I guess some young fellow came passing by . . . I look at her sometimes, pal, and I can't believe that a bottle-nosed drunkard like me has such a treasure. Drop by, talk to her about clever things and—it'll cheer you up. She's an honest, sincere person . . .

> (*Pause.*)

IVANOV   Pasha, dear man, leave me alone . . .

LEBEDEV   I understand, I understand . . . (*Hastily looks at his watch.*) I understand. (*Kisses* IVANOV.) Goodbye. I still have to go to the dedication of a school.[4] (*Goes to the door and stops.*) A clever girl . . . Yesterday Shurochka and I started talking about the gossip. (*Laughs.*) And she blurted out an aphorism: "Papa dear," she says, "glowworms glow in the dark only to make it easier for night birds to see them and eat them, and good people exist so that there can be slander and gossip." How do you like that? A genius, a George Sand![5]

IVANOV   Pasha! (*Stops him.*) What's wrong with me?

LEBEDEV   I've been meaning to ask you about that, yes, but I confess I was too shy. I don't know, pal! On the one hand, I had the impression that you've been suffering all kinds of bad luck; on the other hand, I know that you're not that sort of fellow, that you . . . you

---

4. Elementary schools fell under the jurisdiction of the Rural Board, of which Lebedev is chairman.
5. The pseudonym of Aurore Dudevant (1804–1876), whose overwrought and liberal-minded romantic novels were highly popular in Russia. Turgenev called her "one of our saints," Belinsky "a modern Joan of Arc."

wouldn't let trouble get you down. It's something else, Nikolasha, but what it is—I don't understand.

IVANOV I don't understand either. The way I see it, it's either . . . although, no!

(*Pause.*)

You see, here's what I was about to say. I used to have a work-man Semyon—you remember him. Once, at threshing time, he wanted to show off his strength to the farmgirls, hoisted two sacks of rye on to his back, and got a hernia. He died soon after. The way I see it, I've got my own personal hernia. High school, uni-versity, then farming, district schools, projects . . . I didn't believe the same things as other people; I didn't marry like other people; I'd get enthused, I'd take risks, I'd throw away money, as you well know, right, left and center; I was happy and miserable like no one else in the whole district. Those were all my sacks of rye, Pasha . . . I hoisted a load on my back, and my back caved in. At the age of twenty we're all heroes, we take it all on, can do it all, and by thirty we're already worn out, good for nothing at all. How else can you explain this lassitude? But, maybe I'm wrong . . . Wrong, wrong! . . . God bless you, Pasha, you must be sick and tired of me.

LEBEDEV (*Briskly.*) You know what? Your surroundings, my boy, have got you down!

IVANOV That's stupid, Pasha, and stale. Get out!

LEBEDEV It really is stupid. Now I can see for myself it's stupid. I'm going, I'm going! . . . (*Exits.*)

VI

IVANOV, *then* LVOV.

IVANOV No-good, pathetic, insignificant—that's the kind of man I am. You have to be an equally pathetic, broken-down, flabby-faced drunk, like Pasha, to go on loving and respecting me. How I despise myself, my God! How profoundly I hate my voice, my walk, my hands, my clothes, my thoughts. Well, isn't this ridiculous, isn't this offensive? Barely a year's gone by since I was healthy and strong, I was hale and hearty, indefatigable, impassioned, worked with these very hands, talked so that even ignoramuses were moved to tears, was capable of weeping when I saw misery, feel outraged when I encountered evil. I knew the meaning of inspi-ration, I knew the splendor and poetry of quiet nights, when from dusk to dawn you sit at your desk or beguile your mind with dreams. I had faith, I gazed into the future as into the eyes of a loving mother . . . And now, oh, my God! I'm weary, I have no faith, I waste days and nights in idleness. They don't obey me, brains or hands or feet. The estate goes to rack and ruin, the forests topple beneath the axe. (*Weeps.*) My land stares at me like an orphan. I have no expectations, no compassion for anything, my mind quakes in fear of the day to come . . . And this business with Sarra? I swore everlasting love, I promised happiness, I opened before her eyes a future she had never dreamed of. She believed in it. For the past five years all I could see was how she was flickering out under the weight of her sacrifices, how she was growing exhausted struggling with her conscience, but, God knows, not a single black look at me or word of reproach . . . And then what? I fell out of love with her . . . How? Why? What for? I don't understand. Here she is suffering, her days are numbered; while I, like the lowest of cowards, run away from her pale face, sunken chest, imploring eyes . . . Shameful, shameful!

(*Pause.*)

Sasha, a mere girl, is affected by my misfortunes. She declares her love for me, almost an old man, and I get intoxicated, forget about everything in this world, enchanted as if by music, and I shout: "A new life! Happiness!" But the next day I believe as little in this life and happiness as I do in fairies . . . What's wrong with me? What abyss am I pushing myself into? What is the source of this debility of mine? What has become of my nerves? My sick wife has only to wound my vanity, or a servant-girl get something wrong, or a gun misfire, and I turn rude, nasty, a different person entirely . . .

(*Pause.*)

I don't understand, I don't understand, I don't understand! I simply feel like blowing my brains out! . . .

LVOV (*Enters.*)   I've got to have it out with you, Nikolay Alekseevich!

IVANOV   If we were to have it out every day, Doctor, we'd be too debilitated for anything else.

LVOV   Will you be so good as to listen to me?

IVANOV   I listen to you every day, and so far I can't understand a thing. What do you personally want from me?

LVOV   I speak clearly and firmly, and the only person who could fail to understand me is one without a heart.

IVANOV   My wife is facing death, that I know; I have unpardonably wronged her, that I also know; you're a decent, upright man, I know that too! What more do you want?

LVOV   I am outraged by human cruelty . . . A woman is dying. She has a father and mother whom she loves and would like to see before she dies; they know perfectly well that she will die soon and that she goes on loving them, but, damn their cruelty, they evidently want Jehovah to see how steadfast they are in their religion; they still go on cursing her! You, the man for whom she sacrificed everything—her religion and her parents' home and her peace of mind—in the most blatant manner and with the most blatant intentions, you head over to those Lebedevs every day!

IVANOV Oh, I haven't been there for two weeks now . . .

LVOV (*Not listening to him.*) People such as you have to be spoken to bluntly, with no beating around the bush, and if you don't like what I have to say, then don't listen! I'm used to calling things by their rightful names . . . You need this death in order to carry out new feats of valor, all right, but can't you at least wait? If you were to let her die in the natural scheme of things, without stabbing her with your barefaced cynicism, would the Lebedevs and their dowry disappear? Not now, but in a year or two, you, a wonderful Tartuffe, will manage to turn a young girl's head and make off with her dowry just the same as now. . . . Why are you in such a hurry? Why do you need your wife to die now, and not in a month or a year's time?

IVANOV This is excruciating . . . Doctor, you're a really bad physician if you suppose that a man can control himself forever. It's taking the most appalling willpower not to reply to your insults.

LVOV That's enough, who are you trying to fool? Drop the mask.

IVANOV Clever man, think of this: in your opinion, nothing's easier than understanding me! Right? I married Anna to get a big dowry . . . I didn't get the dowry, I missed the mark, and now I'm driving her to her grave, in order to marry another woman and get that dowry . . . Right? How simple and uncomplicated . . . A man is such a simple and unsophisticated machine . . . No, Doctor, each of us has far more cogs, screws, and valves in him than to enable us to judge one another on first impressions or a few outward signs. I don't understand you, you don't understand me, we don't understand one another. You may be an excellent general practitioner—and still have no understanding of people. Don't be so smug and look at it my way.

LVOV Do you really think that you're so unfathomable, that I am so brainless that I can't tell the difference between disgraceful behavior and decent behavior?

IVANOV Obviously, you and I will never find common ground . . . For the last time I ask you, and, please answer without more ado, what do you personally want from me? What do you hope to achieve? (*Annoyed.*) And whom have I the honor of addressing: the counsel for my prosecution or my wife's physician?

LVOV I am a physician—and, as a physician, I demand that you change your way of life. It is killing Anna Petrovna!

IVANOV   But what am I to do? What? If you understand me better
than I understand myself, then tell me in no uncertain terms: what
am I to do?

LVOV   At least, don't act so openly.

IVANOV   Oh, my God! Do you really understand yourself? (*Drinks
water.*) Leave me alone. I'm a thousand times at fault, I'll answer
for it before God, but no one has entitled you to torture me on a
daily basis . . .

LVOV   And who has entitled you to insult my truth telling, by insulting my person? You have worn me down and poisoned my mind.
Until I wound up in this district, I could deal with the fact that
stupid, inane, self-deluded people existed, but I never believed
there were criminal types who consciously, deliberately used their
intelligence to do evil . . . I respected and loved people, but once
I came in contact with you . . .

IVANOV   I've heard this before!

LVOV   Have you indeed? (*On seeing* SASHA *enter; she is in a riding
habit.*) Now, I hope, we understand one another perfectly well!
(*Shrugs his shoulders and exits.*)

VII

IVANOV *and* SASHA.

IVANOV (*Alarmed.*)   Shura, is that you?

SASHA   Yes, it is. Good afternoon. Weren't you expecting me? Why
haven't you been to see us for so long?

IVANOV   Shura, for God's sake, this is inconsiderate! Your coming
here might have a dreadful effect on my wife.

SASHA   She won't see me. I came in the back way. I'll go right away.
I was worried: are you all right? Why haven't you been to see us
for so long?

IVANOV   My wife's upset even without this, she's almost dying, and
you ride over here. Shura, Shura, this is frivolous and inhuman!

SASHA   What am I supposed to do? You haven't been to see us for
two weeks, don't answer letters. I was in agony. I imagined you
suffering here unbearably, ill, dead. I didn't get a single night's
sleep . . . I'll go right away . . . At least tell me, are you well?

IVANOV   No. I've been tormenting myself, people torment me nonstop . . . I'm at the end of my rope! And now you too! This is so
sick, so abnormal! Shura, so much of this is my fault, my fault!

SASHA   You really do like to say horrible, heartbreaking things! Your
fault? Really? Your fault? Well, then, tell me: how so?

IVANOV   I don't know, I don't know . . .

SASHA That's no answer. Every sinner ought to know how he's sinned. Have you printed counterfeit money or something?

IVANOV That's not funny.

SASHA Your fault you fell out of love with your wife? That may be, but a man isn't master of his feelings. You didn't want to fall out of love. Your fault that she saw us in a loving embrace? No, you didn't want her to see . . .

IVANOV (*Interrupting*). Et cetera, et cetera . . . Fell in love, fell out of love, no master of my feelings . . . these are all clichés, platitudes, they're no help . . .

SASHA It's tiresome to talk to you. (*Looks at a picture.*) How well that dog is painted! Is it done from life?

IVANOV From life. And our whole love affair is a trite cliché: He was downhearted and had lost his bearings. She showed up, strong and bold in spirit, and offered him a helping hand. It's beautiful, but it resembles truth only in novels, not in life. . . .

SASHA It's the same in life.

IVANOV I see you have a sophisticated knowledge of life! My whining inspires you with reverent awe, you imagine you've discovered a second Hamlet in me, but, so far as I'm concerned, this psychosis of mine, and all its symptoms, can serve only as rich material for comedy and nothing else! People should burst out laughing, split their sides at my affectations, but for you—it's a cry for help! Come to my rescue, do a valiant deed! Ah, I really am hard on myself today! I feel that today's nervous tension will come to a head somehow . . . Either I'll break something or . . .

SASHA That's right, that's right, that's just what you need. Break something, smash or scream. You're angry with me, I've done something stupid by deciding to come here. Well, then take it out on me, bawl me out, stamp your feet. Well? Start losing your temper. . . .

(*Pause.*)

Well?

IVANOV Silly girl.

SASHA Excellent! I do believe we're smiling! Be good, deign to smile once more!

IVANOV (*Laughs.*) I've noticed: whenever you try to rescue me and teach me to see sense, common sense, you get a look on your face that's naive, incredibly naive, and your eyes open wide, as if you were staring at a comet. Hold still, your shoulder's covered with dust. (*Wipes the dust off her shoulder.*) A naive man is a fool. But you women manage to be naive so that it comes across as charming and wholesome and affectionate and not so foolish as it might seem. How do you pull that off? When a man is healthy, strong and cheerful, you ignore him, but as soon as he starts sliding downhill and bemoaning his fate, you cling to him. Is it really worse to be the wife of a strong, courageous man than to be the nursemaid of some sniveling loser?

SASHA Much worse!

IVANOV Why is that? (*Laughs loudly.*) Darwin[6] didn't know about that, or else he would have given you hell! You're undermining the human race. Thanks to you soon earth will breed nothing but bellyachers and psychopaths.

SASHA Men just don't get it. Every girl prefers a loser to a success, because every girl is attracted by active love . . . Don't you get it? Active. Men are involved in business and so they shove love far into the background. Talk to his wife, walk around the garden with her, pass the time pleasantly, weep at her grave—that's all. But for us love is life itself. I love you, that means that I dream about how I'll cure you of tedium, how I'll go with you to the ends of the earth . . . You're in the clouds, I'm in the clouds; you're in the dumps, I'm in the dumps. For instance, for me it would be a great joy to stay up nights copying out your papers or to keep watch all night so that no one wakes you, or to walk with you a hundred miles on foot. I remember, three years ago, at threshing time, you once dropped in on us all covered in dust, sunburnt, exhausted, and asked for a drink. I brought you a glass, and you were already stretched out on the sofa, dead to the world. You slept in our house for half a day, and the whole time I stood outside the door and made sure that no one came in. And it made me feel so good! The harder the work, the greater the love—I mean, you understand, the more deeply felt it is.

IVANOV Active love . . . Hmm . . . It's an aberration, a young girl's fancies, or, maybe, that's how things ought to be . . . (*Shrugs his shoulders.*) Who the hell knows? (*Cheerfully.*) Shura, word of honor, I am a respectable man! . . . Judge for yourself: I have always loved to philosophize, but never in my life have I said "our women are depraved" or "a woman's taken the road to perdition." For heaven's sake, I was only grateful and nothing more! Nothing more! My little girl, my pretty, what fun you are! While I, what a ridiculous numbskull! I upset good Christians, bemoan my fate for days on end. (*Laughs.*) Boohoo! Boohoo! (*Quickly walks away from her.*) But go away, Sasha! We've been forgetting . . .

SASHA Yes, it's time to go. Good-bye! I'm afraid that your decent doctor out of a sense of duty will report to Anna Petrovna that I'm here. Listen to me: go to your wife right now and sit, sit, sit . . . If

6. The English scientist Charles Darwin (1809–1882) argued that in natural selection, the females of a species choose for reproduction the strongest or most capable male.

you have to sit for a year, sit for a year. Ten years—sit ten years. Do your duty. And grieve, and ask her forgiveness, and weep—that's how it ought to be. But the main thing is, don't neglect business.

IVANOV I've got that old feeling, as if I've been gorging on toadstools. All over again!

SASHA Well, God bless you! You can stop thinking about me! In two weeks or so you'll drop me a line, and I'll be grateful for it. And I'll write to you . . .

    (BORKIN *looks in at the door.*)

VIII

The same and BORKIN.

BORKIN Nikolay Alekseevich, may I? (*On seeing* SASHA.) Sorry, I didn't see . . . (*Enters.*) *Bonjour!* (*Bows.*)

SASHA (*Embarrassed.*) How do you do? . . .

BORKIN You've got plumper, prettier . . .

SASHA (*to* IVANOV.) I'm leaving now, Nikolay Alekseevich . . . I'm leaving. (*Exits.*)

BORKIN A vision of loveliness! I came about prose, and ran into poetry. . . . (*Sings.*) "Thou didst appear, like a bird flown towards the light . . ."[7] (IVANOV *paces up and down the stage in agitation.* BORKIN *sits.*) There's something about her, *Nicolas*, a certain something that other women haven't got. Am I right? Something special . . . fantastical . . . (*Sighs.*) Actually, the richest eligible girl in the whole district, but her dear mama is such a sourpuss that no one wants to make a match. When she dies, everything will go to Shurochka, but until she dies she'll give ten thousand or so, a curling iron, and a flat iron, and even then she'll make you beg for it on your knees. (*Rummages in his pockets.*) Let's smoke a *de-los-majoros.*[8] Care for one? (*Offers his cigar case.*) They're not bad . . . Quite smokeworthy.

IVANOV (*Walks over to* BORKIN, *choked with rage.*) Don't set foot in my house another minute! Not another minute! (BORKIN *rises a bit and drops the cigar.*) Not another minute!

BORKIN *Nicolas*, what does this mean? What are you angry about?

IVANOV What about? Where did you get those cigars? Do you think I don't know where you take the old man every day, and what for?

BORKIN (*Shrugs his shoulders.*) What's it got to do with you?

IVANOV You're such a crook! Your vulgar schemes, which you broad-

7. From E. S. Shashina's ballad "Three Words" (text by O. P. Pavlova).
8. Spanish, correctly *de los majores*, of the best.

cast through the whole district, have made me a dishonest man in
people's eyes! We've got nothing in common, and I ask you to leave
my home this very minute! (*Walks quickly.*)

BORKIN   I know that you're saying all this out of irritation, and
therefore I won't be angry with you. Insult me as much as you like
. . . (*Picks up the cigar.*) It's time you gave up this melancholy routine. You're no schoolboy . . .

IVANOV   What did I tell you? (*Trembling.*) Are you playing games
with me?

(*Enter* ANNA PETROVNA.)

IX

The same and ANNA PETROVNA.

BORKIN   Well, look, Anna Petrovna's here . . . I'm going. (*Exits.*)
(IVANOV *stops beside the desk and stands, his head bowed.*)

ANNA PETROVNA (*After a pause.*)   Why did she come here just now?
(*Pause.*)
I'm asking you: why did she come here?

IVANOV   Don't question me, Anyuta . . .
(*Pause.*)
I'm much at fault. Think up whatever punishment you want, I'll
bear it, but . . . don't question me . . . I haven't got the strength to
talk.

ANNA PETROVNA (*Angrily.*)   Why was she here?
(*Pause.*)
Ah, so that's what you're like! Now I understand you. Finally I see
what sort of man you are. Dishonorable, vile . . . You remember,
you came and lied to me, saying you loved me . . . I believed it and
left father, mother, religion and followed you . . . You lied to me
about truth, goodness, your honorable intentions; I believed every
word . . .

IVANOV   Anyuta, I never lied to you . . .

ANNA PETROVNA   I lived with you for five years, I broke down and
sickened at the idea that I'd renounced my faith, but I loved you
and never left you for a single minute . . . You were my idol . . .
and now what? All this time you've been deceiving me in the most
shameless manner. . . .

IVANOV   Anyuta, don't tell falsehoods. I was mistaken, yes, but I've
never lied in my life . . . You don't dare reproach me for that . . .

ANNA PETROVNA   Now it's all come out . . . You married me and
thought my father and mother would forgive me, give me money
. . . That's what you thought.

IVANOV   Oh my God! Anyuta, to try my patience like this! (*Weeps.*)

ANNA PETROVNA   Be quiet! When you realized there was no money, you came up with a new game . . . Now I remember it all and I understand. (*Weeps.*) You never loved me and were never faithful to me . . . Never!

IVANOV   Sarra, that's a lie! . . . Say what you want, but don't insult me with lies . . .

ANNA PETROVNA   Dishonorable, vile man . . . You owe Lebedev money, and now, in order to squirm out of your debt, you want to turn his daughter's head, deceive her the way you did me. Is that a falsehood?

IVANOV   (*Choking.*)   Shut up, for God's sake! I can't answer for myself . . . I'm choking with rage, and I . . . I'm liable to insult you . . .

ANNA PETROVNA   You always were a shameless deceiver, and not just of me . . . You pinned all those underhanded actions on Borkin, but now I know whose they really are . . .

IVANOV   Sarra, shut up, get out, or else I'll say something I'll regret! It's all I can do to keep from calling you something horrible, humiliating . . . (*Shouts.*) Shut up, you kike bitch!

ANNA PETROVNA   I will not shut up . . . Too long you've been deceiving me, for me to be able to keep silent . . .

IVANOV   So you won't shut up? (*Struggles with himself.*) For God's sake . . .

ANNA PETROVNA   Now go and cheat the Lebedev girl . . .

IVANOV   Then know that you . . . will die soon . . . The doctor told me that you'll die soon . . .

ANNA PETROVNA   (*Sits down, her voice faltering.*)   When did he say that?
(*Pause.*)

IVANOV   (*Clutching his head.*)   It's all my fault! God, it's all my fault! (*Sobs.*)

CURTAIN

Nearly a year goes by between Acts Three and Four.

Act Four

One of the drawing rooms in the Lebedevs' house. In front an arch separates the drawing room from a reception room, doors at right and left. An antique bronze, family portraits. Decorations for a party. An upright piano, on it a violin, a cello beside it. Throughout the whole act, guests walk through the reception room, dressed for a ball.

I

LVOV.

LVOV (*Enters, looks at his watch.*) Five o'clock. I suppose the benediction will begin any time now[9] . . . They'll give the benediction and drive off to the wedding. There you have it, the triumph of virtue and truth! He didn't manage to rob Sarra, so he tortured her to death and drove her to her grave; now he's found another girl. He'll play the hypocrite with this one too, until he cleans her out and, once he's done that, lays her where poor Sarra is lying. The same old mercenary story . . .

(*Pause.*)

In seventh heaven, a happy man, he'll live beautifully to a ripe old age, and die with a clear conscience. No, I'll strip you bare! When I rip that damned mask off you and everyone learns what kind of bird you are, I'll make you fly down from seventh heaven into such a pit the foul fiend himself won't be able to yank you out of it! I'm a decent person; it's my job to step forward and make the blind to see. I'll do my duty and tomorrow clear out of this damned district! (*Thoughtfully.*) But how can I go about it? Spelling it out to the Lebedevs is a waste of time. Challenge him to a duel? Make a scene? My God, I'm as flustered as a little kid and I've completely lost the ability to analyze the situation. How do I do it? A duel?

II

LVOV *and* KOSYKH.

KOSYKH (*Enters, gleefully to* LVOV.) Yesterday I called a little slam in clubs, and took a grand slam. Only again that Barabanov spoiled the whole shebang for me! We play. I bid: no trumps. He goes pass. Two no trumps. He goes pass. I go two diamonds . . . three clubs . . . and imagine, can you imagine: I call a slam, and he doesn't show his ace. If he'd shown his ace, the bastard, I could have called a grand slam in no-trumps.

LVOV Excuse me, I don't play cards, and so I can't share your enthusiasm. Will the benediction be soon?

KOSYKH I guess so, soon. They're trying to bring Zyuzyushka round. She's wailing like a banshee. She's upset over the dowry.

LVOV And not over her daughter?

KOSYKH Dowry. And she's ticked off. If he gets married, it means he doesn't have to pay back the debt. You can't very well sue your son-in-law for defaulting.

9. In Russian Orthodox wedding ceremonies, the benediction is given before the church ceremony takes place.

III

The same and BABAKINA.

BABAKINA (*Overdressed, pompously crosses the stage between* LVOV *and* KOSYKH; *the latter bursts out laughing up his sleeve; she looks round.*) Idiot! (KOSYKH *touches her waist with his finger and roars with laughter.*) Peasant! (*Exits.*)

KOSYKH (*Roaring with laughter.*) The dame's gone off her rocker! Until she started angling for a title, she was a dame like any dame, but now you can't come near her. (*Mimicks her.*) Peasant!

LVOV (*Upset.*) Listen, tell me truly, what do you think of Ivanov?

KOSYKH A waste of time. He plays like a shoemaker. Last year, during Lent, there was this thing. We sit down to play: me, the Count, Borkin, and him. It's my deal . . .

LVOV (*Interrupting.*) Is he a good man?

KOSYKH What, him? A rogue male! A chiseler like nobody's business. He and the Count are two of a kind. They've got a knack for sniffing out where dirty work is to be done. Came to a dead end with the Jew girl, had to eat crow, but now he's worming his way into Zyuzyushka's strongboxes. I'll bet, or may I be triply damned, in a year's time he'll have Zyuzyushka on the streets. He'll do it to Zyuzyushka, and the Count'll do it to Babakina. They'll snatch the cash and live happily ever after, getting richer and richer. Doctor, why are you so pale today? You look a fright.

LVOV Never mind, that's how it is. I had too much to drink yesterday.

IV

The same, LEBEDEV *and* SASHA.

LEBEDEV (*Entering, with* SASHA.) Let's talk in here. (*To* LVOV *and* KOSYKH.) Go into the other room, you Zulus, and join the young ladies. We have to talk in private.

KOSYKH (*As he passes* SASHA, *snaps his finger in ecstasy.*) Pretty as a picture! The Queen of Trumps!

LEBEDEV Pass by, caveman, pass by!
(LVOV *and* KOSYKH *leave.*)
Sit down, Shurochka, that's right . . . (*Sits and looks around.*) Listen carefully and with due respect. Here's the thing: your mother insisted that I inform you of the following . . . You understand? I'm not talking on my own behalf, but your mother insisted.

SASHA Papa, cut it short!

LEBEDEV You have been granted a dowry of fifteen thousand silver rubles. That's that . . . See that there are no arguments later on!

Hold on, be quiet! That's only for starters, here comes the main course. You've been granted fifteen thousand, but, since Nikolay Alekseevich owes your mother nine thousand, a deduction is being made from your dowry . . . Well now, ma'am, after that, in addition . . .

SASHA Why are you telling me this?

LEBEDEV Your mother insisted!

SASHA Leave me alone! If you had the slightest respect for me or yourself, you wouldn't let yourself talk to me this way. Do I need your dowry? I didn't ask for it then and don't ask for it now!

LEBEDEV What are you taking it out on me for? In Gogol's play the two rats at least sniffed around first, and only then went away,[1] while you, my emancipated lady, don't bother sniffing around, you just take it out on me!

SASHA Do leave me alone, don't humiliate my ears with your nickel-and-diming!

LEBEDEV (Flaring up.) Phooey! The way you're all carrying on, I'll end up sticking a knife in myself or cutting somebody else's throat! That one sets up a fearful howl all the livelong day, nagging, pestering, pinching pennies, while this one, an intelligent, humane, damn it all, emancipated woman, can't understand her own father! I'm humiliating her ears! Well, before coming here to insult your ears, out there (points to the door) I was being cut up into little pieces, drawn and quartered. She can't understand! The two of you have got my head swimming, you've mixed me all up . . . oh, you! (Goes to the door and stops.) I don't like it. I don't like anything about you!

SASHA What don't you like?

LEBEDEV I don't like any of it! Any of it!

SASHA Any of what?

LEBEDEV So now I'm supposed to pull up a chair and start telling you a story. I don't like anything about it, and I don't want to be at your wedding! (Walks over to SASHA, affectionately.) You'll forgive me, Shurochka, maybe your getting married is clever, honorable, uplifting, highly principled; but something about it isn't right, it isn't right! It isn't like other marriages. You're young, fresh, pure as a pane of glass, beautiful; whereas he's a widower, worn to a shadow, to a nub. And I can't figure him out, God bless him. (Kisses his daughter.) Shurochka, forgive me, but something smells rotten. There's already a lot of talk. About how Sarra died at his place, then suddenly for some reason he wanted to marry you . . . (Vigorously.) Anyway, I'm being an old biddy, an old biddy. I'm as bid-

1. At the start of Gogol's comedy *The Inspector General*, the worried mayor tells of a dream in which two rats of "exceptional size" came, sniffed around, and then went away again.

dified as an old hoopskirt . . . Don't listen to me. Don't listen to anybody but yourself.

SASHA   Papa, I feel myself that it's wrong . . . Wrong, wrong, wrong. If only you knew how hard it is for me! Unbearable! It's awkward and painful to me to confess this. Papa, darling, snap me out of this, for God's sake . . . teach me what to do.

LEBEDEV   Such as what? What?

SASHA   I'm more frightened than ever! (*Looks around.*) I feel as if I don't understand him and never will. The whole time we were engaged, not once did he smile, not once did he look directly into my eyes. Constant complaints, remorse over something, hints at some vague fault, trembling . . . I got tired of it. There are even moments when I feel as if I . . . I don't love him as intensely as I should. And when he rides over here or talks to me, I start to get bored. What does all this mean, Papa dear? It's terrifying!

LEBEDEV   My little dove, my only child, listen to your old father. Call it off!

SASHA (*Alarmed.*)   What do you mean, what do you mean?

LEBEDEV   Honestly, Shurochka. There'll be a scandal, the whole district will start wagging their tongues, but, after all, it's better to live through a scandal than destroy your whole life.

SASHA   Don't say that, don't say that, Papa! I won't listen to you. One must fight off these gloomy thoughts. He's a good, unhappy, misunderstood man; I will love him, I will understand him, I will set him on his feet. I will carry out my mission. It's settled!

LEBEDEV   That's not a mission, it's a psychosis.

SASHA   That's enough. I confessed to you something I didn't want to confess even to myself. Don't tell anyone. Let's forget it.

LEBEDEV   I don't understand a thing. Either I've got obtuse in my old age or you all have become so very clever, but, even if you cut my throat, I still don't understand a thing.

V

The same and SHABELSKY.

SHABELSKY (*Entering.*)   To hell with everybody, myself included! It's exasperating!

LEBEDEV   What's got into you?

SHABELSKY   No, seriously, come what may, I'll have to pull off something on my own so lowdown, so vulgar that not only I, but everyone will be nauseated. And I will do the dirty deed. Word of honor. I've already told Borkin to announce my engagement today. (*Laughs.*) Everyone's a lowlife, so I'll be a lowlife too.

LEBEDEV I'm fed up with you! Listen, Matvey, keep talking like that and they'll throw you in the—excuse the expression—booby hatch.

SHABELSKY And why should a booby hatch be any worse than an escape hatch or a nuthatch? Do me a favor, throw me in there right now. You'd be doing me a favor. They're all such petty little, insignificant little, untalented little creatures; I'm a contemptible creature myself, I don't believe a word I say . . .

LEBEDEV You know what, my boy? Put a fuse in your mouth, light it, and breathe fire at people. Or better yet: here's your hat, there's the door. There's a wedding going on here, everybody's celebrating, while you caw-caw like a crow. Yes, honestly. . . . (SHABELSKY *leans on the piano and sobs.*) Good grief! . . . Matvey! . . . Count! . . . What's wrong with you? Dear heart, my love . . . my angel . . . Have I offended you? Well, forgive me, old hound that I am . . . Forgive a drunkard . . . Have some water . . .

SHABELSKY Don't want any. (*Raises his head.*)

LEBEDEV What are you crying for?

SHABELSKY No reason, just because . . .

LEBEDEV No, Matvey, don't lie . . . what for? What's the reason?

SHABELSKY I caught a glimpse of that cello and . . . and I remembered the little Jew girl. . . .

LEBEDEV Oh boy, what a time you picked to remember! May she rest in peace, bless her, but this is no time for reminiscing . . .

SHABELSKY We would play duets together . . . A wonderful, superb woman!

        (SASHA *sobs.*)

LEBEDEV What, you too? Will you stop it? Lord, they're both bawling, while I . . . I . . . At least get out of here, the guests will see!

SHABELSKY Pasha, when the sun shines, it's cheerful even in a graveyard. When there's hope, then it's good even to be old. But I haven't got a hope, not one single one!

LEBEDEV Yes, you're really in a bad way . . . You've got no children, no money, no occupation . . . Well, that's the way it goes. (*To* SASHA.) But what's *your* problem?

SHABELSKY Pasha, give me some money. We'll settle up in the next world. I'll go to Paris, I'll take a look at my wife's grave. In my lifetime I've given away plenty, I squandered half my fortune, and so I've got the right to ask. Besides, I'm asking it from a friend . . .

LEBEDEV (*Dismayed.*) Dear heart, I haven't got a penny! But, all right, all right! I mean, I'm not promising, but you understand . . . fine, fine! (*Aside.*) They've tortured me to death!

VI

The same, BABAKINA *and then* ZINAIDA SAVISHNA.

BABAKINA (*Enters.*)   Now where is my escort? Count, how dare you
   leave me alone? Ooh, you're a disgrace! (*Strikes the Count on the
   arm with her fan.*)
SHABELSKY (*Squeamishly.*)   Leave me alone! I hate you!
BABAKINA (*Dumbfounded.*)   What . . . huh? . . .
SHABELSKY   Please get away from me.
BABAKINA (*Drops into an armchair.*)   Ah! (*Weeps.*)
ZINAIDA SAVISHNA (*Enters, weeping.*)   Someone's arrived . . . I think
   it's the best man. It 's time for the benediction . . . (*Sobs.*)
SASHA (*Pleading.*)   Mamma!
LEBEDEV   Now they've all started blubbering! A quartet! Will you
   please turn off the waterworks? Matvey! . . . Marfa Yegorovna! . . .
   Look, now I . . . I've started crying . . . (*Weeps.*) Good grief !
ZINAIDA SAVISHNA   If you don't need a mother, if you're disobedient
   . . . then do whatever you like, you have my blessing . . .
      (*Enter* IVANOV; *he is wearing a tailcoat and gloves.*)

VII

The same and IVANOV.

LEBEDEV   That's all we need! What's up?
SASHA   Why are you here?
IVANOV   Sorry, ladies and gentlemen. Let me talk to Sasha alone.
LEBEDEV   It isn't proper for the groom to drop in on the bride! It's
   time for you to be at the church!
IVANOV   Pasha, please. . . .
      (LEBEDEV *shrugs his shoulders; he,* ZINAIDA SAVISHNA, *the Count
      and* BABABKINA *leave.*)

VIII

IVANOV *and* SASHA.

SASHA (*Sternly.*)   What do you want?
IVANOV   I'm choking with spite, but I can speak calmly. Listen. Just
   now I was getting dressed for the ceremony; I looked at myself in
   the mirror and the hair at my temples . . . was gray. Shura, we
   mustn't! Shura, while it's not too late, we should call off this mindless farce . . . You're young, pure, you've got your life ahead of you,
   while I . . .
SASHA   None of this is new. I've already heard it a thousand times

and I'm sick and tired of it! Go to the church, don't keep people
waiting.

IVANOV   I'll go home right now, and you can explain to your folks
that there won't be any wedding. Tell them anything. It's time we
came to our senses. I was playing Hamlet, and you the high-
minded damsel—we've had enough of it.

SASHA (*Flaring up.*)   What sort of tone is this? I'm not listening.

IVANOV   But I'm speaking, and I'll go on speaking.

SASHA   Why did you come here? Your whining is becoming ridiculous.

IVANOV   No, I have stopped whining! Ridiculous? Yes, I am ridiculous. And if I could make myself a thousand times more ridiculous
and get the whole world to laugh, I'd do it! I stared at myself in
the mirror—and it was as if a bullet shot me in my conscience! I
laughed at myself and nearly went out of my mind with shame.
(*Laughs.*) Melancholy! Justifiable tedium! Unreasoning grief! The
only thing I left out is writing poetry. To whine, to bemoan my
fate, to drive everyone to distraction, to proclaim that the zest in
life has been squandered forever; that I've gotten rusty, outlived
myself, that I've given in to faintheartedness and am stuck up to
my ears in this foul melancholia—to proclaim this, when the sun
is shining brightly, when even the ants are hauling their loads and
pleased with themselves—thanks but no thanks! To see how some
consider you a charlatan, others pity you, yet others stretch out a
helping hand, a fourth group—the worst of all—heeds your
groans, regards you as a second Mohammed, and waits for you to
preach them a new religion any minute now. No, thank God, I
still have pride and conscience! On the way over here, I laughed
at myself, and I felt as if I need the birds to laugh at me, the trees
to laugh . . .

SASHA   This isn't spite, but insanity!

IVANOV   You think so? No, I'm not insane. Now I see things in their
true light, and my mind is as clear as your conscience. We love
each other, but our wedding cannot be! I can rant and rave and
mope as much as I please, but I have no right to ruin other people!
With my whining I poisoned the last year of my wife's life. While
you've been my fiancée, you've lost the ability to laugh and aged
five years. Your father, for whom everything in life was clear,
thanks to me can't understand people anymore. If I go to a gathering, a party, a hunt; wherever I go, I bring along boredom,
depression, dissatisfaction. Hold on, don't interrupt! I'm being
impetuous, frantic, but, excuse me, spite chokes me, and I cannot
speak any other way. I never used to lie, never used to run down
life, but, ever since I became a grumbler, involuntarily, without
noticing it myself, I do run it down, rail at fate, complain, and

everyone who hears me is infected with a distaste for life and also starts running it down! And what a tone! As if I were doing nature a favor by living. Who the hell do I think I am?

SASHA Hold on . . . What you've just said means that you're fed up with whining and it's time to begin a new life! . . . That's wonderful! . . .

IVANOV I don't see anything wonderful about it. And what's this new life? I'm a hopeless goner! It's time we both understood that. New life!

SASHA Nikolay, come to your senses! What makes you think you're a goner? What is this cynicism? No, I don't want to talk or listen . . . Go to the church!

IVANOV A goner!

SASHA Don't shout that way. The guests will hear!

IVANOV If a reasonably intelligent, educated, and healthy man for no apparent reason starts to bemoan his fate and go downhill, then he's already on the skids without a brake, and there's no escape for him! Well, where's my escape? To what? I can't drink—wine gives me a headache; I don't know how to write bad poetry; I can't romanticize my feeblemindedness and treat it as something sublime. Debility is debility, weakness is weakness—I have no other names for them. I'm a goner, a goner—and it's not worth discussing! (*Looks around.*) They might interrupt us. Listen. If you love me, help me. Right this minute, call it off without delay! Quick . . .

SASHA Oh, Nikolay, if you only knew how you've worn me out! How you've broken my heart! You're a good, intelligent man, so judge: well, can you set these tasks? Every single day, there's a task, each one more difficult than the last . . . I wanted love to be active, not agonizing.

IVANOV And when you become my wife, the tasks will be even more complex. Call it off ! Understand, it's not love speaking through you, but the obstinacy of an honest nature. You set yourself the goal, come what may, of resurrecting the man in me, rescuing me; you flattered yourself that you would do a deed of valor . . . Now you're ready to retreat, but you're prevented by a false feeling. Don't you see?

SASHA What strange, savage logic you use! Well, can I call it off ? How can I call it off ? You don't have a mother, sisters, friends . . . You're a wreck, your estate's been plundered, the people around you speak ill of you . . .

IVANOV I did something stupid coming here. I should have done what I intended . . .

(*Enter* LEBEDEV.)

IX

The same and LEBEDEV.

SASHA (*Runs to meet her father.*)   Papa, for God's sake, he ran over here like a madman and is torturing me! He insists that I call it off, he doesn't want to ruin me. Tell him that I want no part of his magnanimity! I know what I'm doing.

LEBEDEV   I can't figure this out . . . What magnanimity?

IVANOV   There will be no wedding!

SASHA   There will! Papa, tell him there will be a wedding!

LEBEDEV   Hold on, hold on! . . . Why don't you want there to be a wedding?

IVANOV   I've explained why to her, but she refuses to understand.

LEBEDEV   No, don't explain it to her, but to me, and explain it so that I can understand! Ah, Nikolay Alekseevich! God be your judge! You've filled our lives with so much murk and gloom, I feel as if I'm living in a chamber of horrors: no matter where I look, I don't understand a thing . . . It's sheer agony . . . Well, what do you ask me, an old man, to do with you? Challenge you to a duel or what?

IVANOV   No duels are called for. All that's called for is to have a brain in one's head and understand plain Russian.

SASHA (*Walks up and down the stage in agitation.*)   This is horrible, horrible! Just like a child!

LEBEDEV   There's nothing left but to throw up your hands and that's it. Listen, Nikolay. In your opinion, everything you're doing is clever, subtle, in accordance with all the rules of psychology; but in my opinion, it's a scandal and a disaster. Listen to me, an old man, one last time! Here's what I have to say to you: calm your mind! Look at things simply, the way everybody else does! In this world everything is simple. The ceiling is white, boots are black, sugar is sweet. You love Sasha, she loves you. If you love her, stick around; if you don't, go away, we won't hold any grudges. This is simple enough, isn't it? You're both healthy, intelligent, moral, and well-fed, thank God, and clothed . . . What more do you need? No money? Big deal! Money doesn't bring happiness. . . . Of course, I understand . . . your estate is mortgaged, you've got nothing to pay the interest with, but I'm a father, I understand . . . Mother can do as she likes, God bless her; she won't give money—who needs it? Shurochka says you don't need the dowry. Principles, Schopenhauer[2] . . . It's all nonsense . . . I've got ten thousand

---

2. The German philosopher Arthur Schopenhauer (1788–1860) was lodged in the Russian popular imagination as a paragon of systematic pessimism.

stashed in the bank . . . (*Looks around.*) Not a dog in this house knows about it . . . It's Granny's . . . It's for the two of you . . . Take it, only one condition with the money: give Matvey two thousand or so . . .

    (GUESTS *forgather in the reception room.*)

IVANOV   Pasha, this conversation is going nowhere. I act as my conscience dictates.

SASHA   And I act as *my* conscience dictates. You can say what you like, I won't let you go. Papa, the benediction right now! I'm going to get Mama . . . (*Exits.*)

X

IVANOV *and* LEBEDEV.

LEBEDEV   I don't understand a thing . . .

IVANOV   Listen, you poor old soul . . . To explain to you who I am—decent or contemptible, sane or psychopath, I won't even begin. I couldn't get it through your thick skull. I was young, over-enthusiastic, sincere, reasonably intelligent; I loved, hated, and had beliefs different from everyone else's; I worked and hoped for ten men, tilted at windmills, banged my head against walls; without calculating my strength, or reasoning, or knowing life, I hoisted a load on my back, which immediately snapped my spine and strained my sinews; I rushed to consume my one and only youth, I got drunk, got enthused, worked hard; knew no moderation. And tell me: could it be any other way? After all, there aren't many of us and there's plenty of work to be done—plenty! God, what plenty! And here's how life, my adversary, takes its cruel revenge! I wore myself out! Thirty years and the hangover has already set in, I'm old, I already go around in a dressing gown.[3] With a heavy head and an indolent mind, worn out, overtaxed, broken, faithless, loveless, aimless, like a shadow, loitering around people, I don't know: who am I, why am I alive, what do I want? And I've started thinking that love is absurd, caresses are cloying, there's no meaning to hard work; songs and impassioned speeches are vulgar and stale. And wherever I go I bring along tedium, cold boredom, dissatisfaction, distaste for life . . . I'm a hopeless goner! Before you stands a man of thirty-five who's always exhausted, disenchanted, crushed by the insignificance of what he's accomplished; he's burning up with shame, scoffs at his own weakness . . . Oh, how pride mutinies within me, how fury chokes me!

---

3. A reference to Oblomov, the protagonist of Ivan Goncharov's eponymous novel of 1859, an indolent landowner who spends his days in a dressing gown, lolling on a sofa, incapable of making a decision.

(*Swaying.*) Look how I've worn myself out! I'm even staggering . . .
I've gotten weak. Where's Matvey? Let him take me home.

VOICES IN THE RECEPTION ROOM   The best man's here![4]

XI

The same, SHABELSKY, BORKIN, *and then* LVOV *and* SASHA.

SHABELSKY (*Entering.*)   In somebody else's shabby dresscoat . . .
with no gloves . . . and for that reason all those sneering looks,
stupid jokes, vulgar smiles . . . Disgusting pygmies!

BORKIN (*Enters quickly with a bouquet; he is in a tailcoat with a best-
man's favor in his buttonhole.*)   Oof ! Where is he? (*To* IVANOV.)
They've been waiting for you at the church for a long time, and
here you are talking philosophy. What a comedian! Honest to God,
a comedian! After all, you're not supposed to ride with the bride,
but separately with me—then I drive back from the church and
pick up the bride. Can't you even get that right? Positively a comedian!

LVOV (*Enters, to* IVANOV.)   Ah, you're here? (*Loudly.*) Nikolay Alekseevich Ivanov, I declare in the hearing of everyone that you are
a bastard!

IVANOV (*Coldly.*)   Thank you kindly.
    (*General consternation.*)

BORKIN (*To* LVOV.)   My good sir, this is an outrage! I challenge you
to a duel!

LVOV   Mister Borkin, I consider it degrading to talk to you, let alone
fight you! But Mister Ivanov may receive satisfaction, if he so
desires.

SHABELSKY   Dear sir, I'll fight with you!

SASHA (*To* LVOV.)   Why? Why did you insult him? Gentlemen,
please, make him tell me: Why?

LVOV   Aleksandra Pavlovna, I did not insult him without sufficient
reason. I came here as a decent person to open your eyes, and I
beg you to hear me out.

SASHA   What can you say? That you're a decent person? The whole
world knows that! You'd better tell me out of your clear conscience: do you understand what you've done or don't you? You
came in here just now, Mr. Decent Person, and flung a horrible
insult at him, which nearly killed me; in the past, when you dogged
him like a shadow, and kept him from living, you were convinced
that you were doing your duty, that you are a decent person. You

---

4. In Russian Orthodox weddings, there are both a "groom's man" and a "bride's man," who
hold crowns over the couple's heads during the ceremony.

meddled in his private life, badmouthed him and ran him down wherever you could, peppered me and all my friends with anonymous letters—and all the time you thought you were being a decent person. With the idea that it's decent, you, a doctor, didn't even spare his sick wife or give her a moment's peace with your suspicions. And whatever viciousness, whatever nasty act of cruelty you commit, you'll go on thinking that you are an exceptionally decent and progressive person!

IVANOV (*Laughing.*)   This isn't a wedding, it's a debating society! Bravo, bravo!

SASHA (*To* LVOV.)   So think about that now; do you understand what you've done or don't you? Narrowminded, heartless people! (*Takes* IVANOV *by the arm.*) Let's get out of here, Nikolay! Father, let's go!

IVANOV   Where are we to go? Hold on, I'll put an end to this right now! Youth has reawakened in me; the original Ivanov has found his voice! (*He pulls out a revolver.*)

SASHA (*Screams.*)   I know what he wants to do! Nikolay, for heaven's sake!

IVANOV   I've been on the skids too long; now it's time to call a halt! Time to know when you've worn out your welcome! Step aside! Thank you, Sasha!

SASHA (*Cries out.*)   Nikolay, for heaven's sake! Stop him!

IVANOV   Leave me alone!

(*He runs off to one side and shoots himself.*)

CURTAIN

Variants to *Ivanov*

Since the earlier Korsh version is essentially a different play, I have not included any variants from it. The following changes were made in the 1888 revision for the production at the Alexandra Theater in St. Petersburg, and are taken from the censor's copy.

Act Two, Scene VI

SASHA (*Entering through the door at right with* IVANOV.)   Let's go into the garden . . . It's stuffy here.

IVANOV   Here's how things stand, Shurochka. I do nothing and think about nothing, and am weary in body and soul and brain . . . Day and night my conscience aches; I feel that I am profoundly at fault, but precisely where my fault lies, I do not understand . . . On top of that there's my wife's illness, lack of money, constant squabbling, gossip, noise . . . My house has become repulsive to me, and living in it is for me worse than torture . . . I don't know, Shurochka, what's to become of me, but I tell you frankly, for me has become unbearable even the company of my wife, who loves me . . . and such foul, egoistic thoughts crawl into my head, which I couldn't even conceive of before . . .

(*Pause.*)

Vile and nasty . . . I'm distilling tedium from everything, Shurochka; forgive me, but I only can forget it for a moment while I'm talking to you, my friend . . . Next to you I'm like a dog barking at the bright sun. Shurochka, I've known you from the time you were born; I've always loved you, pampered you. . . . I would give a great deal if I had a daughter like you right now . . .

SASHA (*Joking through tears.*)   Nikolay Alekseevich, let's run away to America . . .

IVANOV   I'm too listless to cross this threshold, and you're for America . . .

(*They walk to the entry into the garden.*)

Now then, Shura, is it hard to go on living? I see, I see it all . . . There isn't that air around us . . .

Act Two, Scene X

(ANNA PETROVNA *and* LVOV *enter from the door at right.*)

LVOV   Now why, I ask you, have we come here?

ANNA PETROVNA   Never mind, we'll be glad we did. There's no one here . . . I suppose they're in the garden . . . Let's go into the garden.

(*They go into the garden.*)

Act Three, Scene VII

IVANOV *and* SASHA.

IVANOV (*Alarmed.*) Shura, is that you?

SASHA Yes, it is . . . Didn't you expect me? Why haven't you been to see us for so long?

IVANOV Shura, for god's sake, this is indiscreet . . . Your coming here might have a dreadful effect on my wife . . .

SASHA She won't see me . . . I came by the back door . . . I'll leave right away . . . I'm worried: are you all right? Why haven't you come by for so long?

IVANOV My wife is offended enough without this, she's dying, and you come here . . . Shura, Shura! It's frivolous and . . . and inhuman!

SASHA What's that got to do with me? You haven't been by for two weeks, don't answer my letters . . . I'm in agony. It seemed to me that you were suffering unbearably here, ill, dead . . . Not a single night did I sleep a wink . . . I'll go right away. At least tell me: are you all right?

IVANOV No . . . I was torturing myself, people torture me without end . . . I simply have no more strength. You see, I'm trembling all over. And now on top of it, you . . . Why did you come?

SASHA Nikolay, this is cowardly!

IVANOV It's as if we wish her death . . . How unwholesome this is, how abnormal! Shura, I'm so much at fault, so much at fault!

SASHA Who wants her death? What's the point of those dreadful words? May she live another hundred years and may God grant she live even longer . . . But you're at fault in what? Is it really your fault that you fell out of love with her? Is it your fault that you love me? Think nice thoughts . . .

IVANOV I'm thinking . . .

SASHA It's not your fault, it's the force of circumstance. Buck up . . . I promise you, my dear, here's my hand on it, good days will come and you will be happy.

IVANOV Buck up . . . a time will come . . . in love, out of love—these are all platitudes. Hackneyed phrases, which don't help.

SASHA I talk like everybody else and don't know how else to talk.

IVANOV And this whole love affair of ours is commonplace, trite . . . "He lost heart and lost his bearings . . . She appeared, bold of heart, powerful, and gave him a helping hand." It's nice and appropriate only in novels, but in life—it's wrong, wrong . . . It's not what's needed . . . So you love me, my girl, you've lent a helping hand, and all the same I'm pathetic and helpless . . . And you yourself? You've set out with the goal of salvation, resurrection, doing

a deed of valor, but look at yourself: you're trembling, pale, your
eyes are filled with tears . . . No, Shura, you and I make bad
heroes!

SASHA   You mean to go on like this today, I see . . . Goodbye! Listen
to me: I love you and I'll follow you wherever you wish, even to
Siberia, under whatever clouds you like . . . I'm ready to die for
you. Whatever may happen to you, wherever fate may drive you,
I shall be with you forever and wherever . . .

IVANOV   Yes, yes, yes . . . Talk, talk. (*Presses his face to her shoulder.*)
I've been tormenting you, tormenting myself. Shurochka, in the
name of all that's holy, take me away from her as soon as possible
. . . Let me rest and forget myself for only a moment . . .

First version of the end of Act Three. At the end of the text there
is an additional scene.

Scene X

The same and LVOV.

LVOV (*Enters and, on seeing Anna Petrovna, quickly addresses himself
to her*).   What's going on? (*Looks into her face, to Ivanov.*) What's
been going on with you just now?

IVANOV   God, I'm so much at fault! . . . so much at fault!

LVOV   Anna Petrovna, what's the matter with you? (*To Ivanov.*) Just
you wait! I swear by the honor that isn't in you, you'll pay for her!
I'll put you through hell . . . I'll show you! . . .

IVANOV   I'm so much at fault, so much at fault . . .

CURTAIN

Act Four, VII–XI

SCENE VII

The same and IVANOV.

IVANOV *enters; he is in a tailcoat and gloves; noticeably agitated.*

LEBEDEV   That's all we needed! What's going on? What are you
doing here?

SASHA   Why are you here?

IVANOV   Sorry, ladies and gentlemen, let me speak with Sasha in
private . . .

LEBEDEV   It's improper for the groom to visit the bride. You should
have been at the church long ago!

IVANOV   Sasha, I beg you . . .

(LEBEDEV, *shrugging his shoulders*, ZINAIDA SAVISHNA, SHABEL-SKY, and BABAKINA *leave*.)

SASHA What's the matter with you?

IVANOV (*Getting excited*.) Shurochka, my angel . . .

SASHA You're overexcited . . . What's happened?

IVANOV My happiness, my darling, hear me out . . . Forget that you love me, focus all your attention, and hear me out . . .

SASHA Nikolay, don't frighten me, what's wrong?

IVANOV Just now as I was getting dressed for the ceremony, I looked at myself in the mirror, and my temples were . . . gray . . . Shurochka, this mustn't be . . . While it's still not too late, we mustn't . . . we musn't! (*Clasps her head*.) We mustn't! . . . Call it off! . . . (*Ardently*.) You're young, beautiful, pure, you have your whole life ahead of you, while I . . . gray at the temples, a brokendown wreck, guilt feelings, the past . . . We're no match! . . . I'm no match for you!

SASHA (*Sternly*.) None of this is new, I've heard it all before, and I'm sick and tired of it . . . Drive to the church, don't keep people waiting! . . .

IVANOV (*Takes her hands*.) I love you too much and you're too dear to me for me to dare stand in your way. I won't make you happy . . . I swear to God, I won't! . . . While it's not too late, call it off. It'll be the honorable and intelligent thing to do. I'll go home right now, and you can explain to your folks that there won't be a wedding . . . Explain something to them . . . (*Walks around in agitation*.) My God, my God, I feel that you, Shurochka, don't understand me . . . I'm old, my day is done, I'm covered in rust . . . the vigor of my life is spent forever, there's no future, my memories are gloomy ones. A feeling of guilt grows in me with every passing hour, chokes me . . . Doubts, presentiments . . . Something is going to happen . . . Shurochka, something is going to happen! The dark clouds are gathering, I feel it.

SASHA What do you want then?

IVANOV This very minute, without delay, turn me down. Well? Make up your mind. I beg you, I implore you . . . I see by your eyes you're wavering, you're afraid to speak the truth. Understand, my dear, inexperienced girl: what's speaking in you is not love, but the obstinacy of an honorable nature. You set out with the goal, come what may, of resurrecting the human being in me, saving me; you flattered yourself that you were carrying out a deed of valor . . . yes, yes, yes, don't deny it! Now you're ready to give it up, but a false feeling prevents you. Don't ruin yourself! My joy, listen to the man who loves you more than life itself! Well? Do you agree? Do you?

(*Pause*.)

SASHA   If that's what you want, then please: let's put our wedding off a year.

IVANOV   No, no, right away . . . This very minute! Shurochka, I won't go, I won't leave you in peace, until you call it off . . . Well? Do you agree? Tell me! I'm dying with impatience . . . Do you?

   (*Pause.*)

Do you?

   (SASHA *nods her head.*)

You were even smiling with relief. (*Breathes easily.*) What a weight off my shoulders . . . You're free, and now I'm free. You've taken a ten-ton weight off my conscience.

   (*Pause.*)

And so she called it off . . . If you hadn't agreed, this is what I would have done . . . (*Pulls a revolver out of his pocket.*) I brought it along on purpose . . . (*Hides the revolver.*) It was easier for me to kill myself than to ruin your life . . . She called it off . . . Right? . . . I'm going home . . . I've got weak . . . And I'm ashamed and humiliated and . . . I feel myself to be pathetic . . . Which door should I leave by?

   (*Pause.*)

Why are you silent? Dumbfounded. Yes . . . Don't you see, what a fuss . . . There's something I wanted to say just now and I forgot . . . (*Covers his face with his hands.*)I'm so ashamed!

SASHA   Good-bye, Nikolay Alekseevich. Forgive me! (*Goes to the door.*)

SCENE VIII

The same and LEBEDEV.

LEBEDEV   (*Running into Sasha in the doorway.*) Wait, wait . . . I'll say two words. (*Takes Sasha and Ivanov by the hands, glancing around.*) Listen. This is what mother wants, God bless her. She's not giving any money and there's no need to. Shura, you say that you don't need a dowry. Principles, altruism, Schopenhauer . . . It's all nonsense, but here's what I've got to say to you. I've got ten thousand in a secret bank account (*glancing around*), not a dog in the house knows about it . . . It's Granny's. . . . Grab it! Only one condition goes with money: give Matvey three thousand or so.

SASHA   Let go! (*Pulls away her hand and, swaying a bit, exits.*)

LEBEDEV   What's the meaning of that dream?

IVANOV   There won't be a wedding, Pasha. It's over.

LEBEDEV   How's that again?

IVANOV   Tell the guests. There won't be a wedding. I asked her to call it off.

LEBEDEV   Is this philosophy or the truth?

IVANOV   The truth. I've leaving right now.

> (*Pause.*)

> My God, my God!

LEBEDEV   I don't understand a thing. In other words, I have to go and explain to the guests that there won't be a wedding. Is that right or what?

> (*Pause.*)

> God be your judge, Nikolasha; it's not for me to judge you, but excuse me, we're no longer friends. God bless you, wherever you go. We don't understand one another. Get out!

IVANOV   I should like, Pasha, that now God send me some kind of dreadful misfortune—a disease, hunger, prison, disgrace . . . something of the kind. I can hardly stand on my feet, I'm exhausted . . . Another minute and I think I'll collapse. Where's Matvey? Let him take me home. And I love your Sasha, love her awfully . . . Now I love Sarra too. Poor woman! You remember that thing I called her, in the heat of the moment, when she came into my study? Then I nearly died of horror. For five days I didn't get a moment's sleep, didn't eat a single crumb. And after all she forgave me; forgave me everything when she died!

> (GUESTS *forgather in the reception room.*)

SCENE IX

The same and SHABELSKY.

SHABELSKY (*Enters.*)   Forgive me, Pavel, I won't come to the wedding. I'm going home. My soul is worn out. Good-bye.

IVANOV   Wait. Matvey, let's go together. If only God had sent me a disease, or poverty . . . I think I would have come to life then.

VOICES IN THE RECEPTION ROOM   The best man has arrived!

LEBEDEV (*In a whisper, angrily.*)   Tell the guests yourself, I don't know how. How can I tell them? What shall I tell them? Gentlemen, for God's sake!

SCENE X

The same, BORKIN, *and then* LVOV.

BORKIN (*Enters with a bouquet; he is in a tailcoat and with a best man's boutonniere.*)   Oof! Where is he? (*To* IVANOV.) Why did you come here? They've been waiting for you in the church a long time, and here you are gabbling philosophy. What a comedian! Honest to God, a comedian! After all, you're not supposed to ride with the bride, but separately with me, and then I come back here to bring the bride to church. How can you possibly not know that? Positively a comedian!

LEBEDEV   Well, what shall I say? What words? Dying is easier . . . (*Pulls* IVANOV *by the arm.*) What are you standing there for? Go away! At least get out of our sight!

LVOV (*Enters, to* IVANOV.)   Ah, there you are. (*Loudly.*) Nikolay Alekseevich Ivanov, I declare in the hearing of everyone that you are a bastard!

(*General confusion.*)

IVANOV (*Clutching his head.*)   What for? What for? Tell me, what for?

SHABELSKY (*To* IVANOV.)   Nicolas! Nicolas, for God's sake . . . Pay no attention. Rise above it.

BORKIN (*To* LVOV.)   My dear sir, this is disgraceful! I challenge you to a duel.

LVOV   Mister Borkin, I consider it degrading not only to fight, but even to talk to you. Whereas Mister Ivanov, if he likes, may receive satisfaction at any time.

SHABELSKY   Dear sir, I'll fight you!

IVANOV   Allow me, gentlemen. Let me speak. (*Shaking his head.*) I'm now capable of speaking and I know how to speak like a human being. His insult nearly killed me, but after all, it's not his fault! Put yourself in his shoes! Isn't it ridiculous? He's known me for over two years, but there wasn't a single minute when he could understand what sort of man I am. For two years he conscientiously analyzed me, suffered, didn't give himself or me or my wife a moment's peace, and all the same I remain a riddle and a rebus. I was not understood by my wife or my friends or my enemies or Sasha or these guests. Am I honorable or base? intelligent or stupid? healthy or psychotic? do I love or do I hate? No one knew, and everyone got lost guessing. Truth is as clear and simple as god's daylight, any little kid could understand it, but even intelligent people didn't understand me. Which means that there is no truth in me. Ah, how I understand myself now, how absurd I am to myself! With what indignation I received that "bastard"! (*Roars with laughter.*) Yes, I was honorable, bold, ardent, indefatigable; did the work of three men; knew how to get indignant, weep, love, hate; but to the point that I only wore myself out. Yes, I loved people, loved a woman, like none of you, but my love lasted only two or three years, until my indolent soul wore out; until it began to seem to me that love is rubbish, that affection is cloying, that songs and passionate speeches are vulgar and stale. I was quick to get excited, took on burdens beyond my strength; but quickly grew weak, lost heart, and from a hero turned into a pitiful coward. Now I'm thirty-five, I've accomplished less than a sparrow; but already I'm debilitated, exhausted, my insignificant achievements and sacrifices have crushed me; no faith, passions extinguished, I am disappointed, sick. For what reason? My pretentions were heroic, but my strength was that of a worm. No discipline, no iron in my blood, no willpower. I'm pathetic, insignificant, and destructive as a moth. Woe to those people who respect and love such as I, put them on a pedestal, worship them, excuse them, sympathize! Unhappy those women who, instead of loving brave, magnanimous, strong, healthy, handsome men, love cowardly, feeble, whining, puny men! My young, original Ivanov has begun to speak in me! I despise and hate myself. Don't look at me: I'm ashamed! Don't look! . . . Or are you waiting until I finish my speech? O, I know what to do with myself! There's good reason that I keep trembling with anger and hatred for myself. Just you wait, right now! (*Pulls out the revolver.*) Here you go! (*Shoots himself.*)

CURTAIN

Variants from the censor's copy of 1889, the journal *Northern Herald* (*Severny Vestnik*), and *Plays* (1897).

Act One

Replace first, a young doctor; then a trip to the Crimea; in the Crimea, a native Tatar . . .

with first, a young doctor; then, a trip to the Crimea; in the Crimea, a native Tatar; on the way back, a private train compartment with some dandy, who has lost all his money but is sweet . . . (Censor 1889) (Page 29)

Act Two

Replace (FIRST GUEST *yawns.*)

with FIRST GUEST (*To the* YOUNG LADY *beside him.*)   What, ma'am?

YOUNG LADY   Tell me a story.

FIRST GUEST   What am I supposed to tell you?

YOUNG LADY   Well, something funny.

FIRST GUEST   Funny? (*After a moment's thought.*) A man came up to another man and sees—there's a dog sitting there, you understand. (*Laughs.*) So he asks, "What's your dog's name?" And the other man says, "Liqueurs." (*Roars with laughter.*) Liqueurs . . . Get it? "Like-yours" . . .

YOUNG LADY   Like?

FIRST GUEST   Liqueurs.

YOUNG LADY   There's nothing funny about that.

THIRD GUEST   That's an old joke . . . (*Yawns.*)(Censor 1889) (page 39)

Replace (*Quickly exits into the garden.*)
(*Quickly exits to the terrace and stops near the card table. To* YEGO-RUSHKA.) How much did you put down? What did you put down? Wait . . . thirty-eight multiplied by eight . . . makes . . . eight times eight . . . Ah, the hell with it! . . . (*Goes into the garden.*) (Censor 1889) (Page 41)

After I'm a lowlife too and a slave-owner. — Nikolay doesn't stay home nights—he's a lowlife too: it means he tortures his wife so as to put her in her grave and marry a rich one. (Censor 1889) (Page 47)

After A waste of perfectly good sugar. — I'll take it away, and let Matryona finish it. (Censor 1889) (Page 50)

Act Three

After A virtuoso! — . . . every day he generates thousands of projects, tears the stars out of the sky, but never makes a profit . . . He never has a penny in his pocket . . .
LEBEDEV   Art for art's sake . . . (Censor 1889; *Northern Herald*) (Page 56)

After the stage direction: (*Laughter.*) —
LEBEDEV   Why, he's so addicted to card playing, the dear heart, that instead of good-bye he says pass . . . (Censor 1889; *Northern Herald*)(Page 59)

After (*Greets them.*) — I went through all the rooms, and there's that doctor, like he's been eating loco-weed, he opened his peepers wide and — "What'ya want? Get outta here . . . You'll give the patient a fright," he says . . . As if it's that easy . . . (Censor 1889) (Page 59)

After a George Sand! — I thought only Borkin had great ideas in his head, but now it seems . . . I'm going, I'm going . . . (*Exits.*) (Censor 1889) (Page 62)

After farming, district schools, projects — speeches, cheesemaking that failed, a stud farm, articles, scads of mistakes . . . (Censor 1889) (Page 63)

After. How else can you explain this lassitude? —
All us Russians, at age twenty and twenty-five don't get excited in moderation, we plunge into the fire and mindlessly squander our strength, and nature punishes us for this cruelly: at age thirty, we're already old and worn out. (Censor 1889; *Northern Herald*.) (Page 63)

After brains or hands or feet — as if it weren't Ivanov inside me, but an old, sick horse . . . (Censor 1889) (Page 64)

After Have you indeed? — Well, if it's come to that, then know that I love your wife! I love her as intensely as I hate you! That's my right and that's my privilege! When I first saw her torment, my heart couldn't stand it and . . . (Censor 1889; *Northern Herald*) (Page 66)

After do a valiant deed! — The distinguishing feature of young Russian women is always the fact that they can't tell the difference between a good painting and a caricature. (Censor 1889) (Page 67)

After nothing but bellyachers and psychopaths. — Ah, my little crackpot! What are you laughing at? You're too young to teach me and save me. Little crackpot!

SASHA   If you don't mind, what a thing to say! Really, this won't do at all!

IVANOV   You are my little crackpot!

SASHA   Can we do without the sarcasm?

IVANOV (*Shaking his head.*)   We cannot!

SASHA   All right then! We know how to punish you. How about getting a move on! (*Shoves his shoulder, then pulls him by the arm with all her might.*) Move! Lord, what a heavy lummox! Get a move on, Oblomov!

IVANOV   No, I won't stir from this spot. The likes of you, dear girl, won't get me to budge. You can try with all your might and even send for your dear mamma to help! No, madam, it takes far more strength. A whole houseful of widows and a girl's boarding-school won't move me from this spot.

SASHA   Oof, I'm out of breath . . . I wish you were an empty vessel!

IVANOV   There now, you shameless hussy, that'll teach you to save people! Oh you . . . dark-eyed thing! (Censor 1889; *Northern Herald*) (Page 68)

After Nothing more! — Eh, feed me to the wolves, if only I could smoke the sniveling brat out of myself, I might be a real man! Watch out, here comes the train! (*Chases* SASHA.) Brrr!

SASHA (*Jumps onto the sofa.*)   It's gone, it's gone, it's gone!
IVANOV   Oh frailty, thy name is woman! (*Roars with laughter.*) (Censor 1889; *Northern Herald*) (Page 68)

After what a ridiculous numbskull! — You know, in the reeds along the Dnieper there nests a certain bird — a grayish, very sullen, pitiful little thing, and it's called a bittern. It sits all day in the reeds, dolefully going: boohoo! boohoo! Like a cow locked up in a barn. That's what I'm like. I sit by myself in the reeds and (Censor 1889) (Page 68)

Act Four

After I'm not talking on my own behalf, but your mother insisted. — Listen. Since the best man hasn't gotten here yet and since we still haven't spoken the benediction over you, to avoid any misunderstanding, you should know once and for all that we . . . I mean not we, but your mother . . . (Censor 1889) (Page 73)

After wherever I go, I bring along boredom, depression, dissatisfaction. — My life has become loathsome to me, but that alone does not give me the right to leach the color out of other people's lives. (Censor 1889) (Page 78)

After I have no other names for them. — So wherein lies my salvation? Tell me, in love? That's an old gimmick! Love is that extra stab in the back; it complicates spiritual uplift, it adds a new tedium to tedium. Winning two hundred thousand? The same thing. Stimulating and uplifting my spirit can be achieved only by heaven itself, but the stimulation is followed by the hangover, and my spirit falls even lower than before. You must understand this and not hide from yourself! Our old friend, depression, has only one salvation, and, unfortunately, we are too intelligent for that salvation. (Censor 1889; *Northern Herald*; *Plays*) (Page 79)

After You don't have a mother, sisters, friends . . . — Alone, alone, like an orphan. Whom shall I throw you at? (Censor 1889; *Northern Herald*; *Plays*) (Page 79)

After I should have done what I intended . . . — This is all I wanted . . . (*Shows a revolver and hides it again.*) It's easier to kill myself than to ruin your life. But I thought that you would listen to common sense and . . .
SASHA   Hand over the revolver!
IVANOV   I won't.

SASHA Hand it over, I tell you!

IVANOV Sasha, I have too much love for you and too much anger for small talk. I'm asking you to call it off! It's a final demand in the name of fairness and humane feeling! (Censor 1889) (Page 79)

After how fury chokes me! —

I'll ask you only about one thing. If once in your life you encountered a young man, ardent, sincere, no fool, and you see that he loves, hates and believes not as everyone else does, works and hopes for ten, makes an unusual marriage, tilts at windmills, bangs his head against the wall, if you see how he has hoisted a load which snaps his spine and strains his sinews, then say to him: don't hasten to squander your strength on a single youth, preserve it for your whole life; get drunk, get excited, work, but be temperate, otherwise fate will punish you cruelly! At thirty you will already have a hangover and you will be old. With a heavy head, with an indolent soul, worn out, broken down, without faith, without love, without a goal, like a shadow, you will loiter amidst people and not know: Who are you? Why are you alive? What do you want? And it will seem to you that love is rubbish, affection cloying, that there's no sense in hard work, that songs and passionate speeches are vulgar and stale. And wherever you go, everywhere you will bring with you longing, cold boredom, dissatisfaction, revulsion to life, and there will be no salvation for you. Ruined irrevocably! You'll say, how before you there stood a man of thirty-five already impotent, disappointed, crushed by his insignificant accomplishment, how he burned with shame in your eyes, was mocked for his weakness, how pride was aroused in him, and how stupidly he ended up! How this raving choked him! (Censor 1889; *Northern Herald*) (Page 81)

After Positively a comedian! —

SASHA It doesn't matter, we'll all go together right now. (*Takes* IVA-NOV *by the arm.*) Let's go!

IVANOV An energetic individual! (*Laughs.*) You're marrying a drill sergeant . . . (Censor 1889) (Page 82)

The Wedding

Chekhov characterized *The Wedding* as a "scene in one act," thus distinguishing it from his other one-act comedies, which he called "jokes" (*shutki*). It differs too in being based on real experiences and individuals in Chekhov's past. Chekhov modeled the Greek confectioner Dymba on a clerk in his father's grocery store in Taganrog; he met the flirtatious midwife when serving as best man at an 1887 wedding. Between 1885 and 1886, Chekhov lived in a Moscow flat beneath the quarters of a caterer who rented out room for weddings and balls. At times, Chekhov seemed obsessed with nuptial ceremonials, which are the subject of many of his stories written in the 1880s. This play was first performed at the Art and Literary Society at the Moscow Hunt Club on November 28, 1900, as part of a Chekhov evening. The great writer Leo Tolstoy, who was present, laughed until he cried.

The Wedding masterfully displays the dissolution of social convention. Every pretense kept up by one character is demolished by another. No one's secrets are safe. Over the course of the play, we discover that the groom has married the bride for the sake of a paltry dowry that has yet to be paid; that the bride is totally insensitive to her own situation; that her parents are the most narrowminded and parsimonious of philistines; and that the guests bear no particular goodwill for the newlyweds. The play revolves around one principal deception: to dress out the banquet, a "General"—that is, a high-ranking official, a V.I.P.—is required as guest of honor. The bride's mother has charged a friend with this task; he has pocketed the money and brought a deaf naval captain. The mother discovers the swindle and ejects the old man without further ado. At that moment, the farcical tone of the play alters. The old captain, disabused and stripped of any consideration, can only gasp in horror, "How disgusting! How revolting!" After the old man's exit, the guests and hosts revert to their squabbling. The play's singular moment of genuine feeling has made no dent in their thick hides.

Again, Chekhov employed the comic device of the gap between reality and the characters' aspirations. Hoping to sound refined, they mangle French and mispronounce polysyllabic words. Zmeyukina, a midwife, whose profession is of the earthiest, constantly demands "atmosphere" and delicate feelings. In anticipation of Solyony in *Three Sisters*, she quotes the romantic poet Lermontov. The father of the bride invariably dismisses anything unfamiliar with contempt, branding it "monkey-shines." The main oration of the evening is delivered by a Greek who butchers the Russian language. Yet when a native Russian speaker rises to address the guests, it is the retired Captain, whose naval lingo is every bit as incomprehensible. Assuming that he is entertaining the company, the old salt bores the guests first into stupor and then to mutiny.

A sense of inhumanity hangs over the entire action, with no character ever making true contact with another. A deeply etched caricature in the style of Daumier or Goya, *The Wedding* subjects the lower middle-class to merciless derision. In the process, Chekhov casts a shadow over that stalwart of family value, the institution of holy matrimony.

The Wedding

A Play in One Act

Cast[1]

YEVDOKIM ZAKHAROVICH ZHIGALOV, civil servant, retired
NASTASYA TIMOFEEVNA, his wife
DASHENKA, their daughter
EPAMINOND MAKSIMOVICH APLOMBOV, her bridegroom
FYODOR YAKOVLEVICH REVUNOV-KARAULOV, naval captain second class, retired
ANDREY ANDREEVICH NYUNIN, an insurance agent
ANNA MARTYNOVNA ZMEYUKINA, a midwife, thirty, in a bright crimson dress
IVAN MIKHAILOVICH YAT, a telegraph operator
KHARLAMPI SPIRIDONOVICH DYMBA, a Greek caterer
DMITRY STEPANOVICH MOZGOVOY, sailor in the Volunteer Fleet[2]
GROOM'S MEN,[3] BRIDESMAIDS, WAITERS, ETC.

A brightly-lit reception room. A large table, laid for supper. Tailcoated WAITERS *are fussing around the table. Offstage, a band is playing the last figure of a quadrille.*

ZMEYUKINA, YAT *and the* BEST MAN *cross the stage.*

1. Most of the names are telling names—puns or plays or Russian words. *Zhigalov* recalls *zhigalo*, ringleader, bellwether; *zhigalka*, horsefly, tallow candle; and *zhiga*, invective. *Aplombov* seems to come from the French *aplomb*, self-confidence; *Nyunin*, from *nyuni*, slavering lips; *nyunit*, to moan and groan; *nyunya*, whining child, crybaby; *Zmeukina* from *zmey*, dragon, *zmeya*, snake. *Yat*, the name of a letter in the Cyrillic alphabet, sounded like e but was written otherwise, thus providing a trap for schoolchildren and clerks (it was abolished in the spelling reforms of 1917). *Mozgovoy*, from *mozg*, brain; spinal cord, bone marrow. Revunov-*Karaulov*, one who cries for help (*karaul*).
2. Founded during the Russo-Turkish War (1877–78); its three ships were later ordered to the Pacific to transport prisoners to Vladivostok and the island of Sakhalin.
3. See *Ivanov*, note 48, page 82.

ZMEYUKINA No, no, no!

YAT (*Following her.*) Take pity on me! Take pity on me!

ZMEYUKINA No, no, no!

BEST MAN (*Chasing after them.*) You can't do this, people! Where are you off to? What about the "gran rawn"? "Gran rawn, seel voo playt!"[4]

(*They leave. Enter* NASTASYA TIMOFEEVNA *and* APLOMBOV.)

NASTASYA TIMOFEEVNA Why are you pestering me with this silly talk? You'd better go dance.

APLOMBOV I'm no Spinoza to spin around with my legs bent into a pretzel.[5] I'm a respectable person, with good references, and I derive no amusement from such idle pursuits. But this isn't about dancing. Excuse me, *maman*, but I can't figure out why you act the way you do. For instance, in addition to some indispensable domestic articles, you promised to give me, along with your daughter, two lottery tickets. Where are they?

NASTASYA TIMOFEEVNA I've got such a splitting headache . . . It must be this awful weather . . . we're in for a thaw!

APLOMBOV Don't try to hoodwink me. Today I found out you put those tickets in pawn. Pardon me, *maman*, but the only people who act like that are swindlers. I'm not complaining out of self-ishness—I don't need your lottery tickets, but it's the principle of the thing, and I won't have anybody putting anything over on me. I've procured your daughter happiness, but if you don't hand over those tickets today, I'll make your daughter's life a living hell. On my honor as a gentleman!

NASTASYA TIMOFEEVNA (*Glancing at the table and counting the place settings.*) One, two, three, four, five . . .

A WAITER The chef wants to know how you'd like the ice cream served: with rum, Madeira, or on its own?

APLOMBOV Rum. And tell your boss there's not enough wine. Tell him to serve more "Ho Soturn."[6] (*To* NASTASYA TIMOFEEVNA.) Likewise you promised, and it was fully agreed upon, that there'd be a General at this supper party. Well, where is he, I'd like to know?

NASTASYA TIMOFEEVNA This, my dear, is not *my* fault.

APLOMBOV Whose then?

NASTASYA TIMOFEEVNA It's Andrey Andreevich's fault . . . Yesterday he went and promised to bring the most genuine General. (*Sighs.*)

---

4. Mispronounced French, *Grande ronde, s'il vous plaît*. A "grande ronde" is a round dance, a figure in a quadrille.

5. The Dutch philosopher Benedictus Spinoza (1632–1677) is confused here with the dancer Leone Espinosa (1825–1903), who worked at the Moscow Bolshoy Theater from 1869 to 1872.

6. Mispronunciation of *Haut Sauternes*, a sweet white dessert wine. Drinking this before the meal is another sign of gaucherie.

Must not have run across one anywheres, or he would have brought him . . . Does that mean we're stingy? For our darling daughter we wouldn't stint a thing. You want a General, you'll get a General . . .

APLOMBOV And besides that . . . Everyone, you included, *maman*, knows that before I'd proposed to Dashenka, that telegraph operator Yat was going out with her. Why did you invite him? Didn't you realize it would get on my nerves?

NASTAYA TIMOFEEVNA Ooh, what's your name?—Epaminond Maksimych, you've not been married a full day yet, and already you've tortured both me and Dashenka to death with your blather. What'll it be like after a year? You're such a pest, ooh, a pest!

APLOMBOV You don't like hearing the truth? Aha? Thought so. Then behave like a decent person. That's all I ask of you: behave like a decent person!

(*Couples dancing the grande ronde cross the room from one door to the other. The first couple is the* BEST MAN *and* DASHENKA, *the last* YAT *and* ZMEYUKINA. *These last two fall behind and remain in the room.*

ZHIGALOV *and* DYMBA *enter and walk up to the table.*)

BEST MAN (*Shouting.*) Promenade! M'sewers, promenade! (*Off-stage.*) Promenade!
(*The couples go off.*)

YAT (*To* ZMEYUKINA.) Take pity on me! Take pity, fascinating Anna Martynovna!

ZMEYUKINA Aah, what's wrong with you . . . ? I already told you, I'm not in voice today.

YAT Sing something, I implore you! Just one single note! Take pity on me! Just one note!

ZMEYUKINA You're driving me crazy . . . (*She sits and waves her fan.*)

YAT No, you're simply heartless! That so cruel a creature, pardon the expression, should have so spectacular a voice, spectacular! With a voice like that, excuse the expression, you shouldn't be a midwife, but a singer in concert halls with an audience! For instance, the divine way you handle those trills . . . like this.(*He croons.*) "I loved you once, but ever loved in vain. . . ." Spectacular!

ZMEYUKINA (*Croons.*) "I loved you, and that love might still perhaps. . . ."[7] Is that it?

YAT That's the very thing! Spectacular!

ZMEYUKINA No, I'm not in voice today. Here—fan a breeze my way . . . It's so hot. (*To* APLOMBOV.) Epaminond Maksimych, why so

---

7. The 1829 poem by Aleksandr Pushkin (1799–1837): "I loved you once, perhaps I love still . . . / Love has not fully died out in my heart . . ." was set to music by many composers, including Alyabiev, Bulakhov, Varlamov, and Gurilev.

melancholy? Is that the way a bridegroom should behave? Aren't you ashamed of yourself, you naughty man? Well, a penny for your thoughts!

APLOMBOV   Marriage is a serious step! You've got to consider everything in depth and in detail.

ZMEYUKINA   You're all such naughty cynics! Just being around you smothers me . . . I need atmosphere! You hear? I need atmosphere! (*She croons.*)

YAT   Spectacular! Spectacular!

ZMEYUKINA   Fan me, keep fanning, or I think my heart'll burst. Tell me, please, why do I feel so smothered?

YAT   It's because you're sweating, ma'am . . .

ZMEYUKINA   Phooey, don't be so vulgar! Don't you dare use such expressions!

YAT   Sorry! Of course, you're accustomed, pardon the expression, to aristocratical society and . . .

ZMEYUKINA   Aah, leave me alone! I need poetry, excitement! Fan me, fan me . . .

ZHIGALOV   (*To* DYMBA.)   Shall we have another? (*Pours.*) There's always time for a drink. The main thing, Kharlampy Spiridonych, is don't neglect your business. Drink up, but keep a clear head . . . Though if you want a little nip, why not have a little nip? Always time for a little nip . . . Your health! (*They drink.*) Say, have you got any tigers in Greece?

DYMBA   We got.

ZHIGALOV   How about lions?

DYMBA   And lions we got. In Russia is notting, in Greece is all ting.[8] Dere I got fodder and oncle and brodders, but here is notting.

ZHIGALOV   Hmm . . . any whales in Greece?

DYMBA   All ting we got.

NASTASYA TIMOFEEVNA   (*To her husband.*)   Why are you eating and drinking any old way? It's time we all sat down. Don't stick your fork in the lobsters . . . That's there for the General. He may show up yet . . .

ZHIGALOV   Have you got lobsters in Greece?

DYMBA   We got . . . All ting we got dere.

ZHIGALOV   Hmm . . . have you got senior civil servants too?

ZMEYUKINA   I can imagine what a wonderful atmosphere there is in Greece!

ZHIGALOV   And I'll bet a lot of monkeyshines as well. Greeks are just like Armenians or Gypsies. Can't sell you a sponge or a goldfish without trying to put one over on you. Shall we have another?

8. In Russian, Dymba is not only ungrammatical but also cannot pronounce the sound *ch*.

NASTASYA TIMOFEEVNA   Why keep drinking any old way? It's time to
sit down. Almost midnight! . . .

ZHIGALOV   If it's sitting you want, sitting you'll get. Ladies and gentlemen, please be so kind! Do me the favor! (*He shouts.*) Supper's
on! Young people!

NASTASYA TIMOFEEVNA   Dear guests! Be so kind! Take your seats!

ZMEYUKINA (*Sitting at the table.*)   I need poetry! "But he, the rebel,
seeks the storm, as if a storm could offer peace."[9] I need a storm!

YAT (*Aside.*)   Wonderful woman! I'm in love! Head over heels in love!

>   (*Enter* DASHENKA, MOZGOVOY, BEST MAN, GROOM'S MEN, MAIDS
>   OF HONOR, *etc. Everyone sits noisily at the table. A moment's
>   pause, then the band plays a march.*)

MOZGOVOY (*Rising.*)   Ladies and gentlemen! I'm supposed to say the
following . . . We've got all sorts of toasts and speeches lined up.
So let's not beat around the bush, but start right in! Ladies and
gentlemen, I propose a toast to the newlyweds!

>   (*The band plays a fanfare. Cheers. Clinking glasses.*)

MOZGOVOY   It's bitter! Sweeten it up![1]

EVERYONE   It's bitter! Sweeten it up!

>   (APLOMBOV *and* DASHENKA *kiss.*)

YAT   Spectacular! Spectacular! I must remark, ladies and gentlemen,
and give credit where credit's due, that this room and the whole
affair is magnificent! First-rate, enchanting! But do you know the
one thing missing for absolute perfection? Electric lighting, pardon the expression! Every country has already installed electric
lighting, and only Russia lags behind.

ZHIGALOV (*Weightily.*)   Electricity . . . Hmm . . . Well, in my opinion, electric lighting is just a lot of monkeyshines . . . They shovel
in a little coal and think they've pulled the wool over your eyes!
No, pal, if you're going to light us up, don't give us coal, but something with body to it, something special that a man can sink his
teeth into! Give us fire—got me?—fire, which comes from nature,
not your imagination!

YAT   If you'd ever seen what an electric battery's made out of, maybe
you'd change your mind.

ZHIGALOV   But I don't want to see it. Monkeyshines. They're swin-
dling the common man . . . Squeezing the last drop out of him . . .
We know their kind . . . As for you, young man, why stick up for
monkeyshines? Better have a drink and fill the glasses. That's the
thing to do!

APLOMBOV   I'm in complete agreement, Dad. What's the point of

---

9. Quotation from the poem "The Sail" ("Parus," 1832) by Mikhail Lermontov, which Chekhov also quotes in the last act of *Three Sisters*.
1. The young couple must kiss to "sweeten things up."

trotting out these highbrow conversations? Personally I've got nothing against discussing any kind of invention in a scientific context, but is this the proper time? (*To* DASHENKA.) What's your opinion, "ma chair"?[2]

DASHENKA   The gentleman's just trying to show off his eddication, talking about what nobody understands.

NASTASYA TIMOFEEVNA   We've lived all our life without education, thank God, and this is the third daughter we've married off to a good man. If, according to you, we're so uneducated, why come here? Go back to your educated friends!

YAT   Nastasya Timofeevna, I've always respected your family, so if I bring up the electric light, it doesn't mean I'm showing off. I'll even have a drink. I've always wished Darya Yevdokimovna a good husband from the bottom of my heart. Nowadays, Nastasya Timo-feevna, it's not easy to find a good husband. These days everyone's getting married for what he can make off it, for the money . . .

APLOMBOV   That's an insinuation!

YAT   (*Backing off.*)   No insinuations intended . . . I wasn't talking about present company . . . I just . . . generally speaking . . . For heaven's sake! Everybody knows you're marrying for love . . . The dowry's skimpy enough.

NASTASYA TIMOFEEVNA   No, it is *not* skimpy! You open your mouth, young sir, and pay no mind to what comes out. Besides the thousand rubles cash money, we're giving three lady's coats, a bed, and all the furniture. Just try and dig up such a dowry anywheres else!

YAT   I didn't mean . . . Certainly, furniture's a fine thing and . . . so are coats, of course, but I was concerned about this gentleman's taking offense at my insinuations.

NASTASYA TIMOFEEVNA   Then don't make any. Out of consideration for your parents we invited you to this wedding, and you make all kinds of remarks. If you knew that Epaminond Maksimych was marrying for money, why didn't you say something earlier? (*Tear-fully.*) I reared her, nursed her, cared for her. . . . She was her mother's pride and joy, my little girl . . .

APLOMBOV   So you believe him? Thank you ever so much! Most grateful to you! (*To* YAT.) As for you, Mr. Yat, although you're a friend of mine, I won't have you acting so discourteously in other people's houses! I'll thank you to clear out!

YAT   How's that again?

APLOMBOV   If only you were the same kind of gentleman what I am! In a word, please clear out of here!

(*The band plays a fanfare.*)

2. *Ma chère*, French: my dear.

GROOM'S MEN (*To* APLOMBOV.)   Let it alone! Calm down! Hey, cut it out! Sit down! Take it easy!

YAT   I didn't do a thing . . . I just . . . I certainly don't understand why . . . As you like, I'll go . . . Only first pay me back the five rubles you borrowed last year for a quilted, pardon the expression, waistcoat. I'll have one more drink, and then . . . I'll go, only first you pay me what you owe me.

GROOM'S MEN   Hey, come on, come on! That's enough! Is it worth arguing over nothing?

BEST MAN (*Shouts.*)   To the health of the bride's parents, Yevdokim Zakharych and Nastasya Timofeevna!

(*The band plays a fanfare. Cheers.*)

ZHIGALOV (*Moved, bows in all directions.*)   I thank you! Dear guests! I'm most grateful to you for remembering us and showing up, and not being standoffish! . . . Now don't think that this is a lot of hooey or monkeyshines on my part, for it's strictly from the heart! From the very bottom of my heart! Nothing's too good for decent people! My humble thanks! (*Exchange of kisses.*)

DASHENKA (*To her mother.*)   Mummy dear, why are you crying? I'm so happy!

APLOMBOV   *Maman*'s upset at the imminent parting. But I suggest that she'd better remember what we were talking about before.

YAT   Don't cry, Nastasya Timofeevna! Don't you realize what human tears are? A sign of feebleminded psychiatrics, that's all!

ZHIGALOV   Have you got mushrooms in Greece?

DYMBA   We got. All ting we got dere.

ZHIGALOV   Well, I bet you haven't got the creamy ones.

DYMBA   Krim we got. All ting we got.

MOZGOVOY   Kharlampy Spiridonych, it's your turn to make a speech! Ladies and gentlemen, let him make a speech!

EVERYONE (*to* DYMBA.)   Speech! Speech! Your turn!

DYMBA   Pliss? Not to understanding . . . How is what?

ZMEYUKINA   No, no! Don't you dare turn us down! It's your turn! Stand up!

DYMBA (*Rises, bashful.*)   I talk sometings . . . Is Russia and is Griss. Now in Russia is such a pipples, and in Griss is such a pipples . . . And pipples on ocean is sailing *karávia*, in Russian means sheeps, but on land is all sorts which is railroad trains. I understanding good . . . We Griks, you Russians, and I not needing nottings . . . I can talk also dis . . . Is Russia and is Griss.

(NYUNIN *enters.*)

NYUNIN   Wait a minute, ladies and gentlemen, stop eating! Hold on! Nastasya Timofeevna, step over here a minute! (*Takes* NASTASYA TIMOFEEVNA *aside; out of breath.*) Listen . . . The General's on his way . . . I finally got hold of one . . . Had a perfectly awful time of it . . . The General's genuine, highly respectable, old, must be about eighty, then again maybe ninety. . . .

NASTASYA TIMOFEEVNA   When will he get here?

NYUNIN   Any minute now. You're going to thank me for the rest of your life. Not a general, but a rose garden, a Napoleon![3] Not an ordinary foot soldier, not infantry, but navy! In rank he's a captain second class, but in their lingo, the navy's, that's the same as a major general or in the civil service an actual state councilor. Absolutely the same. Even higher.

NASTASYA TIMOFEEVNA   You're not trying to finagle me, are you, Andryusha sweetie?

NYUNIN   What's that? You think I'm a four-flusher? Don't you worry!

NASTASYA TIMOFEEVNA   (*Sighing.*)   I wouldn't want to throw our money down the drain, Andryusha sweetie . . .

NYUNIN   Don't you worry! He's not just a General, but an oil painting! (*Raising his voice.*) I says to him, "You've quite forgotten us," I says, "your excellency! It's not nice, your excellency, to forget your old friends! Nastasya Timofeevna," I says, "thinks very highly of you!" (*Goes to the table and sits down.*) Then he says, "Excuse me, my friend, how can I go when I don't know the groom?"— "Oh, that's enough of that, your excellency, don't stand on ceremony! The groom," I says, "is a splendid fellow, wears his heart on his sleeve. Works," I says, "as an appraiser in a pawnshop, but don't think, your excellency, that he's some kind of puny little runt or a shifty conman either. Nowadays," I says, "even highborn ladies work in pawnshops." He claps me on the shoulder, we each smoke a panatela, and now he's on his way . . . Wait a bit, ladies and gentlemen, stop eating . . .

APLOMBOV   But when will he get here?

NYUNIN   Any minute now. When I left him, he was putting on his galoshes. Hold on, ladies and gentlemen, don't eat.

APLOMBOV   Then you'd better tell them to play a march . . .

NYUNIN   (*Shouts.*)   Hey, musicians! A march!
(*The band plays a march for a minute.*)

WAITER   (*Announcing.*)   Mister Revunov-Karaulov.
(ZHIGALOV, NASTASYA TIMOFEEVNA, *and* NYUNIN *run to meet him. Enter* REVUNOV-KARAULOV.)

NASTASYA TIMOFEEVNA (*Bowing.*)   Make yourself at home, your excellency! Pleased to meet you!

REVUNOV   Pleasure's all mine!

ZHIGALOV   We're just plain, simple, ordinary people, your excel-

3. In the original, Boulanger: Georges-Ernest-Jean-Marie Boulanger (1837–1891), French Minister of War from 1886 to 1887, an ambitious and reactionary troublemaker, who preached revenge against the Prussians.

lency, but don't suppose that for our part we'd go in for any monkeyshines. We put great stock in decent folks, nothing's too good for 'em. Make yourself at home!

REVUNOV Pleasure's all mine, delighted!

NYUNIN May I introduce, your excellency! The bridegroom, Epaminond Maksimych Aplombov, and his newly-born . . . I mean, his newly-wedded wife! Ivan Mikhailych Yat, who works in the telegraph office! A foreigner of Greek persuasion in the catering line, Kharlampy Spiridonych Dymba! Osip Lukich Babelmandebsky! Et cetera, et cetera . . . All the rest are of no account. Take a seat, your excellency!

REVUNOV Pleasure's all mine! Excuse me, ladies and gentlemen. I'd like to have a word with Andryusha. (*Takes* NYUNIN *aside.*) I'm a little confused, my boy . . . Why do you call me your excellency? For I'm no General, after all! Captain second class—that's even lower than a colonel.

NYUNIN (*Speaks in his ear as if he were deaf.*) I know, Fyodor Yakovlevich, but please allow us to call you your excellency! This here family, y'see, is very old-fashioned, they respect their elders and love to kowtow to people of rank . . .

REVUNOV Oh, if that's the way things are, all right . . . (*Going to the table.*) Pleasure's all mine!

NASTASYA TIMOFEEVNA Take a seat, your excellency! Be so kind! Eat a little something, your excellency! Only forgive us, you must be used to delicacies and we only got plain fare!

REVUNOV (*Not having heard.*) How's that, ma'am? I see . . . Yes'm. (*Pause.*) Yes'm . . . In the olden times people always lived simply and were contented. I'm a man of rank, but even so I live simply . . . Today, Andryusha comes to me and asks me here to the wedding. "How can I go," I ask, "when I don't know 'em? It's awkward!" But he says, "They're simple people, old-fashioned, enjoy entertaining guests . . ." Well, of course, if that's the way things are . . . why not? Happy to oblige. At home, all by my lonesome, it's boring, but if my presence at the wedding can give anybody pleasure, then, I say, let's do 'em a favor . . .

ZHIGALOV You mean, it was from the heart, your excellency? I look up to you! I myself am a simple man, without any monkeyshines, and I look up to others like me. Have a bite, your excellency!

APLOMBOV Have you been in retirement long, your excellency?

REVUNOV Huh? Yes, yes . . . that's right . . . Very true. Yessir. . . . But excuse me, what have we here? The herring's bitter . . . and so's the bread. Have to sweeten it up!

EVERYONE Bitter! Bitter! Sweeten it up!

(APLOMBOV *and* DASHENKA *kiss.*)

REVUNOV Heh, heh, heh . . . Your health. (*Pause.*) Yessir . . . in the

olden days everything was simple and everybody was contented
. . . I love simplicity . . . I'm an old man, you know, went into
retirement in eighteen hundred and sixty-five . . . I'm seventy-two
. . . Yes, indeed. Even so, in the old days, they liked to put on the
dog every once in a while, but . . . (*Noticing* MOZGOVOY.) You there
. . . a sailor, are you?

MOZOGOY   Aye, aye, sir.

REVUNOV   Aha . . . Aye . . . Yes . . . Serving in the navy was always
tough. A man had to keep his wits about him and rack his brains.
The slightest little word had its own special meaning, so to speak!
For instance, "Topmen aloft to the foresail and mainsail yards!"
What does that mean? Never fear, your sailor gets the drift! Heh,
heh. It's as tricky as that arithmetic of yours!

NYUNIN   To the health of his excellency, Fyodor Yakovlevich
Revunov-Karaulov!

　　　(*The band plays a fanfare. Cheers.*)

YAT   Now, your excellency, you've been good enough to mention
how hard it is serving in the navy. But you think telegraphy's any
easier? These days, your excellency, nobody's employed on the
telegraph unless he can read and write French and German. But
the toughest thing we're up against is sending telegrams. Awfully
hard! Just listen to this. (*Taps his fork on the table, in imitation of
sending a telegram in Morse code.*)

REVUNOV   What does it mean?

YAT   It means: "I respect you, your excellency, for your loving kindness." You think that's easy? Here's some more . . . (*Taps.*)

REVUNOV   Make it louder . . . I can't hear . . .

YAT   And that means: "Madam, how happy I am to hold you in my
embrace!"

REVUNOV   What's all this about a madam? Yes . . . (*To* MOZGOVOY.)
Look here, suppose you're running before a full breeze and have
to . . . have to set your topgallants and royals! Then you've got to
give the command, "Crosstrees aloft to the shrouds, the topgallants and royals . . ." And while they're casting loose the sails on
the yards, below they're manning the topgallant and royal sheets,
halyards, and braces . . . [4]

BEST MAN   (*Rising.*)   My dear ladies and kind gentle . . .

REVUNOV   (*Interrupting.*)   Yessiree . . . No end of different commands . . . Aye, aye . . . "In on the top-gallant and royal sheets!
Haul taut the halyards!" Pretty good, eh? But what's it all mean,
what's the sense of it? Why, very simple. They haul, y'see, the

---

4. In his memoirs, Chekhov's brother Mikhail reported that in 1883 Anton had inherited a
book from the late F. F. Popudolgo, *Commands for the Most Important Naval Maneuvers*,
which "provided him material for the role of Revunov-Karaulov."

topgallant and royal sheets and lift off the halyards . . . all together! Next they square the royal sheets and royal halyards as they hoist, and meanwhile, keeping a weather eye out, they ease off the braces from those sails, so that when, as a result, the sheets are taut and all the halyards run right up, then the topgallants and royals are drawing and the yards are braced according to the way the wind's blowing . . .

NYUNIN (*To* REVUNOV.) Fyodor Yakovlevich, our hostess requests you talk about something else. The guests can't make head or tail of this, so they're bored . . .

REVUNOV What? Who's bored? (*To* MOZGOVOY.) Young fellow! Now then, suppose your craft lies close-hauled on the starboard tack under full sail and you've got to wear ship. What command must you give? Why, look here: pipe all hands on deck, wear ship! . . . Heh, heh . . .

NYUNIN Fyodor Yakovlevich, that's enough! Have something to eat.

REVUNOV As soon as they're all on deck, the command is given at once: "Stand by to wear ship!" Ech, what a life! You give the commands, and then you watch the sailors running to their posts like lightning, and they unfurl the topgallants and the braces. And then you can't hold back and you shout, "Well done, my hearties!" (*Chokes and coughs.*)

BEST MAN (*Rushes to take advantage of the consequent pause.*) On this day of days, so to speak, when we are all gathered together to honor our beloved . . .

REVUNOV (*Interrupting.*) Yessiree! And, y'see, you've got to remember all that! For instance: let fly the foresheet, the mainsheet! . . .

BEST MAN (*Offended.*) Why does he keep interrupting? We'll never get through a single speech at this rate!

NASTASYA TIMOFEEVNA We're ignorant folk, your excellency, we can't make head or tail of this, so you'd better talk about something that's more use . . .

REVUNOV (*Not hearing.*) I've already eaten, thanks. You did say: goose? No thanks . . . Aye . . . I was recalling the olden days . . . Those were jolly times, young fellow! You sail the seas, not a care to your name, and . . . (*His voice atremble.*) Remember the excitement when they had to tack about! What seaman doesn't catch fire at the memory of that maneuver?! Why, as soon as the command rings out: Pipe all hands on deck, ready about—you'd think an electric spark was running through the lot of 'em. From the admiral down to the lowliest deckhand—every heart is beating faster . . .

ZMEYUKINA Boring! Boring!
(*General murmur.*)

REVUNOV (*Not hearing.*)   No thanks, I've eaten. (*Carried away.*) They all stand at the ready, and fix their eyes on the first mate . . . "Haul taut the foretop and main braces on the starboard and the mizzen top braces and counterbraces on the port side!" commands the first mate. It's all carried out in an instant . . . "Let fly the foresheet, the jib sheet . . . Hard a'starboard!" (*Rises.*) The craft comes up with the wind, and finally the sails start flapping about. First mate: "The braces, look alive to the braces," and his own eyes are fixed to the main topsail, and when at last even that sail starts to flap; I mean, the moment when the craft comes about, the command rings out like thunder: "Let go the main top bowline, pay out the braces!" Then everything flies, snaps—all hell breaks loose!—it's all carried out with nary a hitch. We've managed to bring her about!

NASTASYA TIMOFEEVNA (*Boiling over.*)   A general, but with no manners . . . You ought to be ashamed at your time of life! It's unreal, stop!

REVUNOV   A veal chop? No, I haven't had one . . . Thanks.

NASTASYA TIMOFEEVNA (*Loudly.*)   I said, you should be ashamed at your time of life! A general, but with no manners!

NYUNIN (*Embarrassed.*)   Ladies and gentlemen, look here . . . what's the difference? Honestly . . .

REVUNOV   In the first place, I'm not a general, I'm a captain second-class, which is equivalent in the military ranking to a lieutenant-colonel.

NASTASYA TIMOFEEVNA   If you're no general, then why did you take the money? We didn't pay you good money so you could act like a hooligan!

REVUNOV (*Bewildered.*)   What money?

NASTASYA TIMOFEEVNA   You know what money. You got twenty-five rubles from Andrey Andreevich, no questions asked . . . (*To* NYUNIN.) As for you, Andryusha sweetie, you're a disgrace! I didn't ask you to hire this sort of thing!

NYUNIN   Come on . . . cut it out! What's the difference?

REVUNOV   Hired? . . . Paid? . . . What is this?

APLOMBOV   Excuse me, just a second . . . you did receive twenty-five rubles from Andrey Andreevich, didn't you?

REVUNOV   What twenty-five rubles? (*Realizing.*) So that's it! Now I understand it all . . . How disgusting! How disgusting!

APLOMBOV   You did take the money, didn't you?

REVUNOV   I never took any money! Get away from me! (*Moves away from the table.*) How disgusting! How revolting! To insult an old man this way, a navy man, an officer who's seen active duty! . . . If you were respectable people, I could challenge someone to a duel, but now what can I do? (*In despair.*) Where's the door? How

do I get out? Waiter, show me the way out! Waiter![5] (*Going out.*)
How revolting! How disgusting! (*Exits.*)

NASTASYA TIMOFEEVNA   Andryusha sweetie, where's the twenty-five
rubles?

NYUNIN   Why bother discussing such trifles? Big deal! Everyone else
is enjoying himself, but who the hell knows what you're on about
. . . (*Shouts.*) To the health of the happy couple! Band, play a
march! Band!

(*The band plays a march.*)

NYUNIN   To the newlyweds' health!

ZMEYUKINA   I'm suffocating! I need atmosphere! I start to suffocate
whenever I'm near you.

YAT (*In ecstasy.*)   Spectacular woman! Spectacular!
(*Noise.*)

BEST MAN (*Trying to make himself heard.*)   My good friends! On this
day of days, so to speak . . .

CURTAIN

---

5. In Russian, *chelovek* can mean both "human being, person" and "waiter." Using this double meaning, the Captain appeals both to a specific person and to humanity in general to
deliver him from this inhuman herd.

Variants to *The Wedding*

Lines come from the two surviving manuscript copies.

After Does that mean we're stingy? — Do me a favor, at least a whole regiment. (Page 99)

After You want a general, you'll get a general . . . — We'll provide it all . . . And if not, then it means Andrey Andreich didn't find a suitable one. It should be time to sit down to supper . . . Twelve o'clock. (Page 99)

After Didn't you realize it would get on my nerves? —
NASTASYA TIMOFEEVNA We didn't invite him, dearie. He came on his own.
APLOMBOV He'd better not make a scene, or else he'll learn from me what it's like to come uninvited. (Page 99)

After: M'sewers, promenade! — Donay mwa toozhoor! (Page 99)

After Have you got senior civil servants too?
YAT Why, I'll bet that in Greece there aren't such beautiful parties of the female sex as certain individuals . . . (Page 100)

Replace Wonderful woman! I'm in love! Head over heels in love! —
with A midwife, no looks to speak of, but give her the once-over, what manners! Right away an obvious aristocrat! (Page 101)

After: Squeezing the last drop out of him. — They should all be hanged. (Page 101)

After A sign of feebleminded psychiatrics, that's all! —
MOZGOVOY (*Rising*.) Ladies and gentlemen! Allow me to say the following. Anna Martynovna is in arrears! When we played forfeits, it fell out that she had to kiss the man who was the most dark-haired of them all. The most dark-haired of us all was Lapkin, but he got embarrassed and left. Now Anna Martynovna has to really pick out another dark-haired man and do what needs to be done . . .
EVERYONE Yes, yes . . . Of course, of course!
ZMEYUKINA How silly! Leave off!
MOZGOVOY Who is the darkest of us all?
BEST MAN Kharlampy Spiridonych!
EVERYONE Yes, yes! Please, Kharlampy Spiridonych!

ZMEYUKINA   I don't want to kiss! (*Hides her face behind a napkin.*)

YAT   No-o, ma'am, no-o, ma'am, Anna Martynovna, please don't be evasive . . . Have a heart, ma'am!

DYMBA (*Confused.*)   Why is what? I notting . . .

ZMEYUKINA   Really, I don't even understand . . . It's even strange . . . (*Aside*). He's so handsome! Such eyes!

YAT (*Rubbing his hands.*)   No-o, no-o! You're obliged!
       (*A fanfare.*)

ZMEYUKINA   Now what? If that was the forfeit that fell to me, then if you please, but . . . it's even extravagantly . . .
       (*Exchanges kisses with* DYMBA. *The kiss is prolonged.* DYMBA, *whose lips were stuck to* ZMEYUKINA's, *staggers back and keeps his balance with his arms.*)

YAT (*Anxious.*)   That's very long! Enough! All right!

EVERYONE (*Anxious.*)   Enough!

DYMBA (*Tearing himself away from* ZMEYUKINA.)   Oof! Why is what? This is who . . . I not understanding.

YAT   }
MOZGOVOY } (*Together.*)   She's faint! Water! Faint!

YAT (*Giving* ZMEYUKINA *water, aside.*)   Right away it's obvious she's an aristocrat! (*To her.*) Calm down! I implore you . . . That's right . . . She's opened her eyes . . . (*Aside.*) Quite the aristocrat!

ZMEYUKINA (*Coming to herself.*)   Where am I? In what ambience am I? Where is he? (*To* DYMBA.) You demon! You have set me afire with your kiss!

DYMBA (*Confused.*)   Why is what? I notting . . . (Page 103)

After Now in Russia is such a pipples, and in Griss is such a pipples — Is good! So is what? (Page 103)

After not infantry, but navy! — He controlled the seas and commanded the storms. (Page 104)

After Be so kind! — (*Aside.*) But what kind of scrawny, what kind of shop-soiled? Not even any epaulets . . . Well, at least there are lots of medals! (*To him.*) (Page 105)

Replace Yes . . . Serving in the navy was always tough . . . Never fear, the sailor gets your drift! —

with I guess it's all newfangled nowadays, not the way it was with us . . . It was all fair-skinned, downy . . . However, the naval service was always a tough one. It had nothing to do with the infantry, or, lets say, the cavalry . . . There's no brainwork to the infantry . . . There even a peasant can figure out what's what . . . You know it yourself: left-right, left-right, or form fours, or right wheel! But what you and I were up against, young man, no sir! You're joking! You and I have to think things over and cudgel our brains. Any insignificant word has, so to speak, its secret . . . eh . . . quandary! For example: topmen to the shrouds, fore- and mainsails! . . . What does that mean? Why, it means that whoever's assigned to look after the topsails has to find himself without fail at that time at the top, otherwise you have to give the order: cross-treemen to the shrouds! There's another meaning as well . . . (Page 106)

Replace (*Not hearing.*) . . . I was recalling the olden days . . . —
with You don't understand because these are . . . terms! Of course! But the young man understands. Yes. I was reminiscing about old times with him . . . (Page 107)

Replace (*Not hearing.*) I've already eaten, thanks . . . We managed to bring her about!
with (*Sobbing.*) Then they raise the jib-halyards, brace the main top-sail and others, at the above mentioned, close-haul the sail, and then they dash to the location of fore and main tack, haul the sheets and haul in the bowline . . . I'm cry . . . I'm crying . . . So glad . . . (Page 107)

The Celebration

In 1891, Russian 116, Private commercial banks were a relatively new feature in Russian life. The state bank itself dated back only to the reforms of 1866. The financial institution in Chekhov's farce is about to celebrate its fifteenth birthday, on which occasion the bank manager Shipuchin will receive a testimonial from grateful shareholders. While he prepares a speech of thanks and his clerk Khirin is, begrudgingly crunching numbers for the thank-you speech, they are interrupted first by Shipuchin's giddy and garrulous wife, and then by old Mrs. Merchutkina, nagging on behalf of her civil-servant husband. The more the women talk, the more the men are driven to distraction. The deputation arrives with its scroll and silver loving cup to behold a vision of chaos: the manager's wife fainting on the sofa, the old lady collapsing in the arms of the babbling Shipuchin, and Khirin threatening the females with murder.

The peculiar position of *The Celebration* lies chronologically halfway between the failed experiment of *The Wood Goblin* and Chekhov's transitional play *The Seagull*. Founded on a published short story, "A Defenseless Creature" (1887), it was written in December 1891 but not performed until a Chekhov evening at the Moscow Hunt Club in 1900. By the time *The Celebration* reached the stage, Chekhov was already known to the public as the author of *The Seagull*, *Uncle Vanya*, and *Three Sisters*. Many were upset by what seemed Chekhov's recession to comic anarchy. *The Moscow News* referred to it as a "strange play" that ends with "the bank manager making an insulting gesture at his bookkeeper, while the latter tears books and files to pieces, tossing the ravaged pieces in the manager's face." Chekhov later rewrote this finale into the Gogolian tableau that greets the astonished delegation of shareholders.

The first St. Petersburg production on the stage of the Alexandra Theater in May 1903 was even more questionably received. Although the audience was dying with laughter at the antics of the elephantine Varlamov as Khirin and the hilarious comedienne Levkeeva as Merchutkina, critics wondered at the crude vulgarity of it all and speculated whether such a piece had a place in a national theater. They could not reconcile its extravagant comedy with the works of Chekhov they had come to expect.

There is a savagery to *The Celebration* that exceeds even the contumely of *The Wedding*. Each member of the comic quartet is despicable: both women are portrayed as idiotic chatterboxes, the clerk is a crabbed

113

misogynist, and the bank manager is an ineffectual fussbudget. The setting enforces hypocrisy. As Shipuchin says, "at home I can be a slob, a
low brow and indulge my bad habits, but here everything has to be on a
grand scale. This is a bank!" The impending ceremony imposes a temporal pressure that propels the mounting hysteria. The result is a hilarious clash of monomanias, not at all what the textbooks call a
"Chekhovian mood."

The Celebration

A Joke in One Act

Characters[1]

SHIPUCHIN, ANDREY ANDREEVICH, Chairman of the Board of the——
    Mutual Credit Society, a middle-aged man, with a monocle
TATYANA ALEKSEEVNA, his wife, twenty-five
KHIRIN, KUZMA NIKOLAEVICH, the bank's bookkeeper, an old man
MERCHUTKINA, NASTASYA FYODOROVNA, an old woman in a baggy over-
    coat
SHAREHOLDERS OF THE BANK
EMPLOYEES OF THE BANK

The action takes place at the —— *Mutual Credit Bank.*

*The office of the Chairman of the Board. A door at left, leading to the
bank's boardroom. Two desks. Pretentious furnishings displaying
refined taste: velvet armchairs, flowers, statues, rugs, a telephone.—
Midday.*

KHIRIN *alone; he is wearing felt boots.*[2]

KHIRIN (*Shouts through the door.*)   Have the pharmacy send over
    fifteen kopeks' worth of valerian drops[3] and tell them to bring fresh
    water to the Chairman's office! I have to tell you a hundred times!
    (*Goes to the desk.*) They'll be the death of me with their torment-
    ing. I've been writing for four days straight without a wink of sleep;
    from morning to night I'm here writing, and I'm home only from
    night to morning. (*Coughs.*) And on top of that there's an inflam-
    mation running through my whole body. Chills, fever, coughing

---

1. The names are suggestive: Shipuchin from *shipat*, to fizzle or sputter; Khirin from *khirit*,
    to be sickly or decay; and Merchutkina from *mertsat*, to flicker, *mertsalka*, nightlight.
2. *Valenki* are lower-class indoor footwear, the equivalent of Khirin wearing mukluks or fuzzy
    house-slippers at the office.
3. See *The Seagull*, note 3, page 152.

jags, my legs ache and swimming before my eyes there's something like . . . exclamation points. (*Sits.*) That fancypants of ours, that skunk, the Chairman of the Board, is going to make a speech to our general assembly today: "Our bank now and in the future." A silver-tongued orator[4], take my word for it . . . (*Writes.*) Two . . . one . . . one . . . six . . . zero . . . seven . . . Then, six . . . zero . . . one . . . six . . . He wants to pull the wool over their eyes, while I sit here and slave for him like a convict! . . . All he's put in this speech is hearts and flowers, not one hard figure, so I have to spend the livelong day clicking the abacus, damn his soul to hell! . . . (*Clicks bead on the abacus.*) I can't stand it! (*Writes.*) Which means, one . . . three . . . seven . . . two . . . one . . . zero . . . He promised to reward my hard work. If everything comes off successfully today and he manages to fool his audience, he's promised me a gold medal and a bonus of three hundred . . . We shall see. (*Writes.*) Well, if my labors go unrewarded, pal, don't be surprised if . . . I've got an explosive temper . . . Pal, when I fly off the handle, I'm liable to do something violent . . . Believe you me!

> (*Offstage noise and applause.*)

SHIPUCHIN'S VOICE Thank you! Thank you! I'm very moved!

> (*Enter* SHIPUCHIN. *He is wearing white tie and tails; he is holding an album that has just been presented to him.*)

SHIPUCHIN (*Standing in the doorway and addressing the boardroom.*) This gift of yours, my dear coworkers, I shall cherish until my dying day as a memento of the happiest hours of my life! Yes, my dear sirs! I thank you once again! (*Blows a kiss and goes to* KHIRIN.) My dear fellow, my most respected Kuzma Nikolaich!

> (*The whole time he is on stage, employees occasionally come in with papers for him to sign and then leave.*)

KHIRIN (*Rising.*) I'm honored to congratulate you on the fifteenth anniversary of our bank and wish that . . .

SHIPUCHIN (*Shakes his hand energetically*). Thank you, my dear man! Thank you! On this very special day, in view of the celebration, I propose that we exchange kisses! . . . (*They exchange kisses.*) Delighted, delighted! Thank you for your work . . . for everything, thanks for everything! If, during the time I have been Chairman of the Board of this bank, I have accomplished anything of use, I am first and foremost obliged to my coworkers. (*Sighs.*) Yes, dear fellow, fifteen years! Fifteen years, or my name's not Shipuchin! (*Livelily.*) Well, how's my speech coming? Any progress?

KHIRIN Yes. There's still about five pages to go.

SHIPUCHIN That's fine. In other words, it'll be ready by three o'clock?

---

4. In the original, *Gambetta*. The French politician Léon Gambetta (1838–1882) was famous as a public speaker.

KHIRIN   If nobody gets in the way, I can finish it. There's only a
trifling amount left to do.

SHIPUCHIN   Splendid. Splendid, or my name's not Shipuchin! The
general assembly begins at four. Please, my dear fellow. Let me
have the first half, I'll give it a once-over . . . Let me have it now
. . . (*Takes the speech.*) I invest enormous hopes in this speech . . .
It is my *profession de foi*,[5] or, to put it more clearly, my display of
fireworks . . . Fireworks, or my name's not Shipuchin! (*Sits and
reads the speech to himself.*) I'm worn out, though, damnably worn
out . . . Last night I had an attack of gout, all morning I've been
hustling and bustling and running around, then this excitement,
ovations, all this commotion . . . I'm worn out!

KHIRIN   (*Writes.*)   Two . . . zero . . . zero . . . three . . . nine . . . two
. . . zero . . . The numbers are turning green before my eyes . . .
Three . . . one . . . six . . . four . . . one . . . five . . . (*Clicks the
beads on the abacus.*)

SHIPUCHIN   Something else unpleasant . . . This morning your wife
came to me and complained about you again. She said that last
night you chased her and your sister-in-law with a knife. Kuzma
Nikolaich, what way is that to behave? Ay-ay!

KHIRIN (*Sternly.*)   In view of the celebration, Andrey Andreich, may
I make a request. Please, at least out of respect for my hard labor
in this penitentiary, don't get involved in my home life. Please
don't!

SHIPUCHIN (*Sighs.*)   You have an impossible temper, Kuzma Nikolaich! You're a splendid fellow, highly respectable, but with women
you behave like some kind of Jack the Ripper.[6] Honestly. What I
don't understand is why you hate them so much.

KHIRIN   And what I don't understand is: why you love them so
much?
   Pause.

SHIPUCHIN   The employees just presented me with an album, and
the shareholders of the bank, so I've heard, want to present me
with a testimonial and a silver loving cup . . . (*Toying with his mon-
ocle.*) Lovely, or my name's not Shipuchin! It's not a meaningless
gesture . . . To uphold the reputation of the bank one needs some
pomp and circumstance, damn it! You're part of the team, so of
course you know what's going on . . . I composed the testimonial
myself, I also bought the silver loving cup myself . . . Why, the
binder for the testimonial cost forty-five rubles, but you can't do
without it. It would never have crossed their minds. (*Looks*

5. French: "my credo."
6. The London murderer and mutilator of prostitutes was frequently discussed in Russian
newspapers in 1890.

around.) What a set of furniture! What interior décor! They do say that I'm too fussy, that all I want is for the doorknobs to be polished, the employees to wear tasteful neckties, yes, and for there to be a stately doorman at the entrance. Well, no, my good sirs. Doorknobs and a stately doorman are not mere baubles. A man may be as much of a slob as he likes at home, eat and sleep like a hog, take too much to drink . . .

KHIRIN Please, I beg you, no insinuations!

SHIPUCHIN Ah, no one's making insinuations! What an impossible temper you have . . . I'm only saying: at home I can be a slob, a lowbrow, and indulge my bad habits, but here everything has to be on a grand scale. This is a bank! Here every little detail has to make an impression, in a manner of speaking, and present a solemn appearance. (*Picks up a piece of paper from the floor and tosses it into the fireplace.*) My great achievement is precisely my upholding the reputation of the bank! . . . The main thing is tone! The main thing, or my name's not Shipuchin. (*After a glance at* KHIRIN.) My dear man, the deputation of shareholders might come in at any moment, and you're wearing felt boots, that muffler . . . some jacket of an uncivilized color . . . You should put on tails, or, at least a black frockcoat . . .

KHIRIN I consider my health more precious than your bank shareholders. I've got inflammation all through my body.

SHIPUCHIN (*Getting excited.*) But you must agree that this is a mess! You're spoiling the effect of the ensemble!

KHIRIN When the deputation arrives, I can always hide. It's no problem . . . (*Writes.*) Seven . . . one . . . seven . . . two . . . five . . . zero. I'm no fan of messes myself! You would have done better not to invite ladies to the celebratory banquet today . . .

SHIPUCHIN What piffle . . .

KHIRIN I know, you've let them in today so you'll have a full house and it'll look chic, but, listen, they'll spoil the whole thing for you. They lead to nothing but stress and mess.

SHIPUCHIN On the contrary, the company of females is uplifting!

KHIRIN Yes . . . Your wife is supposed to be well-bred, but last Wednesday she blurted out something that had me in a dither for the next two days. Suddenly in the presence of bystanders she asks, "Is it true that for our bank my husband bought shares in the Trashko-Pashko bank, and now they've gone down on the stock exchange? Oh, my husband is so worried!" *This* in front of bystanders! And why you confide in her I can't understand! You want them to bring you up on criminal charges?

SHIPUCHIN Now, that'll do, that'll do! For a celebration this is all far too depressing. By the way, you've reminded me. (*Looks at his watch.*) My wifey is supposed to be here any minute. Actually, I should have driven to the station to meet her, poor dear, but there's no time and . . . and I was worn out. To tell the truth, I'm put out with her! I mean, I'm not put out, but I would prefer if she stayed another little day or two at her mother's. She insists that I spend the whole evening with her, today, when they've been planning a little postprandial excursion . . . [7] (*Shudders.*) There now, I've started to get a nervous twitch. My nerves are so frayed that I think the least little trifle is enough to make me burst into tears! No, I have to be firm, or my name's not Shipuchin.

(*Enter* TATYANA ALEKSEEVNA *in a mackintosh,*[8] *with a traveling handbag on a strap across her shoulder.*)

SHIPUCHIN   Bah! Speak of the devil!

TATYANA ALEKSEEVNA   My dear! (*Runs to her husband, a protracted kiss.*)

SHIPUCHIN   Why, we were just talking about you! . . . (*Looks at his watch.*)

TATYANA ALEKSEEVNA (*Panting.*)   Were you bored without me? Are you well? I haven't even been home yet, I came straight from the station. I've got so much to tell you about, so much . . . I can't wait . . . I won't take off my things, I'll only be a minute. (*To* KHIRIN.) How are you, Kuzma Nikolaich! (*To her husband.*) Is everything all right at home?

SHIPUCHIN   Everything. Why, you've got plumper and prettier this past week . . . Well, how was the trip?

TATYANA ALEKSEEVNA   Wonderful. Mamma and Katya send you their regards. Vasily Andreich told me to give you a kiss. (*Kisses him.*) Auntie sent you a pot of jam, and everyone's annoyed that you don't write. Zina told me to give you a kiss. (*Kisses him.*) Oh, if you only knew the things that went on! The things that went on! I'm even terrified to tell you! Ah, the things that went on! But I can tell from your eyes that you're not pleased to see me!

SHIPUCHIN   On the contrary . . . My dearest . . . (*Kisses her.*)

(KHIRIN *coughs angrily.*)

TATYANA ALEKSEEVNA (*Sighs.*)   Oh, poor Katya, poor Katya! I feel so sorry for her, so sorry!

SHIPUCHIN   We're having the celebration today, my dearest; at any moment a deputation of the bank's shareholders might show up, and you're not dressed.

TATYANA ALEKSEEVNA   That's right, the celebration! Congratulations, gentlemen . . . I wish you . . . That means, today is the assembly, the banquet . . . I love it. But you remember, that lovely testimo-

7. All-male testimonial banquets and school reunions often ended with a trip to a brothel.
8. A woman's waterproof cape.

nial, which you took so much trouble to compose for the share-holders? Will they be reading it to you today?

(KHIRIN *coughs angrily.*)

SHIPUCHIN (*Embarrassed.*) My dear, people don't talk about such things . . . Really, you ought to go home.

TATYANA ALEKSEEVNA Right away, right away. It'll take a minute to tell you about it and then I'll go. I'll start the whole story right from the beginning. Well now . . . After you left me off, remember, I sat next to that stout lady and started reading. I never try to make conversation on a train. I went on reading for three stations and not a single word to anybody . . . Well, night came on, and you know, all these gloomy thoughts came with them! Across from me sat a young man, quite proper, not bad at all, dark-haired . . . Well, we started talking . . . A sailor dropped in, then some student or other . . . (*Laughs.*) I told them I wasn't married . . . The way they paid court to me! We chattered away 'til midnight, the dark-haired one told awfully funny stories, and the sailor kept singing. My chest began to hurt from laughing. And when the sailor—oh, those sailors!—when the sailor happened to find out my name is Tatyana, you know what he sang? (*Sings in a bass voice.*) "Onegin, this I cannot hide, Tatyana's my love, she is my bride! . . ."[9] (*Laughs loudly.*)

(KHIRIN *coughs angrily.*)

SHIPUCHIN However, Tatyana, we're disturbing Kuzma Nikolaich. Go home, my dear . . . Later . . .

TATYANA ALEKSEEVNA Never mind, never mind, let him listen, this is very interesting. I'll be done in a minute. At the station Seryozha came for me. Some other young man turned up there, a tax collector, I believe . . . Quite proper, good-looking little fellow, especially his eyes . . . Seryozha introduced him, and all three of us drove off . . . The weather was wonderful . . .

OFFSTAGE VOICES You can't! You can't! What do you want?

(*Enter* MERCHUTKINA.)

MERCHUTKINA (*In the doorway, waving someone away.*) What are you grabbing at? I never! I have to talk to him myself! . . . (*Enters. To* SHIPUCHIN.) I have the honor, your Excellency . . . Wife of a county clerk, Nastasya Fyodorovna Merchutkina, sir.

SHIPUCHIN How can I help you?

MERCHUTKINA If you don't mind, your Excellency, my husband, county clerk Merchutkin, was ailing for five months, and while he was home in bed getting better, they fired him for no reason at all,

9. Prince Gremin's aria in Pyotr Ilich Tchaikovsky's 1879 opera *Evgeny Onegin* (Act III, Scene 1).

your Excellency, and when I went to get his salary, they'd, if you
don't mind, gone and deducted from his salary twenty-four rubles,
thirty-six kopeks. "What for?" I ask. "Well," says they, "he borrowed from the mutual-aid fund and other people vouched for
him." How could that be? Could he borrow anythin' without my
consent? It's impossible, your Excellency! I'm a poor woman, I only
keep body and soul together by taking in lodgers . . . I'm weak,
defenseless . . . I put up with everybody's insults and never hear a
kind word from a soul.

SHIPUCHIN If I may. . . . (*Takes her petition from her and reads it
standing up.*)

TATYANA ALEKSEEVNA (*To* KHIRIN.) But I should begin at the beginning . . . Suddenly last week I got a letter from Mamma. She writes
that my sister Katya was proposed to by a certain Grendilevsky. A
good-looking, unpretentious young man, but without any means
and no fixed occupation. And to make it worse, can you imagine,
Katya was attracted to him. What was there to do? Mamma writes
that I should come without delay and bring my influence to bear
on Katya . . .

KHIRIN (*Severely.*) If you don't mind, you've put me out! You—
Mamma and Katya, and now I'm put out and totally confused.

TATYANA ALEKSEEVNA As if it makes any difference! You listen when
a lady's talking to you! Why are you so touchy today? In love?
(*Laughs.*)

SHIPUCHIN (*To* MERCHUTKINA.) If I may, though, what is this all
about? I don't understand . . .

TATYANA ALEKSEEVNA In love? Aha? He's blushing!

SHIPUCHIN (*To his wife.*) Tanyusha, my dear, step into the boardroom for a minute. I'll be there right away.

TATYANA ALEKSEEVNA All right. (*Exits.*)

SHIPUCHIN I don't understand any of this. Apparently, madam, you
have come to the wrong place. Your request has absolutely nothing
to do with us. You should take care to apply to the department
where your husband worked.

MERCHUTKINA My good sir, I've already been to five different places;
they won't even accept my petition anywheres. I was losing my
mind, but thanks to my son-in-law Boris Matveich, I got the bright
idea to come to you. "Ma, dear," says he, "you appeal to Mister
Shipuchin: he's got pull, that gent can do anything . . ." Help me,
your Excellency!

SHIPUCHIN Mrs. Merchutkina, we can do nothing for you. You
understand: your husband, so far as I can tell, worked in the medical division of the War Office, whereas our institution is entirely
private, mercantile—we're a bank. How can you fail to understand
this?

MERCHUTKINA   Your Excellency, to prove my husband was sick, I got a doctor's certificate. Here it is, your Excellency . . .

SHIPUCHIN (*Annoyed.*)   Lovely, I believe you, but, I repeat, this has nothing to do with us.

(*Offstage,* TATYANA ALEKSEEVNA's *laugh; then, men's laughter.*)

SHIPUCHIN (*After a glance at the door.*)   She's keeping the employees from their work. (*To* MERCHUTKINA.) This is bizarre, even laughable. Your husband knows where to apply, doesn't he?

MERCHUTKINA   He, your Excellency, so far as I'm concerned, knows nothing. All he keeps saying is, "It's none of your business! Get out!" and that's all . . .

SHIPUCHIN   I repeat, madam: your husband worked in the medical division of the War Office, and this is a bank—a private, mercantile institution . . .

MERCHUTKINA   Right, right, right . . . I understand, my good sir. In that case, your Excellency, make them give me at least fifteen rubles! I'll settle for not all at once.

SHIPUCHIN (*Sighs.*)   Oof!

KHIRIN   Andrey Andreich, at this rate I'll never finish the speech!

SHIPUCHIN   Right away. (*To* MERCHUTKINA.) I'm not getting through to you. Try and understand that to apply to us with such a request is as strange as filing for a divorce, for instance, at a drugstore or the Assay Office.[1]

(*Knock at the door.*)

TATYANA ALEKSEEVNA'S VOICE   Andrey, may I come in?

SHIPUCHIN (*Shouts.*)   Wait, my dear, just a minute! (*To* MERCHUTKINA.) They didn't pay you in full, but what's it got to do with us? And besides, madam, we've got a celebration today, we're busy . . . and somebody might come in here at any moment. . . . Excuse me . . .

MERCHUTKINA   Your Excellency, take pity on me, an orphan! I'm a weak, defenseless woman . . . They've been the death of me with their tormenting . . . What with suing my lodgers, and dealing with my husband's stuff, and running around on household chores, and besides that, my son-in-law is out of work.

SHIPUCHIN   Mrs. Merchutkina, I . . . No, excuse me, I cannot talk to you! You've even got my head swimming . . . You are keeping us from work, and wasting time for no good reason . . . (*Sighs, aside.*) Here's a holy terror, or my name's not Shipuchin! (*To* KHIRIN.) Kuzma Nikolaich, will you please explain to Mrs. Merchutkina . . . (*Waves his hand in dismissal and exits into the boardroom.*)

KHIRIN (*Walks over to* MERCHUTKINA. *Sternly.*)   How can I help you?

MERCHUTKINA   I'm a weak, defenseless woman . . . I may look

---

1. Prior to 1896, this government office carried out all testing of gold and silver.

tough, but if you take me to pieces, there's not a single healthy nerve in me! I can barely stand on my feet and I got no appetite. When I had my coffee today, I didn't get the least bit o' satisfaction from it.

KHIRIN   I'm asking you, how can I help you?

MERCHUTKINA   Make them, my good sir, give me fifteen rubles, and the rest at least in a month.

KHIRIN   But I thought you were told in plain Russian: this is a bank!

MERCHUTKINA   Right, right . . . And if necessary, I can produce a doctor's certificate.

KHIRIN   Have you got a brain in your head or not?

MERCHUTKINA   Dearie, I'm asking for what's legally mine, that's all. I don't want nobody else's.

KHIRIN   I'm asking you, madam: have you got a brain in your head or what? Well, damn it all, I haven't got the time to chitchat with you! I'm busy. (*Points to the door.*) Please!

MERCHUTKINA (*Surprised.*)   But what about the money? . . .

KHIRIN   In other words, you haven't got a brain in your head, here's what you've got . . . (*Taps a finger on the desk, then on his forehead.*)

MERCHUTKINA (*Offended.*)   What? Well, never you mind, never you mind . . . Behave that way with your own wife . . . I'm a county clerk's wife . . . With me you better not!

KHIRIN (*Flaring up, in an undertone.*)   Get out of here!

MERCHUTKINA   But, but, but . . . You better not!

KHIRIN (*In an undertone.*)   If you don't get out this second, I'll send for the porter! Out! (*Stamps his feet.*)

MERCHUTKINA   Never you mind, never you mind! I'm not scared o' you! We seen your sort before . . . You empty space!

KHIRIN   I don't think in all my life I've ever laid eyes on anything more repulsive . . . Oof! She's got the blood rushing to my head . . . (*Breathing heavily.*) I'll say it once more . . . Now listen! If you, you old gargoyle, don't clear out of here, I'll grind you into powder! I've got the kind of temper that can make you a cripple for the next century! I might do something violent!

MERCHUTKINA   Hark, hark, the dogs do bark. You blowhard. You don't scare me. We seen your kind before.

KHIRIN (*In despair.*)   I can't look at her! I feel sick! I can't! (*Goes to the desk and sits.*) You've filled the bank with females, so I can't write the speech! I can't!

MERCHUTKINA   I'm not asking for what's somebody else's, just what's legally mine. Look at this shameless creature! In a workplace he sits in felt boots . . . A peasant . . .

(*Enter* SHIPUCHIN *and* TATYANA ALEKSEEVNA.)

TATYANA ALEKSEEVNA (*Following her husband.*)   Then we drove to a soiree at the Berezhnitskys'. Katya was wearing a pale blue cotton-silk dress with light lace and a low neckline . . . A hairdo piled high suits her face very nicely, so I did her hair myself . . . When she was dressed, with her hair done, she was simply bewitching!

SHIPUCHIN (*Already with a migraine.*) Yes, yes . . . bewitching . . . They might come in here any minute.

MERCHUTKINA Your Excellency!

SHIPUCHIN (*Depressed.*) Now what? How can I help you?

MERCHUTKINA Your excellency! . . . (*Points to* KHIRIN.) This here one, this one right here . . . this here one here put his finger to his forehead, and then on the desk . . . You ordered him to deal with my case, but he made fun and talked dirty. I'm a weak, defenseless woman . . .

SHIPUCHIN All right, madam, I'll take care of it . . . I'll take measures . . . Please get out . . . later! . . . (*Aside.*) My gout's flaring up again! . . .

KHIRIN (*Walks over to* SHIPUCHIN, *quietly.*) Andrey Andreich, let me send for the doorman—he'll throw her out in three shakes. What's going on, after all?

SHIPUCHIN (*Alarmed.*) No, no! She'll make an outcry, and there are lots of private apartments in this building.

MERCHUTKINA Your Excellency!

KHIRIN (*In a whining voice.*) But I have to write the speech, don't I? I haven't got the time! . . . (*Goes back to the desk.*) I can't do it!

MERCHUTKINA Your Excellency, when will I get it? I need the money right away.

SHIPUCHIN (*Aside, indignantly.*) No, an ex-tra-or-din-ar-i-ly nasty female! (*To* MERCHUTKINA, *blandly.*) Madam, I've already told you. This is a bank, a private, mercantile establishment . . .

MERCHUTKINA Do me a favor, your Excellency, be a father to me . . . If a doctor's certificate ain't enough, then I can produce a statement from the police too. Tell them to give me the money!

SHIPUCHIN (*Breathing heavily.*) Oof!

TATYANA ALEKSEEVNA (*To* MERCHUTKINA.) Granny, they're telling you you're in the way. How can you, really?

MERCHUTKINA Beautiful lady, be a mother to me; there's not a soul who'll take my part. All I can manage to do is eat and drink, and now I don't get no satisfaction from coffee.

SHIPUCHIN (*Faintly, to* MERCHUTKINA.) How much do you want to receive?

MERCHUTKINA Twenty-four rubles, thirty-six kopeks.

SHIPUCHIN All right! (*Pulls twenty-five rubles out of his wallet and gives them to her.*) Here's twenty-five rubles for you. Take it . . . and get out!

(KHIRIN *angrily coughs.*)

MERCHUTKINA   Thank you kindly, your Excellency . . . (*Puts away the money.*)

TATYANA ALEKSEEVNA (*Sitting beside her husband.*)   Anyway, it's time for me to go home . . . (*After looking at her watch.*) But I still haven't finished. . . . I'll be done in just one little minute and then I'll go . . . The things that went on! Ah, the things that went on! So, we drove to the soiree at the Berezhnitskys' . . . It was all right, it was fun, but nothing special. . . . Of course, Katya's admirer Grendilevsky was there . . . Well, I had a word with Katya, I cried a bit, I worked my influence on her, and that very evening she had it out with Grendilevsky and turned him down. Well, I'm thinking, it's over and done with, all's for the best: it's calmed down mamma, it's saved Katya, and now I myself am calm . . . And what do you think? Just before supper Katya and I are walking down a garden path and suddenly . . . (*Getting excited.*) And suddenly we hear a gunshot . . . No, I can't talk about this in cold blood! (*Fanning herself with her handkerchief.*)

SHIPUCHIN (*Sighs.*)   Oof!

TATYANA ALEKSEEVNA (*Weeps.*)   We run to the summerhouse and there . . . there lies poor Grendilevsky . . . with a pistol in his hand . . .

SHIPUCHIN   No, I can't stand it! I can't stand it! (*To* MERCHUTKINA.) What can I do for you now?

MERCHUTKINA   Your Excellency, is it possible for my husband to get his job back again?

TATYANA ALEKSEEVNA (*Weeping.*)   He'd shot himself right in the heart . . . just there . . . Katya fainted dead away, poor thing . . . And he was awfully scared himself, he's lying there and . . . and asks us to send for a doctor. The doctor came right away and . . . and saved the wretched man . . .

MERCHUTKINA   Your Excellency, it is possible for my husband to get his job back again?

SHIPUCHIN   No, I can't stand it! (*Weeps.*) I can't stand it! (*Extends both his arms to* KHIRIN, *in despair.*) Throw her out! Throw her out, for pity's sake!

KHIRIN (*Walking over to* TATYANA ALEKSEEVNA).   Get out of here!

SHIPUCHIN   Not her, the one over there . . . that dreadful . . . (*points at* MERCHUTKINA.) That one there!

KHIRIN (*Not understanding him, to* TATYANA ALEKSEEVNA.)   Get out of here! (*Stamps his feet.*) Get out now!

TATYANA ALEKSEEVNA   What? What's wrong with you? Have you gone crazy?

SHIPUCHIN   This is horrible! I'm a miserable wretch! Throw her out! Throw her out!

KHIRIN (*To* TATYANA ALEKSEEVNA.)   Out! I'll cripple you! I'll mangle you! I'll do something violent!

TATYANA ALEKSEEVNA (*Runs away from him; he follows her.*)   How dare you! You're being rude! (*Cries out.*) Andrey! Save me! Andrey! (*Screams.*)

SHIPUCHIN (*Runs after them.*)   Stop it! I implore you! Quiet! Spare me!

KHIRIN (*Chasing* MERCHUTKINA.)   Get out of here! Catch her! Smash her! Cut her throat!

SHIPUCHIN (*Shouts.*)   Stop it! Will you please! I implore you!

MERCHUTKINA   Saints alive . . . saints alive! (*Screams.*) Saints alive! . . .

TATYANA ALEKSEEVNA (*Shouts.*)   Save me! Save me! . . . Ah, ah . . . I feel faint! Faint! (*Jumps on to a chair, then falls on the sofa and groans, as if in a swoon.*)

KHIRIN (*Chasing* MERCHUTKINA.)   Smash her! Flog her! Cut her throat!

MERCHUTKINA   Ah, ah . . . saints alive, I'm blacking out! Ah! (*Falls unconscious into* SHIPUCHIN's *arms.*)

(*A knock at the door and a voice offstage: "The deputation!"*)

SHIPUCHIN   Deputation . . . reputation . . . occupation . . .

KHIRIN (*Stamps his feet.*)   Get out, damn it to hell! (*Rolls up his sleeves.*) Hand her over to me! I could do something violent!

(*Enter the five-man* DEPUTATION; *all in tailcoats. One of them is holding the testimonial in a velvet binder, another the loving cup.* EMPLOYEES *look on through the doorway to the boardroom.* TATYANA ALEKSEEVNA *is on the sofa,* MERCHUTKINA *in* SHIPUCHIN's *arms, both women are moaning quietly.*)

SHAREHOLDER (*Reads loudly.*)   Highly respected and cherished Andrey Andreich! On casting a retrospective glance at the past of our financial institution and running our mind's eye over the course of its gradual development, the impression we receive is gratifying to the nth degree. True, in the early days of its existence the limited scope of its original capital, the lack of any profitable operations, as well as the vagueness of its goals gave point to Hamlet's question: "To be or not to be?", and at one time voices were even raised in favor of closing the bank. But then you put yourself at the head of our institution. Your knowhow, energy, and characteristic discretion were reasons for its exceptional success and rare prosperity. The reputation of the bank . . . (*coughs*) the reputation of the bank . . .

MERCHUTKINA (*Groans.*)   Ugh! Ugh!

TATYANA ALEKSEEVNA (*Groans.*)   Water! Water!

SHAREHOLDER (*Carries on.*)   Reputation . . . (*Coughs.*) Reputation

of the bank was raised by you to such a height that our institution
can now compete with the best foreign institutions . . .

SHIPUCHIN   Deputation . . . reputation . . . occupation . . . "Two
friends went for a walk one night and business talked in the moonlight . . ."[2] "Say not that your youth was wasted, that my jealousy
tormented you."[3]

SHAREHOLDER (*Carries on in embarrassment.*)   Then, casting an
objective glance at the present, highly respected and cherished
Andrey Andreich, we . . . (*Lowering his voice.*) Under the circumstances we'll come back later . . . We'd better come back later . . .
(*The* DEPUTATION *leaves in confusion.*)

CURTAIN

---

2. Opening lines of Ivan A. Krylov's fable, "The Passersby and the Dogs."
3. "Gypsy Song," a ballad by Ya. F. Prigozhy to the words of a poem by Nikolay Nekrasov,
"A heavy cross fell to her lot . . ." (1856). Also quoted in *The Seagull*.

Variants to *The Celebration*

Early version of the ending to the play (from the autograph MS.) In this earlier version, Shipuchin is called Kistunov and Merchutkina is Shchukina.

VII

KISTUNOV, KHIRIN, *and* TATYANA ALEKSEEVNA.

(TATYANA ALEKSEEVNA *is lying on the sofa and groaning.*)

KHIRIN (*After a brief pause.*) What did I tell you? What did I tell you? They came, they wrecked the place, they made scenes, one got twenty-five smackers and left, and there's the other baby-doll . . . (*Points at* TATYANA ALEKSEEVNA.) They outdid themselves! I told you a thousand times that you mustn't let them within shooting distance of you.

KISTUNOV Deputation . . . reputation . . . Old bag, wife, felt boots . . . Somebody shot himself . . . "Two friends one night went for a walk and had a private, business talk." (*Rubbing his eyes.*) For two weeks I've being composing this speech for the shareholders, bought on my own account a silver loving cup, paid my own seventy-five rubles for the binder for the speech, five whole days stood in front of the mirror and prepared the pose . . . and now what? It's all failed! All of it! I'm disgraced! Ruined! My reputation gone!

KHIRIN And whose fault is it? Yours! Yours! You ruined the whole business!

KISTUNOV Shut up! It's your fault, not mine!

KHIRIN Yours! Yours!

KISTUNOV No, yours! If it wasn't for your nasty felt boots and your damned insufferable temper, none of this would have happened! Why did you chase my wife? Why did you shout at her? How dare you?

KHIRIN And if you weren't a coquette, and tried to throw a little less dust in their eyes . . . But, to hell with me, I don't want to work here anymore! Please let me have the gold medal and three hundred bonus! Please hand them over!

KISTUNOV You'll get nothing, you old bastard! I'll give you the finger!

KHIRIN Is that right? . . . Then here's your report! (*Tears up the report.*) There! That's for you! I've put you in hot water! Just you wait!

KISTUNOV (*Shouts.*) Clear out of here! (*Rings.*) Hey, throw him out!

KHIRIN (*Stamps his feet.*) Out of my sight! I'm ready to do something violent! I won't answer for myself! Get away!

KISTUNOV Get out!

(*With cries of "Get away! Get out!" they chase one another. Noise. The employees rush in.*)

CURTAIN

Lines from the autograph manuscript.

After while I — do the sums and calculate the percentages and make fair copies, and (Page 115)

After Pause. — KISTUNOV For what . . . Hmm . . . Women, my dear fellow, are . . . the sort of thing . . . it's when . . . it's the aroma of life . . . But go on writing, my dear man . . . Have to make haste.
KHIRIN There are all sorts of aromas.
  (*Pause.*) (p. 116)

Replace You're part of the team, so of course you know what's going on . . . with a portly doorman at the entrance.
with Only I don't know where the ceremony of reading the speech is to take place: at the club before the banquet or else here? I'd like it to be here, and hinted as much to them . . . (*Looks around.*) Such furniture! Neat and tidy! They may say I'm a fussbudget, that all I need is for the doorknobs to be polished, the employees wear fashionable neckties, and that a portly doorman stand at the entrance, but there — and the rest can go to hell. (Page 116)

Before The main thing is tone! — You have to pay attention to public opinion! It's not a bank, they say, but a government department! There, they say, it's awesome to go in! (Page 117) . . .

After What was there to do? — If she marries him, what will they live on? On love alone you don't get fat! (Page 120)

After and that's all . . . — And who has to deal with it? They're all hanging 'round my neck! Mine! (*Weeps.*) (Page 121)

After and besides that, my son-in-law out of work. — It's a wonder that I can eat and drink, and I can barely keep body and soul together. I didn't sleep a wink all night . . . (Page 121)

Replace We seen your sort before . . . —
with KHIRIN Get out of here!
SHCHUKINA We've seen your sort. I'll go to the lawyer Dmitry Karlych, and you'll be out of a job. Three lodgers I've sued, and for your foul mouth I'll strip you down to your felt boots. (Page 128)

The Seagull

The first production of *The Seagull* at the Alexandra Theater in St. Petersburg on October 17, 1896, has gone down in theatrical legend as a classic fiasco. This is an exaggeration, however. The cast was strong, with Davydov, the original Ivanov, as uncle Sorin; the popular comic actor Varlamov (who had already played Lebedev in *Ivanov*) as Shamraev; the handsome *jeune premier* Apollonsky as Treplyov; and the luminous Vera Komissarzhevskaya as Nina. During the scant week of rehearsals, Chekhov was in attendance, prompting the actors and correcting the director. Like most sensitive playwrights, he was dismayed by wasted time and the actors' predilection for superficial characterizations that stunted his brainchildren; but by the last rehearsals, his expectations became more optimistic.

These expectations were dashed on opening night, for the spectators came with expectations of their own, hoping to see their favorite comedienne Levkeeva, whose benefit performance it was.[1] They laughed, booed, and whistled at whatever struck them as funny, from Nina's soliloquy, to Treplyov's entrance with the dead gull, to the actors' ad-libs when they forgot their lines. Chekhov fled the theater, vowing never again to write for the stage. Nevertheless, the ensuing performances, with the actors more secure, played to respectful houses. Before *The Seagull* closed in November, it had become an esteemed success, with Kommissarzhevskaya proclaimed as brilliant. It was successfully revived in Kiev, Taganrog, and other provincial centers, providing Chekhov with handsome royalties.

The writer Nemirovich-Danchenko, an admirer of the play, thought *The Seagull* was just the thing to rescue the flagging fortunes of his newly founded Moscow Art Theater, whose first season was in danger of bankruptcy. He pressed it upon his reluctant colleague Stanislavsky, who at first found the play incomprehensible and unsympathetic. Stanislavsky retired to his country estate to compose a directorial score, which he sent piecemeal to Moscow, where Nemirovich rehearsed the actors.

Stanislavsky's fundamental approach to staging *The Seagull* differed little from his direction of historical drama. He sought in contemporary Russian life the same picturesque groupings, the same telling mannerisms, and the same pregnant pauses that had enthralled audiences in his reconstructions of seventeenth-century Muscovy or Renaissance Venice. Rather than inquiring into Chekhov's intentions, Stanislavsky took the

---

1. A performance given on behalf of a performer who receives the bulk of the box-office takings.

play as romantic melodrama: Nina was an innocent ruined by that "scoundrelly Lovelace" Trigorin, and Treplyov was a misunderstood Byronic genius, the hero of the piece. At this stage of his development, Stanislavsky did not try organically to elicit performances from the actors. Their every move, reaction, and intonation were prescribed by his score and learned by rote.

The opening night, December 17, 1898, despite offstage jitters, was a palpable hit; it insured the theater's success and *The Seagull* became the Moscow Art Theater's trademark production. Chekhov was less than ecstatic. He thought that Stanislavsky misinterpreted Trigorin by making him too elegant and formal; he detested Roksanov's ladylike Nina. Whatever the playwright's misgivings, the educated, middle-class audiences took to the play precisely because, for the first time, Trollope's notion of "the way we live now" was subjected to the same careful counterfeit presentment that had hitherto been applied only to the exotic past. The spectators beheld their own tics and heard their own speech patterns meticulously copied.

Taking advantage of the outdoor settings of the early acts and the dimly lit interior at the end, Stanislavsky laid on climatic and atmospheric effects to create an overpowering mood (*nastroenie*). The method, relying on sound effects, diffused lighting, and a snail's pace, worked so well for *The Seagull* that it became standard operating procedure at the Art Theater for Chekhov's later plays and, indeed, those of almost any author. Retrospectively, it was this pervasive mood that made *The Seagull* a hit. The young actor Meyerhold, who played Treplyov, later credited Stanislavsky with being the first to link the sound of rain on the window and morning light peeping through the shutters with characters' behavior: "At that time, this was a discovery."[2] The dramatist Leonid Andreev called it "panpsychology"—the animation of everything in a Chekhov play from distant music, to the chirp of a cricket, to munching an apple, each contributing equally to the play's total effect.[3]

Chekhov's objections to the Moscow interpretation did not, however, spring from its style, but from the imbalance in meaning that Stanislavsky had induced. Although it contains what Chekhov called "a ton of love," *The Seagull* is neither a soap opera about triangular relationships nor a romantic dramatization of Trigorin's "subject for a short story." It is perhaps Chekhov's most personal play in its treatment of the artist's métier. The theme of the splendors and miseries of artists is plainly struck by Medvedenko at the start, when he enviously refers to Nina and Treplyov sharing in a creative endeavor. Nina picks it up when she explains why her parents will not let her come to Sorin's estate: "They say this place is Bohemia." Years of theatergoing, reviewing, and dealing with performers and managers were distilled by Chekhov into a density of metaphor for the artistic experience, for the contrasts between commercialism and idealism, facility and aspiration, purposeless talent, and

2. A. G. Gladkov, "Meyerhold govorit," *Novy Mir* 8 (1961): 221.
3. Leonid Andreev, "Letters on the Theater," in *Russian Dramatic Theory from Pushkin to the Symbolists*, ed. and trans. L. Senelick (Austin: University of Texas Press, 1981), 238–42.

diligent mediocrity. Of the central characters, one is a would-be play-wright, another a successful author; one is an acclaimed if second-rate star of the footlights, another an aspiring actress.

Stanislavsky's black-and-white vision of the play also ran counter to Chekhov's attempt to create multiple heroes and multiple conflicts. Tre-plyov seems the protagonist because the play begins with his artistic credo and his moment of revolt, and it ends with his self-destruction. In terms of stage time, however, he shares the limelight with many other claimants, whose ambitions cancel one another.

Nina, likewise, cannot be singled out as the survivor who preserves her ideals in spite of all. The character of the victimized young girl, abandoned by her love and coming to a bad end, frequently recurred in Russian literature, from Karamzin's *Poor Liza* (1792) onward. Often, she was depicted as the ward of an old woman who, in her cruelty or wilful egoism, promotes the girl's downfall. Many plays of Ostrovsky and Potekhin feature such a pair, and Turgenev subtly handles the relation-ship in *A Month in the Country* (1850). In *The Seagull*, the relationship is rarefied: it is Arkadina's example, rather than her intention, that sends Nina to Moscow, maternity, and mumming.

The pure-souled, solitary, provincial actress—prey to the jealousy of colleagues, the importunities of admirers, and the scorn of society—was an early avatar of the Poor Liza type. Chekhov's early stories abound with actresses who lead erratic lives and endure slurs and contempt for doing so; but Nina continues to dismiss the shoddiness of the work she is given, determined to develop an inner strength, regardless of old forms or new. Should she be extolled as a shining talent to be contrasted with Arkadina's *routine* activity? Nina's ideas on art and fame are jejune, couched in the bromides of cheap fiction; her inability to see Treplyov's play as other than words and speeches and her offer to eat black bread and live in a garret for the reward of celebrity are obtuse and juvenile. Her dreams do not deserve to be realized, and there is nothing tragic in her having to reconcile them with the ordinary demands of life.

Similarly, Chekhov does not mean us to accept at face value Treplyov's harsh verdicts on his mother and her lover. They may truckle to popular demand, but they are crippled by self-doubt. Arkadina, barnstorming the countryside in the Russian equivalent of *East Lynne*, is convinced that she is performing a public service, her stage name ambivalently refers both to Arcadia and to a garish amusement park in St. Petersburg. Tri-gorin, well aware that he is falling short of his masters Tolstoy and Tur-genev, still plugs away in the tradition of well-observed realism.

Treplyov and Trigorin cannot be set up as hostile antitheses, for as the Soviet critic Chudakov said, they "themselves call their basic theses into question."[4] Treplyov's desire for new forms is a more vociferous and less knowing version of Trigorin's self-deprecation. The younger writer scorns the elder as a hack, but by the play's end, he is longing to find formulas for his own writing. Arkadina may not have read her son's story and Trigorin may not have cut the pages on any story but his own, but Treplyov himself admits he has never read Trigorin's stuff, thus partaking

---

4. A. P. Chudakov, *Chekhov's Poetics*, trans. F. J. Cruise and D. Dragt (Ann Arbor: Ardis, 1983), 193.

of their casual egoism. Since both Treplyov and Trigorin contain elements of Chekhov, a more productive antithesis might be that of idealism and materialism, with Treplyov the romantic at one end and the schoolmaster Medvedenko at the other. The two men are linked by Masha, who loves the one and barely puts up with the other. Each act opens with her statement of the hopelessness of her situation. Even here, though, the antithesis is not complete: Treplyov is as hamstrung by his poverty as Medvedenko, and the teacher cherishes his own wishes to make art with a beloved object.

The literary critic Prince Mirsky pointed out that *bezdarnost* ("lack of talent") is a "characteristically Chekhovian word"[5] in its absence of positive qualities. Chekhov once defined talent as the ability "to distinguish important evidence from unimportant" (to Suvorin, May 30, 1888). In *The Seagull*, "talent" is the touchstone by which the characters evaluate themselves and one another. Treplyov fears "he has no talent at all," but he rebukes Nina for considering him a "mediocrity, a nonentity" and points sarcastically to Trigorin as the "genuine talent." In her anger, Arkadina lashes out at her son by referring to "people with no talent but plenty of pretensions," to which he retaliates, "I'm more talented than the lot of you put together . . ." In Act One, Arkadina encourages Nina to go onstage by saying, "You must have talent," and in the last act, Treplyov grudgingly acknowledges "she showed some talent at screaming or dying." Trigorin complains that his public regards him as no more than "charming and talented," yet when Arkadina caresses him with "You're so talented," he succumbs to her blandishments.

The point is that "talent" exists independently of human relations and can be consummated in isolation. To be talented is not necessarily to be a superior person. As usual, Dr. Dorn sees most acutely the heart of the matter: "You're a talented fellow," he tells Treplyov, "but without a well-defined goal . . . your talent will destroy you." Tactlessly, in Arkadina's presence, he declares, "there aren't many brilliant talents around these days . . . but the average actor has improved greatly," for, sharing Chekhov's distrust of the grand gesture, he prefers a betterment of the general lot to artistic supermen. Even Nina finally realizes that fame and glamour are less important than staying power.

Treplyov's display of talent, his symbolist play located in a void where all things are extinct and the only conflicts are between the Universal Will and the Principle of Eternal Matter, may seem like parody. Chekhov, however, is careful to place the harsh criticism on the lips of Arkadina, whose taste and motives are suspect, and Nina, who is parroting actor's jargon she has heard from the actress. Chekhov is not ridiculing Treplyov for his espousal of a new form, but instead for his inability to preserve the purity of his ideal: his symbolist venture is a garble of popular stage techniques incongruous with his poetic aspirations—"Curtain, first grooves, second grooves, and beyond that, empty space," "special effects." He seems unable to find an original play to express his nebulous ideas; his play, as Chekhov said of the Norwegian Bjørnsen's

5. D. S. Mirsky, *Contemporary Russian Literature 1881–1925* (London: George Routledge and sons, 1926), p. 88.

Beyond Human Power, "has no meaning because the idea isn't clear. It's impossible to have one's characters perform miracles, when you yourself have no sharply defined conviction as to miracles" (to Suvorin, June 20, 1896). In his notebooks, Chekhov stipulated, "Treplyov has no fixed goals, and that's what destroyed him. Talent destroyed him."

Chekhov, for his part, did manage to initiate his own new form in *The Seagull*, inchoate and transitional though it may be. For the first time, he did away with "French scenes," allowing each act to develop not through the entrances and exits of characters, but by a concealed inner dynamic instead. The overall rhythm of the play is also carefully scored. "I began it *forte* and ended it *pianissimo*—contrary to all the rules of dramatic art" (to Suvorin, Nov. 21, 1895). The forte passages occur in the first three acts, which are compressed into a week's time; there is then a lapse of two years before the pianissimo of Act Four. The characters must fill in this long gap by the awkward device of asking one another what's been going on. But this is the result of Chekhov's eagerness to keep offstage what a traditional playwright would have saved for his obligatory scenes. The most intense and sensational actions—Nina's seduction and abandonment, the death of her child, Trigorin's return to Arkadina—are, like Treplyov's two suicide attempts, left to our imagination. We are allowed to see the antecedents and the consequences, but not the acts themselves.

The two-year hiatus between the third and fourth acts stresses the recurrent theme of memory. The past is always idyllic: Arkadina's reminiscence of life along the lakeshore, Polina's evocation of her past fling with the Doctor, Shamraev's evocation of antediluvian actors, and Sorin's rosy picture of an urban existence are all the older generation's forecast of the clashing recollections of Treplyov and Nina. With wry irony, Chekhov divulges each of his characters' insensitivity or obliviousness. "It's too late," insists Dorn when Polina tries to rekindle their earlier affair. "I don't remember," shrugs Arkadina when her charitable behavior is recalled. "I don't remember," says Trigorin, when he is shown the gull he had stuffed in memory of his first conversation with Nina.

Another new form that Chekhov initiated in *The Seagull* is the emblematic progression of localities. The first act is set in "a portion of the park on Sorin's estate," where the path to the lake is blocked off by Treplyov's trestle stage. This particular region is remote from the main house, and Treplyov has chosen it as his private turf: the characters who make up his audience must enter his world of shadows and dampness. They spend only a brief time there before returning to the safe norms evoked by the strains of the piano drifting into the clearing. Treplyov wants his work of art to be seen as coexistent with nature, with what Dorn calls "the spellbinding lake." Ironically, his man-made stage prevents people from walking to the lake, which his mother equates with "laughter, noise, gunshots, and one romance after another," the ordinary recreations Treplyov disdains. The most casual response to the lake comes from Trigorin, who sees it simply as a place to fish.

Act Two moves to Arkadina's territory, a house with a large veranda. The lake can now be seen in the bright sunlight, not the pallid moonshine. The surrounding verdure is a "croquet lawn," as manicured and well-kept as Arkadina herself, who keeps "up to scratch . . . my hair done comme il faut." Notably, Treplyov is the only member of the family circle who does not go into the house in this act. It stands for his mother's hold on life, and from its depths comes the call that keeps Trigorin on the estate.

The dining room of Act Three brings us into the house, but it is a neutral space, used for solitary meals, wound dressing, and farewells. The act is organized as a series of tête-à-têtes that are all the more intense for taking place in a locale which no one can call his own. The last act takes place in a drawing room that Treplyov has turned into a workroom. As the act opens, preparations are being made to convert it into a sick-room. The huddling together of the dying Sorin and the artistically moribund Treplyov implies that they are both "the man who wanted," but who never got what he wanted: a wife and a literary career. Once again, Treplyov has tried to set up a space of his own, only to have it overrun by a bustling form of life that expels him to the margins. To have a moment alone with Nina, he must bar the door to the dining room with a chair; the moment he removes the impediment, the intruders fill his space, turning into a game room. His private act of suicide must occur elsewhere.

This final locale has a Maeterlinckian tinge, for there is a glass door through which Nina enters, romantically draped in a talma, an enveloping cloak named after Napoleon's favorite tragedian. After days spent wandering around the lake, Nina emerges from an aperture no other character uses, to come in from "the garden" where "It's dark . . . that stage . . . stands there bare, unsightly, like a skeleton, and the scene curtain flaps in the wind." Maeterlinck's dramas are full of mysterious windows and doors that serve as entries into another world, beyond which invisible forces are to be intuited and uncanny figures glimpsed. Quoting Turgenev, Nina identifies herself as a "homeless wanderer, seeking a haven." But what is "warm and cozy" to her is claustrophobic and stifling to Treplyov.

In fact, the whole estate is an enclosure for the characters' frustration. This is no Turgenevian nest of gentry, for none of the characters feels at home here. Arkadina would rather be in a hotel room learning lines; Sorin would like to be in his office, hearing street noise. Seeing his nephew withering away on the estate, he tries to pry loose some money for a trip abroad. Nina's are always flying visits, time snatched from her oppressed life elsewhere. Medvedenko is there on sufferance. Shamraev the overseer is a retired military man with no skills as a farm manager. Only Trigorin is loath to depart, because, for him, the estate provides enforced idleness. The lake's enchantment can be felt as the spell of Sleeping Beauty's castle. Everyone who sets foot there is suspended in time, frozen in place. Real life seems to go on somewhere else.

This symbolic use of environment is better integrated than the more obvious symbol of the seagull. In Ibsen's *The Wild Duck*, the title is of essential importance: all the leading characters are defined by their attitude to the bird, and it exists, unseen, as they recreate in their private mythologies. The seagull, however, signifies to only three characters: Treplyov, who employs it as a symbol; Trigorin, who reinterprets its symbolic meaning; and Nina, who adopts and eventually repudiates the symbolism. For Treplyov, it is a means of turning art into life: feeling despised and rejected, he shoots the bird as a surrogate, and, when the surrogate is in turn rejected, he shoots himself. Nina felt "lured to the lake like a gull," but will not accept Treplyov's bird imagery for his self-identification. However, when her idol Trigorin spins his yarn about a girl who lives beside a lake, happy and free as a gull, Nina avidly adopts the persona, even though his notion of her freedom is wholly inaccurate. The story turns out to be false, for the man who ruined the bird is not the one who ruins the girl. Likewise, Nina is not ruined in any real sense. She starts to sign her letters to Treplyov "The Seagull" (or "A Seagull"— Russian has no definite articles); he links this with the mad miller in Pushkin's poem *The Rusalka*, who insanely thought himself a crow after his daughter, seduced and abandoned, drowned herself. Both Treplyov and Trigorin try to recast Nina as a fictional character, the conventional ruined girl who takes her own life. In the last act, however, she refuses this identity: "I'm a seagull. No, not that"—spurning both Treplyov's martyr bird and Trigorin's novelletish heroine. She survives, if only in an anti-romantic, workaday world. Ultimately, Chekhov prefers the active responsibilities contingent on accepting one's lot, even if this means a fate such as Nina's.

The Seagull[1]

A Comedy in Four Acts

Characters

ARKADINA,[2] IRINA NIKOLAEVNA, married name Treplyova, actress
TREPLYOV,[3] KONSTANTIN GAVRILOVICH, her son, a young man
SORIN,[4] PYOTR NIKOLAEVICH, her brother
NINA MIKHAILOVNA ZARECHNAYA,[5] a young woman, daughter of a wealthy landowner

1. Why do *sea*gulls hover over an inland lake on Sorin's estate? In Russian, *chaika* is simply a gull. *Sea* has the connotation of distance and freedom, quite out of keeping with this play. In English, however, *The Seagull* has gained common currency as the play's title, so I have retained it here, but refer simply to the "gull" in the text.
2. Ivan Bunin complained that Chekhov gave the women in his plays names befitting provincial actresses, but since two of the women in *The Seagull* are provincial actresses, no great harm is done. Arkadina is a stage name based on *Arcadia*, with its promise of a blissful pastoral existence (the sort of boring country life Arkadina loathes); but Arcadia was also the name of a garish amusement park in Moscow.
3. *Treplev* hints at *trepat*, to be disorganized or feverish; *trepach*, an idle chatterbox; and *trepetat*, to quiver or palpitate.
4. *Sorin* seems to come from *sorit*, to mess things up, and is indicative of the old man's habitually rumpled state.
5. *Zarechnaya* means "across the river," and suggests Nina's dwelling on the opposite side of the lake, as well as her alien spirit in the world of Sorin's estate.

SHAMRAEV, ILYA AFANASEVICH, retired lieutenant, overseer of Sorin's
    estate
POLINA ANDREEVNA, his wife
MASHA, his daughter
TRIGORIN, BORIS ALEKSEEVICH, a man of letters
DORN, EVGENY SERGEEVICH, a doctor of medicine
MEDVEDENKO,[6] SEMYON SEMYONOVICH, a schoolteacher
YAKOV, a workman
A COOK
A HOUSEMAID

The action takes place on SORIN's *estate. Between Acts Three and Four,
two years elapse.*

Act One

A section of the park on SORIN's *estate. A wide pathway leading from
the audience upstage into the park and towards a lake is blocked by a
platform, hurriedly slapped together for an amateur theatrical, so that
the lake is completely obscured. Bushes to the left and right of the
platform. A few chairs, a small table. The sun has just gone down. On
the platform, behind the lowered curtain, are* YAKOV *and other workmen; we can hear them coughing and hammering.*
MASHA *and* MEDVEDENKO *enter left, on their way back from a walk.*

MEDVEDENKO   How come you always wear black?
MASHA   I'm in mourning for my life. I'm unhappy.
MEDVEDENKO   But how come? (*Thinking about it.*) I don't get it . . .
    You're healthy, and that father of yours may not be rich, but he's
    doing all right. My life's a lot tougher than yours. All I make is
    twenty-three rubles a month, not counting deductions, but you
    don't see me in mourning.
        (*They sit down.*)
MASHA   It's got nothing to do with money. Even a poor person can
    be happy.
MEDVEDENKO   In theory, but in reality it doesn't work that way;
    there's me and my mother and two sisters and my little brother,
    and my pay comes to twenty-three rubles. Got to buy food and
    drink, don't you? And tea and sugar? And tobacco? It gets you
    going in circles.
MASHA (*Looking round at the platform.*)   The show will be starting
    soon.
MEDVEDENKO   Yes. Miss Zarechnaya is going to act in a play written

6. *Medved* means bear, and the name's ending suggests a Ukrainian origin.

by Konstantin Gavrilovich. They're in love, and today their souls will merge in an attempt to present a joint artistic creation. But my soul and yours have no mutual points of convergence. I love you, my longing for you drives me out of the house, every day I walk four miles here and four miles back, and all I ever get from you is apatheticism.[7] No wonder. I've got no money and lots of dependents . . . Who wants to marry a man who can't support himself?

MASHA Don't be silly. (*Takes snuff.*) Your love is touching, but I can't reciprocate, that's all. (*Holding out the snuffbox to him.*) Help yourself.

MEDVEDENKO Don't care for it. (*Pause.*)

MASHA It's so muggy, there's bound to be a storm tonight. All you ever do is philosophize or talk about money. The way you think, there's nothing worse than being poor, but I think it's a thousand times easier to wear rags and beg in the streets than . . . Oh well, you wouldn't understand.

(SORIN *and* TREPLYOV *enter right.*)

SORIN (*Leaning on a stick.*) My boy, this country life kind of has me all—you know—and take my word for it, I'll never get used to it. I went to bed last night at ten, and this morning I woke up feeling as if my brain were glued to my skull from too much sleep, and all the rest. (*Laughs.*) And after supper I accidentally fell asleep again, and now I'm a total wreck, I have nightmares, when all's said and done . . .

TREPLYOV You're right, you ought to be living in town. (*On seeing* MASHA *and* MEDVEDENKO.) Friends, when it starts you'll be called, but you're not supposed to be here now. Please go away.

SORIN (*To* MASHA.) Mariya Ilyinishna, would you kindly ask your dad to have the dog chained up? The way it howls. My sister didn't get a wink of sleep again last night.

MASHA Talk to my father yourself, because I won't. Leave me out of it, if you don't mind. (*To* MEDVEDENKO.) Come on!

(*They both go out.*)

SORIN Which means the dog'll howl all night again. It's the same old story. I never get my way in the country. Used to be, you'd take a month's vacation and come here for relaxation and all the rest, but now they pester you with all sorts of rubbish, so one day of it and you're ready to make your escape. (*Laughs.*) I've always left this place with a sense of deep satisfaction . . . Well, but now I'm retired there's nowhere to escape to, when all's said and done. Like it or not, you stay . . .

YAKOV (*To* TREPLYOV.) Mr. Treplyov, we're going for a swim.

7. He does not use the ordinary Russian word for indifference, *ravnodushie*, but instead the more exotic and pedantic *indifferentizm*.

TREPLYOV   All right, but be in your places in ten minutes. (*Looks at his watch.*) It'll be starting soon.

YAKOV   Yes, sir. (*Exits.*)

TREPLYOV (*Looking over the platform.*)   This is what I call a theater. Curtain, downstage, upstage, and beyond that empty space. No scenery at all. The view opens right on to the lake and the horizon. We'll take up the curtain at eight thirty sharp, just when the moon's rising.

SORIN   Splendid.

TREPLYOV   If Miss Zarechnaya's late, of course, the whole effect will be spoiled. It's high time she got here. Her father and stepmother watch her like hawks, and it's as hard to pry her loose from that house as if it were a prison. (*He straightens his uncle's tie.*) Your hair and beard are a mess. You should get a haircut or something.

SORIN (*Smoothing out his beard.*)   The tragedy of my life. Even when I was young, I looked like I'd been out on a bender—and all the rest. Women never found me attractive. (*Sitting.*) How come my sister's in a bad mood?

TREPLYOV   How come? She's bored. (*Sitting beside him.*) She's jealous. She's already dead-set against me and the performance and my play, because her novelist might take a shine to Miss Zarechnaya.[8] She hasn't seen my play, but she hates it already . . .

SORIN (*Laughs.*)   Can you imagine, honestly . . .

TREPLYOV   She's already annoyed that here on this little stage the success will belong to Miss Zarechnaya and not to her. (*After a glance at his watch.*) A case study for a psychology textbook—that's my mother. No argument she's talented, intelligent, ready to burst into tears over a novel, can rattle off reams of social protest poetry[9] by heart, has the bedside manner of an angel; but just try and praise a star like Duse[1] to her face. Oho ho! You mustn't praise anybody but her; you must write about her, rhapsodize, go into ecstasies over her brilliant acting in flashy vehicles like *Camille* or *Drugged by Life*,[2] but now that that kind of stimulant isn't available

---

8. This line was excised by the censor. It was replaced by "because she isn't acting in it and Miss Zarechnaya is."

9. Literally, "can rattle off all of Nekrasov by heart"—Nikolay Alekseevich Nekrasov (1821–1878), Russian populist poet who called his the "Muse of vengeance and melancholy." His poems about the downtrodden masses, suffering peasants, and appeals for justice were popular parlor recitations at liberal gatherings in the 1880s, but Chekhov uses such recitations to indicate hypocrisy and posing in the reciter.

1. Eleonora Duse (1859–1924), the great Italian actress, first toured Russia in 1891, where Chekhov saw her as Cleopatra. He wrote March 17, 1891): "I don't understand Italian, but she acted so well that I seemed to understand every word. Remarkable actress. I've never seen anything like her." Like Shaw, he preferred her to her rival Bernhardt.

2. Arkadina's repertory consists of rather sensational, fashionably risqué dramas. *Camille* is *La Dame aux camélias* (1852), a play by Alexandre Dumas *fils*, concerning a courtesan with a heart of gold and lungs of tissue paper, who gives up her love and eventually her life to advance her lover. It was first played in Russia in 1867, and later seen there during

here in the country, she gets bored and spiteful, and we're against her, it's all our fault. On top of that, she's superstitious, scared of whistling in the dressing room or the number thirteen.[3] And she's a tightwad. She's got seventy thousand in a bank in Odessa—I know it for a fact. But ask her for a loan and she'll go into hysterics.

SORIN You've got it in your head that your mother doesn't like your play, so you're upset and all the rest. Take it easy, your mother adores you.

TREPLYOV (*Picking the petals from a flower.*) She loves me—she loves me not, she loves me—she loves me not, she loves me—she loves me not. (*Laughs.*) You see, my mother doesn't love me. That's for sure! She wants to live, love, wear bright colors, but I'm twenty-five, and a constant reminder that she's not young any more. When I'm not around, she's only thirty-two; when I am, she's forty-three, and that's why she hates me. She also knows that I don't believe in the theater. She loves the theater; she thinks she's serving humanity, the sacred cause of art, but as far as I'm concerned, the modern theater is trite, riddled with clichés. When the curtain goes goes up on an artificially-lighted room with three walls, and these great talents, acolytes of the religion of art, act out how people eat, drink, make love, walk, wear their jackets; when they take cheap, vulgar plots and cheap, vulgar speeches and try to extract a moral—not too big a moral, easy on the digestion, useful around the house; when in a thousand different ways they serve up the same old leftovers, again and again and again—I run out the exit and keep on running, the way Maupassant ran from the Eiffel Tower,[4] because it was crushing his brain beneath *its* tawdry vulgarity.

SORIN You've got to have theater.

TREPLYOV New forms are what we need. New forms are what we need, and if there aren't any, then we're better off with nothing. (*Looks at his watch.*) I love my mother, love her deeply; but she

tours of Sarah Bernhardt in 1881 and 1892 and Eleonora Duse in 1892. Chekhov loathed *Drugged by Life*, a play by Boleslav Markevich, based on Markevich's novel *The Abyss*, and performed in Moscow in 1884. To quote Chekhov's review, "In general the play is written with a lavatory brush and stinks of obscenity." Its central character is a woman of loose morals, who, after four acts of dissipation and costume changes, dies in the fifth in an odor of sanctity. The connection to Arkadina's life and her expensive wardrobe is clear.

3. Literally, three candles on a table. This is a fatal omen, for at a Russian wake two candles were placed at the corpse's head and one at its feet. Therefore, if three lights are burning, one must be snuffed out.

4. Guy de Maupassant (1850–1893), French writer, whose works began to appear in Russian in 1894 and 1896. He died of syphilis and drugs, not modern technology. The famous landmark, the Eiffel Tower, was erected by Gustave Eiffel in 1889 for the Paris Exposition and at 300 meters, was the highest erection of the time. It was controversial, many persons of taste considering it an eyesore. Maupassant detested it as a symbol of materialism and modern vulgarity; he chose to dine at its restaurant, the only place in Paris from which one could not see the tower.

smokes, drinks, lives openly with that novelist,[5] her name constantly in the papers—it gets me down. Sometimes it's just my plain human ego talking; it's a shame my mother is a famous actress, because I think if she were an ordinary woman, I might be happier. Uncle, can there be a more maddening and ridiculous situation than the one I'm in? Her parties will be packed with celebrities, actors, and writers, and I'll be the only nobody in the room, and they put up with me just because I'm her son. Who am I? What am I? Expelled from the university in my junior year for circumstances that as they say, were beyond the editor's control,[6] with no talent at all, and no money either; according to my passport I'm a bourgeois from Kiev.[7] My father actually *was* a bourgeois from Kiev, but he was also a famous actor. So when all those actors and writers at her parties used to condescend with their kind attentions, I'd feel as if their eyes were sizing up how insignificant I was—I could guess what they were thinking and I'd go through agonies of humiliation.

SORIN   While we're on the subject, tell me, please, what sort of fellow is this novelist? I can't figure him out. He never opens his mouth.

TREPLYOV   Clever enough, easygoing, a bit—what's the word—taciturn. He's all right. He's not even forty, but he's jaded, jaded within an inch of his life . . . Now he only drinks beer and can love only those who are no longer young . . . [8] As for his writing, it's . . . how can I put it? Charming, talented . . . but . . . compared to Tolstoy or Zola,[9] a little Trigorin goes a long way.

SORIN   But I love authors, my boy. There was a time when I desperately wanted two things: I wanted to get married and I wanted to be an author, but I didn't manage to do either one. Yes. It would be nice to be even a second-rate author, when all's said and done . . .

TREPLYOV   (*Listening hard.*) I hear footsteps . . . (*Embraces his uncle.*) I can't live without her . . . Even the sound of her footsteps is musical . . . I'm out of my mind with happiness. (*Quickly goes*

---

5. This phrase was excised by the censor. Chekhov replaced it with "but she leads a disorderly life, constantly carrying on with that novelist."
6. A journalistic euphemism to cover passages deleted by censorship.
7. Literally, a Kievan *meshchanin*, that is, a burgher, townsman, artisan, or small tradesman. The word bears connotations of narrowmindedness, philistinism, and parochialism. By marrying Treplyov's father, Arkadina had come down in station. And although Kiev, the capital of the Ukraine, was the seventh most populous city in Russia, to be associated with it suggests provincialism.
8. This phrase was excised by the censor, and replaced by Chekhov with "already famous and jaded within an inch of his life . . ."
9. Lyov Nikolaevich Tolstoy (1828–1910) was widely considered Russia's greatest author and her moral conscience. The works of Emile Zola (1840–1902), usually appeared in Russian translation shortly after their appearance in French.

to meet NINA ZARECHNAYA *as she enters.*) Enchantress, girl of my dreams . . .

NINA (*Excited.*)   I'm not late . . . I'm sure I'm not late . . .

TREPLYOV (*Kissing her hands.*)   No, no, no . . .

NINA   All day I've been on edge, I've been so worried! I was afraid Father wouldn't let me go . . . But he's just gone out with my step-mother. The sky was red, the moon's already on the rise, so I took a whip to the horses, lashed them. (*Laughs.*) But I'm glad I did. (*Squeezes* SORIN's *hand tightly.*)

SORIN (*Laughs.*)   I do believe your pretty eyes have tears in them . . . Heh-heh! Mustn't do that!

NINA   You're right . . . You see the way I'm panting. In half an hour I've got to go, we must hurry. Don't, don't, for heaven's sake, don't make me late. Father doesn't know I'm here.

TREPLYOV   As a matter of fact, it is time to begin. I have to collect everybody.

SORIN   I'll go fetch 'em and all the rest. Right this minute. (*Crosses right and sings.*) "Back to France two grenadiers . . . [1] (*Looking around.*) Once I started singing just like that, and some assistant D.A.[2] says to me, "Your Honor, that's a powerful voice you've got . . ." Then he thought a bit and added, "Powerful . . . but repulsive." (*Laughs and exits.*)

NINA   Father and his wife won't let me come here. They say this place is bohemian . . . they're afraid I might become an actress . . . But I'm drawn here to the lake, like a gull . . . My heart is filled with all of you. (*Looks around.*)

TREPLYOV   We're alone.

NINA   I think there's someone over there.

TREPLYOV   No one. (*They kiss.*)

NINA   What kind of tree is that?

TREPLYOV   Elm.

NINA   How come it's so dark?

TREPLYOV   It's nightfall; things get dark. Don't leave so soon, for my sake.

NINA   Can't.

TREPLYOV   What if I ride over to your place, Nina? I'll stand all night in the garden and stare at your window.

---

1. The opening lines of a poem by Heinrich Heine, "Die beiden Grenadiere" (1822), set to music by Robert Schumann (1827). The rest of the verse goes:

> They had been imprisoned in Russia.
> And when they got to a German billet,
> They hung their heads.

According to Arthur Ganz, it is ironic that "one of the great romantic evocations of the power of the will (here a will that vows to seize upon its object even from beyond the grave), [is] precisely the quality that Sorin lacks." (*Drama Survey*, Spring 1966).

2. As we learn later, Sorin is an Actual State Councilor, so he's being twitted by an underling.

NINA   Can't—the watchman will catch you. Trésor still isn't used to you and he'll start barking.

TREPLYOV   I love you.

NINA   Ssh . . .

TREPLYOV (*Having heard footsteps.*)   Who's there? That you, Yakov?

YAKOV (*Behind the platform.*)   Right.

TREPLYOV   Got the methylated spirits? And the sulphur? When the red eyes make their entrance, there has to be a smell of sulphur. (*To* NINA.) Go on, they've got it all ready for you. Are you excited?

NINA   Yes, very. Your mama doesn't count. I'm not afraid of her, but then there's Trigorin . . . Acting with him in the audience frightens and embarrasses me . . . A famous writer . . . Is he young?

TREPLYOV   Yes.

NINA   His stories are so wonderful!

TREPLYOV (*Coldly.*)   I wouldn't know; I haven't read them.

NINA   It isn't easy to act in your play. There are no living characters in it.

TREPLYOV   Living characters! Life should be portrayed not the way it is, and not the way it's supposed to be, but the way it appears in dreams.

NINA   There isn't much action in your play. It's like a sitdown read-through.[3] And a play, I think, definitely ought to have love interest . . .

(*They both go behind the platform. Enter* POLINA ANDREEVNA *and* DORN.)

POLINA ANDREEVNA   It's starting to get damp. Go back, put on your galoshes.

DORN   I'm overheated.

POLINA ANDREEVNA   You don't take care of yourself. It's sheer obstinacy. You're a doctor and you know perfectly well that damp air is bad for you, but you want me to suffer; you deliberately sat up all last night on the veranda . . .

DORN (*Sings.*)   "Say not that thy youth was wasted."[4]

POLINA ANDREEVNA   You were so infatuated talking to Irina Nikolaevna . . . you didn't notice the cold. Admit you're attracted to her.

DORN   I'm fifty-five years old.

POLINA ANDREEVNA   Don't be silly, that's not old for a man. You're beautifully preserved and women still find you attractive.

DORN   Then what can I do for you?

POLINA ANDREEVNA   You're all of you ready to fall on your faces at an actress's feet. All of you!

3. *Chitka*, which is theatrical slang. Nina's vocabulary has profited from listening to Arkadina.
4. A line from Nekrasov's poem "A heavy cross fell to her lot" (1856), set to music by Prigozhy.

DORN (*Sings.*)   "Once again I stand before thee . . ."[5] If society loves actors and treats them differently from, say, shopkeepers, it's only natural. It's what's we call idealism.

POLINA ANDREEVNA   Women have always fallen in love with you and flung themselves at you. Do you call that idealism?

DORN (*Shrugging.*)   So what? My relationships with women have always been a good thing. What they really loved was my being a first-class doctor. Ten or fifteen years ago, remember, I was the only competent obstetrician[6] in the whole county. Not to mention, I was honest in my dealings.

POLINA ANDREEVNA (*Seizes him by the hand.*)   My dearest!

DORN   Hush. They're coming.

(*Enter* ARKADINA, *arm in arm with* SORIN; TRIGORIN, SHAMRAEV, MEDVEDENKO, *and* MASHA.)

SHAMRAEV   At the Poltava fair[7] in 1873 she gave a marvelous performance. Sheer delight! Wonderful acting! Would you also happen to know what's become of the comedian Chadin, Pavel Chadin? He was inimitable in *Krechinsky's Wedding*,[8] better than the great Sadovsky,[9] take my word for it, dear lady. Where is he these days?

ARKADINA   You're always asking me about these prehistoric characters. How should I know? (*Sits down.*)

SHAMRAEV (*Sighs.*)   Good old Chadin! You don't see his like nowadays. The stage is going downhill, Irina Nikolaevna! In the old days there were mighty oaks, but now all you see are stumps.

DORN   There's not a lot of brilliant talent around these days, it's true, but the general level of acting has improved considerably.

SHAMRAEV   I can't agree with you there. Still, it's a matter of taste. *De gustibus, pluribus unum.*[1]

(TREPLYOV *enters from behind the platform.*)

ARKADINA (*To her son.*)   My darling son, when are we to begin?

---

5. In full, "stand bewitched before thee," a line from V. I. Krasov's *Stanzas* (1842), set to music by Alyabiev.
6. Dorn uses the French word *accoucheur,* an indication of his refinement.
7. Capital of the *gubernia* of the same name, located in the Ukraine; its main industries were horse trading, slaughterhouses, and machinery manufacture. Its population was largely Little Russians and Jews. Acting companies proliferated in such towns during the fairs.
8. In the original, "as Raspluev." "Ivan Antonovich, a small but thick-set man around fifty," a great comic role in Aleksandr Sukhovo-Kobylin's *Krechinsky's Wedding* (first staged in 1855), the cynical henchman of the confidence-man hero.
9. Stage name of Prov Mikhailovich Yermilov (1818–1872), a famous character actor and member of the Maly Theater troupe in Moscow from 1839 until his death. He was responsible for the growing popularity of Ostrovsky's plays. Sukhovo-Kobylin considered that Sadovsky had vulgarized the part of Raspluev, which the actor created.
1. In the original, *de gustibus, aut bene, aut nihil,* a violent yoking together of three different Latin sayings: *De gustibus non disputantur,* "there's no point arguing over taste"; *De mortuis nil nisi bene,* "Say naught but good of the dead"; and *Aut Caesar aut nihil,* "Either Caesar or nothing."

TREPLYOV   In a minute. Have some patience.

ARKADINA (*Reciting from* Hamlet.)² "My son! Thou turn'st mine eyes into my very soul. And there I see such black and grainéd spots as will not leave their tinct!"

TREPLYOV (*Paraphrasing* Hamlet.) "Then wherefore dost thou yield to sin, seeking love in a morass of crime?" (*A bugle is blown behind the platform.*) Ladies and gentlemen, we're about to begin! Your attention please! (*Pause.*) I'm starting. (*Thumps with a stick and speaks loudly.*) O ye venerable and ancient shades, that nocturnally hover above this lake, put us to sleep and let us dream of what is to be in two hundred thousand years!

SORIN   In two hundred thousand years, there will be nothing.

TREPLYOV   Then let them reveal that nothing.

ARKADINA   Let them. We're asleep already.

> (*The curtain rises; the vista on to the lake is revealed; the moon is over the horizon, reflected in the water; on a large boulder,* NINA ZARECHNAYA *is seated, dressed all in white.*)

NINA   Humans, lions, eagles and partridges, antlered deer, geese, spiders, silent fishes that inhabit the waters, starfish and those beings invisible to the naked eye—in short, all living things, all living things, all living things, having completed the doleful cycle, are now extinct . . . Already thousands of centuries have passed since the earth bore any living creature, and this pale moon to no avail doth light her lamp. No more does the meadow awake to the cries of cranes, and the mayflies are no longer to be heard in the linden groves. Chilly, chilly, chilly. Empty, empty, empty. Ghastly, ghastly, ghastly. (*Pause.*) The bodies of living creatures have crumbled into dust, and Eternal Matter has converted them into stones, water, clouds, and all their souls are mingled into one. The universal soul—'tis I . . . in person. . . . In me are mingled the souls of Alexander the Great, and Caesar, and Shakespeare, and Napoleon, and the lowliest of leeches. In me, human consciousness is mingled with animal instinct, and I remember everything, everything, everything, and I relive each life within my self.

> (*Will-o'-the-wisps appear.*)

ARKADINA (*In a low voice.*) This is something avant-garde.³

TREPLYOV (*Entreating her reproachfully.*) Mama!

NINA   I am alone. Once every hundred years I ope my lips to speak, and my voice echoes dolefully in this void, and no one hears . . .

---

2. A quotation from *Hamlet,* the closet scene, III. iii. In Nikolay Polevoy's Russian translation, Arkadina's quotation is reasonably accurate, but Treplyov's is a loose paraphrase of "making love over the nasty sty." The original image would have been too coarse for nineteenth-century playgoers and censors.

3. Literally, *chto-to dekadentskoe*, something decadent. At this time, symbolist and decadent writing, popularized by Maeterlinck, were considered the cutting edge of literary innovation in Europe, and had began to gain disciples in Russia.

Even ye, pale fires, hear me not . . . Toward morning ye are engendered by the putrescence of the swamp, and roam 'til dawn, but sans thoughts, sans will, sans throbbing life. Fearing lest life spring up in you, the father of Eternal Matter, Satan, at every moment effects in you, as in stones and water, an interchange of atoms, and you transmutate incessantly. Throughout the universe there remains constant and immutable naught but spirit. (*Pause.*) Like a prisoner, flung into a deep empty pit, I know not where I am nor what awaits me. All that is revealed to me is that in the dogged, cruel struggle with Satan, the principle of material forces; it is decreed that I shall conquer, and thereafter matter and spirit will blend in glorious harmony, and the kingdom of universal will is to emerge. But this will come to pass only very gradually, over a long, long series of millennia, when the moon and the twinkling dogstar and the earth are turned to dust . . . But until that time, all will be ghastly, ghastly, ghastly . . . (*Pause; against the background of the lake, two red dots appear.*) Behold, my mighty adversary, Satan, draws nigh. I see his dreadful crimson eyes . . .

ARKADINA   What a stink of sulphur. Is that necessary?

TREPLYOV   Yes.

ARKADINA (*Laughs.*)   Of course, special effects.

TREPLYOV   Mama!

NINA   He grows bored in the absence of human beings. . . .

POLINA ANDREEVNA (*To* DORN.)   You took off your hat. Put it back on or you'll catch cold.

ARKADINA   The doctor's tipping his hat to Satan, the father of eternal matter.

TREPLYOV (*Flaring up, loudly.*)   The play's over! That's enough! Curtain!

ARKADINA   What are you angry about?

TREPLYOV   Enough! Curtain! Ring down the curtain! (*Stamping his feet.*) Curtain! (*The curtain comes down.*) I apologize! I lost sight of the fact that playwriting and playacting are only for the chosen few. I infringed the monopoly! I feel . . . I . . . (*He wants to say something more, but waves his hand dismissively and exits left.*)

ARKADINA   What's come over him?

SORIN   Irina, dear heart, you mustn't treat a young man's self-esteem that way.

ARKADINA   What did I say to him?

SORIN   You offended him.

ARKADINA   He told us beforehand that it was a joke, so I treated his play as a joke.

SORIN   Even so . . .

ARKADINA   Now it turns out that he wrote a masterpiece! Pardon me for living! The real reason he staged this production and asphyxiated us with sulphur was not to make a joke, but to give us an object lesson . . . He wanted to teach us how to write and how to act. This is starting to get tiresome. These constant jabs at me and digs, I don't care what you say, would get on anybody's nerves! Temperamental, conceited little boy.

SORIN   He wanted to give you a treat.

ARKADINA   Really? And yet you'll notice that he didn't pick an ordinary sort of play, but forced us to listen to this avant-garde gibberish. For the sake of a joke I'm willing to listen to gibberish too, but this is all pretentiousness about new forms, a new age in art. So far as I can tell, there's no new forms in it, nothing but a nasty disposition . . .

TRIGORIN   Everyone writes the way he wants and the way he can.

ARKADINA   Let him write the way he wants and the way he can, only let him leave me in peace.

DORN   "Mighty Jove, once angry grown . . ."[4]

ARKADINA   I'm not Jove, I'm a woman. (*Lighting a cigarette.*) I'm not angry, I'm only annoyed that a young man should waste his time in such a tiresome way. I didn't mean to offend him.

MEDVEDENKO   There's no basis for distinguishing spirit from matter, because spirit itself is probably an agglomeration of material atoms. (*Eagerly, to* TRIGORIN.) Now, you know, somebody ought to write a play and get it produced about—our friend the schoolteacher. He leads a tough, tough life!

ARKADINA   That's all very true, but don't let's talk about plays or atoms. What a glorious night! Do you hear the singing, ladies and gentlemen? (*Listening hard.*) How lovely!

POLINA ANDREEVNA   It's on the other side of the lake.

      (*Pause.*)

ARKADINA (*To* TRIGORIN.)   Sit beside me. Some ten or fifteen years ago, here, on the lake, you could hear music and singing nonstop almost every night. There were six country houses along the shore. I can remember laughter, noisemaking, shooting, and one love affair after another . . . The romantic lead and idol of all six houses at that time is among us, may I present: (*nods to* DORN) Doctor Yevgeny Dorn. He's fascinating even now, but in those days he was irresistible. However, my conscience is starting to bother me. Why did I insult my poor little boy? I feel bad about it. (*Loudly.*) Kostya! My child! Kostya!

MASHA   I'll go look for him.

ARKADINA   Please do, darling.

MASHA (*Crosses left.*)   Yoo-hoo! Konstantin! . . . Yoo-hoo! (*Exits.*)

NINA (*Coming out from behind the platform.*)   It looks like we're not

4. A saying that continues "has stopped being Jove" or "is in the wrong."

going to go on, so I can come out. Good evening! (*Exchanges kisses with* ARKADINA *and* POLINA ANDREEVNA.)

SORIN Bravo! Bravo!

ARKADINA Bravo, bravo! We loved it. With such looks, such a wonderful voice it's wrong, it's criminal to vegetate in the country. You probably have talent too. You hear me? You have an obligation to go on the stage!

NINA Oh, that's my fondest dream! (*Sighs.*) But it will never come true.

ARKADINA Who knows? May I introduce: Boris Trigorin.

NINA Ah, I'm delighted . . . (*Embarrassed.*) I read all your things . . .

ARKADINA (*Seating her beside her.*) Don't be embarrassed, darling. He's a celebrity, but he's a simple soul. You see, he's embarrassed himself.

DORN I suppose we can raise the curtain now; it feels spooky this way.

SHAMRAEV (*Loudly.*) Yakov, haul up that curtain, boy!
  (*The curtain is raised.*)

NINA (*To* TRIGORIN.) It's a strange play, isn't it?

TRIGORIN I didn't understand a word. Still, I enjoyed watching it. Your acting was so sincere. And the scenery was gorgeous. (*Pause.*) I suppose there are a lot of fish in that lake.

NINA Yes.

TRIGORIN I love fishing. For me, there's no greater pleasure than sitting on the bank at dusk, watching the float bob up and down.[5]

NINA But I should think anyone who's enjoyed creating a work of art couldn't enjoy anything else.

ARKADINA (*Laughing.*) Don't talk like that. Whenever anyone compliments him, he just shrivels up.

SHAMRAEV I remember at the Moscow Opera House once the famous Silva hit low C. And at the time, as luck would have it, sitting in the gallery was the bass from our church choir, and all of a sudden, you can imagine our intense surprise, we hear from the gallery: "Bravo, Silva!"—a whole octave lower . . . Something like this (*in a basso profundo*): "Bravo, Silva" . . . The audience was dumbfounded.
  (*Pause.*)

DORN An angel of silence flew by.[6]

NINA My time's up. Good-bye.

ARKADINA Where are you off to? So early? We won't let you go.

NINA Papa's waiting for me.

---

5. Chekhov's two favorite pastimes in the country were fishing with a float and gathering mushrooms.
6. A common saying, used whenever a pause suddenly falls over a conversation. Chekhov uses it in his stories frequently.

ARKADINA   That man, honestly . . . (*Exchanges kisses.*) Well, what can we do? It's a shame, a crying shame to let you go.

NINA   If you only knew how hard it is for me to leave!

ARKADINA   Somebody should see you home, you darling girl.

NINA (*Alarmed.*)   Oh, no, no!

SORIN (*To her, imploring.*)   Do stay!

NINA   I can't, Pyotr Nikolaevich.

SORIN   Do stay just one more hour and all the rest. Now, how 'bout it? Come on . . .

NINA (*After thinking it over, tearfully.*)   I can't! (*Shakes hands and exits hurriedly.*)

ARKADINA   The girl's really and truly unhappy. They say her late mother bequeathed her husband her whole huge fortune, down to the last penny, and now this child is left with nothing, because her father's already willed it to his second wife. It's outrageous.

DORN   Yes, her dear old dad is a pedigreed swine. Credit where credit's due.

SORIN (*Rubbing his chilled hands.*)   We'd best be going too, ladies and gentlemen; it's starting to get damp. My legs ache.

ARKADINA   They must be wooden legs—they can hardly move. Well, let's go, you star-crossed old man. (*Takes him by the arm.*)

SHAMRAEV (*Offering his arm to his wife.*)   Madame?

SORIN   I hear that dog howling again. (*To* SHAMRAEV.) Kindly see that he's unchained, Ilya Afanasevich.

SHAMRAEV   Can't be done, Pyotr Nikolaevich; I'm afraid robbers might break into the barn. Got my millet stored there. (*To* MEDVEDENKO, *walking beside him.*) Yes, a whole octave lower: "Bravo, Silva!" Wasn't a professional singer, either, just an ordinary member of the church choir.

MEDVEDENKO   How much does an ordinary member of the church choir make?

(*They all go out, except* DORN.)

DORN (*Alone.*)   I don't know—maybe I'm confused or I'm crazy but I liked the play. There's something in it. When that girl was talking about being lonely and then when Satan's red eyes appeared, my hands trembled with excitement. Fresh, naive . . . Oh, I think he's coming this way. I'd like to tell him the nicest things I can.

TREPLYOV (*Enters.*)   Nobody's here.

DORN   I am.

TREPLYOV   That Masha creature's been looking for me all over the park. Unbearable female.

DORN   Konstantin Gavrilovich, I liked your play very much. It's an unusual piece of work, and I didn't get to hear how it ends, but even so, it makes a powerful impression. You're a talented fellow, you ought to keep at it. (TREPLYOV *squeezes his hand tightly and embraces him impulsively.*) Foo, don't be so high-strung. Tears in his eyes . . . What was I saying? You took a subject from the realm of abstract ideas. That was appropriate, because a work of art definitely ought to express a great idea. The beauty of a thing lies entirely in its seriousness. You're awfully pale!

TREPLYOV   Then what you're saying is—keep at it!

DORN   Yes . . . But write about only what's important and everlasting. You know, I've lived my life with variety and discrimination; I've had it all, but if I ever got the chance to experience the spiritual uplift artists feel at the moment of creation, I think I'd relinquish my physical trappings and all that they entail, and let myself be wafted far away from earth into the empyrean.

TREPLYOV   Sorry, where's Miss Zarechnaya?

DORN   And another thing. Every work of art ought to have a clear, well-defined idea. You ought to know what you're writing for; otherwise, if you travel this picturesque path without a well-defined goal, you'll go astray and your talent will destroy you.

TREPLYOV (*Impatiently.*)   Where's Miss Zarechnaya?

DORN   She went home.

TREPLYOV (*In despair.*)   What am I going to do? I have to see her . . . I've got to see her . . . I'm going . . .

(MASHA *enters.*)

DORN (*To* TREPLYOV.)   Calm down, my friend.

TREPLYOV   But I'm going anyway. I have to go.

MASHA   Come home, Konstantin Gavrilovich. Your mama's waiting for you. She's worried.

TREPLYOV   Tell her I've gone. And will you all please leave me in peace? Stay here! Don't come after me!

DORN   Now, now, now, my dear boy . . . you mustn't act this way . . . isn't nice.

TREPLYOV (*Tearfully.*)   Good-bye, Doctor. Thanks . . . (*Exits.*)

DORN (*Sighs.*)   Youth, youth!

MASHA   When people have nothing better to say, they go: "Youth, youth" . . . (*Takes snuff.*)

DORN (*Takes away her snuffbox and tosses it into the bushes.*)   That's disgusting! (*Pause.*) Sounds like music in the house. Better go in.

MASHA   Wait.

DORN   What?

MASHA   I want to tell you something else. I have to talk to someone . . . (*Getting excited.*) I don't love my father . . . but I feel close to you.[7] Why do I feel so intensely that we have something in com-

7. In the first version of the play, Masha's father was revealed to be Dr. Dorn at this point. When the play was revived at the Moscow Art Theater, Nemirovich-Danchenko advised Chekhov to eliminate this plot element. "I said either this theme has to be developed or

mon? . . . Help me. Help me, or I'll do something stupid, I'll mess
up my life, wreck it . . . I can't stand it any more . . .

DORN   What do you mean? Help you how?

MASHA   I'm in pain. Nobody, nobody knows how much pain I'm in.
(*Lays her head on his chest, quietly.*) I love Konstantin.

DORN   They're all so high-strung! They're all so high-strung! And all
this love . . . Oh, spellbinding lake! (*Tenderly.*) But what can I do,
my child? What? What?

CURTAIN

Act Two

*A croquet lawn. Up right, a house with a wide veranda; at left, the
lake can be seen, with the sun's rays reflected on it. Flowerbeds. Midday. Hot. To one side of the croquet lawn, in the shade of an old linden
tree,* ARKADINA, DORN, *and* MASHA *are sitting on a bench.* DORN *has an
open book on his lap.*

ARKADINA (*To* MASHA.)   Come on, let's get up. (*Both rise.*) Let's stand
side by side. You're twenty-two, and I'm nearly twice that. Yevgeny
Sergeich, which of us is younger?[8]

DORN   You, of course.

ARKADINA   Thank you, kind sir . . . And why? Because I work, I feel
emotions, I'm constantly on the go; while you sit still in the same
place; you don't live . . . And I have a rule: don't peer into the
future. I never give a thought to old age or death. What will be will
be.

MASHA   But I feel as if I were born ages and ages ago; I lug my life
around like a dead weight, like the endless train on a gown . . .
And lots of times I don't feel much like going on living. (*Sits.*) Of
course, this is all silly. I have to shake myself out of it, slough it
off.

---

else entirely removed. Especially since it ends the first act. The end of a first act by its
very nature has to wind up tightly the situation to be developed in the second act.

"Chekhov said, 'The audience does like it when at the end of an act a loaded gun is
aimed at it.'

" 'True enough,' I replied, 'but then it has to go off, and not simply be chucked away
during the intermission.'

"It turns out that later on Chekhov repeated this remark more than a few times.

"He agreed with me. The ending was revised." (Vl. I. Nemirovich-Danchenko, *Out of
the Past* [1938].)

8. In Chekhov's story "Ariadne" (1895), there is a similar passage: "I just wonder, sir, how
you can live without love?', he said. 'You are young, handsome, interesting—in short you
are a fashion plate of a man, but you live like a monk. Ah, these old men of twenty-eight!
I am almost ten years older than you, but which of us is the younger? Ariadne Grigoryevna,
who is younger?'

" 'You, of course,' replied Ariadne."

DORN (*Sings quietly.*) "Tell her of love, flowers of mine . . ."[9]

ARKADINA Besides, I'm as neat and tidy as an English gentleman. Darling, I keep myself up to scratch, if I say so myself, and I'm always dressed and have my hair done comme il faut. Would I ever venture to leave the house, just step into the garden, in a smock or with my hair down? Never. The reason I'm in such good shape is because I was never sloppy, never let myself go, like some people. . . . (*With her hands on her hips, strides up and down the lawn.*) There, you see—light on my feet. Fit to play a girl of fifteen.

DORN Fine and dandy, but regardless of all that I'll go on reading. (*Picks up the book.*) We'd stopped at the grain merchant and the rats.

ARKADINA And the rats. Read away. (*Sits down.*) Actually, give it to me, I'll read it. 'S my turn. (*Takes the book and runs her eyes over it.*) And the rats . . . Here we go . . . (*Reads.*) "And, of course, for people in society to pamper novelists and lure them into their homes is as dangerous as if a grain merchant were to breed rats in his granaries. Meanwhile, they go on loving them. So, when a woman has picked out the writer she wishes to captivate, she lays siege to him by means of compliments, endearments, and flattering attentions . . ."[1] Well, that may be what the French do, but there's nothing of the sort in our country; we have no master plan. In Russia, before a woman captivates a writer, she's usually fallen head over heels in love with him herself, take my word for it. You don't have far to look, just consider me and Trigorin . . .

(*Enter* SORIN, *leaning on a stick, next to* NINA; MEDVEDENKO *wheels an empty armchair behind them.*)

SORIN (*In the tone used to coddle children.*) Are we? Are we having fun? Are we happy today, when's all said and done? (*To his sister.*) We're having fun! Father and Stepmother have gone out of town, and now we're free for three whole days.

NINA (*Sits beside* ARKADINA *and embraces her.*) I'm happy! Now I can be all yours.

SORIN (*Sits in the armchair.*) She's the prettiest little thing today.

ARKADINA Smartly dressed, interesting . . . You're clever at that sort

9. Siébel's song in Act Three, Scene One of Gounod's opera *Faust*. In Russia, quoting it meant "You're talking through your hat."

1. From *Sur l'eau* (1888) by Guy de Maupassant. It is his diary of a Mediterranean cruise, taken to restore his shattered nerves. The passage continues, "Just like water, which, drop by drop, pierces the hardest rock, praise falls, word by word, on the sensitive heart of a man of letters. So, as soon as she sees he is tenderized, moved, won over by this constant flattery, she isolates him, she gradually cuts the connections he might have elsewhere, and insensibly accustoms him to come to her house, to enjoy himself there, to put his mind at ease there. To get him nicely acclimated to her house, she looks after him and prepares his success, puts him in the limelight, as a star, shows him, ahead of all the former habitués of the place, a marked consideration, an unequaled admiration."

of thing. (*Kisses* NINA.) But we mustn't praise her too much, or we'll put a hex on her.[2] Where's Boris Alekseevich?

NINA He's down by the swimming hole fishing.

ARKADINA I'm surprised he doesn't get fed up with it! (*About to go on reading.*)

NINA What have you got there?

ARKADINA *At Sea* by Maupassant, sweetheart. (*Reads a few lines to herself.*) Well, the rest is uninteresting and untrue. (*Closes the book.*) I feel uneasy. Tell me, what's the matter with my son? How come he's so tiresome and surly? He spends whole days on the lake, and I almost never see him.

MASHA He's sick at heart. (*To* NINA, *shyly.*) Please, do recite something from his play!

NINA (*Shrugs.*) You want me to? It's so uninteresting!

MASHA (*With restrained excitement.*) Whenever he recites, his eyes blaze and his face turns pale. He has a beautiful, mournful voice; and the look of a poet.

(SORIN's *snoring is audible.*)

DORN Sweet dreams!

ARKADINA Petrusha!

SORIN Aah?

ARKADINA You asleep?

SORIN Certainly not.

(*Pause.*)

ARKADINA You don't look after yourself, and you should, brother.

SORIN I'd be glad to look after myself, but the doctor here won't prescribe a treatment.

DORN Treatments at age sixty!

SORIN Even at sixty a person wants to go on living.

DORN (*Vexed.*) Oh yeah! Well, take a couple of aspirins.[3]

ARKADINA I think he'd feel better if he went to a health spa.

DORN Think so? Let him go. Then again let him stay here.

ARKADINA Try and figure *that* out.

DORN There's nothing to figure out. It's perfectly clear.

(*Pause.*)

MEDVEDENKO The best thing Pyotr Nikolaevich could do is stop smoking.

SORIN Rubbish.

DORN No, it's not rubbish. Alcohol and tobacco are depersonalizing. After a cigar or a shot of vodka, you're not Pyotr Nikolaevich any more, you're Pyotr Nikolaevich plus somebody else; your sense

2. Literally, "put the evil one on her," presumably by arousing envy.
3. Literally, valerian, a mild sedative, the equivalent of aspirin (which was not widely marketed until 1899). The nervous actors of the Moscow Art Theater, on the opening night of *The Seagull*, dosed themselves heavily with valerian.

of self, your "ego" gets fuzzy around the edges, and you start ta̶
about yourself in the third person—as "that other fellow."

SORIN (*Laughs.*) 'S all right for you to lecture me! You've lived ̶
your lifetime, but what about me? I worked in the Department o̶
Justice for twenty-eight years, but I still haven't lived, haven't had
any experiences, when all's said and done and, take my word for
it, I've still got a lust for life. You're jaded, you don't care, and so
you can be philosophic, but I want to live a little and so I drink
sherry at dinner and smoke cigars and all the rest. So there and
all the rest.

DORN A man should take life seriously, but trying treatments at
sixty, complaining there wasn't enough fun in your youth is, pardon me, ridiculous.

MASHA (*Rises.*) Time for lunch, I guess . . . (*Walks with a sluggish,
unsteady gait.*) Foot fell asleep . . . (*Exits.*)

DORN She'll go and knock down a couple of drinks before lunch.

SORIN The poor thing's got no happiness in her life.

DORN Piffle, your excellency.

SORIN You talk like a man who's had it all.

ARKADINA Ah, what can be more boring that this darling rural boredom! Hot, quiet, nobody lifts a finger, everybody philosophizes . . .
It's nice being with you; my friends, lovely listening to you, but
. . . sitting in my hotel room and learning my lines—what could
be better?

NINA (*Rapturously.*) How wonderful! I know just what you mean.

SORIN Of course, things're better in town. You sit in your office,
the doorman doesn't let anyone in without being announced, the
telephone . . . cabs on every corner and all the rest . . .

DORN (*Sings.*) "Tell her of love, flowers of mine . . ."

(*Enter* SHAMRAEV, *followed by* POLINA ANDREEVNA.)

SHAMRAEV Here's our crowd. Good morning! (*Kisses* ARKADINA's
hand, then NINA's.) The wife tells me you're planning to drive with
her into town today. Is that right?

ARKADINA Yes, that's our plan.

SHAMRAEV Hmm . . . That's just great, but how you do expect to get
there, dear lady? Our rye is being hauled today, all the hired hands
are busy. And which horses will you take, may I ask?

ARKADINA Which? How should I know which?

SORIN We've still got the carriage horses.

SHAMRAEV (*Getting excited.*) Carriage horses? And where am I to
get harnesses? Where am I to get harnesses? This is marvelous!
This is incredible! Dear, dear lady! Forgive me, I bow down to your
talent, I'm ready to give up ten years of my life for your sake, but
horses I cannot give you.

ARKADINA And what if I have to go? A fine how-do-you-do!

lady! You don't know what it means to run a farm!
... *up.*) Here we go again! In that case, I shall leave
... is very day. Have them hire horses for me in town,
... to the station on foot!

... *ing up.*) In that case, I tender my resignation! Go
... self another overseer. (*Exits.*)

... NA   Every summer it's the same thing; every summer I'm
exposed to insults. I'll never set foot in this place again! (*Exits left, where the swimming hole is supposed to be; in a minute she can be seen crossing into the house;* TRIGORIN *follows her with fishing poles[4] and a pail.*)

SORIN (*Flaring up.*)   This is a disgrace! This is—who the hell knows what? This is going to make me lose my temper, when all's said and done. Bring all the horses here this very minute!

NINA (*To* POLINA ANDREEVNA.)   To refuse Irina Nikolaevna, a famous actress! Isn't every one of her wishes, even her whims, more important than your farming? It's just incredible!

POLINA ANDREEVNA (*In despair.*)   What can I do? Put yourself in my position: what can I do?

SORIN (*To* NINA).   Let's go in to my sister. . . . We'll all plead with her not to leave. Isn't that the thing? (*Looking in the direction of* SHAMRAEV's *exit.*) Insufferable fellow! Dictator!

NINA (*Helping him to rise.*)   Sit down, sit down . . . We'll wheel you . . . (*She and* MEDVEDENKO *wheel the armchair.*) Oh, this is just awful!

SORIN   Yes, yes, this is awful . . . But he won't leave; I'll give him a talking-to right now.

(*They leave; only* DORN *and* POLINA ANDREEVNA *remain.*)

DORN   People are so predictable. Ultimately the right thing would simply be to toss your husband out on his ear, but in fact it'll end up with that old fusspot Pyotr Nikolaevich and his sister begging *him* for forgiveness. Wait and see!

POLINA ANDREEVNA   He even sent the carriage horses into the fields. And every day there are squabbles like that. If you only knew how it upsets me! It's making me ill: you see, I'm trembling . . . I can't put up with his crudeness. (*Beseeching.*) Yevgeny, dearest, light of my life, take me with you . . . Time's running out for us; we aren't

---

4. "I was rehearsing Trigorin in *The Seagull*. And Anton Pavlovich invited me himself to talk over the role. I arrived with trepidation.

   "You know,' Anton Pavlovich began, 'the fishing poles ought to be, you know, home-made, bent. He makes them himself with a penknife . . . The cigar is good . . . Maybe it's not even a good one, but it definitely has to have silver paper . . .

   Then he fell silent, thought a bit and said:

   " 'But the main thing is the fishing poles . . . ' " (Vasily Kachalov, *Shipovnik Almanac* 23 [1914].) Chekhov shared Trigorin's love of fishing and wrote in a letter, "To catch a perch! It's finer and sweeter than love!"

young any more; now at least when our lives are over, let's stop hiding, stop lying . . . (*Pause.*)

DORN I'm fifty-five years old; it's too late for me to change my way of life.

POLINA ANDREEVNA I know, you're rejecting me because there are other women you're intimate with too. You can't possibly take all of them in. I understand. Forgive me, I'm getting on your nerves.

(NINA *appears near the house; she is plucking flowers.*)

DORN No, not at all.

POLINA ANDREEVNA I'm sick with jealousy. Of course, you're a doctor, there's no way you can avoid women. I understand . . .

DORN (*To* NINA, *who walks by.*) How are things indoors?

NINA Irina Nikolaevna's crying and Pyotr Nikolaevich is having an asthma attack.

DORN (*Rises.*) I'll go give them both some aspirin . . .

NINA (*Offers him the flowers.*) Please take these!

DORN *Merci bien.* (*Starts towards the house.*)

POLINA ANDREEVNA (*Going with him*). What adorable little flowers! (*Near the house, in a muffled voice.*) Give me those flowers! Give me those flowers! (*Once she gets the flowers, she tears them up and throws them aside.*)

(*They both go into the house.*)

NINA (*Alone.*) How odd to see a famous actress crying, and over such a trivial matter! And isn't it odd, a best-selling author, a favorite with the reading public, written up in all the papers, his portrait on sale, translated into foreign languages; yet he spends the whole day fishing, and he's overjoyed when he catches a couple of perch. I thought that famous people were proud, inaccessible; that they despised the public and their own fame; their celebrity was a kind of revenge for blue blood and wealth being considered more respectable . . . But here they are crying, fishing, playing cards, laughing, and losing their tempers, like anybody else . . .

TREPLYOV (*Enters bareheaded, carrying a rifle and a slain gull.*) You're alone here?

NINA Alone. (TREPLYOV *lays the gull at her feet.*) What does this mean?

TREPLYOV I did something nasty. I killed this gull today. I lay it at your feet.

NINA What's wrong with you? (*Picks up the gull and stares at it.*)

TREPLYOV (*After a pause.*) I'll soon kill myself the very same way.

NINA I don't know who you are any more.

TREPLYOV Yes, ever since I stopped knowing who you are. You've changed toward me; your eyes are cold; my being here makes you tense.

NINA Lately you've been so touchy, and you talk in code, symbols of some kind. And this gull is obviously a symbol too, but, forgive me, I don't understand it . . . (*Lays the gull on the bench.*) I'm too ordinary to understand you.

TREPLYOV It started that night when my play was a stupid fiasco. Women don't forgive failure. I burned everything, everything to the last scrap of paper. If only you knew how unhappy I am! Your coolness to me is horrible, incredible; it's like waking up and seeing that the lake has suddenly dried up or sunk into the ground. You say you're too ordinary to understand me. Oh, what's there to understand? You didn't like my play, you despise my ideas, you've started thinking of me as a mediocrity, a nobody, like all the rest . . . (*Stamping his foot.*) That's something *I* understand; oh, I understand all right! There's a kind of spike stuck in my brain, damn it and damn my vanity, which sucks my blood, sucks it like a snake . . . (*Catching sight of* TRIGORIN, *who is walking and reading a notebook.*) There goes the real genius; he paces the ground like Hamlet, and with a book too. (*Mimicking.*) "Words, words, words . . ."[5] His sun hasn't even shone on you yet, but already you're smiling, your eyes are thawing in his rays. I won't stand in your way. (*He exits quickly.*)

TRIGORIN (*Making notes in the book.*) Takes snuff and drinks vodka . . . Always wears black. Courted by a schoolteacher . . .

NINA Good afternoon, Boris Alekseevich!

TRIGORIN Good afternoon. Circumstances have taken an unexpected turn, so it turns out we leave today. In all likelihood we'll never see one another again. And that's a pity. I don't often get the chance to meet young girls, young and interesting ones; I've long forgotten, I can't quite imagine what it must feel like to be eighteen, nineteen, and that's why in my novellas and stories the young girls are usually stilted. I really would like to be in your shoes, if just for an hour, to find out how your mind works, and more or less what sort of stuff you're made of.

NINA And I should like to be in your shoes.

TRIGORIN What for?

NINA To find out how it feels to be a famous, talented writer. How does fame feel? How do you realize that you're famous?

TRIGORIN How? Nohow, I suppose. I never thought about it. (*Thinking it over.*) It's either-or: either you're exaggerating my fame or there's no real way to realize it.

NINA But what about seeing your name in the papers?

5. *Polonius.* What do you read, my lord?
   Hamlet. Words, words, words. (*Hamlet*, II. ii.) Treplyov's mention of the sun may reflect his unconscious recollection of Hamlet's earlier lines about Ophelia, that she not stand too much i'the sun.

TRIGORIN If it's praise, I feel good; and if it's a scolding, then I'm in a bad mood for a couple of days.

NINA The world's amazing! How I envy you, if you only knew! People's fates are so different. Some people can barely crawl through their boring, obscure existence, the same as everyone else, all unhappy; still others, like you, for instance—you're one in a million—are granted a life that's interesting, brilliant, meaningful . . . You're happy . . .

TRIGORIN Am I? (*Shrugging.*) Hmm . . . You stand here talking about fame, happiness, a brilliant, interesting life,[6] but to me it sounds sweet and gooey, sorry, just like marshmallows, which I never eat. You're very young and very kind.

NINA Your life is so beautiful!

TRIGORIN What's so especially good about it? (*Looks at his watch.*) I ought to get some writing in now. Forgive me, I've got no time . . . (*Laughs.*) You've stepped on my pet corn, as the saying goes,[7] and now I'm starting to get upset and a little bit angry. All right, let me make a statement. Let's talk about my beautiful, brilliant life . . . Well now, where shall we begin? (*After thinking a bit.*) Some people are obsessive-compulsives, a person who thinks all the time, for instance, about the moon; well, I have my own particular moon. All the time, I'm obsessed with one compulsive thought: I have to write, I have to write, I have to . . . I've barely finished one story, when already for some reason I have to write another, then a third, after the third a fourth . . . I write nonstop, like an express train, and I can't help it. What's so beautiful and brilliant about that, I ask you? Oh, what an uncivilized way of life! I'm here talking to you, I'm getting excited, but meanwhile I never forget there's a story of mine waiting to be finished. I see that cloud over there, that looks like a grand piano. I think: have to refer to that somewhere in a story, a cloud drifted by that looked like a grand piano. I catch a whiff of heliotrope,[8] I instantly reel it in on my moustache: cloying smell, widow's color, refer to it in describing a summer evening. I'm angling in myself and you for every phrase, every word, and I rush to lock up all these words and phrases in my literary icebox: sometime or other, they'll come in handy! When I finish work, I run to the theater or go fishing; should be able to relax there, forget myself; oh no, a heavy cannonball has started rolling around in my head—a new subject, and

6. *Cf.* Chekhov's letter to M. V. Kiselyova, September 21, 1886: "It's no great treat to be a great writer. First, the life is gloomy . . . Work from morn to night, and not much profit . . . The money would make a cat weep . . ."
7. An English comic phrase from the works of the humorist Jerome K. Jerome, who was very popular in Russia.
8. *Heliotropium peruvianum*, a small blue or dark-blue flower, with a faint aroma of vanilla.

I'm drawn back to my desk, hurry, hurry, write, write. And so it goes forever and ever and ever, and I know no peace, and I feel that I'm devouring my own life, that to give away honey to somebody out there in space I'm robbing my finest flowers of their pollen, tearing up those flowers and trampling on their roots. Wouldn't you say I'm crazy? Surely my friends and relatives don't behave as if I were sane. "What are you puttering with now?[9] What will you give us next?" The same old same old, and I start thinking that this friendly attention, praise, admiration—it's all a plot, they're humoring me like an invalid, and sometimes I'm afraid that they're just on the verge of creeping up behind me, grabbing me and clapping me into a straitjacket, like the madman in Gogol's story.[1] And years ago, the years of my youth, my best years, when I was starting out, my writing was sheer agony. A second-rate writer, especially when luck isn't with him, sees himself as clumsy, awkward, irrelevant; his nerves are shot, frayed; he can't help hanging around people connected with literature and art, unrecognized, unnoticed by anyone, afraid to look them boldly in the face, like a compulsive gambler who's run out of money. I couldn't visualize my reader, but for that very reason he loomed in my imagination as hostile, suspicious. I was afraid of the public, it terrified me, and every time a new play of mine managed to get produced,[2] I thought the dark-haired spectators disliked it, while the fair-haired spectators couldn't care less. Oh, it's awful! Excruciating![3]

NINA I'm sorry, but surely inspiration and the creative process itself must provide sublime moments of happiness?

TRIGORIN Yes. When I'm writing, it's nice enough. And correcting the proofs is nice too, but . . . it's barely come off the presses, when I can't stand it, and can see that it's not right, a mistake, that it shouldn't have been written just that way, and I'm annoyed, feel rotten inside . . . (*Laughing*.) Then the public reads it: "Yes, charming, talented . . . Charming, but a far cry from Tolstoy," or "Lovely piece of work, but not up to Turgenev's *Fathers and Sons*."[4] And so until my dying day, all I'll hear is charming and talented, charming and talented—and when I die, my friends will file past

9. Rather than the verb *pisat*, to write, Chekhov uses *popisyvat*, which, as George Calderon puts it, "suggests that his writing is a sort of game, something that serves to keep him out of mischief. The critic Mikhailovsky used it, in the early days, of Chekhov's compositions."

1. Poprishchin, the hero of Gogol's "Diary of a Madman," a minor bureaucrat whose frantic scribbling reveals his delusions of adequacy. He falls in love with the daughter of his bureau chief and ends up in a madhouse.

2. See Chekhov's letter to A. S. Suvorin, Jan. 7, 1889 (page 403), which he wrote after the opening of the revised *Ivanov*.

3. Tolstoy considered this speech the only good thing in the play.

4. The most famous novel (1862) of Ivan Sergeevich Turgenev (1818–1883), concerning a generational conflict, and offering a pattern of the "New Man." Chekhov gave the conflict between the generations a new twist in *The Seagull*.

my grave and say, "Here lies Trigorin. He wasn't so bad as a writer, but no Turgenev."

NINA Forgive me, I refuse to accept that. You're simply spoiled by success.

TRIGORIN What do you call success? I'm never satisfied with myself, I don't like myself as a writer. Worst of all is when I'm in some sort of trance and often I don't even understand what I'm writing . . . I love the water over there, the trees, sky, I have a feeling for nature; it inspires me with a passion, the irresistible urge to write. But I'm really more than just a landscape painter;[5] I do have a social conscience as well, I love my country, the people. I feel that if I'm a writer, I have an obligation to discuss the people, their suffering, their future, discuss science, human rights et cetera, et cetera; and I do discuss all of it, trip over myself; I'm attacked from every side, I make people angry, I hurtle back and forth like a fox hunted down by hounds. I see that life and science keep moving farther and farther ahead, while I keep falling farther and farther behind, like a peasant who's missed his train and, when all's said and done, I feel that all I know how to write about is landscapes, and everything else I write is phony, phony to the nth degree!

NINA You've been working too hard, and you've got no time or desire to admit your own importance. Even if you're dissatisfied with yourself, other people think you're great and beautiful! If I were a writer, like you, I would devote my whole life to the public, but I'd realize that their only happiness lay in being brought up to my level, and they would be yoked to my chariot.

TRIGORIN Well, well, a chariot. . . . Am I Agamemnon or something?[6]

(*Both smile.*)

NINA For the joy of being a writer or an actress, I would put up with my family disowning me, poverty, disappointment; I would live in a garret and eat nothing but black bread, suffer dissatisfaction with myself and realize my own imperfection, but in return I would insist on fame . . . real, resounding fame . . . (*Hides her face in her hands.*) My head's spinning. . . . Oof!

ARKADINA'S VOICE (*From the house.*) Boris Alekseevich!

TRIGORIN They're calling me . . . I suppose it's about packing. But I don't feel like leaving. (*Looks around at the lake.*) Just look at this, God's country! . . . It's lovely!

NINA You see the house and garden across the lake?

---

5. Chekhov was the friend and admirer of the landscape painter Isaak Levitan, who tried to commit suicide in October 1895.
6. Agamemnon, leader of the Greek host in the Trojan war, was more familiar to Chekhov from Offenbach's comic opera *La Belle Hélène* (1864) than from Homer's *Iliad.*

TRIGORIN   Yes.

NINA   That's my late mother's country house. I was born there. I've spent my whole life on the shores of this lake and I know every islet in it.

TRIGORIN   Must be nice over at your place! (*Having spotted the gull.*) But what's this?

NINA   A gull. Konstantin Gavrilych killed it.

TRIGORIN   Lovely bird. Honestly, I don't feel like leaving. Look here, go and talk Irina Nikolaevna into staying. (*Jots a note in his notebook.*)[7]

NINA   What's that you're writing?

TRIGORIN   Just jotting down a note . . . A subject came to mind . . . (*Putting away the notebook.*) Subject for a short story: on the shores of a lake a young girl grows up, just like you; loves the lake, like a gull, is happy and free, like a gull. But by chance a man comes along, sees her and, having nothing better to do, destroys her, just like this gull here.

    (*Pause.* ARKADINA *appears in a window.*)

ARKADINA   Boris Alekseevich, where are you?

TRIGORIN   Coming! (*Goes and takes a glance round at* NINA; *at the window, to* ARKADINA.) What?

ARKADINA   We're staying.

    (TRIGORIN *exits into the house.*)

NINA (*Crosses down to the footlights; after a moment's thought.*)   It's a dream!

CURTAIN

Act Three

The dining room in SORIN's *house. Doors right and left. Sideboard. Cupboard with first-aid kit and medicine. Table center. Trunks and cardboard boxes; signs of preparation for a departure.* TRIGORIN *is eating lunch;* MASHA *stands by the table.*

MASHA   I'm telling you all this because you're a writer. You can put it to use. I swear to you: if he'd wounded himself seriously, I wouldn't have gone on living another minute. Not that I'm not brave. I've gone and made up my mind. I'll rip this love out of my heart; I'll rip it up by the roots.

TRIGORIN   How so?

MASHA   I'm getting married. To Medvedenko.

---

7. Chekhov was against the indiscriminate use of notes in creative writing. "There's no reason to write down similes, tidy character sketches or details of landscapes: they should appear of their own accord, whenever needed. But a bare fact, an unusual name, a technical term ought to be put down in a notebook; otherwise it will go astray and get lost."

TRIGORIN   That's that schoolteacher?

MASHA   Yes.

TRIGORIN   I don't see the necessity.

MASHA   Loving hopelessly, waiting and waiting for years on end for something . . . But once I'm married, there'll be no room for love; new problems will blot out the old ones. And anyhow, you know, it makes a change. Shall we have another?

TRIGORIN   Aren't you overdoing it?

MASHA   Oh, go ahead! (*Pours out a shot for each.*) Don't look at me like that. Women drink more often than you think. A few drink openly, like me, but most of them do it on the sly. Yes. And it's always vodka or brandy. (*Clinks glasses.*) Here's to you! You're a nice man. I'm sorry you're going away.
(*They drink.*[8])

TRIGORIN   If it were up to me, I wouldn't be leaving.

MASHA   Then ask her to stay.

TRIGORIN   No, she won't stay now. Her son's been acting very tactlessly. First he tries to shoot himself,[9] and now I hear he intends to challenge me to a duel. And what for? He feuds and fusses, preaches about new forms . . . But there's room enough for everyone, isn't there? New and old—what's the point in shoving?

MASHA   Well, it's jealousy too. Though, that's no business of mine. (*Pause.* YAKOV *crosses left to right with a suitcase.* NINA *enters and stops by a window.*) My schoolteacher isn't very bright, but he's a decent sort, poor, too, and he's awfully in love with me. I feel sorry for him. And I feel sorry for his poor old mother. Well, sir, please accept my best wishes. Think kindly of us. (*Shakes him firmly by the hand.*) Thanks a lot for your consideration. Do send me your book, and be sure there's an inscription. Only don't make it out "To dear madam," but simply "To Mariya, who can't identify her family[1] and lives in this world for no apparent reason." Good-bye. (*Exits.*)

NINA (*Holding out her clenched fist to* TRIGORIN.)   Odds or evens?

TRIGORIN   Evens.

NINA (*Sighing.*)   No. I've only got one bean in my hand. I was guessing whether to become an actress or not. If only someone would give me some advice.

TRIGORIN   You can't give advice about things like that.

8. " 'Look, you know,' Chekhov began, seeing how persistent I was, 'when he, Trigorin, drinks vodka with Masha, I would definitely do it like this, definitely.'
"And with that he got up, adjusted his waistcoat and awkwardly wheezed a couple of times.
" 'There you are, you know, I would definitely do it like that. When you've been sitting a long time, you always want to do that sort of thing' . . ." (Vasily Kachalov, *Shipovnik Almanac* 23 [1914].)
9. The verb form in Russian makes it clear that he failed.
1. A common formula in police reports.

(*Pause.*)

NINA   We're parting and . . . most likely we'll never see one another again. Please take a keepsake of me, here, this little medallion. I had them engrave your initials . . . and on this other side the title of your book: "Days and Nights."

TRIGORIN   How thoughtful! (*Kisses the medallion.*) A charming gift!

NINA   Remember me from time to time.

TRIGORIN   I will. I will remember you as you were on that sunny day—do *you* remember?—a week ago, when you were wearing a brightly-colored dress . . . We were having a long talk . . . and something else, there was a white gull lying on the bench.

NINA   (*Pensively.*)   Yes, a gull . . . (*Pause*) We can't go on talking, someone's coming . . . Before you go, save two minutes for me, please . . . (*Exits left.*)

(*At that very moment,* ARKADINA *enters right, as does* SORIN *in a tailcoat with a star pinned to his chest,*[2] *then* YAKOV, *preoccupied with packing.*)

ARKADINA   You should stay home, you old man. With that rheumatism of yours what are you doing riding around paying calls? (*To* TRIGORIN) Who went out just now? Nina?

TRIGORIN   Yes.

ARKADINA   *Excusez-moi,* we interrupted something . . . (*Sits down.*) I think everything's packed. I'm tired to death.

TRIGORIN   (*Reads the inscription on the medallion.*)   "Days and Nights," page 121, lines eleven and twelve.

YAKOV   (*Clearing the table.*)   Do you want me to pack the fishing poles too?

TRIGORIN   Yes, I can use them again. But the books you can give away.

YAKOV   Yes, sir.

TRIGORIN   (*To himself.*)   Page 121, lines eleven and twelve. What is there in those lines? (*To* ARKADINA.) Are there copies of my books anywhere in the house?

ARKADINA   In my brother's study, the corner bookcase.

TRIGORIN   Page 121 . . . (*Exits.*)

ARKADINA   Honestly, Petrusha, you ought to stay at home . . .

SORIN   You're leaving; with you gone it'll be boring at home . . .

ARKADINA   And what's there to do in town?

SORIN   Nothing special, but even so. (*He laughs.*) They'll be laying the cornerstone for the town hall[3] and all the rest . . . Just for a couple of hours I'd like to stop feeling like a stick-in-the-mud; I've been getting stale, like an old cigarette holder. I told them to send 'round my horses at one; we'll both go at the same time.

2. The decoration is an appurtenance of his status as an Actual State Councilor.
3. In the original, the new *zemstvo* building. See *Ivanov*, note 3, page 24.

ARKADINA (*After a pause.*) Oh, do stay here, don't be bored, don't catch cold. Look after my son. Keep an eye on him. Give him good advice.

(*Pause.*)

Now I've got to go and I still don't know how come Konstantin took a shot at himself. I suppose the main reason was jealousy, so the sooner I take Trigorin away from here, the better.

SORIN How can I put this? There were other reasons too. Take my word for it: a man who's young, intelligent, living in the country, in the sticks, with no money, no position, no future. Nothing to keep him occupied. Gets ashamed of himself and alarmed by his own idleness. I love him dearly and he's very fond of me, but all the same, when all's said and done, he thinks he's unwanted at home, that he's a panhandler here, a charity case. Take my word for it, vanity . . .

ARKADINA He's the cross I bear! (*Musing.*) He could get a desk job in the civil service, or something . . .

SORIN (*Whistles a tune, then tentatively.*) I think it would be best if you . . . gave him some money. First of all, he ought to be dressed like a human being and all the rest. Just look, he's been wearing the same beat-up old frockcoat for the last three years; he has to go out without a topcoat . . . (*Laughs.*) Besides, it wouldn't hurt the boy to live it up a bit . . . Go abroad or something . . . It's not all that expensive.

ARKADINA Even so . . . Possibly, I could manage the suit, but as for going abroad . . . No, at the moment I can't manage the suit either. (*Decisively.*) I have no money! (SORIN *laughs.*) None!

SORIN (*Whistles a tune.*) Yes, ma'am. Sorry, my dear, don't get angry. I believe you . . . You're a generous, selfless woman.

ARKADINA (*Plaintively.*) I have no money!

SORIN If I had any money, take my word for it, I'd let him have it, but I haven't any, not a red cent. (*Laughs.*) The overseer snatches my whole pension from me, and wastes it on farming, livestock, beekeeping, and my money simply melts away. The bees die off, the cows die off, I can never have any horses . . .

ARKADINA Yes, I do have some money, but I'm an actress, aren't I? My costumes alone are enough to ruin me.

SORIN You're kind, affectionate . . . I respect you . . . Yes . . . But something's come over me again . . . (*Staggers.*) My head's spinning. (*Holds on to the table.*) I feel faint and all the rest.

ARKADINA (*Alarmed.*) Petrusha! (*Trying to hold him up.*) Petrusha, dear . . . (*Shouts.*) Help me! Help! (*Enter* TREPLYOV, *a bandage around his head, and* MEDVEDENKO.) He's fainting!

SORIN Never mind, never mind . . . (*Smiles and drinks some water.*) It's all over . . . and all the rest.

TREPLYOV (*To his mother.*)   Don't be alarmed, Mama, it isn't serious. Uncle often gets like this these days. (*To his uncle.*) You ought to lie down for a while, Uncle.

SORIN   For a little while, yes . . . But all the same I'm driving to town . . . I'll go lie down and drive to town . . . Take it from me . . . (*He exits, leaning on his stick.*)

MEDVEDENKO (*Escorting him, holding his arm.*)   Here's a riddle: what goes on four legs in the morning, two at midday, three in the evening . . . [4]

SORIN (*Laughs.*)   I know. And flat on its back at night. Thank you, I can walk on my own.

MEDVEDENKO   Now, now, don't show off . . .

(*He and* SORIN *go out.*)

ARKADINA   He gave me such a fright!

TREPLYOV   Living in the country is bad for his health. He gets depressed. Now, Mama, if only you had a sudden fit of generosity and lent him a couple of thousand or so, he might be able to live in town all year long.

ARKADINA   I have no money. I'm an actress, not a banker.

(*Pause.*)

TREPLYOV   Mama, change my bandage. You do it so well.

ARKADINA (*Gets iodoform and a drawerful of dressings from the first-aid cupboard.*)   The doctor's late.

TREPLYOV   He promised to be here by ten and it's already noon.

ARKADINA   Sit down. (*Removes the bandage from his head.*) Looks like a turban. Yesterday some tramp asked in the kitchen what your nationality was. It's almost completely healed. What's left is nothing. (*Kisses him on the head.*) And when I'm away, you won't do any more *click-click*?

TREPLYOV   No, Mama. It was a moment of insane desperation, when I lost control. It won't happen again. (*Kisses her hands.*) You've got wonderful hands. I remember long, long ago, when you were still working at the National Theater[5]—I was a little boy then—there was a fight in our yard, a washerwoman who lived there got badly beaten up. Remember? She was picked up unconscious . . . You would go and see her, take her medicine, bathe her children in the washtub. Don't you remember?

ARKADINA   No. (*Putting on a fresh bandage.*)

TREPLYOV   At the time there were two ballerinas living in our building . . . They'd come and drink coffee with you . . .

ARKADINA   That I remember.

TREPLYOV   They were so religious. (*Pause.*) Just lately, these last few days, I love you every bit as tenderly and freely as when I was a

4. The classical Greek riddle the Sphinx offers to Oedipus. The answer is *man.*
5. The official Imperial theaters in St. Petersburg and Moscow.

child. Except for you, I've got no one left now. Only why, why do you give in to that man's influence?[6]

ARKADINA You don't understand him, Konstantin. He's a person of the highest refinement.

TREPLYOV But when they told him I was going to challenge him to a duel, his refinement didn't keep him from acting like a coward. He's going away. Retreating in disgrace!

ARKADINA Don't be silly! *I'm* taking him away from here. Of course, I don't expect you to approve of our intimacy, but you're intelligent and sophisticated; I have the right to demand that you respect my independence.[7]

TREPLYOV I do respect your independence, but you've got to let me be independent and treat that man any way I want.[8] The highest refinement! You and I are at one another's throats because of him, while he's somewhere in the drawing room or the garden, laughing at us . . . cultivating Nina, trying to persuade her once and for all that he's a genius.

ARKADINA You enjoy hurting my feelings. I respect that man and must ask you not to say nasty things about him to my face.

TREPLYOV But I don't respect him. You want me to treat him like a genius too. Well pardon me, I cannot tell a lie, his writing makes me sick.

ARKADINA That's jealousy. People with no talent but plenty of pretentions have nothing better to do than criticize really talented people. It's a comfort to them, I'm sure!

TREPLYOV (*Sarcastically.*) Really talented people! (*Angrily.*) I'm more talented than the lot of you put together, if it comes to that! (*Tears the bandage off his head.*) You dreary hacks hog the front-row seats in the arts and assume that the only legitimate and genuine things are what you do yourselves, so you suppress and stifle the rest! I don't believe in any of you! I don't believe in you or him!

ARKADINA Mr. Avant-garde!

TREPLYOV Go back to your darling theatre and act in your pathetic, third-rate plays.

ARKADINA I have never acted in that kind of play. Leave me out of it! You haven't got what it takes to write a miserable vaudeville sketch. You bourgeois from Kiev! You panhandler!

TREPLYOV You skinflint!

ARKADINA You scarecrow! (TREPLYOV *sits down and weeps quietly.*) You nobody! (*Walking up and down in agitation.*) Don't cry. You mustn't cry . . . (*She weeps.*) Don't do it . . . (*She kisses his fore-*

6. This phrase was excised by the censor, and replaced by Chekhov with "Why does that man have to come between us?"
7. These two lines were excised by the censor and replaced with "He'll go right now. I will ask him to leave here myself."
8. This line was excised by the censor.

head, cheeks, head.) My darling boy, forgive me . . . Forgive your wicked mother. Forgive unhappy me.

TREPLYOV (*Embraces her.*)   If only you knew! I've lost everything. She doesn't love me, I can't write any more . . . I've lost all hope . . .

ARKADINA   Don't lose heart. Everything will turn out all right. He'll be leaving soon, she'll love you again. (*Wipes away his tears.*) There now. We're friends again.

TREPLYOV (*Kisses her hands.*)   Yes, Mama.

ARKADINA (*Tenderly.*)   Make friends with him too. There's no need for duels . . . Is there?

TREPLYOV   All right . . . Only, Mama, don't make me see him again. It's too hard for me . . . I can't deal with it . . . (TRIGORIN *enters.*) There he is . . . I'm going . . . (*He rapidly throws the first-aid into the cupboard.*) The doctor will do my bandage later on . . .

TRIGORIN (*Leafing through a book.*)   Page 121 . . . lines eleven and twelve . . . Aha! . . . (*Reads.*) "If ever my life is of use to you, come and take it."[9]

     (TREPLYOV *picks the bandage up off the floor and exits.*)

ARKADINA (*After a glance at her watch.*)   The horses will be here soon.

TRIGORIN (*To himself.*)   If ever my life is of use to you, come and take it.

ARKADINA   You've got all your things packed, I hope?

TRIGORIN (*Impatiently.*)   Yes, yes . . . (*Musing.*) How come this appeal from a pure spirit has sounded a note of sorrow and my heart aches so poignantly? . . . If ever my life is of use to you, come and take it. (*To* ARKADINA.) Let's stay just one more day! (ARKADINA *shakes her head no.*) Let's stay!

ARKADINA   Darling, I know what's keeping you here. But do show some self-control. You're a little tipsy, sober up.

TRIGORIN   Then you be sober too, be understanding, reasonable, please, come to terms with this like a true friend . . . (*Squeezes her hand.*) You're capable of sacrifice . . . Be my friend, let me go.

ARKADINA (*Extremely upset.*)   You're that far gone?

TRIGORIN   I'm attracted to her! Maybe this is just what I need.

9. "While Chekhov was writing this play, the editors of *Russian Thought* sent him a bracelet charm in the shape of a book, on one side of which was engraved the title of his short-story collection and on the other the numbers: P. 247, 1. 6 AND 7. The gift was anonymous. In his collection Anton Pavlovich read: 'You are the most generous, the noblest of men. I am eternally grateful to you. If you ever need my life come and take it.' It is from the story "Neighbors" (1892), in which Grigory Vlasich says these words to his wife's brother. Anton Pavlovich vaguely surmised who had sent him this charm, and thought up an original way to send thanks and a reply: he had Nina give the same medallion to Trigorin and only changed the name of the book and the numbers. The answer arrived as intended at the first performance of *The Seagull*. The actors, of course, never suspected that, as they performed the play, they were simultaneously acting as letter-carriers." (V. I. Nemirovich-Danchenko, *Out of the Past* [1938])

ARKADINA The love of some country girl? Oh, how little you know yourself!

TRIGORIN Sometimes people walk in their sleep; look, I'm here talking to you, but it's as if I'm asleep and seeing her in my dreams . . . I've succumbed to sweet, wonderful visions . . . Let me go.

ARKADINA (*Trembling.*) No, no . . . I'm an ordinary woman, you mustn't talk to me that way . . . Don't tease me, Boris . . . It frightens me.

TRIGORIN If you try, you can be extraordinary. A love that's young, charming, poetical, wafting me to a dream world—it's the one and only thing on this earth that can bring happiness. I've never yet experienced a love like that . . . When I was young I had no time, I was tossing manuscripts over publishers' transoms, fighting off poverty . . . Now it's here, this love, it's come at last, luring me . . . What's the point of running away from it?

ARKADINA (*Angrily.*) You're out of your mind!

TRIGORIN So what?

ARKADINA You've all ganged up today to torture me! (*Weeps.*)

TRIGORIN (*Puts his head in his hands.*) She doesn't understand! She refuses to understand!

ARKADINA Am I now so old and ugly that men don't think twice telling me about other women? (*Embraces and kisses him.*) Oh, you've gone crazy! My gorgeous, fabulous man . . . You're the last chapter in my life story! (*Kneels down.*) My joy, my pride, my blessedness . . . (*Embraces his knees.*) If you desert me for even a single hour, I won't survive. I'll go out of my mind, my incredible, magnificent man, my lord and master . . .

TRIGORIN Somebody might come in. (*He helps her to rise.*)

ARKADINA Let them. I'm not ashamed of my love for you. (*Kisses his hand.*) My precious, headstrong man, you want to do something reckless, but I won't have it, I won't let you . . . (*Laughs.*) You're mine . . . you're mine . . . And this forehead is mine, and these eyes are mine, and this beautiful silky hair is mine too . . . You're all mine. You're so talented, clever, our greatest living writer, you're Russia's only hope . . . You've got so much sincerity, clarity, originality, wholesome humor . . . With a single stroke you can pinpoint the most vital feature in a person or a landscape, your characters are so alive. Oh, no one can read you without going into ecstasy! You think this is soft soap?[1] Am I lying? Well, look into my eyes . . . look . . . Do I look like a liar? There, you see, I'm the only one who knows how to appreciate you; I'm the only one who tells you the truth, my darling, marvelous man . . . You will come? Won't you? You won't desert me?

---

1. *Finiam*: literally, incense; figuratively, gross flattery.

TRIGORIN   I've got no will of my own . . . I never had a will of my own . . . Wishy-washy, spineless, always giving in—how can a woman find that attractive? Take me, carry me off, but don't ever let me out of your sight . . .

ARKADINA (*To herself.*)   Now he is mine. (*Casually, as if nothing had happened.*) Of course, if you want to, you can stay. I'll go by myself, and you can come later, in a week's time. After all, what's your rush?

TRIGORIN   No, let's go together.

ARKADINA   If you say so. Together, whatever you like, together . . . (*Pause.* TRIGORIN *jots something in his notebook.*) What are you up to?

TRIGORIN   This morning I heard a good phrase: "the virgin grove" . . . It'll come in handy. (*Stretching.*) Which means, we're on our way? More train compartments, stations, lunch counters, fried food, smalltalk . . .

SHAMRAEV (*Enters.*)   I have the melancholy honor of announcing that the horses are here. The time has come, dear lady, to go to the station; the train pulls in at two-o-five. By the way, Irina Niko-laevna, do me a favor, you won't forget to find out what's become of the actor Suzdaltsev these days? Is he alive? Is he well? Many's the drink we downed together once upon a time . . . In "The Great Mail Robbery" his acting was inimitable . . . I recall he was acting at the time in Elizavetgrad with the tragedian Izmailov, another remarkable character[2] . . . Don't rush yourself, dear lady, we can spare another five minutes. Once in some melodrama they were playing conspirators, and when they were suddenly caught, the line was supposed to go: "We've fallen into a trap," but Izmailov said, "We've trawlen into a flap" . . . (*Roars with laughter.*) Into a flap!

(*While he is speaking,* YAKOV *fusses around the luggage; a* HOUSEMAID *brings* ARKADINA *her hat, coat, parasol, gloves; everyone helps* ARKADINA *to dress.* THE COOK *peers in through the door left, and after waiting a bit he enters hesitantly.* POLINA ANDREEVNA *enters, then* SORIN *and* MEDVEDENKO.)

POLINA ANDREEVNA (*With a tiny basket.*)   Here are some plums for your trip . . . Nice and ripe. You might want something for your sweet tooth.

ARKADINA   That's very kind of you, Polina Andreevna.

POLINA ANDREEVNA   Good-bye, my dear! If anything wasn't right, do forgive me. (*Weeps.*)

2. Actors invented by Chekhov. *The Great Mail Robbery* is F. A. Burdin's adaptation of the French melodrama *Le courrier de Lyon* (1850) by Eugène Moreau, Paul Siraudin, and Alfred Delacour, well known to Victorian English audiences as *The Lyons Mail.* As an adolescent in Taganrog, Chekhov had seen and loved this play.

ARKADINA (*Embraces her.*) Everything was fine, just fine. Only you mustn't cry.

POLINA ANDREEVNA Time's running out for us!

ARKADINA What can we do?

SORIN (*In an overcoat with a cape, wearing a hat and carrying a walking stick, enters from the door left; crosses the room.*) Sister, it's time. You better not be late, when all's said and done. I'm going to get in. (*Exits.*)

MEDVEDENKO And I'll go to the station on foot . . . to see you off. I'm a fast walker . . . (*He exits.*)

ARKADINA 'Til we meet again, my dears . . . If we're alive and well, we'll see you again next summer . . . (THE HOUSEMAID, YAKOV, *and* THE COOK *kiss her hand.*) Don't forget me. (*Hands* THE COOK *a ruble.*) Here's a ruble for the three of you.

COOK Thank you kindly, ma'am. Have a pleasant trip! Mighty pleased to serve you!

YAKOV God bless and keep you!

SHAMRAEV Brighten our days with a little letter! Good-bye, Boris Alekseevich.

ARKADINA Where's Konstantin? Tell him that I'm going. I've got to say good-bye. Well, think kindly of me. (*To* YAKOV.) I gave a ruble to the cook. It's for the three of you.

> (*Everyone goes out right. The stage is empty. Offstage there is the sort of noise that accompanies people seeing each other off.* THE HOUSEMAID *returns to get the basket of plums from the table, and exits again.*)

TRIGORIN (*Returning.*) I forgot my stick. I think it's out on the veranda. (*Moves left and at the door runs into* NINA, *entering.*) Ah, it's you? We're leaving.

NINA I felt we would meet again. (*Excited.*) Boris Alekseevich, I've made up my mind once and for all, the die is cast, I'm going on the stage. Tomorrow I'll be gone, I'm leaving my father, abandoning everything, starting a new life . . . I'm travelling, like you . . . to Moscow. We shall meet there.

TRIGORIN (*Glancing around.*) Stay at the "Slav Bazaar" Hotel . . . Let me know the minute you're there . . . Molchanovka Street,[3] the Grokholsky Apartments . . . I'm in a hurry . . .

> (*Pause.*)

NINA Just one more minute.

TRIGORIN (*In an undertone.*) You're so beautiful . . . Oh, how wonderful to think that we'll be seeing one another soon! (*She lays her*

---

3. The Slavyansky Bazar, an elegant and fashionable hotel in central Moscow, rated one of the top three and much frequented by Chekhov, was where Stanislavsky and Nemirovich-Danchenko held the epic lunch that resulted in the founding of the Moscow Art Theater. Molchanovka is a street near Arbat Square in Moscow, in the center of the city, within easy walking distance from the Slav Bazaar.

head on his chest.) I'll see these marvelous eyes again, that inde-
scribably beautiful, tender smile . . . these delicate features, this
look of angelic purity . . . My dearest . . . (*A prolonged kiss.*)

CURTAIN

Act Four

Between Acts Three and Four, two years have elapsed.

One of the drawing room in SORIN'S *house, turned by* KONSTANTIN
TREPLYOV *into a workroom. Left and right doors, leading to inner
rooms. Directly facing us, a glass door to the veranda. Besides the usual
drawing-room furniture, in the right corner is a writing desk, near the
left door a Turkish divan, a bookcase full of books, books on the win-
dowsills, on chairs.—Evening. A single lamp with a shade is lit. Semi-
darkness. We can hear the trees rustling and the wind wailing in the
chimney. A watchman raps on a board.*[4] MEDVEDENKO *and* MASHA
enter.

MASHA (*Shouts out.*)   Konstantin Gavrilych! Konstantin Gavrilych!
    (*Looking around.*) Nobody here. The old man never stops asking,
    Where's Kostya? Where's Kostya? . . . Can't live without him . . .
MEDVEDENKO   Afraid to be left alone. (*Listening hard.*) What awful
    weather! For two whole days now.
MASHA (*Igniting the flame in a lamp.*)   There are waves on the lake.
    Enormous ones.
MEDVEDENKO   It's dark outside. Somebody should tell them to pull
    down that stage in the garden. It stands there bare, unsightly, like
    a skeleton, and the scene curtain flaps in the wind. When I was
    going by last night, I thought somebody was on it, crying . . .
MASHA   You don't say . . .
    (*Pause.*)
MEDVEDENKO   Let's go home, Masha!
MASHA (*Shakes her head no.*)   I'll stay and spend the night here.
MEDVEDENKO (*Pleading.*)   Masha, let's go! Our baby's starving, I'll
    bet!
MASHA   Don't be silly. Matryona will feed him.
    (*Pause.*)
MEDVEDENKO   It's a shame. The third night now without his mother.
MASHA   You're getting tiresome. In the old days at least you used to
    talk philosophy, but now it's all baby, home—that's all anybody
    hears out of you.
MEDVEDENKO   Let's go, Masha!

4. See *Ivanov*, note 9, page 37.

MASHA   Go yourself.

MEDVEDENKO   Your father won't give me any horses.

MASHA·   He will. Ask him and he'll give you.

MEDVEDENKO   Maybe so, I'll ask. That means you'll be home tomorrow?

MASHA (*Takes snuff.*)   All right, tomorrow. You're a pest . . .

    (*Enter* TREPLYOV *and* POLINA ANDREEVNA; TREPLYOV *is carrying pillows and a blanket, and* POLINA ANDREEVNA *bedclothes; they lay them on the Turkish divan, after which* TREPLYOV *goes to his desk and sits.*)

MASHA   What's this for, Mama?

POLINA ANDREEVINA   Pyotr Nikolaevich asked for his bed to be made up in Kostya's room.

MASHA   Let me . . . (*Makes the bed.*)

POLINA ANDREEVNA (*Sighs.*)   The old man's like a child. . . . (*Walks over to the writing desk and, leaning on her elbows, looks at the manuscript.*)
    (*Pause.*)

MEDVEDENKO   Well, I'm going. Good-bye, Masha. (*Kisses his wife's hand.*) Good-bye, Mama dear. (*Tries to kiss his mother-in-law's hand.*)

POLINA ANDREEVNA (*Annoyed.*)   Well! Go if you're going.

MEDVEDENKO   Good-bye, Konstantin Gavrilych.

    (TREPLYOV *silently offers his hand;* MEDVEDENKO *exits.*)

POLINA ANDREEVNA (*Looking at the manuscript.*)   Nobody had the slightest idea, Kostya, that you would turn into a real writer. And now look, thank God, they've started sending you money from the magazines. (*Runs her hand over his hair.*) And you're handsome now . . . Dear, good Kostya, be a little more affectionate to my Mashenka.

MASHA (*Making the bed.*)   Leave him be. Mama.

POLINA ANDREEVNA (*To* TREPLYOV).   She's a wonderful little thing. (*Pause.*) Women, Kostya, ask nothing more than an occasional look of kindness. I know from experience.

    (TREPLYOV *gets up from behind the desk and exits in silence.*)

MASHA   Now he's gone and gotten angry. You had to pester him!

POLINA ANDREEVNA   I feel sorry for you, Mashenka.

MASHA   That's all I need!

POLINA ANDREEVNA   My heart bleeds for you. I do see everything, understand everything.

MASHA   It's all nonsense. Unrequited love—that's only in novels. Really silly. Just mustn't lose control or go on waiting for something, waiting for your ship to come in . . . If love ever burrows into your heart, you've got to get rid of it. They've just promised to transfer my husband to another school district. Once we've moved there—I'll forget all about it. . . . I'll rip it out of my heart by the roots.

(*Two rooms away, a melancholy waltz is played.*)

POLINA ANDREEVNA　Kostya's playing. That means he's depressed.

MASHA (*Noiselessly makes a few waltz steps.*)　The main thing, Mama, is to have him out of sight. As soon as they transfer my Semyon, then believe you me, I'll forget in a month. This is all so silly.

(*The door left opens.* DORN *and* MEDVEDENKO *wheel in* SORIN, *in his armchair.*)

MEDVEDENKO　I've got six at home now. And flour, almost two kopeks a pound.

DORN　It gets you going in circles.

MEDVEDENKO　It's all right for you to laugh. You've got more money than you could shake a stick at.

DORN　Money? After thirty years of practice, my friend, on constant call night and day, when I couldn't call my soul my own, all I managed to scrape together was two thousand; besides, I blew it all on my recent trip abroad. I haven't a penny.

MASHA (*To her husband.*)　Haven't you gone?

MEDVEDENKO (*Apologetically.*)　How? If they don't give me horses!

MASHA (*Bitterly annoyed, in an undertone.*)　I wish I'd never set eyes on you!

(*The wheelchair is halted in the left half of the room;* POLINA ANDREEVNA, MASHA, *and* DORN *sit down beside it;* MEDVEDENKO, *saddened, moves away to one side.*)

DORN　So many changes around here, I must say! They've turned the drawing room into a study.

MASHA　It's more comfortable for Konstantin Gavrilych to work here. Whenever he likes, he can go out in the garden and think.

(THE WATCHMAN *taps his board.*)

SORIN　Where's my sister?

DORN　Gone to the station to meet Trigorin. She'll be back any minute.

SORIN　If you found it necessary to write for my sister to come here, it means I'm seriously ill. (*After a silence.*) A fine state of affairs; I'm seriously ill, but meanwhile they won't give me any medicine.

DORN　And what would you like? Aspirin? Bicarbonate? Quinine?

SORIN　Uh-oh, here comes the philosophizing. Oh, what an affliction! (*Nodding his head towards the divan.*) That made up for me?

POLINA ANDREEVNA　For you, Pyotr Nikolaevich.

SORIN　Thank you.

DORN (*Sings.*)　"The moons sails through the midnight sky . . ."[5]

SORIN　There's this subject for a story I want to give Kostya. The

---

5. Beginning of a serenade by K. S. Shilovsky, popular at the time; its sheet music had gone through ten printings by 1882.

title should be: "The Man Who Wanted To." "*L'Homme qui a voulu.*"[6] In my youth I wanted to be an author—and wasn't; wanted to speak eloquently—and spoke abominably (*Mimicking himself.*) "And so on and so forth, this, that, and the other . . ." And in summing up used to ramble on and on, even broke out in a sweat; wanted to get married—and didn't; always wanted to live in town—and now am ending my life in the country and all the rest.

DORN   Wanted to become a senior civil servant[7]—and did.

SORIN (*Laughs.*)   That I never tried for. It came all by itself.

DORN   Complaining of life at age sixty-two is, you must agree—not very gracious.

SORIN   What a pigheaded fellow. Don't you realize I'd like to live?

DORN   That's frivolous. By the laws of nature every life must come to an end.

SORIN   You argue like someone who's had it all. You've had it all, and so you don't care about life; it doesn't matter to you. But even you will be afraid to die.

DORN   Fear of death is an animal fear . . . Have to repress it. A conscious fear of death is only for those who believe in life everlasting, which scares them because of their sins. But in the first place, you don't believe in religion, and in the second—what kind of sins have you got? You worked twenty-seven years in the Department of Justice—that's all.

SORIN (*Laughs.*)   Twenty-eight.

          (TREPLYOV *enters and sits on the footstool at* SORIN's *feet.* MASHA *never takes her eyes off him the whole time.*)

DORN   We're keeping Konstantin Gavrilovich from working.

TREPLYOV   No, not at all.

          (*Pause.*)

MEDVEDENKO   Might I ask, Doctor, which town abroad you liked most?

DORN   Genoa.

TREPLYOV   Why Genoa?

DORN   The superb crowds in the streets there. In the evening when you leave your hotel, the whole street is teeming with people. Then you slip into the crowd, aimlessly, zigzagging this way and that; you live along with it, you merge with it psychically, and you start to believe that there may in fact be a universal soul, much like the one that Nina Zarechnaya acted in your play once.[8] By the way,

6. Chekhov may have been familiar with a series of comic monologues by the eccentric French writer Charles Cros, called *L'Homme Qui*, published between 1877 and 1882.
7. Actual State Councilor, fourth class in the Tsarist table of ranks, equivalent to a Major General and a Rear Admiral, entitled to the title "Your Excellency."
8. Dr. Dorn's pleasure in fleeing the constraints of individual personality into multiple per-

where is Miss Zarechnaya these days? Where is she and how is she?

TREPLYOV She's all right, I suppose.

DORN I'm told she seems to be leading a rather peculiar life. What's that all about?

TREPLYOV That, Doctor, is a long story.

DORN Then you shorten it.

(*Pause.*)

TREPLYOV She ran away from home and went off with Trigorin. You know about that?

DORN I do.

TREPLYOV She had a baby. The baby died. Trigorin fell out of love with her and returned to his previous attachment, as might have been expected. In fact, he had never given up the previous one, but, in his spineless way, somehow maintained both of them. So far as I can make out from my information, Nina's private life has not been a roaring success.

DORN And the stage?

TREPLYOV Even worse, it would seem. She made her debut outside Moscow at a summer theater, then toured the provinces. In those days, I was keeping track of her and for a while wherever she was, I was there too. She would tackle the big roles, but her acting was crude, tasteless; her voice singsong, and her gestures wooden. There were moments when she showed some talent at screaming or dying, but they were only moments.

DORN In other words, she does have *some* talent?

TREPLYOV It was hard to tell. I suppose she has. I saw her, but she didn't want to see me, and her maid wouldn't let me into her hotel room. I understood her mood and didn't insist on meeting. (*Pause.*) What else is there to tell you? Later, by the time I'd returned home, I would get letters from her. The letters were clever, affectionate, interesting; she never complained, but I felt that she was deeply unhappy; not a line but revealed frayed, strained nerves. And a somewhat deranged imagination. She would sign herself *The Gull*. In that play of Pushkin's, the miller says that he's a raven;[9] that's how she'd keep repeating in all her letters that she was a gull.[1] She's here now.

---

sonality echoes Baudelaire: "The pleasure of being in crowds is a mysterious expression of the delight in the multiplication of numbers."

9. *Rusalka* (*The Naiad* or *Nixie*), a fragment of a verse drama by Aleksandr Pushkin (1799–1837), written sometime between 1826 and 1832; the story of a poor miller's daughter, seduced and abandoned by a prince. She drowns herself and turns into a water-nymph, while her father goes mad and calls himself "the local raven." The tale was turned into an opera by A. S. Dargomyzhsky.

1. Since there are no definite or indefinite articles in Russian, this could also be translated "she is *the* gull."

DORN   What do you mean, here?

TREPLYOV   In town, at the railway hotel. About five days now she's been staying in a room there. I've been to see her, and Marya Ilyinishna drove over, but she won't receive anyone. Semyon Semyonych claims that yesterday after dinner he saw her in a field, a mile and a half from here.

MEDVEDENKO   Yes, I did see her. Heading for town. I bowed, asked her how come she didn't pay us a visit. She said she would.

TREPLYOV   She won't. (*Pause.*) Her father and stepmother have disowned her. They've set up watchmen all over so that she can't even get near the estate. (*Moves to the desk with the Doctor.*) How easy, Doctor, to be a philosopher on paper and how hard it is in fact!

SORIN   Splendid girl she was.

DORN   What's that again?

SORIN   Splendid girl, I said, she was. District Attorney Sorin was even a little bit in love with her for a while.

DORN   Old Casanova.[2]

    (SHAMRAEV's *laugh is heard.*)

POLINA ANDREEVNA   I think our folks are back from the station. . . .

TREPLYOV   Yes, I hear Mama.

    (*Enter* ARKADINA *and* TRIGORIN, *followed by* SHAMRAEV.)

SHAMRAEV (*Entering.*)   We're all growing old, weather-beaten by the elements, but you, dear lady, are just as young as ever. . . . Colorful jacket, vivacity . . . grace . . .

ARKADINA   You want to put a hex on me again, you tiresome man!

TRIGORIN (*To* SORIN.)   Good evening, Pyotr Nikolaevich! How come you're still under the weather? That's not good! (*Having seen* MASHA, *jovially.*) Marya Ilyinishna!

MASHA   You recognized me? (*Shakes his hand.*)

TRIGORIN   Married?

MASHA   Long ago.

TRIGORIN   Happy? (*Exchanges bows with* DORN *and* MEDVEDENKO, *then hesitantly walks over to* TREPLYOV). Irina Nikolaevna said that you've let bygones be bygones and no longer hold a grudge.

    (TREPLYOV *extends his hand to him.*)

ARKADINA (*To her son.*)   Look, Boris Alekseevich brought the magazine with your new story.

---

2. Literally, "old Lovelace," the voluptuary hero of Samuel Richardson's *Clarissa* (1748), whose sole purpose in life is to seduce the heroine. Its Russian version was hugely popular in the late eighteenth-century, even among those who, like Tatiana's mother in *Evgeny Onegin*, didn't read it. ("She loved Richardson / Not because she preferred Grandison to Lovelace; / But in the old days Princess Alina, / Her Moscow cousin, / Had often rambled on about them to her" (II. xxx). "Lovelace" gradually became a standard term for a philanderer.

TREPLYOV (*accepting the magazine, to* TRIGORIN.) Thank you. Very kind of you.

(*They sit down.*)

TRIGORIN Your fans send you their best wishes. In Petersburg and Moscow, mostly, they're starting to take an interest in you, and they're always asking me about you. Standard questions: what's he like, how old, dark or fair. For some reason they all think you're not young any more. And nobody knows your real name, since you publish under a pseudonym. You're a mystery, like the Man in the Iron Mask.[3]

TREPLYOV You staying long?

TRIGORIN No, tomorrow I think I'll go back to Moscow. Have to. I'm tripping over myself to finish a novella, and after that I've promised to contribute something to an anthology. In short—the same old story.

(*While they're conversing,* ARKADINA *and* POLINA ANDREEVNA *put a card table in the middle of the room and open it up;* SHAMRAEV *lights candles, arranges chairs. They get a lotto set[4] from a cupboard.*)

TRIGORIN The weather's given me a rude welcome. Ferocious wind. Tomorrow morning, if it's calmed down, I'll head out to the lake and do some fishing. By the way, I have to take a look round the garden and the place where—remember?—your play was performed. I've come up with a theme; just have to refresh my memory on the setting of the action.

MASHA (*To her father.*) Papa, let my husband borrow a horse! He has to get home.

SHAMRAEV (*Mimicking.*) Horse . . . home . . . (*Severely.*) You saw yourself: they've just been to the station. They're not to go out again.

MASHA But there must be other horses . . . (*Seeing that her father is not forthcoming, she waves her hand dismissively.*) I don't want anything to do with either of you . . .

MEDVEDENKO I'll go on foot, Masha. Honestly.

POLINA ANDREEVNA (*Sighs.*) On foot, in weather like this . . . (*Sits at the card table.*) If you please, ladies and gentlemen.

MEDVEDENKO It's really only four miles in all. . . . Good-bye. . . . (*Kisses his wife's hand.*) Good-bye, Mama dear. (*His mother-in-law reluctantly extends her hand for him to kiss.*) I wouldn't have dis-

---

3. A mysterious political prisoner under Louis XIV, whose face was hidden by an iron mask. He was first mentioned in the *Mémoires secrets pour servir à l'histoire de Perse* (Amsterdam, 1745–1746), where he was alleged to be Louis' bastard. He is best known from *Le Vicomte de Bragelonne* (1848–50), the third of Alexandre Dumas' musketeer novels, in which he is supposed to be Louis' twin.

4. An Italian import, known to Americans as "Bingo," the game became fashionable in northern Russia in the 1840s and was briefly banned as a form of gambling.

turbed anybody, except that the baby. . . . (*Bows to them all.*)
Good-bye. . . . (*He exits apologetically.*)

SHAMRAEV   Never fear, he'll get there. He's no V.I.P.

POLINA ANDREEVNA (*Raps on the table.*)   If you please, ladies and
gentlemen. Let's not waste time; they'll be calling us to supper
soon.

    (SHAMRAEV, MASHA, *and* DORN *sit at the table.*)

ARKADINA (*To* TRIGORIN.)   When the long autumn evenings draw on,
they play lotto here. Come and have a look: the old-fashioned lotto
set our late mother used to play with us when we were children.
Wouldn't you like to play a round with us before supper? (*Sits at
the table with* TRIGORIN.) The game's a bore, but once you get used
to it, you don't mind. (*Deals three cards to each.*)

TREPLYOV (*Leafing through the magazine.*)   His own story he's read,
but on mine he hasn't even cut the pages. (*Puts the magazine on
the desk, then starts for the door left; moving past his mother, he
kisses her hand.*)

ARKADINA   What about you, Kostya?

TREPLYOV   Sorry, I don't feel up to it. . . . I'm going for a walk.
(*Exits.*)

ARKADINA   The stakes are ten kopeks. Ante up for me, Doctor.

DORN   Your wish is my command.

MASHA   Everyone's ante'd up? I'm starting. . . . Twenty-two!

ARKADINA   Got it.

MASHA   Three. . . .

DORN   Righto.

MASHA   Got three? Eight! Eighty-one! Ten!

SHAMRAEV   Not so fast.

ARKADINA   The reception they gave me in Kharkov, goodness gracious, my head's still spinning from it!

MASHA   Thirty-four!

    (*A melancholy waltz is played offstage.*)

ARKADINA   The students organized an ovation. . . . Three baskets of
flowers, two bouquets, and look at this. . . . (*Unpins a brooch from
her bosom and throws it on the table.*)

SHAMRAEV   Yes, that's something, all right . . .

MASHA   Fifty! . . .

DORN   Just plain fifty?

ARKADINA   I was wearing a gorgeous outfit. . . . Say what you like,
when it comes to dressing, I'm nobody's fool.

POLINA ANDREEVNA   Kostya's playing. The poor boy's depressed.

SHAMRAEV   The newspaper reviewers give him a hard time.

MASHA   Seventy-seven!

ARKADINA   Who cares about them?

TRIGORIN   He hasn't had any luck. His writing still can't manage to find its proper voice. There's something odd, indefinite about it, sometimes it's like gibberish. . . . Not one living character.

MASHA Eleven!

ARKADINA (*Looking round at* SORIN.) Petrusha, are you bored? (*Pause.*) He's asleep.

DORN Sleep comes to the senior civil servant.

MASHA Seven! Ninety!

TRIGORIN If I lived on an estate like this, by a lake, you think I'd write? I'd kick this addiction and do nothing but fish.

MASHA Twenty-eight!

TRIGORIN To catch a chub or a perch—that's my idea of heaven!

DORN Well, I have faith in Konstantin Gavrilych. There's something there! There's something there! He thinks in images, his stories are colorful, striking, and I have a real fondness for them. It's just a pity he doesn't have well-defined goals. He creates an impression, and leaves it at that, and of course by itself an impression doesn't get you very far. Irina Nikolaevna, are you glad your son's a writer?

ARKADINA Imagine, I still haven't read him. Never any time.

MASHA Twenty-six!

(TREPLYOV *quietly enters and goes to his desk.*)

SHAMRAEV (*To* TRIGORIN.) Hey, Boris Alekseevich, that thing of yours is still here.

TRIGORIN What thing?

SHAMRAEV A while back Konstantin Gavrilych shot a gull, and you asked me to have it stuffed.

TRIGORIN Don't remember. (*Thinking about it.*) Don't remember!

MASHA Sixty-six! One!

TREPLYOV (*Throws open the window, listens.*) So dark! I can't understand how it is I feel so uneasy.

ARKADINA Kostya, shut the window, it's drafty.

(TREPLYOV *closes the window.*)

MASHA Eighty-eight!

TRIGORIN It's my game, ladies and gentlemen.

ARKADINA (*Merrily.*) Bravo! Bravo!

SHAMRAEV Bravo!

ARKADINA This man has the most incredible luck any time, any place. (*Rises.*) And now let's have a bite to eat. Our celebrity didn't have dinner today. After supper we'll resume our game. (*To her son.*) Kostya, put down your writing, we're eating.

TREPLYOV I don't want any, Mama. I'm not hungry.

ARKADINA You know best. (*Wakes* SORIN.) Petrusha, suppertime! (*Takes* SHAMRAEV'S *arm.*) I'll tell you about my reception in Kharkov. . . .

(POLINA ANDREEVNA *blows out the candles on the table, then she and* DORN *wheel out the armchair. Everyone goes out the door left. Only* TREPLYOV *remains alone onstage, at the writing desk.*)

TREPLYOV (*Prepares to write; scans what he's already written.*)   I've talked so much about new forms, but now I feel as if I'm gradually slipping into routine myself. (*Reads.*) "The poster on the fence proclaimed. . . . A pale face, framed by dark hair. . . ." Proclaimed, framed. . . . It's trite.[5] (*Scratches it out.*) I'll start with the hero waking to the sound of rain, and get rid of all the rest. The description of the moonlit night's too long and contrived. Trigorin has perfected a technique for himself, it's easy for him. . . . He has a shard of broken bottle glisten on the dam and a black shadow cast by the millwheel—and there's your moonlit night ready-made.[6] But I've got to have the flickering light, and the dim twinkling of the stars, and the distant strains of a piano, dying away in the still, fragrant air. . . . It's excruciating. (*Pause.*) Yes, I'm more and more convinced that the point isn't old or new forms, it's to write and not think about form, because it's pouring freely out of your soul. (*Someone knocks at the window closest to the desk.*) What's that? (*Looks out the window.*) Can't see anything. . . . (*Opens the glass door and looks into the garden.*) Somebody's running down the steps. (*Calls out.*) Who's there? (*Goes out; he can be heard walking rapidly along the veranda; in a few seconds he returns with* NINA ZARECHNAYA.) Nina! Nina! (NINA *lays her head on his chest and sobs with restraint.*) (*Moved.*) Nina! Nina! it's you . . . you. . . . I had a premonition, all day my heart was aching terribly. (*Removes her hat and knee-length cloak.*[7]) Oh, my sweet, my enchantress, she's here! We won't cry, we won't.

NINA   There's somebody here.

TREPLYOV   Nobody.

NINA   Lock the doors, or they'll come in.

TREPLYOV   No one will come in.

NINA   I know Irina Nikolaevna is here. Lock the doors.

TREPLYOV (*Locks the door at right with a key, crosses left.*)   This one has no lock. I'll put a chair against it. (*Sets a chair against the door.*) Don't be afraid, no one will come in.

5. Chekhov used the same words in criticizing a story by Zhirkevich. "Nowadays ladies are the only writers who use 'the poster proclaimed,' 'a face framed by hair.' ".

6. *Cf.* Chekhov's story "The Wolf" " (1886): "On the weir, drenched in moonlight, there was not a trace of shadow; in the middle the neck of a broken bottle shone like a star. The two millwheels, half sheltered in the shade of an outspread willow, looked angry and bad-tempered. . . ." In a letter to his brother (May 10, 1886), he offers it as a facile technique.

7. In the original, talma. A quilted, knee-length cloak with a wide, turned-down collar and silk lining, named after the French tragedian François Joseph Talma.

NINA (*Stares fixedly at his face.*)   Let me look at you. (*Looking around.*) Warm, pleasant. . . . This used to be a drawing room. Have I changed a great deal?

TREPLYOV   Yes. . . . You've lost weight, and your eyes are bigger. Nina, it feels so strange to be seeing you. How come you didn't let me in? How come you didn't you show up before now? I know you've been living here almost a week. . . . I've been over to your place several times every day, stood beneath your window like a beggar.

NINA   I was afraid you hated me. Every night I have the same dream that you look at me and don't recognize me. If you only knew! Ever since my arrival I keep coming here . . . to the lake. I was at your house lots of times and couldn't make up my mind to go in. Let's sit down. (*They sit.*) We'll sit and we'll talk and talk. It's nice here, warm, cozy. . . . Do you hear—the wind? There's a passage in Turgenev: "Happy he who on such a night sits beneath his roof, and has a warm corner."[8] I'm a gull. . . . No, that's wrong. (*Rubs her forehead.*) What was I on about? Yes. . . . Turgenev. . . . "And the Lord help all homeless wanderers . . ." Never mind. (*Sobs.*)

TREPLYOV   Nina, you still. . . . Nina!

NINA   Never mind, it makes me feel better. . . . For two years now I haven't cried. Late last night I went to look at the garden, to see if our stage was still there. And it's standing to this day. I burst into tears for the first time in two years, and I felt relieved, my heart grew lighter. You see, I've stopped crying. (*Takes him by the hand.*) And so, now you're a writer. You're a writer, I'm an actress. . . . We've both fallen into the maelstrom.[9] . . . I used to live joyously, like a child—wake up in the morning and start to sing; I loved you, dreamed of fame, and now? First thing tomorrow morning I go to Yelets[1], third class . . . traveling with peasants, and in Yelets art-loving businessmen will pester me with their propositions. A sordid kind of life!

TREPLYOV   Why Yelets?

NINA   I took an engagement for the whole winter. Time to go.

TREPLYOV   Nina, I cursed you, hated you, tore up your letters and photographs, but every moment I realized that my soul is bound to you forever. I haven't the power to stop loving you. From the time I lost you and began publishing, life for me has been unbearable—I'm in pain. . . . My youth was suddenly somehow snatched away, and I felt as if I'd been living on this earth for ninety years.

8. The last sentence is slightly misquoted from the Epilogue of Turgenev's novel *Rudin* (1856).
9. *Omut* can also be translated "millrace," which would connect back to *The Rusalka* imagery.
1. The Des Moines of Tsarist Russia, a rapidly growing provincial trade center in the Oryol gubernia, south of Tula, noted for its grain elevators, tanneries, and brickyards, with a population of 52,000.

I appeal to you, kiss the ground you walk on; wherever I look, everywhere your face rises up before me, that caressing smile that shone on me in the best years of my life. . . .

NINA (*Perplexed.*)   Why does he say such things, why does he say such things?

TREPLYOV   I'm alone, unwarmed by anyone's affection. I'm cold as in a dungeon, and, no matter what I write, it's all arid, stale, gloomy. Stay here, Nina, I beg you, or let me go with you! (NINA *quickly puts on her hat and cloak.*) Nina, why? For God's sake, Nina. . . . (*Watches her put on her wraps.*)
      (*Pause.*)

NINA   My horses are standing at the gate. Don't see me out, I'll manage by myself. . . . (*Tearfully.*) Give me some water. . . .

TREPLYOV (*Gives her something to drink.*)   Where are you off to now?

NINA   To town. (*Pause.*) Is Irina Nikolaevna here?

TREPLYOV   Yes. . . . On Thursday Uncle wasn't well; we wired for her to come.

NINA   Why do you tell me you'd kiss the ground I walk on? I should be killed. (*Leans over the desk.*) I feel so tired! Have to get some rest . . . rest! (*Lifts her head.*) I'm a gull. . . . That's wrong, I'm an actress. Ah, yes! (*Having heard* ARKADINA's *and* TRIGORIN's *laughter, she listens, then runs to the door left and peeks through the keyhole.*) He's here too. . . . (*Returning to* TREPLYOV.) Ah, yes. . . . Never mind. . . . Yes. . . . He had no faith in the theater, he'd laugh at my dreams, and little by little I lost faith in it too, lost heart. . . . But then the anxiety over our affair, jealousy, constant worrying about the baby. . . . I became petty, trivial, acted mindlessly. . . . I didn't know what to do with my hands, didn't know how to stand on stage, couldn't control my voice. You can't imagine what that's like, when you realize your acting is terrible. I'm a gull. No, that's wrong. . . . Remember, you shot down a gull? By chance a man comes along, sees, and with nothing better to do destroys. . . . Subject for a short story. That's wrong. . . . (*Rubs her forehead.*) What was I saying? . . . I was talking about the stage. I'm not like that now. . . . Now I'm a real actress, I like acting, I enjoy it, I'm intoxicated when I'm on stage and feel that I'm beautiful. And now that I'm living here, I go walking and walking and thinking and thinking and feel every day my spirit is growing stronger. . . . Now I know, understand, Kostya, that in our work—it doesn't matter whether we act or we write—the main thing isn't fame, glamour, the things I dreamed about, it's knowing how to endure. I know how to shoulder my cross and I have faith. I have faith and it's not so painful for me, and when I think about my calling, I'm not afraid of life.

TREPLYOV (*Mournfully.*)   You've found your path, you know where you're going, but I'm still drifting in a chaos of day dreams and

images, without knowing what or whom it's for. I have no faith
and I don't know what my calling is.[2]

NINA (*Listening hard.*)   Ssh . . . I'm going. Good-bye. When I
become a great actress, come to the city and have a look at me.
Promise? But now. . . . (*Squeezes his hand.*) Now it's late. I'm dead
on my feet. . . . I'm famished, I'd like a bite to eat . . .

TREPLYOV   Stay here, I'll bring you some supper . . .

NINA   No, no. . . . Don't show me out, I'll manage by myself. . . . My
horses are close by. . . . That means, she brought him with her?
So what, it doesn't matter. When you see Trigorin, don't say anything to him. . . . I love him. I love him even more than before.
. . . Subject for a short story. . . . I love, love passionately, love to
desperation. It used to be nice. Kostya! Remember? What a bright,
warm, joyful, pure life, what feelings—feelings like tender, fragile
flowers. . . . Remember? . . . (*Recites.*) "Humans, lions, eagles and
partridges, antlered deer, geese, spiders, silent fishes that inhabit
the waters, starfish and those beings invisible to the naked eye—
in short, all living things, all living things, all living things, having
completed the doleful cycle, are now extinct. . . . Already
thousands of centuries have passed since the earth bore any living
creature, and this pale moon to no avail doth light her lamp. No
more does the meadow awake to the cries of cranes, and the may
flies are no longer to be heard in the linden groves. . . ." (*Embraces*
TREPLYOV *impulsively and runs to the glass door.*)

TREPLYOV (*After a pause.*)   I hope nobody runs into her in the garden
and tells Mama. It might distress Mama. . . . (*Over the course of*
two minutes, he silently tears up all his manuscripts and throws them
under the desk, then unlocks the door and exits.)

DORN (*Trying to open the door left.*)   Funny. Door seems to be
locked. . . . (*Enters and puts the chair in its proper place.*) Obstacle
course.

(*Enter* ARKADINA, POLINA ANDREEVNA, *followed by* YAKOV *with*
bottles and MASHA, *then* SHAMRAEV *and* TRIGORIN.)

ARKADINA   Put the red wine and the beer for Boris Alekseevich here
on the table. We'll drink while we play. Let's sit down, ladies and
gentlemen.

POLINA ANDREEVNA (*To* YAKOV.)   And bring the tea now. (*Lights the*
candles, sits at the card table.)

SHAMRAEV (*Leads* TRIGORIN *to the cupboard.*)   Here's that thing I was
talking about before. . . . (*Gets a stuffed gull out of the cupboard.*)
You ordered it.

---

2. From Chekhov's notebook: "Treplyov has no well-defined aims, and this is what destroyed
him. His talent destroyed him. He says to Nina at the end: 'You have found your path,
you are saved, but I am ruined.' "

TRIGORIN (*Staring at the gull.*)   Don't remember! (*Thinking about it.*) Don't remember!

    (*A shot offstage right; everyone shudders.*)

ARKADINA (*Alarmed.*)   What's that?

DORN   Nothing. I suppose something exploded in my first-aid kit. Don't worry. (*Exits through the door right, returns in a few seconds.*) That's what it is. A vial of ether exploded. (*Sings.*) "Once again I stand bewitched before thee. . . ."

ARKADINA (*Sitting at the table.*)   Phew, I was terrified. It reminded me of the time. . . . (*Hides her face in her hands.*) Things even went black before my eyes. . . .

DORN (*Leafing through the magazine, to* TRIGORIN.)   About two months ago there was a certain article published in here . . . a letter from America, and I wanted to ask you, among other things. . . . (*Takes* TRIGORIN *'round the waist and leads him down to the footlights.*) because I'm very interested in this matter. . . . (*Lowering his voice.*) Take Irina Nikolaevna somewhere away from here. The fact is, Konstantin Gavrilovich *has* shot himself. . . .

CURTAIN

Variants to *The Seagull*

These lines appeared in the censorship's copy (Cens.), the first publication in the journal *Russian Thought* (*Russkaya Mysl*, 1896) (RT), and the 1897 edition of Chekhov's plays (1897)

Act One

After And tobacco? — Yesterday, ma'am, I had to get some flour, we look for the bag high and low, and beggars had stolen it. Had to pay fifteen kopeks for another one. (Cens.) (Page 136)

Before Talk to my father yourself, because I won't. —
MASHA Tell him yourself. The barn is full of millet now, and he says that if it weren't for the dogs, thieves would carry it off.
TREPLYOV To hell with him and his millet! (Cens.) (Page 137)

After I never get my way in the country. — It's all millet one time, dogs another, no horses another, because they've gone to the mill and so on and so forth.(Cens.) (Page 137)

Before You've got it in your head [. . .] — Horace said: *genus irritabele vatum*. (Cens., RT) (Page 139)

After When all's said and done. — Once, about ten years ago, I published an article about trial lawyers, I just remembered, and, you know, it was pleasant, and meanwhile when I begin to remember that I worked twenty-eight years in the Justice Department, it's the other way 'round, I'd rather not think about it . . . (*Yawns.*) (Cens.) (Page 140)

Before (TREPLYOV *enters from behind the platform.*)
MEDVEDENKO (*To* SORIN.) And before Europe achieves results, humanity, as Flammarion writes, will perish as a consequence of the cooling of the earth's hemispheres.
SORIN God bless us.
MASHA (*Offering her snuffbox to* TRIGORIN.) Do have some! You're always so silent. Do you ever talk?
TRIGORIN Yes, I talk sometimes. (*Takes snuff.*) Disgusting. How can you?
MASHA Well, you've got a nice smile. I suppose you're a simple man. (Cens.) (Page 143)

After I didn't mean to offend him. —
NINA (*Peering out from behind the curtain.*) Is it over already? We won't be going on?

ARKADINA   The author left. I suppose it is over. Come on out, my dear, and join us.

NINA   Right away. (*Disappears.*)

MEDVEDENKO (*To* MASHA.)   It all depends on the substantiality of psychic matter and (Cens.) (Page 146)

After but in those days he was irresistible. —
          (POLINA ANDREEVNA *weeps quietly.*)

SHAMRAEV (*Reproachfully.*)   Polina, Polina . . .

POLINA ANDREEVNA   Never mind . . . Forgive me . . . I suddenly got so depressed! (Cens.) (Page 146)

After Yes. — SHAMRAEV Bream and pike, for the most part. There are pike perch as well, but not many. (Cens.) (Page 147)

After Credit where credit's due. —

MEDVEDENKO   A deplorable manifestation of atavism, worthy of the attention of Lombroso.

DORN (*Teasing.*)   "Lombroso" . . . You can't live without pedantic words. (Cens.) (Page 148)

After (*Takes him by the arm.*) — In some play there's a line, "Come to your senses, old man!" (Cens.) (Page 148)

Replace And will you all please leave me in peace? Stay here! Don't come after me! —

with MASHA On what? My father will tell you that all the horses are occupied.

TREPLYOV   (*Angrily.*) He hasn't got the right! I don't keep anyone from living, so they can leave me in peace. (Cens.) (Page 149)

Act Two

After You don't live . . .

MASHA   My mama brought me up like that girl in the fairy tale who lived in a flower. I don't know how to do anything. (Cens.) (Page 150)

After just consider me and Trigorin . . . — I didn't pick out Boris Alekseevich, didn't lay siege, didn't enthrall, but when we met, everything in my head went topsy-turvy, my dears, and things turned green before my eyes. I used to stand and look at him and cry. I mean it, I'd howl and howl. What kind of master plan is that? (Cens.) (Page 151)

After At Sea by Maupassant, sweetheart. —
MEDVEDENKO   Never read it.
DORN   You only read what you don't understand.
MEDVEDENKO   Whatever books I can get, I read.
DORN   All you read is Buckle and Spencer, but you've got no more
   knowledge than a night watchman. According to you, the heart is
   made out of cartilage and the earth is held up by whales.
MEDVEDENKO   The earth is round.
DORN   Why do say that so diffidently?
MEDVEDENKO   (*Taking offense.*)   When there's nothing to eat, it
   doesn't matter if the earth is round or square. Stop pestering me,
   will you please?
ARKADINA   (*Annoyed.*)   Stop it, gentlemen. (Cens.) (Page 152)

After It's so uninteresting! — (*Recites.*) Humans, lions, eagles and
   partridges, antlered deer, geese, spiders, silent fishes that inhabit
   the waters, starfish and those beings invisible to the naked eye —
   in short, all living things, all living things, all living things, having
   completed   the   doleful   cycle,   are   now   extinct . . . Already
   thousands of centuries have passed since the earth bore any living
   creature, and this pale moon to no avail doth light her lamp. No
   more does the meadow awake to the cries of cranes, and the mayflies are no longer to be heard in the linden groves. (Cens.) (Page
   152)

After Stop smoking. — DORN   You should have done it long ago.
   Tobacco and wine are so disgusting! (Cens.) (Page 152)

Replace You've lived in your life time, but what about me? I worked
   in the Department of Justice for twenty-eight years, but still
   haven't lived.
   with You've lived your life, your room is full of embroidered pillows, slippers and all that, like some kind of museum, but I still
   haven't lived. (Cens.) (Page 153)

Replace So there and all the rest.
   with Everyone's right according to his own lights, everyone goes
   wherever his inclinations lead him. (Cens.) (Page 153)

Before A man should take life seriously[. . .] — It's precisely
   because everyone is right according to his own lights, that everyone suffers. (Cens.) (Page 153)

After Ridiculous. — It's time to think about eternity.
   (TREPLYOV *walks past the house without a hat, a gun in one
   hand, and a dead gull in the other.*)

ARKADINA   (*To her son.*) Kostya, come join us!
    (TREPLYOV *glances at them and exits.*)
DORN (*Singing quietly.*)   "Tell her my tale, flowers of mine . . ."
NINA   You're off-key, doctor.
DORN   It doesn't matter. (*To* SORIN.) As I was saying, your excel-
    lency. It's time to think about eternity. (*Pause.*) (Cens.) (Page 153)

Replace DORN (*Sings quietly.*)   "Tell her of love, flowers of mine . . ."
with DORN   Well, say what you like, I cannot do without nature.
ARKADINA   What about books? In poetic images, nature is more mov-
    ing and refined than as is. (Cens.) (Page 153)

Replace Carriage horses?
    with A carriage horse? Did you say a carriage horse? Go out there
    and see for yourself: the roan is lame, Cossack Lass is bloated with
    water . . . (Cens.) (Page 153)

After This is incredible! —
POLINA ANDREEVNA (*To her husband.*)   Stop it, I implore you.
ARKADINA   Horse collars or rye are nothing to do with me . . . I am
    going and that's that.
SHAMRAEV   Irina Nikolaevna, have a heart, on what? (Cens.) (Page
    153)

After what can I do? —
SORIN   He's going. He's leaving the farmwork at the busiest time
    and so on. I won't let him do it! I'll force him to stay!
DORN   Pyotr Nikolaevich, have a least a penny's worth of character!
    (Cens.) (Page 154)

After He even sent the carriage horses into the fields — He does
    what he likes. His third year here, he told the old man to mortgage
    the estate . . . What for? What was the need? He bought pedigreed
    turkeys and suckling pigs and they all died on his hands. He set
    up expensive beehives and in winter all the bees froze to death.
    The entire income from the estate he wastes on building, and on
    top of that takes the old man's pension away and sends Irina Niko-
    laevna six hundred rubles a year out of the old man's money, as if
    it were part of the income, and she's delighted because she's
    stingy.
DORN (*Distractedly.*)   Yes. (*Pause.*) (Cens.) (Page 154)

Replace stop lying . . . (*Pause.*) —
with stop lying . . . Twenty years I've been your wife, your friend . . .
    Take me into your home. (Page 155)

Replace Forgive me, I'm getting on your nerves.
DORN (*To* NINA.) —
with DORN (*Sings quietly.*)   "At the hour of parting, at the hour of
farewell . . ."
     (NINA *appears near the house; she picks flowers.*)
POLINA ANDREEVNA (*To* DORN, *in an undertone.*)   You spent all morn-
ing again with Irina Nikolaevna!
DORN   I have to be with somebody.
POLINA ANDREEVNA   I'm suffering from jealousy. Forgive me. You're
sick and tired of me.
DORN   No, not at all.
POLINA ANDREEVNA   Of course, you're a doctor, there's no way you
can avoid women. That's how it is. But you know that this is tor-
ture. Be with women, but at least try so that I don't notice it.
DORN   I'll try. (*To* NINA.) (Cens.) (Page 155)

After like anybody else . . . — They're modest. Yesterday I asked him
for an autograph, and he was naughty and wrote me bad poetry,
deliberately bad, so that everyone would laugh . . . (Cens.) (Page
155)

Act Three

After I can never have any horses. — (*Enter* MEDVEDENKO) (Cens.)
(Page 163)

Replace SORIN   You're kind, affectionate . . . I respect you . . . Yes
. . . (*Staggers.*)
with MEDVEDENKO (*Smokes a fat hand-rolled cigarette; addressing no
one in particular.*)   The schoolteacher at Telyatyev bought hay at
a very good price. Nine kopeks for thirty-five pounds, delivery
included. And just last week I paid eleven. It gets you going in
circles. (*Noticing the star on* SORIN'S *chest.*) What's that you've got?
Hmm . . . I received a medal too, but they should have given me
money.
ARKADINA   Semyon Semyonych, be so kind, allow me to talk with
my brother. We would like to left in private.
MEDVEDENKO   Ah, fine! I understand . . . I understand . . . (*Exits.*)
SORIN   He comes here at the crack of dawn. Keeps coming and talking about something. (*Laughs.*) A kind man, but already a bit . . .
makes you sick and tired. (*Staggers.*) (Cens.) (Page 163)

Act Four

Replace MEDVEDENKO   Might I ask, Doctor, which town abroad you
liked most?

with MEDVEDENKO (*To* DORN.)   Allow me to ask you, doctor, how much does a ream of writing paper cost abroad?

DORN   I don't know — I never bought any.

MEDVEDENKO   And what town did you like most? (Cens.) (Page 173)

After the setting of the action . . .

SHAMRAEV   (*To* ARKADINA.) Are they alive?

ARKADINA   I don't know.

SHAMRAEV   She was a highly talented actress, I must remark. Her like is not around nowadays! In *The Murder of Coverley*, she was just . . . (*Kisses the tips of his fingers.*) I'd give ten years of my life. (Cens.) (Page 176)

After with either of you . . .

SHAMRAEV (*Flaring up, in an undertone.*)   Well, cut my throat! Hang me! Let him go on foot! (Cens.) (Page 176)

After he's no V.I.P.!

DORN   You get married — you change. What's happened to atoms, substantiality, Flammarion? (*Sits at the card table.*) (Cens.) (Page 177)

After the stage direction (TREPLYOV *closes the window.*)

SHAMRAEV   The wind's up. The wind's getting up . . . A certain young lady is standing by a window, conversing with an amorous young man, and her mama says to her, "Come away from the window, Dashenka, or else you'll get the wind up . . ." The wind up! (*Roars with laughter.*)

DORN   Your jokes smell like an old, shabby waistcoat. (Cens.) (Page 178)

Replace Then she and DORN *wheel the wheelchair. Everyone goes out the door at left; only* TREPLYOV *remains alone on stage at the desk.* —
with Everyone goes out left; on stage remain only SORIN *in his chair and* TREPLYOV *at the desk.* (Cens.) (Page 179)

Replace Nobody. —
with It's uncle. He's asleep. (Cens.) (Page 179)

Replace (*Looking around.*)
with And now at him. (*Walks over to* SORIN.) *He's asleep.* (Cens.) (Page 180)

After Time to go. — (*Nodding at* SORIN.) Is he badly?

TREPLYOV   Yes. (*Pause.*) (Cens.) (Page 180)

Replace (Recites.) —
with (Sits on the little bench and swathes herself in the bedsheet, which
 she has taken from the bed.) (Cens.) (Page 182)

Replace Embraces TREPLYOV *impulsively* —
with tears off the sheet, embraces TREPLYOV *impulsively, then* SORIN
 (Cens.) (Page 182)

After Obstacle course.
POLINA ANDREEVNA   (*Following him.*) You looked at her the whole
 time. I beg you, I entreat you by all that's holy, stop torturing me.
 Don't look at her, don't talk to her for so long.
DORN   All right, I'll try.
POLINA ANDREEVNA   (*Squeezing his hand to her breast.*) I know, my
 jealousy's foolish, mindless, I'm embarrassed by it myself. You're
 fed up with me.
DORN   No, not at all. If it's hard for you to keep still, go on talking.
 (Cens.) (Page 182)

Uncle Vanya

Many of Chekhov's contemporaries considered *Uncle Vanya* to be simply *The Wood Goblin* revised. For that reason, the Society for Russian Dramatic Authors denied it a prestigious prize in 1901. Scholars assume that Chekhov finished the play sometime in late 1896, after he had written *The Seagull* but before that comedy had suffered the hapless opening that turned him off playwriting for years. When, in 1897, Nemirovich-Danchenko requested *Uncle Vanya* for the Moscow Art Theater, fresh from its success with *The Seagull*, Chekhov had to explain that he had already promised it to the Maly Theater. However, the literary-advisory committee there, whose members included a couple of professors, was offended by the slurs on Serebryakov's academic career and what it saw as a lack of motivation, and demanded revisions. Chekhov coolly withdrew *Uncle Vanya* and turned it over to the Art Theater, which opened it on October 26, 1899. The opening night audience was less than enthusiastic, but the play gained in favor during its run. It became immensely popular in the provinces, where the audiences could identify with the plight of Vanya and Astrov. Gorky wrote to Chekhov, "I do not consider it a pearl, but I see in it a greater subject than others do; its subject is enormous, symbolic, and in its form it's something entirely original, something incomparable."[1]

A useful way of approaching *Uncle Vanya*, and indeed all of Chekhov's late plays, is that suggested by the poet Osip Mandelshtam in an unfinished article of 1936: starting with the cast list.

> What an inexpressive and colorless rebus. Why are they all together? How is the privy counselor related to anybody? Try and define the kinship or connection between Voinitsky, the son of a privy counselor's widow, the mother of the professor's first wife and Sofiya, the professor's young daughter by his first marriage. In order to establish that somebody happens to be somebody else's uncle, one must study the whole roster . . .
>
> A biologist would call this Chekhovian principle ecological. Combination is the decisive factor in Chekhov. There is no action in his drama, there is only propinquity with its resultant unpleasantness.[2]

What Mandelshtam calls "propinquity" is more important than the causal connections usually demanded by dramatic necessity, and distinct

1. M. Gorky and A. Chekhov, *Stati, vyskazyvaniya, perepiska* (Moscow: Goslitizdat, 1951), 63–65.
2. O. Mandelshtam, "O pyese A. Chekhova 'Dyadya Vanya,'" *Sobranie sochineniya* (Paris: YMCA Press), IV: 107–109.

from naturalistic "environment." Chekhov brings his people together on special occasions to watch their collisions and evasions. Conjugal or blood ties prove to be a lesser determinant of the characters' behavior than the counter-irritants of their proximity to one another. They are rarely seen at work in their natural habitats: Arkadina was not on stage or Trigorin at his desk; the officers in *Three Sisters* are not in camp; here the Professor has been exiled from his lecture hall.

The principle is especially conspicuous in *Uncle Vanya*, in which Chekhov stripped his cast down to the smallest number in any of his full-length plays. He achieved this primarily by conflating the cast of *The Wood Goblin*, combining the traits of two characters into one. By limiting the dramatis personae to eight (if we exclude the workman), Chekhov could present doublets of each character, to illustrate contrasting reactions to circumstances. Take the Serebryakov / Waffles dyad: the Professor, fond of his academic honors and perquisites, is an old man married to a young woman too repressed to betray him, yet he jealously tyrannizes her. Waffles, whose pompous language aspires to erudition, and whose wife abandoned him almost immediately after their wedding, responded with loving generosity. His life, devoid of honors, is devoted to others. He feels strongly the opprobrium of being a "freeloader," while the Professor is oblivious to his own parasitism.

Of the old women, Marina is earthy, stolid in her obedience to the natural cycle, her life narrowly focused on the practical matters of barnyard and kitchen. Still, she is capable of shrewd commentary on human behavior. Mariya Vasilyevna is equally static and narrow, but her eyes never rise from the pages of a pamphlet; she is totally blind to what goes on inside her fellow men. Her reading and Marina's knitting are both palliatives. One, meant for the betterment of all mankind, is sterile; the other, meant for the comfort of individuals, is not.

The contrasts are more complex but just as vivid in the younger characters. Sonya and Yelena are both unhappy young women on the threshold of wasted lives; both are tentative and withdrawn in matters of the heart. Sonya, however, indulges in daydreams while eagerly drugging herself with work. Yelena is too inhibited to yield to her desires, managing to be both indolent and clumsily manipulative in her dealings with others. She declares her affinity to Vanya because they are both "exasperating" people.

Astrov and Vanya are the only two "educated persons in the district," who started, like Ivanov, with exceptional promise, but grew disillusioned. Astrov's disillusionment was gradual, developing over years of drudgery as a country doctor; he has turned into a toper and a cynic, but can still compartmentalize vestiges of his idealism in his reforestation projects. Vanya's disillusionment came as a thunderclap with the Professor's arrival; its suddenness negated any possibility of maintaining an ideal. Instead, he is diverted to fantasies of bedding Yelena and, even at a moment of crisis, considering himself a potential Dostoevsky or Schopenhauer. His impossible dreams are regularly deflated by Astrov's sarcasm, but both men are, to use a word repeated throughout the play, "crackpots" (*chudaki*).

Thus, the propinquity of the characters brings out their salient features: the existence of each puts the other in relief. As in *The Seagull*, Chekhov locates them on an estate where they are displaced persons. The estate has been in the family for little more than a generation. Vanya relinquished his patrimony to provide his sister's dowry, giving up his own career to cut expenses and to work the estate on the Professor's behalf, taking his mother with him. Vanya and his mother are acclimatized without being naturalized. The Professor and Yelena are obvious intruders, who disrupt the estate's settled rhythms and cannot accommodate themselves to it. Even Astrov seldom pays a call; he prefers his forests. Only Sonya, Marina, and Waffles are rooted in the estate's soil.

Again, the physical progression of the stage setting serves as an emblem of the inner development of the action. The play begins outside the house, with a tea table elaborately set to greet the Professor, who, on his entrance, walks right past it to closet himself in his study. The eruption of these dining-room accessories into a natural setting suggests the upheaval caused by the Petersburgers' presence. Moreover, the samovar has gone cold during the long wait; it fails to serve its purpose. As is usual with Chekhov, the play begins with a couple of characters onstage, waiting for the others to precipitate an event. When it comes, the event—the tea party—is frustrated.

The second act moves indoors, its sense of claustrophobia enhanced by the impending storm and Yelena's need to throw open the window. The dining room too has been usurped by the Professor, who has turned it into a study cum sickroom, his medicine littering the sideboard. No family gathers to share a meal: midnight snacks, a clandestine glass of wine, tête-à-têtes rather than group encounters are standard. Nanny, who has already grumbled at the altered meal times, complains that the samovar has still not been cleared. Later, she rejoices that plain noodles have replaced the Professor's spicy curries.

In Act Three, the Professor thrusts the family into unfamiliar surroundings when he convenes them in a rarely used reception room. Cold, formal, empty, it suits the Professor's taste for his missing podium and further disorients the others. Nanny, cowed by the ambience, must be asked to sit down; for the sake of the occasion, she had been prepared to stand by the door like a good servant. Anyone can wander through, as Vanya does when he intrudes upon Astrov and Yelena wit his bunch of roses—another property rendered useless by circumstance.

Finally, in Act Four, we move, for the first time, to a room actually lived in, Vanya's combination bedchamber and estate office. The real life of the house has migrated to this small, cluttered area where day-to-day tasks are carried out, where Astrov keeps his drawing table, Sonya her ledgers. There is even a mat for peasants to wipe their feet on. Vanya, like Treplyov, has no personal space that is not encroached on, and none of his objects bespeaks a private being. Once the Professor and Yelena, the disruptive factor, are gone, the family comes together in this atmosphere of warmth generated by routine. For them to do so, however, Vanya must abandon his personal desires and ambitions; for good reason a caged starling chirps by the worktable. The absence of conversation is

noteworthy in this symbiosis. Were it not for Vanya's impassioned outburst and Sonya's attempts to console him, the characters would write,
yawn, read and strum the guitar voicelessly, with no need to communicate aloud, bound together by propinquity.

The more inward the play moves in terms of locale, the more the sense
of oppression mounts. Chekhov uses weather and seasons along with
certain verbal echoes to produce this feeling. In the first few lines of
dialogue, Astrov declares, "It's stifling" (*dushno*), and variations on that
sentiment occur regularly. Vanya repeats it and speaks of Yelena's
attempt to muffle her youth; the Professor begins Act Two by announcing that he cannot breathe, and Vanya speaks of being choked by the
idea that his life is wasted. Astrov admits he would be suffocated if he
had to live in the house for a month. The two young women fling open
windows to be able to breathe freely. During the first two acts, a storm
is brewing and then rages; Vanya spends the last act moaning *Tyazhelo
mene*—literally "It is heavy on me," "I feel weighed down." At the very
end, Sonya's "We shall rest" (*My otdokhnyom*) is etymologically related
to *dushno* and connotes "breathing freely."

Cognate is Yelena's repeated assertion that she is "shy," in Russian
zastenchivaya, a word that suggests "hemmed in" or "walled up," and
might, in context, be better translated "inhibited." The references to the
Professor's gout, clouded vision, blood poisoning, and morphine contribute to the numbing atmosphere. This is intensified by the sense of
isolation: constant reference is made to the great distances between
places. Only Lopakhin in *The Cherry Orchard* is as insistent as Astrov
on how many miles it takes to get somewhere. The cumulative effect is
one of immobility and stagnation, oppression and frustration.

Time also acts as a pressure. "What time is it?" or a statement of the
hour is voiced at regular intervals, along with mention of years, months,
seasons, and mealtimes. The play begins with Astrov asking Marina,
"how long have we known one another?"—simple exposition but also an
initiation of the motif of lives eroded by the steady passage of time.
(Chekhov was to reuse this device to open *Three Sisters* and *The Cherry
Orchard*.) *Uncle Vanya* opens at summer's end, proceeds through a wet
and dismal autumn, and concludes with a bleak winter staring the characters in the face. The suggestion of summer's evanescence and the
equation of middle age with the oncoming fall may seem hackneyed.
Vanya certainly leaps at the obvious, with his bouquet of "mournful
autumn roses" and his personalization of the storm as the pathetic fallacy
of his own despair. Chekhov, however, used storms in his short stories
as a favorite premonition of a character's mental turmoil, and, in stage
terms, the storm without and the storm within Vanya's brain effectively
collaborate.

The play ends with Sonya's vision of "a long, long series of days, no
end of evenings" to be lived through before the happy release of death.
The sense of moments ticking away inexorably is much stronger here
than in Chekhov's other plays, because there are no parties, balls, the-
atricals, railway journeys, or fires to break the monotony. The Professor
and Yelena have destroyed routine, supplanting it with a more troubling

sense of torpid leisure. Without the narcotic effect of their daily labor, Astrov, Vanya, and Sonya toy with erotic fantasies that make their present all the grimmer.

Beyond these apparent devices, Chekhov is presenting a temporal sequence that is only a segment of a whole conspectus of duration. Another bond with the symbolists is that time in Chekhov's plays resembles Henri Bergson's concept of *temps-fleuve*: ("the current of time) human beings can measure duration, but they cannot stand outside the flow. The action of *Uncle Vanya* really began when Vanya gave up his inheritance for his sister's dowry years before the action of the play begins; the consequences of that action fill Acts One through Four, but its further consequences remain unrevealed. Chekhov used the provincial university town of Kharkov often as a symbol of nowhere: in *The Seagull*, it adores Arkadina's acting and in *The Cherry Orchard* it is one of Lopakhin's destinations. How will the Professor and Yelena get on together? How will Astrov manage to avoid dipsomania without the balm of Vanya's conversation and Sonya's solicitude? How will Vanya and Sonya salve their emotional wounds over the course of a lifetime? These questions are left to our imaginations.

Samuel Beckett, describing habit as a blissful painkiller, referred to "the perilous zones in the life of an individual, dangerous, precarious, painful, mysterious and fertile, when for a moment the boredom of living is replaced by the suffering of being."[3] Throughout *Uncle Vanya*, the characters, divorced from habit, suffer painful confrontations with being, and, by the final curtain, must try hard to return to the humdrum but safe addiction to living.

Although the tautness of the play's structure, its triangles and confidants, might suggest neoclassic tragedy, it comes closest to comedy, because no passion is ever pushed to an irremediable fulfillment. Yelena's name may refer to Helen of Troy but, if so, Chekhov had Offenbach, not Homer, in mind. He may also have been thinking of the Russian fairy tale of "Yelena the Fair," a Cinderella story in which the sniveling booby Vanya woos and wins the beautiful princess with the aid of his dead father. Folklore has other echoes here: the Russian version of "Snow White" is quoted ("the fairest in the land") and Vanya characterizes Yelena as a *rusalka*, a water-nymph of voluptuous beauty and destructive tendencies. Others may regard her as a dynamic force in their life, but she describes herself as a "secondary character," without any real impact. Her acceptance of a fleeting kiss and a souvenir pencil as trophies of a romantic upsurge is comically reductive.

The anti-tragic tendency of the play is apparent in the title. Most serious Russian drama at the turn of the nineteenth century bore titles of symbolic import: *Gold* and *The Price of Life* (Nemirovich-Danchenko), *Chains* (Sumbatov), *At Bottom* (*The Lower Depths*) (Gorky), *Walls* (Naidyonov), or else the name of its protagonist (Suvorin's *Tatyana Repina*) or a central relationship (Naidyonov's *Vanyushin's Children*). As a rule, Chekhov follows this convention.

In *Uncle Vanya*, though, the title reveals that the center of attention

3. Samuel Beckett, *Proust* (London: Chatto and Windus, 1931), 8.

is not Astrov, whose attractive qualities can upstage the title role in performance, but the self-pitying Voinitsky instead. Our Uncle Jack, as he might be in English, sounds peripheral, the archetype of mediocrity. Such a man is not serious enough to be called by a grownup name; he counts chiefly in his relationship to others. But who calls him Uncle Vanya? To the Professor, Yelena, and Astrov, he is Ivan Petrovich, except when they mean to be slighting. "That Uncle Vanya" is how Yelena dismisses him in Act Three, and in Act Four Astrov flippantly calls for an embrace before "Uncle Vanya" comes in. To his mother, he is Jean, the "shining light" of his youth. He is Vanya primarily to Sonya and Waffles, who love him. Therefore, if Voinitsky matters most when he is Uncle Vanya, his self-realization lies not in competing with the Professor or winning Yelena, but instead in his dealings with his dependents. He gave up trying to be Jean long ago; when he stops trying to be Iran Petrovich and fulfills himself as Uncle Vanya, a new life might commence.

Uncle Vanya

Scenes from Country Life[1]

In Four Acts

Characters[2]

SEREBRYAKOV, ALEKSANDR VLADIMIROVICH, retired professor
YELENA ANDREEVNA, his wife
SOFIYA ALEKSANDROVNA (SONYA), his daughter by his first marriage
VOINITSKAYA, MARIYA VASILYEVNA, widow of a government official,[3] and
  mother of the Professor's first wife
VOINITSKY, IVAN PETROVICH, her son
ASTROV, MIKHAIL LVOVICH, a physician
TELEGIN, ILYA ILYICH, an impoverished landowner
MARINA, an old nanny[4]
A WORKMAN
The action takes place on SEREBRYAKOV's *estate.*

1. Also the subtitle of Turgenev's play *A Month in the Country.*
2. The names are suggestive but not explicit in their meanings. Serebryakov "silvery"; Voinitsky "warrior"; Astrov "starry"; Telegin "cart"; "Yelena" is Helen, with hints at Helen of Troy (Offenbach's rather than Homer's); and Sofiya is Greek for "wisdom."
3. Literally, a privy councilor, a relatively high civilian position in the table of official ranks, equivalent to a lieutenant-general in the army.
4. The *nyanya* was the children's nursemaid, who would live in the household until her death, even when the children were grown up, and might care for their children in turn. *Cf.* Anfisa in *Three Sisters* and the deceased Nanny in *The Cherry Orchard.*

Act One

The garden. Part of the house and its veranda are visible. Along the path beneath an old poplar there is a table set for tea. Benches, chairs; a guitar lies on one of the benches. Not far from the table is a swing.— Between two and three in the afternoon. Overcast.

(MARINA, *a corpulent, imperturbable old woman, sits by the samovar knitting a stocking, while* ASTROV *paces nearby.*)

MARINA (*Pours a glass of tea.*)   Have a bite to eat, dearie.

ASTROV (*Reluctantly takes the glass.*)   Somehow I don't feel like it.

MARINA   Maybe you'll have a nip of vodka?

ASTROV   No. I don't drink vodka all the time. Besides, it's stifling. (*Pause.*) Nanny old girl, how long have we known one another?

MARINA (*Thinking it over.*)   How long? God help my memory . . . You came here to these parts . . . when? . . . Vera Petrovna was still alive, dear little Sonya's mother. In her time you visited us two winters . . . Well, that means nigh on eleven years have gone by. (*After giving it some thought.*) Could be even more . . .

ASTROV   Have I changed terribly since then?

MARINA   Terribly. In those days you were young, good-looking, and now you're old. And your good looks are gone too. And it's got to be said—you like a nip of vodka.

ASTROV   Yes . . . In ten years' time I've turned into another man. And what's the reason? I've been working too hard, nanny old girl. Morning to night, always on my feet, not a moment's rest, at night you lie under the blanket afraid you'll be hauled off to some patient.[5] In all the time we've known one another, I haven't had a single day to myself. Why wouldn't a man grow old? Besides, life itself is dreary, silly, filthy . . . It drags you down, this life. You're surrounded by crackpots, nothing but crackpots; you live with them for two, three years and little by little, without noticing it, you turn into a crackpot yourself. (*Twirling his long moustache.*) Look at this interminable moustache I've been cultivating. A silly moustache. I've turned into a crackpot, nanny old girl . . . Speaking of silly, I'm still in my right mind, thank God, my brain's still intact, but my feelings are sort of numb. There's nothing I want, nothing I need, no one I love . . . Present company excepted. (*Kisses her on the head.*) When I was a child I had a dear old nanny just like you.

MARINA   Maybe you'd like a bite to eat?

5. In the early 1890s the rural boards increased the number of medical outposts in small villages, with several beds for inpatients and a dispensary for outpatients. Doctors were expected to look after all the peasants in a given district.

ASTROV   No. In Lent, third week, I went to Malitskoe to deal with
an epidemic . . . Spotted typhus[6] . . . In the huts the peasants were
packed side by side . . . Mud, stench, smoke, bull calves on the
floor right next to the sick . . . Piglets too . . . I was at it all day
long, never sat down for a second, not a blessed drop passed my
lips, and when I did get home, they wouldn't let me rest—they
brought over a signalman from the railway; I put him on the table
to operate, and he goes and dies on me under the chloroform. And
just when they're least wanted, my feelings came back to life, and
I felt a twinge of conscience, just as if I'd killed him on purpose
. . . Down I sat, closed my eyes—just like this, and started thinking: the people who'll live one or two hundred years from now, the
people we're blazing a trail for, will they remember us, have a kind
word for us? Nanny, old girl, they won't remember a thing!

MARINA   People won't remember, but God will remember.

ASTROV   Thank you for that. Just the right thing to say.

(VOINITSKY *emerges from the house; he has been napping after
lunch and looks rumpled; he sits on the bench, adjusts his fancy
tie.*)[7]

VOINITSKY   Yes . . . (*Pause.*) Yes . . .

ASTROV   Had enough sleep?

VOINITSKY   Yes . . . Plenty. (*Yawns.*) Ever since the Professor and his
lady have been living here, our life's been shunted on to a siding
. . . I sleep at odd hours, for lunch and dinner eat all kinds of spicy
food,[8] drink wine. . . . unhealthy, that's what I call it! Before, there
wasn't a moment's leisure, Sonya and I were always at work—now,
lo and behold, Sonya does the work on her own and I sleep, eat,
drink . . . It's not right!

MARINA   (*After shaking her head.*)   No sense to it! The Professor gets
up at twelve o'clock, though the samovar's[9] been boiling away from
early morning, waiting on him. Before they came we always had
dinner between noon and one, like everybody else, but now they're

---

6. A highly contagious fever distinguished by purple spots, extreme prostration, and delirium.
7. "Chekhov got very angry when a certain provincial theatre depicted Uncle Vanya as a
   landowner on the skids, dirty, tattered, and in greased boots.
   " 'Well, what should he be like?' he was asked.
   " 'It's all written down in my play!' he replied.
   "And this is in the stage direction with the remark that Uncle Vanya is wearing a fancy
   necktie. Chekhov considered that this was quite enough to designate his dress." (Aleksandr
   Vishnevsky, *Keys to Memory,* 1928.)
   Chekhov described Voinitsky as "an elegant, cultivated man. It is counter to the truth
   to say that our country squires walk around in boots that stink of grease." (Stanislavsky,
   My Life in Art, 1924). The tie is mentioned specifically, because it is put on to impress
   Yelena Andreevna.
8. *Kabuli,* highly-spiced Caucasian stews similar to curries. Evidently, the Professor's biliousness derives in part from his diet.
9. A metal urn, heated by charcoal, to keep water on the boiling point for making tea. The
   pot with leaves would be kept warm on top of the samovar and filled with water from the
   tap as necessary.

here it's going on seven. At night the Professor reads and writes, and all of a sudden, round about two, the bell rings . . . What's the matter, goodness gracious? Tea! Wake folks up for him, set up the samovar . . . No sense to it!

ASTROV   And how much longer are they staying here?

VOINITSKY (*Whistles.*)   A century. The Professor has decided to take root here.

MARINA   Just like now. The samovar's on the table two hours, and they go off for a walk.

VOINITSKY   Here they come, here they come . . . Don't fret yourself. (*Voices are heard: from the bottom of the garden, returning from a walk, come* SEREBRYAKOV, YELENA ANDREEVNA, SONYA, *and* TELEGIN.)

SEREBRYAKOV   Beautiful, beautiful . . . Magnificent vistas.

TELEGIN   Outstanding, your excellency.

SONYA   Tomorrow we'll go to the forest preserve, Papa. Would you like that?

VOINITSKY   Ladies and gentlemen, it's teatime!

SEREBRYAKOV   My dear friends, send my tea to the study, if you'll be so kind! I have something more to do today.

SONYA   And you're sure to enjoy a visit to the forest preserve . . . (YELENA ANDREEVNA, SEREBRYAKOV, *and* SONYA *go into the house;* TELEGIN *goes to the table and sits beside* MARINA.)

VOINITSKY   The weather's hot, stifling, but our prodigy of learning wears an overcoat and galoshes with an umbrella and gloves.[1]

ASTROV   Which shows he takes care of himself.

VOINITSKY   But isn't she fine! Really fine! In all my life I've never seen a more beautiful woman.

TELEGIN   I may be riding in the fields, Marina Timofeevna, or strolling in a shady garden, or looking at this table, and I have this feeling of inexplicable bliss![2] The weather is enchanting, the birdies are singing, we live, all of us, in peace and harmony—what more could we ask? (*Accepting a glass.*) My heartfelt thanks!

VOINITSKY (*dreamily.*)   Her eyes . . . Wonderful woman!

ASTROV   Talk about something else, Ivan Petrovich.

VOINITSKY (*Listlessly.*)   What am I supposed to talk about?

ASTROV   Nothing new?

VOINITSKY   Not a thing. The same old stuff. I'm just the same as ever I was, no, worse, I've gotten lazy, all I do is growl like an old grouch. My old magpie of a *maman* goes on babbling about women's rights;

---

1. Chekhov wrote in a notebook entry of August 20, 1896, "M[enshikov] in dry weather goes around in galoshes, carries an umbrella, so as not to die of sunstroke, is afraid to wash with cold water, complains about heart trouble."
2. Telegin's flowery way of speaking is typical of the old-fashioned landowner, trying to seem courtly and well-educated. Chekhov uses a similar device in his first published story of 1879: "Letter of a Landowner to his Learned Neighbor Dr. Friedrich."

one eye peers into the grave, while the other pores over her high-minded pamphlets, looking for the dawn of a new life.

ASTROV   And the Professor?

VOINITSKY   And the Professor as usual sits alone in the study from morn to darkest night and writes. "With straining brain and fur-rowed brow, We write for nights and days, Yet all our poetry some-how Can never meet with praise."[3] I feel sorry for the paper! He'd be better off writing his autobiography. What a first-rate subject that is! A retired professor, you know what that means, a pedantic old fossil, a guppy with a terminal degree . . . Gout,[4] rheumatism, migraine, his poor old liver's bloated with envy and jealousy . . . Now this guppy lives on his first wife's estate, lives there reluc-tantly because he can't afford to live in town—Endlessly griping about his bad luck, although as a matter of fact he's incredibly lucky. (*Jittery.*) Just think about the luck he's had! The son of a humble sexton, a seminary student on a tuition scholarship, he's acquired academic degrees and chairs, the title Your Excellency, married the daughter of a senator[5] and so on and so forth. That's not the important thing, though. Check this out. For precisely twenty-five years the man reads and writes about art, although he understands absolutely nothing about art. For twenty-five years he chews over other people's ideas about realism, naturalism, and the rest of that rubbish; for twenty-five years he reads and writes about stuff that intelligent people have known for ages and fools couldn't care less about—which means, for twenty-five years he's been pouring the contents of one empty bottle into another emptier bottle. And add to that, his conceit! His pretensions! He's gone into retirement and not a single living soul has ever heard of him, he is totally obscure; which means, for twenty-five years he took up someone else's place. But look at him! He struts about like a demigod!

ASTROV   Sounds like you're jealous.

VOINITSKY   Of course I'm jealous! Look at his success with women! Not even Don Juan enjoyed such unqualified success! His first wife, my sister, a beautiful, gentle creature, pure as that blue sky overhead, noble, openhearted, with more admirers than he had students—loved him as only pure angels can love beings as pure and beautiful as themselves. My mother, his mother-in-law, adores him to this day, and to this day he inspires her with awe and rev-erence. His second wife, a woman with looks, brains—you saw her

---

3. Quotation from the satirical poem "At Second Hand" (*Chuzhoy tolk*, 1794) by Ivan Dim-itriev (1760–1837). The poem, which mocks the rhetorical form of the ode, was one of the standard texts of the pre-Pushkin era.
4. A periodic painful swelling in the lower joints, owing to the accumulation of uric acid; often a result of rich diet, heavy drinking, and a sedentary life.
5. If Yelena Andreevna's father is a senator, he ranks higher than a general in the military.

just now—married him when he was an old man, made him a gift of her youth, beauty, independence, her brilliance. What for? Why?

ASTROV   She's faithful to the Professor?

VOINITSKY   Sorry to say she is.

ASTROV   Why sorry?

VOINITSKY   Because this faithfulness is phony from start to finish. It's all sound and no sense. To cheat on an old husband you can't stand—that's immoral; to try and stifle the vestiges of youth and vital feeling in yourself—that's not immoral.

TELEGIN (*In a plaintive voice.*)   Vanya, I don't like it when you say things like that. Why, now, honestly . . . Anybody who cheats on a wife or husband is, I mean, a disloyal person, someone who might even betray his country!

VOINITSKY (*Annoyed.*)   Turn off the waterworks,[6] Waffles!

TELEGIN   Excuse me, Vanya. My wife ran away with the man she loved the day after our wedding on account of my unprepossessing looks. I didn't shirk my duty despite it all. I love her to this day, and I'm faithful to her, I help however I can, and sold my estate to educate the kiddies she bore to the man she loved. Happiness was denied me, but what I did have left was my pride. What about her? Her youth has gone now, her beauty, subject to the laws of nature, has faded, the man she loved has passed away . . . What does she have left?

(*Enter* SONYA *and* YELENA ANDREEVNA; *after a while, enter* MARIYA VASILYEVNA *with a book; she sits and reads; they give her tea and she drinks it without looking.*)

SONYA (*Hastily, to the nanny.*)   Nanny dear, some peasants have come. Go and talk to them, and I'll do the tea . . . (*Pours tea.*)

(MARINA *exits.* YELENA ANDREEVNA *takes her cup and sits in the swing, as she drinks.*)

ASTROV (*To* YELENA ANDREEVNA.)   I came here to treat your husband. You wrote that he's very ill, rheumatism and something else, but it turns out he's as healthy as a horse.

YELENA ANDREEVNA   Last night he was moping, complaining of pains in his legs, but today they're gone . . .

ASTROV   And I was breaking my neck, forty-five miles at a gallop. Well, never mind, it's not the first time. So it won't be a total loss, I'll stay the night here, at least I'll get some sleep "to be taken as needed."[7]

---

6. From the "Thoughts and Aphorisms" of the poet Kozma Prutkov, a fictional creation of A. K. Tolstoy and the brothers Zhemchuzhnikov, "published" between 1854 and 1863. One of his synthetic aphorisms is "If you have waterworks, turn them off; give the waterworks a rest too."

7. In the original, Astrov uses a Latin term often found in prescriptions: *quantum satis*, "as much as necessary."

SONYA Why, that's lovely. It's so seldom you stay over with us. I don't suppose you've had dinner?

ASTROV No, ma'am, I have not.

SONYA Then you're just in time for some. Nowadays we dine between six and seven. (*Drinks.*) Tea's cold!

TELEGIN There's been a perceptible drop in temperature in the samovar.

YELENA ANDREEVNA Never mind, Ivan Ivanych, we'll drink it cold.

TELEGIN Excuse me, ma'am . . . Not Ivan Ivanych, but Ilya Ilyich, ma'am . . . Ilya Ilyich Telegin, or, as some call me on account of my pockmarked face, Waffles. I once stood godfather to little Sonya, and His Excellency, your spouse, knows me very well. I'm now living with you, ma'am, on this estate, ma'am[8]. . . . If you will kindly notice, I dine with you every day.

SONYA Ilya Ilyich is our assistant, our right-hand man. (*Affectionately.*) Here, Godfather, I'll pour you some more.

MARIYA VASILYEVNA Ah!

SONYA What's the matter, Granny?

MARIYA VASILYEVNA I forgot to tell *Alexandre*[9] . . . I must be losing my memory . . . today I got a letter from Kharkov from Pavel Alekseevich . . . He sent his new pamphlet.

ASTROV Interesting?

MARIYA VASILYEVNA Interesting, but rather peculiar. He opposes the very thing he was promoting seven years ago. It's appalling!

VOINITSKY It's not at all appalling. Drink your tea, *Maman*.

MARIYA VASILYEVNA But I want to talk!

VOINITSKY For fifty years now we've been talking and talking, and reading pamphlets. It's high time we stopped.

MARIYA VASILYEVNA For some reason you don't like to listen when I talk. Pardon me, *Jean*, but this last year you have changed so much that I utterly fail to recognize you . . . You used to be a man of steadfast convictions, a shining light . . .

VOINITSKY Oh yes! I was a shining light but no one ever basked in my rays . . . *Pause.* I was a shining light . . . Don't rub salt in my wounds! Now I'm forty-seven. Before last year I was the same as you, deliberately trying to cloud my vision with this booklearning of yours, to keep from seeing real life—and I thought I was doing the right thing. And now, if you had the least idea! I don't sleep nights out of frustration, out of spite for having wasted my time so stupidly when I could have had everything that's withheld from me now by my old age!

8. *Ma'am* is to indicate that Telegin adds an s for *sudar* (sir) or *sudarinya* (madam) to his words, an old-fashioned and obsequious manner of speaking.
9. Mariya Vasilyevna belongs to a generation of educated persons who conversed in French and referred to one another by the French forms of their names: hence, *Alexandre, Jean*.

SONYA   Uncle Vanya, this is boring!

MARIYA VASILYEVNA (*To her son.*)   You seem to be blaming your former convictions for something . . . But they aren't to blame, *you* are. You have forgotten that convictions per se mean nothing, they're a dead letter . . . One must take action.[1]

VOINITSKY   Take action! Not everyone is capable of being a perpetual motion writing machine like your Herr Professor.

MARIYA VASILYEVNA   What do you mean by that?

SONYA (*Pleading.*)   Granny! Uncle Vanya! For pity's sake!

VOINITSKY   I'm mute. I'm mute and I apologize.
    (*Pause.*)

YELENA ANDREEVNA   Lovely weather today . . . Not too hot . . .
    (*Pause.*)

VOINITSKY   Good weather for hanging oneself . . .
    (TELEGIN *strums his guitar.* MARINA *walks near the house and calls chickens.*)

MARINA   Chick, chick, chick . . .

SONYA   Nanny dear, what did the peasants come for?

MARINA   The same old thing, still on about those untilled fields. Chick, chick, chick . . .

SONYA   Who're you calling?

MARINA   Speckles's gone off with her chicks . . . The crows might get 'em. (*Exits.*)
    (TELEGIN *plays a polka; all listen in silence. Enter a* WORKMAN.)

WORKMAN   Is Mister Doctor here? (*To* ASTROV.) 'Scuse me, Dr Astrov, there's some folks here to fetch you.

ASTROV   Where from?

WORKMAN   The factory.[2]

ASTROV (*Vexed.*)   Thanks a lot. That's that, got to go . . . (*Looking around for his peaked cap.*) What a nuisance, damn it . . .

SONYA   How unpleasant, honestly . . . After the factory you'll come to dinner.

ASTROV   No, it'll be too late. Now where in the world . . . where oh where?[3] . . . (*To* THE WORKMAN.) Listen, my boy, bring me a shot of vodka, anyway.
    (WORKMAN *exits.*)
    Now where in the world . . . where oh where . . . (*He has found his cap.*) In one of Ostrovsky's plays there's a man who's long on mous-

---

1. *Nado delo delat*, "one must do something," "be active," "committed," "get involved." A motto of liberalism in the 1860s, it does *not* mean "One must work," as it is often translated.
2. Between 1887 and 1900, the number of factory workers in Russia increased from one million to 2.5 million. Sanitary and housing conditions were very bad, since employers were not compelled to protect workers against dangerous machinery and few factories provided medical attention.
3. Astrov imitates the manner of speaking of Anfusa Tikhonovna in Ostrovsky's 1875 comedy *Wolves and Sheep.*

tache and short on brains[4] ... That's me all over. Well, my respects, ladies and gents ... (*To* YELENA ANDREEVNA.) If you drop in on me some time, along with Sofiya Aleksandrovna of course, I'd be really delighted. I have a smallish estate, no more than eighty acres in all, but if you're interested, there's an experimental orchard and a tree nursery, the likes of which you'll not find a thousand miles around. Next door I've got the state forest preserve ... The forester there is old, always ailing, so, as a matter of fact, I do all the work.

YELENA ANDREEVNA I've been told you're very fond of forests. Of course, they may be admirable, but really, don't they get in the way of your true calling? After all, you are a doctor.

ASTROV God alone knows what our true calling is.

YELENA ANDREEVNA And is it interesting?

ASTROV Yes, the work is interesting.

VOINITSKY (*Sarcastically.*) Very!

YELENA ANDREEVNA (*To* ASTROV.) You're still a young man, you look ... well, thirty-six, thirty-seven ... and I don't suppose it's as interesting as you say. Nothing but forest and more forest. I suppose it's monotonous.

SONYA No, it's remarkably interesting. Mikhail Lvovich plants a new forest every year, and they've already honored him with a bronze medal and a testimonial. He's had a hand in preventing them from destroying the old-growth areas. If you hear him out, you'll agree with him completely. He says that forests beautify the land, that they teach people to understand beauty and inspire them with a sense of grandeur. Forests alleviate a harsh climate. In lands where the climate is mild, less energy is spent on the struggle with nature, and therefore human beings there are milder and more delicate; there people are beautiful, athletic, very sensitive, their speech is refined, their movements graceful. There art and sciences flourish, their philosophy is not gloomy, their attitude to women is full of exquisite chivalry ...

VOINITSKY (*Laughing.*) Bravo, bravo! ... Which is all very charming, but not convincing, so (*to* ASTROV) allow me, my friend, to go on stoking my stoves with logs and building my sheds out of wood.

ASTROV You can stoke your stoves with peat[5] and build sheds of stone. Well, all right, chop down forests when it's absolutely necessary, but why destroy them? Russian forests are toppling beneath the axe, the habitats of birds and beasts are dwindling, tens of thousands of trees are perishing, rivers are running shallow

4. The popular dramatist Aleksandr Ostrovsky (1823–1886). The character is Paratov in *The Girl without a Dowry* (1879), who, in Act two, scene IX, says, "We already know one another (*Bows.*) A man long on moustache and short on abilities."
5. In Chekhov's *The Wood Goblin*, the title character, Dr. Khrushchyov, a liberal ecologist, says much the same thing.

and drying up, gorgeous natural scenery is disappearing irretrievably, and all because lazy human beings can't be bothered to bend
down and pick up fuel from the earth. (*To* YELENA ANDREEVNA.)
Am I right, madam? A person has to be an unreasoning barbarian
to destroy what cannot be re-created. Human beings are endowed
with reason and creative faculties in order to enhance what is
given to them but so far they have not created but destroyed. Forests are ever fewer and fewer, rivers dry up, wildlife is wiped out,
the climate is spoiled, and every day the earth grows more impoverished and ugly. (*To* VOINITSKY.) There you go, staring at me sarcastically, nothing I say is taken seriously, and . . . and, maybe I
am talking like a crackpot, but, when I walk through the peasants'
forests that I have saved from being chopped down, or when I hear
the wind rustling in my stand of saplings, planted by my own
hands, I realize that the climate is to some slight degree in my
control, and if, a thousand years from now, humanity is happy,
then I will be partially responsible. When I plant a birch tree, and
then see how it grows green and sways in the wind, my soul swells
with pride, and I . . . (*Having seen* THE WORKMAN, *who brings in a
shot of vodka on a tray.*) Anyway . . . (*Drinks.*) My time's up. This
is, most likely, crackpot talk, when's all said and done. And so I
take my leave! (*Goes to the house.*)

SONYA (*Takes him by the arm and accompanies him.*)   When *are* you
coming back to see us?

ASTROV   Don't know . . .

SONYA   A whole month again? . . .

>   (ASTROV *and* SONYA *go into the house.* MARIYA VASILYEVNA *and*
>   TELEGIN *remain near the table.* YELENA ANDREEVNA *and* VOIN-
>   ITSKY *walk towards the veranda.*)

YELENA ANDREEVNA   Well, Ivan Petrovich, you behaved impossibly
again. You had to provoke Mariya Vasilyevna with talk about perpetual motion! And today after lunch you picked a fight with Aleksandr again. It's all so petty!

VOINITSKY   And what if I hate him?

YELENA ANDREEVNA   There's no point in hating Aleksandr, he's the
same as anybody else. No worse than you.

VOINITSKY   If you could see your face, your movements . . . What an
indolent life you lead! Ah, the indolence of it!

YELENA ANDREEVNA   Ah, indolent and boring as well! Everyone
insults my husband, everyone is so sympathetic with me: unhappy
creature, she's got an old husband! This compassion for me—oh,
how well I understand it! It's what Astrov was saying just now: you
all recklessly chop down forests, and soon nothing will be left on
earth. The very same way you recklessly destroy a human being,
and soon, thanks to you, there won't be any loyalty or purity or

capacity for self-sacrifice left on earth. Why can't you look at a
woman with indifference if she isn't yours? Because—that doctor's
right—inside all of you there lurks a demon of destruction. You
have no pity for forests or birds or women or one another . . .

VOINITSKY   I don't like this philosophizing!

(*Pause.*)

YELENA ANDREEVNA   That doctor has a weary, sensitive face. An
interesting face. Sonya, it's obvious, likes him, she's in love with
him, and I understand why. Since I've been here, he's dropped by
three times now, but I'm inhibited and haven't once had a proper
chat with him, didn't show him much affection. He went away
thinking I'm ill tempered. No doubt, Ivan Petrovich, that's why
we're such friends, you and I; we're both exasperating, tiresome
people! Exasperating! Don't look at me that way, I don't like it.

VOINITSKY   How else can I look at you if I love you? You're my happiness, life, my youth! I know, my chances of reciprocity are minute, practically nil, but I don't want anything; just let me look at
you, hear your voice . . .

YELENA ANDREEVNA   Hush, they can hear you! (*Goes into the house.*)

VOINITSKY (*Following her.*)   Let me talk about my love, don't drive
me away, and that alone will be my greatest joy . . .

YELENA ANDREEVNA   This is agony . . .

(*They go into the house.*)

(TELEGIN *strums the strings and plays a polka;* MARIYA VASI-
LYEVNA *jots a note in the margin of the pamphlet.*)

CURTAIN

Act Two

The dining room in SEREBRYAKOV's *house.—Night.—We can hear* THE
WATCHMAN *tapping in the garden.*[6]

(SEREBRYAKOV *sits in an armchair before an open window and
drowses; and* YELENA ANDREEVNA *sits beside him and drowses
too.*)

SEREBRYAKOV (*Waking.*)   Who's there? Sonya, you?

YELENA ANDREEVNA   I'm here.

SEREBRYAKOV   You, Lenochka . . . The pain's unbearable!

YELENA ANDREEVNA   Your lap rug's fallen on the floor. (*Wraps up his
legs.*) Aleksandr, I'll close the window.

SEREBRYAKOV   No, I'm suffocating . . . I just now started to doze off
and dreamed that my left leg belonged to somebody else. I woke

6. See *Ivanov*, note 9, page 37.

up with the agonizing pain. No, it isn't gout, more like rheumatism.
What's the time now?

YELENA ANDREEVNA   Twenty past twelve.

(*Pause.*)

SEREBRYAKOV   In the morning, see if we've got a Batyushkov[7] in the
library. I think we have him.

YELENA ANDREEVNA   Huh? . . .

SEREBRYAKOV   Look for Batyushkov's poems in the morning. I seem
to remember we had a copy. But why am I finding it so hard to
breathe?

YELENA ANDREEVNA   You were tired. Second night without sleep.

SEREBRYAKOV   They say that Turgenev had gout that developed into
angina pectoris.[8] I'm afraid I may have it too. Wretched, repulsive
old age. Damn it to hell. When I got old, I began to disgust myself.
Yes, and all the rest of you, I daresay, are disgusted to look at me.

YELENA ANDREEVNA   You talk about your old age as if it was our fault
you're old.

SEREBRYAKOV   You're the first one to be disgusted by me.

(YELENA ANDREEVNA *moves away and sits at a distance.*)
Of course, you're in the right. I'm no fool and I understand. You're
young, healthy, beautiful, enjoy life, while I'm an old man, practically a corpse. That's it, isn't it? Have I got it right? And, of
course, it was stupid of me to live this long. But wait awhile, I'll
soon liberate you all. I can't manage to hang on much longer.

YELENA ANDREEVNA   I'm worn out . . . For God's sake be quiet.

SEREBRYAKOV   It turns out that thanks to me you're all worn out,
bored, wasting your youth, I'm the only one enjoying life and
having a good time. Oh yes, of course!

YELENA ANDREEVNA   Do be quiet! You've run me ragged!

SEREBRYAKOV   I've run all of you ragged. Of course.

YELENA ANDREEVNA (*Through tears.*)   This is unbearable! Say it, what
do you want from me?

SEREBRYAKOV   Not a thing.

YELENA ANDREEVNA   Well then, be quiet. For pity's sake.

SEREBRYAKOV   Funny, isn't it? Let Ivan Petrovich start talking or that
old she-idiot Mariya Vasilyevna—and nothing happens, everyone
listens, but let me say just one word, watch how they all start
feeling sorry for themselves. Even my voice is disgusting. Well,
suppose I am disgusting, I'm selfish, I'm a tyrant—but surely in

---

7. Konstantin Nikolaevich Batyushkov (1787–1855), Russian Romantic poet, an immediate
forerunner of Pushkin and author of the best Anacreontic verse in Russian. Evidently the
Professor wants to read about wine, woman, and song.

8. Latin for "a frog on the chest." Severe chest pain caused by deficient oxygenation of the
heart muscles. The novelist Ivan Turgenev (1818–1883), who suffered from gout, actually
died of spinal cancer.

my old age haven't I got a right to be selfish? Surely I've earned it? Surely, I ask you, I've earned the right to a peaceful old age, to have people pay me some attention?

YELENA ANDREEVNA   No one is disputing your rights. (*The window rattles in the wind.*) The wind's rising, I'll close the window. (*Closes it.*) It'll rain presently. No one is disputing your rights.

(*Pause.* THE WATCHMAN *in the garden taps and sings a song.*)

SEREBRYAKOV   To labor all one's life in the cause of learning, to grow accustomed to one's study, to the lecture hall, to esteemed colleagues—and suddenly, with no rhyme or reason, to find oneself in this mausoleum, to spend every day seeing stupid people, listening to trivial chitchat . . . I want to live, I love success, I love celebrity, fame, and here—it's like being in exile. Every minute yearning for the past, watching the successes of others, fearing death . . . I can't do it! I haven't got the strength! And on top of that they won't forgive me my old age!

YELENA ANDREEVNA   Wait, be patient! In five or six years I too shall be old.

(*Enter* SONYA.)

SONYA   Papa, you specifically asked us to send for Doctor Astrov, and when he came, you refused to let him in. That is discourteous. To disturb a man for no reason . . .

SEREBRYAKOV   What do I care about your Astrov? He understands as much about medicine as I do about astronomy.

SONYA   Just for your gout, we can't send for a whole medical school.

SEREBRYAKOV   I won't even give that maniac[9] the time of day.

SONYA   Have it your way. (*Sits.*) It's all the same to me.

SEREBRYAKOV   What's the time now?

YELENA ANDREEVNA   Past twelve.

SEREBRYAKOV   It's stifling . . . Sonya, get me the drops from the table!

SONYA   Right away. (*Gives him the drops.*)

SEREBRYAKOV (*Aggravated.*)   Ah, not those! A person can't ask for a thing!

SONYA   Please don't be crotchety. Some people may care for it, but don't try it on me, for goodness' sake! I do not like it. And I have no time, I have to get up early tomorrow, I have hay to mow.

(*Enter* VOINITSKY *in a dressing gown, holding a candle.*)

VOINITSKY   Outside there's a storm brewing. (*Lightning.*) Clear out now! Hélène and Sonya, go to bed. I've come to take over for you.

SEREBRYAKOV (*Terrified.*)   No, no! Don't leave me with him! No. He'll talk me blue in the face.

9. In the original, *yurodivy*, a holy fool, a feebleminded beggar considered to be touched by God and hence licensed to speak the truth.

VOINITSKY But they've got to get some rest! This is the second night they've had no sleep.

SEREBRYAKOV Let them go to bed, but you go away too. Thank you. I implore you. For the sake of our former friendship, don't protest. We'll talk later.

VOINITSKY (*With a sneer.*) Our *former* friendship . . . Former . . .

SONYA Be quiet, Uncle Vanya.

SEREBRYAKOV (*To his wife.*) My dear, don't leave me alone with him! He'll talk me blue in the face!

VOINITSKY This is starting to get ridiculous.

(*Enter* MARINA *with a candle.*)

SONYA You should be in bed, nanny dear. It's very late.

MARINA The samovar's not cleared from the table. Not likely a body'd be in bed.

SEREBRYAKOV Nobody sleeps, everybody's worn out; I'm the only one who's deliriously happy.

MARINA (*Walks over to* SEREBRYAKOV; *tenderly.*) What is it, dearie? Achy? These legs o'mine got twinges too, such twinges. (*Adjusts the lap rug.*) This complaint o'yours goes back a long ways. Vera Petrovna, rest in peace, little Sonya's mother could never sleep nights, wasting away . . . Oh, how she loved you.

(*Pause.*)

Old folks're like little 'uns, they want a body to feel sorry for 'em, but old folks got no one to feel sorry for 'em. (*Kisses* SEREBRYAKOV *on the shoulder.*[1]) Let's go, dearie, bedtime . . . Let's go, my sunshine . . . Some limeflower tea I'll brew for you, your li'l legs I'll warm . . . God I'll pray to for you . . .

SEREBRYAKOV (*Moved.*) Let's go, Marina.

MARINA These legs o'mine got twinges too, such twinges. (*Leads him with* SONYA's *help.*) Vera Petrovna never stopped wasting away, never stopped crying . . . You, Sonya darlin', were just a little 'un then, a silly . . . Come, come, dearie . . .

(SEREBRYAKOV, SONYA, *and* MARINA *leave.*)

YELENA ANDREEVNA I've worried myself sick over him. Can hardly stand on my feet.

VOINITSKY He makes you sick and I make myself sick. This is the third night now I haven't slept.

YELENA ANDREEVNA There's something oppressive about this house. Your mother hates everything except her pamphlets and the Professor; the Professor is irritable, won't trust me, is afraid of you;

1. A traditional form of greeting used by inferiors to their betters that survived from the days of serfdom.

Sonya's nasty to her father, nasty to me, and hasn't spoken to me for two weeks now; you hate my husband and openly despise your mother; I'm irritable and today some twenty times I was ready to burst into tears . . . There's something oppressive about this house.

VOINITSKY   Let's drop the philosophizing!

YELENA ANDREEVNA   Ivan Petrovich, you're an educated, intelligent man; I should think you'd understand that the world is being destroyed not by criminals, not by fires, but by hatred, animosities, all this petty bickering . . . You shouldn't be growling, you should be bringing everyone together.

VOINITSKY   First bring the two of us together! My darling . . . (*Clutches her hand.*)

YELENA ANDREEVNA   Stop it! (*Extricates her hand.*) Go away!

VOINITSKY   Any moment now the rain will end, and everything in nature will be refreshed and breathe easy. I'll be the only thing not refreshed by the storm. Day and night, like an incubus, the idea chokes me that my life has been wasted irretrievably. I've got no past; it's been stupidly squandered on trivialities, and the present is horrible in its absurdity. Here, take my life and my love; what am *I* to do with them? My better feelings are fading away for no reason at all, like a sunbeam trapped at the bottom of a mineshaft, and I'm fading along with them.

YELENA ANDREEVNA   Whenever you talk to me about your love, it's as if I go numb and don't know what to say. Forgive me, there's nothing I can say to you. (*About to go.*) Good-night.

VOINITSKY   (*Blocks her path.*)   And if only you had any idea how I suffer at the thought that right beside me in this house another life is fading away—yours! What are you waiting for? What damned philosophizing stands in your way? Seize the day, seize it . . .

YELENA ANDREEVNA   (*Stares fixedly at him.*)   Ivan Petrovich, you're drunk!

VOINITSKY   Could be, could be . . .

YELENA ANDREEVNA   Where's the doctor?

VOINITSKY   He's in there . . . spending the night in my room. Could be, could be . . . Anything could be!

YELENA ANDREEVNA   So you were drinking today? What for?

VOINITSKY   It makes me feel alive somehow . . . Don't stop me, Hélène!

YELENA ANDREEVNA   You never used to drink and you never used to talk so much . . . Go to bed! You're boring me.

VOINITSKY   (*Clutching her hand.*)   My darling . . . wonderful woman!

YELENA ANDREEVNA   (*Annoyed.*)   Leave me alone. Once and for all, this is disgusting. (*Exits.*)

VOINITSKY (*Alone.*)   She walked out on me . . . (*Pause.*) Ten years ago I met her at my poor sister's. Then she was seventeen and I was thirty-seven. Why didn't I fall in love with her then and propose to her? After all, it could have been! And now she'd be my wife . . . Yes . . . Now both of us would be awakened by the storm; she'd be frightened by the thunder and I'd hold her in my arms and whisper, "Don't be afraid, I'm here." Oh, marvelous thoughts, wonderful, it makes me laugh . . . but, my God, the thoughts are snarled up in my head . . . Why am I old? Why doesn't she understand me? Her speechifying, indolent morality, indolent drivel about destroying the world—it makes me profoundly sick.

(*Pause.*)

Oh, how I've been cheated! I idolized that professor, that pathetic martyr to gout, I worked for him like a beast of burden! Sonya and I squeezed every last drop out of this estate; like grasping peasants, we drove a trade in vegetable oil, peas, cottage cheese; stinted ourselves on crumbs so we could scrape together the pennies and small change into thousands and send them to him. I was proud of him and his learning; I lived, I breathed for him! Everything he wrote or uttered seemed to me to emanate from genius . . . God, and now? Now that he's retired you can see what his whole life adds up to: when he goes, not a single page of his work will endure; he is utterly unknown, he's nothing! A soap bubble! And I've been cheated . . . I see it—stupidly cheated . . .

(*Enter* ASTROV *in a frockcoat without a waistcoat or necktie; he is tipsy;* TELEGIN *follows him with a guitar.*)

ASTROV   Play!

TELEGIN   They're all asleep, sir!

ASTROV   Play!

(TELEGIN *plays quietly.*)

ASTROV (*To* VOINITSKY.)   You alone here? No ladies? (*Arms akimbo, sings softly.*) "My shack is fled, my fire is dead, I've got no place to lay my head . . ."[2] Well, the storm woke *me* up. An impressive little downpour. What's the time now?

VOINITSKY   How the hell should I know?

ASTROV   Could have sworn I heard the voice of Yelena Andreevna.

VOINITSKY   She was here a moment ago.

ASTROV   Magnificent woman. (*Spots the medicine bottles on the table.*) Medicine. Prescriptions galore! From Kharkov, from Moscow, from Tula . . . Every town in Russia must be fed up with his gout. Is he sick or faking?

2. A folk song.

VOINITSKY   Sick.

(*Pause.*)

ASTROV   Why're you so sad today? Sorry for the Professor or what?

VOINITSKY   Leave me alone.

ASTROV   Or else, maybe, in love with Mrs. Professor?

VOINITSKY   She's my friend.

ASTROV   Already?

VOINITSKY   What's that mean—already?

ASTROV   A woman can be a man's friend only in the following sequence: first, an acquaintance; next, a mistress; and thereafter a friend.

VOINITSKY   A vulgar philosophy.

ASTROV   What? Yes . . . Have to admit—I am turning vulgar. Y'see, I'm even drunk. Ordinarily I drink like this once a month. When I'm in this state, I become insolent and impertinent to the nth degree. Then nothing fazes me! I take on the most intricate operations and perform them beautifully; I outline the broadest plans for the future; at times like that, I stop thinking of myself as a crackpot and believe that I'm doing humanity a stupendous favor . . . stupendous! And at times like that, I have my own personal philosophy, and all of you, my little brothers, seem to me to be tiny insects . . . microbes. (*To* TELEGIN.) Waffles, play!

TELEGIN   Dearest friend, I'd be glad to play for you with all my heart, but bear in mind—the family's asleep!

ASTROV   Play!

(TELEGIN *plays quietly.*)

ASTROV   A drink's what I need. Let's go back in; I think we've still got some cognac left. And when it's light, we'll head over to my place. Want to go for a rod? I've got an orderly[3] who never says "ride," always says, "rod."[4] Terrible crook. So, want to go for a rod? (*Seeing* SONYA *enter.*) 'Scuse me, I'm not wearing a tie. (*Quickly exits;* TELEGIN *follows him.*)

SONYA   So, Uncle Vanya, you and the Doctor got drunk together again. Birds of a feather flock together. Well, he's always been like that, but why should you? At your age it doesn't suit you at all.

VOINITSKY   Age has nothing to do with it. When there's no real life, people live on illusions. After all it's better than nothing.

SONYA   All our hay is mown, it rains every day, everything's rotting, and you're obsessed with illusions. You've given up farming for

3. *Feldsher* (from the German, *Feldscher*, an assistant medical officer), a medical attendant without a doctor's degree; in rural areas of Russia, the *feldsher* often stood in for a licensed physician.

4. In Russian, the wordplay is on *idet,* "let's go, let's pay a visit" and *idyot,* which sounds like *idiot,* "imbecile," a joke Chekhov often used privately, especially in letters to his brother Aleksandr.

good . . . I'm the only one working, I'm completely worn out . . . (*Alarmed.*) Uncle, there are tears in your eyes!

VOINITSKY   What tears? Nothing of the sort . . . don't be silly . . . Just now the way you looked like your poor mother. My precious . . . (*Avidly kisses her hands and face.*) My dear sister . . . my darling sister . . . Where is she now? If only she knew! Ah, if only she knew!

SONYA   What? Uncle, knew what?

VOINITSKY   Oppressive, wrong . . . Never mind . . . Later . . . Never mind . . . I'm going . . . (*Goes.*)

SONYA (*Knocks on the door.*)   Mikhail Lvovich! Are you asleep? May I see you for a moment!

ASTROV (*Behind the door.*)   Right away! (*After a slight delay, he enters; he is now wearing a waistcoat and a necktie.*) What can I do for you?

SONYA   Go ahead and drink, if it doesn't make you sick, but, please, don't let Uncle drink. It's no good for him.

ASTROV   Fine. We won't drink any more. (*Pause.*) I'll go home right now. No sooner said than done. By the time the horses are hitched, dawn'll be coming up.

SONYA   It's raining. Wait 'til morning.

ASTROV   The storm's passing over, we'll only catch the tail end of it. I'm going. And, please, do not invite me to visit your father any more. I tell him it's gout, and he says it's rheumatism; I ask him to lie down, he sits up. And today he wouldn't even see me.

SONYA   He's spoiled. (*Looks in the sideboard.*) Would you like a bite to eat?

ASTROV   I suppose so, sure.

SONYA   I love midnight snacks. I think there's something in the sideboard. In his lifetime, they say, he was a great success with women, and the ladies have spoiled him. Here, have some cheese.
    (*Both stand at the sideboard and eat.*)

ASTROV   I didn't eat a thing today, just drank. Your father has a oppressive nature. (*Gets a bottle from the sideboard.*) May I? (*Drinks a shot.*) There's nobody around, so a man can speak frankly. You know, I have the feeling I wouldn't last a month in your house, I'd suffocate in this atmosphere . . . Your father, all wrapped up in his gout and his books, Uncle Vanya with his biliousness, your grandmother, lastly your stepmother . . .

SONYA   What about my stepmother?

ASTROV   Everything about a human being ought to be beautiful: face, dress, soul, ideas. She's the fairest in the land,[5] no argument

---

5. Literally, "Fair is she," an allusion to the "Tale of the Tsar's Dead Daughter and the Seven Warriors," a Russian version of "Snow White" by Aleksandr Pushkin (1833). The evil

there, but . . . all she does is eat, sleep, go for walks, enchant us all with her beauty—and that's it. She has no responsibilities, others work for her . . . Am I right? And a life of idleness cannot be pure.

(*Pause.*)

Anyway, maybe I'm being too hard on her. I'm dissatisfied with life same as your Uncle Vanya, and we're both turning into grouches.

SONYA So you're dissatisfied with life?

ASTROV Life in the abstract I love, but our life, rural, Russian, humdrum, I cannot stand, and I despise it with every fiber of my being. And as to my own private life, honest to God, there's absolutely nothing good about it. You know how, when you walk through a forest on a dark night, if all the time in the distance there's a glimmer of light, you don't mind the fatigue or the dark or the prickly branches hitting you in the face . . . I work—as you know—harder than anyone else in the district, fate never stops hitting me in the face, at times I suffer unbearably, but in the distance there's no light glimmering for me. I've stopped expecting anything for myself, I don't love people . . . For a long time now I've loved no one.

SONYA No one?

ASTROV No one. I do feel a certain affection for your dear old nanny—for old time's sake. The peasants are very monotonous, backward, they live in filth; and it's hard to get on with educated people. They're tedious. All of them, our good friends and acquaintances, think petty thoughts, feel petty feelings, and don't see beyond their noses—fools, plain and simple. And the ones who are a bit cleverer and a bit more earnest are hysterical, hung up on categories and clichés . . . Their sort whines, foments hatred, spreads contagious slander; they sidle up to a man, peer at him out of the corner of their eye and decide, "Oh, he's a psychopath!" or "He's a windbag!" And when they don't know what label to stick on my brow, they say, "He's weird, really weird!" I love forests— that's weird; I don't eat meat—that's weird too. A spontaneous, unpolluted, open relationship to nature and human beings no longer exists . . . Oh no, no! (*Is about to drink.*)

SONYA (*Stops him.*)   No, for my sake, please, don't drink anymore.

ASTROV Why not?

Tsarina turns to her mirror with the question whether she is really the fairest in the land, and the mirror replies, "Fair art thou, no contest there; but the Tsar's daughter's still more fair . . ."

ACT TWO

SONYA It's so out of character for you! You're refined, you have such a gentle voice . . . Besides, you, unlike anyone I know—you're beautiful. Why do you want to be like ordinary people who drink and play cards? Oh, don't do that, for my sake! You're always saying that people don't create, they only destroy what is given them from on high. Why then are you destroying yourself? You mustn't, you mustn't, I beg you, I implore you.

ASTROV (*Extends a hand to her.*) I won't drink anymore.

SONYA Give me your word.

ASTROV Word of honor.

SONYA (*Squeezes his hand firmly.*) Thank you!

ASTROV *Basta!*[6] I've sobered up. You see, I'm quite sober and will remain so to the end of my days. (*Looks at his watch.*) Well now, let's proceed. As I was saying: my time's long gone, it's too late for me . . . I'm growing old, overworked, coarsened, all my feelings are numb, and I don't believe I could form an attachment to anyone any more. I love no one and . . . have stopped falling in love. What still gets through to me is beauty. I'm not indifferent to it. It seems to me that if Yelena Andreevna here wanted to, she could turn my head in no time at all . . . But of course that's not love, not affection . . . (*Covers his eyes with his hand and shudders.*)

SONYA What's wrong?

ASTROV Just . . . In Lent, a patient of mine died under the chloroform.

SONYA It's time to forget that. (*Pause.*) Tell me, Mikhail Lvovich . . . If I happened to have a girl friend or a younger sister, and you were to learn that she . . . well, let's suppose, she loves you, how would you deal with that?

ASTROV (*With a shrug.*) I don't know, nohow, I suppose. I'd let her understand that I could not love her . . . besides, it's not the sort of thing that's on my mind. Anyway, if I'm to go, the time's come. Good-bye, my dear, otherwise we'll be at it 'til morning. (*Presses her hand.*) I'll go through the parlor, if you don't mind, or else I'm afraid your uncle will detain me. (*Exits.*)

SONYA (*Alone.*) He didn't say anything to me . . . His heart and soul are still hidden from me, so why do I feel so happy? (*Laughs with delight.*) I said to him: you're refined, noble, you have such a gentle voice . . . Was that uncalled for? His voice throbs, caresses . . . I can feel it here in the air. And when I mentioned a younger sister, he didn't understand . . . (*Wringing her hands.*) Oh, it's an awful thing to be unattractive! Simply awful! And I know I'm unattractive, I know, I know . . . Last Sunday, when we were coming out of church, I heard the way they talked about me, and one woman

6. Italian, "enough."

said, "She's kind and good-natured, what a pity she's so unattractive . . ." Unattractive . . .

(*Enter* YELENA ANDREEVNA.)

YELENA ANDREEVNA (*Opens a window.*) The storm has passed. What lovely air! (*Pause.*) Where's the doctor?

SONYA Gone. (*Pause.*)

YELENA ANDREEVNA *Sophie!*

SONYA What?

YELENA ANDREEVNA How long are you going to keep glowering at me? We haven't done one another any harm. Why do we have to be enemies? Enough is enough.

SONYA I wanted to myself . . . (*Embraces her.*) No more tantrums.

YELENA ANDREEVNA Splendid.

(*Both are agitated.*)

SONYA Is Papa in bed?

YELENA ANDREEVNA No, he's sitting in the parlor . . . We don't talk to one another for weeks on end and God knows why . . . (*Noticing the open sideboard.*) What's this?

SONYA Mikhail Lvovich had some supper.

YELENA ANDREEVNA And there's some wine . . . Let's pledge one another as sisters.[7]

SONYA Let's.

YELENA ANDREEVNA Out of the same glass . . . (*Pours.*) That's better. Well, here goes—friends?

SONYA Friends.[8] (*They drink and kiss.*) For a long time now I've wanted to make it up, but somehow I was embarrassed . . . (*Weeps.*)

YELENA ANDREEVNA What are you crying for?

SONYA No reason; it's the way I am.

YELENA ANDREEVNA Well, never mind, never mind . . . (*Weeps.*) You little crackpot,[9] now you've got me crying . . .

(*Pause.*)

You're angry with me because you think I married your father for ulterior motives . . . If you'll believe an oath, I'll swear to you—I married him for love. I was attracted to him as a scholar and a celebrity. The love was unreal, artificial, but at the time I thought it was real. It's not my fault. But from the day we got married, you've gone on punishing me with your shrewd, suspicious eyes.

SONYA Well, truce, truce! We'll put it behind us.

---

7. In the original, Yelena Andreevna uses the German word *Bruderschaft*, "brotherhood" or "fellowship." They are pledging, arms linked, out of one glass, like fraternity brothers.
8. Literally, *na ty*, meaning their relationship will now be on a "thou" basis, rather than the formal "you."
9. Yelena has picked one of Astrov's favorite words; she's clearly been listening to him.

YELENA ANDREEVNA   You mustn't look at people that way—it doesn't suit you. You must trust everyone; otherwise life becomes unlivable.
        (*Pause.*)

SONYA   Tell me truthfully, friend to friend . . . Are you happy?

YELENA ANDREEVNA   No.

SONYA   I knew that. One more question. Tell me frankly—would you like to have a young husband?

YELENA ANDREEVNA   What a little girl you are still. Of course I would! (*Laughs.*) Go on, ask me something else, ask me . . .

SONYA   Do you like the Doctor?

YELENA ANDREEVNA   Yes, very much.

SONYA (*Laughs.*)   I have a funny face . . . don't I? Now he's gone, but I keep hearing his voice and footsteps, and I look out the dark window—and his face appears to me. Let me say what's on my mind . . . But I can't say it out loud, I'm embarrassed. Let's go to my room, we'll talk there. Do you think I'm being silly? Admit it . . . Tell me something about him . . .

YELENA ANDREEVNA   Such as?

SONYA   He's intelligent . . . He knows how to do everything, can do everything . . . He practices medicine and plants forests . . .

YELENA ANDREEVNA   Forests and medicine have nothing to do with it . . . Darling, what you have to understand is, he's got talent![1] Do you know the meaning of talent? Daring, an uncluttered mind, breadth of vision . . . He plants a tree and already he's planning ahead, what the result will be in a thousand years, he's already imagining the happiness of generations to come. People like that are rare, one must love them . . . He drinks, he's uncouth—but what's the harm in that? A talented man in Russia cannot be a puritan. Just consider the life this doctor leads! Mud up to his waist on the roads; frosts; blizzards; vast distances; coarse, savage people; all-around poverty; disease; and it's hard for a man working and struggling in surroundings like that day after day to reach the age of forty spotless and sober . . . (*Kisses her.*) I wish you happiness from the bottom of my heart, you deserve it . . . (*Rises.*) But mine is a dreary walk-on part . . . In the field of music and in my husband's house, in any of life's dramas—no matter where, in short, I've only had a walk-on part. Personally speaking, Sonya, when you think about it, I'm very, very unhappy! (*Walks nervously around the stage.*) No happiness for me in this world. No! Why are you laughing?

1. "Talent" is one of Chekhov's favorite words of praise, equivalent almost to "genius." His characters name it as a positive quality, when they are otherwise unable to specify someone's virtues. The opposite is "untalented."

SONYA (*Laughs, covering her face.*)   I'm so happy . . . happy!

YELENA ANDREEVNA   I'd like to play the piano . . . I want to play something right now.

SONYA   Do play. (*Embraces her.*) I can't sleep. Play.

YELENA ANDREEVNA   Presently. Your father isn't asleep. When he's ill, music irritates him. Go and ask. If he doesn't object, I'll play. Go on.

SONYA   Right this minute. (*Exits.*)

(*In the garden,* THE WATCHMAN *is tapping.*)

YELENA ANDREEVNA   It's been a long time since I played. I'll play and weep, weep like a fool. (*Out the window.*) Is that you tapping, Yefim?

WATCHMAN'S VOICE   It's me!

YELENA ANDREEVNA   Don't tap; the master's not well.

WATCHMAN'S VOICE   I'll go right now! (*Whistles under his breath.*) Here, boys, Blackie, Laddie! Blackie!²

(*Pause.*)

SONYA (*Returning.*)   The answer's no!

CURTAIN

Act Three

Parlor in SEREBRYAKOV'S *house. Three doors: right, left, and center.—Daytime.* VOINITSKY *and* SONYA *are sitting;* YELENA ANDREEVNA *walks about the stage with something on her mind.*

VOINITSKY   Herr Professor has graciously expressed the desire that today we all congregate in this parlor at one o'clock P.M. (*Looks at his watch.*) A quarter to one. He's got something he wants to tell the world.

YELENA ANDREEVNA   Probably some business matter.

VOINITSKY   He has no business. He writes drivel, moans and groans, and oozes envy, that's all.

SONYA (*Reproachfully.*)   Uncle!

VOINITSKY   All right, sorry. (*Indicates* YELENA ANDREEVNA.) Wonder at her: she can't walk without tottering from sheer indolence. Very charming! Very!

YELENA ANDREEVNA   All you do all day is buzz, buzz—how come you don't get sick of it! (*Languorously.*) I'm dying of boredom, I don't know what I'm to do.

2. *Zhuchka*, from *zhuk*, beetle, a common name for a black dog.

SONYA (*Shrugging.*) How about a little work? Only the lady has to make an effort.

YELENA ANDREEVNA For instance?

SONYA Get involved in running the farm, teach, tend the sick. Isn't that enough? Around here, before you and Papa arrived, Uncle Vanya and I used to go to the fair ourselves to market the flour.

YELENA ANDREEVNA I don't know how. Besides, it's not interesting. Only in social-purpose novels do people teach and tend peasants, and how am I, out of the blue, supposed to go tend them or teach them?

SONYA But then I can't understand what's prevents you from going and teaching them. After a while it'll become second nature. (*Embraces her.*) Don't be bored, dear. (*Laughs.*) You're bored; you can't find a niche for yourself, but boredom and idleness are catching. Look: Uncle Vanya does nothing but follow you around, like a shadow; I've given up my chores and come running to you for a chat. I've got lazy, I can't help it! The Doctor used to stay with us very seldom, once a month, it wasn't easy to ask him, but now he rides over every day, he's abandoned his forests and his medicine. You must be a witch.

VOINITSKY Why are you mooning about? (*Vigorously.*) Come, my elegant darling, show how clever you are! The blood of water nymphs courses through your veins, be a water-nymph! Satisfy your desires at least once in your life, fall in love as fast as you can, head over heels, with some water sprite[3]—plop! take a nose-dive into a whirlpool, so that Herr Professor and the rest of us throw up our hands in amazement!

YELENA ANDREEVNA (*Angrily.*) Leave me alone! This is sadistic! (*About to go.*)

VOINITSKY (*Doesn't let her go.*) There, there, my sweet, forgive me . . . I apologize. (*Kisses her hands.*) Truce.

YELENA ANDREEVNA You'd try the patience of a saint, you must admit.

VOINITSKY As a token of peace and harmony, I'll bring you a bouquet of roses this very minute; I put it together for you this morning . . . Autumnal roses—superb, mournful roses . . . (*Exits.*)

SONYA Autumnal roses—superb, mournful roses . . .
      (*Both women look out the window.*)

YELENA ANDREEVNA Here it is September already. How are we to get through the winter here?
      (*Pause.*)

3. A water-nymph or *rusalka* is not a mermaid, for although she is dangerous and sexy, she is also undead, usually the spirit of a drowned girl. A water sprite or *vodovoy* is more benign, the aquatic equivalent of a wood sprite or *leshy*. Astrov can be considered a wood sprite.

Where's the doctor?

SONYA   In Uncle Vanya's room. He's writing something. I'm glad
Uncle Vanya went out, I have to talk to you.

YELENA ANDREEVNA   What about?

SONYA   What about? (*Lays her head on* YELENA's *breast*.)

YELENA ANDREEVNA   There, there . . . (*Smoothes* SONYA's *hair*.)
That'll do.

SONYA   I'm unattractive.

YELENA ANDREEVNA   You have beautiful hair.

SONYA   No! (*Looks around to view herself in a mirror*.) No! Whenever
a woman's unattractive, they tell her, "You have beautiful eyes,
you have beautiful hair!" . . . I've loved him now for six years, love
him more than my own mother; every minute I can hear him, feel
the pressure of his hand; and I stare at the door and wait, I get
the sense he's just about to walk in. There, you see, I keep coming
to you to talk about him. He's here every day now, but he doesn't
look at me, doesn't see . . . It's so painful! There's no hope at all,
no, none! (*In despair*.) Oh, God, my strength is gone . . . I was up
all night praying . . . Lots of times I'll walk up to him, start to
speak, look him in the eyes . . . I've got no pride left, no willpower
. . . I couldn't help it and yesterday I confessed to Uncle Vanya
that I love him . . . Even all the servants know I love him. Everyone
knows.

YELENA ANDREEVNA   Does he?

SONYA   No. He doesn't notice me.

YELENA ANDREEVNA   (*Musing*.)   A weird sort of man . . . You know
what? Let me talk to him . . . I'll be discreet, I'll hint . . . (*Pause*.)
Honestly, how long can a person go on not knowing . . . Let me!
(SONYA *nods her head yes*.) That's splendid. Whether or not he's in
love shouldn't be too hard to find out. Now don't be embarrassed,
my pet, don't be upset—I'll question him discreetly, he won't even
notice. All we have to find out is: yes or no? (*Pause*.) If no, then
he should stop coming here. Right? (SONYA *nods her head yes*.) It's
easier when you don't see him. We won't file and forget it, we'll
question him right now. He was planning to show me some drawings . . . Go and tell him I'd like to see him.

SONYA   (*Intensely excited*.)   You'll tell me the whole truth?

YELENA ANDREEVNA   Yes, of course. I should think that the truth,
whatever it turns out to be, is nowhere near as awful as not knowing. Depend on me, my pet.

SONYA   Yes, yes . . . I'll say that you want to see his charts . . . (*Goes
but stops near the door*.) No, not knowing is better . . . Then there's
hope . . .

YELENA ANDREEVNA   What's that?

SONYA   Nothing. (*Exits*.)

YELENA ANDREEVNA (*Alone.*)   Nothing's worse than knowing someone else's secret and being unable to help. (*Pondering.*) He's not
in love with her—that's obvious, but why shouldn't he marry her?
She's no beauty, but for a country doctor, at his age, she'd make
a fine wife. A good head on her shoulders, so kind, unspoiled . . .
No, that's not it, that's not it . . . (*Pause.*) I understand the poor
girl. In the midst of howling boredom, when all she sees prowling
around her are gray blurs, not people, all she hears are banalities,
all they know is eating, drinking, sleeping; once in a while he'll
show up, different from the others, handsome, interesting, attractive, like a full moon emerging from dark clouds . . . To yield to
the embrace of such a man, to forget oneself . . . Apparently I'm
a wee bit attracted myself. Yes, when he's not here, I'm bored—
look, I'm smiling as I think about him . . . Uncle Vanya was saying
the blood of water-nymphs courses through my veins. "Satisfy your
desires at least once in your life" . . . Should I? Maybe I have to.
. . . If I could fly like an uncaged bird away from you all, from your
drowsy expressions, from idle chatter, forget your very existence
on earth . . . But I'm a coward, inhibited . . . I'm having an attack
of conscience . . . There, he shows up every day, I can guess why
he's here, and I'm starting to feel guilty; any minute now I'll drop
to my knees and beg Sonya's forgiveness, burst into tears . . .

ASTROV (*Enters with a diagram.*)   Good afternoon! (*Shakes her
hand.*) You wanted to see my drawing?

YELENA ANDREEVNA   Yesterday you promised to show me your work
. . . You're free?

ASTROV   Oh, definitely. (*Unrolls the diagram on a card table and fas-
tens it with thumb tacks.*) Where were you born?

YELENA ANDREEVNA (*Helping him.*)   In Petersburg.

ASTROV   And educated?

YELENA ANDREEVNA   At the Conservatory.[4]

ASTROV   Then you'll probably find this uninteresting.

YELENA ANDREEVNA   Why? True, I'm not familiar with country life,
but I've read quite a lot.

ASTROV   Here in the house I have my own table . . . In Ivan Petrovich's room. When I'm utterly exhausted, to the point of total leth-
argy, I drop everything and hurry over here, and then I amuse
myself with this stuff for an hour or two . . . Ivan Petrovich and
Sofiya Aleksandrovna plug away at the accounts, while I sit next
them at my table and putter—and I feel warm, relaxed, and the
cricket chirps. But I don't allow myself this indulgence very often,
once a month . . . (*Pointing to the diagram.*[5]) Now look at this. A

4. The St. Petersburg Conservatory, founded in 1862 by Anton Rubinstein, was an outstanding nursery of brilliant musicians.
5. See Chekhov's letter to Dr. P. I. Kurkin (May 24, 1899), p. 425. Kurkin sent him a survey

picture of our district, as it was fifty years ago. The dark green and
light green indicate forest; half the total area is covered with forest.
Where the green is crosshatched with red lines, there used to be
elks, goats . . . I show both flora and fauna on this. In this lake
lived swans, geese, ducks and, as the old-timers say, a power of
birds of every description, more than the eye could see: they sailed
by like a cloud. Besides hamlets and villages, you see, scattered
here and there are different settlements, little farmsteads, monasteries of Old Believers,[6] watermills . . . Horned cattle and horses
were numerous. The light blue tells us that. For instance, in this
county, the light blue is laid on thick; there were whole herds of
cattle, and in every stable there was an average of three horses.
    (*Pause.*)
Now let's look further down. What it was like twenty-five years
ago. Now only one-third the total area is under forestation. There
are no more goats, but there are elks. The green and light blue are
much fainter. And so on and so on. Let's move to part three: a
picture of the district at the present moment. The green is there
in patches; the elks and swans and wood-grouse have disappeared
. . . Of the earlier settlements, small farmsteads, monasteries,
mills, not a trace. Over all, a picture of gradual and indisputable
decline, which will apparently take another ten or fifteen years to
be complete. You will say that this is the result of civilization, that
the old life must naturally give way to the new. Yes, I'd understand
that, if these depleted forests were replaced by paved highways,
railroads, if there were factories, mills, schools—if the lower classes had become healthier, more prosperous, more intelligent, but
there's certainly nothing like that here! In the district there're the
same swamps, mosquitoes, the same impassable roads, indigence,
typhus, diphtheria, fires . . . Here we're dealing with decline
resulting from a struggle for survival beyond human strength; it's
a decline caused by stagnation, ignorance, the most total absence
of self-awareness, when a frostbitten, starving, sickly man, to preserve the last vestiges of life, to protect his children, instinctively,
unthinkingly grabs hold of whatever can possibly satisfy his hunger, to warm himself he destroys everything, with no thought of
the morrow . . . The destruction to date has been almost total, but
to make up for it nothing has yet been created. (*Coldly.*) I see from
your face that you find this uninteresting.

YELENA ANDREEVNA But I understand so little of it.

ASTROV There's nothing to understand; it's simply uninteresting.

---

map of the Serpukhov region with the village of Melikhovo, where Chekhov lived, in the
middle. Chekhov liked it and had it used in the Moscow Art Theater production.
6. Schismatics from the Russian Orthodox church, persecuted by the authorities from the
seventeenth century, sought refuge in the countryside and split into many sects.

YELENA ANDREEVNA To tell the truth, my mind wasn't on it. Forgive me, I have to subject you to a slight interrogation, and I'm embarrassed, I don't know how to begin . . .

ASTROV Interrogation?

YELENA ANDREEVNA Yes, interrogation, but . . . quite a harmless one. Let's sit down. (*They sit.*) This concerns a certain young person. Let's talk openly, like friends, and not beat around the bush. All right?

ASTROV All right.

YELENA ANDREEVNA It concerns my stepdaughter Sonya. Do you like her?

ASTROV Yes, I respect her.

YELENA ANDREEVNA Do you like her as a woman?

ASTROV (*Not immediately.*) No.

YELENA ANDREEVNA A few words more—and it's all over. Have you noticed anything?

ASTROV No.

YELENA ANDREEVNA (*Takes him by the hand.*) You don't love her, I see it in your eyes . . . She is suffering . . . Understand that and . . . stop coming here.

ASTROV (*Rises.*) My time's up now . . . Actually, there's never any time . . . (*After a shrug.*) When could I? (*He is embarrassed.*)

YELENA ANDREEVNA Oof! What a disagreeable conversation! I'm as relieved as if I'd been lugging around a twenty-ton weight. Well, thank goodness that's over. We'll forget we ever had a talk and . . . and you will go away. You're an intelligent man, you understand . . . (*Pause.*) I'm blushing all over.

ASTROV If you had said something a month or two ago, maybe I might have considered it, but now . . . (*Shrugs.*) But if she's suffering, well, of course . . . The only thing I don't understand is: why did *you* have to conduct this interrogation? (*Stares her in the face and wags his finger at her.*) You are a sly fox!

YELENA ANDREEVNA What's that supposed to mean?

ASTROV (*Laughing.*) A sly fox! Suppose Sonya is suffering, I'm ready to accept that; but what's the point of your interrogation? (*Not letting her speak, energetically.*) Come now, don't act so surprised, you know perfectly well why I'm here every day . . . Why and for whose sake I'm here, you know very well indeed. Cunning little vixen, don't look at me like that, this chicken's an old hand . . .

YELENA ANDREEVNA (*Bewildered.*) Cunning vixen? I don't understand.

ASTROV A beautiful, fluffy weasel . . . You need victims! For a whole month now I've done nothing, let everything slide, seek you out greedily—and you're awfully pleased by it—awfully . . . Well, what of it? I'm beaten, you knew that even without an interrogation.

(*Crossing his hands over his chest and bowing his head.*) I surrender.
Go ahead, eat me up.

YELENA ANDREEVNA   You're out of your mind!

ASTROV (*Laughs through his teeth.*)   You're inhibited . . .

YELENA ANDREEVNA   Oh, I'm a better, more decent person than you
think! I swear to you. (*About to go.*)

ASTROV (*Blocking her path.*)   I will go today, I won't come here any
more, but . . . (*Takes her by the arm, looks around.*) where shall we
get together? Tell me quickly: where? Here someone might come
in, tell me quickly . . . (*Passionately.*) What a wonderful, elegant
. . . One kiss . . . Just let me kiss your fragrant hair . . .

YELENA ANDREEVNA   I swear to you . . .

ASTROV (*Not letting her speak.*)   Why swear? There's no need to
swear. There's no need for more words . . . Oh, what a beauty!
What hands! (*Kisses her hands.*)

YELENA ANDREEVNA   That's enough, once and for all . . . go away . . .
(*Extricates her hands.*) You're out of control.

ASTROV   Then tell me, tell me where we'll get together tomorrow?
(*Takes her by the waist.*) You see, it's inevitable, we have to get
together. (*Kisses her; at that moment,* VOINITSKY *enters with a bouquet of roses and stops in the doorway.*)

YELENA ANDREEVNA (*Not seeing* VOINITSKY.)   For pity's sake . . . let go
of me . . . (*Puts* ASTROV'S *head on her chest.*) No! (*Tries to go.*)

ASTROV (*Restraining her by the waist.*)   Drive tomorrow to the forest
preserve . . . around two o'clock . . . Yes? Yes? Will you?

YELENA ANDREEVNA (*Having seen* VOINITSKY?)   Let go! (*In intense
embarrassment walks over to the window.*) This is horrible.

VOINITSKY (*Puts the bouquet on a chair; agitated, wipes his face and
the inside of his collar with a handkerchief.*)   Never mind . . . Yes
. . . never mind . . .

ASTROV (*Peeved.*)   Today, my dear Mr. Voinitsky, the weather's not
too bad. It was overcast this morning, as if it was going to rain,
but now it's sunny. To tell the truth, autumn's turned out lovely
. . . and the winter wheat's doing all right. (*Rolls the diagram into
a cylinder.*) Only trouble is: the days are getting shorter. (*Exits.*)

YELENA ANDREEVNA (*Quickly goes over to* VOINITSKY.)   You will make
every effort, you will use all your influence to get my husband and
me to leave here this very day! You hear? This very day!

VOINITSKY (*Mopping his brow.*)   Huh? Well, yes . . . fine . . . *Hélène*,
I saw it all, all of it . . .

YELENA ANDREEVNA (*On edge.*)   You hear? I must leave here this very
day!

(*Enter* SEREBRYAKOV, SONYA, TELEGIN, *and* MARINA.)

TELEGIN   Your Excellency, I'm not in the best of health either. Why, for two days now, I've been under the weather. My head feels sort of, y'know . . .

SEREBRYAKOV   Where are the others? I do not like this house. Just like a labyrinth. Twenty-six enormous rooms, everyone scatters, and you can never find anyone. (*Rings.*) Request Mariya Vasilyevna and Yelena Andreevna to come here!

YELENA ANDREEVNA   I'm here.

SEREBRYAKOV   Please, ladies and gentlemen, be seated.

SONYA (*Going over to* YELENA ANDREEVNA, *impatiently.*)   What did he say?

YELENA ANDREEVNA   Later.

SONYA   You're trembling? You're upset? (*Looks searchingly into her face.*) I understand . . . He said he won't come here any more . . . Right? (*Pause.*) Tell me: am I right?

(YELENA ANDREEVNA *nods her head yes.*)

SEREBRYAKOV (*To* TELEGIN.)   Ill health one might be reconciled to, if the worse came to the worst, but what I cannot stomach is this regimen of rustication. I have the feeling I've dropped off the earth on to some alien planet. Sit down, ladies and gentlemen, please. Sonya!

(SONYA *does not hear him, she stands with her head bowed in sorrow.*)

Sonya!

(*Pause.*)

She's not listening. (*To* MARINA.) And you sit down too, Nanny.

(THE NANNY *sits down and knits a stocking.*)

Please, my friends. Lend me your ears, as the saying goes.(*Laughs.*)

VOINITSKY (*Getting excited.*)   Maybe I'm not needed. I can go?

SEREBRYAKOV   No, you are needed here more than anyone.

VOINITSKY   What do you want from me, sir?[7]

SEREBRYAKOV   Sir? . . . Why are you getting angry? (*Pause.*) If I've offended you in any way, then please forgive me.

VOINITSKY   Drop that tone. Let's get down to business . . . What do you want?

(*Enter* MARIYA VASILYEVNA.)

SEREBRYAKOV   And here's *Maman*. I shall begin, ladies and gentlemen. (*Pause.*) I have invited you here, my friends, to inform you that we are about to be visited by an Inspector General.[8] However, joking aside. The matter is a serious one. Ladies and gentlemen,

---

7. In the original, Voinitsky uses the formal "you," *vy*, whereas the Professor addresses him with the informal *ty*.

8. The famous opening line of the Mayor in Gogol's classic comedy *The Inspector General*, Act One, Scene I, to the officials who have gathered in his house. A cliché joke of pedagogues.

I have convened you in order to solicit your aid and advice and, knowing your customary civility, I trust to receive them. I am a man of learning, a bookworm, and have ever been a stranger to practical life. I cannot do without the counsel of informed individuals, and so I ask you, Ivan Petrovich, and you too, Ilya Ilyich, you, *Maman*. . . . What it comes down to is *manet omnes una nox*,[9] we are all mortal in the sight of God; I am old, ill, and therefore deem it appropriate to regulate my material concerns insofar as they relate to my family. My life is over now; it's not myself I'm thinking of, but I have a young wife, an unmarried daughter.

(*Pause.*)

To go on living in the country I find impossible. We were not made for country life. To live in town on those funds which we earn from this estate is equally impossible. If we were to sell, say, our forest, that is an extraordinary measure which could not be repeated annually. We must seek out measures which will guarantee us a regular, more or less fixed amount of income. I have thought of one such measure and I have the honor to submit it for your discussion. Leaving aside the details, I set it forth in its general outlines. Our estate yields on average no more than two percent. I propose to sell it. If we turn the money thus acquired into interest-bearing securities, we shall receive from four to five percent, and I think there may even be a surplus of a few thousand that will enable us to buy a small cottage in Finland.

VOINITSKY   Hold on . . . my ears seem to be deceiving me. Repeat what you just said.

SEREBRYAKOV   Turn the money into interest-bearing securities and with the surplus left over buy a cottage in Finland.[1]

VOINITSKY   Not Finland . . . You said something else.

SEREBRYAKOV   I propose to sell the estate.

VOINITSKY   There, that's it. You'll sell the estate, splendid, good thinking . . . And where do you propose I go with my old mother and Sonya there?

SEREBRYAKOV   All that will be discussed in due time. Not everything at once.

VOINITSKY   Hold on. Obviously, up to now I didn't have a grain of common sense. Up to now I was stupid enough to think that this estate belongs to Sonya. My late father bought this estate as a dowry for my sister. Up to now I was naive, I didn't interpret the laws like a heathen, and I thought the estate passed from my sister to Sonya.

---

9. Latin, "The same night awaits us all," from Horace's *Odes*, Book I, ode XXVIII.
1. Since Finland was part of the Russian Empire, its rural areas within easy reach of St. Petersburg were dotted with summer cottages and villas. The Professor is trying to find a cheap way of returning to the scene of his celebrity.

SEREBRYAKOV Yes, the estate belongs to Sonya. Who disputes it? Without Sonya's consent I will not resolve to sell it. Besides, I'm proposing to do this on Sonya's behalf.

VOINITSKY This is incomprehensible, incomprehensible! Either I've gone out of my mind, or . . . or . . .

MARIYA VASILYEVNA *Jean*, don't contradict *Alexandre*. Believe me, he knows better than we what is right and what is wrong.

VOINITSKY No, give me some water. (*Drinks water.*) Say what it is you want. What do you want?

SEREBRYAKOV I don't understand why you're getting so worked up. I don't say my project is ideal. If everyone finds it infeasible, I shall not insist.

   (*Pause.*)

TELEGIN (*Embarrassed.*) Your Excellency, I cherish for learning not just reverence, but even a kindred feeling. My brother Grigory's wife's brother, maybe you deign to know him, Konstantin Trofimovich Spartakov,[2] had a master's degree . . .

VOINITSKY Hold on, Waffles, we're talking business . . . Wait, later . . . (*To* SEREBRYAKOV.) You go ahead and ask *him*. This estate was bought from his uncle.

SEREBRYAKOV Ah, why should I ask him? What for?

VOINITSKY This estate was bought at that time for ninety-five thousand. Father paid only seventy down, so there was a mortgage of twenty-five thousand left. Now listen . . . This estate would not be free and clear if I hadn't relinquished an inheritance in favor of my sister, whom I loved devoutly. Moreover, for ten years I worked like an ox and paid off the whole debt . . .

SEREBRYAKOV I'm sorry I brought up the subject.

VOINITSKY The estate is clear of debt and not in a mess thanks only to my personal efforts. And now, when I'm growing old, they want to throw me out of here on my ear!

SEREBRYAKOV I can't understand what you're driving at!

VOINITSKY For twenty-five years I ran this estate, worked hard, sent you money like the most conscientious bookkeeper, and in all that time not once did you thank me. The whole time—both in my youth and now—you paid me a salary of five hundred rubles a year—a pittance!—and not once did you have the decency to raise it by even one ruble!

SEREBRYAKOV Ivan Petrovich, how was I to know? I'm not a man of business and I have no head for such things. You could have raised it yourself as much as you liked.

VOINITSKY Why didn't I steal? Why don't you all despise me because

---

2. In the original, *Lakedaimonov*, a joke name based on Lacedæmon, land of the Spartans.

I didn't steal? That would have been the thing to do! and now I wouldn't be a pauper!

MARIYA VASILYEVNA (*Sternly.*)   *Jean!*

TELEGIN (*Getting upset.*) Vanya, dear friend, you mustn't, you mustn't. . . . I'm all atremble . . . Why spoil good relations? (*Kisses him.*) You mustn't.

VOINITSKY For twenty-five years I and my mother here, like moles, sat between these four walls . . . All our thoughts and feelings concerned no one but you. Days we talked about you, about your work, took pride in you, uttered your name with reverence; nights we wasted reading periodicals and books, which I now deeply despise!

TELEGIN You mustn't, Vanya, you mustn't . . . I can't take it . . .

SEREBRYAKOV (*Angrily.*)   I don't understand, what do you want?

VOINITSKY To us you were a creature of a higher order, and we learned your articles by heart . . . But now my eyes have been opened! I see it all! You write about art, but not one thing do you understand about art! All your work, which I loved, isn't worth a tinker's dam! You bamboozled us!

SEREBRYAKOV My friends! Try and calm him down, once and for all! I'm going!

YELENA ANDREEVNA Ivan Petrovich, I insist that you keep quiet! You hear me?

VOINITSKY I won't keep quiet! (*Blocking* SEREBRYAKOV's *path.*) Stop, I haven't finished! You ruined my life! I haven't lived, I haven't lived! Thanks to your charity I blighted, destroyed the best years of my life! You are my deadliest enemy!

TELEGIN I can't take it . . . can't take it . . . I'm going. (*Exits in extreme consternation.*)

SEREBRYAKOV What do you want from me? And what right do you have to take such a tone with me? A nobody! If the estate is yours, then take it, I have no use for it!

YELENA ANDREEVNA I'm getting out of this hellhole this very minute! (*Screams.*) I can't take any more of this!

VOINITSKY My life is wasted! I'm talented, intelligent, audacious . . . If I had had a normal life, I might have evolved into a Schopenhauer, a Dostoevsky[3] . . . What a damn fool thing to say! I'm losing my mind . . . Mommy, I'm desperate! Mommy!

MARIYA VASILYEVNA (*Sternly.*) Do as *Alexandre* says!

SONYA (*Kneels before the nanny and clings to her.*)   Nanny dear! Nanny dear!

3. Arthur Schopenhauer, German philosopher (1788–1860), apostle of pessimism, and Fyodor Mikhailovich Dostoevsky, Russian novelist (1821–1881), apostle of salvation through Slavic Christianity.

VOINITSKY   Mommy! What am I to do? Don't, don't say anything! I know what I have to do! (*To* SEREBRYAKOV.) You're going to remember me! (*Goes to the center door.*)

(MARIYA VASILYEVNA *goes after him.*)

SEREBRYAKOV   Ladies and gentlemen, what is all this, I mean really? Get that madman away from me! I cannot live under the same roof with him! He lives right there (*indicates the center door*), practically on top of me . . . Move him into the village, to the servants' quarters, or I'll move, but to stay in the same house with him is out of the question . . .

YELENA ANDREEVNA (*To her husband.*)   We will leave here today! It is imperative you arrange it this very minute.

SEREBRYAKOV   The most insignificant creature!

SONYA (*Kneeling, turns to her father; nervously, through tears.*)   Open your heart, Papa! Uncle Vanya and I are so unhappy! (*Mastering her despair.*) Open your heart![4] Remember when you were younger, Uncle Vanya and Granny would spend nights translating books for you, copying out your writings . . . every night, every night! Uncle Vanya and I worked without a rest, afraid to spend a penny on ourselves, and sent everything to you . . . We had to pay our own way! I'm not saying this right, it's not what I mean, but you understand us, papa. Open your heart!

YELENA ANDREEVNA (*Distraught, to her husband.*)   Aleksandr, for heaven's sake, have it out with him . . . Please.

SEREBRYAKOV   Very well, I'll have it out with him . . . I'm not accusing him of anything, I'm not angry, but, you must agree, his behavior is just the slightest degree peculiar. If you insist, I'll go to him. (*Goes out the center door.*)

YELENA ANDREEVNA   Be gentler with him, calm him down . . . (*Goes out behind him.*)

SONYA (*Clinging to the nanny.*)   Nanny dear! Nanny dear!

MARINA   Never mind, child. *Honk, honk*, go the geese—and then they stop . . . *Honk, honk, honk*—then they stop . . .

SONYA   Nanny dear!

MARINA (*Smoothes her hair.*)   You're shivery-shaky, just like you had a chill! Well, well, little orphan, God is merciful. Some limeflower

---

4. "Anton Pavlovich was once watching *Uncle Vanya.*

"In the third act, Sonya, at the words, "Papa, open your heart," got on her knees and kissed her father's hand.

" 'She mustn't do that, that's really not drama,' said Anton Pavlovich. 'All the sense, all the drama of a human being is inward, and not expressed in outward manifestations. There was drama in Sonya's life up to that moment, there will be drama after that, but this is simply an incident, the consequence of the gunshot. And a gunshot is really not drama, but an incident." (Nadezhda Butova, "From Memories of A. P. Chekhov at the Art Theater," *Shipovnik Almanac* 23 [1914].)

tea or raspberry, it'll pass . . . Don't grieve, little orphan . . . (*Looking at the center door, angrily.*) Fly off the handle, will you, you geese, dern ya all!

>   (*Offstage a gunshot; we hear* YELENA ANDREEVNA *scream;* SONYA *shudders.*)

Ooh, what're you up to!

SEREBRYAKOV (*Runs in, stumbling in fear.*)   Restrain him! Restrain him! He's gone out of his mind!

>   (YELENA ANDREEVNA *and* VOINITSKY *are struggling in the doorway.*)

YELENA ANDREEVNA (*Trying to wrest the revolver away from him.*) Give it to me! Give it to me, I tell you!

VOINITSKY   Let go, *Hélène*! Let go of me! (*Pulling loose, he runs in and looks around for* SEREBRYAKOV.) Where is he? Ah, there he is! (*Fires at him.*) Bang! (*Pause.*) Missed him? Another fiasco?! (*Angrily.*) Oh, hell, hell . . . damn it to hell . . . (*Throws the revolver on the floor and sits exhausted on a chair.*)

>   (SEREBRYKOV *is stunned;* YELENA ANDREEVNA *is leaning against the wall, feeling faint.*)

YELENA ANDREEVNA   Take me away from here! Take me away, kill me, but . . . I cannot stay here, I cannot!

VOINITSKY (*In desperation.*)   Oh, what am I doing! What am I doing!

SONYA (*Quietly.*)   Nanny dear! Nanny dear!

CURTAIN

Act Four

IVAN PETROVICH's *room; it is both his bedroom and the office of the estate. By the window are a large table with ledgers and papers of all sorts, a writing desk, cupboards, scales. A somewhat smaller table for* ASTROV; *on this table implements for drawing, paints; beside it a cardboard portfolio. A starling in a cage. On the wall a map of Africa, apparently of no use to anyone here. An enormous divan, covered in oilcloth. At left, a door leading to the bedroom; at right, a door in the wall. Beneath the right door is a doormat to keep the peasants from tracking in mud.—Autumn evening. Stillness.*

>   (TELEGIN *and* MARINA *are seated face to face, winding a ball of knitting yarn.*)

TELEGIN   You be quick, Marina Timofeevna, or before you know it they'll call us to say good-bye. They've already ordered the horses brought 'round.

MARINA (*Trying to wind more quickly.*)   There's just a bit left.

TELEGIN   Kharkov's where they're going.[5] That's where they'll live.

MARINA   Good riddance.

TELEGIN.   They got a scare . . . Yelena Andreevna says, "Not one more hour," she says, "will I live here . . . let's go, let's go . . . We'll live," she says, "in Kharkov, we'll give it the once-over and then we'll send for our things . . ." Traveling light. Which means, Marina Timofeevna, they weren't destined to live here. Not destined . . . Preordained by fate.

MARINA   Good riddance. Just now they were raising a rumpus, shooting guns—a downright disgrace!

TELEGIN   Yes, a scene that deserves treatment by a painter of shipwrecks and tempests.[6]

MARINA   That my eyes should see such a sight. (*Pause.*) Once again we'll live as we used to, the old way. Tea in the morning between seven and eight, dinner between noon and one, sit down to supper in the evening; everything in its place, the way folks do it . . . like Christians. (*With a sigh.*) It's a long time, bless my soul, since I've had noodles.

TELEGIN   Yes, it's quite a little while since they served us noodles. (*Pause.*)

Quite a little while . . . This morning, Marina Timofeevna, I go to the village and the shopkeeper yells at me, "Hey, you freeloader!" And it made me feel so bitter!

MARINA   You pay it no mind, dearie. We're all freeloaders on God. You and Sonya and Ivan Petrovich—no one sits idle, everyone gets down to work! Everyone . . . where *is* Sonya?

TELEGIN   In the garden. She and the doctor are on the move, looking for Ivan Petrovich. They're afraid he might lay hands on himself.

MARINA   And where's the pistol?

TELEGIN (*In a whisper.*)   I hid it in the cellar!

MARINA (*With a broad grin.*)   Bless us sinners!

(*Enter from outside* VOINITSKY *and* ASTROV.)

VOINITSKY   Leave me alone. (*To* MARINA *and* TELEGIN.) Get out of here—leave me alone for just an hour! I can't stand being spied on.

TELEGIN.   This minute, Vanya. (*Tiptoes out.*)

MARINA   Goosie-goosie-gander, honk, honk, honk! (*Gathers up the yarn and exits.*)

5. Capital of the Kharkov *gubernia* in the Ukraine, a university town of 220,000 inhabitants, famous for its annual cattle and wool market. In the view of a Petersburgher, Kharkov was back of the beyond; Chekhov often uses it to suggest a humdrum way of life.
6. In the original, "worthy of the brush of Aivazovsky." Ivan Konstantinovich Aivazovsky (1817–1900) was a Russian painter famous for his seascapes, particularly storms and naval battles, whom Chekhov had met in Feodosiya on the Black Sea in 1888.

VOINITSKY   Leave me alone!

ASTROV   With the greatest of pleasure, I should have left here long ago, but, I repeat, I will not leave until you return what you took from me.

VOINITSKY   I took nothing from you.

ASTROV   I'm in earnest—don't detain me. It was time for me to leave hours ago.

VOINITSKY   Nothing, that's what I took from you.
   (*Both sit down.*)

ASTROV   Is that so? All right, I'll wait a little longer, and then, sorry, I'll have to use force. We'll tie you up and frisk you. I mean this quite seriously.

VOINITSKY   Whatever you like. (*Pause.*) To act like such a fool; to shoot twice and miss both times! That's something I'll never forgive myself for!

ASTROV   When the urge to shoot came over you, you should have blown out your own brains.

VOINITSKY   (*After a shrug.*)   'S funny. I attempted murder, but they don't arrest me, they don't put me on trial. Which means they think I'm insane. (*A malicious smile.*) I am insane, and the sane are the ones who disguise themselves as professors, learned sages, to conceal their lack of talent, their obtuseness, their blatant heartlessness. The sane are the ones who marry old men and then cheat on them in broad daylight, I saw, I saw the way you embraced her!

ASTROV   Yes, sir, embraced, sir,[7] what's it to you? (*Thumbs his nose at him.*)

VOINITSKY   (*Glancing at the door.*)   No, the earth is insane for supporting you.

ASTROV   Now, that's just stupid.

VOINITSKY   So what? I'm insane, not responsible in the eyes of the law. I have the right to say stupid things.

ASTROV   An old trick. You're not insane, you're just a crackpot. A baggy-pants clown.[8] There was a time when I considered every crackpot to be psychotic, abnormal, but now I'm of the opinion that the normal human condition is to be a crackpot.[9] You're perfectly normal.

VOINITSKY   (*Covers his face with his hands.*)   The shame! If you only knew the shame I feel! This stabbing sense of shame can't be

---

7. Astrov picks up Telegin's affected style of talking.
8. *Gorokhy shut*, literally "a pea-green jester," a generic term for a buffoon, like Shakespeare's "motley fool."
9. *Cf.* Chekhov's notebooks: "He used to consider that a ridiculous crackpot was ill, but now he is of the opinion that it is the normal condition of mankind to be a ridiculous crackpot."

compared to any pain there is. (*Plaintively.*) It's unbearable. (*Leans on the table.*) What am I to do? What am I to do?

ASTROV Not a thing.

VOINITSKY Give me something! Oh my God . . . I'm forty-seven; suppose I live to be sixty, I still have another thirteen years to get through. A long time! How can I live through those thirteen years! What will I do, how will I fill them? Oh, you understand . . . (*Convulsively squeezes* ASTROV's *hand.*) you understand, if only one could live out the rest of one's life in a new way somehow. If one could wake up on a bright, still morning and feel that life had begun anew, that all the past is forgotten, has blown away like smoke. (*Weeps.*) To begin a new life . . . Write me a prescription, how to begin . . . where to begin . . .

ASTROV (*Annoyed.*) Aw, cut it out! What new life? Our condition, yours and mine, is hopeless.

VOINITSKY Is it?

ASTROV I'm convinced of it.

VOINITSKY Give me something . . . (*Indicating his heart.*) It's searing inside.

ASTROV (*Shouts in anger.*) Stop it! (*Assuaging him.*) Those who will live a hundred, two hundred years from now and who will despise us because we lived our lives so stupidly and so gracelessly—they may find a way to be happy, but we . . . For you and me there's only one hope. The hope that when we lie in our coffins, we'll be haunted by visions, maybe even pleasant ones. (*After a sigh.*) Yes, my boy. In the whole district there were only two decent, cultured men: you and I. But it took no more than ten years for humdrum life, despicable life, to drag us down; its pestilential fumes poisoned our blood, and we became just as vulgar as everybody else. (*Vigorously.*) But don't try to charm away the toothache with talking. You give back what you took from me.

VOINITSKY I didn't take anything from you.

ASTROV What you took out of my portable medicine chest was a little jar of morphine. (*Pause.*) Listen, if you insist on putting an end to your life, no matter what, go out in the forest and shoot yourself there. But give back the morphine or else there'll be talk, inquests, they'll think I gave it to you . . . It'll be bad enough having to perform your autopsy . . . You think that'll be interesting?

(*Enter* SONYA.)

VOINITSKY Leave me alone.

ASTROV (*To* SONYA.) Sofiya Aleksandrovna, your uncle pilfered a little jar of morphine from my medicine chest and won't give it back. Tell him that it is . . . basically not an intelligent thing to do.

SONYA Uncle Vanya, did you take the morphine?

(*Pause.*)

ASTROV   He took it. I'm sure of it.

SONYA   Give it back. Why do you terrorize us? (*Tenderly.*) Give it
back, Uncle Vanya. I may be just as unhappy as you are, but I
don't give in to despair. I am patient and will be patient until my
life comes to an end on its own . . . You be patient too.

(*Pause.*)

Give it back! (*Kisses his hands.*) Dear, wonderful uncle, dearest,
give it back! (*Weeps.*) You're kind, you'll feel sorry for us and give
it back. Have patience, uncle! Have patience!

VOINITSKY (*Gets a little jar from the table and gives it to* ASTROV.)   Go
on, take it! (*To* SONYA.) But we must go to work quickly, do something quickly, or else I can't . . . I can't . . .

SONYA   Yes, yes, to work. As soon as we see them off, we'll get down
to work . . . (*Nervously riffles through papers on the table.*) We've
let everything go.

ASTROV (*Puts the jar in the medicine chest and straps it tightly shut.*)
Now a man can be on his way.

YELENA ANDREEVNA (*Enters.*)   Ivan Petrovich, you're here? We're
leaving right away. Go to Aleksandr, he has something to say to
you.

SONYA   Go, Uncle Vanya. (*Takes* VOINITSKY *by the arm.*) Let's go.
Papa and you ought to be reconciled. That's absolutely necessary.

(SONYA *and* VOINITSKY *leave.*)

YELENA ANDREEVNA   I'm leaving. (*Gives* ASTROV *her hand.*) Good-bye.

ASTROV   So soon?

YELENA ANDREEVNA   The horses have already been brought 'round.

ASTROV   Good-bye.

YELENA ANDREEVNA   You promised me today that you would leave
here.

ASTROV   I remember. I'm just leaving. (*Pause.*) Was the lady frightened? (*Takes her by the hand.*) Is this really so terrifying?

YELENA ANDREEVNA   Yes.

ASTROV   Otherwise the lady would have stayed! Ah? Tomorrow in
the forest preserve . . .

YELENA ANDREEVNA   No . . . it's been settled . . . And that's why I
can look at you so fearlessly, because our departure is definite . . .
All I ask of you is: have a higher opinion of me. I would like you
to respect me.

ASTROV   Ay! (*Gesture of impatience.*) Do stay, please. Admit it, you've
got nothing to do in this world, no purpose in life, nothing to
engage your attention, and sooner or later, make no mistake, you'll
give in to your feelings—it's inevitable. So it's far better not to let
it happen in Kharkov or somewhere like Kursk but here, in the lap
of nature . . . Poetically speaking, at least, autumn is a beautiful

season . . . There are forest preserves, half-dilapidated manor houses out of a Turgenev novel[1] . . .

YELENA ANDREEVNA What a funny man you are . . . I'm angry with you, but still . . . I'll remember you with pleasure. You're an interesting, original person. Never again will we meet, and so—why hide it? I was attracted to you a little . . . Well, let's shake hands and part as friends. Keep a kind thought for me.

ASTROV (*Has shaken her hand.*) Yes, go away . . . (*Pensively.*) You seem to be a decent, sincere person, but there also seems to be something odd about your basic nature. You and your husband show up, and everyone around here who used to work or putter or create things was compelled to lay aside his work and all summer long concentrate on nothing but your husband's gout and you. The two of you infected all the rest of us with your idleness. I was attracted, did nothing for a whole month, while people were falling ill, peasants grazed their cattle in my forest and stands of young trees . . . And so, wherever you and your husband set foot, destruction follows in your wake . . . I'm joking, of course, but all the same . . . it's odd, and I'm convinced that if you were to stay, the havoc wreaked would be stupendous. I would perish, and you would . . . wouldn't get off scot-free. Well, go away. *Finita la commedia!*[2]

YELENA ANDREEVNA (*Takes a pencil from the table and quickly conceals it.*) I'll take this pencil to remember you by.

ASTROV It's kind of strange . . . We were getting to know one another and all of a sudden for no good reason . . . we'll never meet again. It's the way of the world . . . While nobody's here, before Uncle Vanya comes in with a bouquet, let me . . . kiss you . . . As a farewell . . . All right? (*Kisses her on the cheek.*) There now . . . Well done.

YELENA ANDREEVNA I wish you the best of everything. (*Looking around.*) Whatever the cost, for once in my life! (*Embraces him impulsively, and both immediately and rapidly move away from one another.*) It's time to go.

ASTROV Go quickly. Now that the horses have been brought 'round, you'll be off.

YELENA ANDREEVNA Here they come, I think.
      (*Both listen hard.*)
ASTROV *Finita!*
      (*Enter* SEREBRYAKOV, VOINITSKY, MARIYA VASILYEVNA *with a book,* TELEGIN, *and* SONYA.)

1. An allusion to the novels of Ivan Turgenev, such as as *A Nest of Gentry* (1859), which were proverbial by Chekhov's time.
2. Italian, "The play is over," an expression Chekhov often used in his letters to mean "it's all played out."

SEREBRYAKOV (*To* VOINITSKY.)   Let the dead Past bury its dead.[3] After what has occurred in these last few hours, I have experienced so much and done so much thinking that I believe I could write a whole treatise on the art of living for the edification of posterity. I gladly accept your apologies and in turn ask you to forgive me. Good-bye! (*Exchanges three kisses with* VANYA.)

VOINITSKY   You will punctually receive the same amount as before. Everything will be as it was before.

     (YELENA ANDREEVNA *embraces* SONYA.)

SEREBRYAKOV (*Kisses* MARIYA VASILYEVNA's *hand.*)   Maman . . .

MARIYA VASILYEVNA (*Kissing him.*)   Alexandre, have another picture taken and send me your photograph. You know how dear you are to me.

TELEGIN   Good-bye, your excellency! Don't forget us!

SEREBRYAKOV (*After kissing his daughter.*)   Good-bye . . . Good-bye, all! (*Giving his hand to* ASTROV.) Thank you for your pleasant company . . . I respect your way of thinking, your enthusiasms, effusions, but allow an old man to add to his valediction this one observation: one must take action, my friends! One must take action! (*Bows all round.*) My very best wishes! (*Exits, followed by* MARIYA VASILYEVNA *and* SONYA.)

VOINITSKY (*Soundly kisses* YELENA ANDREEVNA's *hand.*)   Good-bye . . . Forgive me . . . We'll never meet again.

YELENA ANDREEVNA (*Moved.*)   Good-bye, my pet. (*Kisses him on the head and exits.*)

ASTROV (*To* TELEGIN.)   Waffles, tell them to bring 'round my horses too while they're at it.

TELEGIN   Right you are, dear friend. (*Exits.*)

     (*Only* ASTROV *and* VOINITSKY *are left.*)

ASTROV (*Takes the paints from the table and stuffs them into his suitcase.*)   Why don't you go and see them off?

VOINITSKY   Let them go, but I . . . I cannot. I feel depressed. Have to hurry and get involved in something . . . To work, to work! (*Burrows into the papers on the table.*)

     (*Pause. The sound of harness bells.*)

ASTROV   They're gone. The Professor's relieved, I'll bet. You couldn't lure him back here again for all the tea in China.

MARINA (*Enters.*)   They're gone. (*Sits in the easy chair and knits a stocking.*)

SONYA (*Enters.*)   They're gone. (*Wipes her eyes.*) Pray God it's for the best. (*To* UNCLE.) Well, Uncle Vanya, let's do something.

VOINITSKY   To work, to work . . .

---

3. I have chosen a quotation from Longfellow (from his *Psalm of Life*) to indicate the hackneyed nature of the Professor's remark. In the original Russian, Serebryakov quotes a proverb, "He who bears a grudge should have a eye plucked out."

SONYA It's been ever so long since we sat together at this table. (*Lights a lamp on the table.*) There doesn't seem to be any ink . . . (*Takes the inkwell to the cupboard and fills it.*) But I feel down now that they're gone.

MARIYA VASILYEVNA (*Enters slowly.*) They're gone! (*Sits and gets absorbed in reading.*)

SONYA (*Sits at the table and leafs through the ledgers.*) First of all, Uncle Vanya, let's write up all the accounts. It's funny the way we've let things go. They sent for a bill again today. Write. You write one bill, I'll do another . . .

VOINITSKY (*Writes.*) "Account . . . of Mister . . ."
     (*Both write in silence.*)

MARINA (*Yawns.*) Beddy-bye for me . . .

ASTROV Stillness. The pens scratch, the cricket chirps. Warm, cozy . . . I don't feel like leaving here. (*The sound of harness bells.*) There, they've brought the horses . . . All that's left, therefore, is to say good-bye to you, my friends, to say good-bye to my table and—off we go! (*Places the diagram in the portfolio.*)

MARINA Now what are you fussing for? You should sit a while.

ASTROV Can't be done.

VOINITSKY (*Writes.*) "And carried over from the old debt two seventy-five . . ."
     (*Enter* THE WORKMAN.)

WORKMAN Mikhail Lvovich, the horses are ready.

ASTROV I heard. (*Gives him the medicine chest, suitcase, and portfolio.*) Here, take this. See that you don't crumple the portfolio.

WORKMAN Yes sir. (*Exits.*)

ASTROV Well, now . . . (*Goes to say good-bye.*)

SONYA When shall we see you again?

ASTROV Not until summer, I should think. Hardly this winter . . . Naturally, if anything comes up, let me know—I'll stop by. (*Shakes hands.*) Thanks for the hospitality, the kindness . . . everything, in short. (*Goes to the nanny and kisses her on the head.*) Good-bye, old woman.

MARINA So you're going without tea?

ASTROV I don't want any, Nanny old girl.

MARINA Maybe you'd like a nip of vodka?

ASTROV (*Hesitantly.*) Could be . . .
     (MARINA *exits.*)

ASTROV (*After a pause.*) For some reason my trace-horse[4] started limping. I noticed it again yesterday when Petrushka was leading him to water.

VOINITSKY Needs a new shoe.

_____
4. A troika consists of three horses harnessed together; the two harnessed by straps or traces to the outside shafts are called trace-horses.

ASTROV   Have to stop at Rozhdestvennoe and look in at the blacksmith's. Can't be helped . . . (*Walks over to the map of Africa and
looks at it.*) I suppose there must be a heatwave over in Africa right
now—something awful!

VOINITSKY   I suppose so.

MARINA (*Returning with a saucer holding a shot glass of vodka and a
little piece of bread.*)   Here you are. (ASTROV *drinks the vodka.*)
Your health, dearie. (*Bows low.*) But you should have a bit o'bread.

ASTROV   No, this'll do . . . So, the best of everything! (*To* MARINA.)
Don't see me off, Nanny old girl, there's no need.

　　　(*He leaves.* SONYA *follows with a candle to see him off;* MARINA
　　　sits in her easy-chair.)

VOINITSKY (*Writes.*)   "February second vegetable oil twenty pounds
. . . February sixteenth another twenty pounds vegetable oil . . .
buckwheat groats . . ."

　　　(*Pause. The sound of harness bells.*)

MARINA   He's gone!

　　　(*Pause.*)

SONYA (*Returning, puts the candle on the table.*)   He's gone . . .

VOINITSKY (*Checking over the accounts and making notations.*)   Total
. . . fifty . . . twenty-five . . .

　　　(SONYA *sits and writes.*)

MARINA (*Yawns.*)   Uh, bless us sinners . . .

　　　(TELEGIN *tiptoes in, sits by the door, and quietly strums the
　　　guitar.*)

VOINITSKY (*To* SONYA, *running his hand through her hair.*)   Dearest
child, how hard it is! Oh, how hard it is!

SONYA   What can be done? We have to go on living!

　　　(*Pause.*)

Uncle Vanya, we will live. We will live through a long, long series
of days, no end of evenings; we will patiently bear the ordeals that
Fate sends us; we will labor for others both now and in our old
age, knowing no rest; but when our time comes, we will die
meekly, and beyond the grave we will tell how we suffered, how
we wept, how bitter we felt, and God will take pity on us, and you
and I, Uncle Vanya, dear Uncle, shall see a life bright, beautiful,
exquisite; we shall rejoice and look upon our present unhappiness
with forbearance, with a smile—and we shall be at rest.[5] I believe,
Uncle, I believe intensely, passionately . . . (*Kneels before him and
lays her head on his hands; in a weary voice.*) We shall be at rest!

　　　(TELEGIN *quietly plays the guitar.*)

We shall be at rest! We shall hear the angels, we shall see heaven
all diamonds, we shall see how all earthly woes, all our suffering

5. The Russian, *my otdokhnyom*, connotes "We shall breathe easily" and is connected etymologically to words such as *dushno*, used by characters to say that conditions are stifling.

will be submerged in a compassion that will fill up the world, and our life will grow serene, tender, sweet as a caress. I believe, believe . . . (*Wipes his tears away with a handkerchief.*) Poor, poor Uncle Vanya, you're crying . . . (*Through tears.*) You've known no joy in your life, but wait, Uncle Vanya, wait . . . We shall be at rest . . . (*Embraces him.*) We shall be at rest!

(THE WATCHMAN *taps.*)

(TELEGIN *quietly goes on playing;* MARIYA VASILYEVNA *writes in the margin of a pamphlet;* MARINA *knits a stocking.*)

We shall be at rest!

(*Curtain slowly falls.*)

Variants to *Uncle Vanya*

Lines come from *Plays* (1897)

Act One

After my time's up—
VOINITSKY (*To* ELENA ANDREEVNA). He doesn't eat meat either.
ASTROV Yes, I consider it a sin to kill living things. (Page 205)

Three Sisters

At the urging of the Moscow Art Theater, Chekhov set out to write them a play. With specific actors in mind for given roles and mindful of the Art Theatre's strengths, Chekhov spent more time in the composition of *Three Sisters* than on any of his earlier dramas. He was especially anxious to cut out superfluities in monologues and to provide a sense of movement.

Unfortunately, when the Art Theater actors heard the author read the play for the first time in October 1900, they were sorely disappointed. "This is no play; it's only an outline" was the immediate reaction. Chekhov sedulously reworked all of it, and in the process added many striking touches. The ironic counterpoint of Tusenbach's and Chebutykin's remarks in Acts One and Four, most of Solyony's pungent lines, and Masha's quotation from *Ruslan and Lyudmila* about the curved seashore all were added at this stage. It is amazing to think that only in revising the play did Chekhov decide to leave Masha on stage for the final tableau. He sat in on early rehearsals and insisted that a colonel be in attendance to instruct the actors in proper military deportment; Chekhov also personally orchestrated the firebell sound effects for Act Three. He put the greatest emphasis on that act, which, he insisted, must be performed quietly and wearily.

Three Sisters opened at the Art Theater on January 31, 1901, with Stanislavsky as Vershinin, Olga Knipper as Masha, and the young Vsevolod Meyerhold as Tusenbach. Although many critics were put off by what struck them as the play's hopelessness and vague motivation in the characters, the production was acclaimed by the public. "It's music, not acting," asserted Maksim Gorky.[1]

The writer Leonid Andreev attended the thirtieth performance, despite a friend's warning that its effect would be suicidally depressing. Quite against expectation, he found himself totally drawn into the play by the middle of Act One. No longer appraising the scenery or the actors, he became convinced that "the story of the three sisters . . . is not a fiction, not a fantasy, but a fact, an event, something every bit as real as stock options at the Savings Bank." By the end, he, with the rest of the audience, was in tears, but his dominant impression was not pessimistic. For Andreev, the residual effect, the pervasive mood, the play's basic "tragic melody" was a yearning for life. "Like steam, life can be compressed into a narrow little container, but, also like steam, it will endure

---

1. Maksim Gorky, *Sobranie sochineniya* (Moscow: Akademiya Nauk SSR, 1958), XXVIII: 159.

pressure only to a certain point. And in *Three Sisters*, this pressure is brought to the limit, beyond which it will explode—and don't you actually hear how life is seething, doesn't its angrily protesting voice reach your ears?"[2]

This reaction was due in part to the play's early run coinciding with student riots. Consequently, the characters' aspirations were identified with topical political protest. It was due as well to the theater's remarkably veristic production and its careful transmission of mood. Eventually, theatergoers would say not that they were going to the Art Theater to view *Three Sisters*, but that they were "paying a call on the Prozorovs." Chekhov's technique, however, provided the premises of this illusion of reality.

The American poet Randall Jarrell has compared Chekhov's technique in *Three Sisters* to that of the painter Édouard Vuillard.

> In certain of his indoor and outdoor scenes of French domestic life, the foundation areas on the canvas are made less emphatic by the swarms of particles that mottle the walls with rose-printed paper, the rugs from swirls, the lawns with pools of sun and shade. From such variation and variegation comes his cohesion. Vuillard commingles plaids and dappled things as non sequitur as the jottings in Chebutykin's notebook.[3]

And Jarrell made lists of what he called "Vuillard spots" in the play: apparently random speech habits, mannerisms, personality traits, and incidents that add up to a character of an action.

It is a stimulating analogy, useful in revealing what is new about *Three Sisters*. To extend the metaphor, this is the first time Chekhov employs a broad canvas devoid of exclusively foreground figures—no Ivanovs, not even Treplyovs or Vanyas. The sisters must share their space, in every space, with Natasha, Tusenbach, and Solyony. There are no more soliloquys: a character is almost never left alone on stage. Andrey must pour out his discontents to deaf Ferapont, and Masha must proclaim her adulterous love to the stopped-up ears of her sister Olga. Tête-à-têtes are of the briefest: no more Trigorin spinning out a description of a writer's career or Astrov explicating maps to prospective paramours. Vershinin and Tusenbach spout their speeches about work and the future to a room full of auditors.

Those rhetorical paeans have been cited as Utopian alternatives to the dreary provincial life depicted on stage. True, the men who formulate them are ineffectual, with no chance of realizing their "thick-coming fantasies." But the monologues do work as a meliorative element. Unable in a play to use the narrative to offer a contrasting vision, Chekhov must put into the mouths of his characters visions of an improved life. The

---

2. Leonid Andreev, "Tri sestry" *Polnoe sobranie sochineny* (St. Petersburg: A. F. Marks, 1913), VI: 321–25.
3. Randall Jarrell, "About *The Three Sisters*. Notes," in *The Three Sisters* (London: Macmillan, 1969), 105–06. There was an impressionist show in Moscow in 1896, and Tolstoy characterized Chekhov's technique as a storywriter as impressionism. Edouard Vuillard (1868–1940), a Parisian painter, enjoyed a long and successful career; his domestic interiors use the linear techniques and vibrant colors of Japanese prints.

imagery of birds of passage, birch trees, and flowing rivers sound a note of freshness and harmony that highlights all the more acutely the characters' inability to get in touch with the spontaneous and the natural. The cranes are programmed to fly, "and whatever thoughts, sublime or trivial, drift through their heads, they'll go on flying, not knowing what for or where to."

The most blatant call for an alternative is the sisters' recurrent plaint, "To Moscow, to Moscow!" Almost from the play's premiere, critics wondered what was stopping the Prozorovs from buying a ticket to the big city. Obviously, Moscow is an imaginary site, envisaged differently by each character. Andrey sees it not only as a university town, but also as the site of great restaurants, while for old Ferapont it marks the locale of a legendary pancake feast. Vershinin gloomily recalls a grim bridge and roaring water there, Solyony has invented a second university for it, and Olga looks back to a funeral. No clear image emerges from the medley of impressions, so Moscow remains somewhere over the rainbow, just out of sight.

Because the sisters are fixated on this distant point, commentators and directors have regularly inflated them into heroines. Too frequently, the play is reduced to a conflict between three superwomen and a ravening bitch: the sensitive and high-strung Prozorov sorority can be no match for the ruthless life force embodied in Natasha, so they succumb, albeit preserving their ideals. This common interpretation is not borne out by a close examination of the play, which Chekhov said has *four* heroines. As the Rumanian critic Jovan Hristić has shrewdly noted, the three of the title are "true spiritual sisters of Hedda Gabler, who corrupt everything around them by dint of thinking themselves superior."[4] The analogy works on several levels, from the military upbringing (Masha's scorn of civilians is bitter) to the ultimate downfall, engineered partly by an instinctual bourgeoise (Natasha for Thea Elvsted), second-rate academics (Andrey and Kulygin for Tesman), and inept idealists (Vershinin and Tusenbach for Løvborg). Like Hedda, the three sisters are at variance with their environment, which, for them, represents common vulgarity.

The play maps the town's encroachment on their lives, as Olga becomes embedded in the educational hierarchy, Irina turns into a cog in the civil bureaucracy, Andrey becomes a fixture on the County Council, and Masha becomes a recalcitrant faculty wife. By the last act, the stage direction informs us that their backyard has become a kind of empty lot, across which the townsfolk tramp when necessary. It is the next step after the fire, when the townsfolk invaded their home and bore off their old clothes. And, of course, Natasha's depredations and those of her lover and the town's de facto head, the unseen Protopopov, began earliest of all.

To protect themselves against this encroachment, the sisters have erected a paling of culture, and into it they have invited the military. For once, Chekhov does not use outsiders as a disruptive force; for the sis-

---

4. Jovan Hristić, *Le théâtre de Tchékhov*, trans. H. and F. Wybrands (Lausanne: L'Âge d'homme, 1982), 166.

ters, the soldiers spell color, excitement, and life. But the factitiousness of this glamour quickly becomes apparent: a peacetime army is a symbol of idleness and pointless expense. Men trained to fight while away their time philosophizing and playing the piano, teaching gymnastics and reading the paper, carrying on backstairs love affairs and fighting duels. The sisters have pinned their hopes on a regiment of straw men. It is hard to determine who is weakest: Vershinin, forecasting future happiness while unable to cope with his psychotic wife; Tusenbach, whose noble sentiments are belied by his unprepossessing looks and unassertive manner; or Solyony, veering crazily between blustering egotism and crippling introspection. These are carpet knights, suitable for dressing out a party, but not for salvaging anyone's life. That the sisters should make such a fuss abut them reveals at once the unreality of their values.

If culture, in the sense of refined feelings revealed through sensitivity and a cultivated understanding of art, is the touchstone for the Prozorovs, it will not sustain scrutiny either. The Prozorov family prides itself on the Russian *intelligent's* virtues of political awareness, social commitment, and artistic discrimination, and the family judges others by them. Many of the play's major characters are connected with the educational system. When tested by the realities of life, however, the fabric of their culture soon falls to pieces. They and their circle cling to shreds and patches—Latin tags for Kulygin, quotations from Russian classics for Masha and Solyony, and amateur musicmaking. Andrey's "sawing away" at the violin and Masha's untested prowess at the keyboard are mocked in the last act by Natasha's offstage rendition of the "Maiden's Prayer." Irina grieves that she cannot remember the Italian for *window*, as if a foreign vocabulary could buoy her in a sea of despair. Solyony poses as the romantic poet Lermontov, but his behavior shows him to be more like Martynov, the bully who killed Lermontov in a duel. During the fire, it is Natasha who must remind Olga of the *intelligent's* duty "to help the poor. It's an obligation of the rich." Philosophizing (always a pejorative word for Chekhov) passes for thought, newspaper filler passes for knowledge, and a superior attitude passes for delicacy of feeling; yet everyone's conduct sooner or later dissolves into rudeness or immorality.

Three Sisters does not try to show how three gifted women are defeated by a philistine environment, but rather illustrates that their unhappiness is of their own making. If they are subjugated and evicted by the Natashas of this world, it is because they have not recognized and dealt with their own shortcomings. At some point in the play, each sister is as callous and purblind as Natasha herself. Olga cattily criticizes Natasha's dress sense at a party, although Olga has been told that the girl is shy in company; in Act Three, Olga refuses to listen to Masha's avowal of love, refusing to face facts. Her very removal to a garret is as much avoidance of involvement as it is an exile imposed by Natasha. Irina is remarkably unpleasant to both her suitors, Tusenbach and Solyony; as a telegraph clerk, she is brusque with a grieving mother, and at the very last refuses to say the few words of love that might lighten the Baron's last moments, even though, as Chekhov informed Olga Knipper, she is prescient of the impending catastrophe. Masha swears like a trooper, drinks, and abuses the old nanny nearly as badly and with less excuse than Natasha does. Her flagrant adultery with Vershinin may ultimately be more destructive than Natasha's with Protopopov, for Kulygin genuinely loves his wife, whereas Andrey tries to forget he has one.

This litany of faults is not meant to blacken the sisters or to exonerate Natasha, Solyony, and the others. It is meant to redress the balance: Chekhov selects the Prozorov family (who, along with the officers, were based on Chekhov's personal acquaintances) to sum up a way of life. With all the benefits of education, a loving home, and creature comforts, the sisters stagnate, not simply because they live in the sticks, but because they keep deferring any activity that might give meaning to their existence. The ennobling labor that Tusenbach and Vershinin rhapsodize over and that inspires Irina seems to have nothing in common with doing a job every day. Olga's teaching, Irina's work at the Council and the telegraph office, and the position at the mines to which Tusenbach retires offer a prospect of meaningless drudgery.

The prevalent state of mind is to be "sick and tired," "fed up" (*nadoelo*). In his brief moment alone with Masha in Act Two, Vershinin claims that the average local "educated man" for being "sick and tired of his wife, sick and tired of his home, sick and tired of his estate, sick and tired of his horses"; but he is clearly characterizing himself, for he soon draws a picture of his own wretched marriage. Masha, whom Vershinin would exempt as an exceptional person, is "sick and tired of winter," and when her husband proclaims his love with "I'm so happy," she bitterly spits back, "I'm sick and tired, sick and tired, sick and tired." Even the genteel Olga pronounces herself "sick and tired" of the fire. The unanimous response to this spiritual malaise is a commonplace fatalism. Chebutykin's dismissive "It doesn't matter" (*Vsyo ravno*) is echoed by most of the characters. Vershinin quotes it when denying differences between the military and civilians; Tusenbach describes his resignation from the army in those words; Solyony denigrates his love for Irina with the phrase. According to Irina, Andrey's debts "don't matter" to Natasha. This deliberate insouciance is the counterbalance to the equally deliberate velleities about the future.

To represent the slow disintegration of these lives, *Three Sisters* unfolds over a longer period of time than any of Chekhov's other plays. It begins on the fifth of May, Irina's twentieth name day, and ends in autumn four years later. The characters talk incessantly about time, from the very first line. The passage of time is denoted by such obvious tokens as Natasha's growing children, Andrey's problem with his weight and debts, and Olga's promotions. However, this is more than a family chronicle. Chekhov insists on the subjectivity of time. Each act indicates that what had gone before is now irrevocably swallowed up, not lost simply in the distant past, but in what had been yesterday. The sisters' rosy retrospect of their youth in Moscow, so aglow with promise, is tarnished when it comes in contact with someone who shared that youth, Vershinin. The party in Act One is spoken of in Act Two, which takes place only a few months later, as if it belonged to a bygone Golden Age. By Act Three, Tusenbach is referring to it as "Back in those days." Time measures the increasing negativity of life; it has been two years since the doctor took a drink, three (or maybe four) years since Masha played the piano. It's been a long time since Andrey played cards—the few months since Act Two. If time passes in a steady process of diminution, perspectives into the future are not enough to replace the losses. Chebutykin smashes a valuable clock, demolishing time, but his chiming watch in the last act continues to announce fresh departures.

Setting up markers for time, Chekhov constructs each act around a special event that catalyzes routine responses and sticks in the memory. Irina's name day celebration serves a number of dramatic functions: it commemorates a date, assembles all the characters in one place, and is the high water mark for the sisters' hopes. It is the last time we see them as sole mistresses in their own domain: each of them is on the verge of a promising situation. Coming of age opens the world to Irina; the arrival of Vershinin enlivens Masha; Olga still enjoys teaching. The Shrovetide party in Act Two is in sharp contrast: it takes place after dark, with several habitués absent (Olga and Kulygin must work late; Vershinin is delayed by his wife's suicide attempt). Twice the party is broken up by the usurper Natasha, from whom no masqueraders are forthcoming, any more than carriage horses were from Shamraev in The Seagull. Finally, the revelers realize that amusement must now be sought outside this home.

The eating at these events, a metaphor for shared experience, disintegrates as the play proceeds. Act One ends with the cast gathered round the table, regaling themselves with roast turkey, apple pie, and too much vodka. The odd men out are Natasha and Andrey, furtively conducting their romance removed from the teasing family. In Act Two, however, Natasha is seated at the festive board, criticizing the table manners of others and withholding tea; Solyony has eaten up all the chocolates. Once Natasha gains a foothold, the indiscriminate feeding ends. Vershinin goes hungry.

The fire in Act Three is a real coup de théâtre: physical danger, mass hysteria, and crowd movement, though kept offstage, have forced the characters into their present situation, both locally and emotionally. Like Andreev's image of steam rising in a boiler, they gradually are forced upwards into the compressed space beneath the eaves. Even though the conflagration does not singe the Prozorov house, it creates this thermodynamic effect. Exhausted or drunken, in some way pushed to an extreme by the calamity, the characters pour out their feelings and then leave. It is the most hysterical and most confessional act. Olga protests to no avail, "I'm not listening, I'm not listening!" Unlike purifying fires in Ibsen and Strindberg, this blaze leaves the sisters uncleansed, as their world is rapidly being consumed. Amidst the desolation, they are simply charred.

Once again, Chekhov constrains his characters to come in contact by preventing privacy. One would expect the bedroom of an old-maid schoolmarm and a young virgin to be the most sacrosanct of chambers, but a concatenation of circumstances turns it into Grand Central Station, from which intruders like Solyony and Chebutykin must be forcibly ejected. The space is intimate, just right for playing out personal crises; but the secrets are made to detonate in public. The doctor's drunken creed of nihilism, Andrey's exasperation with his wife, and Masha's blurting out of her adultery all become public events.

Or else the private moment is neutralized by submersion in minutiae. Masha makes up her mind to elope with Vershinin. Traditionally, this should be a major dramatic turning point, the crux when the heroine undergoes her peripeteia. Here, the decision is muffled by plans for a charity recital, Tusenbach's snoring, and other people's personal problems. The chance tryst offered by the fire trivializes Masha's and Vershinin's love because it projects it against a background of civic crisis. Even their lovesong has been reduced to "Trom-tom-tom," humming a theme from an operatic aria. What is crucial to some characters is always irrelevant or unknown to others, much as the seagull had been in that play. As Chebutykin says, "It doesn't matter." Chekhov, however, does not insist on the impossibility of values and communication; he simply believes that the attribution of value is hard for myopic mortals to make.

The last act adjusts the angle of vantage. There is very little recollection in it, but a good deal of futile straining towards the future. A brief time has elapsed between Act Three, when the regiment's departure is offhandedly mentioned, and Act Four, when it takes place. The departure is so abrupt an end to the sisters' consoling illusion that they cannot bring themselves to allude to the past. Henceforth, they will be thrown on their own resources. The play began with them lording it over the drawing room, but now they are cast into the yard. Olga lives at the school, Masha refuses to go into the house, and Andrey wanders about with the baby carriage like a soul in limbo. Food has lost its ability to comfort. The Baron must go off to his death without his morning coffee, while Andrey equates goose and cabbage with the deadly grip of matrimony. Each movement away is accompanied by music: the regiment leaves to the cheerful strains of a marching band, the piano tinkles to the cozy domesticity of Natasha and Protopopov, and the Doctor mockingly sings "Tarara-boom-de-ay." The bereft sisters standing in the yard are made to seem out of tune.

The final tableau, with the sisters clinging to one another, intoning "If only we knew, if only we knew!" has been played optimistically, as if the dawn of a bright tomorrow does lie just beyond the horizon. But Olga's evocation of time to come has lost the rosy tinge of Vershinin's and Tusenbach's improvisation. Like Sonya's threnody in *Uncle Vanya*, it is whistling in the dark, predicting a void that must be filled. The disillusionment of the four hours' traffic on the stage and the four years' passage of time has aged the sisters, but not enlightened them. In William Blake's words, they still "nurse unacted desires."

Directors who want an upbeat ending eliminate Dr. Chebutykin from this moment, but Chekhov placed him there to prevent this final descant from being taken at face value. The music-hall chorus he sings had Russian lyrics that would have been known to everyone in the original audience: "I'm sitting on a curbstone / Bitterly crying / 'Cause I don't know much." The implied mockery shows Olga's "If only we knew" to be an absurd wish. It is a laconic equivalent of the final chorus in *Oedipus the King*:

> . . . none of us mortals
> can truly be thought of as happy
> until he is granted deliverance from life . . .

Sophocles warned human beings not to assume they knew their place in the divine scheme. Chekhov's antiphony of Olga and Chebutykin carols the impossibility of such awareness, and the need to soldier on, despite that disability.

Three Sisters

A Drama in Four Acts

Characters[1]

PROZOROV, ANDREY SERGEEVICH

NATALYA IVANOVNA, his fiancée, afterwards his wife

OLGA
MASHA } his sisters
IRINA

KULYGIN, FYODOR ILYICH, high school teacher, Masha's husband

VERSHININ, ALEKSANDR IGNATYEVICH, Lieutenant Colonel, battery commander

TUSENBACH, NIKOLAY LVOVICH, Baron, Lieutenant

SOLYONY, VASILY VASILYEVICH, Staff Captain

CHEBUTYKIN, IVAN ROMANOVICH, army doctor

FEDOTIK, ALEKSEY PETROVICH, Second Lieutenant

RODÉ, VLADIMIR KARLOVICH, Second Lieutenant

FERAPONT, messenger for the County Council,[2] an old timer

ANFISA, nanny, an old woman of eighty

The action takes place in a county seat.[3]

1. There are fewer "speaking names" in this play than in the others: Ironically, Prozorov suggests "insight, perspicuity," and Vershinin suggests "heights, summit." Solyony means "salty." The name of the unseen Protopopov hints at descent from a line of archpriests.
2. *Zemskaya uprava*, the permanent executive council of the *zemstvo* or Rural Board, elected from among the members, not unlike a cabinet in its operations. For *zemstvo*, see *Ivanov*, note 3, page 24.
3. The capital of the *guberniya* and hence the seat of the regional government.

Act One

In the Prozorovs' home. A drawing room with columns, behind which a large reception room can be seen. Midday: outside it's sunny and bright.[4] *In the reception room, a table is being set for lunch.*

OLGA, *wearing the dark blue uniform of a teacher at a high school for girls,*[5] *never stops correcting students' examination books, both standing still and on the move.* MASHA, *in a black dress, her hat in her lap, sits reading a book.* IRINA, *in a white dress, stands rapt in thought.*

OLGA Father died just a year ago, this very day, the fifth of May, your saint's day,[6] Irina. It was very cold—snowing, in fact. I never thought I'd live through it; you had fainted dead away. But a year's gone by now, and we don't mind thinking about it, you're back to wearing white, your face is beaming. (*The clock strikes twelve.*) The clock struck then too. I remember, when Father was carried to his grave, there was music playing, they fired a salute at the cemetery. He was a general, commanded a whole brigade, but very few people showed up. Of course, it was raining at the time. Pelting rain and snow too.

IRINA Why remember?

(*Behind the columns, in the reception room near the table,* BARON TUSENBACH, CHEBUTYKIN, *and* SOLYONY *appear.*)

OLGA Today it's warm, the windows can be thrown open, and the birch trees aren't even budding yet. Father was put in charge of a brigade and we all left Moscow eleven years ago, and I distinctly remember, it was early May; why, just this time of year, everything in Moscow would already be in bloom, warm, everything would be bathed in sunlight. Eleven years have gone by, but I can remember everything there as if we'd left yesterday. Oh my goodness! I woke up this morning, saw the light pouring in, the springtime, and joy began to quicken in my heart; I began to long passionately for my beloved home.

4. "In *Three Sisters* on the rise of the curtain, as Stanislavsky's concept has it, birds are singing. These sounds were usually produced by Stanislavsky himself, A. L. Vishnevsky, I. M. Moskvin, V. F. Gribunin, N. G. Aleksandrov, and I, standing in the wings and cooing like doves. [Chekhov] listened to all these shenanigans, and, walking over to me, said: 'Listen, you bill and coo wonderfully, only it's an Egyptian dove!' And of the portrait of the sisters' father—General Prozorov (me in the makeup of an old general) he remarked, 'Listen, that's a Japanese general, we don't have that kind in Russia.' " (V. V. Luzhsky, *Solntse Rossii* 228 / 25 [1914])

5. Olga and Kulygin teach at a *gymnasium* or four-year provincial school, open to all classes of society; in 1876, to slow down the upward mobility of the lower classes, a heavy dose of Latin, Greek, and Old Church Slavonic replaced the more dangerous subjects of history, literature and geography in the extremely rigorous curriculum. Hence Kulygin's frequent citations from the classics.

6. Also known as a name day. Orthodox Russians celebrate the day of the saint after whom a person was named more commonly than their birthdays. St. Irina's day is May 5 in the Orthodox calendar.

CHEBUTYKIN   To hell with both of you!

TUSENBACH   You're right, it's ridiculous.

>   (MASHA, *brooding over her book, quietly whistles a tune under her breath.*[7])

OLGA   Don't whistle, Masha. How can you!

>   (*Pause.*)

Because I'm at the high school all day long and then have to give tutorials well into the night, I've got this constant headache, and my thoughts are those of an old woman. As a matter of fact, the four years I've been working at the high school, I've felt as if every day my strength and youth were draining from me drop by drop. While that same old dream keeps growing bigger and stronger . . .

IRINA   To go to Moscow. To sell the house, wind up everything here and—go to Moscow . . .

OLGA   Yes! Quick as you can to Moscow.

>   (CHEBUTYKIN *and* TUSENBACH *laugh.*)

IRINA   Brother will probably become a professor, he certainly won't go on living here. The only thing holding us back is our poor old Masha.

OLGA   Masha will come and spend all summer in Moscow, every year.

>   (MASHA *quietly whistles a tune.*)

IRINA   God willing, everything will work out. (*Looking out the window.*) Lovely weather today. I don't know why my heart feels so light! This morning I remembered that it was my saint's day, and suddenly I felt so happy, and remembered my childhood, when Mama was still alive. And such wonderful thoughts ran through my head, such thoughts!

OLGA   You're simply radiant today, you look especially pretty. And Masha's pretty too. Andrey'd be good-looking, only he's putting on too much weight and it doesn't suit him. And I'm aging just a bit and getting terribly thin; I suppose because I get cross with the girls at school. Well, today I'm free, I'm home, and my head doesn't ache; I feel younger than I did yesterday. I'm only twenty-eight . . . Everything is for the best, everything is God's will, but I do think that if I were married and could stay home all day, things might be better.

>   (*Pause.*)

I'd love my husband.

TUSENBACH (*To* SOLYONY.)   You talk such rubbish, a person gets sick and tired just listening to you. (*Entering the drawing room.*) I for-

---

7. See Chekhov's letter to Olga Knipper, January 2 (15), 1901, page 433.

got to mention. Today you'll be getting a visit from our new battery commander, Vershinin. (*Sits at the baby grand piano.*)

OLGA Is that so? That'll be nice.

IRINA Is he old?

TUSENBACH No, not really. Forty at most, forty-five. (*Quietly plays by ear.*) A splendid fellow, by all accounts. And no fool, that's for sure. Only he does talk a lot.

IRINA Is he interesting?

TUSENBACH Yes, so-so, but he's got a wife, a mother-in-law, and two little girls. His second wife at that. He goes visiting and tells everybody that he's got a wife and two little girls. He'll tell it here too. The wife's some kind of half-wit, with a long braid, like a school-girl, only talks about highfalutin stuff, philosophy, and she makes frequent attempts at suicide, apparently in order to give her husband a hard time. I would have left a woman like that ages ago, but he puts up with it and settles for complaining.

SOLYONY (*Entering the drawing room from the reception room with* CHEBUTYKIN.) With one hand I can't lift more than fifty pounds, but with both it goes up to two hundred pounds. Which leads me to conclude that two men are not twice as strong as one, but three times as strong, even stronger . . .

CHEBUTYKIN (*Reads the paper as he walks.*) For loss of hair . . . eight and a half grams of naphthalene in half-a-bottle of grain alcohol . . . dissolve and apply daily[8] . . . (*Makes a note in a memo book.*) Let's jot that down, shall we? (*To* SOLYONY.) Listen, as I was saying, you stick a tiny little cork in a tiny little bottle, and pass a tiny little glass tube through it . . . Then you take a tiny little pinch of the most common, ordinary alum . . .

IRINA Ivan Romanych, dear Ivan Romanych!

CHEBUTYKIN What, my darling girl, light of my life?

IRINA Tell me, why am I so happy today? I feel as if I'm skimming along at full sail, with the wide blue sky above me and big white birds drifting by. Why is that? Why?

CHEBUTYKIN (*Kissing both her hands, tenderly.*) My own white bird . . .

IRINA When I woke up today, I got out of bed and washed, and suddenly it dawned on me that I understand everything in the world and I know how a person ought to live. Dear Ivan Romanych, I know everything. A person has to work hard, work by the sweat of his brow, no matter who he is, and that's the only thing

---

8. Letter of Olga Knipper to Chekhov (September 12, 1900): "I'm going to give you a wonderful remedy to keep hair from falling out. Take half a bottle of methylated spirits and mix in eight grams of naphtalin and rub in regularly—it's a big help. Will you do it? Because it's not a good idea to come to Moscow bald—people will think I pulled your hair out."

that gives meaning and purpose to his life, his happiness, his moments of ecstasy. Wouldn't it be great to be a manual laborer who gets up while it's still dark out and breaks stones on the road, or a shepherd, or a schoolteacher, or an engineer on the railroad? . . . My God, what's the point of being human? You might as well be an ox, an ordinary horse, so long as you're working, rather than a young woman who gets up at noon, has her coffee in bed, and takes two hours to dress . . . oh, isn't that awful! Sometimes when the weather's sultry, the way you long for a drink; well, that's the way I long for work. And if I don't get up early and work hard, stop being my friend, Ivan Romanych.

CHEBUTYKIN (*Tenderly.*) I will, I will . . .

OLGA Father drilled us to get up at seven. Nowadays, Irina wakes up at seven and stays in bed at least 'til nine, thinking about things. And the serious face on her! (*Laughs.*)

IRINA You're used to treating me like a little girl, so you think it's strange when I put on a serious face. I'm twenty years old!

TUSENBACH The longing for hard work, oh dear, how well I understand it! I've never worked in my life. I was born in Petersburg, cold, idle Petersburg, to a family that didn't know the meaning of hard work or hardship. I remember, whenever I came home from school, a lackey would pull off my boots, while I'd fidget and my mother would gaze at me in adoration and be surprised when anyone looked at me any other way. They tried to shield me from hard work. And they just about managed it, only just! The time has come; there's a thundercloud looming over us, there's a bracing, mighty tempest lying in wait, close at hand, and soon it will blow all the indolence, apathy, prejudice against hard work, putrid boredom out of our society. I shall work, and in twenty-five or thirty years everyone will be working. Every last one of us!

CHEBUTYKIN I won't work.

TUSENBACH You don't count.

SOLYONY In twenty-five years you won't be on this earth, thank God. In two or three years you'll die of apoplexy, or I'll fly off the handle and put a bullet through your brain, angel mine. (*Takes a flask of perfume from his pocket and sprinkles his chest and hands.*)

CHEBUTYKIN (*Laughs.*) As a matter of fact, I've never done a thing. Ever since I left the university, I haven't lifted a finger, not even read a book, nothing but newspapers . . . (*Takes from his pocket a second newspaper.*) You see . . . I know by the papers that there was, let's say, somebody named Dobrolyubov,[9] but what he wrote—I don't know . . . God knows . . . (*Someone can be heard*

9. Nikolay Aleksandrovich Dobrolyubov (1836–1861), Russian journalist of the radical democratic camp and proponent of realistic literature. He invented the concept of the "superfluous man."

knocking on the floor from a lower story.) There . . . They're calling for me downstairs, someone's come for me. I'll be right there . . . hold on. . . . (*Leaves hurriedly, combing his beard.*)

IRINA   This is something he's cooked up.

TUSENBACH   Yes. He went out with a look of triumph on his face; I'll bet he's about to deliver a present.

IRINA   How unpleasant!

OLGA   Yes, it's awful. He's always doing something silly.

MASHA   "On the curved seashore a green oak stands, a golden chain wound 'round that oak . . . A golden chain wound 'round that oak . . ."[1] (*Rises and hums quietly.*)

OLGA   You're in a funny mood today, Masha. (MASHA, *humming, adjusts her hat.*)
Where are you off to?

MASHA   Home.

IRINA   Strange . . .

TUSENBACH   Leaving a saint's day party!

MASHA   Doesn't matter. I'll be back this evening. Good-bye, my dearest . . . (*Kisses* IRINA.) Best wishes once more, good health, be happy. In the old days, when Father was alive, every time we celebrated a saint's day, some thirty or forty officers would show up, there was lots of noise; but today there's only a man and a half, and it's as desolate as a desert . . . I'm off . . . I'm melancholeric[2] today, I don't feel very cheerful, and you musn't mind me. (*Laughs through tears.*) Later we'll have a talk, but good-bye for now, my darling, I'm off.

IRINA (*Put out.*)   Well, that's just like you . . .

OLGA (*Plaintively.*)   I understand you, Masha.

SOLYONY   If a man philosophizes, you could call it philosophistry or even sophisticuffs, but if a woman philosophizes or two women, that you could call—Polly want a cracker!

MASHA   What do you mean by that, you dreadfully awful man?

SOLYONY   Not a thing. "He scarcely had time to gasp, When the bear had him in its grasp."[3]

---

1. Masha quotes from the opening lines of the famous poetic fable *Ruslan and Lyudmila* by Aleksandr Pushkin, a classic love story. On her wedding night, Lyudmila is abducted by a wizard and Ruslan finds her only after many adventures. The lines are: "On the curved seashore a green oak stands, / A golden chain wound round that oak; / And night and day a learned cat / Walks 'round and 'round upon that chain. / When he goes right a song he sings, / When he goes left a tale he tells." An English equivalent might be Edward Lear's "The owl and the pussycat went to sea, In a beautiful pea-green boat . . . A beautiful pea-green boat . . ."

2. *Merlekhyundiya*, instead of *melankholiya*. A favorite word of Chekhov's, often used in private correspondence, as well as in "The Examining Magistrate" and *Ivanov*. "[Y]our nerves are in bad shape, and you're under the sway of a psychiatric semi-ailment, which seminarians call melancholera." (To A. A. Suvorin, August 23, 1893).

3. Quotation from the fable "The Peasant and the Farmhand" by Ivan Krylov (1768–1844), which Chekhov also quotes in the story "With Acquaintances" (1898): "He had a habit,

(*Pause.*)

MASHA (*To* OLGA, *angrily.*)   Stop snivelling!

(*Enter* ANFISA *and* FERAPONT *with a layer cake.*)

ANFISA   Over here, dearie. Come on in, your feet're clean. (*To* IRINA.) From the County Council, from Protopopov, from Mikhail Ivanych . . . A cake.

IRINA   Thank you. Thank him. (*Takes the cake.*)

FERAPONT   How's that?

IRINA (*Louder.*)   Thank him!

OLGA   Nanny dear, give him some pie. Ferapont, go on, out there they'll give you some pie.

FERAPONT   How's that?

ANFISA   Let's go, dearie, Ferapont Spiridonych. Let's go . . . (*Exits with* FERAPONT.)

MASHA   I do not like Protopopov, that bear bearing gifts. It isn't right to invite him.

IRINA   I didn't invite him.

MASHA   Good girl.

(*Enter* CHEBUTYKIN, *followed by* A SOLDIER *carrying a silver samovar; a low murmur of astonishment and displeasure.*)

OLGA (*Hides her face in her hands.*)   A samovar! How dreadfully inappropriate.[4] (*Goes to the table in the reception room.*)

IRINA   Ivan Romanych, you darling, what are you doing? ⎫

TUSENBACH (*Laughs.*)   I told you so. ⎬ (*Together.*)

MASHA   Ivan Romanych, you're simply shameless! ⎭

CHEBUTYKIN   My dears, my darlings, you're the only ones I have; for me you're more precious than anything on this earth. I'll be sixty soon, I'm an old man; a lonely, insignificant old man . . . There's nothing good about me, except this love for you, and if it weren't for you, I'd be dead and gone long ago . . . (*To* IRINA.) My dearest child, I've known you since the day you were born . . . I held you in my arms . . . I loved your poor mama . . .

IRINA   But why such expensive presents?

CHEBUTYKIN (*Through tears, angrily.*)   Expensive presents . . . You're the limit! (*To* THE ORDERLY.) Put the samovar over there . . . (*Mimicks.*) Expensive presents . . .

(THE ORDERLY *takes the samovar into the reception room.*)

ANFISA (*Crossing the drawing room.*)   My dears, a strange colonel! He's already taken off his overcoat; boys and girls, he's coming in

---

unsettling for his interlocutor, of pronouncing as an exclamation a certain phrase which had no relation to the conversation, while snapping his fingers."

4. A samovar was traditionally given by a husband to his wife on their silver or golden anniversary.

here. Arinushka, now you be a charming, polite little girl . . .
(*Going out.*) Lunch should have been served a long time ago now
. . . Honest to goodness . . .

TUSENBACH   Vershinin, I suppose. (*Enter* VERSHININ.) Lieutenant
Colonel Vershinin.

VERSHININ (*To* MASHA *and* IRINA.)   May I introduce myself: Vershinin.[5] Very, very pleased to meet you at long last. How you've
grown! My! my!

IRINA   Do sit down, please. We're glad to have you.

VERSHININ (*Merrily.*)   I am delighted, delighted. But weren't you
three sisters? I remember three little girls. I've stopped remembering faces, but your father, Colonel Prozorov, had three little
girls; that I distinctly remember, and I saw them with my own eyes.
How time flies. Dear, dear, how time flies!

TUSENBACH   The Colonel is from Moscow.

IRINA   From Moscow? You're from Moscow?

VERSHININ   Yes, that's where I'm from. Your late father was battery
commander there; I was an officer in the same brigade. (*To*
MASHA.) Now your face I do seem to remember.

MASHA   And I remember yours—not at all!

IRINA   Olya! Olya! (*Shouts into the reception room.*) Olya, come
here! (OLGA *enters the drawing room from the reception room.*)
Lieutenant Colonel Vershinin, it turns out, is from Moscow.

VERSHININ   You must be Olga Sergeevna, the eldest . . . And you're
Masha . . . And you're Irina—the youngest . . .

OLGA   You're from Moscow?

VERSHININ   Yes. I was at school in Moscow and entered the service
in Moscow, served a long time there, was finally given a battery
here—I've been transferred here, as you see. I don't remember
you individually, I only remember that you were three sisters. Your
father's stuck in my memory; why, I can close my eyes and see
him as if he were alive. I used to visit you in Moscow . . .

OLGA   I was sure I remembered everyone, and suddenly . . .

VERSHININ   My name is Aleksandr Ignatyevich . . .

IRINA   Aleksandr Ignatyevich, you're from Moscow . . . That's a
coincidence!

OLGA   In fact, we'll be moving there.

IRINA   We think we'll be there as soon as autumn. Our home town,
we were born there . . . On Old Basmanny Street . . .
         (*Both women laugh for joy.*)

MASHA   We've unexpectedly come across someone from our neck of

5. "When I played Vershinin, Chekhov said: 'Good, very good. Only don't salute like that,
it's not like a colonel. You salute like a lieutenant. You have to do it more firmly, more
confidently' . . ." (Vasily Kachalov, *Shipovnik Almanac* 23 [1914].)

the woods! (*Vivaciously.*) Now I remember! I do remember. Olya, at home they used to talk about "the lovesick major." You were a lieutenant then and in love with someone, and everybody teased you, calling you major for some reason . . .

VERSHININ (*Laughs.*) That's right, that's right! . . . "The lovesick major," right you are . . .

MASHA Then you only had a moustache . . . Oh, how you've aged! (*Plaintively.*) How you've aged!

VERSHININ Yes, in those days they called me the lovesick major; I was still young and in love. It's not the same now.

OLGA But you don't have a single gray hair yet. You've aged, but you haven't grown old.

VERSHININ Nevertheless, I am forty-three. Have you been away from Moscow a long time?

IRINA Eleven years. Why, what's wrong, Masha? You're crying, you crazy . . . (*Plaintively.*) Now I'm starting to cry . . .

MASHA I'm all right. And what street did you live on?

VERSHININ Old Basmanny.

OLGA Why, we lived there too . . .

VERSHININ At one time, I lived on German Street. I'd walk from German Street to the Red Barracks. On the way there's this grim-looking bridge, with the water roaring beneath it. A lonely man begins to feel his heart bowed down.

(*Pause.*)

But here there's such a broad, such a fertile river! A wonderful river!

OLGA Yes, only it's cold. It's cold here and there are mosquitoes . . .

VERSHININ Why should you care? Here there's such a wholesome, bracing Russian climate. A forest, a river . . . and birch trees here, too. Dear, humble birches, I love them more than any other tree. It's a good place to live. Only it's odd—the train station is over thirteen miles away . . . And nobody knows why that is.

SOLYONY I know why that is. (*Everyone stares at him.*) Because if the station were nearby, it wouldn't be far away, and if it were far away, obviously it wouldn't be nearby.

(*An awkward silence.*)

TUSENBACH Always clowning, Solyony.

OLGA Now I've remembered you too. I do remember.

VERSHININ I knew your dear mother.

CHEBUTYKIN She was a good woman, rest her soul.

IRINA Mama is buried in Moscow.

OLGA In Novodevichy churchyard . . . [6]

6. Graveyard attached to the historic Moscow "New Virgin" convent, where many celebrities of politics, society, and culture, including Chekhov and his father, are buried.

MASHA Just imagine, I'm already beginning to forget what she looked like. No one will remember about us either. They'll forget.

VERSHININ Yes. They'll forget. Such is our fate, nothing you can do about it. The things we take to be serious, meaningful, of great importance—a time will come when they will be forgotten or seem of no importance.

(*Pause.*)

And the interesting thing is, we have absolutely no way of knowing just what will be considered sublime and important, and what trivial and absurd. Didn't the discoveries of Copernicus or, say, Columbus at first sound pointless, absurd, while some inane nonsense written by a crank sounded true? And it may come about that our current life, which we're so used to, will in time seem strange, uncomfortable, unintelligent, devoid of purity, maybe even depraved . . .

TUSENBACH Who knows? Maybe they'll call our life sublime and remember us with respect. Nowadays we don't have torture, executions, invasions; and yet, there's so much suffering.

SOLYONY (*Shrilly.*) Cheep, cheep, cheep . . . Don't feed the Baron birdseed, just let 'im philosophize.

TUSENBACH Solyony, please leave me in peace . . . (*Moves to another seat.*) It gets to be a bore, after a while.

SOLYONY (*Shrilly.*) Cheep, cheep, cheep . . .

TUSENBACH (*To* VERSHININ.) The suffering you can observe nowadays—and there's so much of it!—nevertheless betokens a certain moral progress that society has already achieved . . .

VERSHININ Yes, yes, of course.

CHEBUTYKIN You said just now, Baron, they'll call our life elevated, but all the same people are low . . . (*Rises.*) Look how low I am. My only consolation is you telling me my life is elevated and makes sense.

(*Offstage, someone is playing a violin.*)

MASHA That's Andrey playing, our brother.

IRINA He's the scholar of the family. He's meant to be a professor. Papa was a military man, but his son chose an academic career.

MASHA As Papa wished.

OLGA Today we were teasing the life out of him. He's a bit infatuated, it seems.

IRINA With a certain local miss. She'll show up here today, most likely.

MASHA Ah, the way she dresses! It's not so much unbecoming or unfashionable as simply pathetic. Some strange, gaudy, yellowish skirt with a vulgar little fringe and a red jacket. And her cheeks are scrubbed so raw! Andrey is not in love—I won't allow that,

after all he has taste—but he's simply, well, teasing us, playing the
fool. Yesterday I heard she's marrying Protopopov, the chairman
of the County Council. And a good thing, too . . . (*Out the side
door.*) Andrey, come here! Just for a second, dear!

(*Enter* ANDREY.)

OLGA This is my brother, Andrey Sergeich.

VERSHININ Vershinin.

ANDREY Prozorov. (*Wipes his sweating face.*) You're here as battery
commander?

OLGA Imagine, the Colonel is from Moscow.

ANDREY Really? Well, congratulations, now my sisters won't give
you a moment's peace.

VERSHININ I've had plenty of time already to bore your sisters.

IRINA Just look at the portrait frame Andrey gave me today! (*Displays the frame.*) He made it himself.

VERSHININ (*Looking at the frame and not knowing what to say.*) Yes
. . . quite something . . .

IRINA And there's that picture frame over the baby grand, he made
that too.

(ANDREY *waves his hand in dismissal and moves away.*)

OLGA He's the scholar in the family and plays the violin and makes
all sorts of things with his fretsaw—in short, a Jack of all trades.
Andrey, don't go away! He's funny that way—always wandering
off. Come over here!

(MASHA *and* IRINA *take him by the arms and laughingly escort
him back.*)

MASHA Come on, come on!

ANDREY Leave me alone, for pity's sake.

MASHA Don't be ridiculous! They used to call the Colonel the lovesick major and he didn't get the tiniest bit angry.

VERSHININ Not the tiniest bit!

MASHA And I want to call you: the lovesick fiddler!

IRINA Or the lovesick professor! . . .

OLGA He's lovesick! Andryusha's lovesick!

IRINA (*Applauding.*) Bravo, bravo! Encore! Little Andryusha's lovesick!

CHEBUTYKIN (*Comes up behind* ANDREY *and puts both arms around his
waist.*) "For love alone did Nature put us on this earth!"[7] (*Roars
with laughter; he's still holding onto his newspaper.*)

ANDREY All right, that's enough, that's enough . . . (*Wipes his face.*)
I didn't get a wink of sleep last night and now I'm not quite myself,

---

7. The opening of Taisiya's "Russian aria" in the old opera-vaudeville *Reversals* by Pyotr
Kobryakov (1808): "For love alone did Nature / Put us on this earth; / As comfort to
the mortal race / She gave the gift of tender feelings!"

as they say. I read until four, then I went to bed, but it was no good. I kept thinking about this and that, and the next thing I knew it's dawn and the sun's creeping into my bedroom. This summer, while I'm still here, I want to translate a certain book from the English.

VERSHININ So you read English?

ANDREY Yes. Father, rest in peace, overstocked us with education. It sounds silly and absurd, but still I must admit, after his death I started putting on weight and, well, I put on so much weight in one year, it's as if my body were freeing itself of its constraints. Thanks to Father, my sisters and I know French, German and English, and Irina also knows a little Italian. But what good is it?

MASHA In this town knowing three languages is a superfluous luxury. Not even a luxury, but a kind of superfluous appendage, a bit like a sixth finger. We know a lot of useless stuff.

VERSHININ Well, I'll be. (*Laughs.*) I don't think there is or can be a town so boring and dismal that an intelligent, educated person isn't of use. Let's assume that among the one hundred thousand inhabitants of this town, which is, I grant you, backward and crude, there are only three such as you. Naturally, it's not up to you to enlighten the benighted masses that surround you. In the course of your lifetime, you must gradually surrender and be swallowed up in the crowd of a hundred thousand, you'll be smothered by life, but even so you won't disappear, won't sink without a trace. In your wake, others like you will appear, maybe six, then twelve and so on, until at last the likes of you will be the majority. In two hundred, three hundred years life on earth will be unimaginably beautiful, stupendous. Man needs a life like that, and if it isn't here and now, then he must look forward to it, wait, dream, prepare himself for it, and that's the reason he must see and know more than his father and grandfather saw and knew. (*Laughs.*) And you complain you know a lot of useless stuff.

MASHA (*Takes off her hat.*) I'm staying for lunch.

IRINA (*With a sigh.*) Honestly, I should have taken notes . . .

(ANDREY's *gone; he left unnoticed.*)

TUSENBACH Many years from now, you say, life on earth will be beautiful, stupendous. That's true. But to take part in it now, even remotely, a person has to prepare for it, a person has to work . . .

VERSHININ (*Rises.*) Yes. By the way, you have so many flowers! (*Looking around.*) And wonderful quarters! I'm jealous! All my life I've knocked around in cramped quarters with two chairs, the same old sofa, and stoves that invariably smoke. The main thing missing in my life has been flowers like these . . . (*Waves his hand in dismissal.*) Oh well! That's how it is!

TUSENBACH Yes, a person has to work. I suppose you're thinking: he's gushing all over the place like a typical sentimental German.[8] But, word of honor, I'm a Russian, I don't even speak German. My father belongs to the Orthodox Church . . .

(*Pause.*)

VERSHININ (*Paces the stage back and forth.*) I often think: what if a man were to begin life anew, and fully conscious at that? If one life, which has already been lived out, were—how shall I put it?—a rough draft, and the other—a final revision! Then each of us, I think, would, first of all, try hard not to repeat himself; at least we'd create a different setting for our life, we'd furnish quarters like these for ourselves with flowers, great bunches of flowers . . . I have a wife, two little girls, in addition my wife's not a well woman, et cetera, et cetera, yes, but if one were to begin life from the beginning, I wouldn't get married . . . No, no!

(*Enter* KULYGIN *in a uniform dress coat.*)

KULYGIN (*Comes up to* IRINA.) Dearest sister, may I congratulate you on your saint's day and sincerely wish you, from the bottom of my heart, the best of health and all those things proper to wish a young girl of your years. (*Gives her the book.*) The history of our high school over the past fifty years, written by yours truly. A frivolous little book, written when I had nothing better to do, but you go ahead and read it all the same. Greetings, ladies and gentlemen! (*To* VERSHININ.) Kulygin, teacher in the local high school. Civil servant, seventh class. (*To* IRINA.) In that book, you'll find a list of all the alumni of our high school for the past fifty years. *Feci quod potui, faciant meliora potentes.*[9] (*Kisses* MASHA.)

IRINA But didn't you give me this book last Easter?

KULYGIN (*Laughs.*) Impossible! In that case give it back, or better yet, give it to the Colonel. Here you are, Colonel. Someday you'll read it when you're bored.

VERSHININ Thank you. (*Prepares to go.*) I'm most happy to have made your acquaintance . . .

OLGA You're going? No, no!

IRINA You'll stay and have lunch with us. Please.

OLGA I insist!

VERSHININ (*Bows.*) I seem to have dropped in on a saint's day party. Forgive me, I didn't know, I haven't congratulated you . . . (*Goes into the reception room with* OLGA.)

KULYGIN Today, ladies and gentlemen, is Sunday, the day of rest; therefore, let us rest, let us make merry each according to his age

---

8. Tusenbach further explains his German ancestry in Act Two. In Chekhov's notebooks, Tusenbach's patronymic is Karlovich (son of Karl), which was later changed to Lvovich (son of Leo, a more Russian name).

9. Latin, "I have done what I could, let those who can do better." A paraphrase of Cicero, when the Roman consulate conferred his powers on his successors.

and station in life. The rugs will have to be taken up for summer
and put away until winter . . . With mothballs or naphthalene . . .
The Romans were a healthy people because they knew how to
work hard and they knew how to relax; they had *mens sana in
corpore sano*.[1] Their life moved according to a set pattern. Our
headmaster says: the main thing in every man's life is its pattern
. . . Whatever loses its pattern ceases to exist—and in our everyday
life the same holds true. (*Takes* MASHA *'round the waist, laughing.*)
Masha loves me. My wife loves me. And the window curtains too
along with the rugs . . . Today I'm cheerful, in splendid spirits.
Masha, at four o'clock today we have to go to the headmaster's.
An outing's been arranged for the faculty and their families.

MASHA I'm not going.

KULYGIN (*Mortified.*) Masha dear, whyever not?

MASHA We'll discuss it later . . . (*Angrily.*) Very well, I'll go, but do
leave me alone, for pity's sake . . . (*Walks away.*)

KULYGIN And then we'll spend the evening at the headmaster's.
Despite his failing health, that man strives above all to be sociable.
An outstanding, brilliant personality. A magnificent man. Yesterday after our meeting he says to me, "I'm tired, Fyodor Ilyich! I'm
tired!" (*Looks at the clock on the wall, then at his watch.*) Your
clock is seven minutes fast. Yes, says he, I'm tired!

(*Offstage, someone is playing the violin.*)

OLGA Ladies and gentlemen, please come to the table! There's a
meat pie!

KULYGIN Ah, my dear Olga, my dear! Yesterday I worked from morn
to eleven at night; I was exhausted, and today I feel happy. (*Goes
to the table in the reception room.*) My dear . . .

CHEBUTYKIN (*Puts the newspaper in his pocket, combs out his beard.*)
A meat pie? Splendid!

MASHA (*Sternly, to* CHEBUTYKIN.) Just watch your step; don't have
anything to drink today. You hear? Drinking's bad for you.

CHEBUTYKIN Bah! That's over and done with. Two years since I last
was drunk. (*Impatiently.*) Anyways, lady, it don't make no never
mind!

MASHA All the same, don't you dare drink. Don't you dare. (*Angrily,
but so her husband can't hear.*) Damn it to hell, another boring
evening at the headmaster's!

TUSENBACH If I were in your shoes, I wouldn't go . . . Plain and
simple.

CHEBUTYKIN Don't go, my lovely!

MASHA 'Sall very well to say "don't go" . . . This damned life is
unbearable . . . (*Goes into the reception room.*)

1. Latin, "A healthy mind in a healthy body," quotation from the *Satires* of Juvenal.

CHEBUTYKIN (*Following her.*)   Now, now!

SOLYONY (*Crossing into the reception room.*)   Cheep, cheep, cheep . . .

TUSENBACH   That's enough, Solyony. Cut it out!

SOLYONY   Cheep, cheep, cheep . . .

KULYGIN (*Merrily.*)   Your health, Colonel! I'm an educator, and here in this house one of the family, Masha's hubby . . . She's a kind-hearted creature, really kind . . .

VERSHININ   I'll have some of that dark vodka[2] there . . . (*Drinks.*) Your health! (*To* OLGA.) I feel so good being here with you! . . .

          (*In the drawing room,* IRINA *and* TUSENBACH *remain.*)

IRINA   Masha's in a funny mood today. She married at eighteen, when he seemed to her to be the cleverest of men. And now he doesn't. He's the kindest, but not the cleverest.

OLGA (*Impatiently.*)   Andrey, are you coming?

ANDREY (*Offstage.*)   Right away.(*Enters and goes to the table.*)

TUSENBACH   What are you thinking about?

IRINA   This. I don't like that Solyony of yours, I'm afraid of him. Everything he says is stupid . . .

TUSENBACH   He's a strange fellow. I feel sorry for him, and I get annoyed by him, but mostly sorry. I think he's shy . . . When we're alone together, he's often clever and pleasant enough, but in company he's rude, a bully. Don't go, let them sit at the table a little. Let me be near you for a while. What are you thinking about? (*Pause.*) You're twenty, I'm not yet thirty. How many years there are ahead of us, ahead of us, a long, long series of days, filled with my love for you . . .

IRINA   Nikolay Lvovich, don't talk to me about love . . .

TUSENBACH (*Not listening.*)   I thirst so passionately for life, struggle, hard work, and this thirst of my heart has blended with my love of you, Irina, and it all seems to fit, because you're beautiful and life looks just as beautiful to me! What are you thinking about?

IRINA   You say: life is beautiful. Yes, but what if it only seems that way! For us three sisters, life hasn't been beautiful; it's choked us, like weeds . . . There are tears running down my face. That's not what we need . . . (*Quickly wipes her face, smiles.*) What we need is work, work. That's why things look so gloomy to us, why we take such a dim view of life, because we don't know what hard work is. We're the children of people who despised hard work . . .

          (NATALIYA IVANOVNA *enters, wearing a pink dress with a green belt.*)

2. Vodka is traditionally flavored with herbs and spices such as buffalo grass, cardamom and peppercorns.

NATASHA They've already sat down to lunch . . . I'm late . . . (*Catches a glimpse of herself in a mirror, sets herself to rights.*) My hairdo looks all right . . . (*On seeing* IRINA.) Dear Irina Sergeevna, congratulations! (*Kisses her energetically and at length.*) You've got a lot of guests, honestly, I'm embarrassed . . . Good afternoon, Baron!

OLGA (*Entering the drawing room.*) Why, here's Nataliya Ivanovna too. Good afternoon, my dear!
(*They exchange kisses.*)

NATASHA With the party girl. You've got such a lot of company, I'm awfully nervous . . .

OLGA Don't be silly, it's all family. (*In an undertone, shocked.*) You're wearing a green belt! My dear, that's a mistake!

NATASHA Is it bad luck?

OLGA No, it simply doesn't go . . . It's all wrong somehow . . .

NATASHA (*On the verge of tears.*) Really? But actually it's not green, it's more a sort of beige.
(*Follows* OLGA *into the reception room.*)
(*In the reception room, everyone is seated at the table; not a soul is left in the drawing room.*)

KULYGIN I wish you, Irina, a proper fiancé. It's high time you got married.

CHEBUTYKIN Nataliya Ivanovna, I wish you a tiny little fiancé.

KULYGIN Nataliya Ivanovna already has a tiny little fiancé.

MASHA (*Raps a fork on a plate.*) I'll have a glass of wine! What the hell, life's for living, so let's live dangerously!

KULYGIN Your conduct gets C-minus.

VERSHININ My, this is a tasty cordial. What's it flavored with?

SOLYONY Cockroaches.

IRINA (*On the verge of tears.*) Ick! Ick! That's disgusting! . . .

OLGA For supper we're having roast turkey and apple pie.[3] Thank God, I'm home all day today, home this evening . . . Gentlemen, do come again this evening.

VERSHININ May I come in the evening too?

IRINA Please do.

NATASHA It's do as you please around here.

CHEBUTYKIN "For love alone did Nature put us on this earth." (*Laughs.*)

ANDREY (*Angrily.*) Will you stop it, gentlemen! Don't you get sick of it?
(FEDOTIK *and* RODÉ *enter with a large basket of flowers.*)

3. American though this sounds, the turkey would have been stuffed with liver and walnuts, sliced, and served with a Madeira sauce. The open-face apple pie would contain almonds, cherry jam, and raisins.

FEDOTIK They're already eating lunch.

RODÉ (*Loudly, rolling his r's.*) They're already eating? Yes, they are already eating . . .

FEDOTIK Wait just a minute! (*Takes a snapshot.*) One! Hold it just a bit more . . . (*Takes another snapshot.*) Two! Now we're through!
   (*They take the basket and go into the reception room, where they are greeted boisterously.*)

RODÉ (*Loudly.*) Congratulations! I wish you the best of everything, the best of everything! Enchanting weather today, simply splendid. All this morning I was out on a hike with the high-school students. I teach gymnastics at the high school . . .

FEDOTIK You may move now, Irina Sergeevna, yes you may! (*Takes a snapshot.*) You are an interesting model today. (*Pulls a humming top out of his pocket.*) And in addition, look, a humming top . . . Makes a wonderful sound . . .

IRINA What a treasure!

MASHA "On the curved seashore a green oak stands, a golden chain wound 'round that oak . . . A golden chain wound 'round that oak . . ." (*Tearfully.*) Now, why do I keep saying that? Those lines have been stuck in my head since this morning . . .

KULYGIN Thirteen at table!

RODÉ (*Loudly.*) Ladies and gentlemen, how can you possibly lend credence to superstitions?
   (*Laughter.*)

KULYGIN If there are thirteen at table, that means there are lovers here. Might you be one, Doctor? Perish the thought . . .
   (*Laughter.*)

CHEBUTYKIN I've been a sinner from way back, but look, why Nataliya Ivanovna should get embarrassed is something I simply cannot understand.
   (*Loud laughter.* NATASHA *runs out of the reception room into the drawing room, followed by* ANDREY.)

ANDREY Never mind, don't pay any attention! Wait . . . Stop, please . . .

NATASHA I'm embarrassed . . . I don't know what to do with myself, and they're all poking fun at me. I just left the table, and I know it's impolite, but I can't . . . I can't . . . (*Hides her face in her hands.*)

ANDREY My dearest, please, I beg you, don't get upset. I swear to you, they're only joking, it's all in good fun. My dearest, my own, they're all kind, loving people and they love me and you. Come over here to the window where they can't see us . . . (*Looking around.*)

NATASHA I'm so unaccustomed to being in society! . . .

ANDREY   Oh youth, wonderful, beautiful, youth. My dearest, my own, don't get so upset! . . . Believe me, believe me . . . I feel so good, my heart is brimming over with love, delight . . . Oh, they can't see us! They can't see! Why I fell in love with you, when I fell in love with you—oh, I have no idea. My dearest, good, pure love, be my wife! I'd love you, love you . . . like no one ever . . . (*A kiss.*)

>   (TWO OFFICERS *enter and, on seeing the kissing couple, stop in amazement.*)

CURTAIN

Act Two

Same set as in Act One.
Eight o'clock at night. From offstage, as if from the street, one can faintly hear a concertina playing. No lights.

>   (*Enter* NATALIYA IVANOVNA *in a housecoat and carrying a candle; she walks around and stops by the door leading to* ANDREY's *room.*)

NATASHA   Andryusha, what're you doing? Reading? Never mind, I'm just . . . (*Walks around, opens another door and, after peeping in, closes it again.*) Seeing if there's a light . . .

ANDREY (*Enters, holding a book.*)   You what, Natasha?

NATASHA   I'm checking to see if there's a light . . . Now that it's carnival week,[4] the servants are out of control, you have to keep a sharp lookout to see that nothing goes wrong. Last night at midnight, I was walking through the dining room and there was a candle burning. Who lit it, I never did manage to find out. (*Puts down the candle.*) What time is it?

ANDREY (*After a look at his watch.*)   Quarter past eight.

NATASHA   And Olga and Irina not back yet. They aren't here. Still at work, poor things. Olga at the faculty meeting, Irina at the telegraph office . . . (*Sighs.*) Just this morning I was saying to your sister, "Take care of yourself," I say, "Irina, love." But she doesn't listen. A quarter past eight, you said? I'm worried our Bobik[5] isn't at all well. Why is he so cold? Yesterday he had a fever and today he's cold all over . . . I'm so worried!

ANDREY   It's nothing, Natasha. The boy's healthy.

---

4. *Maslennitsa* or Butter Week, the week preceding Lent, was traditionally devoted to parties and carousing. The consumption of butter-soaked pancakes (*blini*) and the invitation of musicians into homes were traditional activities. Evidently a year and nine months have passed since Act One.
5. Natasha is being pretentious, but gets it wrong. An English name such as Bob was fashionable in high society, but at this time Bobik was usually applied to dogs.

NATASHA But even so, we'd better put him on a diet. I'm worried. And at nine o'clock tonight, they were saying, the masqueraders[6] will be here. It'd be better if they didn't put in an appearance, Andryusha.

ANDREY I really don't know. After all, they were sent for.

NATASHA This morning, the little darling woke up and looks at me, and suddenly he smiled, which means he recognized me. "Bobik," I say, "morning! morning! darling!" And he laughs. Children do understand, they understand perfectly well. So, in that case, Andryusha, I'll tell the servants not to let the masqueraders in.

ANDREY (*Indecisively.*) But after all, that's up to my sisters. They're in charge here.

NATASHA Oh, they are too, I'll tell them. They're considerate . . . (*Walks around.*) For supper I ordered some yogurt. Doctor says you shouldn't eat anything but yogurt, otherwise you won't lose weight. (*Stops.*) Bobik is cold. I'm worried, it's too cold for him in his room, most likely. At least until the weather gets warmer we should put him in another room. For instance, Irina's room is just right for a baby, it's dry and sunny all day long. I'll have to tell her, meanwhile she can double up with Olga in the same room . . . It doesn't matter, she's not at home during the day, only spends the night here . . . (*Pause.*) Andryusha, sweetie pie, why don't you say something?

ANDREY No reason, I was thinking . . . Besides, there's nothing to be said . . .

NATASHA Right . . . Something I wanted to tell you . . . Oh yes. Ferapont's out there, sent by the council; he's asking to see you.

ANDREY (*Yawns.*) Send him in.

     (NATASHA *exits;* ANDREY, *hunched over the candle she's forgotten, reads a book. Enter* FERAPONT; *he is wearing an old threadbare overcoat with a turned-up collar, his ears covered by a kerchief.*)

ANDREY 'Evening, old timer. What have you got to say for yourself ?

FERAPONT Chairman sent a book and a paper of some sort. Here . . . (*Hands over a book and a paper.*)

ANDREY Thanks. Fine. But why didn't you get here earlier? After all it's past eight already.

FERAPONT How's that?

ANDREY (*Louder.*) I said, you've come so late, it's already past eight.

FERAPONT Right you are. When I got here it was still light, but they

---

6. *Ryazhenye* were well-behaved amateur performers in carnival costume who, after dusk, would go from house to house at Shrovetide, dancing and receiving food in return. Trick-and-treaters and carolers combined, they might be joined by professional bear-leaders, storytellers, and beggars.

wouldn't let me in all this time. The master, they say, is busy. Well, that's that. Busy's busy, I got no cause to rush. (*Thinking that* ANDREY *is asking him something.*) How's that?

ANDREY Nothing. (*Examining the book.*) Tomorrow's Friday, we don't meet, but I'll go there all the same . . . I'll find something to do, it's boring at home . . .

(*Pause.*)

You dear old man, it's funny the way things change, the way life isn't fair! Today out of boredom, with nothing to do, I picked up this book here—my old university lecture notes, and I had to laugh . . . Good grief, I'm secretary to the County Council, the council Protopopov presides over, I'm secretary and the most I can hope for—is to become a full member of the County Council! Me, a member of the local County Council; me, who dreams every night that I'm a professor at Moscow University, a famous scholar, the pride of Russia!

FERAPONT I couldn't say . . . I'm hard o' hearing . . .

ANDREY If your hearing was good, I probably wouldn't be talking to you. I have to talk to someone, and my wife doesn't understand me, my sisters scare me for some reason, I'm afraid they'll make fun of me, embarrass me . . . I don't drink, I've no great fondness for barrooms, but I'd love to be sitting in Moscow at Testov's tavern right now or the Grand Moscow restaurant, my friend.

FERAPONT Why, in Moscow, a contractor at the Council was saying the other day, there was some shopkeepers eating pancakes;[7] one ate forty pancakes and like to died. May ha' been forty, may ha' been fifty. I don't rec'llect.

ANDREY You sit in Moscow in the vast main dining room of a restaurant, you don't know anyone and no one knows you, and at the same time you don't feel like a stranger. Whereas here you know everyone and everyone knows you, but you're a stranger, a stranger . . . A stranger and alone.

FERAPONT How's that?

(*Pause.*)

And that same contractor was saying—lying too, mebbe—as how there's a rope stretched acrost all Moscow.

ANDREY What for?

FERAPONT How do I know? The contractor said so.

ANDREY Don't be silly. (*Reads the book.*) Were you ever in Moscow?

FERAPONT (*After a pause.*) I was not. 'Tweren't God's will.

(*Pause.*)

Can I go?

ANDREY You may go. Keep well.

7. The classical dish for Butter Week is pancakes made of flour or buckwheat, fried in plenty of butter and filled with cottage cheese.

(FERAPONT *exits.*)

Keep well. (*Reading.*) Come back tomorrow morning, pick up the paper . . . Go on . . .

(*Pause.*)

He's gone. (*The doorbell rings.*) Yes, business . . . (*Stretches and unhurriedly goes back into his room.*)

(*Offstage,* A NURSEMAID *is singing a lullaby to a baby. Enter* MASHA *and* VERSHININ. *Later, during their dialogue,* THE PARLOR MAID *lights a lamp and candles.*)

MASHA   I don't know. (*Pause.*) I don't know. Of course, habit has a lot to do with it. After Father died, for instance, it was a long time before we could get used to not having orderlies any more. But habit aside, I think I'm being impartial. Maybe it isn't like this in other places, but in our town the most decent, most honorable and cultured people are the military.

VERSHININ   I'd like something to drink. I could use some tea.

MASHA (*After a glance at the clock.*)   They'll bring some soon. They married me off when I was eighteen, and I was afraid of my husband because he was a schoolteacher and at the time, I'd just graduated. At the time he seemed to me to be terribly clever, learned and important. But that's no longer the case, sad to say.

VERSHININ   Is that so? . . . yes.

MASHA   I'm not including my husband, I'm used to him, but among civilians in general there are so many crude, uncongenial, uncouth people. I get upset, I'm offended by crudeness, it pains me to see a man who's not as refined or sensitive or congenial as he should be. When I have to be with schoolteachers, my husband's colleagues, I'm just in agony.

VERSHININ   Yes, ma'am . . . But I don't think it matters much; civilian or military, they're equally uninteresting, at least in this town. Makes no difference! If you listen to any educated man in this town, civilian or military, he's sick and tired of his wife, sick and tired of his home, sick and tired of his estate, sick and tired of his horses . . . A Russian is highly capable of coming up with advanced ideas, so tell me, why is his aim in life so low? Why?

MASHA   Why?

VERSHININ   Why is he sick and tired of his children, sick and tired of his wife? And why are his wife and children sick and tired of him?

MASHA   You're in a bad mood today.

VERSHININ   Could be. I haven't had dinner today, I've eaten nothing since this morning. One of my daughters is under the weather, and when my little girls are ill, anxiety gets the better of me. My conscience pricks me for giving them such a mother. Oh, if only

you could have seen her today! So petty! We started bickering at
seven in the morning, and at nine I slammed the door and went
out.

    (*Pause.*)

I never talk about this, and it's strange, you're the only one I complain to. (*Kisses her hand.*) Don't be angry with me. Except for you,
only you, I have no one, no one . . .

    (*Pause.*)

MASHA What a racket in the stove! Not long before Father died,
there was a whistling in our stovepipe. It was exactly like that.

VERSHININ You're superstitious?

MASHA Yes.

VERSHININ 'Sfunny. (*Kisses her hand.*) You're a superb, a marvelous
woman. Superb, marvelous woman! It's dark in here, but I can see
the sparkle in your eyes.

MASHA (*Moves to another chair.*) There's more light over here . . .

VERSHININ I love, love, love . . . I love your eyes, your movements,
which come to me in my dreams . . . Superb, marvelous woman!

MASHA (*Laughing quietly.*) When you talk to me that way, for some
reason I have to laugh, even though I feel terrified. Don't say it
again, please don't . . . (*In an undertone.*) Go on, do talk, it doesn't
matter to me . . . (*Hides her face in her hands.*) To me it doesn't
matter. Someone's coming in here, talk about something else . . .

    (IRINA *and* TUSENBACH *enter through the reception room.*)

TUSENBACH I have a tripartite name. I'm called Baron Tusenbach-
Krone-Altschauer, but I'm a Russian, of the Orthodox faith, same
as you. There's only a bit of German left in me—actually, only the
dogged obstinacy I pester you with. I escort you home every single
night.

IRINA I'm so tired!

TUSENBACH And every single night I'll come to the telegraph office
and escort you home, I will for ten, twenty years, until you chase
me away . . . (*On seeing* MASHA *and* VERSHININ, *gleefully.*) Is that
you? Good evening.

IRINA Here I am, home at last. (*To* MASHA.) Just now a lady comes
in, wires her brother in Saratov[8] to say that her son has died,
and she couldn't manage to remember the address. So she sent it
without an address, simply to Saratov. Crying the whole time. And
I was rude to her for no reason at all. "I haven't got the time," I
said. It sounded so stupid. Are the masqueraders dropping by
tonight?

MASHA Yes.

___

8. A city on the Volga.

IRINA (*Sits in an armchair.*)   Have to rest. I'm tired.

TUSENBACH (*With a smile.*)   Whenever you come home from work, you look so small, such a puny little thing . . .
     (*Pause.*)

IRINA   I'm tired. No, I don't like the telegraph office, I don't like it.

MASHA   You're getting thinner . . . (*Whistles under her breath.*) And younger, for your face looks just like a sweet little boy's.

TUSENBACH   It's the way she does her hair.

IRINA   I've got to look for another job, this one's not for me. What I so wanted, what I dream of is definitely missing in this one. Drudgery without poetry, without thought . . . (*A knock on the floor.*) The doctor's knocking. (*To* TUSENBACH.) Knock back, my dear. I can't . . . I'm tired . . . (TUSENBACH *knocks on the floor.*) He'll be here in a minute. Somebody ought to do something about him. Yesterday the Doctor and Andrey were at the club and lost again. They say Andrey lost two hundred rubles.

MASHA (*Indifferently.*)   What can you do now!

IRINA   Two weeks ago he lost, back in December he lost. If only he'd hurry up and lose everything, maybe we'd leave this town. Honest to God, I dream of Moscow every night, I'm getting to be a regular obsessive. (*Laughs.*) We'll move there in June, and 'til June there's still . . . February, March, April, May . . . almost half a year!

MASHA   Just so long as Natasha hasn't found out about his losses.

IRINA   I shouldn't think it matters to her.
     (CHEBUTYKIN, *who only just got out of bed—he was napping after dinner—enters the reception room and combs out his beard, then sits at the table and pulls a newspaper out of his pocket.*)

MASHA   Here he comes . . . Has he paid his room rent?

IRINA (*Laughs.*)   No. For eight months, not the slightest kopek. Apparently he's forgotten.

MASHA (*Laughs.*)   How pompously he sits!
     (*They all laugh; pause.*)

IRINA   Why are you so silent, Colonel?

VERSHININ   I don't know. I'd like some tea. Half my kingdom for a glass of tea![9] I haven't had anything to eat since this morning . . .

CHEBUTYKIN   Irina Sergeevna!

IRINA   What do you want?

CHEBUTYKIN   Please come over here. *Venez ici!*[1] (IRINA *goes and sits at the table.*) I can't live without you. (IRINA *lays out a game of solitaire.*)

---

9. Paraphrase of the famous line from Shakespeare's *Richard III:* "A horse! a horse! my kingdom for a horse!" (V. iv).
1. French, "Come here."

VERSHININ   What do you say? If there's no tea, let's at least philosophize.

TUSENBACH   Let's. What about?

VERSHININ   What about? Let's dream a little . . . for instance, about
the life to come after us, some two hundred or three hundred years
from now.

TUSENBACH   How about this? The people who come after us will fly
in hot-air balloons, suit jackets will be cut in a different style,
maybe they'll discover a sixth sense and put it to use; but life will
stay just the same, life will be hard, full of mysteries and happy.
And a thousand years from now men will sigh in just the same
way: "Ah, life is a burden!"—and just as they do now, they'll be
scared and resist having to die.

VERSHININ (*After giving it some thought.*)   How I can put this? I have
the impression that everything on earth should be changing little
by little and is already changing before our very eyes. In two hundred, three hundred, all right, a thousand years—the time span's
of no importance—a new and happy life will come into being. This
life is something we won't take part in, of course, but we're living
for it now, we work, oh and we suffer, we are creating it—and this
is the one and only purpose of our existence and, if you like, our
happiness.

       (MASHA *laughs quietly.*)

TUSENBACH   What's come over you?

MASHA   I don't know. All day long I've been laughing, ever since this
morning.

VERSHININ   I finished school at the same grade you did, I didn't go
to the Military Academy; I read a great deal, but I don't know how
to choose books and maybe I don't read what I should, and yet the
more I live, the more I want to know. My hair's turning gray, any
day now I'll be an old man, but I know so little, ah, so little! But
even so, I think what's most important, what really matters I do
know, and know it through and through. If only I could prove to
you that there is no happiness, there shouldn't be and will not be
for any of us . . . All we should do is work and go on working, as
for happiness, that's the lot of future generations.

       (*Pause.*)

Not my lot but that of future generations of future generations.

       (FEDOTIK *and* RODÉ *appear in the reception room; they sit down
       and sing quietly, strumming on the guitar.*)

TUSENBACH   To your way of thinking, a person's not supposed to
dream of happiness! But what if I am happy?

VERSHININ   No.

TUSENBACH (*Clasping his hands together and laughing.*)   Obviously,
we're not communicating. Well, how can I convince you?

(MASHA *laughs quietly.*)

TUSENBACH (*Wagging a finger at her.*)   Go ahead and laugh! (*To* VER-
SHININ.) Not just two hundred or three hundred, but even a million
years from now, life will be the same as it's always been; it won't
change, it will stay constant, governed by its own laws, which are
none of our business or, at least, which we'll never figure out. Birds
of passage, cranes, for instance, fly on and on, and whatever
thoughts, sublime or trivial, may drift through their heads, they'll
keep on flying and never know what for or where to. They fly and
will keep on flying, whatever philosopher they may hatch; and let
them philosophize to their heart's content, so long as they keep
on flying . . .

MASHA   Then what's the point?

TUSENBACH   The point . . . Look, there's snow falling. What's the
point of that?
   (*Pause.*)

MASHA   It seems to me, a person ought to believe in something or
look for something to believe in; otherwise his life is empty, empty
. . . To live and not know why cranes fly, why children are born,
why stars are in the sky . . . Either you know why you live or else
it's all senseless, gobbledygook.
   (*Pause.*)

VERSHININ   Still it's a pity that youth has flown . . .

MASHA   In one of Gogol's stories, he says, "It's a sad world, my masters!"[2]

TUSENBACH   And I say: it's hard to argue with you, my masters!
You're too much . . .

CHEBUTYKIN (*Reading the paper.*)   Balzac was married in Berdichev.[3]
   (IRINA *sings quietly.*)
That's something to jot down in the book. (*Jots it down.*) Balzac
was married in Berdichev. (*Reads the paper.*)

IRINA (*Laying out a game of solitaire; pensively.*)   Balzac was married
in Berdichev.

TUSENBACH   The die is cast.[4] You know, Mariya Sergeevna, I've
turned in my resignation.

MASHA   So I've heard. And I doubt anything good will come of it. I
don't like civilians.

TUSENBACH   Doesn't matter . . . (*Rises.*) I'm not good-looking, what

2. Masha is quoting the last sentence of Gogol's "Story of How Ivan Ivanovich and Ivan
Nikiforovich Fell Out" (1832): "It's boring in this world, gentlemen." Like Gogol's heroes,
Tusenbach and Vershinin will never agree.
3. The French novelist Honoré de Balzac (1799–1850) married the Polish landowner Ewe-
lyna Hanska in Berdichev a few months before he died. Berdichev, a city in the Kiev
gubernia in the Ukraine, was almost entirely populated by Jews, hence the incongruity.
4. Spoken by Julius Caesar on crossing the Rubicon, as related in Suetonius' *Lives of the
Twelve Caesars.*

kind of military figure do I cut? Besides, it doesn't matter, anyway
. . . I'll go to work. At least once in my life I'll do some work, so I
can come home at night, collapse on my bed exhausted, and fall
fast asleep in an instant. (*Going into the reception room.*) I suppose
workingmen sleep soundly!

FEDOTIK (*To* IRINA.) Just now on Moscow Street at Pyzhikov's I
bought you some colored pencils. And here's a little penknife.

IRINA You're used to treating me like a child, but I really am grown
up now . . . (*Takes the pencils and penknife; with delight.*) What
fun!

FEDOTIK And for myself I bought a jackknife . . . here, have a look
at it . . . one blade, then another blade, a third, that's for cleaning
out the ears, this is a tiny scissors, this one's for trimming nails . . .

RODÉ (*Loudly.*) Doctor, how old are you?

CHEBUTYKIN Me? Thirty-two.

            (*Laughter.*)

FEDOTIK Now I'm going to show you another kind of solitaire . . .
            (*Deals out a game of solitaire.*)

            (*The samovar is brought in.* ANFISA *is by the samovar; a bit of
            a wait and then* NATASHA *enters and also fusses around the sam-
            ovar.* SOLYONY *enters and, after exchanging greetings, sits at the
            table.*)

VERSHININ Incidentally, that's quite a wind!

MASHA Yes. I'm sick and tired of winter. I've already forgot what
summer's like.

IRINA The solitaire's coming out, I see. We'll be in Moscow.

FEDOTIK No it isn't. You see, the eight was on top of the deuce of
spades. (*Laughs.*) That means, you won't be in Moscow.

CHEBUTYKIN (*Reads the paper.*) Tsitsikar.[5] Smallpox is raging there.

ANFISA (*Coming over to* MASHA). Masha, have some tea, dearie. (*To*
VERSHININ.) Please, your honor . . . forgive me, dearie, I've forgot
your name . . .

MASHA Bring it here, Nanny. I refuse to go in there.

IRINA Nanny!

ANFISA Com-uming!

NATASHA (*To* SOLYONY). Breast-fed children understand one perfectly. "Good morning," I'll say, "Good morning, Bobik darling!"
He'll stare at me in a special sort of way. You probably think that's
the mother in me talking but no, no, absolutely not! He's an exceptional baby.

SOLYONY If that baby were mine, I'd fry him in a pan and eat him.
            (*Takes his glass into the drawing room and sits in a corner.*)

NATASHA (*Hiding her face in her hands.*) Rude, uncouth man!

5. Or Tsitihar or Qiqihar or Ch'i-ch'i-ha-erh, a province of Chinese Manchuria.

MASHA   Happy the man who doesn't notice whether it's summer or winter. I think if I were in Moscow, I wouldn't pay any attention to the weather . . .

VERSHININ   A few days ago I was reading the diary of a French cabinet minister, written in prison. The cabinet minister had been sentenced for taking bribes in the Panama scandal.[6] With what intoxication, what ecstasy he recalls the birds he sees from his prison window, and which he failed to notice before when he was a cabinet minister. Of course, now that he's released and at liberty, he's stopped noticing birds, just as before. And you'll stop noticing Moscow once you're living there. We have no happiness, there is none, we only long for it.

TUSENBACH   (*Takes a little box from the table.*)   Where are the chocolates?

IRINA   Solyony ate them.

TUSENBACH   All of 'em?

ANFISA   (*Handing around the tea.*)   There's a letter for you, dearie.

VERSHININ   For me? (*Takes the letter.*) From my daughters. (*Reads.*) Yes, naturally . . . Excuse me, Mariya Sergeevna, I'll leave ever so quietly. I won't have any tea. (*Rises in great agitation.*) These everlasting scenes . . .

MASHA   What is it? Not a secret?

VERSHININ   (*Quietly.*)   My wife poisoned herself again. I've got to go. I'll slip out without being noticed. Awfully unpleasant all this. (*Kisses* MASHA's *hand.*) My dear, wonderful, lovely woman . . . I'll slip out of here ever so quietly . . . (*Exits.*)

ANFISA   Where's he off to? Why, I gave him tea . . . What a one.

MASHA   (*Losing her temper.*)   Stop it! Forever badgering us, you never give us a moment's peace . . . (*Goes with her cup to the table.*) I'm sick and tired of you, old woman!

ANFISA   Why are you so touchy? Sweetheart!

ANDREY'S VOICE   Anfisa!

ANFISA   (*Mimicks.*)   Anfisa! There he sits . . . (*Exits.*)

MASHA   (*In the reception room at the table, angrily.*)   Do let me sit down! (*Messes up the cards on the table.*) Sprawling around with your cards. Drink your tea!

IRINA   Mashka, you're being nasty.

MASHA   If I'm nasty, don't talk to me. Don't touch me!

CHEBUTYKIN   (*Laughing.*)   Don't touch her, don't touch . . .

MASHA   You're sixty years old, but you're like a snotty little boy, nobody knows what the hell you're babbling about.

6. *Impressions cellulaires* by Charles Baïhaut (1834–1905), French Minister for Panama, who was condemned to two years in prison in 1893. Chekhov had read this book during his stay in Nice in 1897. The bankruptcy in 1888 of the company organized to build the Panama Canal resulted in the conviction for fraud of several French politicians.

NATASHA (*Sighs.*) Masha dear, what's the point of using such expressions in polite conversation? With your lovely looks you'd be simply enchanting in decent society, I'll say that straight to your face, if it weren't for that vocabulary of yours. *Je vous prie, pardonnez moi, Marie, mais vous avez des manières un peu grossières.*[7]

TUSENBACH (*Restraining his laughter.*) Let me . . . let me . . . I think there's some cognac . . .

NATASHA *Il paraît, que mon Bobik déjà ne dort pas,*[8] he woke up. He isn't well today. I'll go to him, excuse me . . . (*Exits.*)

IRINA But where has the Colonel gone?

MASHA Home. His wife again—something unexpected.

TUSENBACH (*Goes to* SOLYONY, *carrying a decanter of cognac.*) You always sit by yourself, thinking about something—and you have no idea what. Well, let's make peace. Let's have some cognac. (*They drink.*) I'll have to tickle the ivories all night tonight, I suppose, play all sorts of trash . . . Come what may!

SOLYONY Why make peace? I haven't quarrelled with you.

TUSENBACH You always make me feel that something has happened between us. You've got a strange personality, you must admit.

SOLYONY (*Declaiming.*) "Strange I may be, but then who is not?"[9] "Contain your wrath, Aleko!"[1]

TUSENBACH What's Aleko got to do with it? . . .

(*Pause.*)

SOLYONY When I'm alone with anyone, it's all right, I'm like everybody else, but in company I'm dejected, inhibited and . . . I talk all sorts of rubbish. But all the same, I'm more honest and decent than lots and lots of people. And I can prove it.

TUSENBACH I often get angry with you; you're constantly needling me when we're in public, but all the same for some reason I have an affinity for you. Come what may, I'll get drunk tonight. Let's drink!

SOLYONY Let's drink. (*They drink.*) I don't have anything against you, Baron. But my temperament is like Lermontov's. (*Quietly.*) I even look a little like Lermontov[2] . . . so they say . . . (*Takes the flask of perfume from his pocket and sprinkles it on his hands.*)

---

7. French, "Please, forgive me, Marie, but you have rather rude manners." French was common in Russian intellectual circles, but it is pretentious on the part of Natasha, who makes frequent mistakes. Correctly, it would be *"je vous en prie."*

8. Bad French: "It seems my Bobik is already not asleep." Natasha uses Russian word order, not French.

9. Quotation from the classic comedy *Woe from Wit* by Aleksandr Griboedov, a line of the protagonist Chatsky (Act Three, Scene I), who is in opposition to Moscow's high society and its blind Francophilia.

1. Aleko is the hero of the romantic verse tale "The Gypsies" by Aleksandr Pushkin (1824), heavily influenced by Byronic romanticism. A Russian depressed by civilization, Aleko turns his back on elegant Petersburg and lives with gypsies; he falls in love with a gypsy girl and commits murder out of jealousy. Rachmaninov turned it into an opera (1892).

2. Mikhail Yuryevich Lermontov (1814–1841), after Pushkin the most important lyric poet

TUSENBACH   I've turned in my resignation. *Basta!*[3] For five years I
   kept turning it over in my mind and finally I came to a decision. I
   shall go to work.

SOLYONY (*Declaiming.*)   "Contain your wrath, Aleko . . . Forget, forget your dreams . . ."
            (*While they talk,* ANDREY *enters with a book and sits by the
            candles.*)

TUSENBACH   I shall go to work.

CHEBUTYKIN (*Going into the drawing room with* IRINA.)   And the
   refreshments were also authentic Caucasian dishes: onion soup
   and for the roast—chekhartma, a meat dish.

SOLYONY   Cheremsha[4] isn't meat at all, but a vegetable related to
   our onion.

CHEBUTYKIN   No sir, angel mine. Chekhartma is not an onion, but
   roast mutton.

SOLYONY   And I tell you, cheremsha is onion.

CHEBUTYKIN   And I tell you, chekhartma is mutton.

SOLYONY   And I tell you, cheremsha is onion.

CHEBUTYKIN   Why should I argue with you? You were never in the
   Caucasus and never ate chekhartma.

SOLYONY   I never ate it because I can't stand it. Cheremsha reeks as
   badly as garlic.

ANDREY (*Pleading.*)   That's enough, gentlemen! For pity's sake!

TUSENBACH   When do the masqueraders get here?

IRINA   They promised to be here by nine, which means any minute
   now.

TUSENBACH (*Embraces* ANDREY.)   "Ah you gates, my gates, new
   gates . . ."

ANDREY (*Dances and sings.*)   "New gates, made of maple . . ."

CHEBUTYKIN (*Dances.*)   "Lattice-grates upon my gates!"[5]
            (*Laughter.*)

TUSENBACH (*Kisses* ANDREY.)   Damn it, let's have a drink. Andryusha,
   let's drink to being old pals. And I'm going with you, Andryusha,
   to Moscow, to the University.

SOLYONY   Which one? In Moscow there are two universities.

ANDREY   In Moscow there is one university.

SOLYONY   And I tell you—two.

ANDREY   Make it three. The more the merrier.

SOLYONY   In Moscow there are two universities! (*Grumbling and*

---

of Russian Romanticism. As an officer, Lermontov was twice exiled to the Caucasus and
killed in a duel. See Chekhov's letter to I. A. Tikhomirov of January 14, 1901 (page 434).
3. Italian: "enough!"
4. *Chekhartma*, correctly *chikhartma*, is a Caucasian soup of lamb or chicken, flavored with
coriander and saffron. *Cheremsha* may refer to either *cheremitsa* (masculine, *Allium angu-
losum*), the sharp-edged leek, or *cheremitsa* (feminine, *Allium ursinum*), wild garlic.
5. A folk song sung as accompaniment to vigorous dancing.

hissing.) In Moscow there are two universities: the old one and the new one. And if you don't enjoy listening to me, if my words annoy you, then I can stop talking. I can even go off into another room . . . (*Exits through one of the doors.*)

TUSENBACH   Bravo, bravo! (*Laughs.*) Gentlemen, proceed, I shall commence to play! Laughable, that Solyony . . . (*Sits down at the baby grand, plays a waltz.*)

MASHA (*Dances a waltz by herself.*)   Baron's drunk, baron's drunk, baron's drunk!

(*Enter* NATASHA.)

NATASHA (*To* CHEBUTYKIN.)   Ivan Romanych! (*Mentions something to* CHEBUTYKIN, *then quietly exits.*)

(CHEBUTYKIN *taps* TUSENBACH *on the shoulder and whispers something to him.*)

IRINA   What is it?

CHEBUTYKIN   Time for us to go. Be well.

TUSENBACH   Good night. Time to go.

IRINA   Excuse me . . . But what about the masqueraders? . . .

ANDREY (*Embarrassed.*)   There won't be any masqueraders. You see, my dear, Natasha says that Bobik isn't very well, and so . . . To make a long story short, I don't know anything about it, it doesn't matter to me in the least.

IRINA (*Shrugging.*)   Bobik isn't well!

MASHA   Now we've had it! They're kicking us out, so I suppose we've got to go. (*To* IRINA.) It's not Bobik that's sick, it's her . . . Here! (*Taps her forehead with a finger.*) Suburban slut![6]

(ANDREY *exits through the door right, to his room,* CHEBUTYKIN *follows him; those in the reception room say good-bye.*)

FEDOTIK   What a shame! I'd counted on spending a full night here, but if the little baby's ill, then, of course . . . Tomorrow I'll bring him a little toy . . .

RODÉ (*Loudly.*)   I deliberately took a nap after dinner today; I thought I'd be up all night dancing. After all, it's only nine o'clock now!

MASHA   Let's go out in the street and discuss it there. We'll come up with something to do. (*"Good-bye! Keep well!" can be heard, as well as the merry laughter of* TUSENBACH. ANFISA *and* THE PARLOR MAID *clear the table and extinguish the lights.* THE NURSEMAID *can be heard singing. Enter quietly* ANDREY *in an overcoat and hat and* CHEBUTYKIN.)

CHEBUTYKIN   I didn't have the time to get married because life flashed by me like a streak of lightning, and besides I was madly in love with your dear mother, who was married already . . .

6. *Meshchanka*, literally petty bourgeois female, commoner. Natasha is a social inferior to the Prozorovs, who come from the gentry.

ANDREY   There's no reason to get married. No reason, because it's
a bore.

CHEBUTYKIN   That may be so, but then there's the loneliness. However you philosophize, loneliness is a terrible thing, my boy . . .
Although, basically . . . Of course, it doesn't matter!

ANDREY   Let's go quickly.

CHEBUTYKIN   What's the rush? We've got time.

ANDREY   I'm afraid the wife might stop me.

CHEBUTYKIN   Ah!

ANDREY   I won't play tonight, I'll just sit and watch. I don't feel well
. . . Doctor, what should I do for shortness of breath?

CHEBUTYKIN   Why ask? I don't remember, my boy. I don't know.

ANDREY   Let's go through the kitchen.

> (*They leave.*)
> (*The doorbell rings, then rings again, voices and laughter are
> heard.*)

IRINA (*Enters.*)   What's that?

ANFISA (*In a whisper.*)   Masqueraders!

> (*The doorbell.*)

IRINA   Nanny dear, say no one's at home. Make excuses.

> (ANFISA *exits.* IRINA *walks about the room in a revery; she is on
> edge. Enter* SOLYONY.)

SOLYONY (*Bewildered.*)   No one's here . . . But where are they all?

IRINA   They went home.

SOLYONY   Strange. You're alone here?

IRINA   Alone. (*Pause.*) Good-bye.

SOLYONY   A while ago I behaved without proper restraint and discretion. But you aren't like the rest; you're exalted and pure, you
can discern the truth . . . You alone, only you can understand me.
I love, I love profoundly, incessantly . . .

IRINA   Good-bye! Go away.

SOLYONY   I can't live without you. (*Following her around.*) Oh, my
heaven on earth! (*Plaintively.*) Oh, happiness! Exquisite, wonderful, bewitching eyes, I've never seen their like in any other
woman . . .

IRINA (*Coldly.*)   Stop it, Vasily Vasilich!

SOLYONY   For the first time I'm talking to you of love, and it's exactly
like being out of this world, on another planet. (*Rubs his forehead.*)
Well, still, it doesn't matter. You can't be compelled to be affectionate, of course . . . But I won't tolerate any successful rivals . . .
Won't tolerate it . . . I swear to you by all that's holy, I'll kill any
rival . . . Oh, wonderful woman!

> (NATASHA *passes through with a candle.*)

NATASHA (*Peers through one door, then another, and passes the door
leading to her husband's room.*)   Andrey's in there. Let him read.

Do forgive me, Vasily Vasilich, I didn't know you were here; I'm in a housecoat.

SOLYONY   It doesn't matter to me. Good-bye! (*Exits.*)

NATASHA   And you're tired, darling, my poor little girl. (*Kisses* IRINA.) You should have gone to bed much sooner.

IRINA   Is Bobik asleep?

NATASHA   He's asleep. But he sleeps so·restlessly. By the way, darling, I wanted to tell you, but you're never around, or I never have the time . . . Bobik's present nursery seems to me to be cold and damp. But your room is so right for a baby. Dearest, sweetheart, move in with Olya for a while!

IRINA (*Confused.*)   Where?

(*A troika with harness bells can be heard pulling up to the house.*)

NATASHA   You and Olya can be in one room for a while, and your room will go to Bobik. He's such a little darling, today I say to him, "Bobik, you're mine! All mine!" And he stares at me with his pretty little peepers. (*Doorbell.*) That's Olga, I suppose. Isn't she late! (THE PARLOR MAID *walks to* NATASHA *and whispers in her ear.*) Protopopov? What a character. Protopopov's here and wants me to go for a ride with him in the troika. (*Laughs.*) How funny men are . . . (*Doorbell.*) Someone's ringing . . . Olga's back, I suppose. (*Exits.*)

(THE PARLOR MAID *runs out;* IRINA *sits rapt in thought; enter* KULYGIN *and* OLGA, *followed by* VERSHININ.)

KULYGIN   Would you look at this? But they said they'd be having a party.

VERSHININ   Strange; I left not long ago, half an hour, and they were waiting for the masqueraders . . .

IRINA   They've all gone.

KULYGIN   Masha's gone too? Where did she go? And why is Protopopov downstairs waiting in a troika? Who's he waiting for?

IRINA   Don't give me a quiz . . . I'm tired.

KULYGIN   My, what a scatterbrain . . .

OLGA   The meeting only just ended. I'm exhausted. Our headmistress is ill, and I'm taking her place now. My head, my head aches, my head . . . (*Sits.*) Andrey lost two hundred rubles at cards yesterday . . . The whole town's talking about it.

KULYGIN   Yes, the meeting wore me out too. (*Sits.*)

VERSHININ   My wife just now took it into her head to give me a scare; she all but poisoned herself. It's all blown over, and I'm relieved, I can take it easy now . . . So, I suppose we've got to go? Well then, let me wish you all the best. Fyodor Ilyich, walk somewhere with me! I can't stay at home, I simply cannot . . . Let's go for a walk!

KULYGIN I'm tired. I'm going nowhere. (*Rises.*) I'm tired. Did my wife go home?

IRINA I suppose so.

KULYGIN (*Kisses* IRINA's *hand.*) Good-bye. Tomorrow and the day after, I've got the whole day to relax in. All the best! (*Goes.*) I'd really like some tea. I counted on spending the evening in congenial company and—o, fallacem hominum spem![7] . . . Accusative case, used in the vocative . . .

VERSHININ Which means I'm on my own. (*Exits with* KULYGIN, *whistling.*)

OLGA My head aches, my poor head . . . Andrey lost . . . the whole town's talking . . . I'll go lie down. (*Goes.*) Tomorrow I'm free . . . Oh, goodness, how nice it'll be! Free tomorrow, free the day after . . . My head aches, my poor head . . . (*Exits.*)

IRINA (*Alone.*) They've all gone. No one's left.

(*In the street there's a concertina.* THE NURSEMAID *sings a song.*)

NATASHA (*Wearing a fur coat and hat, walks through the reception room, followed by* THE PARLOR MAID). I'll be back in half an hour. Just going for a little ride. (*Exits.*)

IRINA (*Alone, yearning.*) To Moscow! To Moscow! To Moscow!

CURTAIN

Act Three

OLGA's *and* IRINA's *room. Beds at left and right, fenced 'round with screens. Between two and three o'clock in the morning. Offstage, an alarum bell is ringing to fight a fire that started much earlier. Quite clearly, no one in the house has been to bed yet. On a sofa lies* MASHA, *dressed, as usual, in black.*

(*Enter* OLGA *and* ANFISA.)

ANFISA They're sitting downstairs now under the staircase . . . And I says, "Please go upstairs," I says, " 'tain't right for you to sit here"—they're crying. "Papa," they says, "we don't know where he's at. God forbid," they says, "he ain't burned up." Where they'd get a notion like that! And there's some more in the yard . . . undressed too.

OLGA (*Pulls dresses out of a wardrobe.*) Here, take this gray one . . . And this one too . . . The housecoat as well . . . And take this skirt, my dear . . . What a thing to happen, dear God! Kirsanov Lane is burnt to the ground, it seems. (*Flings the dresses into her arms.*) The poor Vershinins are in a panic . . . Their house was nearly burned down. Have them spend the night with us . . . we can't let

---

7. Latin, "Oh, vain is human hope!" from Cicero, *The Orator* (III.11).

them go home . . . At poor Fedotik's, everything was burned, nothing was saved . . .

ANFISA   You'd better call Ferapont, Olyushka, otherwise I can't handle it all . . .

OLGA (*Rings.*)   I'm not getting through . . . (*Out the door.*) Come in
here, somebody!

> (*Through the open door can be seen a window, red with the
> glow in the sky, and the fire brigade can be heard driving past
> the house.*)

How horrible. And I'm sick and tired of it!

> (*Enter* FERAPONT.)

Here, take this and carry it downstairs . . . The young Kolotilin
ladies are standing under the stairs . . . give it to them. And give
them this . . .

FERAPONT   Yes ma'am. In the year '12, Moscow was burned down
too. Lord God almighty! It sure surprised the Frenchies.[8]

OLGA   Go, go on . . .

FERAPONT   Yes ma'am. (*Exits.*)

OLGA   Nanny dear, darling, give it all away. We don't need any of it,
give it all away, nanny dear . . . I'm worn out, can barely stand on
my feet . . . we can't let the Vershinins go home . . . The little girls
will sleep in the drawing room, have the Colonel go to the baron's
. . . Fedotik can go to the Baron's too, or let him stay here with us
in the reception room . . . The doctor, as if he did it on purpose,
is drunk, hideously drunk, and no one can be put in with him.
And Vershinin's wife in the drawing room too.

ANFISA (*Faintly.*)   Olyushka darling, don't drive me away! Don't drive
me away!

OLGA   Don't be silly, nanny. No one's going to drive you away.

ANFISA (*Lays her head on* OLGA's *bosom.*)   My love, my precious, I
toil, I work . . . I'm getting feeble, everybody says, get out! And
where am I to go? Where? In my eighties. My eighty-second
year . . .

OLGA   You sit down, nanny dear . . . You're tired, poor thing . . .
(*Helps her sit down.*) Have a rest, my dear. How pale she is!

> (NATASHA *enters.*)

NATASHA   Downstairs, they're saying somebody ought to hurry and
organize a committee in aid of the fire victims. Why not? It's a
lovely idea. As a rule, one ought to help the poor; it's an obligation
of the rich. Bobik and Sophiekins are asleep, asleep as if nothing
had happened. We've got so many people all over the place,
wherever you go, the house is packed. There's flu going around
town now; I'm worried the children might catch it.

---

8. Ferapont alludes to the burning of Moscow in 1812 during its occupation by Napoleon's
troops. No one knows for sure, but rumor had it that the Russians started the fire.

OLGA (*Not listening to her.*) You can't see the fire from this room; it's peaceful here . . .

NATASHA Yes . . . I suppose I look a mess. (*Before a mirror.*) They say I'm putting on weight . . . it's not true! Not a bit of it! And Masha's asleep, worn out, poor thing . . . (*To* ANFISA, *coldly.*) Don't you dare sit in my presence! Stand up! Get out of here! (ANFISA *exits; pause.*) And why you hold on to that old woman I cannot understand!

OLGA (*Startled.*) Excuse me, I can't understand either . . .

NATASHA There's no reason for her to be here. She's a peasant, she ought to live in the country . . . It's pampering them! I like a house to be in order! There shouldn't be any useless people in a house. (*Stroking* OLGA's *cheek.*) You're tired, poor dear! Our headmistress is tired! Why, when my Sophiekins is a big girl and goes to high school, I'll be afraid of you.

OLGA I'm not going to be headmistress.

NATASHA They'll pick you, Olga sweetie. The decision's made.

OLGA I'll turn it down. I cannot . . . I haven't the strength for it . . . (*Drinks some water.*) Just now, you abused Nanny so rudely . . . Forgive me, I'm in no condition to put up with . . . It's going dark before my eyes . . .

NATASHA (*Agitated.*) Forgive me, Olya, forgive . . . I didn't mean to upset you.

(MASHA *gets up, takes a pillow, and exits angrily.*)

OLGA Try to understand, dear . . . Perhaps we've had a strange upbringing, but I cannot tolerate this. That sort of behavior depresses me, it makes me ill . . . My heart just sinks!

NATASHA Forgive me, forgive me . . . (*Kisses her.*)

OLGA Any coarseness, even the slightest, an indelicately spoken word upsets me . . .

NATASHA I often say too much, that's true, but you must agree, my dear, she could live in the country.

OLGA She's been with us thirty years.

NATASHA But she's incapable of working now! Either I don't understand you or else you refuse to understand me. She's not fit for housework; she only sleeps or sits.

OLGA Then let her sit.

NATASHA (*In wonderment.*) What do you mean, let her sit? Why, she's a servant, isn't she? (*Plaintively.*) I don't understand you, Olya. I have a nursemaid, I have a wetnurse, I have a parlor maid, a cook . . . what do we need this old woman for? What for?

(*Offstage, the alarum is rung.*)

OLGA I've aged ten years tonight.

NATASHA We've got to thrash this out, Olya, once and for all . . . You're at the high school, I'm at home; you have your teaching, I

have my housework. And when I put in a word about servants, I know what I'm talking about; I know what I am talking about . . . And so tomorrow will see the last of that thieving old crow, that nasty old hag . . . (*Stamps her foot.*) That witch! . . . Don't you dare provoke me! Don't you dare! (*Recollecting herself.*) Honestly, if you don't move downstairs, why, we'll always be quarreling. It's awful.
    (*Enter* KULYGIN.)

KULYGIN Where's Masha? It's high time we went home. They say the fire's dying out. (*Stretching.*) Only one ward was burned, but the wind was so strong that it looked at first as if the whole town would go up in flames. (*Sits down.*) I'm worn out. Olechka, my dear . . . I often think: if it hadn't been for Masha, I would have married you, Olechka. You're very good . . . I'm exhausted. (*Hearkening to something.*)

OLGA What?

KULYGIN As if he did it on purpose, the doctor's on a bender, he's awfully drunk. As if he did it on purpose! (*Stands up.*) There, sounds like he's coming in here . . . You hear him? Yes, in here . . . (*Laughs.*) What a one, honestly . . . I'll hide. (*Goes in the corner next to the wardrobe.*) What a delinquent!

OLGA For two years he hasn't touched a drop, and now all of a sudden he goes and gets drunk . . . (*Goes with* NATASHA *to the back of the room.*)
    (CHEBUTYKIN *enters; not staggering, seemingly sober, he crosses the room, stops, looks, then walks over to the washbasin and starts to wash his hands.*)

CHEBUTYKIN (*Surly.*) Damn 'em all to hell . . . ram 'em all . . . [9] They think I'm a doctor, know how to treat all sorts of ailments, but I don't know a blessed thing, forgot anything I ever knew, don't remember a thing, not a blessed thing.
    (OLGA *and* NATASHA *leave, unnoticed by him.*)
To hell with 'em. Last Wednesday I treated a woman at Zasyp—she died, and it's my fault she died. Yes . . . I did know something twenty-five years ago or so, but now I don't remember a thing. Not a thing . . . My head's empty, my soul's frozen. Maybe I'm not even a human being, but just seem to have arms and legs . . . and a head; maybe I don't even exist at all, but it just seems to me I walk, eat, sleep. (*Weeps.*) Oh, if only I didn't exist! (*Stops weeping, surly.*) Who the hell knows . . . Day before yesterday, talk at the club; they're dropping names, Shakespeare, Voltaire . . . I haven't read 'em, haven't read 'em at all, but I made a face to show I'd read 'em. And the others did the same as me. Shabby and vulgar and vile! And that woman that died on Wednesday, I remembered her

---

9. Rhyming wordplay in Russian *"chyort by pobral . . . podral"* (May the devil carry you off, may the devil thrash you soundly).

. . . and remembered it all, and my soul turned all twisted, repulsive, foul . . . I went out, started drinking . . .

> (IRINA, VERSHININ, *and* TUSENBACH *enter*; TUSENBACH *is wearing civilian clothes, new and fashionable.*)

IRINA   Let's sit down here. No one will come in here.

VERSHININ   If it hadn't been for the soldiers, the whole town would have burned down. Fine lads! (*Rubs his hands in satisfaction.*) Sterling fellows! Ah, what fine lads!

KULYGIN (*Walking over to them.*)   What time is it, gentlemen?

TUSENBACH   Four o'clock already. Getting light.

IRINA   Everyone's sitting in the reception room, no one will leave. That Solyony of yours is sitting there too . . . (*To* CHEBUTYKIN.) You should be in bed, Doctor.

CHEBUTYKIN   Never mind, ma'am . . . Thank you, ma'am. (*Combs out his beard.*)

KULYGIN (*Laughs.*)   You're sploshified, Doctor! (*Claps him on the shoulder.*) Attaboy! *In vino veritas,*[1] said the ancients.

TUSENBACH   They keep asking me to organize a concert on behalf of the fire victims.

IRINA   Why, who could . . .

TUSENBACH   A person could organize one, if a person wanted to. Your sister Mariya, for instance, plays the piano marvelously.

KULYGIN   Marvelously is the way she plays!

IRINA   By now she's forgotten. She hasn't played for three years . . . or four.

TUSENBACH   Absolutely no one in this town understands music, not a single soul, but I do understand it and I give you my word of honor, your sister Mariya plays magnificently; there's talent there.

KULYGIN   You're right, Baron. I love her very much, my Masha. She's superb.

TUSENBACH   To be able to play so splendidly and at the same time to realize that no one, absolutely no one understands you!

KULYGIN (*Sighs.*)   Yes . . . But is it proper to her to take part in a concert? (*Pause.*) Of course I know nothing about it, gentlemen. Perhaps it might even be a good thing. Still I must confess, our headmaster is a good man, a very good man indeed, the most intelligent of men, but the views he holds . . . Of course, it's none of my business, but even so, if you like, I can probably talk to him about it.

> (CHEBUTYKIN *picks up a porcelain clock in both hands and scrutinizes it.*)

VERSHININ   I got covered in filth at the fire, must look a sight.

1. Latin, "in wine lies truth."

(*Pause.*) Yesterday I heard in passing that they intend to transfer our brigade somewhere far away. Some say, to the Kingdom of Poland, others—possibly to Chita.[2]

TUSENBACH   I heard that too. Then what? The town will be quite empty.

IRINA   And we shall go away!

CHEBUTYKIN (*Drops the clock which shatters in pieces*).   Smithereens!

    (*Pause; everyone is distressed and embarrassed.*)

KULYGIN (*Picks up the fragments.*)   To break such an expensive object—ah, Ivan Romanych, Ivan Romanych! You get F-minus for conduct![3]

IRINA   That clock was our poor Mama's.

CHEBUTYKIN   Could be . . . If it's Mama's, then it's Mama's. Could be I didn't break it, it only seems like I broke it. Maybe it only seems to us that we exist, but as a matter of fact we don't. I don't know anything, nobody knows anything. (*At the door.*) What are you staring at? Natasha's having a cute little affair with Protopopov, and you don't see it . . . There you sit and don't see a thing, while Natasha's having a little affair with Protopopov . . . (*Sings.*) "A fig for you and tell me how you like it . . ."[4] (*Exits.*)

VERSHININ   Yes . . . (*Laughs.*) How altogether strange this is! When the fire broke out, I rushed home at once; I get there, take a look— our house is intact and unharmed and out of danger, but my two little girls are standing on the doorstep in nothing but their underwear, their mother's missing, people are milling about, horses running, dogs, and their little girl faces register alarm, panic, entreaty, I don't know what; my heart clenched when I saw those faces. My God, I think, what else will those girls have to live through in the course of a long life! I grab them, run and keep thinking that thought: what else will they have to live through in this world!

    (*Alarum bell; pause.*)

I get here, and their mother's here, shouting, throwing a tantrum.

    (MASHA *enters with a pillow and sits on the sofa.*)

And when my little girls were standing on the doorstep in nothing but their underwear, barefoot, and the street was red with flame, and there was a terrible racket, it occurred to me that things like that used to happen many years ago when there'd be a sudden

---

2. Poland at this time was a vice regency of the Russian Empire. Chita was far away in the opposite direction, the capital of the region of Transbaikal, Siberia, on the Chinese frontier.
3. In Russian schools, grades ran from five to one, with five being highest. In Chekhov's original, Kulygin gives Chebutykin "Zero minus."
4. See Chekhov's letter to I. A. Tikhomirov (January 14, 1901), page 434.

enemy invasion, looting and burning . . . And yet, what a fundamental difference there is between how things are now and how
they were then! And a little more time will go by, say two hundred,
three hundred years, and our present life will be regarded in the
same way with horror and contempt, everything that exists now
will seem awkward and clumsy and very uncomfortable and
strange. Oh, for all we know, what a life that's going to be, what
a life! (*Laughs.*) Forgive me, I've started philosophizing again. Do
let me go on, ladies and gentlemen. I very much want to philosophize, the fit is on me now.

   (*Pause.*)

   Absolutely everyone's asleep. As I was saying: what a life that's
going to be! Can you imagine . . . in town now there are only three
like you, in generations to come there'll be more, ever more and
more, and there'll come a time when everything will change to be
your way, people will live your way, and then even you will get
obsolete, people will evolve and be superior to you . . . (*Laughs.*)
There's a certain special fit come over me today. I want like hell
to live . . . (*Sings.*) "All ages bend the knee to love, its pangs are
blessings from above . . ."[5]

MASHA   Trom-tom-tom.

VERSHININ   Trom-tom . . .

MASHA   Tra-ra-ra?

VERSHININ   Tra-ta-ta. (*Laughs.*)

   (*Enter* FEDOTIK.)

FEDOTIK (*Dances.*)   All burned up, all burned up! Every last thing!
   (*Laughter.*)

IRINA   What's so funny about that? Everything's burned?

FEDOTIK (*Laughs.*)   Every last thing. Nothing's left. Even the guitar
   was burned, and the camera equipment burned, and all my letters
   . . . And the notebook I wanted to give you—burned too.

   (*Enter* SOLYONY.)

IRINA   No, please, go away, Vasily Vasilich. You can't come in here.

SOLYONY   Why can the Baron, and not me?

VERSHININ   We'd all better leave, in fact. How's the fire?

SOLYONY   They say it's dying down. No, I find this particularly odd,
   why can the Baron and why can't I? (*Takes out the flask of perfume
   and sprinkles it about.*)

VERSHININ   Trom-tom-tom.

MASHA   Trom-tom.

VERSHININ (*Laughs; to* SOLYONY.)   Let's go into the reception room.

SOLYONY   All right, sir, but we're making a note of it. "I'd make my

---

5. Vershinin sings the opening of Gremin's aria in Tchaikovsky's opera *Evgeny Onegin* (1877)
   from Pushkin's verse novel.

meaning crystal clear, But 'twould upset the geese, I fear . . ."[6]
(*Looking at* TUSENBACH.) Cheep, cheep, cheep . . .

    (*He exits with* VERSHININ *and* FEDOTIK.)

IRINA   That Solyony's smoked up the place . . . (*Startled.*) The
Baron's asleep! Baron! Baron!

TUSENBACH (*Coming to.*)   I was tired, though . . . The brickworks
. . . I'm not raving, as a matter of fact I'll be going to the brickworks
soon, I'll start working there . . . There's been some talk about it
already. (*To* IRINA, *tenderly.*) You're so pale, beautiful, bewitching
. . . I feel as if your pallor brightens the dark atmosphere like a
beacon . . . You're sad, you're dissatisfied with life . . . Oh, come
away with me, come away to work together!

MASHA   Nikolay Lvovich, get out of here.

TUSENBACH (*Laughing.*)   You're here? I didn't see you. (*Kisses* IRINA*'s
hand.*) Good-bye, I'll be going . . . I look at you now and call to
mind how once, long ago, on your saint's day, you were confident
and carefree and talked of the joys of hard work . . . And what a
happy life flashed before me then! Where is it? (*Kisses her hand.*)
You've got tears in your eyes. Go to bed, it's daylight already . . .
here comes the morning . . . If only I might give my life for you!

MASHA   Nikolay Lvovich, go away! Now really, what . . .

TUSENBACH   I'm going . . . (*Exit.*)

MASHA (*Lies down.*)   You asleep, Fyodor?

KULYGIN   Huh?

MASHA   You should go home.

KULYGIN   My dearest Masha, my dearest Masha . . .

IRINA   She's worn out. You should let her rest, Fedya.

KULYGIN   I'll go right away . . . My wife's lovely, splendid . . . I love
you, my one and only . . .

MASHA (*Angrily.*)   *Amo, amas, amat, amamus, amatis, amant.*[7]

KULYGIN (*Laughs.*)   No, really, she's marvelous. I've been married to
you for seven years, but it feels as if we were wed only yesterday.
Word of honor. No, really, you're a marvelous woman. I'm content,
I'm content, I'm content!

MASHA   I'm sick and tired, sick and tired, sick and tired . . . (*Rises to
speak in a sitting position.*) I just can't get it out of my head . . . it's
simply appalling. Stuck in my brain like a spike, I can't keep quiet.
I mean about Andrey . . . He's mortgaged this house to the bank,
and his wife snatched all the money, but in fact the house belongs
not just to him but to the four of us! He ought to know that, if
he's a decent human being.

---

6. The moral of Ivan Krylov's fable *The Geese* (1811), in which the barnyard fowl boast of
their ancestors, the geese who saved Rome, but have no / merits of their own.
7. Latin, the basic conjugation of the verb *amare*, to love: I love; thou lovest; he, she, or it
loves; we love; you love; they love.

KULYGIN   Why bother, Masha? What's it to you? Andryusha's in debt all around, so God be with him.

MASHA   It's appalling in any case. (*Lies down.*)

KULYGIN   You and I aren't poor. I work, I'm at the high school, later in the day I give lessons . . . I'm an honest man. A simple man . . . *Omnia mea mecum porto,*[8] as the saying goes.

MASHA   It's not that I need the money, but the unfairness of it galls me.

   (*Pause.*)

   Get going, Fyodor.

KULYGIN (*Kisses her.*)   You're tired; rest for just half an hour while I sit outside and wait. Get some sleep . . . (*Goes.*) I'm content, I'm content, I'm content. (*Exits.*)

IRINA   As a matter of fact, our Andrey's become so shallow, so seedy and old living with that woman! He used to make plans to be a professor, but yesterday he was boasting that he's finally managed to make member of the County Council. He's a Council member, but Protopopov's the chairman . . . The whole town's talking, laughing, and he's the only one who sees and knows nothing . . . Here again, everybody runs off to the fire, but he sits by himself in his room and pays no attention. All he does is play the violin. (*On edge.*) Oh, it's horrible, horrible, horrible! (*Weeps.*) I cannot, cannot stand it any more! . . . I cannot, I cannot! . . .

   (OLGA *enters and tidies her night table.*)

   (*Sobs loudly.*) Throw me out, throw me out, I can't stand it any more! . . .

OLGA (*Alarmed.*)   What's wrong, what's wrong? Dearest!

IRINA (*Sobbing.*)   Where? Where has it all gone? Where is it? Oh, my God, my God! I've forgotten everything, forgotten . . . It's all tangled up in my mind . . . I can't remember the Italian for window or, uh, ceiling . . . I forget everything, every day I forget, and life goes on and won't ever, ever come back, we'll never get to Moscow . . . I can see that we won't . . .

OLGA   Dearest, dearest . . .

IRINA (*Under control.*)   Oh, I'm unhappy . . . I cannot work, I will not go on working. Enough, enough! I used to be a telegraph operator, now I work for the Town Council and I hate, despise whatever they give me to do . . . I'm twenty-four already, I've been working for a long time now, and my brain has dried up; I've got skinny and ugly and old, and I've got nothing, nothing, no sort of satisfaction, while time marches on, and I keep feeling that I'm

---

8. Latin, "I carry all my goods on my person," from Cicero is *Paradoxa.* Expression of a member of the family of the philosopher Bias fleeing their country before the Persians and refusing to take any worldly goods with him (ca. 570 B.C.).

moving away from a genuine, beautiful life, moving ever further and further into some kind of abyss. I'm desperate, I'm desperate! And why I'm still alive, why I haven't killed myself before now, I don't understand . . .

OLGA Don't cry, my little girl, don't cry . . . It pains me.

IRINA I'm not crying, not crying . . . Enough . . . There, look, I'm not crying anymore. Enough . . . Enough!

OLGA Dearest, I'm speaking to you as a sister, as a friend; if you want my advice, marry the Baron! (IRINA *weeps quietly.*) After all, you do respect him, think highly of him . . . True, he's not good-looking but he's so decent, so pure . . . After all, people don't marry for love, but just to do their duty. At least that's how I think of it, and I would marry without love. Anyone who came courting, I'd marry him all the same, I mean if he were a decent man. I'd even marry an old man . . .

IRINA I kept waiting for us to move to Moscow, there my true love would find me, I would dream about him, love him . . . But it's all turned out to be foolishness, nothing but foolishness . . .

OLGA (*Embraces her sister.*) My darling, lovely sister, I understand it all; when the Baron resigned from military service and came calling on us in a suit jacket, he looked so homely I even started to cry . . . He asked me, "What are you crying for?" How could I tell him? But if it were God's will that he marry you, I'd be very happy. That would make a change, a complete change.

(NATASHA, *carrying a candle, crosses the stage from the door right to the door left, in silence.*)

MASHA (*Sits up.*) She prowls around as if she were the one who'd set the fire.

OLGA Don't be silly, Masha. The silliest in our family, that's you. Forgive me, please. (*Pause.*)

MASHA I want to make a confession, dear sisters. My heart is heavy, I'll confess to you and never again to anyone, ever . . . I'll speak my piece right now. (*Quietly.*) This is my secret, but you ought to know it all . . . I can't keep still . . . (*Pause.*) I love, love . . . I love that man . . . You just saw him . . . Well, there you have it. In short, I love Vershinin.

OLGA (*Goes behind her screen.*) Stop it. It doesn't matter, I'm not listening.

MASHA What can I do? (*Clutches her head.*) At first he struck me as peculiar, then I felt sorry for him . . . then I fell in love . . .

OLGA (*Behind the screen.*) I'm not listening, it doesn't matter. Whatever silly things you say, it doesn't matter, I'm not listening.

MASHA Ay, you're incredible, Olya. I love—which means, it's my fate. Which means, such is my lot . . . And he loves me . . . it's all terrible. Right? it's no good, is it? (*Takes* IRINA *by the hands and draws her to her.*) Oh my dear . . . How are we to get through our lives, what's to become of us . . . When you read a novel, it all seems so trite and so easy to understand, but when you fall in love yourself, you realize that no one knows anything about it and everyone has to decide for herself . . . My dears, my sisters . . . I've confessed to you, now I'll keep still . . . Now I'll be like that madman in Gogol's story . . . [9] still . . . still . . .

    (*Enter* ANDREY, *followed by* FERAPONT.)

ANDREY (*Angrily.*) What d'you want? I don't understand.

FERAPONT (*In the doorway, indecisively.*) Andrey Sergeich, I already said ten times or so.

ANDREY In the first place, I'm not Andrey Sergeich to you, I'm Your Honor!

FERAPONT The firemen, your highness, want to know if you'll let 'em drive across the garden to the river. Otherwise, they got to ride 'round and 'round in a circle—wears the daylights out of 'em.

ANDREY All right. Tell them it's all right. (FERAPONT *exits.*) They make me sick. Where's Olga? (OLGA *appears from behind her screen.*) I came here to get the key to the bookcase, I've lost mine. You've got one of those tiny little keys. (OLGA *gives him the key in silence.* IRINA *goes behind her screen; pause.*) What a terrific fire, eh! It's starting to die down now. Dammit, that Ferapont got on my nerves, I was talking nonsense . . . Your Honor . . .

    (*Pause.*)

Why don't you say something, Olga?

    (*Pause.*)

It's about time you stopped being so silly, pouting like this, acting so high and mighty . . . You're here, Masha, Irina's here, well, that's just fine—let's clear this up right in the open, once and for all. What do you have against me? What?

OLGA Drop it, Andryusha. We'll clear it up tomorrow. (*Distraught.*) What an excruciating night!

ANDREY (*He's very embarrassed.*) Don't get upset. I'm asking this perfectly calmly:what do you have against me? Say it straight out.

VERSHININ'S VOICE Trom-tom-tom!

MASHA (*Rises; loudly.*) Tra-ta-ta! (*To* OLGA.) Good-bye, Olya, God bless you. (*Goes behind the screen, kisses* IRINA.) Sleep in peace . . . Good-bye, Andrey. Go away, they're exhausted . . . tomorrow you can clear things up . . . (*Leaves.*)

OLGA Really, Andryusha, let's put it off 'til tomorrow . . . (*Goes behind her screen.*) It's time for bed.

9. Poprishchin, hero of Gogol's story *Diary of a Madman* (1835), is a victim of unrequited love. He continually repeats the phrase "Never mind, never mind . . . silence."

ANDREY   I'll just say this and then I'll go. Right away . . . In the first
place, you've got something against Natasha, my wife, and I've
noticed it from the very day of our wedding. If you want to know,
Natasha is a beautiful, honest person, forthright and upstanding—
that's my opinion. I love and respect my wife—understand me—
respect her, and I demand that she be respected by others as well.
I repeat, she's an honest, upstanding person, and all your criticism,
if you don't mind my saying so, is simply frivolous . . .

    (*Pause.*)

In the second place, you seem to be angry because I'm not a professor, don't have scholarly pursuits. But I serve the county, I'm a
member of the County Council, and I consider this service of mine
just as dedicated and exalted as service to scholarship. I'm a member of the County Council and proud of it, if you want to know . . .

    (*Pause.*)

In the third place . . . I've got something else to say . . . I mortgaged the house, without asking your permission . . . There I am
at fault, yes, and I beg you to forgive me. I was driven to it by my
debts . . . thirty-five thousand . . . I've stopped playing cards, I
gave it up a long time ago, but the main thing I can say in my
defense is that you're girls, you get Father's pension, but I don't
have . . . any income, so to speak . . .

    (*Pause.*)

KULYGIN   (*In the doorway.*)   Masha's not here? (*Alarmed.*) Where is
she? This is odd . . . (*Exits.*)

ANDREY   They aren't listening. Natasha is an excellent, honest person. (*Paces the stage in silence, then stops.*) When I got married, I
thought we'd be happy . . . everybody happy . . . But my God . . .
(*Weeps.*) My dear sisters, precious sisters, don't believe me, don't
believe me . . . (*Exits.*)

KULYGIN   (*In the doorway, worried.*)   Where's Masha? Isn't Masha
here then? Amazing. (*Exits.*)

    (*Alarum bell; the stage is empty.*)

IRINA   (*Behind a screen.*)   Olya! Who's that knocking on the floor?

OLGA   It's the Doctor. He's drunk.

IRINA   What a crazy night!

    (*Pause.*)

Olya! (*Peers out from behind her screen.*) Did you hear? They're
taking the brigade away from us; they're transferring it somewhere
far away.

OLGA   That's mere rumor.

IRINA   We'll be here all alone then . . . Olya!

OLGA   Well?

IRINA   Dearest, precious, I respect, I think highly of the Baron; he's
a fine man, I will marry him, agreed; only, let's go to Moscow!

Only please, please, let's go! There's nothing on earth better than Moscow! Let's go, Olya! Let's go!

Act Four

An old garden attached to the Prozorovs' house. A long path lined with fir trees, at whose end a river can be seen. On the farther bank of the river is a forest. To the right, the veranda of the house; here on a table are bottles and glasses; apparently, someone has been drinking champagne. Twelve o'clock noon. Passersby occasionally cut through the garden from the street to the river; five or so soldiers pass quickly by.

> (CHEBUTYKIN, *in an affable mood that stays with him throughout the whole act, is sitting in an armchair in the garden, waiting to be called; he wears a forage cap and has a walking stick.* IRINA, KULYGIN *with a medal around his neck and without his moustache, and* TUSENBACH, *sitting on the veranda, are seeing off* FEDOTIK *and* RODÉ, *who are coming down the steps, both officers in field kit.*)

TUSENBACH (*Exchanging kisses with* FEDOTIK.) You're a good man; we were such friends. (*Exchanges kisses with* RODÉ.) One more time . . . Good-bye, my dear friend!

IRINA See you soon!

FEDOTIK It isn't "see you soon," it's good-bye, we'll never meet again!

KULYGIN Who knows! (*Wipes his eyes, smiles.*) Look, I'm starting to cry.

IRINA We'll meet someday.

FEDOTIK In, say, ten or fifteen years? But then we'll barely recognize one another, we'll say a formal how-d'you-do. (*Takes a snapshot.*) Hold still . . . Once more, the last time.

RODÉ (*Embraces* TUSENBACH.) We won't meet again . . . (*Kisses* IRINA's *hand.*) Thanks for everything, everything!

FEDOTIK (*Annoyed.*) Just hold still!

TUSENBACH God willing, we shall meet. Do write to us. Be sure and write.

RODÉ (*Casts a glance around the garden.*) Good-bye, trees! (*Shouts.*) Hop to it! (*Pause.*) Good-bye, echo!

KULYGIN You'll get married out there in Poland, perish the thought . . . Your Polish wife will throw her arms around you and say, "Kochany!"[1] (*Laughs.*)

FEDOTIK (*After a glance at his watch.*) There's less than a hour left.

---

1. Polish, "beloved, dearest."

Solyony's the only one from our battery going on the barge, we're with the line unit. Three batteries are leaving today in battalions, another three tomorrow—and the town will surrender to peace and quiet.

TUSENBACH   And god-awful boredom.

RODÉ   And where's Mariya Sergeevna?

KULYGIN   Masha's in the garden.

FEDOTIK   Have to say good-bye to her.

RODÉ   Good-bye, got to go, or else I'll start bawling . . . (*Quickly embraces* TUSENBACH *and* KULYGIN, *kisses* IRINA's *hand.*) We had a wonderful time here . . .

FEDOTIK   (*To* KULYGIN.) Here's a souvenir for you . . . a notebook with a tiny little pencil . . . We'll go through here to the river . . .
          (*They move away, both looking around.*)

RODÉ   (*Shouts.*) Hop to it!

KULYGIN   (*Shouts.*) Good-bye!
          (*Very far upstage,* FEDOTIK *and* RODÉ *run into* MASHA *and say good-bye to her; she exits with them.*)

IRINA   They've gone . . . (*Sits on the bottom step of the veranda.*)

CHEBUTYKIN   And forgot to say good-bye to me.

IRINA   And what about *you*?

CHEBUTYKIN   Yes, I forgot too somehow. However, I'll soon be seeing them, I leave tomorrow. Yes . . . Just one day left. In a year they'll let me retire, I'll come back here again and live out my life beside you. I've just got one little year left before my pension . . . (*Puts the newspaper in his pocket, takes out another.*) I'll come back here to you and I'll change my way of living through and through. I'll turn into such a nice, quiet, beni . . . benignant, well-behaved little fellow . . .

IRINA   Well, you ought to change your way of life, my love. You ought to somehow.

CHEBUTYKIN   Yes. I can feel it. (*Sings quietly.*) "Tarara . . . boom-de-ay . . . I sit in gloom all day . . ."[2]

KULYGIN   Incorrigible, that's our Doctor! Incorrigible!

CHEBUTYKIN   Well then, it's up to you to teach me better. Then I'd be corrigible.

IRINA   Fyodor shaved off his moustache. I can't look at him!

KULYGIN   Why not?

CHEBUTYKIN   I'd love to tell you what your face looks like now, but I'd better not.

KULYGIN   So what? It's comfortable this way, it's the *modus vivendi*.[3]

2. *Tarara boom-de-ay. Cf.* Chekhov's story "Volodya the Great and Volodya the Little" (1893). In the Russian translation, it goes, "Tarara boom-de-ay / I'm sitting on a curbstone / Bitterly crying / 'Cause I don't know much." The second verse is slightly racy.
3. Latin, "a means of living, a temporary compromise."

Our headmaster never lets his moustache grow, so, when I was made school inspector, I shaved mine off. Nobody likes it but it doesn't matter to me. I'm content. Moustache or no, I'm just as content . . . (*Sits down.*)

    (*Far upstage,* ANDREY *is wheeling a sleeping infant in a baby carriage.*)

IRINA Ivan Romanych, my dear, my darling, I'm awfully worried. You were downtown yesterday. Tell me, what happened there?

CHEBUTYKIN What happened? Nothing. Trivia. (*Reads the paper.*) Doesn't matter.

KULYGIN The story goes that Solyony and the Baron met yesterday downtown outside the theater. . . .

TUSENBACH Stop! Well, really. . . . (*Waves his hand in dismissal and goes inside the house.*)

KULYGIN Outside the theater. . . . Solyony started needling the baron, and the baron wouldn't stand for it, and said something insulting . . .

CHEBUTYKIN I wouldn't know. 'S all hokum.

KULYGIN In a seminary once a teacher wrote "Hokum" on a composition, and the student thought it was Latin, started to conjugate it—hokum, hokium, hokii, hokia.[4] (*Laughs.*) Wonderfully funny. They say Solyony's in love with Irina and sort of developed a hatred for the Baron . . . That's understandable. Irina's a very nice girl. She even resembles Masha, the same sort of moodiness. Only you've got the milder temper, Irina. Although Masha has a very nice temper too, of course. I do love her, my Masha.

    (*Offstage, at the bottom of the garden:* "Yoo-hoo! Hop to it!")

IRINA (*Startled.*)   Somehow everything frightens me today.

    (*Pause.*)

All my things are already packed, after dinner I'll send them off. Tomorrow the Baron and I will be married, tomorrow we move to the brickworks, and by the day after tomorrow I'll be in school, starting a new life. Somehow God will help me. When I took the qualifying exam for the teaching certificate, I even wept for joy, at the integrity of it . . .

    (*Pause.*)

Any minute now, the horse and wagon will come by for my things . . .

KULYGIN Well, that's how it goes, but somehow it isn't serious. Nothing but abstract idealism, and very little seriousness. Still, I wish you good luck from the bottom of my heart.

CHEBUTYKIN (*Affectionately.*) My miracle, my dearest . . . My trea-

---

4. The Russian joke is that *chepukha* ("nonsense," "rot") written out in Cyrillic script looks like a nonexistent but ostensible Latin word, *renixa*.

sure . . . You've moved far away from me, I can't catch up with you. I'm left far behind, like a bird of passage that's too old to fly. Fly away, my darlings, fly and God bless you!

(*Pause.*)

It was a mistake to shave off your moustache, Fyodor Ilyich.

KULYGIN   That's enough out of you! (*Sighs.*) So today the military departs and everything will go on again as it did in the past. Say what you like; Masha's a good, honorable woman, I love her very much and thank my lucky stars. People have such different fates . . . There's a certain Kozyryov[5] who works for internal revenue. He went to school with me, was expelled his senior year in high school because he could never manage to learn the *ut consecutivum* construction.[6] Now he's awfully poor, ill, and whenever we meet, I say to him, "Greetings, *ut consecutivum*"—"Yes," he says, "*consecutivum* indeed . . ." and then he coughs. But I've been lucky all my life, I'm happy, look, I've even got the Order of Stanislas second class[7] and now I'm teaching others that same *ut consecutivum*. Of course, I'm a clever man, cleverer than a great many others, but that's not what happiness is all about . . .

(*In the house, "The Maiden's Prayer"[8] is played on the piano.*)

IRINA   And tomorrow night I won't have to listen to "The Maiden's Prayer," I won't have to meet Protopopov. . . .

(*Pause.*)

There's Protopopov sitting in the drawing room; he came by again today . . .

KULYGIN   The headmistress still isn't here?

(*Far upstage,* MASHA *saunters quietly across the stage.*)

IRINA   No. She's been sent for. If only you knew how hard it is for me to live here alone, without Olya . . . She lives at the high school; she's headmistress, busy with her work all day, while I'm alone, I'm bored, nothing to do, and the hateful room I live in . . . So I came to a decision: if it's not my fate to live in Moscow, so be it. After all, it must be fate. Nothing to be done about it . . . Everything is God's will, true enough. The Baron proposed to me . . . Then what? I thought it over and decided. He's a good man, a wonderful man really, so good . . . And suddenly, just as if my

---

5. A telling name, since *kozyr* means "ace."
6. The rule in Latin grammar that demands the use of the subjunctive mood in subordinate clauses beginning with the conjunction *ut* (that, so that). Chekhov had trouble with this rule as a schoolboy.
7. One of the decorations bestowed in pre-Revolutionary Russia on civil servants and military men. The least important, the Stanislas Third Class, was bestowed on Chekhov in 1899 for his work in educating the peasants.
8. Sentimental piano piece by the Polish composer Tekla Badarzewska-Baranowskaa (1839–1862), "La prière d'une vierge." Anyone who could read a note could play it. In Brecht and Weill's opera *The Rise and Fall of the City of Mahogonny* (1929), after it is played by a whore in a brothel, a customer sighs deeply and says, "Ah! that is eternal art."

heart had sprouted wings, I cheered up, I felt relieved, and once
again I started wanting to work, work . . . Only something happened yesterday; a kind of mystery has been hanging over me . . .

CHEBUTYKIN   Hokium. Hokum.

NATASHA (*Out the window.*)   The headmistress!

KULYGIN   The headmistress is here . . . Let's go in.
(*Exits into the house with* IRINA.)

CHEBUTYKIN (*Reads the papers and sings softly.*)   "Tara-ra . . . boom-
de-ay . . . I sit in gloom all day . . ."
(MASHA *comes up; upstage,* ANDREY *wheels the baby carriage.*)

MASHA   Sitting by himself, taking it easy . . .

CHEBUTYKIN   So what?

MASHA (*Sits down.*)   Nothing . . .
(*Pause.*)
Did you love my mother?

CHEBUTYKIN   Very much.

MASHA   And she loved you?

CHEBUTYKIN (*After a pause.*)   I can't remember any more.

MASHA   Is my man here? That's how our cook Marfa used to refer
to her policeman: my man. Is my man here?

CHEBUTYKIN   Not yet.

MASHA   When you get happiness in bits and pieces, in snatches, and
then you lose it, as I do, you gradually toughen up, you get bitchy.
(*Points to her bosom.*) I'm seething inside . . . (*Looking at her
brother* ANDREY, *wheeling the baby carriage.*) Look at our Andrey,
our baby brother . . . All hope is lost. Thousands of people were
hoisting a bell, a lot of energy and money was expended, and all
of a sudden it fell to the ground and smashed. All of a sudden,
without rhyme or reason. 'S just the same with Andrey . . .

ANDREY   When will the house finally quiet down? Such a rumpus.

CHEBUTYKIN   Soon. (*Looks at his watch, then winds it; the watch
chimes.*) I've got an antique watch, with a chime. . . . The first,
second, and fifth batteries are leaving at one on the dot.
(*Pause.*)
And I go tomorrow.

ANDREY   Forever?

CHEBUTYKIN   I don't know. Maybe I'll be back within the year. Who
the hell knows, though . . . Doesn't matter . . .
(*Somewhere far away, a harp and a fiddle can be heard playing.*)

ANDREY   The town's emptying out. Just as if a dustcover had been
dropped over it.
(*Pause.*)
Something happened yesterday outside the theater: they're all talking about it, but I don't know what it was.

CHEBUTYKIN   Nothing. Trivia. Solyony started needling the baron, so the baron flared up and insulted him, and what with one thing and another in the end Solyony was obliged to challenge him to a duel. (*Looks at his watch.*) It's about time now, I think . . . Half-past twelve, in the state forest preserve, that one over there, the one you can see on the far side of the river . . . Bing-bang. (*Laughs.*) Solyony imagines he's Lermontov, and even writes poetry. Look, a joke's a joke, but this is his third duel by now.

MASHA   Whose?

CHEBUTYKIN   Solyony's!

MASHA   And what about the Baron?

CHEBUTYKIN   What *about* the Baron?
        (*Pause.*)

MASHA   My thoughts are all snarled . . . Even so, I say it's not right to let him do it. He might wound the Baron or even kill him.

CHEBUTYKIN   The Baron's all right, but one baron more or less—does it really matter? Let it be! It doesn't matter! (*Beyond the garden, a shout: "Yoo-hoo! Hop to it!"*) You wait. That's Skvortsov shouting, one of the seconds. He's sitting in a rowboat.

ANDREY   In my opinion, even taking part in a duel, even being present at one, if only in the capacity of a medical man, is simply immoral.

CHEBUTYKIN   It only seems that way . . . There's nothing on this earth, we aren't here, we don't exist, but it only seems that we exist . . . So what does it matter?

MASHA   So they waste the whole day here talking and talking . . . (*Walks.*) You live in a climate like this, expecting it to snow any minute, and you still carry on these conversations . . . (*Stops.*) I won't go inside the house, I can't go in there . . . When Vershinin comes, let me know . . . (*Walks up the path.*) And the birds of passage are already on the wing . . . (*Looks upward.*) Swans, or geese . . . My lovelies, my happy creatures . . . (*Exits.*)

ANDREY   Our house is emptying out. The officers are going, you're going, sister's getting married, and I'll be left alone in the house.

CHEBUTYKIN   What about your wife?
        (FERAPONT *enters with papers.*)

ANDREY   A wife is a wife. She's honest, decent, oh and kind, but for all that there's something in her that reduces her to a petty, blind sort of bristly animal. In any case, she's not human. I'm talking to you as a friend, the only person I can open my heart to. I love Natasha, I do, but sometimes she seems to me incredibly vulgar, and then I get mixed up; I don't understand how and why I love her so, or, at least, loved her . . .

CHEBUTYKIN (*Rises.*)   My boy, I'll be leaving tomorrow, maybe we'll never meet again, so here's my advice to you. Look, put on your hat, take up your stick, and leave . . . leave and go away, go without looking back. And the further you go, the better.

> (SOLYONY *passes by upstage with* TWO OFFICERS; *catching sight of* CHEBUTYKIN, *he turns towards him;* THE OFFICERS *walk further on.*)

SOLYONY   Doctor, it's time! Half-past twelve already. (*Exchanges greetings with* ANDREY.)

CHEBUTYKIN   Right away. You all make me sick. (*To* ANDREY.) If anyone asks for me, Andryusha, say I'll be right back . . . (*Sighs.*) Oy-oy-oy!

SOLYONY   "He scarcely had time to gasp, when the bear had him in its grasp." (*Walks with him.*) What are you groaning about, old man?

CHEBUTYKIN   Oh!

SOLYONY   Feeling healthy?

CHEBUTYKIN   (*Angrily.*)   Like a rich man's wealthy.

SOLYONY   The old man's getting upset for no good reason. I'll indulge myself a bit, I'll only wing him, like a woodsnipe. (*Takes out the perfume and sprinkles his hands.*) Look, I've poured a whole flask on them today, but they still smell. My hands smell like a corpse.

> (*Pause.*)

So, sir . . . You remember the poem? "But he, the rebel, seeks the storm, As if a storm could give him peace . . ."[9]

CHEBUTYKIN   Yes. "He scarcely had time to gasp, when the bear had him in its grasp."

> (*Exits with* SOLYONY.)

FERAPONT   Papers to sign . . .

ANDREY (*Jittery.*)   Get away from me! Get away! For pity's sake! (*Exits with the baby carriage.*)

FERAPONT   But that's what papers is for, to be signed. (*Exits upstage.*)

> (*Enter* IRINA *and* TUSENBACH *wearing a straw hat.*)

KULYGIN (*Crossing the stage, shouting*)   Yoo-hoo, Masha, yoo-hoo!

TUSENBACH   It looks like he's the only man in town who's glad the military are leaving.

IRINA   That's understandable.

> (*Pause.*)

Our town is emptying out now.

TUSENBACH   I'll be back in a minute, dear.

IRINA   Where are you off to?

TUSENBACH   I have to go downtown to . . . to see my comrades off.

9. Familiar quotation from the poem "The Sail" ("Parus," 1832) by Mikhail Lermontov. Chekhov also quotes it in *The Wedding*.

IRINA   That's not true . . . Nikolay, why are you so on edge today?
(*Pause.*)
What happened yesterday outside the theater?

TUSENBACH (*Gesture of impatience.*)   I'll be back in an hour and we'll
be together again. (*Kisses her hand.*) Light of my life . . . (*Looks
into her face.*) It's five years now since I started loving you, and I
still can't get used to it, and you seem ever more beautiful to me.
What lustrous, wonderful hair! What eyes! I'll take you away
tomorrow, we shall work, we'll be rich, my dreams will come true.
You shall be happy. There's just one thing, though, just one thing:
you don't love me!

IRINA   It's not in my power! I'll be your wife, and a true one, an
obedient one; but there's no love, what can I do? (*Weeps.*) I've
never loved even once in my life. Oh, I've dreamt so much about
love, I've been dreaming about it for a long time now, day and
night, but my heart is like an expensive piano, locked tight, and
the key is lost.
(*Pause.*)
You seem restless.

TUSENBACH   I didn't sleep all night. There's never been anything in
my life so terrible that it could frighten me, and yet this lost key
tears my heart to pieces, won't let me sleep. Tell me something.
(*Pause.*)
Tell me something . . .

IRINA   What? What? Everything around us is so mysterious, the old
trees stand in silence . . . (*Puts her head on his chest.*)

TUSENBACH   Tell me something.

IRINA   What? What am I to say? What?

TUSENBACH   Something.

IRINA   Stop it! Stop it!
(*Pause.*)

TUSENBACH   What trivia, what foolish trifles sometimes start to matter in our lives, all of a sudden, for no good reason. At first you
laugh at them, treat them as trifles, and all the same you go on
and feel you haven't the power to stop. Oh, let's not talk about it!
I feel cheerful, as if I'm seeing those spruces, maples, birches for
the first time in my life, and they all take a curious look at me and
wait. What beautiful trees, and, really, the life we lead in their
shade ought to be so beautiful! (*A shout: "Yoo-hoo! Hop to it!"*) I
have to go, it's time now . . . There's a tree that's withered and
dead, but all the same it sways with the others in the breeze. So,
I guess, if I die too, I'll still take part in life one way or another.
Goodbye, my dear . . . (*Kisses her hand.*) Those papers you gave
me are in my desk, under the almanac.

IRINA   I'll go with you.

TUSENBACH   (*Alarmed.*)   No, no. (*Goes quickly, stops on the path.*)
Irina!

IRINA   What?

TUSENBACH   (*Not knowing what to say.*)   I haven't had any coffee
today. Ask them to make me some . . . (*Exits quickly.*)

　　　(IRINA *stands rapt in thought, then walks far upstage and sits
　　　on a swing. Enter* ANDREY *with the baby carriage.* FERAPONT
　　　appears.)

FERAPONT   Andrey Sergeich, these here papers ain't mine, they're
official. I didn't dream 'em up.

ANDREY   Oh, where is it, where has my past gone to, when I was
young, cheerful, intelligent, when my dreams and thoughts were
refined, when my present and future glistened with hope? Why,
when we've barely begun to live, do we get boring, gray, uninteresting, lazy, apathetic, useless, unhappy . . . Our town has existed
for two hundred years, it contains a hundred thousand inhabitants, and not one who isn't exactly like the others, not one dedicated person, past or present, not one scholar, not one artist, not
one even faintly remarkable person who might stir up envy or a
passionate desire to emulate him. All they do is eat, drink, sleep,
then die . . . others are born and they too eat, drink, sleep and, to
keep from being stultified by boredom, vary their lives with vicious
gossip, vodka, cards, crooked deals, and the wives cheat on the
husbands while the husbands lie, pretend to notice nothing, hear
nothing, and an irresistibly vulgar influence is brought to bear on
the children, and the divine spark in them flickers out, and they
become the same miserable, identical dead things as their fathers
and mothers . . . [1] (*To* FERAPONT, *angrily.*) What d'you want?

FERAPONT   How's that? Papers to sign.

ANDREY   You make me sick.

FERAPONT   (*Handing him the papers.*)   A while ago the doorman at
the town hall was saying . . . Looks like, says he, this winter in
Petersburg there was ten degrees o'frost.

ANDREY   The present is repulsive, but when, on the other hand, I
think of the future, it's so fine! I start to feel so relieved, so expansive; and a light begins to dawn in the distance, I can see freedom,
I can see how my children and I will be freed from idleness, from
beer-drinking, from goose and cabbage, from after-dinner naps,
from degrading sloth . . .

FERAPONT   Two thousand people froze, seems like. The common

---

1. "[Chekhov] demanded that in the last monologue Andrey be very excited. 'He should
almost threaten the audience with his fists!' " (V. V. Luzhsky, *Solntse Rossii* 228 / 25
[1914].)

folks, says he, was scared to death. Either Petersburg or Moscow—
I don't rec'llect.

ANDREY (*Caught up in a feeling of tenderness.*)   My dear sisters, my
wonderful sisters! (*Plaintively.*) Masha, sister dear . . .

NATASHA (*Out the window.*)   Who's talking so loudly out there? Is
that you, Andryusha? You'll wake up Sophiekins. *Il ne faut pas
faire du bruit, la Sophie est dormée déjà. Vous êtes un ours.*[2] (*Losing
her temper.*) If you want to talk, then give the buggy and the baby
to somebody else. Ferapont, take the baby buggy from the master!

FERAPONT   Yes'm. (*Takes the carriage.*)

ANDREY (*Embarrassed.*)   I'm talking softly.

NATASHA (*Back of the window, petting her little boy.*)   Bobik! Cunning Bobik! Naughty Bobik!

ANDREY (*Glancing at the papers.*)   All right, I'll look them over and
sign what's necessary, and you take them back to the council . . .
(*Exits into the house, reading the papers;* FERAPONT *wheels the
carriage.*)

NATASHA (*Back of the window.*)   Bobik, what's your mommy's name?
Cutie, cutie! And who's this? It's Auntie Olya. Say to Auntie: Afternoon, Olya!

(*Itinerant musicians, a man and a girl, play the fiddle and the
harp. Out of the house come* VERSHININ, OLGA, *and* ANFISA, *and
listen a moment in silence;* IRINA *comes up to them.*)

OLGA   Our garden's like an empty lot; people walk and drive right
through it. Nanny, give those musicians something! . . .

ANFISA (*Gives something to the musicians.*)   God bless you, sweet-
hearts. (*The musicians bow and leave.*) Hard-luck folks. When your
belly's full, you don't have to play. (*To* IRINA.) Afternoon, Arisha!
(*Kisses her.*) My, my, child, lookit the way I live now! The way I
live! In the high school in government housing, grand rooms, along
with Olyushka—the Lord decreed that for my old age. I've not
lived like that in all my born days, sinner that I am . . . The housing's big, on the government money, and I've got a whole little
room and a little bed to myself. All on the government. I wake up
at night and—oh Lord, oh Mother o'God, there's nobody happier'n
me!

VERSHININ (*After a glance at his watch.*)   We'll be leaving any minute, Olga Sergeevna. My time's up.

(*Pause.*)

I wish you the best of luck, the best . . . Where's Mariya Sergeevna?

IRINA   She's somewhere in the garden. I'll go find her.

2. Bad French for "Don't make any noise, Sophie is already asleep. You are a bear!"

VERSHININ Please do. I'm in a hurry.

ANFISA I'll go and look too. (*Shouts.*) Mashenka, yoo-hoo! (*Goes with* IRINA *to the bottom of the garden.*) Yoo-hoo, yoo-hoo!

VERSHININ Everything must come to an end. Here we are saying good-bye. (*Looks at his watch.*) The town gave us a kind of lunch, we drank champagne, the mayor delivered a speech, I ate and listened, but in spirit I was here with you . . . (*Looks around the garden.*) I've grown accustomed to you.

OLGA Will we ever meet again?

VERSHININ I don't suppose so.

(*Pause.*)

My wife and both my little girls will stay on here another two months or so; please, if anything happens or if anything's needed . . .

OLGA Yes, yes, of course. Don't worry.

(*Pause.*)

Tomorrow there won't be a single military man left in town, it will all have turned into a memory, and, of course, a new life will begin for us . . .

(*Pause.*)

Nothing works out the way we'd like it to. I didn't want to be a headmistress, but even so I am one. Which means, not being in Moscow.

VERSHININ Well . . . Thank you for everything. Forgive me, if anything wasn't right . . . I talked a lot, an awful lot—and forgive me for it, don't think badly of me.

OLGA (*Wipes away tears.*) What's keeping Masha? . . .

VERSHININ What more is there to say at parting? How about philosophizing? . . . (*Laughs.*) Life is hard. It appears to many of us to be lackluster and hopeless, but even so, you must admit, it will grow ever brighter and easier, and apparently the time's not far off when it will be very bright. (*Looks at his watch.*) My time's up, it's time! In olden days humanity was preoccupied with wars, its whole existence filled with campaigns, invasions, victories; now all that's out of date, but it's left behind an enormous vacuum, which so far has been impossible to fill; humanity is passionately seeking and will find it at last. Ah, the sooner the better!

(*Pause.*)

You know, if only hard work were supplemented by education, and education by hard work. (*Looks at his watch.*) However, my time's up . . .

OLGA Here she comes.

(MASHA *enters.*)

VERSHININ I came to say good-bye . . .

(OLGA *draws somewhat apart, as not to intrude on their farewells.*)

MASHA (*Gazes into* VERSHININ's *face.*)   Good-bye . . . (*A long, drawn-
out kiss.*)

OLGA   That'll do, that'll do . . .

(MASHA *sobs vehemently.*)

VERSHININ   Write to me . . . Don't forget! Let me go . . . it's time . . .
Olga Sergeevna, take her, I have to . . . It's time . . . I'm late . . .
(*Much affected, he kisses* OLGA's *hand, then embraces* MASHA *once
again and leaves quickly.*)

OLGA   That'll do, Masha! Stop it, dear . . .

(*Enter* KULYGIN.)

KULYGIN (*In consternation.*)   Never mind, let her go on crying, let
her . . . My good Masha, my kind Masha . . . You're my wife, and
I'm happy, no matter what went on here . . . I'm not complaining,
I'm not reproaching you in the least . . . Olya there is a witness
. . . Let's start over again living as we used to, and I won't say a
single word to you, no recriminations . . .

MASHA (*Controlling her sobbing.*)   On the curved seashore a green
oak stands, a golden chain wound 'round that oak . . . A golden
chain wound 'round that oak . . . I'm losing my mind . . . On the
curved seashore . . . a green oak stands . . ."[3]

OLGA   Calm down, Masha . . . Calm down . . . Get her some water.

MASHA   I'm not crying any more.

KULYGIN   She's not crying any more . . . she's being considerate . . .

(*A muffled shot is heard in the distance.*)

MASHA   On the curved seashore a green oak stands, a golden chain
wound 'round that oak . . . A golden chain wound 'round that oak
. . . A green cat stands . . . A green oak stands . . . I'm raving . . .
(*Drinks some water.*) Life's a failure . . . I don't want anything now
. . . I'll be all right presently . . . Doesn't matter . . . What does
that mean, on the curved seashore? Why is that phrase in my
head? My thoughts are running wild.

(IRINA *enters. The harp- and fiddle-playing can be heard far
away down the street.*)

OLGA   Calm down, Masha. Now, there's a good girl . . . Let's go
inside.

MASHA (*Angrily.*)   I will not go in there. (*Sobs, but instantly stops.*) I
don't go in that house anymore and I won't go . . .

IRINA   Let's sit down together, at least let's not say anything. After
all, I'm going away tomorrow . . .

3. The images are from the opening lines of Pushkin's *Ruslan and Lyudmila.* See note 1,
page 253. Masha changes the rhyme words "green oak" (*dub zelyony*) and "learned cat"
(*kot uchyony*) to "green cat" (*kot zelyony*).

(*Pause.*)

KULYGIN   Yesterday in the sophomore class I took this moustache and beard away from some smart aleck . . . (*Puts on the moustache and beard.*) Looks like the German teacher . . . (*Laughs.*) Doesn't it? Those kids are a scream.

MASHA   Actually, it does look like your German.

OLGA (*Laughs.*)   Yes.

(MASHA *weeps.*)

IRINA   That's enough, Masha!

KULYGIN   A lot like him . . .

(*Enter* NATASHA.)

NATASHA (*To* THE PARLOR MAID.)   What? Protopopov's going to sit with Sophiekins for a while—Mikhail Ivanych—and Andrey Sergeich can take Bobik for an airing. So much fuss over children . . . (*To* IRINA.) You're going away tomorrow, Irina—such a shame. Do stay just another little week at least. (*Shrieks on seeing* KULYGIN; *he laughs and removes the moustache and beard.*) Why, you gave me quite a shock! (*To* IRINA.) I've got used to you and do you think parting from you is easy for me? I've told them to move Andrey and his violin into your room—he can saw away in there!—and we'll put Sophiekins in his room. A wonderful, fantastic baby! Such a little cutie! Today she stared at me with her little peepers and went—"Mama."

KULYGIN   A beautiful baby, true enough.

NATASHA   In other words, I'll be all on my own here tomorrow. (*Sighs.*) First of all I'll have them chop down that row of fir trees, then that maple over there. In the evenings it's so eerie, unattractive . . . (*To* IRINA.) Dear, that belt doesn't suit your coloring at all . . . it's in bad taste. You need something perkier. And then I'll have them plant posies everywhere, posies, and they'll give off such a fragrance . . . (*Sternly.*) Why is there a fork lying on this bench? (*Crossing into the house, to* THE PARLOR MAID.) Why is there a fork lying on a bench, I'm asking you? (*Shouts.*) Hold your tongue!

KULYGIN   She's on the warpath again!

(*Offstage, the music plays a march; everyone listens.*)

OLGA   They're leaving.

(*Enter* CHEBUTYKIN.)

MASHA   Our boys are leaving. Well, that's that . . . Happy journey to them! (*To her husband.*) We ought to go home . . . Where's my hat and cape? . . .

KULYGIN   I took them into the house . . . I'll fetch 'em right away. (*Exits into the house.*)

OLGA   Yes, now we can head for home. It's time.

CHEBUTYKIN   Olga Sergeevna!

OLGA   What?
          (*Pause.*)
      What?

CHEBUTYKIN   Nothing . . . I don't know how to tell you . . . (*Whispers in her ear.*)

OLGA (*In shock.*)   That's impossible!

CHEBUTYKIN   Yes . . . what a fuss . . . I'm worn out, exhausted, that's all I'll say . . . (*Annoyed.*) Anyway, it doesn't matter!

MASHA   What happened?

OLGA (*Embraces* IRINA.)   Today is a dreadful day . . . I don't know how to tell you, my precious . . .

IRINA   What? Tell me quickly, what? For God's sake! (*Weeps.*)

CHEBUTYKIN   The Baron was just killed in a duel.

IRINA   I knew it, I knew it . . .

CHEBUTYKIN (*Sits far upstage on a bench.*)   I'm worn out . . . (*Pulls a newspaper out of his pocket.*) Let 'em have a good cry . . . (*Sings quietly.*) Ta-ra-ra-boom-de-ay . . . I sit in gloom all day . . . What does it matter?

          (*The three sisters stand, clutching one another.*)

MASHA   Oh, how the music plays! They're leaving us, one of them has gone forever and ever, we're left alone to begin our life anew. One has to go on living . . . One has to go on living . . .

IRINA (*Lays her head on* OLGA's *bosom*).   A time will come when everyone will realize why all this is, what these sufferings are for, there won't be any mysteries, but in the meantime a person has to live . . . has to work, nothing but work! Tomorrow I'll go away by myself, I'll teach school and I'll devote my whole life to anyone who may possibly need it. It's autumn now, winter will be here soon, the snow will cover everything up, but I shall work, I shall work . . .

OLGA (*Embraces both sisters.*)   The music is playing so gaily, cheerfully, and I feel like living! Oh, dear Lord! Time will pass, and we'll be gone forever, people will forget us, they'll forget our faces, voices and how many of us there were, but our suffering will turn to joy for those who live after us, happiness and peace will come into being on this earth, and those who live now will be remembered with a kind word and a blessing. Oh, dear sisters, this life of ours is not over yet. Let's go on living! The music plays so gaily, so cheerfully, and it looks like just a little while longer and we shall learn why we're alive, why we suffer . . . If only we knew, if only we knew!

          (*The music plays ever more quietly;* KULYGIN, *smiling cheerfully, brings in the hat and cape;* ANDREY *wheels a different baby carriage, in which Bobik is sitting.*)

CHEBUTYKIN (*Sings quietly.*)   Tara . . . ra . . . boom-de-ay . . . I sit in gloom all day . . . (*Reads the paper.*) Doesn't matter! Doesn't matter!

OLGA   If only we knew, if only we knew!

CURTAIN

Variants to *Three Sisters*

Lines come from the censor's copies (Cens.), the fair copy (A), the publication in *Russian Thought* (*Russkaya Mysl* — RT), and the separate publication as *Three Sisters* (1901 — TS)

Act One

Replace you've gone back to wearing white, your face is beaming. — *with* you're in white, there's a smile on your face. (A) (Page 249)

After such thoughts! — I'm twenty, already grown up, how nice it is! (Cens.) (Page 250)

Replace from hard work. And they just about managed it, only just [. . .]a healthy, mighty
with from hard work, but they haven't protected us from the influence of this massive thing advancing on all of us, this glorious healthy (Cens.) (Page 252)

Before In twenty-five years — No offense meant, (Cens.) (Page 252)

Replace If a man philosophizes . . . Polly want a cracker! —
with All this is philosophistics, it's your sophistics, mystics, excuse me, not worth a tinker's dam. It's all crapistics. (Cens.) (Page 253)

Replace SOLYONY (*Shrilly*) . . . VERSHININ Yes, yes, of course. —
with SOLYONY Suffering . . . For instance, bugs bite one another . . . (*Gets embarrassed.*)
OLGA (*Embarrassed, aside.*) He's talking vulgarity.
VERSHININ (*To* TUSENBACH.) Of course, he may be right. (Cens.) (Page 257)

Replace Ah, the way she dresses! It's not so much —
with You're from Moscow, you understand. I can't look at the way they dress here; the local fashion plates simply offend me. It's not that. (A, RT) (Page 258)

Replace Well, I'll be[. . .]It don't think there is
with Superfluous? Who knows! Who among us has a sufficiently accurate point of view to tell what's superfluous from what's necessary? I don't think we do . . . (A, RT) (Page 259)

After even remotely — to look forward to it. (Cens.) (Page 259)

After that invariably smoke. — Never in my life have I had such flowers . . . (A) (Page 260)

Replace TUSENBACH   [. . .]I wouldn't go[. . .]Don't go, my lovely.
with TUSENBACH   So don't go.
CHEBUTYKIN   Certainly not. (Cens.) (Page 262)

Replace SOLYONY   (*Crossing into the reception room.*) Cheep, cheep, cheep . . .
with SOLYONY   You're always singing, it's business, well now let's dance. (*Goes in the reception room.*) (Cens.) (Page 262)

Act Two

Replace Come back tomorrow morning[. . .](*unhurriedly goes back into his room.*)
with I remember everything, I haven't forgotten a thing. I have a phenomenal memory; with a memory like mine another man in my place would long ago have stretched himself and not a rope across all Moscow . . . Across all Russia . . . I don't think anything can provides greater, sweeter pleasure than fame . . .
    (*The doorbell rings.*)
Yes, business . . . Once I dreamed of fame . . . yes . . . (*Stretches.*) And it was so possible . . . (*Unhurriedly goes into his room.*) (Cens., A, RT) (Page 268)

Replace I pester you with. I escort you home every single night.
with I'm waiting for my own happiness. I've been waiting for you four years now and I'm ready to wait at least another ten. (Cens.) (Page 269)

Replace And every single night I'll[. . .]until you chase me away . . .
with And ten years running I'll come to the telegraph office every night and escort you home! (Cens.) (Page 269)

After this town. — Not a town, but a pathetic little hamlet . . . (Cens.) (Page 270)

After (*Laughs*). How pompously he sits! — Attaboy, Doctor! (Page 270)

After our happiness. — If not mine, then at least that of my posterity's posterity. (Cens.) (Page 272)

After will not be for any of us — and we mustn't waste time and strength chasing after it. (Cens.) (Page 272)

After strumming on the guitar. —
"Did you know my soul's unrest.") (Page 272)

After Well, how can I convince you? — We live our own real life, the future will live its own life, just the same as ours — no better, no worse . . . (A, RT) (Page 272)

After Balzac was married in Berdichev. —
      (FEDOTIK *shuffles the cards.*)
IRINA (*Angrily.*)   What are you doing?
FEDOTIK   Don't mess up my wheeling-dealing.
IRINA   I'm fed up with you and your jokes.
FEDOTIK   Makes no difference, the solitaire wouldn't have come out.
    I shall now show you another kind . . . (*Deals out a hand of soli-
    taire.*)
RODÉ (*Loudly.*)   Doctor, how old are you?
CHEBUTYKIN   Me? Thirty-two.
      (*Laughter.*)
IRINA (*Looking at the cards.*)   But what was Balzac doing in Russia?
(*Pause.* (Cens.) (Page 273)

Before VERSHININ   Incidentally, that's quite a wind! —
IRINA   The solitaire is coming out, I see . . . I don't believe in telling
    fortunes by cards, but my heart is filled with joy. We will live in
    Moscow.
FEDOTIK   No, the solitaire is not coming out. You see, the eight was
    lying on the two of spades. (*Laughs.*) Which means, you won't live
    in Moscow. (Cens.) (Page 273)

Replace SOLYONY (*Declaiming*)   [. . . .]forget your dreams . . ." —
with SOLYONY   It's all right, no matter what you say.
TUSENBACH   I shall work. (Cens.) (Page 275)

After Baron's drunk! — (*Dances a waltz by herself.*) (Cens.) (Page
    277)

Replace What a shame![. . .]I'll bring him a little toy . . . —
with Where can I go now with a guitar? (Cens.) (Page 278)

After I'm tired. — (*Hides his face in his hands.*) (Cens., A, RT) (Page
    280)

Act Three

After what a life that's going to be! — What a pity that my little girls won't live long enough to see that time! They're special creatures, and I devote all my strength to making sure they will be beautiful and strong. (Cens.) (Page 286)

After and be superior to you . . . (*Laughs.*) — How I'd like to live, if only you knew. (Cens.) (Page 286)

Replace is simply frivolous . . . —
with are only the whims of old maids. Old maids never love their sisters-in-law — that's a rule. (A, RT, TS) (Page 291)

Act Four

Replace (*Casts a glance around the garden.*) —
with (*Casts a glance around the garden.*) Today I destroyed my guitar, there's nowhere to play it any more, and I don't feel like it. (Cens.) (Page 293)

Replace TUSENBACH And god-awful boredom[. . .]And where's Mariya Sergeevna? —
with IRINA Aleksey Petrovich, what happened yesterday on the boulevard near the theater? Tell me frankly.
FEDOTIK Nothing happened.
IRINA Word of honor?
　　　(*Pause.*)
FEDOTIK Nothing happened . . . Well, trivia . . . It'll all blow over. But where's Mariya Sergeevna? (Cens.) (Page 293)

Replace Good-bye, got to go[. . .]*she exits with them.*) —
with Let's go, or else I'll start to cry.
　　　(*They both walk out, glancing around.*)
　　We had a fine life here . . . (*Shouts.*) Mariya Sergeevna! Hop to it! (*They leave.*) (Cens.) (Page 293)

Replace She even resembles Masha[. . .]I do love her, my Masha. —
with When I was engaged to Masha, sometimes I'd simply walk around like a crazy person, like a drunk, and talk hokum, hokium . . . I'm happy now too, but in those days I was delirious with happiness. Well, the Baron is probably the same way . . . (Cens.) (Page 295)

After shave off your moustache, Fyodor Ilyich. —
KULYGIN That's enough out of you.

CHEBUYTKIN   Now your wife will be scared of you. (Cens; A, RT) (Page 295)

After that's not what happiness is all about . . . — (*Pause.*) Strange, the fates people have. (Cens.); (*Pause.*) You don't understand anything in this world. (A, RT); (*Pause.*) (TS) (Page 296)

After you get bitchy. — like a cook. (Page 297)

Replace Looking at her brother[. . .]Look at our Andrey, our baby brother —

with The one I'd like to give a good thrashing is Andrushka over there, our baby brother. Ridiculous dummy! (Page 297)

Replace (*Reads the papers and sings softly.*)[. . .]I sit in gloom all day . . . —

with Yes, say what you like, Ivan Romanych, but it's high time to change your way of life. (*Sings quietly.*) "Ah, you, Sashka, my mischiefmaker, change my blue notes . . . They're all brand-new notes . . ." (Cens.) (Page 296)

After I'll be left alone in the house. — I don't consider a wife a person.
(*Enter* FERAPONT *with papers.*)
CHEBUTYKIN   Why not? (Cens.) (Page 298)

After the further you go, the better. — (*Pause.*) Or, whatever you like! Doesn't matter . . . (TS) (Page 298)

Replace SOLYONY   The old man's getting upset for no good reason [. . .]ANDREY *and* FERAPONT *enter.* —
with SOLYONY   And what's the Baron doing? Writing his will? Saying good-bye to his beloved, pledging her eternal love, or already on the battlefield?
      (*Pause.*)
I'll plug him all the same, like a sitting duck . . .
      (*They leave. Cries are heard of "Hop to it! Yoo-hoo!"* ANDREY *and* FERAPONT *enter.* (Cens.) (Page 298)

Replace FERAPONT   Papers to sign[. . .]Yoo-hoo, Masha, yoo-hoo! —
with ANDREY   Oh, where is it, where has my past gone to, when I was young, cheerful, clever, when I dreamed and had refined thoughts, when both my present and my future lit up with hope? Why do we, having barely begun life, become boring, gray, unin-

teresting, lazy, indifferent, useless . . . Our town has been in existence for two hundred years, in it — it's a joke! — are a hundred
thousand inhabitants, and not one who isn't like another, neither
in the past or the present, not a single enthusiast, not a single
scholar, not a single artist, not the least remarkable person, who
might arouse envy or a passionate desire to emulate him . . . They
only eat, drink, sleep, then die; others are born and they too eat,
drink, sleep, and, in order not to be stupefied with boredom, vary
their lives with nasty gossip, vodka, cards, and the women cheat
on their husbands, and the husbands lie, pretend they don't see
anything, don't hear anything, and irresistibly a vulgar influence
weighs on the children — and the divine spark dies out in them,
and they become the same pitiful, indistinguishable corpses as
their fathers and mothers . . . (*To* FERAPONT.) Whadda you want?

FERAPONT   Howzat? Papers to be signed.

ANDREY (*Caught up in a feeling of tenderness.*)   My dear sisters, my
wonderful sisters!

FERAPONT (*Handing over the papers.*)   The doorman at the gummint
offices was just saying. Seems, he says, winter in Petersburg there
was two hundred degrees of frost. Two thousand people froze to
death. Folks, he says, was scared to death. Could be Petersburg,
could be Moscow — I don't rec'llect.

ANDREY   Every night now I lie awake and think . . . I think about
how in two or three years, I'll end up drowning in unpaid debts,
I'll become a pauper, this house will be sold, my wife will run out
on me — suddenly my soul becomes so buoyant, so airy, and in
the distance a light begins to dawn, I have a presentiment of freedom, and then I'd like to run to my three sisters, run to them, and
shout out: sisters, I'm saved, I'm saved!

NATASHA (*Through the window.*)   You're making too much noise
there, Andryusha. You'll wake Sophiekins. (*Losing her temper.*) If
you want to talk, give the baby carriage to somebody else. Ferapont, take the carriage from the master!

FERAPONT   Yes, ma'am. (*Takes the carriage.*)

ANDREY (*Embarrassed.*)   I'll talk quietly.

NATASHA (*Behind the window, petting her little boy.*)   Bobik!
Naughty Bobik! Bad Bobik!

ANDREY (*Glancing at the papers.*)   I'll look over this mishmash right
now and sign whatever I have to, and you can take it back to the
office . . .

(*He exits into the house, reading the papers;* FERAPONT *pushes
the baby carriage; in the garden in the distance* IRINA *and* TUS-
ENBACH *appear, the Baron is dressed foppishly, in a straw hat.*)

NATASHA (*Behind the window.*)   Bobik, what's your mommy's name?

Darling, darling! And who's that? That's Auntie Olya. Say to
Auntie: afternoon, Olya!
    (*Enter* KULYGIN.)
KULYGIN (*To* IRINA.)   Where's Masha?
IRINA   Somewhere in the garden.
KULYGIN   I haven't seen her since this morning . . . She's in a bad
mood today . . . (*Shakes his head.*) And they still haven't painted
that bench! What a bunch, really . . . (*Shouts.*) Yoo-hoo! Masha,
yoo-hoo! (*Exits into the garden.*) (Cens.) (Page 299)

After in life one way or another. — *Wandering musicians, a man and
a girl, play the fiddle and the harp.* (Cens.) (Page 302)

Replace Which means, not being in Moscow[. . . .](*Laughs.*) Life is
hard. —
with It's not up to me . . . I'll do a bit of work and, I suppose, I'll go
to Moscow.
VERSHININ   Now where . . .
    (*Pause.*)
Life follows its own laws, not ours. Yes. (Cens.) (Page 303)

Replace KULYGIN   She's not crying any more[. . .]*Enter* NATASHA —
with MASHA   "We took the town of Turtukay, And all of us were
standing by, We beat the English, beat the Turks . . ." Damn it,
I'm raving. (*Drinks water.*) I don't need anything . . . I'll be calm
right away . . . It doesn't matter . . . "We took the town of Turtukay, And all of us were standing by . . ." The ideas are whirling
around in my head.
    (*Enter* IRINA; *in the distance, in the street a harp and fiddle are
    heard playing.*)
OLGA   Calm down, Masha. Let's go to my room.
MASHA   It's passed me by. There's nothing now. (*Smiles.*) Which
means, fate does what it wants, there's nothing you can do about
it . . . (*Sobs and immediately stops.*) Let it be.
    (*A distant gunshot is heard.*)
IRINA   (*Shudders.*) Let's go to the bottom of the garden; we'll sit
together, not saying a word . . .
(*A distant gunshot is heard.* NATASHA *enters.* (Cens.)

Replace OLGA   What?[. . .]For God's sake! (*Weeps.*) —
with OLGA   What?
CHEBUYTKIN   (*Whispers in her ear.*) Yes . . . what a fuss . . . Well, sir,
now I'll have a bit of a sitdown, rest, then pack it up . . . (*Sits far*

upstage on the bench.) I'm worn out. (*Pulls a newspaper out of his pocket.*)

OLGA   (*Embraces* IRINA.) I don't know what to say . . . Today is a dreadful day . . .

IRINA   What's been going on? Tell me, what? I won't faint, I won't. I'll endure it all . . . (Cens.) (Page 304)

After Let's go on living! — I shall live, sisters! . . . A person has to live . . . (*Looks upwards.*) The birds of passage are overhead, they fly by every spring and fall, for a thousand years now, and they don't know why but they'll go on flying for a long, long time to come, many thousands of years — until God finally reveals the mystery to them . . . (Page 306)

After plays ever more quietly; — very far upstage a commotion, a crowd can be seen watching as the body of the Baron, slain in the duel, is borne past. (Cens.) (Page 306)

The Cherry Orchard

"The next play I write will definitely be funny, very funny, at least in concept," Chekhov declared to his wife on March 7, 1901, after *Three Sisters* had opened. This concept, as the author sketched it to Stanislavsky, would incorporate a footman mad about fishing, a garrulous one-armed billiard player, and a situation in which a landowner is continually borrowing money from the footman. He also envisaged a branch of flowering cherry thrust through a window of the manor house.

Chekhov's notebooks reveal that *The Cherry Orchard* had taken root even earlier, with his concepts of the governess Charlotta, another farcical type, and the idea that "the estate will soon go under the hammer" as the next ramification. The theme had a personal application. For the boy Chekhov, the sale of his home after his father's bankruptcy had been desolating. The imminent loss of one's residence looms over his early plays, becomes the (literal) trigger of *Uncle Vanya*, and gives an underlying dynamic to *Three Sisters*.

The endangered estate, in Chekhov's early plans, was to belong to a liberal-minded old lady who dressed like a girl, smoked, and could not do without society; a sympathetic sort, tailored to the Maly Theater's Olga Sadovskaya, who specialized in biddies and beldams. When the Maly Theater refused to release her, Chekhov reshaped the role until it was suitable for someone of Olga Knipper's age. Only then did he conceive of Lopakhin. Varya first appeared as a grotesquely comic name, Varvara Nedotyopina (Varvara Left-in-the-Lurch): *nedotyopa* eventually became the catchphrase of old Firs.

As Chekhov's letters reveal, he stressed the play's comic nature and was put out when the Moscow Art Theater saw it as a tearful tragedy. Even if some of Chekhov's complaints can be dismissed as a side effect of his physical deterioration, there is no doubt that the Art Theater misplaced many of his intended emphases. He seems to have meant the major role to be the peasant-turned-millionaire Lopakhin, played by Stanislavsky. However, Stanislavsky, a millionaire of peasant origins, preferred the part of the feckless aristocrat Gaev, and handed Lopakhin over to Leonidov, a less experienced actor. Olga Knipper, whom the author saw in the grotesque role of the German governess, was cast as the elegant Ranevskaya. Immediately, the central focus shifted to the genteel family of landowners because the strongest actors were in those parts. Later on, fugitives from the Revolution identified so closely with Ranevskaya and Gaev that they disseminated a nostalgic view of the gentry's plight throughout the West. Soviet productions then went to the opposite extreme, reinterpreting Lopakhin as a man of the people capable of building a progressive society, and the student Trofimov as an eloquent harbinger of that brave new world.

Choosing sides immediately reduces the play's complexity and ambiguity. Chekhov had no axe to grind, not even the axe that hews down the orchard. Neither Lopakhin nor Trofimov is invested with greater validity than is Ranevskaya or Gaev. Trofimov is constantly undercut by comic devices: after a melodramatic exit line, "All is over between us," he falls downstairs; and, despite his claim to be in the vanguard of progress, he is too absentminded to locate his own galoshes. Even his earnest speech about the idle upper classes and the benighted workers is addressed to the wrong audience: how can Ranevskaya possibly identify with the Asiatic bestiality that Trofimov indicts as a Russian characteristic? Only in the hearing of the infatuated Anya do Trofimov's words seem prophetic; at other times, his inability to realize his situation renders them absurd.

Chekhov was anxious to avoid the stage clichés of the *kulak*, the hardhearted, hard-fisted, loudmouthed merchant, in his portrayal of Lopakhin; after all, Lopakhin shares Chekhov's own origins as a man of peasant background who worked his way up in a closed society. He can be the tactless boor that Gaev insists he is, exulting over his purchase of the orchard and starting its decimation even before the family leaves. But, in the same breath, he is aware of his shortcomings, longs for a more poetic existence, and has, in the words of his antagonist Trofimov, "delicate, gentle fingers, like an artist . . . a delicate, gentle soul." And for all his pragmatism, he too is comically inept when it comes to romance. His halfhearted wooing of Varya may result from a more deep-seated love of her foster mother.

Ironically, it is the impractical Ranevskaya who pricks Lopakhin's dreams of giants and vast horizons and suggests that he examine his own gray life rather than build castles in the air. She may be an incorrigible romantic about the orchard and totally scatterbrained about money, but on matters of sex she is more clearsighted than Lopakhin, Trofimov, or Gaev, who considers her "depraved." Prudish as a young Komsomol, Trofimov is as scandalized by her advice that he take a mistress as he had been annoyed that Varya should distrust his moments alone with Anya.

In short, any attempt to grade Chekhov's characters as "right-thinking" or "wrongheaded" ignores the multifaceted nature of their portrayal. It would be a mistake to adopt wholeheartedly either the sentimental attitude of Gaev and Ranevskaya to the orchard or the pragmatic and "socially responsible" attitude of Lopakhin and Trofimov. By 1900, there was any number of works about uprooted gentlefolk and estates confiscated by *arrivistes*. Pyotr Nevezhin's *Second Youth* (1883), a popular melodrama dealing with the breakup of a nest of gentry, held the stage until the Revolution, and Chekhov had seen it. That same year brought Nikolay Solovyov's *Liquidation*, in which an estate is saved by a rich peasant marrying the daughter of the family. Chekhov would not have been raking over these burned-out themes if he did not have a fresh

angle. *The Cherry Orchard* is the play in which Chekhov most successfully achieved a "new form," the amalgam of a symbolist outlook with
the appurtenances of social comedy.

Perhaps the Russian critic A. R. Kugel was right when he wrote, "All
the inhabitants of *The Cherry Orchard* are children and their behavior
is childish."[1] Certainly, Chekhov seems to have abandoned his usual
repertory company: there is no doctor, no mooning *intelligent* complaining of a wasted life (Yepikhodov may be a parody of that), no love triangles except for the comic one of Yepikhodov-Dunyasha-Yasha. The
only pistol is wielded by the hapless dolt Yepikhodov, and Nina's mysterious enveloping *"talma"* in *The Seagull* has dwindled into Dunyasha's
talmochka, a fancy term for a shawl. Soliloquies have been replaced by
monologues that are patently ridiculous (Gaev's speeches to the bookcase and the sunset) or misdirected (Trofimov's speech on progress). The
absurdly-named Simeonov-Pishchik, his "dear daughter Dashenka," and
his rapid mood shifts would be out of place in *Three Sisters*. The upstart
valet Yasha, who smells of chicken coops and cheap perfume, recalls
Chichikov's servant Petrushka in Gogol's *Dead Souls*, who permeates the
ambience with his effluvium. Gogol, rather than Turgenev, is the pre-
siding genius of this comedy.

The standard theme of New or Roman comedy, the source of modern
domestic drama, is that of the social misfit—miser or crank or misanthrope—creating a series of problems for young lovers. Confounded
by a crafty servant who, protected by comedy's holiday spirit, oversteps
his rank, the misfit is either reintegrated into society or expelled from it.
The result is an affirmation of society's ideals and conventions. By the
late eighteenth century, this formula was beginning to break down: in
Beaumarchais' *Marriage of Figaro*, the clever servant finds his master's
aims too much in conflict with his own. The dissolution of the social
fabric is prefigured by the growing tension within the comic framework.

The Cherry Orchard carries forward this dissolution. All the characters
are misfits, from Lopakhin, who dresses like a rich man but feels like a
pig in a pastry shop; to Yasha and Dunyasha, servants who ape their
betters; to the expelled student Trofimov, aimlessly hustled from place
to place; to Yepikhodov, who puts simple ideas into inappropriate language; to Varya, who is an efficient manager but longs to be a pilgrim;
to the most obvious example, the uprooted governess Charlotta, who has
no notion who she is. Early on, we hear Lopakhin protest, "Got to
remember who you are!" Jean-Louis Barrault, the French actor and
director, suggested that the servants are satiric reflections of their master's ideals:[2] old Firs is the senile embodiment of the rosy past over which
Gaev waxes lyrical; Yasha, that pushing young particle, with his taste for
Paris and champagne, is a parody of Lopakhin's upward mobility and
Ranevskaya's sophistication; Trofimov's dreams of social betterment are
mocked by Yepikhodov reading Buckle and beefing up his vocabulary.

1. A. R. Kugel, *Russkie dramaturgi* (Moscow: Mir, 1934), 120.
2. Jean-Louis Barrault, "Pourquoi *La Cerisaie*?", *Cahiers de la Compagnie Barrault-Renaud*
   6 (July 1954): 87–97. See p. 620 in this volume for a translation of this essay.

If there is a norm here, it exists offstage, in town, at the bank, in the restaurant; in Mentone and Paris, where Ranevskaya's lover entreats her return; or in Yaroslavl, where Great Aunt frowns on the family's conduct. Chekhov peoples this unseen world with what Vladimir Nabokov might call "homunculi." Besides the lover and Auntie, there are Ranevskaya's alcoholic husband and drowned son; Pishchik's daughter and the Englishmen who find clay on his land; rich Deriganov, who might buy the estate; the Ragulins, who hire Varya; the famous Jewish orchestra; Gaev's deceased parents and servants; the staff eating beans in the kitchen; and a host of others—indicating that the cherry orchard is a desert island in a teeming sea of life. Chekhov had used the device in *Uncle Vanya* and *Three Sisters*, where Vanya's dead sister, the prepotent Protopopov, Mrs. Colonel Vershinin, and Kulygin's headmaster shape the characters' fates but are never seen. In *The Cherry Orchard*, the plethora of invisible beings fortifies the sense of the estate's vulnerability, transience, and isolation.

Barrault also pointed out that "the action" of the play is measured by the outside pressures on the estate. In Act One, the cherry orchard is in danger of being sold; in Act Two, it is on the verge of being sold; in Act Three, it is sold; and in Act Four, it has been sold. The characters are defined by their responses to these "events," which, because they are spoken of, intuited, feared, and longed-for, but never seen, automatically make the sale equivalent to Fate or Death in a play of Maeterlinck or Andreev. As Henri Bergson insisted,[3] anything living that tries to stand still in fluid, evolving time becomes mechanical and thus comic. How do the characters take a position in the temporal flow? Are they delayed? Do they move with it? Do they try to outrun it? Those who refuse to join in (Gaev and Firs) or who rush to get ahead of it (Trofimov) can end up looking ridiculous.

Viewed as traditional comedy, *The Cherry Orchard* thwarts our expectations: the lovers are not threatened except by their own impotence; the servants are uppity and of no help to anyone; all the characters are expelled at the end, but their personal habits have undergone no reformation. Ranevskaya returns to her lover; Gaev, at his most doleful moment, pops another candy in his mouth; Lopakhin and Trofimov are back on the road, one on business, the other on a mission. Even the abandonment of Firs hints that he cannot exist off the estate, but is, as Ranevskaya's greeting to him implies, a piece of furniture like "my dear little table." This resilience in the face of change, with the future yet to be revealed, is closest to the symbolist sense of human beings trapped in the involuntary processes of time, their own mortality insignificant within the broader current. A Bergsonian awareness that reality stands outside time, dwarfing the characters' mundane concerns, imbues Chekhov's comedy with its bemused objectivity.

It also bestows on *The Cherry Orchard* its sense of persons suspended for the nonce. The present barely exists, elbowed aside by memory and

---

3. Henri Bergson, *Laughter: An Essay on the Meaning of the Comic*, trans. C. Brereton and F. Rothwell (New York: Macmillan, 1911), 88–89.

nostalgia on the one hand and by expectation and hope on the other. When the play first opened, the critic Nevedomsky remarked that the characters are simultaneously "living persons, painted with the colors of vivid reality, and at the same time schemata of that reality, as it were its foregone conclusions." Or as Kugel put it more succinctly, "the inhabitants of *The Cherry Orchard* live, as if half asleep, spectrally, on the border line of the real and the mystical."[4]

Chekhov's friend, the writer Ivan Bunin, pointed out that there were no such cherry orchards in Russia, that Chekhov was inventing an imaginary landscape.[5] The estate is a wasteland in which the characters drift among the trivia of their lives while expecting something dire or important to occur. As in Maeterlinck, the play opens with two persons waiting in a dimly-lit space, and closes with the imminent demise of a character abandoned in emptiness. Chekhov's favorite scenarios of waiting are especially attenuated here, since the suspense of "What will happen to the orchard?" dominates the first three acts, and in the last act the wait for carriages to arrive and to effect the diaspora frames the conclusion.

However, the symbolism goes hand-in-glove with carefully observed reality: they coexist. Hence the uneasiness caused by what seem to be humdrum characters or situations. Act Two, with its open-air setting, demonstrates this concurrence of reality and super-reality. Chekhov's people are seldom at ease in the open. The more egotistic they are, like Arkadina and Serebryakov, the sooner they head for the safe haven of the house or, like Natasha, renovate nature to suit their taste. The last act of *Three Sisters* literally strands its protagonists in an uncongenial vacancy, with "yoo-hoos" echoing across the expanse.

By removing the characters in *The Cherry Orchard* from the memory-laden atmosphere of the nursery (where children should feel at home), Chekhov strips them of their habitual defenses. In Act Two, the characters meet on a road, one of those indeterminate locations halfway between the railway station and the house, but, symbolically, halfway between past and future, birth and death, being and nothingness. Something here impels them to deliver their innermost thoughts in monologues: Charlotta complains of her lack of identity, Yepikhodov declares his suicidal urges, Ranevskaya describes her "sinful" past, Gaev addresses the sunset, Trofimov speechifies on what's wrong with society, and Lopakhin paints his hopes for Russia. As if hypnotized by the sound of their voices reverberating in the wilderness, they deliver quintessences of themselves.

At this point comes the portentous moment of the snapped string:

> (*Everyone sits, absorbed in thought. The only sound is* FIRS, *softly muttering. Suddenly a distant sound is heard, as if from the sky; the sound of a breaking string, dying away, mournfully.*)

4. M. Nevedomsky, "Simvolizm v posledney drame A. P. Chekhova," *Mir bozhy* 8, 2 (1904): 18–19. Kugel, *op.cit.*, 125.

5. Ivan Bunin, *O Chekhove* (About Chekhov) (New York: Chekhov Publishing House, published posthumously in 1955), 216.

LYUBOV ANDREEVNA   What's that?

LOPAKHIN   I don't know. Somewhere far off in a mineshaft the rope broke on a bucket. But somewhere very far off.

GAEV   Or perhaps it was some kind of bird . . . something like a heron.

TROFIMOV   Or an owl . . .

LYUBOV ANDREEVNA (*Shivers.*)   Unpleasant anyhow.
      (*Pause.*)

The moment is framed by those pauses that evoke the gaps in existence that Bely claimed were horrifying, and that Beckett was to characterize as the transitional zone in which being made itself heard. Chekhov's characters again recall Maeterlinck's, faintly trying to surmise the nature of the potent force that hovers just outside the picture. The thought-filled pause, then the uncanny sound and the ensuing pause, conjure up what lies beyond.

Even then, however, Chekhov does not forgo a realistic prextext for the inexplicable. Shortly before the moment, Yepikhodov crosses upstage, strumming his guitar. Might not the snapped spring be one broken by the clumsy bookkeeper? At the play's end, before we hear the sound plangently dying away, Lopakhin says that he has left Yepikhodov on the grounds as a caretaker. Chekhov always overlays any symbolic inference with a patina of irreproachable reality.

The party scene in Act Three is the supreme example of Chekhov's intermingling of subliminal symbol and surface reality. Bely saw it as a "crystallization of Chekhov's devices." It so struck the imagination of the young director Meyerhold that he wrote to Chekhov (May 8, 1904) that "the play is abstract like a symphony by Tchaikovsky . . . in (the party scene) there is something Maeterlinckian, terrifying." He later referred to "this nightmarish dance of puppets in a farce" in "Chekhov's new mystical drama."[6]

The act takes place in three dimensions: the forestage, with its brief interchanges by individual characters; the forced gaiety of the dancing in the background, and the offstage auction whose outcome looms over it all. Without leaving the sphere of the mundane, we have what Novalis called "a sequence of ideal events running parallel to reality." Characters are thrust out from the indistinct background, and then return to it. Scantily identified, the postal clerk and the stationmaster surge forward, unaware of the main characters' inner lives, and make unwitting ironic comments. The stationmaster recites Aleksey Tolstoy's orotund poem, "The Sinful Woman," about a courtesan's conversation by the Christ at a lavish orgy in Judaea. The opening lines, describing a sumptuous banquet, cast a sardonic reflection on the frumps gathered on this dismal occasion. They also show the subsequent interview between the puri-

6. Andrey Bely, "The Cherry Orchard." See the full essay on pages 579–82. Vsevolod Meyerhold, *Perepiska* (Moscow: Iskusstvo, 1976), 45, and "Teatr (k istorii tekhnike)," in *Teatr: kniga o novom teatre* (St. Petersburg: Shipovnik, 1908), 143–45.

tanical Trofimov and the self-confessed sinner Ranevskaya to be a parodic confrontation between a messiah in eyeglasses and a Magdalene in a Parisian ballgown. Charlotta is described in the stage directions as a "figure in a gray top hat and checked trousers," waving its arms and jumping up and down—a nameless, ambiguously sexed phantasm erupting out of nowhere. All her irrelevant tricks point up the arbitrary nature of human action. The act culminates in the moving juxtaposition of Ranevskaya's weeping and Lopakhin's laughter, as the unseen musicians play loudly at his behest.

A party as a playground for contrasting moods was a staple of romantic stagecraft, especially in Russian drama. In Griboedov's *Woe from Wit*, the hectic tempo of the hero's despair is scored against the inanity of a high society soirée. Pushkin's *Feast in Plaguetime* mordantly contrasted libertinage and fatality. Lermontov's *Masquerade* made a costume ball the setting for betrayal and murder. Chekhov's innovation is to reduce the romantic element to banality in consonance with his own favored method. So the ball in *The Cherry Orchard* is a sorry congregation of provincial nobodies, upstart servants, and a klezmer band. The gaiety becomes even more hollow and the pervasion of the grotesque more pungent.

The return to the nursery, now stripped of its evocative trappings, in Act Four, confirms the inexorable expulsion. In Act One, it has been a room in which to linger; now, it is a cheerless space in which characters loiter only momentarily on their way to somewhere else. The old Russian tradition of sitting for a moment before taking leave becomes especially meaningful when there are no chairs, only trunks and bundles to perch on. The ghosts that Gaev and Ranevskaya had seen in the orchard in the first act have now moved indoors, in the person of Firs, who is doomed to haunt the scene of the past, since he has no future.

"Ladies in white dresses" had been one of Chekhov's earliest images for the play. Visually, the dominant note is etiolation, from Ranevskaya confusing the clusters of white blossoms in the garden with her late mother in a white dress, to the final tableau of Firs in his white waistcoat recumbent on the sofa. Achromatism is ambivalent: it is vernal and virginal, and at the same time the hue of dry bones and sterility. The white is set in relief by Varya's nun-like costume. The American actress Eva Le Gallienne astutely noted Chekhov's repetitive use of a young woman in black. "Just as in painting there is a note of black in one of his female characters . . . the wearing of black is an outward manifestation of an inner state of mind, especially when worn by young women."[7] *The Seagull*'s Masha, "in mourning for her life," and Masha in *Three Sisters*, wearing black on a festive occasion, are shown up as poseurs. Varya fancies herself tramping the country from shrine to shrine, but on the belt of her black gown hangs a ring of keys: the emblem of a bustling, officious nature ill-suited to spiritual withdrawal. When she gives up her keys, it is to fling them, in unholy anger, at Lopakhin.

7. Eva Le Gallienne, *At 33* (New York: Longmans Green, 1934), 224.

The consummate mastery of *The Cherry Orchard* is revealed in an authorial shorthand that is both impressionistic and theatrical. The pull on Ranevskaya to return to Paris takes shape in the telegram prop: in Act One, she tears up the telegrams; by Act Three, she has preserved them in her handbag; in Act Four, the lodestones draw her back. The dialogue is similarly telegraphic, as in Anya's short speech about her mother's flat in Paris. "Mama is living on the sixth floor; I walk all the way up, there are some French people there, ladies, an old Catholic priest with a pamphlet, and it's full of cigarette smoke, not nice at all." In a few strokes, a past is encapsulated: a high walk-up, signifying Ranevskaya's reduced circumstances, her toying with religious conversion, a louche atmosphere.

Each character is distinguished by an appropriate speech pattern. Ranevskaya constantly employs diminutives and terms of endearment; for her everyone is *golubchik,* "dovie." She is also vague, using adjectives like "some kind of" (*kakoi-to*). Gaev is a parody of the after-dinner speaker: emotion can be voiced only in fulsome oration, thick with platitudes. When his flow is stanched, he falls back on billiard terms or stops his mouth with candy and anchovies. Pishchik has high blood pressure, so Chekhov the doctor makes sure he speaks in short, breathless phrases, a hodgepodge of old-world courtesy, hunting terms, and newspaper talk. Lopakhin's language is more varied, according to his interlocutor: blunt and colloquial with servants, more respectful with his former betters. As suits a businessman, his language is concise and well-structured, citing exact numbers and a commercial vocabulary, with frequent glances at his watch. Only in dealing with Varya does he resort to ponderous facetiousness and even bleating.

Memorably, Firs's "half-baked bungler" is the last line in the play. Its periodic repetition suggests that Chekhov meant it to sum up all the characters. They are all inchoate—some, like Anya and Trofimov, in the process of taking shape; others, like Gaev and Yepikhodov, never to take shape. The whole play has been held in a similar state of contingency until the final moments, when real chopping begins in the orchard and, typically, it is heard from offstage, mingled with the more cryptic and reverberant sound of the snapped string.

The Cherry Orchard[1]

A Comedy[2]

Characters[3]

RANEVSKAYA, LYUBOV ANDREEVNA, a landowner
ANYA, her daughter, seventeen
VARYA, her foster-daughter, twenty-four
GAEV, LEONID ANDREEVICH, Ranevskaya's brother
LOPAKHIN, YERMOLAY ALEKSEICH, a businessman
TROFIMOV, PYOTR SERGEEVICH, a university student
SIMEONOV-PISHCHIK, BORIS BORISOVICH, a landowner
CHARLOTTA IVANOVNA, a governess
YEPHIKHOV, SEMYON PANTELEEVICH, a bookkeeper
DUNYASHA, a parlor maid
FIRS[4] NIKOLAEVICH, a valet, an old-timer of eighty-seven
YASHA, a young valet
A VAGRANT
THE STATIONMASTER
A POSTAL CLERK
GUESTS, SERVANTS

The action takes place on RANEVSKAYA'*s estate.*[5]

Act One

A room, which is still known as the Nursery. One of the doors opens into ANYA'*s bedroom. Dawn, soon the sun will be up. It is already May, the cherry trees are in bloom; but it is chilly in the orchard, there is a*

---

1. According to Stanislavsky, Chekhov wavered between the pronunciations *Vishnevy sad* (accentuated on the first syllable, "an orchard of cherries") and *Vishnyovy sad* (accentuated on the second syllable, "a cherry orchard"). He decided on the latter. "The former is a market garden, a plantation of cherry trees, a profitable orchard that still had value. But the latter offers no profit, it does nothing but preserve within itself and its snow-white blossoms the poetry of the life of the masters of olden times." (*My Life in Art*)
2. This subtitle was used in the Marks edition of 1904. On the posters and publicity, the play was denominated a drama.
3. To a Russian ear, certain associations can be made with the names. Lyubov means love, and a kind of indiscriminate love characterizes Ranevskaya. Gaev suggests *gaer*, buffoon, while Lopakhin may be derived from either *lopata*, shovel, or *lopat*, to shovel food down one's gullet—both earthy-sounding. Simeonov-Pishchik combines a noble boyar name with a silly name reminiscent of *pishchat*, to chirp, something like De Montfort-Tweet.
4. He is named for the Orthodox Saint Thyrsus (martyred 251).
5. For a description of the house, see Chekhov's letters to O. L. Knipper (October 14, 1903 page 448) and K. S. Stanislavsky (November 5, 1903, page 453). Stanislavsky decided that the estate was located in the Oryol province near Kursk, possibly because the area is rich in potter's clay, and would justify the Englishmen in Act Four finding "some kind of white clay" on Pishchik's land.

frost. The windows in the room are shut. Enter DUNYASHA *carrying a candle and* LOPAKHIN *holding a book.*

LOPAKHIN   Train's pulled in, thank God. What time is it?

DUNYASHA   Almost two. (*Blows out the candle.*) Light already.

LOPAKHIN   But just how late was the train? A couple of hours at least. (*Yawns and stretches.*) That's me all over, had to do something stupid! Drove over here on purpose, to meet them at the station, and spent the time fast asleep. . . . Sat down and dropped off. Annoying . . . Though you should have woke me up.

DUNYASHA   I thought you'd gone. (*Listening.*) There, sounds like they're driving up.

LOPAKHIN   (*Listening.*)   No . . . the luggage has to be loaded, one thing and another . . . (*Pause.*) Lyubov Andreevna's been living abroad five years now, I don't know what she's like these days . . . A good sort of person, that's her. A kindhearted, unpretentious person. I remember, when I was just a kid about fifteen,[6] my late father—he kept a shop in this village back then—punched me in the face with his fist, blood was gushing from my nose . . . We'd come into the yard back then for some reason, and he'd been drinking. Lyubov Andreevna, I remember as though it was yesterday, still a youngish lady, so slender, brough me to the washstand, here in this very room, the nursery. "Don't cry," she says, "my little peasant, you'll live long enough to get married . . ."

(*Pause.*)

My little peasant . . . My father, true, was a peasant, and here I am in a white waistcoat, yellow high-button shoes. Like a pig's snout on a tray of pastry[7] . . . Only difference is I'm rich, plenty of money, if you think it over and work it out, once a peasant, always a peasant[8] . . . (*Leafs through the book.*) I was reading this book here and couldn't make head or tail of it. Reading and nodding off.

(*Pause.*)

DUNYASHA   The dogs didn't sleep all night, they can sense the mistress is coming home.

---

6. In an earlier version, the boy's age was five or six. At that time Chekhov still saw Ranevskaya as an old woman. He reduced her age when it became clear that his wife Olga Knipper would play the part.

7. Literally, "with a pig's snout in White-Bread Row," the street in any city market where fine baked goods are sold.

8. For a description of Lopakhin, see Chekhov's letters to Olga Knipper (October 30, 1903, page 451), Stanislavsky (October 30, 1903, page 451), and Nemirovich-Danchenko (November 2, 1903, page 452).

"[Chekhov] told me that Lopakhin externally should either be like a merchant or like a medical professor at Moscow University. And later, at the rehearsals, after Act Three he said to me:

" 'Listen, Lopakhin doesn't shout. He is rich, and rich men never shout.' . . .

"When I inquired of Chekhov how to play Lopakhin, he replied: 'In yellow high-button shoes.' " (L. M. Leonidov, "Past and Present," *Moscow Art Theater Yearbook for 1944*, Vol. 1 [1946].)

LOPAKHIN   What's got into you, Dunyasha? You're so . . .

DUNYASHA   My hands are trembling. I'm going to swoon.

LOPAKHIN   Much too delicate, that's what you are, Dunyasha.
Dressing up like a young lady, fixing your hair like one too. Mustn't
do that. Got to remember who you are.

> (YEPIKHODOV[9] *enters with a bouquet; he is wearing a jacket and
> brightly polished boots, which squeak noisily. On entering, he
> drops the bouquet.*)

YEPIKHODOV (*Picks up the bouquet.*)   Here, the gardener sent them,
he says stick 'em in the dining room. (*He hands* DUNYASHA *the
bouquet.*)

LOPAKHIN   And bring me some kvas.[1]

DUNYASHA   Yes, sir. (*Exits.*)

YEPIKHODOV   There's a morning frost now, three degrees of it, but
the cherries are all in bloom. I can't condone our climate. (*Sighs.*)
I can't. Our climate cannot be conducive in the right way. Look,
Yermolay Alekseich, if I might append, day before yesterday I
bought myself some boots and they, I venture to assure you,
squeak so loud, it's quite out of the question. What's the best kind
of grease?

LOPAKHIN   Leave me alone. You wear me out.

YEPIKHODOV   Every day I experience some kind of hard luck. But I
don't complain, I'm used to it. I even smile.

> (DUNYASHA *enters and gives* LOPAKHIN *a glass of kvas.*[2])

YEPIKHODOV   I'm on my way. (*Bumps into a chair, which falls over.*)
Look . . . (*As if in triumph.*) There, you see, pardon the expression,
what a circumstance, one of many . . . It's simply incredible! (*He
exits.*)

DUNYASHA   I have to confess, Yermolay Alekseich, Yepikhodov proposed to me.

YEPIKHODOV   Ah!

DUNYASHA   I don't know how to handle it . . . He's a quiet sort, but
sometimes he just starts talking, and you can't understand a word.
It's nice and it's sensitive, only you can't understand a word. I kind

---

9. A parody of the self-made man represented by Lopakhin. Chekhov first envisaged the
character as plump and elderly, but revised this to fit one of his favorite actors, Ivan
Moskvin, who was young and trim. The character had several originals. Yepikhodov's auto-
didacticism, reading abstruse books to better his mind, originated when Chekhov suggested to one of his attendants in Yalta that he go in for self-improvement. The man went
out, bought a red tie, and announced his intention of learning French. Yepikhodov's clum-
siness derives from a conjuring clown Chekhov saw perform at the Hermitage gardens.
The act consisted of disasters: juggled eggs smashing on the clown's forehead and dishes
crashing to the ground while the woebegone wizard stood with an expression of bewilderment and embarrassment. Chekhov kept shouting, "Wonderful! It's wonderful!" (Stanislavsky, *Teatralnaya gazeta*, November 27, 1914.)
1. See *The Bear*, note 6, page 9.
2. On the servants' relation to Lopakhin, see Chekhov's letter to Stanislavsky, November 10,
1903, on page 454.

of like him. He's madly in love with me. As a person he's always
in trouble, something goes wrong every day. So around here we've
taken to calling him Tons of Trouble[3] . . .

LOPAKHIN (*Hearkening.*)   Listen, I think they're coming . . .

DUNYASHA   They're coming! What's the matter with me? . . . I've got
cold chills.

LOPAKHIN   They're coming. Let's go meet them. Will she recognize
me? It's five years since last we met.

DUNYASHA (*Flustered.*)   I'll faint this minute . . . Ah, I'll faint!
(*We hear the sound of two carriages drawing up to the house.*
LOPAKHIN *and* DUNYASHA *go out quickly. The stage is empty.*
Noise begins in the adjoining rooms. FIRS, *leaning on a stick,*
hurries across the stage; he has just been to meet LYUBOV
ANDREEVNA; *he is wearing an old suit of livery and a top hat;*
he mutters something to himself but no words can be made out.
A voice: "Let's go through here." LYUBOV ANDREEVNA,[4] ANYA, *and*
CHARLOTTA IVANOVNA *with a lapdog on a leash, all three dressed*
in travelling clothes, VARYA *in an overcoat and kerchief,* GAEV,
SIMEONOV-PISHCHIK, LOPAKHIN, DUNYASHA *with a bundle and*
parasol, servants carrying suitcases—all pass through the room.)

ANYA[5]   Let's go through here. Mama, do you remember what room
this is?

LYUBOV ANDREEVNA (*Joyfully, through tears.*)   The nursery!

VARYA   It's cold, my hands are numb. (*To* LYUBOV ANDREEVNA.) Your
rooms, the white and the violet, are still the same as ever, Mama
dear.

LYUBOV ANDREEVNA   The nursery, my darling, beautiful room . . . I
slept here when I was a little girl . . . (*Weeps.*) And now I feel like
a little girl . . . (*She kisses her brother and* VARYA *and then her*
brother again.) And Varya is just the same as ever, looks like a nun.
And I recognized Dunyasha . . . (*Kisses* DUNYASHA.)

GAEV   The train was two hours later. What'd y' call that? What kind
of system is that?

CHARLOTTA (*To* PISHCHIK.)   My dog eats nuts even.[6]

---

3. *Dvadtsat-dva neschastye*, literally means twenty-two misfortunes, "twenty-two" being a
number indicating "lots." *Neschastye* is a recurrent word throughout the play.
4. See Chekhov's letter to Olga Knipper, October 25, 1903, page xxx.
5. For descriptions of Anya and Varya, see Chekhov's letters to Nemirovich-Danchenko,
October 24 (page 450) and November 2, 1903 (page 453).
6. "Muratova, who played Charlotta, asks Anton Pavlovich, might she wear a green necktie.
" 'You may but it's not necessary,' " the author answers. (L. M. Leonidov, "Past and
Present," *Moscow Art Theater Yearbook for 1944*, Volume 1 [1946]).
    For a description of Charlotta, see Chekhov's letters to Nemirovich-Danchenko,
November 2, 1903, on page 452. The character was based on an eccentric English gov-
erness, whom Chekhov had met while staying on Stanislavsky's estate. This acrobatic Miss
Prism would leap up on Chekhov's shoulders and salute passersby by taking off his hat
and forcing him to bow. (*My Life in Art*, Russian edition.)

PISHCHIK (*Astounded.*)[7] Can you imagine!

(*They all go out, except for* ANYA *and* DUNYASHA.)

DUNYASHA We're worn out with waiting. . . . (*Helps* ANYA *out of her overcoat and hat.*)

ANYA I couldn't sleep the four nights on the train . . . now I'm so frozen.

DUNYASHA You left during Lent, there was snow then too, frost, and now? My darling! (*She laughs and kisses her.*) We're worn out with waiting for you, my pride and joy . . . I'll tell you now, I can't hold it back another minute . . .

ANYA (*Weary.*) Always something . . .

DUNYASHA Yepikhodov the bookkeeper right after Easter proposed to me.

ANYA You've got a one-track mind . . . (*Setting her hair to rights.*) I've lost all my hairpins . . . (*She is very tired, practically staggering.*)

DUNYASHA I just don't know what to think. He loves me, loves me so much!

ANYA (*Peering through the door to her room, tenderly.*) My room, my windows, as if I'd never gone away. I'm home! Tomorrow morning I'll get up, run through the orchard . . . Oh, if only I could get some sleep! I couldn't sleep the whole way, I was worried to death.

DUNYASHA Day before yesterday, Pyotr Sergeich arrived.

ANYA (*Joyfully.*) Petya!

DUNYASHA The gent's sleeping in the bathhouse, the gent's staying there. "I'm afraid," says the gent, "to be a nuisance." (*Looking at her pocket watch.*) Somebody ought to wake the gent up, but Varvara Mikhailovna gave the order not to. "Don't you wake him up," she says.

(*Enter* VARYA, *with a keyring on her belt.*)

VARYA Dunyasha, coffee right away . . . Mama dear is asking for coffee.

DUNYASHA Right this very minute. (*She exits.*)

VARYA Well, thank God you're here. You're home again. (*Caressing her.*) My darling's here again! My beauty's here again!

ANYA What I've been through.

VARYA I can imagine!

ANYA I left during Holy Week, it was so cold then. Charlotta kept talking the whole way, doing tricks. Why you stuck me with Charlotta . . .

VARYA You couldn't have travelled by yourself, precious. Seventeen years old!

ANYA We get to Paris, it was cold there too, snowing. My French is

7. For a description of Pishchik, see Chekhov's letter to Nemirovich-Danchenko, November 2, 1903, on page 452.

awful. Mama is living on the sixth floor; I walk all the way up, there are some French people there, ladies, an old Catholic priest with a pamphlet, and it's full of cigarette smoke, not nice at all. And suddenly I started to feel sorry for Mama, so sorry for her, I took her head in my hands and couldn't let go. Then Mama kept hugging me, crying . . .

VARYA (*Through tears.*)   Don't talk about it, don't talk about it . . .

ANYA   The villa near Mentone[8] she'd already sold, she had nothing left, nothing. And I hadn't a kopek left either, we barely got this far. And Mama doesn't understand! We sit down to dinner at a station, and she orders the most expensive meal and gives each waiter a ruble tip. Charlotta's the same. Yasha insists on his share too, it's simply awful. Of course Mama has a manservant, Yasha; we brought him back.

VARYA   I saw the lowlife . . .

ANYA   Well, how are things? Have we paid the interest?

VARYA   What with?

ANYA   Oh dear, oh dear . . .

VARYA   In August, the estate's to be auctioned off . . .

ANYA   Oh dear . . .

LOPAKHIN (*Sticking his head in the doorway and bleating.*)   Me-e-eh . . . (*Exits.*)

VARYA (*Through tears.*)   I'd like to smack him one . . . (*Shakes her fist.*)

ANYA (*Embraces* VARYA, *quietly.*)   Varya, has he proposed? (VARYA *shakes her head no.*) He *does* love you . . . Why don't you talk it over, what are you waiting for?

VARYA   I don't think it will work out for us. He has so much business, can't get around to me . . . and he pays me no mind. Forget about him, I can't even get to see him . . . Everybody talks about our getting married, everybody says congratulations, but as a matter of fact, there's nothing to it, it's all like a dream . . . (*In a different tone.*) You've got a brooch like a bumblebee.

ANYA (*Sadly.*)   Mama bought it. (*Goes to her room, speaks cheerfully, like a child.*) And in Paris I went up in a balloon!

VARYA   My darling's here again! My beauty's here again!

(DUNYASHA *has returned with a coffeepot and is brewing coffee.*)

(*Stands near the door.*) The whole day long, darling, while I'm doing my chores, I keep dreaming. If only there were a rich man for you to marry, even I would be at peace, I'd go to a hermitage,

8. Or Menton, a resort area on the Mediterranean coast of France.

then to Kiev . . . to Moscow, and I'd keep on going like that to holy
shrines . . . I'd go on and on. Heaven! . . . [9]

ANYA   The birds are singing in the orchard. What time is it now?

VARYA   Must be three. Time for you to be asleep, dearest. (*Going
into* ANYA's *room.*) Heaven!

   (YASHA *enters with a lap rug and a travelling bag.*)

YASHA (*Crosses the stage; in a refined way.*)   May I come through,
ma'am?

DUNYASHA   A person wouldn't recognize you, Yasha. You've really
changed abroad.

YASHA   Mmm . . . who are you?

DUNYASHA   When you left here, I was so high . . . (*Measures from the
floor.*) Dunyasha, Fyodor Kozoedov's daughter. You don't remember!

YASHA   Mmm . . . Tasty little pickle! (*Glances around and embraces
her, she shrieks and drops a saucer.* YASHA *exits hurriedly.*)

VARYA (*In the doorway, crossly.*)   Now what was that?

DUNYASHA (*Through tears.*)   I broke a saucer . . .

VARYA   That's good luck.

ANYA (*Entering from her room.*)   We ought to warn Mama that
Petya's here . . .

VARYA   I gave orders not to wake him.

ANYA (*Thoughtfully.*)   Six years ago father died; a month later, our
brother Grisha drowned in the river, a sweet little boy, seven years
old. Mama couldn't stand it, she went away, went away without
looking back . . . (*Shivers.*) How well I understand her, if only she
knew!

   (*Pause.*)

Since Petya Trofimov was Grisha's tutor, he might remind her . . .

   (*Enter* FIRS *in a jacket and white waistcoat.*)

FIRS (*Goes to the coffeepot; preoccupied.*)   The mistress will take it
in here . . . (*Putting on white gloves.*) Cawrfee ready? (*Sternly, to*
DUNYASHA.) You! What about cream?

DUNYASHA   Oh, my goodness . . . (*Exits hurriedly.*)

FIRS (*Fussing with the coffeepot.*)   Eh you, half-baked bungler[1] . . .

---

9. Becoming a *bogomolets* or pilgrim was a common avocation in pre-Revolutionary Russia,
   especially for the rootless and outcast. A pilgrim would trek from shrine to shrine, putting
   up at monasteries and living off alms. Varya's picture of such a life is highly idealized. Its
   picaresque side can be glimpsed in Nikolay Leskov's stories, such as "The Enchanted
   Pilgrim" and in the ambiguous figure Luka in Maksim Gorky's 1902 play *The Lower
   Depths.*
1. *Nedotyopa* was not a Russian word when Chekhov used it; it was Ukrainian for an incompetent, a mental defective. Chekhov may have remembered hearing it in his childhood; it
   doesn't appear in Russian dictionaries until 1938, and then Chekhov is cited as the source.
   George Calderon perceived the etymology to derive from *ne*, not, and *dotyapat*, to finish
   chopping, which makes great sense in the context of the play. Translators grow gray over
   the word: earlier English versions have "good-for-nothing," "rogue," "duffer," "job-lot,"

THE CHERRY ORCHARD

330

(*Mumbles to himself.*) Come home from Paris . . . And the master went to Paris once upon a time . . . by coach and horses . . . (*Laughs.*)

VARYA Firs, what are you on about?

FIRS What's wanted, miss? (*Joyfully.*) My mistress has come home! I've been waiting! Now I can die . . . (*Weeps with joy.*)

(*Enter* LYUBOV ANDREEVNA, GAEV, LOPAKHIN, *and* SIMEONOV-PISHCHIK, *the last in a long-waisted coat of expensive cloth and baggy pantaloons.* GAEV, *on entering, moves his arms and torso as if he were playing billiards.*)

LYUBOV ANDREEVNA How does it go? Let me remember . . . Yellow in the corner! Doublette in the center![2]

GAEV Red in the corner! Once upon a time, sister, we used to sleep together here in this room, and now I've turned fifty-one, strange as it seems . . .

LOPAKHIN Yes, time marches on.

GAEV How's that?[3]

LOPAKHIN Time, I say, marches on.

GAEV It smells of cheap perfume[4] in here.

ANYA I'm going to bed. Good night, Mama. (*Kisses her mother.*)

LYUBOV ANDREEVNA My dazzling little princess.[5] (*Kisses her hands.*) Are you glad you're home? I can't get over it.

ANYA Good night, uncle.

GAEV (*Kisses her face, hands.*) God bless you. How like your mother you are! (*To his sister.*) Lyuba, at her age you were just the same.

(ANYA *gives her hand to* LOPAKHIN *and* PISHCHIK, *exits, and shuts the door behind her.*)

LYUBOV ANDREEVNA She's utterly exhausted.

PISHCHIK Must be a long trip.

VARYA (*To* LOPAKHIN *and* PISHCHIK.) Well, gentlemen? Three o'clock, by this time you've worn out your welcome.

LYUBOV ANDREEVNA (*Laughing.*) And you're still the same too,

---

"lummox," "silly young cuckoo," "silly old nothing," "nincompoop," "muddler," "silly galoot," "numbskull," and "young flibbertigibbet." The critic Batyushkov considered the whole play to be a variation on the theme of "nedotyopery," each of the characters representing a different aspect of life unfulfilled.

2. In pre-Revolutionary Russia, billiards was played with five balls, one of them yellow. A doublette occurs when a player's ball hits the cushion, rebounds, and sinks the other player's ball. George Calderon ventured that Gaev "always plays a declaration game at billiards, no flukes allowed." Chekhov himself did not play billiards and asked the actor who was to play Gaev to brush up on the terminology and to add the proper phrases in rehearsal. See letters to Olga Knipper, October 10 (page 446) and October 14, 1903 (page 447).

3. The colloquial "*Kogo*?" (literally, "Whom?") instead of "*chego*?" ("What's that?"), the quirky locution of an aristocrat.

4. Literally, patchouli, an oil made from an Asian plant, which has a very powerful aroma, prized in the Orient but insufferable to many Westerners.

5. *Nenaglyadnaya ditsyusya moya*, literally, "blindingly beauteous bairn of mine," a formula found in fairy tales.

Varya. (*Draws* VARYA *to her and kisses her.*) First I'll have some coffee, then everybody will go.

   (FIRS *puts a cushion under her feet.*)

Thank you, dear. I've grown accustomed to coffee. I drink it night and day. Thank you, my old dear. (*Kisses* FIRS.)

VARYA I've got to see if all the luggage was brought in . . . (*Exits.*)

LYUBOV ANDREEVNA Can I really be sitting here? (*Laughs.*) I feel like jumping up and down and swinging my arms. (*Covers her face with her hands.*) But suppose I'm dreaming! God knows, I love my country, love it dearly, I couldn't look at it from the train, couldn't stop crying. (*Through tears.*) However, we should have some coffee. Thank you, Firs, thank you, my old dear. I'm so glad you're still alive.

FIRS Day before yesterday.

GAEV He's hard of hearing.

LOPAKHIN I've got to leave for Kharkov right away, around five. What a nuisance! I wanted to feast my eyes on you, have a chat . . . You're still as lovely as ever.

PISHCHIK (*Breathing hard.*) Even prettier . . . Dressed in Parisian fashions . . . "lost my cart with all four wheels . . ."[6]

LOPAKHIN Your brother, Leonid Andreich here, says that I'm an oaf, I'm a money-grubbing peasant,[7] but it doesn't make the least bit of difference to me. Let him talk. The only thing I want is for you to believe in me as you once did, for your wonderful, heartbreaking eyes to look at me as they once did. Merciful God! My father was your grandfather's serf, and your father's, but you, you personally did so much for me once that I forgot all that and love you like my own kin . . . more than my own kin.

LYUBOV ANDREEVNA I can't sit still, I just can't . . . (*Leaps up and walks about in great excitement.*) I won't survive this joy . . . Laugh at me, I'm silly . . . My dear little cupboard. (*Kisses the cupboard.*) My little table.

GAEV While you were away, Nanny died.

LYUBOV ANDREEVNA (*Sits and drinks coffee.*) Yes, rest in peace. They wrote me.

GAEV And Anastasy died. Cross-eyed Petrusha left me and now he's working in town for the chief of police. (*Takes a little box of hard candies out of his pocket and sucks one.*)

PISHCHIK My dear daughter Dashenka . . . sends her regards. . . .

LOPAKHIN I'd like to tell you something you'd enjoy, something to cheer you up. (*Looking at his watch.*) I have to go now, never time for a real conversation . . . well, here it is in a nutshell. As you

---

6. The rest of the folk song verse goes "lost my heart head over heels."
7. *Kulak*, literally, a fist, but figuratively a tightfisted peasant or small dealer. See Chekhov's letter to Stanislavsky of October 30, 1903, on page 451.

already know, the cherry orchard will be sold to pay your debts, the auction is set for August twenty-second, but don't you worry, dear lady, don't lose any sleep, there's a way out . . . Here's my plan. Your attention please! Your estate lies only thirteen miles from town, the railroad runs past it, and if the cherry orchard and the land along the river were subdivided into building lots and then leased out for summer cottages, you'd have an income of at the very least twenty-five thousand a year.

GAEV   Excuse me, what rubbish!

LYUBOV ANDREEVNA   I don't quite follow you, Yermolay Alekseich.

LOPAKHIN   You'll get out of the summer tenants at least twenty-five rubles a year for every two and a half acres, and if you advertise now, I'll bet whatever you like that by fall there won't be a single lot left vacant; they'll all be snapped up. In short, congratulations, you're saved. The location's wonderful, the river's deep. Only, of course, it'll have to be spruced up, cleared out . . . for example, tear down all the old sheds, and this house, say, which is absolutely worthless, chop down the old cherry orchard . . .

LYUBOV ANDREEVNA   Chop it down? My dear, forgive me, but you don't understand at all. If there's anything of interest in the entire district, even outstanding, it's none other than our cherry orchard.[8]

LOPAKHIN   The only outstanding thing about this orchard is it's very big. The cherries grow once in two years, and then there's no way to get rid of them; nobody buys them.

GAEV   The *Encyclopedia* has a reference to this orchard.

LOPAKHIN   (*After a glance at his watch.*)   If we don't think up something and come to some decision, then on the twenty-second of August the cherry orchard and the whole estate will be sold at auction. Make up your mind! There's no other way out, I promise you. Absolutely none.

FIRS   In the old days, forty-fifty years back, cherries were dried, preserved, pickled, made into jam, and sometimes . . .

GAEV   Be quiet, Firs.

FIRS   And used to be whole cartloads of dried cherries were sent to Moscow and Kharkov. Then there was money! And in those days

---

8. Chekhov's close friend, the writer Ivan Bunin, objected to this feature of the play. "I grew up in just such an impoverished 'nest of gentry,'" he wrote. "It was a desolate estate on the steppes, but with a large orchard, not cherry, of course, for, Chekhov to the contrary, nowhere in Russia were there orchards comprised *exclusively* of cherries; only *sections* of the orchards on these estates (though sometimes very vast sections) grew cherries, and nowhere, Chekhov to the contrary again, could these sections be *directly beside* the main house, nor was there anything wonderful about the cherry trees, which are quite unattractive, as everyone knows, gnarled with puny leaves, puny blossoms when in bloom (quite unlike those which blossom so enormously and lushly right under the very windows of the main house at the Art Theater) . . ." *O Chekhove* (New York, 1955), 215–16.

the dried cherries were tender, juicy, sweet, tasty . . . They had a recipe then . . .

LYUBOV ANDREEVNA And where's that recipe today?

FIRS It's forgot. Nobody remembers.

PISHCHIK (*To* LYUBOV.) What's going on in Paris? What was it like? You eat frogs?

LYUBOV ANDREEVNA I ate crocodiles.

PISHCHIK Can you imagine . . .

LOPAKHIN So far there's only been gentry and peasants in the country, but now there's these vacationers. Every town, even the smallest, is surrounded these days by summer cottages. And I'll bet that over the next twenty-odd years the summer vacationer will multiply fantastically. Now all he does is drink tea on his balcony, but it might just happen that on his two and a half acres he starts growing things, and then your cherry orchard will become happy, rich, lush . . .

GAEV (*Getting indignant.*) What drivel!

(*Enter* VARYA *and* YASHA.)

VARYA Mama dear, there are two telegrams for you. (*Selects a key; with a jangle opens the antique cupboard.*) Here they are.

LYUBOV ANDREEVNA They're from Paris. (*Tears up the telegrams without reading them.*) I'm through with Paris . . .

GAEV Lyuba, do you know how old that cupboard is? A week ago I pulled out the bottom drawer, took a look, and there are numbers branded on it. This cupboard was built exactly one hundred years ago. How d'you like that? Eh? Maybe we ought to celebrate its centenary. An inanimate object, but all the same, any way you look at it, this cupboard is a repository for books.

PISHCHIK (*Astounded.*) A hundred years . . . Can you imagine!

GAEV Yes . . . This thing . . . (*Stroking the cupboard.*) Dear, venerated cupboard! I salute your existence, which for over a century has been dedicated to enlightened ideals of virtue and justice; your unspoken appeal to constructive endeavor has not faltered in the course of a century, sustaining (*through tears*) in generations of our line, courage, faith in a better future and nurturing within us ideals of decency and social consciousness.[9]

(*Pause.*)

LOPAKHIN Right . . .

LYUBOV ANDREEVNA You're still the same, Lyonya.

9. Chekhov is making fun of the Russian mania for celebrating anniversaries. Stanislavsky reports that on the twenty-fifth anniversary of Chekhov's literary career, held during the third performance of *The Cherry Orchard*, "One of the men of letters began his speech of tribute with the same words that Gaev addresses to the old cupboard in Act One of *The Cherry Orchard*, 'Dear, venerated.' Only instead of cupboard, the orator said 'Anton Pavlovich.' Chekhov winked at me and smiled a wicked smile." (*Letters*)

GAEV (*Somewhat embarrassed.*) Carom to the right corner! Red in the center!

LOPAKHIN (*Glancing at his watch.*) Well, my time's up.

YASHA (*Handing medicine to* LYUBOV.) Maybe you'll take your pills now . . .

PISHCHIK Shouldn't take medicine, dearest lady . . . It does no good, or harm . . . Hand 'em over . . . most respected lady. (*He takes the pills, shakes them into his palm, blows on them, pops them into his mouth, and drinks some kvas.*) There!

LYUBOV ANDREEVNA (*Alarmed.*) You've gone crazy!

PISHCHIK I took all the pills.

LOPAKHIN He's a bottomless pit!

(*They all laugh.*)

FIRS The gent stayed with us Holy Week, ate half a bucket of pickles . . . (*Mumbles.*)

LYUBOV ANDREEVNA What is he on about?

VARYA For three years now he's been mumbling like that. We're used to it.

YASHA Second childhood.

(CHARLOTTA IVANOVNA *crosses the stage in a white dress. She is very slender, tightly laced, with a pair of pince-nez on a cord at her waist.*)

LOPAKHIN Excuse me, Charlotta Ivanovna, I haven't had time yet to welcome you back. (*Tries to kiss her hand.*)

CHARLOTTA (*Pulling her hand away.*) If I let you kiss a hand, next you'd be after a elbow, then a shoulder . . .

LOPAKHIN My unlucky day.

(*Everybody laughs.*)

Charlotta Ivanovna, show us a trick!

LYUBOV ANDREEVNA Charlotta, show us a trick!

CHARLOTTA Nothing doing. I want to go to bed. (*Exits.*)

LOPAKHIN Three weeks from now we'll meet again. (*Kisses* LYUBOV ANDREEVNA's *hand.*) Meanwhile, good-bye. It's time. (*To* GAEV.) Be suing you.[1] (*Exchanges kisses with* PISHCHIK.) Be suing you. (*Gives his hand to* VARYA, *then to* FIRS *and* YASHA.) I don't want to go. (*To* LYUBOV ANDREEVNA.) If you reconsider this cottage business and come to a decision, then let me know; I'll arrange a loan of fifty thousand or so. Give it some serious thought.

VARYA (*Angrily.*) Well, go if you're going!

LOPAKHIN I'm going, I'm going . . . (*He leaves.*)

GAEV Oaf. All right, *pardon* . . . Varya's going to marry him, that's our Varya's little intended!

VARYA Don't say anything uncalled for, Uncle dear.

1. Instead of *Do svidaniya,* "Be seeing you," Lopakhin facetiously says *Do svidantsiya.*

LYUBOV ANDREEVNA   So what, Varya? I'll be very glad. He's a good man.

PISHCHIK   A man, you've got to tell the truth . . . most worthy . . . And my Dashenka . . . also says that . . . says all sorts of things. (*Snores, but immediately wakes up.*) But by the way, most respected lady, lend me. . . . two hundred and forty rubles . . . tomorrow I've got to pay the interest on the mortgage . . . [2]

VARYA (*Alarmed.*)   We're all out, all out!

LYUBOV ANDREEVNA   As a matter of fact, I haven't a thing.

PISHCHIK   It'll turn up. (*Laughs.*) I never lose hope. There, I think, all is lost, I'm a goner, lo and behold!—the railroad runs across my land and . . . pays me for it. And then, watch, something else will happen sooner or later . . . Dashenka will win two hundred thousand . . . she's got a lottery ticket.

LYUBOV ANDREEVNA   The coffee's finished; now we can go to bed.

FIRS (*Brushes GAEV's clothes, scolding.*)   You didn't put on them trousers again. What am I going to do with you?

VARYA (*Quietly.*)   Anya's asleep. (*Quietly opens a window.*) The sun's up already, it's not so cold. Look, Mama dear, what wonderful trees! My goodness, the air! The starlings are singing!

GAEV (*Opens another window.*)   The orchard's all white. You haven't forgotten, Lyuba? There's that long pathway leading straight on, straight on, like a stretched ribbon, it glistens on moonlit nights. You remember? You haven't forgotten?

LYUBOV ANDREEVNA (*Looks through the window at the orchard.*)   O, my childhood, my innocence! I slept in this nursery, gazed out at the orchard, happiness awoke with me every morning, and it was just the same then, nothing has changed. (*Laughs with joy.*) All, all white! O, my orchard! After the dark, drizzly autumn and the cold winter, you're young again, full of happiness, the angels in heaven haven't forsaken you . . . If only I could lift off my chest and shoulders this heavy stone, if only I could forget my past!

GAEV   Yes, and the orchard will be sold for debts, strange as it seems . . .

LYUBOV ANDREEVNA   Look, our poor Mama is walking through the orchard . . . in a white dress! (*Laughs with joy.*) There she is.

GAEV   Where?

VARYA   God keep you, Mama dear.

LYUBOV ANDREEVNA   There's nobody there, it just seemed so to me. On the right, by the turning to the summer house, a white sapling was bending, it looked like a woman . . .

2. By 1903, almost one half of all private land in Russia (excluding peasant land) was mortgaged, forcing the landed gentry to sell their estates and join the professional or commercial classes—as Gaev does at the end of this play.

(*Enter* TROFIMOV, *in a shabby student's uniform and eye-glasses.*[3])

What a marvelous orchard! White bunches of blossoms, blue sky . . .

TROFIMOV   Lyubov Andreevna! (*She has stared around at him.*) I'll just pay my respects and then leave at once. (*Kisses her hand fervently.*) They told me to wait 'til morning, but I didn't have the patience . . .

(LYUBOV ANDREEVNA *stares in bewilderment.*)

VARYA (*Through tears.*)   This is Petya Trofimov.

TROFIMOV   Petya Trofimov, used to be tutor to your Grisha . . . Can I have changed so much?

(LYUBOV ANDREEVNA *embraces him and weeps quietly.*)

GAEV (*Embarrassed.*)   Come, come, Lyuba.

VARYA (*Weeps.*)   Didn't I tell you, Petya, to wait 'til tomorrow?

LYUBOV ANDREEVNA   My Grisha . . . my little boy . . . Grisha . . . my son . . .

VARYA   There's no help for it, Mama dear; God's will be done.

TROFIMOV (*Gently, through tears.*)   There, there . . .

LYUBOV ANDREEVNA (*Quietly weeping.*)   A little boy lost, drowned . . . What for? What for, my friend? (*More quietly.*) Anya's asleep in there, and I'm so loud . . . making noise . . . Well now, Petya? Why have you become so homely? Why have you got old?

TROFIMOV   On the train, a peasant woman called me "that scruffy gent."

LYUBOV ANDREEVNA   You were just a boy in those days, a dear little student, but now your hair is thinning, eyeglasses. Are you really still a student? (*Goes to the door.*)

TROFIMOV   I suppose I'll be a perpetual student.[4]

LYUBOV ANDREEVNA (*Kisses her brother, then* VARYA.)   Well, let's go to bed . . . You've got old too, Leonid.

PISHCHIK (*Follows her.*)   That means it's time for bed . . . Ugh, my gout. I'll stay over with you . . . And if you would, Lyubov Andreevna, dear heart, tomorrow morning early . . . two hundred and forty rubles . . .

GAEV   He never gives up.

PISHCHIK   Two hundred and forty rubles . . . to pay the interest on the mortgage.

LYUBOV ANDREEVNA   I have no money, darling . . .

---

3. On Trofimov's expulsion, see Chekhov's letter to Olga Knipper, October 19, 1903, on page 448.
4. Radical student dropouts were far from uncommon. The saying went, "It takes ten years to graduate—five in study, four in exile, and one wasted while the university is shut down."

PISHCHIK We'll pay it back, dear lady . . . The most trifling sum.

LYUBOV ANDREEVNA Well, all right, Leonid will let you have it . . . Let him have it, Leonid.

GAEV I'll let him have it; hold out your pockets.

LYUBOV ANDREEVNA What can we do? Let him have it . . . He needs it . . . He'll pay it back.

> (LYUBOV ANDREEVNA, TROFIMOV, PISHCHIK, *and* FIRS *go out.* GAEV, VARYA, *and* YASHA *remain.*)

GAEV My sister still hasn't outgrown the habit of squandering money. (*To* YASHA.) Out of the way, my good man; you smell like a chicken coop.

YASHA (*With a sneer.*) But you, Leonid Andreich, are just the same as you were.

GAEV How's that? (*To* VARYA.) What did he say?

VARYA (*To* YASHA.) Your mother's come from the village; since yesterday she's been sitting in the servant's hall, she wants to see you . . .

YASHA To hell with her!

VARYA Ah, disgraceful!

YASHA That's all I need. She could have come tomorrow. (*Exits.*)

VARYA Mama dear is just as she was before, she hasn't changed a bit. If it were up to her, she'd give away everything.

GAEV Yes . . .

> (*Pause.*)

If a large number of cures is suggested for a particular disease, it means the disease is incurable. I think, wrack my brains, I've come up with all sorts of solutions, all sorts, which means, actually, none. It would be nice to inherit a fortune from somebody, nice if we married our Anya to a very rich man, nice to go to Yaroslavl and try our luck with our Auntie the Countess. Auntie's really very, very wealthy.

VARYA (*Weeps.*) If only God would come to our aid.

GAEV Stop snivelling. Auntie's very wealthy, but she isn't fond of us. In the first place, Sister married a lawyer, not a nobleman . . .

> (ANYA *appears in the doorway.*)

Married a commoner and behaved herself, well, you can't say very virtuously. She's a good, kind, splendid person, I love her very much; but, no matter how you consider the extenuating circumstances, you still have to admit she's depraved. You can feel it in her slightest movement.

VARYA (*Whispering.*) Anya's standing in the doorway.

GAEV How's that?

> (*Pause.*)

Extraordinary, something's got in my right eye . . . my sight's beginning to fail. And Thursday, when I was at the county court-house . . .

(ANYA *enters.*)

VARYA   Why aren't you asleep, Anya?

ANYA   I can't fall asleep. I can't.

GAEV   My teeny-weeny. (*Kisses* ANYA's *face, hands.*) My little girl . . . (*Through tears.*) You're not my niece, you're my angel, you're every-thing to me. Believe me, believe . . .

ANYA   I believe you, Uncle. Everybody loves you, respects you . . . but dear Uncle, you must keep still, simply keep still. What were you saying just now about my Mama, your own sister? How come you said that?

GAEV   Yes, yes . . . (*Hides his face in his hands.*) It's an awful thing to say! My God! God help me! And today I made a speech to the cupboard . . . like a fool! And as soon as I'd finished, I realized what a fool I'd been.

VARYA   True, Uncle dear, you ought to keep still. Just keep still, that's all.

ANYA   If you keep still, you'll be more at peace with yourself.

GAEV   I'll keep still. (*Kisses* ANYA's *and* VARYA's *hands.*) I'll keep still. Only this is business. Thursday I was at the county courthouse, well, some friends gathered 'round, started talking about this and that, six of one, half a dozen of the other, and it turns out a person can sign a promissory note and borrow money to pay the interest to the bank.

VARYA   If only God would come to our aid!

GAEV   I'll go there on Tuesday and have another talk. (*To* VARYA.) Stop snivelling. (*To* ANYA.) Your Mama will talk to Lopakhin, he won't refuse her, of course . . . And you, after you've had a rest, will go to Yaroslavl to the Countess, your great aunt. That way, we'll have action on three fronts—and our business is in the bag! We'll pay off the interest, I'm sure of it . . . (*Pops a candy into his mouth.*) Word of honor, I'll swear by whatever you like, the estate won't be sold! (*Excited.*) I swear by my happiness! Here's my hand on it, call me a trashy, dishonorable man if I permit that auction! I swear with every fiber of my being!

ANYA   (*A more peaceful mood comes over her, she is happy.*)   You're so good, Uncle, so clever! (*Embraces her uncle.*) Now I feel calm! I'm calm! I'm happy!

(*Enter* FIRS.)

FIRS   (*Scolding.*)   Leonid Andreich, have you no fear of God? When are you going to bed?

GAEV   Right away, right away. Go along, Firs. Have it your own way, I'll undress myself. Well, children, beddy-bye . . . Details tomorrow, but for now go to bed. (*Kisses* ANYA *and* VARYA.) I'm a man of the eighties . . . People don't put much stock in that period[5], but all the same I can say I've suffered for my convictions to no small degree in my time. There's a good reason peasants love me. You've got to study peasants! You've got to know what . . .

ANYA You're at it again, Uncle!

VARYA Uncle dear, you must keep still.

FIRS (*Angrily.*) Leonid Andreich!

GAEV Coming, coming . . . You two go to bed. Two cushion carom to the center! I sink the white . . . (*Exits followed by* FIRS, *who is hobbling.*)

ANYA Now I'm calm. I don't want to go to Yaroslavl. I don't like my great aunt, but all the same, I'm calm. Thanks to Uncle. (*Sits down.*)

VARYA Got to get some sleep. I'm off. Oh, while you were away, there was a bit of an uprising. There's nobody living in the old servants' hall, as you know, except the old servants: Yefimushka, Polya, Yevstigney, oh, and Karp. They started letting these vagabonds spend the night there—I held my peace. Only then, I hear, they've spread the rumor that I gave orders to feed them nothing but beans. Out of stinginess, you see . . . And this was all Yevstigney's doing . . . Fine, I think. If that's how things are, I think, just you wait. I send for Yevstigney . . . (*Yawns.*) In he comes . . . What's wrong with you, I say, Yevstigney . . . you're such an idiot . . . (*Glancing at* ANYA.) Anechka!
(*Pause.*)
Fast asleep! . . . (*Takes* ANYA *by the arm.*) Let's go to bed . . . Let's go! . . . (*Leads her.*) My darling is fast asleep! Let's go! . . .
(*They go out.*)
(*Far beyond the orchard a shepherd is playing his pipes.*)
(TROFIMOV *crosses the stage, and, seeing* ANYA *and* VARYA, *stops short.*)
Ssh . . . She's asleep . . . asleep . . . Let's go, dearest.

ANYA (*Softly, half-asleep.*) I'm so tired . . . all the sleigh bells . . . Uncle . . . dear . . . and Mama and Uncle . . .

VARYA Let's go, dearest, let's go . . . (*They go into* ANYA's *room.*)

TROFIMOV (*Moved.*) My sunshine! My springtime!

CURTAIN

5. Under Alexander III, political reaction to reforms set in, the police and censorship became extremely repressive, and anti-Semitic pogroms broke out. Large-scale political reform became impossible, so that liberal intellectuals devoted themselves to local civilizing improvements in the villages, Tolstoyan passive resistance, and dabbling in "art for art's sake." This feeling of social and political impotence led to the torpid aimlessness common to Chekhov's characters.

Act Two

A field. An old, long-abandoned chapel leaning to one side, beside it a well, large slabs which were once, apparently, tombstones, and an old bench. A road into GAEV's estate can be seen. At one side, towering poplars cast their shadows; here the cherry orchard begins. Farther off are telegraph poles, and way in the distance, dimly sketched on the horizon, is a large town, which can be seen only in the best and clearest weather. Soon the sun will set. CHARLOTTA, YASHA, and DUNYASHA are sitting on the bench. YEPIKHODOV stands nearby and strums a guitar; everyone is rapt in thought. CHARLOTTA is wearing an old peaked cap with a visor; she has taken a rifle off her shoulder and is adjusting a buckle on the strap.

CHARLOTTA (*Pensively.*)   I haven't got a valid passport,[6] I don't know how old I am, and I always feel like I'm still oh so young. When I was a little girl, my father and mama used to go from fairground to fairground, giving performances, pretty good ones. And I would do the death-defying leap[7] and all sorts of stunts. And when Papa and Mama died, a German gentlewoman took me home with her and started teaching me. Fine. I grew up, then turned into a governess. But where I'm from and who I am—I don't know . . . Who my parents were, maybe they weren't married . . . I don't know. (*Pulls a pickle out of her pocket and eats it.*) I don't know anything.
(*Pause.*)
It would be nice to talk to someone, but there is no one . . . I have no one.

YEPIKHODOV (*Strums his guitar and sings.*)   "What care I for the noisy world, what are friends and foes to me . . ." How pleasant to play the mandolin!

DUNYASHA   That's a guitar, not a mandolin. (*Looks in a hand mirror and powders her nose.*)

YEPIKHODOV   To a lovesick lunatic, this is a mandolin . . . (*Sings quietly.*) "Were but my heart aflame with the spark of requited love . . ."
(YASHA *joins in.*)

CHARLOTTA   Horrible the way these people sing . . . Phooey! A pack of hyenas.

DUNYASHA (*To* YASHA.)   Anyway, how lucky to spend time abroad.

YASHA   Yes, of course. I can't disagree with you there. (*Yawns, then lights a cigar.*)

---

6. In the sense of an "internal passport," an identity document carried when travelling through the Russian empire.
7. In the original, Italian, *salto mortale.*

YEPIKHODOV   Stands to reason. Abroad everything long ago attained its complete complexification.

YASHA   Goes without saying.

YEPIKHODOV   I'm a cultured person, I read all kinds of remarkable books, but somehow I can't figure out my inclinations, what I want personally, to live or to shoot myself, speaking on my own behalf, nevertheless I always carry a revolver on my person. Here it is . . . (*Displays a revolver.*)

CHARLOTTA   I'm done. Now I'll go. (*Shoulders the gun.*) Yepikhodov, you're a very clever fellow, and a very frightening one; the women ought to love you madly. Brrr! (*On her way out.*) These clever people are all so stupid there's no one for me to talk to . . . No one . . . All alone, alone, I've got no one and . . . who I am, why I am, I don't know. (*Exits.*)

YEPIKHODOV   Speaking on my own behalf, not flying off on tangents, I must express myself about myself, among others, that Fate treats me ruthlessly, like a small storm-tossed ship. If, suppose, I'm wrong about this, then why when I woke up this morning, to give but a single example, I look and there on my chest is a ghastly enormity of a spider . . . Like so. (*Uses both hands to demonstrate.*) Or then again, I'll take some kvas, so as to drink it, and lo and behold, there'll be something indecent to the nth degree, along the lines of a cockroach . . .

  (*Pause.*)

Have you read Buckle?[8]

  (*Pause.*)

I should like to distress you, Avdotya Fyodorovna, with a couple of words.

DUNYASHA   Go ahead.

YEPIKHODOV   I would be desirous to see you in private . . . (*Sighs.*)

DUNYASHA (*Embarrassed.*)   All right . . . only first bring me my wrap[9] . . . It's next to the cupboard . . . it's a bit damp here.

YEPIKHODOV   Yes ma'am . . . I'll fetch it, ma'am. . . . Now I know what I have to do with my revolver . . . (*Takes the guitar and exits playing it.*)

YASHA   Tons of Trouble! Pretty stupid, take it from me. (*Yawns.*)

DUNYASHA   God forbid he should shoot himself.

---

8. Henry Thomas Buckle (1821–1862), pronounced Buckly, whose *History of Civilization in England* (translated into Russian in 1861) posited that skepticism is the handmaiden of progress and that religion retards the advance of civilization. His materialist approach was much appreciated by progressive Russians in the 1870s, and Chekhov had read him as a student. By the end of the century Buckle's theories seemed outmoded, so the reference suggests that Yepikhodov's efforts at self-education are behind the times.

9. Literally, *talmochka*, or little talma, a smaller version of the garment Nina wears in the last act of *The Seagull*.

(*Pause.*)

I've gotten jittery, nervous all the time. Just a little girl, they brought me to the master's house, now I'm out of touch with ordinary life, and my hands are white as white can be, like a young lady's. I've gotten sensitive, so delicate, ladylike, afraid of every little thing . . . Awfully so. And, Yasha, if you deceive me, then I don't know what'll happen to my nerves.

YASHA (*Kisses her.*)   Tasty little pickle! Of course, a girl ought to know how far to go, and if there's one thing I hate, it's a girl who misbehaves.

DUNYASHA   I love you ever so much, you're educated, you can discuss anything.

(*Pause.*)

YASHA *Yawns.*)   Yes'm . . . The way I look at it, it's like this: if a girl loves somebody, that means she's immoral.

(*Pause.*)

Nice smoking a cigar in the fresh air . . . (*Listening.*) Someone's coming this way . . . The masters . . .

(DUNYASHA *impulsively embraces him.*)

Go home, pretend you'd been to the river for a swim, take this bypath or you'll run into them, and they'll think I've been going out with you. I couldn't stand that.

DUNYASHA (*Coughs quietly.*)   Your cigar's given me a headache . . . (*Exits.*)

(YASHA *remains, seated beside the shrine. Enter* LYUBOV ANDREEVNA, GAEV, *and* LOPAKHIN.)

LOPAKHIN   You've got to decide once and for all—time won't stand still. The matter's really simple, after all. Do you agree to rent land for cottages or not? Give me a one-word answer: yes or no? Just one word!

LYUBOV ANDREEVNA   Who's been smoking those revolting cigars around here? . . . (*Sits.*)

GAEV   Now that there's a railroad, things are convenient.[1] (*Sits.*) You ride to town and have lunch . . . yellow in the center! I should go home first, play one game . . .

LYUBOV ANDREEVNA   You'll have time.

LOPAKHIN   Just one word! (*Pleading.*) Give me an answer!

GAEV (*Yawning.*)   How's that?

LYUBOV ANDREEVNA (*Looking into her purse.*)   Yesterday I had lots of money, but today there's very little left. My poor Varya feeds everybody milk soup to economize, in the kitchen the old people get nothing but beans, and somehow I'm spending recklessly . . .

---

1. There was a railway boom in Russia in the 1890s, although, owing to bribery and corruption, the stations were often some distance from the towns, and service was far from efficient.

(*Drops the purse, scattering gold coins.*) Oh dear, they've spilled all over . . . (*Annoyed.*)

YASHA   Allow me, I'll pick them up at once. (*Gathers the money.*)

LYUBOV ANDREEVNA   That's sweet of you, Yasha. And why did I go out to lunch? . . . That nasty restaurant of yours with its music, the tablecloths smelled of soap . . . Why drink so much, Lyonya? Why eat so much? Why talk so much? Today in the restaurant you started talking a lot again and all beside the point. About the seventies, about the decadents.[2] And who to? Talking to waiters about the decadents!

LOPAKHIN   Yes.

GAEV (*Waves his hand in dismissal.*)   I'm incorrigible, it's obvious . . . (*Irritably, to* YASHA.) What's the matter? Forever whirling around in front of us . . .

YASHA (*Laughing.*)   I can't hear your voice without laughing.

GAEV (*To his sister.*)   Either he goes or I do . . .

LYUBOV ANDREEVNA   Go away, Yasha, run along . . .

YASHA (*Handing the purse to* LYUBOV ANDREEVNA.)   I'll go right now. (*Barely keeping from laughing.*) Right this minute . . .
(*Exits.*)

LOPAKHIN   Deriganov the rich man intends to purchase your estate. They say he's coming to the auction in person.

LYUBOV ANDREEVNA   Where did you hear that?

LOPAKHIN   They were talking about it in town.

GAEV   Our Auntie in Yaroslavl promised to send something, but when or how much she'll send, we don't know . . .

LOPAKHIN   How much is she sending? A hundred thousand? Two hundred?

LYUBOV ANDREEVNA   Well . . . around ten or fifteen thousand, and we're glad to have it . . .

LOPAKHIN   Excuse me, such frivolous people as you, my friends, such unbusinesslike, peculiar people I've never run into before. Somebody tells you in plain words your estate is about to be sold, and you act as if you don't understand.

LYUBOV ANDREEVNA   But what are we supposed to do? Teach us, what?

LOPAKHIN   I teach you every day. Every day I tell you one and the same thing. Both the cherry orchard and the land have got to be leased as lots for cottages, do it right now, immediately—the auction is staring you in the face! Can't you understand? Decide once and for all that there'll be cottages, they'll lend you as much money as you want, and then you'll be saved.

2. A period when the intelligentsia formed the *Narodniki*, or Populists, who preached a socialist doctrine and tried to educate the peasants. They were severely repressed in 1877–78. *Decadents* here refers to writers of symbolist literature.

LYUBOV ANDREEVNA   Cottages and vacationers—it's so vulgar, excuse me.

GAEV   I absolutely agree with you.

LOPAKHIN   I'll burst into tears or scream or fall down in a faint. It's too much for me! You're torturing me to death! (*To* GAEV.) You old biddy!

GAEV   How's that?

LOPAKHIN   Old biddy! (*Starts to exit.*)

LYUBOV ANDREEVNA (*Frightened.*)   No, don't go, stay, dovie. Please. Maybe we'll think of something.

LOPAKHIN   What's there to think about?

LYUBOV ANDREEVNA   Don't go, please. With you here somehow it's more fun . . .
    (*Pause.*)
I keep anticipating something, as if the house were about to collapse on top of us.

GAEV (*Rapt in thought.*)   Off the cushion to the corner . . . doublette to the center . . .

LYUBOV ANDREEVNA   We've sinned so very much . . .

LOPAKHIN   What kind of sins have you got? . . .

GAEV (*Pops a hard candy into his mouth.*)   They say I've eaten up my whole estate in hard candies . . . (*Laughs.*)

LYUBOV ANDREEVNA   Oh, my sins . . . I've always thrown money around wildly, like a maniac, and married a man who produced nothing but debts. My husband died of champagne—he was a terrible drunkard—and, then, to add to my troubles, I fell in love with another man, had an affair, and just at that time—this was my first punishment, dropped right on my head—over there in the river . . . my little boy drowned, and I went abroad, went for good, never to return, never to see that river again . . . I shut my eyes, ran away, out of my mind, and *he* came after me . . . cruelly, brutally. I bought a villa near Mentone, because he fell ill there, and for three years I didn't know what it was to rest day or night: the invalid wore me out, my heart shrivelled up. But last year, when the villa was sold to pay my debts, I went to Paris, and there he robbed me, ran off, had an affair with another woman, I tried to poison myself . . . so silly, so shameful . . . and suddenly I was drawn back to Russia, to my country, to my little girl . . . (*Wipes away her tears.*) Lord, Lord, be merciful, forgive me my sins! Don't punish me any more! (*Takes a telegram out of her pocket.*) I received this today from Paris . . . He begs my forgiveness, implores me to come back . . . (*Tears up telegram.*) Sounds like music somewhere. (*Listens.*)

GAEV   That's our famous Jewish orchestra. You remember, four fiddles, a flute and a double bass.

LYUBOV ANDREEVNA   Does it still exist? We ought to hire them some time and throw a party.

LOPAKHIN (*Listening.*)   I don't hear it . . . (*Sings softly.*) "And for cash the Prussians will frenchify the Russians." (*Laughs.*) That was some play I saw at the theater yesterday, very funny.

LYUBOV ANDREEVNA   And most likely there was nothing funny about it. You have no business looking at plays, you should look at yourselves more. You all live such gray lives, you talk such nonsense.

LOPAKHIN   That's true, I've got to admit, this life is of ours is idiotic . . .

(*Pause.*)

My dad was a peasant, an imbecile, he didn't understand anything, didn't teach me, all he did was get drunk and beat me with the same old stick. Deep down, I'm the same kind of blockhead and imbecile. I never studied anything, my handwriting is disgusting; I write, I'm ashamed to show it to people, like a pig.

LYUBOV ANDREEVNA   You ought to get married, my friend.

LOPAKHIN   Yes . . . that's true.

LYUBOV ANDREEVNA   You should marry our Varya; she's a good girl.

LOPAKHIN   Yes.

LYUBOV ANDREEVNA   She came to me from peasant stock, she works all day long, but the main thing is she loves you. Besides, you've been fond of her a long time.

LOPAKHIN   Why not? I'm not against it . . . She's a good girl.

(*Pause.*)

GAEV   They're offering me a position at the bank. Six thousand a year . . . Have you heard?

LYUBOV ANDREEVNA   You indeed! Stay where you are . . .

(FIRS *enters, carrying an overcoat.*)

FIRS (*To* GAEV.)   Please, sir, put it on, or you'll get wet.

GAEV (*Putting on the overcoat.*)   You're a pest, my man.

FIRS   Never you mind . . . This morning you went out, didn't tell me. (*Inspects him.*)

LYUBOV ANDREEVNA   How old you're getting, Firs!

FIRS   What's wanted?

LOPAKHIN   The mistress says, you're getting very old!

FIRS   I've lived a long time. They were making plans to marry me off, long before your daddy even saw the light . . . (*Laughs.*) And when freedom came,[3] I was already head footman. I didn't go along with freedom then, I stayed by the masters . . .

(*Pause.*)

And I recollect they was all glad, but what they was glad about, that they didn't know.

3. Alexander II emancipated the serfs in 1861.

LOPAKHIN   It used to be nice all right. In those days you could at least get flogged.

FIRS (*Not having heard.*)   I'll say. The peasants stood by the masters, the masters stood by the peasants, but now it's every which way, you can't figure it out.

GAEV   Keep quiet, Firs. Tomorrow I have to go to town. They promised to introduce me to some general, who might make us a loan on an I.O.U.

LOPAKHIN   Nothing'll come of it. And you won't pay the interest, never fear.

LYUBOV ANDREEVNA   He's raving. There are no such generals.

(*Enter* TROFIMOV, ANYA, *and* VARYA.)

GAEV   Look, here comes our crowd.

ANYA   Mama's sitting down.

LYUBOV ANDREEVNA (*Tenderly.*)   Come here, come . . . My darlings . . . (*Embracing* ANYA *and* VARYA.) If only you both knew how much I love you. Sit beside me, that's right.

(*Everyone sits down.*)

LOPAKHIN   Our perpetual student is always stepping out with the young ladies.

TROFIMOV   None of your business.

LOPAKHIN   Soon he'll be fifty and he'll still be a student.

TROFIMOV   Stop your idiotic jokes.

LOPAKHIN   What are you getting angry about, you crank?

TROFIMOV   Stop pestering me.

LOPAKHIN (*Laughs.*)   And may I ask, what do you make of me?

TROFIMOV   This is what I make of you, Yermolay Alekseich: you're a rich man, soon you'll be a millionaire. And just as an essential component in the conversion of matter is the wild beast that devours whatever crosses its path, you're essential.

(*Everyone laughs.*)

VARYA   Petya, tell us about the planets instead.

LYUBOV ANDREEVNA   No, let's go on with yesterday's discussion.

TROFIMOV   What was that about?

GAEV   Human pride.[4]

TROFIMOV   Yesterday we talked for quite a while, but we didn't get anywhere. Human pride, as you see it, has something mystical about it. Maybe you're right from your point of view, but if we reason it out simply, without frills, what's the point of human pride, what's the sense of it, if man is poorly constructed physiologically, if the vast majority is crude, unthinking, profoundly

---

4. A reference to Gorky's "Proud man" in *The Lower Depths*. "Hu-man Be-ing! That's magnificent! That sounds . . . proud!" "Man is truth . . . He is the be-all and the end-all. Nothing exists but man, all the rest is the work of his hands and his brain. Man is something great, proud, man is."

wretched. We should stop admiring ourselves. We should just work.

GAEV All the same you'll die.

TROFIMOV Who knows? What does that mean—you'll die? Maybe man has a hundred senses and in death only the five we know perish, the remaining ninety-five live on.

LYUBOV ANDREEVNA Aren't you clever, Petya! . . .

LOPAKHIN (*Ironically.*) Awfully!

TROFIMOV Mankind is advancing, perfecting its powers. Everything that's unattainable for us now will someday come within our grasp and our understanding, only we've got to work, to help the truth-seekers with all our might. So far here in Russia, very few people do any work. The vast majority of educated people, as I know them, pursues nothing, does nothing, and so far isn't capable of work. They call themselves intellectuals, but they refer to the servants by pet names,[5] treat the peasants like animals, are poorly informed, read nothing serious, do absolutely nothing, just talk about science, barely understand art. They're all earnest, they all have serious faces, they all talk only about major issues, they philosophize; but meanwhile anybody can see that the working class is abominably fed, sleeps without pillows, thirty or forty to a room; everywhere bedbugs, stench,[6] damp, moral pollution . . . So obviously all our nice chitchat serves only to shut our eyes to ourselves and to others. Show me, where are the daycare centers we talk so much about, where are the reading rooms? People only write about them in novels; in fact, there aren't any. There's only dirt, vulgarity, Asiatic inertia[7] . . . I'm afraid of, I don't like very earnest faces, I'm afraid of earnest discussions. It's better to keep still!

LOPAKHIN You know, I get up before five every morning. I work from dawn to dusk, well, I always have money on hand, my own and other people's, and I can tell what the people around me are like. You only have to go into business to find out how few decent, honest people there are. Sometimes, when I can't sleep, I think: Lord, you gave us vast forests, boundless fields, the widest horizons, and living here, we really and truly ought to be giants . . .

LYUBOV ANDREEVNA So you want to have giants . . . They're only good in fairy tales; anywhere else they're scary.

---

5. Literally, "they address the servant girl with the familiar form of 'you,' " as Lopakhin does Dunyasha. It is typical of Trofimov's intellectual astigmatism that he demands token respect for the servant class, but cannot foresee doing away with it entirely.

6. The line beginning "Anyone can see" and ending "moral pollution" was deleted by Chekhov to accommodate the censor, and restored only in 1917. It was replaced by a line reading, "the vast majority of us, ninety-nine percent, live like savages, at the least provocation swearing and punching one another in the mouth, eating nauseating food, sleeping in mud and foul air."

7. *Aziatchina*, a pre-Revolutionary term of abuse, referring to negative qualilites in the Russian character such as laziness and inefficiency.

(Far upstage, YEPIKHODOV crosses and plays his guitar.)

LYUBOV ANDREEVNA *(Dreamily.)*   There goes Yepikhodov . . .

ANYA *(Dreamily.)*   There goes Yepikhodov . . .

GAEV   The sun has set, ladies and gentlemen.

TROFIMOV   Yes.

GAEV *(Quietly, as if declaiming.)*   Oh Nature, wondrous creature, aglow with eternal radiance, beautiful yet impassive, you whom we call Mother, merging within yourself Life and Death, you nourish and you destroy . . .

VARYA *(Pleading.)*   Uncle dear!

ANYA   Uncle, you're at it again!

TROFIMOV   You'd better bank the yellow in the center doublette.

GAEV   I'll be still, I'll be still.

(Everyone sits, absorbed in thought. The only sound is FIRS, softly muttering. Suddenly, a distant sound is heard, as if from the sky; the sound of a breaking string, dying away, mournfully.)

LYUBOV ANDREEVNA   What's that?

LOPAKHIN   I don't know. Somewhere far off in a mineshaft the rope broke on a bucket.[8] But somewhere very far off.

GAEV   Or perhaps it was some kind of bird . . . something like a heron.

TROFIMOV   Or an owl . . .

LYUBOV ANDREEVNA *(Shivers.)*   Unpleasant anyhow.

     (Pause.)

FIRS   Before the troubles, it was the same: the screech owl hooted and the samovar never stopped humming.

GAEV   Before what troubles?

FIRS   Before freedom.[9]

     (Pause.)

LYUBOV ANDREEVNA   You know, everyone, we should go home. Evening's drawing on. *(To ANYA.)* You've got tears in your eyes . . . What it is, little girl? *(Kisses her.)*

ANYA   Nothing special, Mama. Never mind.

TROFIMOV   Someone's coming.

     (A VAGRANT appears in a shabby white peaked cap and an overcoat; he is tipsy.)

VAGRANT   May I inquire, can I get directly to the station from here?

GAEV   You can. Follow that road.

VAGRANT   Obliged to you from the bottom of my heart. *(Coughs.)*

---

8. This was a sound Chekhov remembered hearing as a boy. In his story "Happiness" (1887), he uses it ironically as a spectral laugh, presaging disappointment.

9. Under the terms of the Emancipation Act, field peasants were allotted land but had to pay back the government in annual installments the sum used to indemnify former landowners. House serfs, on the other hand, were allotted no land. Both these conditions caused tremendous hardship and were responsible for great unrest among the newly manumitted.

Splendid weather we're having . . . (*Declaims.*) "Brother mine, suffering brother . . . come to the Volga, whose laments . . ."[1] (*To*
VARYA.) Mademoiselle, bestow a mere thirty kopeks on a famished
fellow Russian . . .

     (VARYA *is alarmed, screams.*)

LOPAKHIN (*Angrily.*)   There's a limit to this kind of rudeness!

LYUBOV ANDREEVNA (*Flustered.*)   Take this . . . here you are . . .
(*Looks in her purse.*) No silver . . . Never mind, here's a gold piece
for you . . .

VAGRANT   Obliged to you from the bottom of my heart! (*Exits.*)
     (*Laughter.*)

VARYA (*Frightened.*)   I'm going . . . I'm going . . . Oh, Mama dear,
there's nothing in the house for people to eat, and you gave him
a gold piece.

LYUBOV ANDREEVNA   What can you do with a silly like me? I'll let
you have all I've got when we get home. Yermolay Alekseich, lend
me some more! . . .

LOPAKHIN   At your service.

LYUBOV ANDREEVNA   Come along, ladies and gentlemen, it's time.
And look, Varya, we've made quite a match for you; congratulations.

VARYA (*Through tears.*)   It's no joking matter, Mama.

LOPAKHIN   I'll feel ya,[2] get thee to a nunnery. . . .

GAEV   My hands are trembling; it's been a long time since I played
billiards.

LOPAKHIN   I'll feel ya, o nymph, in thy horizons be all my sins
remembered![3]

LYUBOV ANDREEVNA   Come along, ladies and gentlemen. Almost time
for supper.

VARYA   He scared me. My heart's pounding.

LOPAKHIN   I remind you, ladies and gentlemen, on the twenty-
second of August the estate will be auctioned off. Think about
that! . . . Think! . . .

     (*Everyone leaves except* TROFIMOV *and* ANYA.)

ANYA (*Laughing.*)   Thank the vagrant, he scared off Varya, now we're
alone.

TROFIMOV   Varya's afraid we'll suddenly fall in love, so she hangs
around us all day. Her narrow mind can't comprehend that we're
above love. Avoiding the petty and specious—that keeps us from

---

1. The Vagrant quotes from a popular and populist poem of 1881 by Semyon Yakovlevich
   Nadson (1862–1887) and from Nekrasov's "Reflections at the Main Gate" (1858). The
   laments come from barge-haulers along the Volga. Quoting Nekrasov is always a sign of
   insincerity in Chekhov.
2. *Okhmeliya,* from *okhmelyat,* to get drunk; instead of Ophelia.
3. Lopakhin is misquoting Hamlet, "Nymph, in thy orisons, be all my sins remember'd" (III.
   1).

being free and happy, that's the goal and meaning of our life. Forward! We march irresistibly toward the shining star, glowing there in the distance! Forward! No dropping behind, friends!

ANYA (*Stretching up her arms.*)   You speak so well!

(*Pause.*)

It's wonderful here today.

TROFIMOV   Yes, superb weather.

ANYA   What have you done to me, Petya, why have I stopped loving the cherry orchard as I used to? I loved it so tenderly, there seemed to me no finer place on earth than our orchard.

TROFIMOV   All Russia is our orchard. The world is wide and beautiful and there are many wonderful places in it.

(*Pause.*)

Just think, Anya: your grandfather, great-grandfather, and all your ancestors were slave-owners; they owned living souls, and from every cherry in the orchard, every leaf, every tree trunk there must be human beings watching you, you must hear voices . . . They owned living souls—it's corrupted all of you, honestly, those who lived before and those living now, so that your mother, you, your uncle, no longer notice that you're living in debt, at other people's expense, at the expense of those people whom you wouldn't even let beyond your front hall . . . [4] We're at least two hundred years behind the times, we've still got absolutely nothing, no definite attitude to the past; we just philosophize, complain of depression or drink vodka. It's so clear, isn't it, that before we start living in the present, we must first atone for our past, put an end to it, and we can atone for it only through suffering—only through extraordinary, unremitting labor. Understand that, Anya.

ANYA   The house we live in hasn't been our house for a long time, and I'll go away, I give you my word.

TROFIMOV   If you have the housekeeper's keys, throw them down the well and go away. Be free as the wind.

ANYA (*Enraptured.*)   You speak so well!

TROFIMOV   Believe me, Anya, believe! I'm not yet thirty, I'm young. I'm still a student, but I've already undergone so much! When winter comes, I'm starved, sick, anxious, poor as a beggar and—where haven't I been chased by Fate, where haven't I been! And yet always, every moment of the day and night, my soul has been full of inexplicable foreboding. I foresee happiness, Anya, I can see it already . . .

---

4. The line beginning "They owned human souls" and ending "your front hall" was deleted by Chekhov to accommodate the censor and restored only in 1917. It was replaced with this line: "Oh, it's dreadful; your orchard is terrifying. At evening or at night when you walk through the orchard, the old bark on the trees begins to glow, and it seems as if the cherry trees are dreaming of what went on one or two hundred years ago, and painful nightmares make them droop. Why talk about it?"

ANYA (*Dreamily.*)   The moon's on the rise.

(*We can hear* YEPIKHODOV *playing the same gloomy tune as before on his guitar. The moon comes up. Somewhere near the poplars,* VARYA *is looking for* ANYA *and calling, "Anya! Where are you?"*)

TROFIMOV   Yes, the moon's on the rise.

(*Pause.*)

Here's happiness, here it comes, drawing closer and closer, I can already hear its footsteps. And if we don't see it, can't recognize it, what's wrong with that? Others will see it!

VARYA'S VOICE   Anya! Where are you?

TROFIMOV   That Varya again! (*Angrily.*) Aggravating!

ANYA   So what? Let's go down to the river. It's nice there.

TROFIMOV   Let's go.

(*They leave.*)

VARYA'S VOICE   Anya! Anya!

CURTAIN

Act Three

The drawing room, separated from the ballroom by an arch. A chandelier is alight. We can hear a Jewish orchestra, the same as mentioned in Act Two, playing in the hallway. Evening. A grande ronde is being danced in the ballroom. SIMEONOV-PISHCHIK's *voice: "Promenade à une paire!" The drawing room is entered by: the first couple* PISHCHIK *and* CHARLOTTA IVANOVNA, *the second* TROFIMOV *and* LYUBOV ANDREEVNA, *the third* ANYA *and the* POSTAL CLERK, *the fourth* VARYA *and the* STATIONMASTER, *etc.* VARYA *is weeping quietly and, as she dances, she wipes away the tears. In the last couple,* DUNYASHA. *They go around and through the drawing room.* PISHCHIK *calls out, "Grand-rond balançez!" and "Les cavaliers à genoux et remerciez vos dames!"*[5]

(FIRS *in a tailcoat crosses the room with a seltzer bottle on a tray.* PISHCHIK *and* TROFIMOV *enter the room.*)

PISHCHIK   I've got high blood pressure, I've already had two strokes, it's tough dancing, but, as the saying goes, when you run with the pack, whether you bark or not, keep on wagging your tail. Actually, I've got the constitution of a horse. My late father, what a card, rest in peace, used to talk of our ancestry as if our venerable line, the Simeonov-Pishchiks, was descended from the very same horse

5. Figures in a quadrille. *Promenade à une paire!*: Promenade with your partner! *Grand rond, balançez!*: reel around, swing your arms! *Les cavaliers à genoux et remerciez vos dames!*: Gentlemen, on your knees and salute your ladies!

Caligula made a senator . . . [6] (*Sits down.*) But here's the problem:
no money! A hungry dog believes only in meat . . . (*Snores and
immediately wakes up.*) Just like me . . . I can't think of anything
but money . . .

TROFIMOV   As a matter of fact, your build has something horsey
about it.

PISHCHIK   So what? . . . A horse is a noble beast . . . you could sell
a horse . . .

(*We hear billiards played in the next room.* VARYA *appears in
the archway to the ballroom.*)

TROFIMOV (*Teasing.*)   Madam Lopakhin! Madam Lopakhin!

VARYA (*Angrily.*)   Scruffy gent!

TROFIMOV   Yes, I'm a scruffy gent and proud of it!

VARYA (*Brooding bitterly.*)   Here we've hired musicians, and what are
we going to pay them with? (*Exits.*)

TROFIMOV (*To* PISHCHIK.)   If the energy you've wasted in the course
of a lifetime tracking down money to pay off interest had been
harnessed to something else, you probably, ultimately could have
turned the world upside-down.

PISHCHIK   Nietzsche . . . a   philosopher . . . the   greatest, most
famous . . . a man of immense intellect, says in his works that it's
all right to counterfeit money.

TROFIMOV   So you've read Nietzsche?[7]

PISHCHIK   Well . . . Dashenka told me. But now I'm in such straits
that if it came to counterfeiting money . . . Day after tomorrow
three hundred rubles to pay . . . I've already borrowed a hundred
and thirty . . . (*Feeling his pockets, alarmed.*) The money's gone!
I've lost the money! (*Through tears.*) Where's the money? (*Gleefully.*) Here it is, in the lining . . . I was really sweating for a minute . . .

(*Enter* LYUBOV ANDREEVNA *and* CHARLOTTA IVANOVNA.)

LYUBOV ANDREEVNA (*Humming a lezginka.*[8])   Why is Lyonya taking
so long? What's he doing in town? (*To* DUNYASHA.) Dunyasha, offer
the musicians some tea . . .

6. "To one of his chariot-steeds named Incitatus . . . besides a stable all-built of marble stone
for him, and a manger made of ivory, over and above his caparison also and harness of
purple . . . he allowed a house and family of servants, yea, and household stuff to furnish
the same . . . It is reported, moreover, that he meant to prefer him into a consulship."
Suetonius, *History of Twelve Caesars*, trans. Philemon Holland (1606).
7. Friedrich Wilhelm Nietzsche (1844–1900), whose philosophy encourages a new "master"
morality for supermen and instigates revolt against the conventional constraints of Western civilization in his *Morgenröthe. Gedanken über die moralischen Vorurtheile* (*Dawns.
Reflections on moral prejudices*, 1881). This recalls Chekhov's statement in a letter (February 25, 1895): "I should like to meet a philosopher like Nietzsche somewhere on a train
or a steamer, and spend the whole night talking to him. I don't think his philosophy will
last very long, though. It's more sensational than persuasive."
8. A lively Caucasian dance in two-four time, popularized by Glinka, and also by Rubinstein
in his opera *The Demon*.

TROFIMOV   The auction didn't take place, in all likelihood.

LYUBOV ANDREEVNA   And the musicians showed up at the wrong time and we scheduled the ball for the wrong time . . . Well, never mind . . . (*Sits down and hums softly.*)

CHARLOTTA (*Hands* PISHCHIK *a deck of cards.*)   Here's a deck of cards for you; think of a card, any card.

PISHCHIK   I've got one.

CHARLOTTA   Now shuffle the deck. Very good. Hand it over, oh my dear Mister Pishchik. *Ein, zwei, drei!*[9] Now look for it, it's in your side pocket . . .

PISHCHIK (*Pulling a card from his side pocket.*)   Eight of spades, absolutely right! (*Astounded.*) Can you imagine!

CHARLOTTA (*Holds deck of cards on her palm, to* TROFIMOV.)   Tell me quick, which card's on top?

TROFIMOV   What? Why, the queen of spades.

CHARLOTTA   Right! (*To* PISHCHIK.) Well? Which card's on top?

PISHCHIK   The ace of hearts.

CHARLOTTA   Right! (*Claps her hand over her palm, the deck of cards disappears.*) Isn't it lovely weather today!

(*She is answered by a mysterious female voice, as if from beneath the floor: "Oh yes, marvelous weather, Madam."*)

You're so nice, my ideal . . .

VOICE   "*Madam, I been liking you very much too.*"[1]

STATIONMASTER (*Applauding.*)   Lady ventriloquist, bravo!

PISHCHIK (*Astounded.*)   Can you imagine! Bewitching Charlotta Ivanovna . . . I'm simply in love with you . . .

CHARLOTTA   In love? (*Shrugging.*) What do you know about love? *Guter Mensch, aber schlechter Musikant.*[2]

TROFIMOV (*Claps* PISHCHIK *on the shoulder.*)   Good old horse . . .

CHARLOTTA   Your attention please, one more trick. (*Takes a laprug from a chair.*) Here is a very nice rug. I'd like to sell it . . . (*Shakes it out.*) What am I offered?

PISHCHIK (*Astounded.*)   Can you imagine!

CHARLOTTA   *Ein, zwei, drei!* (*Quickly lifts the lowered rug.*)

(*Behind the rug stands* ANYA, *who curtsies, runs to her mother, embraces her, and runs back to the ballroom amid the general delight.*)

LYUBOV ANDREEVNA (*Applauding.*)   Bravo, bravo!

CHARLOTTA   One more time! *Ein, zwei, drei!* (*Lifts the rug.*)

(*Behind the rug stands* VARYA, *who bows.*)

---

9. German, "one, two, three."
1. In the Russian, Charlotta confuses her genders, using the masculine singular instead of the feminine plural.
2. German, "A good man, but a bad musician." A catch phrase from the comedy *Ponce de Leon* by Clemens von Brentano (1804), meaning an incompetent, another version of *nedotyopa*.

PISHCHIK (*Astounded.*)   Can you imagine!

CHARLOTTA   The end! (*Throws the rug at* PISHCHIK, *curtsies, and runs into the ballroom.*)

PISHCHIK (*Scurrying after her.*)   You little rascal! . . . How do you like that! How do you like that! (*Exits.*)

LYUBOV ANDREEVNA   And Leonid still isn't back. I don't understand what he can be doing in town all this time! Everything must be over there, either the estate is sold or the auction didn't take place, but why keep us in suspense so long?

VARYA (*Trying to comfort her.*)   Uncle dear bought it, I'm sure of it.

TROFIMOV (*Sarcastically.*)   Sure.

VARYA   Great-aunt sent him power of attorney so he could buy it in her name and transfer the debt. She did it for Anya. And I'm sure, God willing, that Uncle dear bought it.

LYUBOV ANDREEVNA   Your great-aunt in Yaroslavl sent fifty thousand to buy the estate in her name—she doesn't trust us—but that money won't even pay off the interest. (*Hides her face in her hands.*) Today my fate will be decided, my fate . . .

TROFIMOV (*Teases* VARYA.)   Madam Lopakhin! Madam Lopakhin!

VARYA (*Angrily.*)   Perpetual student! Twice already you've been expelled from the university.

LYUBOV ANDREEVNA   Why are you getting angry, Varya? He teases you about Lopakhin, what of it? You want to—then marry Lopakhin, he's a good, interesting person. You don't want to—don't get married; darling, nobody's forcing you.

VARYA   I take this seriously, Mama dear; I've got to speak frankly. He's a good man, I like him.

LYUBOV ANDREEVNA   Then marry him. What you're waiting for I cannot understand!

VARYA   Mama dear, I can't propose to him myself. For two years now people have been talking to me about him, everyone's talking, but he either keeps still or cracks jokes. I understand. He's getting rich, busy with his deals, no time for me. If only I'd had some money, even a little, just a hundred rubles, I'd have dropped everything, and gone far away. I'd have entered a convent.

TROFIMOV   Heaven!

VARYA (*To* TROFIMOV.)   A student ought to be intelligent! (*In a gentle voice, tearfully.*) You've gotten so homely, Petya, grown so old! (*To* LYUBOV ANDREEVNA, *no longer weeping.*) Only I can't do without work, Mama dear. I have to have something to do every minute.

(*Enter* YASHA.)

YASHA (*Can hardly keep from laughing.*)   Yepikhodov broke a billiard cue!

(*He exits.*)

VARYA   What's Yepikhodov doing here? Who gave him permission to play billiards? I don't understand these people . . . (*Exits.*)

LYUBOV ANDREEVNA   Don't tease her, Petya; can't you see she's miserable enough without that?

TROFIMOV   She's just too officious, poking her nose into other people's affairs. All summer long she couldn't leave us in peace, me or Anya, she was afraid a romance might break out. What business is it of hers? And anyway, I didn't show any signs of it, I'm so removed from banality. We're above love!

LYUBOV ANDREEVNA   Well then, I must be beneath love. (*Extremely upset.*) Why isn't Leonid back? If only I knew: is the estate sold or not? Imagining trouble is so hard for me I don't even know what to think, I'm at a loss . . . I could scream right this minute . . . I could do something foolish. Save me, Petya. Say something, tell me . . .

TROFIMOV   Whether the estate's sold today or not—what's the difference? It's been over and done with for a long time now, no turning back, the bridges are burned. Calm down, dear lady. You mustn't deceive yourself; for once in your life you've got to look the truth straight in the eye.

LYUBOV ANDREEVNA   What truth? You can see where truth is and where falsehood is, but I seem to have lost my sight. I can't see anything. You boldly solve all the major problems, but tell me, dovie, isn't that because you're young, because you haven't had time to suffer through any of your problems? You boldly look forward, but isn't that because you don't see, don't expect anything awful, because life is still hidden from your young eyes? You're more courageous, more sincere, more profound than we are, but stop and think, be indulgent if only in the tips of your fingers, spare me. This is where I was born, after all, this is where my father and my mother lived, my grandfather, I love this house, without the cherry orchard I couldn't make sense of my life, and if it really has to be sold, then sell me along with the orchard . . . (*Embraces* TROFIMOV, *kisses him on the forehead.*) Remember, my son was drowned here . . . (*Weeps.*) Show me some pity, dear, kind man.

TROFIMOV   You know I sympathize wholeheartedly.

LYUBOV ANDREEVNA   But you should say so differently, differently . . . (*Takes out a handkerchief, a telegram falls to the floor.*) My heart is so heavy today, you can't imagine. I can't take the noise here, my soul shudders at every sound, I shudder all over, but I can't go off by myself, I'd be terrified to be alone in silence. Don't blame me, Petya . . . I love you like my own flesh and blood. I'd gladly let you marry Anya, believe me, only, dovie, you've got to study, got to finish your degree. You don't do anything, Fate simply tosses you from place to place, it's so odd . . . Isn't that right? Isn't it? And something's got to be done about your beard, to make it grow somehow . . . (*Laughs.*) You look so funny!

TROFIMOV (*Picks up the telegram.*) I make no claim to be good-looking . . .

LYUBOV ANDREEVNA This telegram's from Paris. Every day I get one. Yesterday too and today. That wild man has fallen ill again, something's wrong with him again . . . He begs my forgiveness, implores me to come back, and actually I ought to go to Paris, stay with him a while. You look so disapproving, Petya, but what's to be done, dovie, what am I to do? He's ill, he's lonely, unhappy, and who's there to look after him, who'll keep him out of mischief, who'll give him his medicine at the right time? And what's there to hide or suppress, I love him, it's obvious, I love him, I love him . . . It's a millstone round my neck, it's dragging me down, but I love that stone and I can't live without it. (*Squeezes* TROFIMOV's *hand.*) Don't judge me harshly, Petya, don't say anything, don't talk . . .

TROFIMOV (*Through tears.*) Forgive my frankness, for God's sake, but he robbed you blind!

LYUBOV ANDREEVNA No, no, no, you mustn't talk that way . . . (*Covers her ears.*)

TROFIMOV Why, he's a scoundrel, you're the only one who doesn't realize it! He's a petty scoundrel, a nobody . . .

LYUBOV ANDREEVNA (*Getting angry, but under control.*) You're twenty-six or twenty-seven, but you're still a sophomoric school-boy!

TROFIMOV Is that so?

LYUBOV ANDREEVNA You should act like a man—at your age you should understand people in love. And you should be in love yourself . . . you should fall in love! (*Angrily.*) Yes, yes! And there's no purity in you, you're simply a puritan, a funny crackpot, a freak . . .

TROFIMOV (*Aghast.*) What is she saying?

LYUBOV ANDREEVNA "I am above love!" You're not above love, you're simply, as our Firs says, a half-baked bungler. At your age not to have a mistress! . . .

TROFIMOV (*Aghast.*) This is horrible! What is she saying? (*Rushes to the ballroom, clutching his head.*) This is horrible . . . I can't stand it, I'm going . . . (*Exits, but immediately returns.*) All is over between us! (*Exits to the hall.*)

LYUBOV ANDREEVNA (*Shouting after him.*) Petya, wait! You funny man, I was joking! Petya!

(*We hear in the hallway someone running up the stairs and*

suddenly falling back down with a crash. ANYA *and* VARYA *shriek, but immediately there is the sound of laughter.*

LYUBOV ANDREEVNA   What's going on in there?

   (ANYA *runs in.*)

ANYA (*Laughing.*)   Petya fell down the stairs! (*Runs out.*)

LYUBOV ANDREEVNA   What a crackpot that Petya is . . .

   (THE STATIONMASTER *stops in the middle of the ballroom and recites Aleksey Tolstoy's "The Sinful Woman."*[3] *The guests listen, but barely has he recited a few lines, when the strains of a waltz reach them from the hallway and the recitation breaks off. Everyone dances. Enter from the hall* TROFIMOV, ANYA, VARYA, *and* LYUBOV ANDREEVNA.)

LYUBOV ANDREEVNA   Well, Petya . . . well, my pure-in-heart . . . I apologize . . . let's dance . . . (*Dances with* TROFIMOV.)

   (ANYA *and* VARYA *dance.*)

   (FIRS *enters, leaves his stick by the side door.* YASHA *also enters the drawing room, watching the dancers.*)

YASHA   What's up, Gramps?

FIRS   I'm none too well. In the old days we had generals, barons, admirals dancing at our parties, but now we send for the postal clerk and the stationmaster; yes, and they don't come a-running. Somehow I got weak. The late master, the grandfather, doctored everybody with sealing wax for every ailment. I've took sealing wax every day now for twenty-odd years, and maybe more; maybe that's why I'm still alive.[4]

YASHA   You bore me stiff, Gramps. (*Yawns.*) How about dropping dead?

FIRS   Eh, you . . . half-baked bungler! (*Mutters.*)

   (TROFIMOV *and* LYUBOV ANDREEVNA *dance in the ballroom, then in the drawing room.*)

LYUBOV ANDREEVNA   Merci. I'm going to sit for a bit . . . (*Sits down.*) I'm tired.

   (*Enter* ANYA.)

3. Aleksey Tolstoy (1817–1875), Russian poet; his fustian ballad "*Greshnitsa*"(1858) was frequently recited at public gatherings and even inspired a painting. It is about a Magdalen and her repentance at a feast in Judaea under the influence of Christ. Chekhov, who had a low opinion of Tolstoy's poetry, cites it in his stories to ironic effect. The title refers back to Ranevskaya's catalogue of sins in Act Two. The opening lines of the poem also comment by contrast on the dowdiness of her ball:

   The people seethe; joy, laughter flash
   The lute is twanged, the cymbals clash.
   Fern fronds and flowers are strewn about,
     And twixt the columns in th'arcade
     In heavy folds the rich brocade
   With ribbon broderie is decked out . . .

4. The treatment is to soak the wax in water and then drink the water.

ANYA (*Upset.*)   Just now in the kitchen some man was saying the cherry orchard's been sold already.

LYUBOV ANDREEVNA   Sold to whom?

ANYA   He didn't say. He left. (*Dances with* TROFIMOV; *they both go into the ballroom.*)

YASHA   There was some old man muttering away. Not one of ours.

FIRS   And Leonid Andreich still isn't back, still not home. That top-coat he's got on's too flimsy for between seasons—see if he don't catch cold. Eh, when they're young, they're green!

LYUBOV ANDREEVNA   I'll die this instant! Yasha, go and find out to whom it's been sold.

YASHA   He went away a long time ago, that old man. (*Laughs.*)

LYUBOV ANDREEVNA (*Somewhat annoyed.*)   Well, what are you laughing about? What's made you so happy?

YASHA   Yepikhodov's awfully funny. The man's incompetent. Tons of Trouble.

LYUBOV ANDREEVNA   Firs, if the estate is sold, then where will you go?

FIRS   Wherever you order, there I'll go.

LYUBOV ANDREEVNA   Why is your face like that? Aren't you well? You know you ought to be in bed . . .

FIRS   Yes . . . (*with a grin*) I go to bed, and with me gone, who'll serve, who'll look after things? I'm the only one in the whole house.

YASHA (*To* LYUBOV ANDREEVNA.)   Lyubov Andreevna! Let me ask you a favor, be so kind! If you go off to Paris again, take me with you, please. For me to stick around here is absolutely out of the question. (*Glances around, lowers his voice.*) It goes without saying, you can see for yourself, the country's uncivilized, the people are immoral; not to mention the boredom, in the kitchen they feed us garbage, and there's that Firs going around, muttering all kinds of improper remarks. Take me with you, be so kind!

(*Enter* PISHCHIK.)

PISHCHIK   May I request . . . a teeny waltz, loveliest of ladies . . . (LYUBOV ANDREEVNA *goes with him.*) Enchanting lady, I'll borrow a hundred and eighty little rubles off you just the same . . . Yes I will . . . (*Dances.*) A hundred and eighty little rubles . . .

(*They have passed into the ballroom.*)

YASHA (*Singing softly.*)   "Wilt thou learn my soul's unrest . . ."[5]

(*In the ballroom, a figure in a gray top hat and checked trousers waves its arms and jumps up and down; shouts of "Bravo, Charlotta Ivanovna!"*)

DUNYASHA (*Stops to powder her nose.*)   The young mistress orders me to dance—lots of gentlemen and few ladies—but dancing

5. Title and opening line of a ballad by N. S. Rzhevskaya (1869).

makes my head swim, my heart pound. Firs Nikolaevich, and just
now the postal clerk told me something that took my breath away.
(*Music subsides.*)

FIRS Well, what did he tell you?

DUNYASHA You, he says, are like a flower.

YASHA (*Yawns.*) How uncouth . . . (*Exits.*)

DUNYASHA Like a flower . . . I'm such a sensitive girl, I'm awfully
fond of compliments.

FIRS You'll get your head turned.

(*Enter* YEPIKHODOV.)

YEPIKHODOV Avdotya Fyodorovna, you don't wish to see me . . . as
if I were some sort of bug. (*Sighs.*) Ech, life!

DUNYASHA What can I do for you?

YEPIKHODOV Indubitably you may be right. (*Sighs.*) But, of course,
if it's considered from a standpoint, then you, if I may venture the
expression, pardon my outspokenness, positively drove me into a
state of mind. I know my lot, every day I run into some kind of
trouble, and I've grown accustomed to that long ago, so I look upon
my destiny with a smile. You gave me your word, and even though
I . . .

DUNYASHA Please, let's talk later on, but leave me alone for now.
I'm dreaming now. (*Toys with her fan.*)

YEPIKHODOV Every day I run into trouble, and I, if I may venture
the expression, merely smile, even laugh.

(*Enter* VARYA *from the ballroom.*)

VARYA Haven't you gone yet, Semyon? Honestly, you are the most
disrespectful man. (*To* DUNYASHA.) Clear out of here, Dunyasha.
(*To* YEPIKHODOV.) If you're not playing billiards and breaking the
cue, you're lounging around the drawing room like a guest.

YEPIKHODOV To take me to task, if I may venture the expression,
you can't.

VARYA I'm not taking you to task, I'm just telling you. But you know
all you do is walk around instead of attending to business. We
keep a bookkeeper but nobody knows what for.

YEPIKHODOV (*Offended.*) Whether I work or whether I walk or
whether I eat or whether I play billiards may be criticized only by
my elders and betters who know what they're talking about.

VARYA How dare you say such things to me? (*Flying into a rage.*)
How dare you? You mean I don't know what I'm talking about?
Get out of here! This minute!

YEPIKHODOV (*Alarmed.*) Please express yourself in a more refined
manner.

VARYA (*Beside herself.*) This very minute, out of here! Out! (*He goes
to the door, she follows him.*) Tons of Trouble! Don't draw another
breath here! Don't let me set eyes on you!

(YEPIKHODOV *has gone, behind the door his voice: "I'm going to complain about you."* So, you're coming back? (*Seizes the stick* FIRS *left near the door.*) Come on . . . come on . . . come on, I'll show you . . . Well, are you coming? Are you coming? Here's what you get . . . (*Swings the stick.*)

(*At the same moment,* LOPAKHIN *enters.*)

LOPAKHIN   My humble thanks.

VARYA (*Angrily and sarcastically.*)   Sorry!

LOPAKHIN   Never mind, ma'am. Thank you kindly for the pleasant surprise.

VARYA   Don't mention it. (*Starts out, then looks back and asks gently.*) I didn't hurt you?

LOPAKHIN   No, it's nothing. The bump is going to be enormous, though.

(*Voices in the ballroom: "Lopakhin's here, Yermolay Alekseich!"*)

PISHCHIK   Sights to be seen, sounds to be heard . . . (*He and* LOPAKHIN *exchange kisses.*) There's cognac on your breath, my dear boy, apple of my eye. But we were making merry here too.

(*Enter* LYUBOV ANDREEVNA.)

LYUBOV ANDREEVNA   Is that you, Yermolay Alekseich? Why the delay? Where's Leonid?

LOPAKHIN   Leonid Andreich came back with me, he's on his way . . .

LYUBOV ANDREEVNA (*Agitated.*)   Well, what? Was there an auction? Say something!

LOPAKHIN (*Embarrassed, afraid to reveal his glee.*)   The auction was over by four o'clock . . . We missed the train, had to wait 'til half-past nine. (*Sighs heavily.*) Oof! My head's a little woozy . . .

(*Enter* GAEV; *his right hand is holding packages, his left is wiping away tears.*)

LYUBOV ANDREEVNA   Lyonya, what? Well, Lyonya? (*Impatiently, tearfully.*) Hurry up, for God's sake . . .

GAEV (*Not answering her, only waves his hand to* FIRS, *weeping.*) Here, take this . . . There's anchovies, smoked herring . . . I haven't had a thing to eat all day . . . What I've been through!

(*The door to the billiard room opens. We hear the click of the balls and* YASHA's *voice: "Seven and eighteen!"* GAEV's *expression alters, he stops crying.*)

I'm awfully tired. Firs, help me change. (*Exits through the ballroom, followed by* FIRS.)

PISHCHIK   What about the auction? Tell us!

LYUBOV ANDREEVNA   Is the cherry orchard sold?

LOPAKHIN   Sold.

LYUBOV ANDREEVNA   Who bought it?

LOPAKHIN   I bought it.

> (*Pause.* LYUBOV ANDREEVNA *is overcome; she would fall, were she not standing beside an armchair and a table.* VARYA *removes the keys from her belt, throws them on the floor in the middle of the drawing room and exits.*)

LOPAKHIN   I bought it! Wait, ladies and gentlemen, do me a favor, my head's swimming, I can't talk . . . (*Laughs.*) We got to the auction, Deriganov's there already. Leonid Andreich only had fifty thousand, and right off Deriganov bid thirty over and above the mortgage. I get the picture, I pitched into him, bid forty. He forty-five, I fifty-five. I mean, he kept upping it by fives, I by tens . . . Well, it ended. Over and above the mortgage I bid ninety thousand, it was knocked down to me. Now the cherry orchard's mine. Mine! (*Chuckling.*) My God, Lord, the cherry orchard's mine! Tell me I'm drunk, out of my mind, that I'm making it all up . . . (*Stamps his feet.*) Don't laugh at me! If only my father and grandfather could rise up from their graves and see all that's happened, how their Yermolay, beaten, barely literate Yermolay, who used to run around barefoot in the wintertime; how this same Yermolay bought the estate, the most beautiful thing in the world. I bought the estate where my grandfather and father were slaves, where they weren't even allowed in the kitchen. I'm dreaming, it's a hallucination, it only looks this way . . . This is a figment of your imagination, veiled by shadows of obscurity[6] . . . (*Picks up the keys, smiles gently.*) She threw down the keys, she wants to show that she's no longer in charge here . . . (*Jingles the keys.*) Well, it doesn't matter.

> (*We hear the orchestra tuning up.*)

Hey, musicians, play, I want to hear you! Come on, everybody, see how Yermolay Lopakhin will swing an axe in the cherry orchard, how the trees'll come tumbling to the ground! We'll build cottages, and our grandchildren and great-grandchildren will see a new life here . . . Music, play!

> (*The music plays;* LYUBOV ANDREEVNA *has sunk into a chair, crying bitterly.*)

LOPAKHIN   (*Reproachfully.*)   Why, oh, why didn't you listen to me? My poor, dear lady, you can't undo it now. (*Tearfully.*) Oh, if only this were all over quickly; if somehow our ungainly, unhappy life could be changed quickly.

PISHCHIK   (*Takes him by the arm; in an undertone.*)   She's crying.

---

6. George Calderon states that this phrase is "a cant jocular phrase, a literary tag. Lopakhin is quoting out of some bad play, as usual when he is lively." Chekhov uses this phrase in his correspondence.

Let's go into the ballroom, leave her alone . . . Let's go . . . (*Drags him by the arm and leads him into the ballroom.*)

LOPAKHIN   So what? Music, play in tune! Let everything be the way I want it! (*Ironically.*) Here comes the new landlord, the owner of the cherry orchard! (*He accidentally bumps into a small table and almost knocks over the candelabrum.*) I can pay for everything! (*Exits with* PISHCHIK.)

(*No one is left in the ballroom or drawing room except* LYUBOV ANDREEVNA *who is sitting, all hunched up, weeping bitterly. The music is playing softly.* ANYA *and* TROFIMOV *hurry in.* ANYA *goes to her mother and kneels before her.* TROFIMOV *remains at the entrance to the ballroom.*)

ANYA   Mama! . . . Mama, you're crying? Dear, kind, good Mama, my own, my beautiful, I love you . . . I bless you. The cherry orchard's sold, it's gone now, that's true, true, true, but don't cry, Mama, you've still got your life ahead of you, you've still got your good, pure heart . . . Come with me, come, dearest, let's go away from here, let's go! . . . We'll plant a new orchard, more splendid than this one, you'll see it, you'll understand, and joy, peaceful, profound joy will sink into your heart, like the sun when night falls, and you'll smile, Mama! Let's go, dearest! Let's go! . . .

CURTAIN

Act Four

First act setting. Neither curtains on the windows, nor pictures on the wall, a few sticks of furniture remain, piled up in a corner as if for sale. A feeling of emptiness. Near the door to the outside and at the back of the stage are piles of suitcases, travelling bags, etc. The door at left is open, and through it we can hear the voices of VARYA *and* ANYA. LOPAKHIN *stands, waiting.* YASHA *is holding a tray of glasses filled with champagne. In the hallway,* YEPIKHODOV *is tying up a carton. Offstage, at the back, a murmur. It's the peasants come to say good-bye.*

GAEV'S VOICE   Thank you, friends, thank you.

YASHA   The common folk have come to say good-bye. I'm of the opinion, Yermolay Alekseich, that they're decent enough people, but not very bright.

(*The murmur subsides. Enter through the hall* LYUBOV ANDREEVNA *and* GAEV. *She isn't crying, but is pale, her face twitches, she can't talk.*)

GAEV   You gave them your purse, Lyuba. You shouldn't have! You shouldn't have!

LYUBOV ANDREEVNA   I couldn't help it! I couldn't help it!

    (*They go out.*)

LOPAKHIN (*Through the door, after them.*)   Please, I humbly beseech you! A little drink at parting! It didn't occur to me to bring any from town, and at the station I only found one bottle. Please!

    (*Pause.*)

How about it, ladies and gentlemen? Don't you want any? (*Walks away from the door.*) If I'd known, I wouldn't have bought it. Well, I won't drink any either.

    (YASHA *carefully sets the tray on a chair.*)

Drink up, Yasha, you have some.

YASHA   To those departing! And happy days to the stay-at-homes! (*Drinks.*) This champagne isn't the genuine article, you can take it from me.

LOPAKHIN   Eight rubles a bottle.

    (*Pause.*)

It's cold as hell in here.

YASHA   They didn't stoke up today; it doesn't matter, we're leaving. (*Laughs.*)

LOPAKHIN   What's that for?

YASHA   Sheer satisfaction.

LOPAKHIN   Outside it's October, but sunny and mild, like summer. Good building weather. (*Glances at his watch, at the door.*) Ladies and gentlemen, remember, until the train leaves, there's forty-seven minutes in all! Which means, in twenty minutes we start for the station. Get a move on.

    (*Enter from outdoors* TROFIMOV *in an overcoat.*)

TROFIMOV   Seems to me it's time to go now. The horses are at the door. Where the hell are my galoshes? Disappeared. (*Through the door.*) Anya, my galoshes aren't here! I can't find them!

LOPAKHIN   And I have to be in Kharkov. I'll go with you on the same train. I'm spending all winter in Kharkov. I've been hanging around here with you, I'm worn out with nothing to do. I've got to be doing something, I don't even know where to put my hands; they dangle this funny way, like somebody else's.

TROFIMOV   We'll be going soon, and you can return to your productive labors.

LOPAKHIN   Do have a little drink.

TROFIMOV   None for me.

LOPAKHIN   In other words, back to Moscow now?

TROFIMOV   Yes, I'll go with them as far as town, but tomorrow back to Moscow.

LOPAKHIN   Yes . . . Hey, the professors are on a lecture strike, I'll bet they're waiting for you to show up!

TROFIMOV   None of your business.

LOPAKHIN   How many years have you been studying at the University?

TROFIMOV   Think up something fresher. That's old and stale. (*Looks for his galoshes.*) You know, it's unlikely we'll ever meet again, so let me give you a piece of advice as a farewell: don't wave your arms! Break yourself of that habit—arm-waving. And cottage-building as well, figuring that vacationers will eventually turn into property owners; figuring that way is just the same as arm-waving . . . Anyhow, I can't help liking you. You've got delicate, gentle fingers, like an artist, you've got a delicate, gentle heart.[7]

LOPAKHIN   (*Hugs him.*)   Good-bye, my boy. Thanks for everything. If you need it, borrow some money from me for the trip.

TROFIMOV   What for? Don't need it.

LOPAKHIN   But you don't have any!

TROFIMOV   I do. Thank you. I got some for a translation. Here it is, in my pocket. (*Anxiously.*) But my galoshes are missing!

VARYA   (*From the next room.*)   Take your nasty things! (*She flings a pair of rubber galoshes on stage.*)

TROFIMOV   What are you upset about, Varya? Hmm . . . But these aren't my galoshes!

LOPAKHIN   Last spring I planted nearly three thousand acres of poppies, and now I've cleared forty thousand net. And when my poppies bloomed, it was like a picture! So look, what I'm getting at is, I cleared forty thousand, which means I offer you a loan because I can afford it. Why turn up your nose? I'm a peasant . . . plain and simple.

TROFIMOV   Your father was a peasant, mine a druggist, and it all adds up to absolutely nothing.

(LOPAKHIN *pulls out his wallet.*)

Don't bother, don't bother . . . Even if you gave me two hundred thousand, I wouldn't take it. I'm a free man. And everything that you all value so highly and fondly, rich men and beggars alike, hasn't the slightest effect on me; it's like fluff floating in the air. I can manage without you, I can pass you by, I'm strong and proud. Humanity is moving toward the most sublime truth, the most sublime happiness possible on earth, and I'm in the front ranks!

LOPAKHIN   Will you get there?

TROFIMOV   I'll get there.

    (*Pause.*)

I'll get there, or I'll blaze a trail for others to get there.

    (*We hear in the distance an axe striking a tree.*)

LOPAKHIN   Well, good-bye, my boy. Time to go. We turn up our noses at one another, while life keeps slipping by. When I work a

---

7. These lines did not exist in the first version of the play, but Chekhov added them to support his view of Lopakhin as a decent person.

long time nonstop, then my thoughts are clearer, and I even seem
to know why I exist. But, pal, how many people there are in Russia
who don't know why they exist? Well, what's the difference? That's
not what makes the world go 'round. Leonid Andreich, they say,
took a job, he'll be in the bank, six thousand a year . . . Only he
won't keep at it, too lazy . . .

ANYA (*In the doorway.*)   Mama begs you, until she's gone, not to chop
down the orchard.

TROFIMOV   I mean really, haven't you got any tact . . . (*Exits through
the hall.*)

LOPAKHIN   Right away, right away . . . These people, honestly! (*Exits
after him.*)

ANYA   Did they take Firs to the hospital?

YASHA   I told them to this morning. They took him, I should think.

ANYA (*To* YEPIKHODOV, *who is crossing through the room.*)   Semyon
Panteleich, please find out whether Firs was taken to the hospital.

YASHA (*Offended.*)   I told Yegor this morning. Why ask ten times?

YEPIKHODOV   Superannuated Firs, in my conclusive opinion, is past
all repairing; he should be gathered to his fathers. And I can only
envy him. (*Sets a suitcase on top of a cardboard hatbox and crushes
it.*) Well, look at that, typical. I should have known.

YASHA (*Scoffing.*)   Tons of Trouble . . .

YEPIKHODOV   Well, it could have happened to anybody.[8] (*Exits.*)

VARYA (*From behind the door.*)   Have they sent Firs to the hospital?

ANYA   They have.

VARYA   Then why didn't they take the letter to the doctor?

ANYA   We'll have to send someone after them . . . (*Exits.*)

VARYA (*From the next room.*)   Where's Yasha? Tell him his mother's
here, wants to say good-bye to him.

YASHA (*Waves his hand in dismissal.*)   They simply try my patience.
    (DUNYASHA *in the meantime has been fussing with the luggage;
    now that* YASHA *is alone, she comes up to him.*)

DUNYASHA   If only you'd take one little look at me, Yasha. You're
going away . . . you're leaving me behind . . . (*Weeps and throws
herself on his neck.*)

YASHA   What's the crying for? (*Drinks champagne.*) In six days I'll
be in Paris again. Tomorrow, we'll board an express train and dash
away, we'll be gone in a flash. Somehow I can't believe it. *Veev lah
Franz!* . . . It doesn't suit me here, I can't live . . . nothing going
on. I've had an eyeful of uncouth behavior—I'm fed up with it.

8. This line does not appear in any printed edition, but was improvised in performance by
Ivan Moskvin. It got a laugh, and he asked if he could keep it in. See Chekhov's affirmative
response (letter to O. L. Knipper, March 20 1904, page 457). Somehow, Chekhov never
did insert the line in the proofs as he intended, but it appears penciled into the Moscow
Art Theater prompt script.

(*Drinks champagne.*) What's the crying for? Behave respectably, then you won't have to cry.[9]

DUNYASHA (*Powdering her nose, looks in a hand mirror.*) Drop me a line from Paris. I really loved you, Yasha, loved you so! I'm a soft-hearted creature, Yasha!

YASHA Someone's coming in here. (*Fusses with the luggage, humming softly.*)

(*Enter.* LYUBOV ANDREEVNA, GAEV, ANYA, *and* CHARLOTTA IVA-NOVNA.)

GAEV We should be off. Not much time left. (*Looking at* YASHA.) Who's that smelling of herring?

LYUBOV ANDREEVNA In about ten minutes, we ought to be getting into the carriages. (*Casting a glance around the room.*) Good-bye, dear old house, old Grandfather. Winter will pass, spring will come again, but you won't be here any more, they'll tear you down. How much these walls have seen! (*Kissing her daughter ardently.*) My precious, you're radiant, your eyes are sparkling like two diamonds. Are you happy? Very?

ANYA Very! A new life is beginning, Mama!

GAEV (*Gaily.*) As a matter of fact, everything's fine now. Before the sale of the cherry orchard, we were all upset, distressed, but then, once the matter was settled finally, irrevocably, everyone calmed down, even cheered up . . . I'm a bank employee, now I'm a financier. . . . Yellow in the center—and you, Lyuba, anyway, you're looking better, that's for sure.

LYUBOV ANDREEVNA Yes. My nerves are better, that's true.

(*They help her on with her hat and coat.*)

I sleep well. Carry my things out, Yasha. It's time. (*To* ANYA.) My little girl, we'll be back together soon . . . I'm off to Paris, I'll live there on that money your great-aunt in Yaroslavl sent us to buy the estate—hurray for Auntie!—but that money won't last long.

ANYA Mama, you'll come back soon, soon . . . won't you? I'll study, pass the examination at the high school, and then I'll work to help you. Mama, we'll be together and read all sorts of books . . . Won't we? (*Kisses her mother's hand.*) We'll read in the autumn evenings, we'll read lots of books, and before us a new, wonderful world will open up . . . (*Dreamily.*) Mama, come back . . .

LYUBOV ANDREEVNA I'll come back, my precious. (*Embraces her daughter.*)

(*Enter* LOPAKHIN. CHARLOTTA *is quietly singing a song.*)

GAEV Charlotta's happy! She's singing!

CHARLOTTA (*Picks up a bundle that looks like a swaddled baby.*) "Rock-a-bye, baby, on the tree top" . . .

9. Another echo of Hamlet to Ophelia: "If you are honest and fair, your honesty could admit no props to your fairness" (II. i).

(*We hear a baby crying:* "Waa! Waa!")

Hush, my sweet, my dear little boy.

("Waa! . . . Waa! . . .")

I'm so sorry for you! (*Throws down the bundle.*) Will you please find me a position? I can't keep on this way.

LOPAKHIN   We'll find one, Charlotta Ivanovna, don't worry.

GAEV   Everyone's dropping us, Varya's leaving . . . we've suddenly become superfluous.

CHARLOTTA   There's nowhere for me to live in town. Have to go away . . . (*Hums.*) What difference does it make?

(*Enter* PISHCHIK.)

LOPAKHIN   The freak of nature!

PISHCHIK (*Out of breath.*)   Oy, let me catch my breath . . . I'm winded . . . my most honored . . . Give me some water . . .

GAEV   After money, I suppose? Your humble servant, deliver me from temptation . . . (*Exits.*)

PISHCHIK (*Out of breath.*)   I haven't been to see you for the longest time . . . loveliest of ladies . . . (*To* LOPAKHIN.) You here . . . glad to see you . . . a man of the most enormous intellect . . . take . . . go on . . . (*Hands money to* LOPAKHIN.) Four hundred rubles . . . I still owe you eight hundred and forty . . .

LOPAKHIN (*Bewildered, shrugs.*)   It's like a dream . . . Where did you get this?

PISHCHIK   Wait . . . Hot . . . Most amazing thing happened. Some Englishmen[1] stopped by my place and found on my land some kind of white clay . . . (*To* LYUBOV ANDREEVNA.) And four hundred for you . . . beautiful lady, divine creature . . . (*Hands her money.*) The rest later. (*Drinks water.*) Just now some young man on the train was telling about some sort of . . . great philosopher who recommends jumping off roofs . . . "Jump!"—he says, and that solves the whole problem. (*Astounded.*) Can you imagine! Water! . . .

LOPAKHIN   Who were these Englishmen?

PISHCHIK   I leased them the lot with the clay for twenty-four years . . . But now, excuse me, no time . . . Have to run along . . . I'm going to Znoikov's . . . Kardamonov's . . . I owe everybody . . . (*Drinks.*) Your good health . . . On Thursday I'll drop by . . .

LYUBOV ANDREEVNA   We're just about to move to town, and tomorrow I'll be abroad.

PISHCHIK   What? (*Agitated.*) Why to town? Goodness, look at the furniture . . . the suitcases . . . well, never mind . . . (*Through tears.*) Never mind. Persons of the highest intelligence . . . those

---

1. The British appear in nineteenth-century Russian fiction as progressive and enterprising businessmen. They were often hired as estate managers, land surveyors, or experts in animal husbandry. The uncle of the writer Nikolay Leskov was a Scotsman who managed several vast Russian estates for their aristocratic owners.

Englishmen . . . Never mind . . . Be happy . . . God will come to your aid . . . Never mind . . . Everything in this world comes to an end . . . (*Kisses* LYUBOV ANDREEVNA's *hand.*) And should rumor reach you that my end has come, just remember this very thing—a horse, and say: "Once there lived so-and-so . . . Simeonov-Pishchik . . . rest in peace" . . . The most incredible weather . . . yes . . . (*Exits, overcome with emotion, but immediately reappears in the doorway and says*) Dashenka sends you her regards! (*Exits.*)

LYUBOV ANDREEVNA　Now we can go. I'm leaving with two things on my mind. First—that Firs is ill. (*Glancing at her watch.*) There's still five minutes . . .

ANYA　Mama, they've already sent Firs to the hospital. Yasha sent him this morning.

LYUBOV ANDREEVNA　My second anxiety is Varya. She's used to rising early and working, and now, without work, she's like a fish out of water. She's lost weight, she's got pale, she cries, poor soul . . .
(*Pause.*)
You know this perfectly well, Yermolay Alekseich; I had dreamt . . . of marrying her to you, yes, and it certainly looked as if you were going to get married. (*Whispers to* ANYA, *who nods to* CHARLOTTA, *and both leave.*) She loves you, you're fond of her, I don't know, I just don't know why you seem to sidestep one another. I don't understand!

LOPAKHIN　I don't understand either, I admit. It's all strange somehow . . . If there's still time, then I'm ready right now . . . Let's get it over with right away—and that'll be that, but if it wasn't for you, I have the feeling I wouldn't be proposing.

LYUBOV ANDREEVNA　That's wonderful. One little minute is all it takes. I'll call her right now . . .

LOPAKHIN　And there's champagne for the occasion. (*Looks in the glasses.*) Empty—somebody drank it already.
(YASHA *coughs.*)
I should say, lapped it up . . .

LYUBOV ANDREEVNA　(*Lively.*)　Fine! We'll go outside . . . Yasha, *allez!*[2] I'll call her . . . (*In the doorway.*) Varya, drop everything, come here. Come on! (*Exits with* YASHA.)

LOPAKHIN　(*Glancing at his watch.*)　Yes . . .
(*Pause.*)
(*Behind the door a stifled laugh, whispering, finally* VARYA *enters.*)

VARYA　(*Inspects the luggage for a long time.*)　That's funny, I just can't find it . . .

LOPAKHIN　What are you looking for?

2. French: "go on!"

VARYA   I packed it myself and can't remember.
    (*Pause.*)
LOPAKHIN   Where are you off to now, Varvara Mikhailovna?
VARYA   Me? To the Ragulins' . . . I've agreed to take charge of their
    household . . . as a housekeeper, sort of.
LOPAKHIN   That's in Yashnevo? About fifty miles from here.
    (*Pause.*)
So ends life in this house . . .
VARYA (*Examining the luggage.*)   Where in the world is it? . . . Or
    maybe I packed it in the trunk . . . Yes, life in this house is over
    . . . there won't be any more . . .
LOPAKHIN   And I'll be riding to Kharkov soon . . . by the same train.
    Lots of business. But I'm leaving Yepikhodov on the grounds . . .
    I hired him.
VARYA   Is that so!
LOPAKHIN   Last year by this time, it was already snowing, if you
    remember, but now it's mild, sunny. Except that it's cold . . .
    About three degrees of frost.
VARYA   I haven't noticed.
    (*Pause.*)
And besides our thermometer is broken . . .
    (*Pause.*)
VOICE FROM OUTSIDE (*Through the door.*)   Yermolay Alekseich!
LOPAKHIN (*As if expecting this call for a long time.*)   Right away!
    (*Rushes out.*)
        (VARYA, *sitting on the floor, laying her head on a pile of dresses,*
        quietly sobs. The door opens and LYUBOV ANDREEVNA *enters cau-*
        tiously.)
LYUBOV ANDREEVNA   Well?
    (*Pause.*)
We've got to go.
VARYA (*Has stopped crying, wipes her eyes.*)   Yes, it's time, Mama
    dear. I'll get to the Ragulins' today, provided I don't miss the
    train . . .
LYUBOV ANDREEVNA (*In the doorway.*)   Anya, put your things on!
        (*Enter* ANYA, *then* GAEV *and* CHARLOTTA IVANOVNA. GAEV *has on*
        a heavy overcoat with a hood. The SERVANTS *and* COACHMEN
        gather. YEPIKHODOV *fusses around the luggage.*)
Now we can be on our way.
ANYA (*Joyously.*)   On our way!
GAEV   My friends, my dearly beloved friends! Abandoning this house
    forever, can I be silent, can I refrain from expressing at parting
    those feelings which now fill my whole being . . .
ANYA (*Entreating.*)   Uncle! . . .
VARYA   Uncle dear, you mustn't!

GAEV (*Downcast.*)   Bank the yellow in the center . . . I'll keep
   still . . .
        (*Enter* TROFIMOV, *then* LOPAKHIN.)
TROFIMOV   Well, ladies and gentlemen, time to go!
LOPAKHIN   Yepikhodov, my overcoat!
LYUBOV ANDREEVNA   I'll sit just one little minute.[3] It's as if I never
   saw before what the walls in this house are like, what the ceilings
   are like, and now I gaze at them greedily, with such tender love . . .
GAEV   I remember when I was six, on Trinity Sunday I sat in this
   window and watched my father driving to church . . .
LYUBOV ANDREEVNA   Is all the luggage loaded?
LOPAKHIN   Everything, I think. (*Putting on his overcoat, to* YEPIKHO-
   DOV.) You there, Yepikhodov, see that everything's in order.
YEPIKHODOV (*In a hoarse voice.*)   Don't worry, Yermolay Alekseich!
LOPAKHIN   What's the matter with you?
YEPIKHODOV   I just drank some water, swallowed something.
YASHA (*Contemptuously.*)   How uncouth . . .
LYUBOV ANDREEVNA   We're going—and there won't be a soul left
   here.
LOPAKHIN   Not until spring.
VARYA (*Pulls a parasol out of a bundle, looking as if she is about to hit
   someone.*)
        (LOPAKHIN *pretends to be scared.*)
   What are you, what are you doing . . . it never entered my
   mind . . .
TROFIMOV   Ladies and gentlemen, let's get into the carriages . . . It's
   high time! The train'll be here any minute!
VARYA   Petya, here they are, your galoshes, next to the suitcase.
   (*Tearfully.*) And yours are so muddy, so old . . .
TROFIMOV (*Putting on his galoshes.*)   Let's go, ladies and gentlemen!
GAEV (*Overcome with emotion, afraid he'll cry.*)   The train . . . the
   station . . . Follow shot to the center, white doublette to the cor-
   ner . . .
LYUBOV ANDREEVNA   Let's go!
LOPAKHIN   Everybody here? Nobody there? (*Locking the side door at
   the left.*) Things stored here, have to lock up. Let's go! . . .
ANYA   Good-bye, house! Good-bye, old life!
TROFIMOV   Hello, new life! (*Exits with* ANYA.)
        (VARYA *casts a glance around the room and exits unhurriedly.*
        YASHA *and* CHARLOTTA *with her lapdog go out.*)
LOPAKHIN   Which means, 'til spring. Come along, ladies and gentle-
   men . . . 'Til we meet again! . . . (*Exits.*)
        (LYUBOV ANDREEVNA *and* GAEV *are left alone. As if they had been*

---

3. Sitting down for a brief while before leaving for a journey was an old Russian custom.

waiting for this, they throw their arms around one another's neck and sob with restraint, quietly, afraid of being heard.)

GAEV (*In despair.*)   Sister dear, sister dear . . .

LYUBOV ANDREEVNA   Oh, my darling, my sweet, beautiful orchard! . . . My life, my youth, my happiness, good-bye! . . . Good-bye! . . .

ANYA'S VOICE (*Gaily, appealing.*)   Mama! . . .

TROFIMOV'S VOICE (*Gaily, excited.*)   Yoo-hoo!..

LYUBOV ANDREEVNA   One last look at the walls, the windows . . . Our poor mother loved to walk in this room . . .

GAEV   Sister dear, sister dear! . . .

ANYA'S VOICE   Mama! . . .

TROFIMOV'S VOICE   Yoo-hoo! . . .

LYUBOV ANDREEVNA   We're coming! . . .

(*They go out.*)

(*The stage is empty. We hear all the doors being locked with a key, and then the carriages driving off. It grows quiet. In the stillness, there is the dull thud of an axe against a tree, sounding forlorn and dismal.*)

(*We hear footsteps. From the door at right, FIRS appears. He's dressed, as always, in a jacket and white waistcoat, slippers on his feet. He is ill.*)

FIRS (*Crosses to the door, tries the knob.*)   Locked. They've gone . . . (*Sits on the sofa.*) Forgot about me . . . Never mind . . . I'll sit here a spell . . . And Leonid Andreich, I'll bet, didn't put on his fur coat, went out in his topcoat . . . (*Sighs, anxiously.*) I didn't see to it . . . When they're young, they're green! (*Mutters something that cannot be understood.*) This life's gone by like I ain't lived. (*Lies down.*) I'll lie down a spell . . . Not a bit o' strength left in you, nothing left, nothing . . . Eh you . . . half-baked bungler! . . . (*Lies immobile.*)

(*We hear the distant sound, as if from the sky, the sound of a breaking string, dying away mournfully. Silence ensues, and all we hear far away in the orchard is the thud of an axe on a tree.*)

CURTAIN

Variants to *The Cherry Orchard*

Lines come from the original manuscript version (A1), a subsequent set of corrections (A2), the manuscript with the addition to Act Two (AA), and the first publication in the anthology *Knowledge* (*Znanie*) (K).

Act One

Replace Everyone talks about our getting married [. . .] it's all like a dream . . . —

with Everyone talks about our getting married, everyone offers congratulations, and he looks just as if he were about to propose any minute now, but in fact there's nothing to it, it's all like a dream, an unsettling, bad dream . . . Sometimes it even gets scary, I don't know what to do with myself . . . (A2) (Page 328)

Replace I'd like to tell you [. . .] Here's my plan.

with This is what I want to say before I go. (*After a glance at his watch.*) Now about the estate . . . in two words . . . I want to propose to you a means of finding a way out. So that your estate doesn't incur losses, you'd have to get up every day at four in the morning and work all day long. For you, of course, that's impossible, I understand . . . But there is another way out. (A1) (Page 331)

Replace Nothing doing. I want to go to bed. (*Exits.*)

with (*Walking over to the door.*) Who is that standing in the doorway? Who's there? (*Knock on the door from that side.*) Who's that knocking? (*Knock.*) That gentleman is my fiancé. (*Exits.*) *Everyone laughs.* (A1&2) (Page 334)

After He's a good man. — By the way, how much do we owe him?

GAEV   For the second mortgage just a trifle — about forty thousand. (A1) (Page 335)

Stage direction: a peaceful mood has returned to her, she is happy. (A1 & 2) (Page 338)

Act Two

Opening stage direction

(YASHA *and* DUNYASHA *are sitting on a bench,* YEPIKHODOV *stands nearby. From the estate along the road,* TROFIMOV *and* ANYA *pass by.*)

ANYA Great Aunt lives alone. She's very rich. She doesn't like Mamma. At first, it was hard for me staying with her, she didn't talk much to me. Then nothing, she relented. She promised to send the money, gave me and Charlotta Ivanovna something for the trip. But how awful, how hard it is to feel that one is a poor relation.

TROFIMOV There's somebody here already, it looks like . . . They're sitting down. In that case, let's walk along a little further.

ANYA Three weeks I've been away from home. I missed it so much! (*They leave.*) (A1 & 2) (Page 340)

After Tasty little pickle! — (*Pause.*) (A2, AA) (Page 342)

After a girl who misbehaves. — (*Sings quietly and, because he has no ear, extremely off-key.*) "Would you know my soul's unrest." (A2) (Page 342)

After The masters . . . — (*Rapidly.*) Come here today when it gets dark. Be sure to come . . . (A1&2) (Page 342)

After Maybe we'll think of something! —
        (VARYA *and* CHARLOTTA IVANOVNA *pass by on the road from the estate.* CHARLOTTA *is in a man's cap with a gun.*)

VARYA She's an intelligent, well-bred girl, nothing can happen, but all the same it's not right to leave her alone with a young man. Supper's at nine, Charlotta Ivanovna.

CHARLOTTA I don't want to eat. (*Quietly hums a ditty.*)

VARYA It doesn't matter. You have to for decency's sake. There, you see, they're sitting there on the riverbank . . .
        (VARYA *and* CHARLOTTA *leave.*) (A1 & 2) (Page 344)

After (*Inspects him.*) — Today should be the lightweight gray suit, but this one's a disgrace. (A1) (Page 345)

After ANYA (*Dreamily.*) There goes Yepikhodov . . . —

VARYA How come he's living with us? He only eats on the run and drinks tea all day long . . .

LOPAKHIN And makes plans to shoot himself.

LYUBOV ANDREEVNA But I love Yepikhodov. When he talks about his troubles, it gets so funny. Don't discharge him, Varya.

VARYA There's no other way, Mamma dear. We have to discharge him, the good-for-nothing. (Page 348)

Replace TROFIMOV Believe me, Anya, believe! [. . .]

CURTAIN

with TROFIMOV Tsss . . . Someone's coming. That Varya again! (*Angrily.*) Exasperating!

ANYA So what? Let's go to the river. It's nice there . . .

TROFIMOV Let's go . . .

    They start out.

ANYA Soon the moon will rise.

    They leave.

    (*Enter* FIRS, *then* CHARLOTTA IVANOVNA. FIRS, *muttering, is looking for something on the ground near the bench; he lights a match.*)

CHARLOTTA That you, Firs? What are you up to?

FIRS (*Mutters.*) Eh, you half-baked bungler!

CHARLOTTA (*Sits on the bench and removes her cap.*) That you, Firs? What are you looking for?

FIRS Mistress mislaid her purse.

CHARLOTTA (*Looking.*) Here's a fan . . . And here's a hanky . . . smells of perfume.

    (*Pause.*)

Nothing else. Lyubov Andreevna is constantly mislaying things. She's even mislaid her own life. (*Quietly sings a little song.*) I haven't got a valid passport, granddad, I don't know how old I am, and I always feel like I'm still oh so young . . . (*Puts her cap on* FIRS; *he sits motionless.*) O, I love you, my dear sir! (*Laughs.*) *Ein, zwei, drei!* (*Takes the cap off* FIRS *and puts it on herself.*) When I was a little girl, my father and mamma used to go from fairground to fairground, giving performances, pretty good ones. And I would be dressed as a boy and do the death-defying leap and all sorts of stunts, and so forth. And when Poppa and Mamma died, a German lady took me home with her and started teaching me. Fine. I grew up, then turned into a governess. But where I'm from and who I am — I don't know . . . Who my parents were, maybe they weren't married . . . I don't know. (*Pulls a pickle from her pocket and eats it.*) I don't know anything.

FIRS I was twenty or twenty-five, we're goin' along, me and the deacon's son and Vasily the cook, and there's this here man sittin' on a stone . . . a stranger like, don't know 'im . . . Somehow I git skeered and clear off, and when I'm gone they up and killed him . . . There was money on him.

CHARLOTTA Well? *Weiter.*

FIRS Then, I mean, comes a trial, they start askin' questions . . . They convict 'em . . . And me too . . . I sit in the penal colony two years or so . . . Then nothing, they let me go . . . A long time ago this was.

    Pause.

You can't rec'llect all of it . . .

CHARLOTTA   It's time for you to die, Granddad. (*Eats the pickle.*)

FIRS   Huh? (*Mutters to himself.*) And then, I mean, we're all riding together, and there's a rest stop . . . Uncle leaped out of the wagon . . . took a sack . . . and in that sack's another sack. And he looks, and there's something in there — jerk! jerk!

CHARLOTTA (*Laughs, quietly.*)   Jerk, jerk! (*Eats the pickle.*)

> (*We hear someone quickly walking along the road, playing a balalaika . . . The moon comes up . . . Somewhere near the poplars,* VARYA *is looking for* ANYA *and calling, "Anya! Where are you?"*

CURTAIN

(A1 & 2) (Page 350)

Act Three

After You're so nice, my ideal . . . —

How are you?

VOICE   *O, when I seen you, my heart got very sore.* (A) (Page 353)

After Guter Mensch aber schlechter Musikant. —

PISHCHIK   Well, I don't understand your schlechter-mechter. Lyubov Andreevna will favor me today with a loan of one hundred and eighty rubles . . . that I do understand . . .

LYUBOV ANDREEVNA   What sort of money do I have? Leave off. (A) (Page 353)

After Here is a very nice rug. —

there are no moth holes in it, no little stains. Very nice. (A) (Page 353)

After in a gray top hat — *in a tailcoat* (A) (Page 358)

After to powder her nose. — *tries to do it without being noticed.* (A) (Page 358)

After my head swim . . . — *We've been drinking cognac.* (A) (Page 359)

After Don't laugh at me! — *There's no need, no need, no need!* (A) (Page 363)

Act Four

After but that money won't last long. — *Well, uncle got a job at the bank . . .* (A) (Page 366)

After singing a song.) — CHARLOTTA Would you know my soul's unrest . . . (A) (Page 366)

After twenty-four years . . . — (*Astounded.*) Can you imagine! (A) (Page 367)

After fill my whole being? . . . — My friends, you, who feel this as keenly as I do, who know . . . (A) (Page 369)

After I'll sit just one little minute. — I'll sit a while . . . This feels good, it feels grand . . . (A) (Page 370)

CHEKHOV'S LETTERS

Translations are based on the texts in *Polnoe sobraniya sochineny i pisem v tridtsati tomakh* (Moscow: Nauka, 1974–83).

Comments in brackets are the translator's.

. . . indicates Chekhov's ellipsis; [. . .] indicates the editor's ellipsis.

Salutations have been omitted. Dates are given in Old Style (the Julian Calendar), except when Chekhov is writing from Europe, in which case both styles are given.

To M. V. Kiselyova,[1] Moscow, September 13, 1887

[. . .] I've been to Korsh's theater twice, and both times Korsh[2] insistently asked me to write him a play. I replied: glad to. The actors are convinced that I will write a good one, because I know how to play on people's nerves. I answered: *merci*.[3] And, of course, I won't write a play. Let Golokhvostova[4] write, but I will have absolutely nothing to do with theatres or humanity . . . To blazes with them!

To Al. P. Chekhov,[5] Moscow, October 6 or 7, 1887

[. . .] Ask Fyodorov or Bezhetsky[6] to insert the following notice in the theatrical news:

"*Ivanov*, a comedy by A. P. Chekhov, in four acts. Read to one of the Moscow literary circles (or something of that kind), it made the strongest impression. The plot is an original one, the characters are boldly outlined, etc."

This is a commercial notice. The play slipped out of me easy as pie, without a single tedious patch. The subject matter is unusual. I will stage it, probably, at Korsh's (if the latter isn't stingy).

[. . .] There's no need to praise the play in this notice, but stick to commonplaces. [. . .]

To Al. P. Chekhov, Moscow, October 10 or 12, 1887

[. . .] I wrote the play inadvertently, after a conversation with Korsh. Went to bed, thought up a theme, and wrote it down. Spent less than two weeks on it, or, more accurately, ten days, because in those

1. Mariya Vladimirovna Kiselyova (1850–1921), writer and close family friend of Chekhov, who vacationed at her estate Babkino. She and her husband, intimates of the composer Tchaikovsky, introduced Chekhov to classical music.
2. Fyodor Abramovich Korsh (1852–1923), founder and manager of the Moscow theatre that bore his name. Despite his fondness for audience-pleasing drama, he also staged innovative new plays and classics at special matinees.
3. French: Chekhov uses the word to indicate "thanks but no thanks."
4. Olga Andreevna Golokhvostova (d. 1894), writer and dramatist, a neighbor of the Kiselyovs at Babkino.
5. Aleksandr Pavlovich Chekhov (1855–1913), Anton's older brother, a writer and journalist.
6. Mikhail Pavlovich Fyodorov (1839–1900), journalist and nominal editor of the Petersburg newspaper *New Times*. A. Bezhetsky was the pseudonym of A. N. Maslov; see note 1, page 388.

two weeks there were days when I didn't work or wrote something else. I cannot judge the merits of the play. It has come out in a suspiciously short time. Everybody likes it. Korsh did not find a single error and sin against the stage,—proof of how sound and shrewd my judges are. It's the very first time I've written a play, *ergo*,—there are bound to be mistakes. The plot is complicated and not stupid. I finish up each act as if it were a story: I conduct all the action quietly and peacefully, and at the end I sock the audience in the snoot. All my energy was spent on a few really forceful and striking passages, but the bridges linking these passages are trivial, shaky and trite. All the same, I am pleased; no matter how bad the play is, I've created a type that has literary significance, I have produced a role which only a talent as great as Davydov[7] will undertake to play, a role in which an actor can show off, and display true ability . . . It's a pity that I can't read my play to you. [. . .]

The play has fourteen characters, five of them women. I feel that my ladies, with the exception of one, are not thoroughly worked out. [. . .]

To Al. P. Chekhov, Moscow, October 21, 1887

[. . .] My play will go on at Korsh's at the end of November or the beginning of December at somebody's benefit. Contract: no less than 8% of the box-office takings. A sold-out house at Korsh's comes to 1100–1500, and at benefits 2400. The play will be put on many times. The praise lavished on it, along with the forthcoming deal, have cheered me up a bit. All the same, you keep expecting something's going to go wrong . . . If the censor doesn't pass it, which is doubtful, then I . . . probably won't shoot myself, but it will be hard to take. [. . .]

To Al. P. Chekhov, Moscow, October 24, 1887

[. . .] Modern playwrights pack their plays with angels, cads, and buffoons exclusively,—well, go find those elements anywhere in Russia! If you look, you'll find them, but not in such extreme forms as playwrights need. Against your better judgment, you begin to squeeze them out of your brain, you sweat and strain, and give it up . . . I wanted to create something original: I did not portray a single villain or angel (though I could not refrain when it came to buffoons), did not indict anyone or acquit anyone . . . Whether I succeeded in this, I do not know . . . The play will definitely come off,—Korsh and the actors are sure about that. But I am not sure. The actors do not

---

7. Vladimir Nikolaevich Davydov (pseudonym of Ivan Nikolaevich Gorelov, 1849–1925), leading actor at the Maly Theater, who had transferred to Korsh in 1886.

understand, they talk nonsense, don't take the roles that suit them, but I soldier on in the belief that if the play does not go on the way I've cast it, it will perish. If they don't do what I want, then, to avoid disgrace, I'll have to withdraw the play. In general it's an unsettling and extremely unpleasant sort of thing. If I had known, I wouldn't have had anything to do with it. [. . .]

To N. M. Yezhov,[8] *Moscow, October 27, 1887*

[. . .] I consider it of some import to inform you, the best man to my *Ivanov*, of the following. *Ivanov* will definitely be put on at the end of November or the beginning of December. The contract with Korsh is already signed. Ivanov is to be played by Davydov, who, to my great satisfaction, is in ecstasies over the play, has set to work on it enthusiastically and has understood my Ivanov exactly as I could wish. Yesterday I sat with him until three in the morning and was convinced that he is really the most terrific artist.

If one is to believe such a judge as Davydov, I know how to write a play [. . .] It seems that I instinctively, intuitively, even unconsciously, wrote a completely finished piece of work and did not make *a single* theatrical mistake. Whence cometh the moral: "Young people, go to it!" [. . .]

To Al. P. Chekhov, Moscow, October 29, 1887

[. . .] Because Suvorin[9] is interested in the fate of my play, let him know that Davydov has taken to it passionately and enthusiastically. I so pleased him with the role that he dragged me off to his place, kept me till three o'clock in the morning and the whole time, gazing affectionately at my kisser, assured me that he has never lied in all his born days and that in the play from A to ω (that's not a ж—but an omega) everything is subtle, correct, decorous and noble. He asserts that my play has *five* excellent roles and that therefore it will flop with a thud at Korsh's, because there's no one to act it.

[. . .] The contract with Korsh (that crook!) is already signed. I get 8% of the box-office gross, i.e., 2% per act. [. . .]

---

8. Nikolay Mikhailovich Yezhov (1862–1942), writer and journalist.
9. Aleksey Sergeevich Suvorin (1834–1912), journalist and publisher, had risen from peasant origins to become a millionaire and influence-monger in the conservative camp; he and Chekhov were good friends until they took different sides in the Dreyfus Affair. The Theatre of the Literary-Artistic Society in St. Petersburg had been founded by Suvorin, who edited the powerful newspaper *New Times*.

To N. A. Leikin,[1] Moscow, November 4, 1887

[. . .] My play, beyond all expectations,—damn and blast it!—has so overtaxed and exhausted me that I have lost the ability to keep track of time, am weak in the knees, and will probably soon turn into a psychopath. It wasn't hard to write, but the staging requires not only spending money on cabs and time, but also masses of nerve-jangling work. Judge for yourself: 1. In Moscow there is not a single sincere person who knows how to tell the truth; 2. The actors are capricious, vain, half of them uneducated, conceited; they can't stand one another, and a certain N is ready to sell his soul to the devil to keep his comrade Z from getting a good part; 3. Korsh is a businessman, and what he wants is not success for the actors and the play, but sold-out houses; 4. There are no women in the company, and I have two fine women's roles which will be spoiled without rhyme or reason.

5. Of the male cast, only Davydov and Kiselevsky[2] will get it right; all the rest will come out bland.

6. After I signed the contract with Korsh, they let me know that the Maly Theatre (the State theater) would have been glad to accept my play.

7. In Davydov's opinion, which I trust, my play is better than all the plays written in the current season, but it is bound to fail thanks to the weakness of Korsh's acting company.

8. Yesterday I wanted to take back my play, but Korsh began to twitch hand and foot. [. . .]

I'd need another twenty points, but eight is enough. Now you can judge what the situation of a "neophyte playwright" is like, who for no good reason got into the wrong pew and involved in something that isn't his business.

I am comforted only by the fact that Davydov and Kiselevsky will be brilliant. Davydov is setting to work on his role with enthusiasm.

From Korsh, I did not take fifty rubles per performance, as you advised, but more: 8% of the box-office gross, i.e., 2% per act. Such is the contract. [. . .]

To N. A. Leikin, Moscow, November 15, 1887

[. . .] Your lines about staging plays have put me in a quandary. You write: "The author only impedes the staging, inhibits the actors, and in most cases makes only stupid comments." Let answer you thusly: 1. The play is the author's property, not the actors'; 2. Everywhere,

---

1. Nikolay Aleksandrovich Leikin (1841–1906), humorist and editor of the comic journal *Splinters* (*Oskolki*), to which Chekhov contributed from 1882 to 1887.
2. Ivan Platonovich Kiselevsky (1839–1898), a famous provincial actor, created the role of Count Shabelsky.

casting the play is the author's responsibility, if he is around; 3. To date, *all* my comments have been useful, and have all been put into practice, as I indicated; 4. The actors themselves ask for my comments; 5. Along with my play, the Maly Theater is rehearsing a new play by Shpazhinsky,[3] who has changed the furniture *three* times and got the management to lay out money for new set-pieces *three* separate times. Etc. If you reduce author participation to zero, what the hell will be the result? . . . Remember how Gogol raged when they put on his play![4] And wasn't he right? [. . .]

To Al. P. Chekhov, Moscow, November 20, 1887

Well, the play went on . . . I will describe everything in order. First of all, Korsh promised me ten rehearsals, and held only four, of which only two could be called rehearsals, for the other two turned out to be bouts in which Messrs. Performers practiced verbal sparring and quarrelling. Davydov and Glama[5] were the only ones who knew their lines, and the rest performed following the prompter and their own inner conviction.

Act One. I am backstage in a little cubicle like a prisoner's dock. The family is in an orchestra box: they tremble. Contrary to expectation, I am cool, and experience no agitation. The actors are excited, tense and cross themselves. Curtain up. Enter the actor whose benefit night it is.[6] His uncertainty, his unfamiliarity with his role, and the presentation of a wreath make me fail to recognize the play from the very first lines. Kiselevsky, in whom I had placed great expectations, did not deliver a single phrase accurately. Literally, *not a single one.* In spite of this and the stage manager's blunders, the first act was a great success. Lots of curtain calls.

Act Two. On the stage a mass of people. The guests. They don't know their lines, get confused, talk nonsense. Every word stabs me like a knife in the back. But—O Muse!—this act, too, was a success. They called out everybody, even called me out twice. Congratulations and success.

Act Three. They do not play badly. Enormous success. I am called before the curtain three times, Davydov shakes my hand, and Glama, in the manner of Manilov,[7] squeezes my other hand to her heart. The triumph of talent and virtue.

3. Ippolit Vasilievich Shpazhinsky (1844–1917), a popular playwright, whose *Princess Kurakina* was a big hit of the season.
4. Nikolay Gogol was very upset by the sloppy staging of his play *The Inspector General* at its premiere at the St. Petersburg Alexandra Theater in 1836, and he spent a great deal of effort writing instructions and corrections to improve later productions.
5. Aleksandra Yakovlevna Glama-Meshcherskaya (1856–1942) appeared as Sarra. She and Davydov were the two biggest names in the all-star cast.
6. Nikolay Vladimirovich Svetlov (real name Potyomkin, d. 1909), the character actor who played Borkin.
7. A sickly-sweet sentimentalist in Gogol's *Dead Souls.*

Act Four, Scene One. It does not go badly. More curtain calls. Then the longest, most tiresome intermission. The audience, not accustomed to getting up and going for refreshments between two scenes, murmurs. The curtain goes up. Beautiful: through the arch is seen the supper table (the wedding). The band plays fanfares. Enter the groom's men: they are drunk, and therefore, you see, they have to clown around and kick up their heels. A sideshow and a pothouse, which horrifies me. Then enter Kiselevsky: a soul-stirring, poetic passage, but this Kiselevsky of mine does not know his lines, is drunk as a skunk, and a short little poetical dialogue is transformed into something drawn-out and disgusting. The audience is baffled. At the end of the play the hero dies because he cannot endure an insult he has received. The audience, grown cold and tired, does not understand this death (which the actors imposed on me; I have a different version). The actors and I are called out again. During one of these curtain-calls, I hear sounds of open hissing, drowned out by the clapping and stamping of feet.

In general, weariness and a feeling of annoyance. It's disgusting, although the play was a solid success (denied by Kicheev[8] and Co.) . . .

Theater people say that they had never seen such a commotion in a theatre, such general applause cum hissing, and that never before had they heard so many arguments as they saw and heard at my play. And at Korsh's no author has ever before been called out after the second act.

The play will be performed a second time on the 23rd, with a variant and other changes—I banish the grooms' men. [. . .]

To Al. P. Chekhov, Moscow, November 24, 1887

[. . .] You can't imagine what it was like! From such a meaningless turd of a playlet [. . .] there's been a hell of a development. I have already written you that at the premiere there was such excitement among the audience and backstage, that the prompter, who has worked in the theater for thirty-two years, declared he had never seen anything like it in all his born days. They made an uproar, they yelled the house down, they clapped, they hissed; at the refreshment counter they almost came to blows, and in the gallery students wanted to throw someone out, and two persons were ejected by the police. It was complete bedlam. Sister almost fainted; Dyukovsky, who was overcome by palpitation of the heart, fled, while Kiselyov[9]

---

8. Pyotr P. Kicheev, a journalist, who, in the *Moscow Broadside*, called the play "profoundly immoral," "an insolent and cynical confusion of ideas," and "incoherent."

9. Mikhail Mikhailovich Dyukovsky, a school inspector, friend of the Chekhov family. Aleksey Sergeevich Kiselyov (d.1910), a landowner whose estate may later have been the model for the one in *The Cherry Orchard*.

clutched his head for no rhyme or reason and vociferated most earnestly, "Well, what will I do now?"

The actors were in a state of nervous tension. Everything I wrote to you [. . .] about their acting and attitudes to the matter, must not, of course, go any further. There is much to excuse and understand . . . It turns out that the actress who played the leading part in my play has a little daughter at death's door—how could she be up to acting?

Kurepin[1] was right to praise the actors. The day after the performance there was a review by Pyotr Kicheev in the *Moscow Broadside*. He calls my play impudently cynical and immoral rubbish. The *Moscow Intelligencer* praised it.

The second performance didn't go badly, though not without surprises. Replacing the actress whose little daughter was sick was another (who'd had no rehearsal). Again there were curtain calls after Act Three (twice) and after Act Four, but no more hisses.

And that's all. On Wednesday, my *Ivanov* will be presented again. Now everyone has calmed down and goes about his business.

[. . .] If you read the play, you will not understand the excitement I have described; you will find nothing special in it. Nikolay, Shekhtel, and Levitan[2]—all of them artists—assure me that on the stage it is so original that it is quite strange to look at. In reading one does not notice this.

N.B. If it comes to your notice that anybody at *New Times* wants to pan the actors who took part in my play, ask them to refrain from carping. In the second performance they were splendid. [. . .]

[. . .] insert a notice in the paper saying that "*Ivanov* has its second performance on November 23rd at the Korsh Theater. The actors, especially Davydov, Kiselevsky, Gradov-Sokolov, and Kosheva,[3] won many curtain calls. The author was called out after Acts Three and Four." Something along those lines . . . A notice like that will make them do the play again, and I'll get an extra fifty or a hundred smackers. [. . .]

—YOUR SCHILLER SHAKESPEAROVICH GOETHE

1. Aleksandr Dmitrievich Kurepin, editor of *The Alarm Clock* and a contributor to *New Times*.
2. Nikolay Pavlovich Chekhov (1858–1889), an elder brother of the dramatist, and a gifted painter and caricaturist. Frants Osipovich Shekhtel (1859–1926), an architect, who designed the Moscow Art Theater building and the Chekhov Library in Taganrog. Isaak Ilyich Levitan (1861–1900), landscape artist and one of Chekhov's closest friends.
3. Leonid Ivanovich Gradov-Sokolov (1840–1890), a popular provincial comedian, played Kosykh. Bronislava Eduardovna Kosheva, a lively provincial actress, played Babakina.

To V. N. Davydov, St. Petersburg, December 1, 1887

As I write you this letter, my play is being passed from hand to hand and read. Beyond all expectation (I went to St. Pete terrified and did not expect much good to come of it), it generally makes a very decent impression here. Suvorin, who took the liveliest, most feverish interest in my childish nonsense, spends whole hours keeping me at his home and lecturing about *Ivanov*. So do other people. There's a bit less talk than in Moscow, but all the same there's enough to make me fed up with my *Ivanov*. Briefly I shall inform you of the verdict of my judges, which comes down to the following points:

1. The play is written carelessly. Its form has called down fiery Gehenna from the Sanhedrin.[4] The language is irreproachable.

2. There is no objection to the title.

3. The idea that there is an immoral and insolently cynical element in the play provokes laughter and bewilderment.

4. The personalities are sufficiently contrasted, the characters are alive, and the life depicted in the play is not contrived. Fault-finding and misunderstanding on this point has not been heard for a while, although I undergo the most nitpicking examination on a daily basis.

5. Ivanov *is adequately delineated*. Nothing needs to be added or subtracted. Suvorin, however, stuck to his personal opinion: "I understand Ivanov well, because, it seems, I myself am Ivanov, but the masses, which every actor should keep in mind, will not understand him; it wouldn't hurt to give him a soliloquy."

6. Burenin[5] doesn't like the fact that there is no climax in Act One,—it doesn't go according to the rules.

7. The very best and most essential passage in terms of Ivanov's characterization is granted by most persons to be the one in Act Four, where Ivanov comes running to Sasha before the wedding. Suvorin is in raptures over this passage.

8. A certain constriction is felt in the play owing to the abundance of characters: characters abound to the detriment of Sarra and Sasha, who are not allotted enough stagetime and who therefore are colorless in places.

9. The end of the play does not sin against truth, but nevertheless constitutes a "theatrical falsehood." It can satisfy the spectator only on one condition: through exceptionally good acting. They say to me:

"If you can guarantee that such actors as Davydov will play Ivanov everywhere, then leave that ending, otherwise we'll be the first to hiss you."

[. . .] To sum up: the sparks have been blown into a conflagration.

---

4. The highest court of justice in ancient Jerusalem. This is equivalent to saying, "The church of art anathematized it."

5. Viktor Petrovich Burenin (1842–1926), journalist and dramatist, a conservative who later savagely parodied Chekhov's plays.

A bagatelle has somehow wound up as a strange, garbled Day of Judgment.

As for me, I have regained my composure in the interests of bread-winning and feel completely content. You have portrayed my Iva-nov—all my ambition is encompassed by that. Thank you and all the actors [. . .]

To the Chekhov family, St. Petersburg, December 3, 1887

[. . .] Everyone is vying in invitations and lavishing flattery on me. They are all absolutely enraptured by my play, although they scold me for carelessness. My only copy is passing from hand to hand, and I cannot get hold of it to give it to the censorship.

Suvorin is angry because I gave my play to Korsh; in his opinion, neither Korsh's company nor the Moscow audience (?) can under-stand Ivanov. The Moscow reviews raise laughs here. Everyone is waiting for me to stage the play in St. Pete, and is sure of its success, but after Moscow my play has become so repulsive to me that I cannot force myself to think about it: I'm lazy and out of sorts. As soon as I recall how Korsh's shitheads played practical jokes, how they mangled and fractured it, how nauseating it became than you start to feel sorry for the audience, which left the theater with empty stomachs. I'm sorry for myself and Davydov.

Suvorin is excited about my play. It's remarkable: after Korsh's acting not one person in the audience understood Ivanov, they abused and pitied me, yet here everyone unanimously asserts that my Ivanov was adequately delineated, that nothing needs to be added or subtracted. [. . .]

It's hardly likely my play will go on at Korsh's again. Some nitwit on *New Times* who overheard my conversation with Suvorin and Co. and failed to understand so thumbed his nose in the paper at Korsh's acting company that I cried bloody murder. Suvorin called the nitwit "an unprincipled beast," but Korsh probably passed out. The nitwit wanted to do me a good turn, but who the hell knows what will come of it. If Korsh removes my play from the repertory, all the better. What's the point of being disgraced? To hell with them! [. . .]

To Ya. P. Polonsky,[6] Moscow, February 22, 1888

. . . Just to while away the time I wrote a vapid little, Frenchified vaudeville, *The Bear.* [. . .]

Ah, if they find out at *The Northern Herald* that I write vaudevilles they will excommunicate me! What am I to do, if my hands get to

---

6. Yakov Petrovich Polonsky (1819–1898), writer who nominated Chekhov for the Pushkin Prize, even before they first met in St. Petersburg in 1887.

itching and want to commit something ooh-la-la? All my efforts to be serious come to nothing, and my earnestness invariably alternates with vulgarity. I suppose it is my horoscope. But seriously speaking, this "horoscope" may be symptomatic of the fact that I can never turn into a serious thoroughgoing craftsman. [. . .]

To A. I. Maslov,[7] Moscow, April 7, 1888

[. . .] I advised you to write a comedy and advise you once again. It won't do you any harm, but will provide an income. My *Ivanov*, can you imagine, is played even in Stavropol. As to the execution, there's nothing to fear. First of all, you have a wonderful flair for dialogue, second, ignorance of stage technique will be fully compensated by the literary qualities of the play. Only don't stint on the women and don't give vent to your spleen. [. . .]

To A. S. Suvorin, Moscow, October 2, 1888

[. . .] I have been reading my *Ivanov*. It seems to me if I were to write a different Act Four, delete portions, and stick in a monologue that is already fixed in my mind, the play will be finished and extremely effective. I'll correct it by Christmas and send it to the Alexandrinka.

The Bear has been passed by the censor (apparently, not unconditionally)[8] and will be put on at Korsh's. Solovtsov[9] is slavering to play it. [. . .]

To A. S. Suvorin, Moscow, between October 5 and 6, 1888

[. . .] In *Ivanov*, I have radically refashioned Acts Two and Four. I gave *Ivanov* a monologue, touched up Sasha, and so on. If they don't understand my *Ivanov* now, I'll throw it on the fire and write a short story called "Enough!" I'm not changing the title. It's awkward. If the play had not been performed before, it would be another story. [. . .]

To A. S. Suvorin, Moscow, October 27, 1888

[. . .] Tomorrow, my *Bear* will be put on at Korsh's. I've written another vaudeville: two male roles, one female. [. . .][1]

7. Aleksey Nikolaevich Maslov (b. 1853), writer and dramatist under the pseudonym A Bezhetsky, who contributed to *New Times*.
8. The censor demanded the suppression of certain "coarse expressions."
9. Nikolay Nikolaevich Solovtsov (Fyodorov, 1856–1902), a childhood friend of Chekhov and the actor who created Smirnov in *The Bear*.
1. Probably *The Proposal*.

To M. V. Kiselyova, Moscow, November 2, 1888

[. . .] I succeeded in writing a silly vaudeville, which, because of its silliness, is meeting with great success. Vasiliev in the *Moscow Intelligencer* tore me to pieces, the rest of them and the audience are in seventh heaven. There is a constant roar of laughter in the theatre. You never can tell what is going to take! [. . .]

To I. L. Leontyev (Shcheglov),[2] Moscow, November 2, 1888

[. . .] Now about *The Bear*. Solovtsov played phenomenally. Rybchinskaya[3] was appropriate and charming. The theater was in a constant roar of laughter; the soliloquies were interrupted by applause. At the first and second performances, the actors and the author were called forth. All the newspaper scribblers praised it, except Vasiliev[4] . . . But, old pal, Solovtsov and Rybch. are inartistic, with no nuances; they harp on one note, don't take risks, and so on. The acting is rough-hewn.

After the first performance there was an accident. A coffeepot killed my bear. Rybchinskaya was drinking coffee, the coffeepot exploded from the steam, and scalded her whole face. At the second performance Glama took her place, very decently. Now Glama has gone to St. Pete, and that's how my fuzzy bear unwillingly dropped dead, after barely three days of life. Rybchinskaya promises to be well by Sunday.

[. . .] Am I turning into a popular writer of vaudevilles? Goodness gracious, the way they clamor for them! If in my lifetime I just manage to scribble a dozen airy trifles for the stage, I'll be thankful for it. I have no love for the stage. I'll write *The Power of Hypnosis*[5] during the summer—I don't feel like it right now. This season I'll write one little vaudeville and then rest until summer. Can you call this labor? Can you call this passion? [. . .]

To N. A. Leikin, Moscow, November 2, 1888

[. . .] That farce of mine, *The Bear*, is meeting with great success at Korsh's. In all probability, this bear is going to stay in the repertory for a long time, and will be frequently divided up on the provincial and amateur stages. I regret that I have neither the time nor the enthusiasm to write comic skits for the stage. [. . .]

2. Ivan Leontievich Leontyev (pseud. Shcheglov, 1856–1911), writer and dramatist, close friend and sometime collaborator of Chekhov.
3. Natalya Dmitrievna Rybchinskaya (d. 1920), noted as a comic ingenue.
4. Pseudonym of Sergey Vasilievich Flerov (1841–1901), theater critic.
5. Chekhov never wrote the play, but Shcheglov left a very full synopsis of the plot and in 1910 published a play over his own and Chekhov's names. See Laurence Senelick, "The Department of Missing Plays, Chekhov Division," *Theater* (Spring 1991): 33–39.

To I. L. Leontyev (Shcheglov), Moscow, November 7, 1888

[. . .] If you still so magnanimously agree to take on convict labor—
to deal with the friendly commissions, you've only yourself to blame.
On Thursday at 3 P.M. you will receive three copies of *The Bear*,
which I ask you to hand-deliver ASAP. On Saturday you will take it
into your head that you need an outing, and you'll drive over to the
Committee. If they approve the play, take the extra copy and hand
it over to an actor or actress at your discretion. You recommend
Savina[6] and Sazonov[7] Fine. Tikhonov recommends Dalmatov and
Vasilyeva[8] . . . That's good too. That is, it doesn't make the least bit
of difference to me, because I don't know the acting company in St.
Pete. Do what you like, and if you don't do it, I won't bear a grudge.
[. . .]

To A. S. Suvorin, Moscow, November 7, 1888

[. . .] Everyone advised me to send *The Bear* to the Alexandrinka.
So I'm sending it. The audience at Korsh's roars with laughter nonstop, although the acting of Solovtsov and Rybchinskaya is far from
artistic. My sister and I could give better performances. [. . .]

To I. L. Leontyev (Shcheglov), Moscow, November 11, 1888

[. . .] I learned of Savina's desire to play *The Bear* two days before
Abarinova's wish, and so before I got your letter I had already has-
tened to send my agreement to the highly talented and divine Mariya
Gavrilovna. The confusion occurred despite our best intent. I am
afraid that it will put somebody in an awkward situation. If your keen
eye observes embarrassment in someone's mind (your own or the
actress's), perform a quick maneuver: take back my *Bear*, giving as
your reason my wish not to make my debut on the State stage with
a vaudeville or something similar. I am not worried about such a
maneuver. [. . .]

You want to argue with me about the theater. Do what you must,
but you won't argue me out of my dislike for the scaffold on which
they execute dramatists. The modern theater is a world of dimwits,
Karpovs,[9] obtuseness, and idle gossip. [. . .]

6. Mariya Gavrilovna Savina (1850–1915), leading lady at the Alexandra Theater in St.
Petersburg, specialized in dramatic roles. A diva of imperious taste, she disliked Chekhov's
later plays, and he in turn found her inferior to the Italian star Eleonora Duse.
7. Nikolay Fyodorovich Sazonov (1843–1902), an actor who prided himself more on his
technique and experience than on his artistic goals.
8. Vladimir Alekseevich Tikhonov (1857–1914), a fellow playwright, later reviewed *Ivanov*.
Vasily Panteleimonovich Dalmatov (1845–1912) was best in the role of fops, though he
fancied himself in heavy dramatic parts. Nadezhda Sergeevna Vasilyeva (1852–1920),
actress at the Alexandra Theater, served on the selection committee for plays.
9. Yevtikhy Pavlovich Karpov (1857–1926), a director on the staff of the Alexandra Theater,
was later assigned to stage the premiere of *The Seagull*. Chekhov later referred him as "an

To A. N. Pleshcheev,[1] Moscow, November 13, 1888

[...] Savina wants to play my *Bear*—she was at Suvorin's, took my address and the issue with *The Bear* in it. In Moscow it's going like a house afire, and is about to move smartly in the provinces. You never know where you'll win and where you'll lose. [...]

To Al. P. Chekhov, Moscow, November 16, 1888

[...] In case any of my plays accidentally winds up on the State stage or if some private stage wishes to put on a "novelty" I've written, I fully authorize the administrators, managers, and impresarios to do their deals with you, sign contracts with you and pay you the royalties. If my *Bear* goes on at the Alexandrinka, you can use the power of attorney: the manager will sign the contract with you. Take note once and for all: if any management wishes to buy any of my plays, decline such a wish, even if they offer you a million. I wish to receive percentages of the box office (2% per each act). You will receive the fee each time by my special behest. [...]

A play performed on the State stage can in no event go to a private theater. Consequently, what is put on at the Alexandrinka or is about to be put on there cannot not even be allowed one performance in a private theater. I will inform you about any new play. As to the number of plays proposed for production on the State stage, two exist at the moment: *The Bear* and *Swan Song* (*Calchas*). Keep my theatrical dealings private. Not a whisper to a soul ... One more precept: in theatrical dealings do not go anywhere yourself or take action yourself, but wait until they address or summon you. You may demand, if necessary, as much as you like, but you may not make a request.

Plays not contracted to the State management are under the control of the Dramatic Society, and therefore, if on the poster of a private theater you spy something like *The Soft-boiled Crocodile, or Ooh-la-la Papa!* billed as a work of mine, don't sound the alarum, but sit quietly on the toilet. [...]

To A. S. Suvorin, Moscow, November 18, 1888

[...] One can dislike the theater and curse it out and at the same time enjoy staging plays. I like staging a play in the same way that I fish or catch crayfish: you cast your line and wait to see if anything

---

untalented playwright who entertains unfathomable delusions of grandeur" (letter to Chekhov's wife, April 22, 1904).
1. Aleksey Nikolaevich Pleshcheev (1825–1893), a poet and radical reformer, had been a prisoner in Siberia with Dostoevsky; he was the editor of the liberal paper *The Northern Herald*.

will turn up. But you go to the Society [for Russian Dramatic Authors] to collect your royalties with the same feeling with which you go to a fishtrap or an eelpot: overnight, did you snag a perch or a lot of crayfish? It's a pleasant recreation. [. . .]

To A. S. Suvorin, Moscow, December 19, 1888

[. . .] I've finished my *Moronov*[2] and am sending it along with this letter. I'm as fed up with it as Shcheglov is with actors. If you feel like it, read it, and if not, send it immediately to Potekhin.[3] I promised to send him my play by December 22 [. . .] I haven't thrown out a single hint about the production and I won't. Don't say anything to him. I shall pretend that I need neither the glory nor the money. Now my Mr. Ivanov is much easier to understand. The ending doesn't quite satisfy me (except for the gunshot, it's all flabby), but I am comforted by the fact that it's still in an unfinished form. If they want to stage it and ask who is to act it, convey to them my inviolable will:

Ivanov—Davydov.

Sarra—Savina.

Shabelsky—Svobodin.[4]

Lvov—Sazonov.

Lebedev—Varlamov.[5]

Sasha—Take your pick.

You may inform Potekhin of this list even now, so that our mutual friend Davydov won't run ahead bunny-like and make a mess of things. I consign Ivanov to Davydov—there's nothing else to do: Davydov played this role in Moscow. Sazonov, Svobodin, and Varlamov will play well, so well that they will shake up Davydenka and break him of taking the drama on himself. You see what subtle schemes I hatch!

[. . .] Don't you find that I manage plays rather efficiently? I barely laid a finger on *Ivanov* and it's ready. I'll have to go in for being Krylov.[6]

[. . .] I give you my word that I shall write no more of such intellectual and foul plays as *Ivanov*. If *Ivanov* does not succeed I shall

2. In Russian, *Bolvanov*, i.e., Blockhead.
3. Aleksey Anisimovich Potekhin (1829–1908), dramatist and chief of the repertory at the Alexandra Theater in the 1880s.
4. Pavel Matveevich Svobodin (Kozhenko, 1850–1892), a prominent actor whose performance in *Ivanov* so pleased Chekhov that they became good friends.
5. Konstantin Aleksandrovich Varlamov (1848–1915), an elephantine comic actor.
6. Viktor Aleksandrovich Krylov (1838–1906), widely produced playwright, a hack whom Chekhov detested.

not be surprised, and shall not attribute it to intrigues and plots.
[. . .]

Tell Svobodin if you see him, that Count Shabelsky is his role.
Make him this promise before Davydov snatches this role for the
wooden Dalmatov.

To A. S. Suvorin, Moscow, December 23, 1888

[. . .] I just got your letter. The absence of Sasha in the fourth act
leapt sharply to your eyes. So it should. Let the whole audience
notice that Sasha is not there. You insist on her appearing: the laws
of the stage, saith thou, demand it. All right, let her appear, but what
is she to say? What words? Such young ladies (she is not a girl but
a young lady) cannot and should not speak. The original Sasha could
speak and be sympathetic, but the new one will only irritate the
public by making an appearance. After all, she cannot really fall on
Ivanov's neck and say, "I love you!" After all, she does not love and
has said as much. To bring her onstage at the end she would have
to be remodeled from the word go. You say that there is not a single
woman and that this shrivels up the ending. I agree. The only women
who could appear at the end and stand up for Ivanov are the two
who really loved him: his mother and the kike girl. But as both of
them are dead, that is out of the question. An orphan he is and an
orphan he shall stay, and to hell with him.

The Bear has gone into a second printing. And you say that I am
not a first-rate dramatist. I've dreamed up for Savina, Davydov, and
the ministers a vaudeville entitled *Thunder and Lightning*. During a
thunderstorm at night I will have the country doctor Davydov drop
in on the old maid Savina. Davydov's teeth will ache, and Savina will
have an insufferable personality. Interesting dialogue, interrupted by
thunder. At the end—I marry them. When I'm all written out, I'll
start to write vaudevilles and live off them. I think I could write a
hundred a year. Vaudeville plots gush up in me like oil in the wells
of Baku. Why can't I give my oil fields to Shcheglov?[. . .]

To A. S. Suvorin, Moscow, December 26, 1888

[. . .] You want me no matter what to unleash Sasha. But *Ivanov* is
unlikely to prove a success. If it is, then as you wish, I shall act
according to your opinion, but, pardon me, I shall let her have it, the
bitch! You say that women love out of compassion, that they marry
out of compassion . . . What about men? I do not like it when realistic novelists slander women, but I dislike it even more when they
hoist woman by the shoulders, as Yuzhin[7] does, and try to show that

7. Pseudonym of Prince Aleksandr Ivanovich Sumbatov (1857–1925), actor and dramatist,
   who tried with little success to get Chekhov's plays staged at the Maly Theater in Moscow.

even if she is worse than man, man is still a lowlife bastard and woman is an angel. Neither women nor men are worth a cent, but man is more intelligent and more just. [. . .]

To A. S. Suvorin, Moscow, December 30, 1888

[. . .] The director[8] considers *Ivanov* a superfluous man, in the Turgenev style; Savina asks, "Why is Ivanov a blackguard?" You write: "You have to add something to Ivanov to make it clear why two women are attracted to him, and why he is a blackguard, and the doctor is a great man." If that's how the three of you have understood me, it means my *Ivanov* is no good at all. I've probably lost my wits and common sense, and written something other than what I intended. If Ivanov comes across as a blackguard or a superfluous man, and the doctor as a great man, if it is not clear why Sarra and Sasha love Ivanov, then evidently the play has not come off, and a production of it is out of the question.

This is how I understand my leading characters. Ivanov is a gentleman, a university man, not remarkable in any way: his nature is easily aroused, hotheaded, powerfully prone to enthusiasm, honest and straightfoward, like most of the educated gentry. He has lived on his estate and served on the rural council. What he has been doing and how he has behaved, what has interested and attracted him can be seen from the following words of his to the doctor (Act One, Scene V): "Don't marry Jewish girls or neurotics or intellectuals . . . don't wage war singlehanded against thousands, don't tilt at windmills, don't batter your head against the wall . . . God forbid you go in for any experimental farming methods, alternative schools, impassioned speeches." This is what he has in his past. Sarra, who has seen his progressive farming and other fads, says of him to the doctor: "Doctor, he is a remarkable man, and I'm sorry you didn't get to know him two or three years ago. Now he's depressed, taciturn, doesn't do anything, but in the past . . . Such splendor!" (Act One, Scene VII). His past is resplendent, as with most cultured Russians. There is not, or there hardly is, a single Russian aristocrat or university man who does not boast of his past. The present is always worse than the past. Why? Because Russian excitability has one specific characteristic: it is quickly replaced by exhaustion. In the heat of the moment, a man, barely off the schoolbench, rushes to take up a burden beyond his strength; all at once tackles the schools, and the peasants, and progressive farming, and the *Messenger of Europe*; makes speeches, writes to the minister, grapples with evil, applauds good; falls in love, not in any old ordinary way, but invariably with

---

8. Fyodor Aleksandrovich Fyodorov-Yurkovsky (1842–1915), actor and stage director of the Alexandra Theater in St. Petersburg.

either a bluestocking, or a psychopath, or a kike girl, or even a prostitute whom he rescues, and so on, and so on . . . But he's barely thirty or thirty-five when he begins to feel tired and bored. He hasn't got a decent moustache yet, but he already says with authority: "Don't get married, my dear fellow . . . Trust my experience." Or "After all, what does Liberalism amount to? Between ourselves, Katkov[9] was often right . . ." He is ready to reject the rural council and progressive farming, and science and love . . . My Ivanov says to the doctor (Act One, Scene V): "You took your degree only last year, my dear friend, you are still young and vigorous, while I am thirty-five. I have a right to advise you . . ." That's the tone these prematurely exhausted people take. Later on, sighing authoritatively, he advises: "Don't you marry in this or that way (see one of the quotations above), but choose something commonplace, gray, with no vivid colors or superfluous sounds . . . Altogether, build your life according to the conventional pattern. The grayer and more monotonous the background, the better . . . The life that I have led, how tiresome it is! . . . ah, how tiresome!"

Sensing physical exhaustion and boredom, he does not undertand what is the matter with him, and what has happened. In a panic, he says to the doctor (Act One, scene III): "Here you tell me she is going to die and I feel neither love nor pity, but a sort of emptiness, weariness . . . If one looks at me from outside it probably must be horrible, I myself don't understand what is happening to my soul . . ." Having fallen into such a situation, shallow and unconscientious people generally throw the whole blame on their environment, or characterize themselves as superfluous men and Hamlets and take comfort in that. But Ivanov, a straightforward man, openly states to the doctor and to the audience that he does not understand himself. "I don't understand, I don't understand . . ." That he really doesn't understand can be seen from his long soliloquy in Act Three, where, tête-à-tête with the audience and making a confession to it, he even weeps!

The change that has taken place within him offends his sense of propriety. He looks for the causes outside himself and fails to find them; he begins to look for them inside and finds only a vague feeling of guilt. It is a Russian feeling. A Russian—whether there's a death in the family, or someone's fallen ill, or he owes money or lends it to someone—always feels guilty. Ivanov talks all the time about being to blame in some way, and the feeling of guilt increases in him with every jolt. In Act One, he says, "Suppose I am terribly to blame, yet my thoughts are in a tangle, my soul is fettered to some kind of sloth, and I am incapable of understanding myself . . ." In Act Three, he

---

9. Mikhail Nikiforovich Katkov (1818–1887), an influential reactionary journalist who opposed the reforms of the 1860s.

says to Sasha, "My conscience aches day and night, I feel that I am profoundly to blame, but just how I have done wrong I do not understand."

To exhaustion, boredom, and the feeling of guilt, add one more enemy. This is loneliness. Were Ivanov a civil servant, an actor, a priest, a professor, he would have grown used to his situation. But he lives on his estate. He is in the country. Other people are either drunkards or card addicts, or the same as the doctor . . . None of them cares about his feelings or the change in him. He is lonely. Long winters, long evenings, an empty garden, empty rooms, the grouchy Count, the ailing wife . . . He has nowhere to go. This is why he is tortured every minute by the question: where is he to turn?

Now the fifth enemy. Ivanov is tired, does not understand himself, but life has nothing to do with that! It makes its legitimate demands upon him, and whether he will nor no, he must solve problems. His sick wife is a problem, his heap of debts is a problem, Sasha flinging herself at him is a problem. The way in which he solves all these problems must be evident from his monologue in Act Three, and from the contents of the last two acts. Men like Ivanov do not solve problems, but instead collapse under their weight. They lose their heads, wave their arms, get nervous, complain, do silly things, and finally, giving rein to their flabby, undisciplined nerves, lose the ground under their feet and enter the ranks of the "brokendown" and "misunderstood."

Disappointment, apathy, flabby nerves, and exhaustion appear to be the inevitable consequences of extreme excitability, and such excitability is characteristic of our young people to a great degree. Take literature. Take the present day . . . Socialism is one of the forms of this excitement. But where is it? [. . .] Where is Liberalism? [. . .] And what are all the Russian enthusiasms worth? The war has wearied us, Bulgaria[1] has wearied us to the point of irony. Zucchi[2] has wearied us and so has comic opera.

Being overtired (Dr. Bertenson[3] will confirm this too) is expressed not only in complaining or the sensation of boredom. The life of an overtired man cannot be represented like this: ~~~~~~~~~~~~~/. It is very uneven. Overtired people never lose the capacity for becoming extremely excited, but not for very long, and each excitement is followed by still greater apathy . . . Graphically, it could be depicted like this:

---

1. Russia and Bulgaria were involved in a diplomatic conflict over an invitation to a German prince to occupy the Bulgarian throne.
2. The Imperial Ballet created a scandal by refusing to renew the contract of the dancer Virginia Zucchi.
3. Lyov Bertonson, a popular St. Petersburg physician.

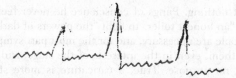

The decline, as you see, does not follow an inclined plane, but takes a somewhat different course. Sasha declares her love. Ivanov cries out in ecstasy, "A new life!", and next morning he believes in this life as little as he does in fairies (the monologue in Act Three); his wife insults him, he is beside himself with anger, he gets worked up and flings a cruel insult at her. He is called a scoundrel. If this doesn't kill his flabby brain, it arouses him and he passes sentence on himself.

Not to tire you out altogether, I move to Dr. Lvov. He is the type of an honest, straightforward, hotheaded but narrowminded and inflexible man. Clever people say of such men, "He's a fool, but his feelings are honorable." Anything like breadth of outlook or spontaneous feeling is foreign to Lvov. He is platitudes personified, tendentiousness on two legs. He peers through a narrow frame at every phenomenon or individual, he judges everything according to preconceived notions. Someone who shouts, "Make way for honest labor!" he worships; anyone who doesn't is a bastard and a moneygrubber. There is no middle ground. He has been brought up on Mikhailov's novels[4]; at the theater he has seen on the stage "new men," i.e., moneygrubbers and sons of our age, painted by modern playwrights. [. . .] He has reeled this in on his moustache, but wound it so tightly that when he reads *Rudin*,[5] he is sure to be asking himself, "Is Rudin a bastard or not?" Literature and the stage have so conditioned him that he approaches every character in real life and in fiction with this question. [. . . .] It is not enough that all men are sinners. You must provide him with saints and bastards!

He was prejudiced before he came to the district. He at once classified all the well-off peasants as moneygrubbers, and Ivanov, whom he could not understand, immediately as a bastard. The man has a sick wife and he goes to see a rich neighbor-lady—well, he must be a bastard! It is obvious that he is killing his wife in order to marry a rich girl . . .

Lvov is honest, direct, and deals straight from the shoulder, not counting the cost. If necessary, he will throw a bomb under a coach, punch a school inspector in the kisser, or call a man a bastard. He

4. The pseudonym of Aleksandr Konstantinovich Sheller (1838–1900), author of many ideologically progressive novels popular in the 1870s and 1880s.
5. The leading character in Turgenev's novel of that name, a young man whose idealism is expressed in rhetoric rather than action.

will stop at nothing. Pangs of conscience he never feels—it is his mission as "an honest toiler" to fight "the powers of darkness"!

Such people are necessary, and for the most part sympathetic. To caricature them, even in the interests of the stage, is dishonorable and serves no purpose. True, a caricature is more striking, and therefore easier to understand, but it is better to leave the sketch unfinished than to lay it on with a trowel . . .

Now about the women. What's the reason they love? Sarra loves Ivanov because he is a good man, because he's fiery, brilliant, and speaks as passionately as Lvov (Act One, Scene VII). She loves him while he is exciting and interesting; but when he begins to grow misty in her eyes, and his sharply-defined profile blurs, she ceases to understand him, and by the end of Act Three she speaks out plainly and sharply.

Sasha is a young woman shaped in the latest mould. She is well-educated, intelligent, honest, and so on. When you're out of fish, even a shrimp counts as a fish, so she favors Ivanov in spite of his being thirty-five. He is better than anyone else. She knew him when she was a child and saw his activism close at hand, in the period before he was worn out. He is a friend of her father's.

What we have here is a female who is won not by the bright plumage of the males, not by their agility, their courage, but by their complaints, whining, failures. She is the sort of woman who loves a man in the period of his decline. No sooner has Ivanov lost heart when the young lady is there on cue. That's just what she was waiting for. For goodness' sake, she now has such a gratifying, sacred mission! She will raise up the fallen one, set him on his feet, make him happy . . . It is not Ivanov she loves, but this mission. D'Argenton in Daudet's book[6] said, "Life is not a novel!" Sasha does not know this. She does not know that for Ivanov love is only an unwelcome complication, one more stab in the back. And what comes of it? Sasha contends with Ivanov for a whole year and, instead of being uplifted, he keeps sinking lower and lower.

My fingers ache, I'll finish up . . . If all of this is not in the play, there can be no question of producing it. It seems that I did not write what I wished. Take it off the boards. I do not want to preach heresy on the stage. If the audience leaves the theater with the conviction that Ivanovs are scoundrels and that Doctor Lvovs are great men, then I'll have to give up and fling my pen to the devil. You won't get anywhere with revisions and insertions. No revisions can knock a great man off his pedestal, and no insertions can change a scoundrel into an ordinary sinful mortal. You may bring Sasha on the stage at the end, but to Ivanov and Lvov I can add nothing more. I simply

6. D'Argenton is a vapid and melancholic poet and schoolteacher in Alphonse Daudet's mildly Dickensian novel *Jack* (1876).

don't know how. And if I should add anything, it will spoil the effect still more. Trust in my intuition; it is an author's, you know.

[. . .] Frankly speaking, what tempted me about the production of the play was neither fame nor Savina . . . I was counting on earning about a thousand rubles. But it is better to borrow this thousand than risk doing something stupid.

Don't tempt me with success! Success in my case, provided I don't die, still lies ahead. I'll bet that, sooner or later, I shall fleece the management to the tune of six or seven thousand. Want to bet?

On no account will Kiselevsky give up playing the count! As if my play didn't give him enough grief in Moscow! He went around everywhere and complained that they were forcing him to play such a sonofabitch as my count. Why should I give him more grief?

They say, it's awkward: he's already played it . . . But then why should it be easy to give Ivanov to Sazonov or Dalmatov? After all, Davydov has already played Ivanov!

[. . .] In my character sketch of Ivanov, I often dropped the word "Russian." Don't let it annoy you. When I was writing the play, I had in mind only the things that really matter—that is, only typically Russian traits. Thus, the deep-seated excitability, the feeling of guilt, the proneness to exhaustion are purely Russian.

Germans never get excited, and that is why Germany knows nothing of disappointed, superfluous, or overtired people . . . The excitability of the French is always maintained at one and the same level, and makes no sudden leaps or drops, and so a Frenchman is normally excitable down to a decrepit old age. In other words, the French do not have to waste their energy in overenthusiasm; they spend their powers sensibly, and do not go bankrupt.

Be it understood that in the play I did not use such terms as Russian, excitability, overtired, etc., in full expectation that the reader and spectator would be attentive and have no need of such signs as "This ain't no punkin, it's a plum." I tried to express myself simply, did not try to be clever, and was far from suspecting that the readers and spectators would label my characters with a phrase, focus on the dialogue about the dowry, etc.

I don't know how to write a play. Of course, it's a pity. Ivanov and Lvov appear to my imagination to be living people. I tell you sincerely, in all conscience, these men were born in my head, not out of sea foam, not out of "cogitation," not by accident. They are the result of observing and studying life. They exist in my brain, and I feel that I have not falsified the truth one centimeter or exaggerated it one iota. If on paper they have not come out clear and living, the fault lies not in them but my inability to express my thoughts. It means it's too soon for me to take up playwriting.

To I. L. Leontyev (Shcheglov), Moscow, December 31, 1888

[. . .] The director of your theater Fyodorov-Yurkovsky has stated a desire to stage my *Ivanov* at his benefit with Strepetova and Savina. This is, of course, flattering to me and I am pleased and gratified. Evidently, even Potekhin wants to be nice to me and prove to you for the 1001th time, that I'm not Chekhov but Potyomkin.[7] The play is already cast, but . . . but the production is unlikely to take place. I am so worried about the defects in my play and these defects are so important that I cannot in all conscience be indifferent. Today I sent a letter in which I listed a few conditions; if in the opinion of those to whom I wrote, my play fails to satisfy only one of those conditions, then I have seriously asked that my play be withdrawn. You will agree, my dear fellow, that a play, which in the eyes of all St. Pete is to be promoted ahead of plays by Mey[8] and Victor Hugo (*Hernani*)[9] has to be exceptional; I agree, and you will understand that I am not putting on airs and acting the coquette. I am doing what you and Suvorin and any man who was the slightest degree touchy and who rarely writes plays would do in my place.

But the defects in my play are irreparable. It's not just I who sees them, but also persons in whom I fully trust and whose competence I rate higher than my own. Wait 'til I write another play, but don't waste time on *Ivanov*. [. . .]

To A. N. Pleshcheev, Moscow, January 2, 1889

[. . .] It makes absolutely no difference to me when you publish the play: July and even if you don't publish it—I don't like it. The later you publish it the better—closer to the season. Besides, I have a malicious intention: when my *Ivanov* flops in St. Pete, I'll read a paper at the Literary Society about how not to write a play, and I shall read excerpts from my play on the characteristics of my leading characters, whom I, no matter what, consider to be novel in Russian literature and still untreated by anyone else. The play is bad, but the characters are alive and not contrived.

That's why I feel that *Ivanov* won't succeed. I'm flattered and touched that the director wants to stage it, but the production does not promise me anything good. I sent to St. Pete my sincere opinion of the play, listed conditions which it has to satisfy and which, so I hear, it does not satisfy; if this opinion of mine is not foolish and is taken into consideration, the play won't go on. [. . .]

7. Leontyev jokingly called Chekhov *Potyomkin*, after Catherine the Great's favorite and prime minister, because of his literary successes.
8. Lyov Aleksandrovich Mey (1822–1862), poet and author of historical dramas.
9. The great success of Hugo's romantic tragedy at the Maly Theater was due to the acting of Aleksandr Lensky as Ruy Gomez de Silva and Mariya Yermolova as Dona Sol.

To A. S. Suvorin, Moscow, January 3, 1889

[. . .] Let Arabinova[1] play Babakina, Svobodin play Shabelsky, Apollonsky[2] play Doctor Lvov. I agree and thank you.

Davydov wants to play Lebedev? I'd be delighted. But then who is to play Ivanov, if Sazonov is occupied?

[. . .] Of course, I'm not my own enemy and I want my play to succeed. But, to tell you a secret, I don't like my play and I'm sorry that it was written by me and not by some more intelligent and rational person. [. . .]

To V. N. Davydov, Moscow, January 4, 1889

[. . .] My deceased Ivanov, as you know, has been exhumed from the grave and is again exposed to the experts. When the higher powers demanded that I cast the roles, then I, obedient to your will, which you expressed in one of our last chats, wrote that Ivanov is definitely to be played by you. Yesterday I got a telegram from Suvorin, in which Aleksey Sergeevich informs me that, so he's heard, you want to play Lebedev. Your every wish in the realm of *Ivanov* is for me a law. If you were to agree to assume two or three roles at once, all there would for me to do would be rejoice for the sake of my play. Therefore—there is still plenty of time to make whatever changes you might like. If in fact you wish to play Lebedev, do write to me. In my casting I assigned Lebedev to Mr. Varlamov—you advised me to do so. Because Mr. Varlamov, probably, is still uninformed about this, I don't think it will create any awkwardness, if I decide to grant your wish.

But who will play Ivanov then? Mr. Sazonov, they say, is busy with another play. [. . .]

To A. S. Suvorin, Moscow, January 4, 1889

I am sending you for transmission to Fyodorov two insertions and one revision. If my play drags on an extra half-hour, print this letter so that everyone knows whose fault it is. It's your fault! If it weren't for you, there'd be no insertions.

Advise me what Fyodorov-Yurkovsky's first name and patronymic are; I shall stop bothering you and send my corrections straight to the address of the party responsible for the happy event. Tell him that there will be more corrections and insertions, but only if they send me a copy of my play. I have no Act Four, almost no Two, and

1. Antonina Ivanovna Arabinova (1842–1901), actress who specialized in playing elderly society ladies.
2. Roman Borisovich Apollonsky (1864–1928), romantic leading man at the Alexandra Theater, whose Treplyov at the premiere of *The Seagull* was so hackneyed as to evoke laughter in the most dramatic passages.

a piece of Three. Ask in such a way that the corrections I sent will
be taken into consideration when the roles are copied out. I am
sending them to the censor not now, but ten to fifteen along with
those revisions which I still intend to commit. I am definitely despoil-
ing this play of its virginity!

Ask them to print on the posters that the author is not to be called
before the curtain at the end of the play. Three acts will go smoothly,
but four will be its undoing. [. . .]

To A. S. Suvorin, Moscow, January 7, 1889

[. . .] I sent you two variants for my *Ivanov* today. If an agile, energetic actor were to play Ivanov, I would have added and changed a
lot of things. And I would have had a free hand. But alas! Davydov
plays Ivanov. This means that one must write more concisely and
more drably, bearing in mind that all halftones and "nuances" will
be smeared into one gray blur and be boring. Can Davydov be tender
at times, furious at others? When he plays serious parts it is as if a
grindstone were in his throat—a monotonous, creaky one, that acts
instead of him . . . I pity poor Savina that she has to play sallow
Sasha. For Savina I'd be glad to help with all my heart, but as long
as Ivanov keeps on mumbling, no matter how I polish up Sasha,
nothing I do will work. I am just ashamed that Savina must play such
a hell of a mess. Had I known in time that she would play Sasha and
Davydov Ivanov, I would have named my play *Sasha* and constructed
the entire work on this basis, and shunted Ivanov to a siding; but
who knew?

Ivanov has two long monologues that are crucial to the play: one
in Act three; the other in Act four . . . The first needs to be sung, the
second delivered ferociously. Both the one and the other are impossible for Davydov. He will deliver both of them "ingeniously," that
is, with infinite flabbiness.

[. . .] I have been cherishing the bold dream of summing up all
that has hitherto been written about whining, despondent people,
and with my *Ivanov* putting an end to such writing. It seemed to me
that all Russian novelists and playwrights felt an obligation to depict
depressed people, and that they all wrote instinctively, having no
definite images or views on the subject. As far as my concept goes I
was pretty much on the right track, but the execution isn't worth a
good goddam. I ought to have waited! [. . .] Besides an abundance
of material and talent, one needs something else no less important.
One needs maturity—in the first place; and in the second, a *feeling
of personal freedom* is essential, and that feeling has only recently
begun to develop in me. Earlier I didn't have it; its place was suc-

cessfully filled by my frivolity, carelessness, and lack of respect for my work.

What writers of gentle birth take from nature for free, commoners purchase at the cost of their youth. How about writing a story, about how a young man, the son of a serf, a former shop clerk, a chorister, a high-school pupil and university student, brought up to respect rank, to kiss the hands of priests, to truckle to the ideas of others, who gave thanks for every crust of bread, was frequently whipped, went out to give lessons without his galoshes, got into fistfights, tortured animals, loved dining with rich relatives, was hypocritical to God and man for no good reason, solely out of an awareness of his own insignificance—write how this young man squeezes the slave out of himself, drop by drop, and how, on waking one fine morning, he feels that the blood coursing through his veins is no longer that of a slave but that of a real human being. [. . .]

To F. A. Fyodorov-Yurkovsky, Moscow, January 8, 1889

M. G. Savina has agreed to play Sasha in my play, yet the role of Sahsa is extremely bland and offers scant material for acting. When I wrote it one and a half years ago, I attached no special importance to it. Now, in view of the honor that M. G. is bestowing on my play, I have decided to refashion this role in a fundamental way and in places I have already refashioned it as powerfully as the framework of the play allows. I ask you earnestly not to rush the copying-out of the roles and *as soon as* possible to send me a copy of my play. The role for Act Three is almost ready now, I can do it for Act Four, only when I have the play in hand. You will receive all the corrections and variants two days after I have received the play. So, if I get the copy by the fifteenth, you will get the corrections no later than the seventeenth. But I should like to have a copy of play before the fifteenth.

All the corrections and variants will be submitted to the censor in good time. You can rest assured about this. I won't delay. [. . .]

To A. S. Suvorin, Moscow, January 8, 1889

[. . .] I'm waiting for a copy of my play. I wrote Fyodorov a flattering letter with the request to hurry up and send the play. Otherwise a great deal will go uncorrected. Know what? In my Act Three, Sasha is spinning like a top—that's how much I changed it! Entirely for Savina. Tell Savina that I am so flattered that she has agreed to take a bland and ungratifying role in my play, so flattered that I'll roll up my sleeves and change the role in a fundamental way, so far as the framework of the plays allows. Savina in my play will spin like a top, and jump on a sofa, and recite monologues. To keep the audience from being bored by whining, I have depicted in one scene a merry, guffawing, sprightly Ivanov, and with him a merry Sasha . . . This isn't pointless, is it? I think I'm on the right track . . . But how hard it is to be careful! I write, but I tremble at every word, so as not to spoil the figure of Ivanov.

Let's write a second play in the summer! Now that we've had experience. We've grasped the devil by the tail. [. . .] Only you mustn't write plays in the winter, not amidst conversations, not under the influence of city air, but in the summer, when everything urban and wintery looks laughable and unimportant. In summer authors are free and objective. Never write a play in the winter; do not write a single line for the theater, if it isn't a thousand miles away from you. [. . .]

To A. N. Pleshcheev, Moscow, January 15, 1889

I am writing you after serving my term of hard labor. Oh, why did you approve my *Ivanov* in committee? What brainless demons put it into Fyodorov's head to choose my play for his benefit performance? I am tortured to death, and no fee can make up for the convict-like stress I suffered all last week. I never used to attach any importance to my play and regarded it with condescending irony; it was written, forsooth, and to hell with it. But now that unexpectedly and suddenly it's back in business, I realized what a scrappy job it was. The last act is particularly bad. All week long I've been tinkering with the play, scribbling revisions, corrections, insertions, fashioned a new Sasha (for Savina), changed Act Four beyond recognition, polished up Ivanov himself, and was so tortured to death and started my play to such a degree, that I was ready it end it with the line from *Kean*, "Give Ivanov the stick, the stick!"[3]

[. . .] To compose a good play for the theater, you must have a special talent (one can be a splendid novelist and at the same time write plays like a shoemaker), but to compose a bad play and then attempt to make a good one out of it, to try all kinds of hocus-pocus, cross out, write in, insert monologues, resurrect the dead, bury the living—for this you must have much greater talent. This is as difficult as buying an old pair of military pants and trying, at all costs, to turn them into a swallowtail coat. [. . .]

---

3. A line from Alexandre Dumas *père*'s play *Kean*, about the English tragic actor: "The stick, give Kean the stick." On the Russian stage it was a popular vehicle for romantic leading men.

To M. P. Chekhov,[4] Petersburg, end of January 1889

[. . .] The actors are playing badly, and nothing will come of the play; with that pest Davydov I quarrel and make up ten times a day. It's tiresome. There absolutely nothing to be done. The play won't go on more than four times: the game's not worth the candle. There's no reason for Masha to come here.

To D. T. Savelyev,[5] Moscow, February 4, 1889

[. . .] My play had an enormous success, and I returned crowned with laurels. You can learn the details from New Times. [. . .]

To A. S. Suvorin, Moscow, February 4, 1889

[. . .] Maslov calls actors buffoons and lowlifes. That's because they seldom perform his plays. After actors performed my Ivanov, they all seemed to be members of my family. They were as close to me as patients I was treating or those children I used to teach. I cannot forget that Strepetova[6] wept after Act Three and that all the actors were milling about with joy, like shadows; I cannot forget a great deal, even though earlier even I was cruel enough to agree that it is not respectable for a man of letters to walk down the street arm-in-arm with an actor and nod to the fans. To hell with aristocratic feeling if it tells lies. [. . .]

To A. S. Suvorin, Moscow, February 6, 1889

Your idea about moving the lines about slander from one place to another came too late; I approve of it, but I cannot use it. The only thing I can do for the theater at the present time is to receive the fee for my play, for anything else I feel too glutted. To refashion, organize, write a new play now is as lacking in appeal for me as soup after a rich dinner. The future, when I take on The Wood Goblin[7] and vaudevilles, looks to me to be far in the distance.

The point you used to puncture my vanity as an author I accept with indifference. You are right. In my letter, Ivanov is probably clearer than on the stage. This is because a fourth of Ivanov's lines were censored. I would gladly offer half of my success to be allowed to make my play twice as boring. The public extols the theater as a

4. Mikhail Pavlovich Chekhov (1865–1936), the dramatist's youngest brother, who left many memoirs of Anton.
5. Dmitry Timofeevich Savelyev (1857–1909), physician, a schoolmate of Chekhov's from high school and university.
6. Pelageya Antipyevna Strepetova (1850–1903), noted for her moving performances of suffering Russian women; she played Sarra in Ivanov.
7. The Wood Goblin, a play Chekhov intended to write in collaboration with Suvorin but eventually composed himself alone. It was performed unsuccessfully in October 1889.

school. If it is not being hypocritical, then let it put up with boredom. Schools, after all, are no fun.

[. . .] Incidentally, how the gutter press worries my *Ivanov*! Wherever you look he is not so much Ivanov as Boulanger.[8] [. . .]

To A. S. Suvorin, Moscow, February 8, 1889

[. . .] You think I shouldn't have regarded Ivanov as "ready." Please imagine that you are the author of my play, so that instinct will hint to you how wrong you are. [. . .] The outlines of my Ivanov are accurately drawn, he is begun in the proper way—my intuition does not intuit anything phony; the halftones got blurred, and because of that the shading is bad. Your suspicions concern the outlines.

Women are not needed in my play. My chief concern was to keep the females from obscuring the center of gravity, which is located outside them. If I succeeded in making them beautiful, I would count my mission in their regard absolutely achieved. Women have been involved in the downfall of Ivanov . . . Well, what of that? Must this involvement really be cleared up at length, when it is well understood and has been treated so thoroughly a thousand times before me?

Concerning *Ivanov*, I receive anonymous and un-anonymous letters. Some socialist (I assume) gets indignant in his anonymous letter and sends me a bitter reproach; he writes that after my play some young person will perish, that my play is harmful and so on. All the letters interpret *Ivanov* the same way. Obviously, they have understood, which makes me very happy. [. . .]

To A. N. Pleshcheev, Moscow, February 11, 1889

[. . .] Of course, I take much less money for a play than for prose. I set the price when I know the size of the play. The longer it is, the less I take per page. I have never published a play and don't know the prices. If you were to give me advice—what sort of price to set, so that no one is offended—I would be very grateful to you. Name a figure. [. . .]

To A. S. Suvorin, Moscow, February 14, 1889

[. . .] I got a letter from Svobodin, full of complaints about his working conditions and colleagues. The letter is long and sincere. I replied to him at length that the dissatisfaction arises only from the fundamental attributes of all real talent, and, maliciously, with my characteristic hypocrisy, requested him to be forever dissatisfied. I am very sorry that at the present time Russian writers never take the

8. See *The Wedding*, note 3, page 104.

time to write and Russian readers never take the time to read about actors, otherwise it would be a good thing to stir up their emotions. So far our novelists are interested only in bohemian actors, but haven't wanted to know those actors who have legitimate families, live in very respectable drawing rooms, read, criticize, but—the most important thing—earn a bigger salary than a governor. Davydov and Svobodin are very, very interesting. Both talented, intelligent, sensitive, and both unquestionably innovative. Their domestic life is extremely appealing. [. . .]

The whole mob is planning to come to St. Pete in Shrovetide to see *Ivanov*, but the Shrovetide schedule has spoiled the whole picnic. When should we come if *Ivanov* is put on for the last time at a Wednesday matinee? That's why my sister can't come; her boarding school doesn't let out until Wednesday. [. . .]

To A. S. Suvorin, Moscow, February 14, 1888

[. . .] Davydov and Svobodin are extremely interesting. Both of them are talented, intelligent, high-strung, and both are undoubtedly original [. . .]

To M. V. Kiselyova, Moscow, February 17, 1889

[. . .] My *Ivanov* continues to have a colossal, phenomenal success. In St. Pete now there are two heroes of the day: Semiradsky's naked Phryne[9] and my fully-dressed self. Both are making a stir. But for all that how bored I am and how glad I would be to fly to dear old Babkino! [. . .]

To I. L. Leontyev (Shcheglov), February 1889,

[. . .] In your letter, you console me for *Ivanov*. Thank you, but I assure you on my word of honor, I am calm and completely satisfied with what I've done and got. I have done what I could and knew how to do—therefore, it's true: you don't have eyes on the top of your head; I didn't get what I deserved, but more than was necessary. Even Shakespeare didn't manage to hear such speeches as I had to listen to. What the hell use is this to me? And if there are a hundred people in St. Pete who shrug their shoulders, smirk scornfully, cast aspersions, fling mud or lie hypocritically, I actually don't see any of this and don't let it bother me. In Moscow, you can't even smell Petersburg. Every day I see a hundred people, but don't hear a single word about *Ivanov*, just as if I hadn't written the play, and the St. Pete ovations and success seem to me an unsettling dream, from which I have had a healthy awakening. [. . .]

9. Semiradsky's painting of the courtesan "Phryne at the Festival of Poseidon at Eleusis" had a great success when exhibited in January 1889 at the Academy of Arts in Petersburg.

To N. A. Leikin, Moscow, February 21, 1889

Ivanov, sold with *The Bear*, has earned me a thousand or a bit under a thousand rubles. And I'm going to get about two or three hundred from the Society of Dramatic Authors. It's profitable to write plays, but it's unsettling to be a dramatist and not in my nature. I don't care about ovations, backstage panics, successes and failures, and I have a lazy soul and can't stand abrupt rises and falls in temperature. A smooth and even career as a writer of fiction looks to me to be much more appealing and soothing. That's why it's hardly likely I shall turn into a decent dramatist. [. . .]

To Al. P. Chekhov, Moscow, February 21, 1889

[. . .] The season is over. Go to Suvorin's and ask him how to get the money from the theatre managements. He will explain it to you. When you get the explanation, go to the management and demand the money for *Ivanov* and *The Bear*. If they won't hand it over or they cheat, tell them that you will appeal to the commercial middleman Bykov. Wire me the money, and then send the accounting by post. You should get around a thousand in cash. I want you to drop dead from black envy or else to be compelled by jealousy to sit down and write a play, which isn't hard to do. You ought to write a couple of plays. It will profit the children. A play is a pension.

This spring I shall collect the money from all my sources in order to buy a farm in the summer—a place, where the Chekhov family can practice domestic intimacy. [. . .]

To Al. P. Chekhov, Moscow, March 2, 1889

Man!

I got the money—994 rubles and thank you for not embezzling it. Next season, when I earn 3444 rubles for a new play, I'll send you to the management to pick up that sum with nothing less than a military escort—it's more reassuring, otherwise I'd be worrying the whole time. [. . .]

To A. S. Suvorin, Moscow, March 5, 1889

[. . .] Svobodin dropped by and said, among other things, that you allegedly had a letter from some parent whose son had shot himself after my *Ivanov*. If this letter isn't a myth, send it to me, please. I will add it to those letters which I've already got concerning my *Ivanov*. I haven't read *The Citizen*, for 1. I don't get that newspaper and 2. I am so dreadfully sick and tired of *Ivanov*; I cannot read about it and I get quite beside myself when people start discussing it wittily and cleverly. [. . .]

To I. M. Kondratyev,[1] March 6, 1889

A slight error has crept into the account which I received yesterday. My *Bear* was performed at Korsh's eighteen times, but in the account it is listed as seventeen times. This error has occurred, probably, because *The Bear* was performed once at Korsh's instead of Turgenev's *Evening in Sorrento* and was not advertised on the playbill. [. . .]

To V. A. Tikhonov, Moscow, March 7, 1889

[. . .] I am not writing a play and won't write one soon, for I have neither plots nor enthusiasm. In order to write for the theater, one must love the work, and without love nothing that makes sense will result. When there's no love, even success won't flatter you. Starting next season, I shall visit the theater regularly and educate myself in stage ways. [. . .]

To N. A. Leikin, Moscow, April 10, 1889

[. . .] Bilibin[2] wrote me that he read somewhere that I'm supposed to be going to Kiev to stage my *Ivanov* there. Yes, all I need is to gallop from town to town staging my plays. They sickened me even in the capitals. [. . .]

To Al. P. Chekhov, Moscow, April 11, 1889

[. . .] My advice: in a play try to be original and as intelligent as possible, but don't be afraid to look like a fool; you need to be a free-thinker, but only the kind of free-thinker who isn't afraid to write nonsense. Don't lick everything clean, don't polish it up, but be clumsy and audacious. Brevity is the sister of talent. Remember, by the way, that love scenes, wives and husbands cheating on one another, widows, orphans and all the rest of the tearjerking have long since been described. The topic [*syuzhet*] has to be a new one, but a plot [*fabula*] isn't necessary [. . .]

To V. A. Tikhonov, Sumy, May 31, 1889

[. . .] I was starting a comedy, but wrote two acts and gave it up. It came out boring. There's nothing more boring than a boring play, but now, it would seem, I am capable of writing only boring stuff, so it's better to give it up.

1. Ivan Maksimovich Kondratyev (1841–1924), secretary to the Society for Russian Dramatic Authors and Opera Composers, to whom Chekhov often applied concerning his performance royalties.
2. Viktor Viktorovich Bilibin (1859–1908), a humorist and journalist, was an expert at writing one-act farces.

To I. L. Leontyev (Shcheglov), Moscow, September 18, 1889

A whole revolution has broken out over my vaudevilles. *The Proposal* was going on at Goreva's—I took it out of the repertory; on account of *The Bear*, Korsh and Abramova[3] are at loggerheads: the former pointlessly proves his exclusive rights to this play, while Abramova's Solovtsov says that *The Bear* belongs to him, because he's already played it 1817 times. The devil himself couldn't sort it out! The Maly Theater is offended, because *Ivanov* is going on at Korsh's, and Lensky[4] so far still hasn't paid me a call—I suppose he's angry. Woe unto you, Messrs. Theater People!

To A. N. Pleshcheev, Moscow, September 24, 1889

[. . .] Everyone tells me and writes to me that I should write a play. The Maly Theater actors pass a motion that I should write one without fail. Ah, if only there were time! A good play wouldn't get written, but it would be enough to make a little bit of money. [. . .]

To A. S. Suvorin, Moscow, November 25, 1889

[. . .] Sazonov plays vilely in *The Bear*. It's easy to understand. Actors never observe ordinary people. They don't know landowners or merchants or priests or civil servants. On the other hand, they are excellent at portraying billiard hustlers, kept women, haggard cardsharps—in general, all those individuals whom they accidently observe as they stagger their way through taverns and bachelor parties. The ignorance is appalling. [. . .]

To A. N. Sumbatov-Yuzhin, Moscow, December 14, 1889

I am sending you the play [*The Wedding*], that we've already discussed. Yesterday I got it from the censor, read it over, and now I find that after *Macbeth*, when the audience is keyed up to the Shakespearean pitch, this play will risk seeming outrageous. Truly, after splendid Shakespearean villains, watching the petty, shoddy riffraff that I depict is quite unappetizing.[5]

Read it. I don't think it will be to Fedotova's[6] taste. [. . .]

3. Yelizaveta Nikolaevna Goreva (1859–1917), actress who in 1889 opened her own theater in Moscow. Mariya Moritsevna Abramova (Geynrikh, 1865–1892), actress who opened a theater in Moscow in 1889, where she put on the first production of Chekhov's *The Wood Goblin*.
4. Aleksandr Pavlovich Lensky (Vervitsiotti, 1847–1908), actor at the Maly Theater and close friend of Chekhov; best in classical roles, he never performed in a Chekhov play.
5. It had been proposed that *The Wedding* be played as an afterpiece to *Macbeth* at the Maly Theater at a benefit performance for Glikeriya Fedotova.
6. Glikeriya Nikolaevna Fedotova (1846–1925), one of Russia's greatest actresses, was beloved in comic and pathetic roles at the Moscow Maly Theater.

To the Chekhovs, Naples, April 7 (19), 1891

[. . .] All summer, Messrs. Gentry, we will have no money, and the thought of this spoils my appetite. For the trip, which *solo* I should have completed for three hundred rubles, I have gone into debt for a thousand. All my hopes lie in the idiotic amateurs who will perform my *Bear*. [. . .]

To A. S. Suvorin, Bogimovo, August 30, 1891

[. . .] I shall go to Moscow, collect from the Society about 150–200 rubles for *The Bear*, that's how God provides for our fellow man the loafer. [. . .]

To A. S. Suvorin, Melikhovo,[7] June 4, 1892

[. . .] I have an interesting subject for a comedy, but I have not yet thought of an ending. Anyone who invents new endings for plays will open a new era. The lousy endings won't come! The hero either marries or shoots himself, there is no other way out. My comedy-to-be is called *The Cigar Case*. I won't start to write it until I think up an ending as ingenious as the beginning. And when I do come up with the ending, I shall write it in two weeks. [. . .]

To V. V. Bilibin, Moscow, January 18, 1895

[. . .] I am not writing a play and, altogether, I have no inclination to write any. I am grown old, and I have lost my burning ardor. I should like to write a novel a hundred miles long. When your play is ready, write me—do you need any pull with Korsh? [. . .]

To A. S. Suvorin, Melikhovo, May 5, 1895

[. . .] If what you write about the play is serious, I am glad and shall come without fail in order to attend rehearsals along with you. Then I too will write a play especially designed for your circle, where you staged *Hannele*,[8] and where, maybe, you will put me on, if my play is not too bad. I will write something strange. For the State and for money I have no desire to write. For the time being I am comfortable, and can afford to write a play for which I shall get nothing; if circumstances alter, then, of course, it'll be a different tune [. . .]

---

7. In 1891, Chekhov bought the farmstead of Melikhovo, fifty miles south of Moscow, where he settled his parents and siblings, planted a cherry orchard, and set about humanitarian reforms.

8. Gerhardt Hauptmann's dream play *Hannele's Ascension* was presented at Suvorin's Theater of the Literary-Artistic Circle in St. Petersburg. This letter might include the first mention of *The Seagull*.

To A. S. Suvorin, Melikhovo, October 21, 1895

[. . .] Can you imagine? I am writing a play which I shall probably not finish before the end of November. I am writing it not without pleasure, though I swear horribly at the conventions of the stage. A comedy, three women's parts, six men's, four acts, a landscape (view of a lake); a great deal of conversation about literature, little action, five tons of love. [. . .]

To A. S. Suvorin, Moscow, November 2, 1895

[. . .] Why don't you try to stage Maeterlinck[9] in your theater? If I were the manager of your theater, in two years I would have made it decadent or tried to do so. The theater, perhaps, would look strange, but all the same it would have a distinct profile.

And why don't you stage Zola's plays? After all, his *Thérèse Raquin*[1] is very acceptable play. [. . .]

To A. S. Suvorin, Moscow, November 10, 1895

[. . .] My play is moving forward; meanwhile everything's going swimmingly, but what is to come, towards the end, I know not. I'll finish in November. Pchelnikov,[2] through Nemirovich,[3] has promised to give me an advance in January (if the play is found suitable), so they must be considering a postponement of the play's production until the following season. It must be because of the play that my pulse is more frequently intermittent; I fall asleep at a late hour and, in general, feel wretched, although since my return from Moscow I have been leading a life of moderation in all respects. [. . .]

To I. L. Leontiev (Shcheglov), November 14, 1895

[. . .] Can you imagine? I'm writing a play! I'm finishing it now. A comedy in four acts. I shall try to have it staged at the Moscow Maly Theater, but it's God's will! [. . .]

---

9. Maurice Maeterlinck (1862–1949), Belgian dramatist of mystical, symbolist plays. Suvorin followed Chekhov's advice and staged *La Princesse lointaine*.
1. As a naturalist, Emile Zola (1850–1902) was at the opposite end of the scale from Maeterlinck; his *Thérèse Raquin* was a study of a relationship disintegrating under the influence of a crime.
2. Pavel Mikhailovich Pchelnikov (1851–1913), business manager of the Moscow Imperial Theaters.
3. Vladimir Ivanovich Nemirovich-Danchenko (1858–1943), playwright and cofounder of the Moscow Art Theater, one of Chekhov's greatest boosters.

To E. M. Shavrova-Yust,[4] Melikhovo, November 18, 1895

[. . .] I have finished a play. It is called *The Seagull*. It turned out not so bad at that. Generally speaking, as a dramatist I'm minor-league. [. . .]

To A. S. Suvorin, Melikhovo, November 21, 1895

Well sir, I have now finished the play. I began it *forte* and ended it *pianissimo*—contrary to all the rules of dramatic art. It has turned into a novella. I am more dissatisfied than satisfied with it, and reading over my newborn play, I am more convinced than ever that I am not a dramatist. The acts are very short, there are four of them. Though it is so far only the skeleton of a play, a blueprint which will be altered a million times before the coming season, I have nevertheless ordered two copies to be typed on a Remington (the machine prints two copies at once)—and I'll send you one. Only don't let anyone else read it [. . .]

To A. S. Suvorin, Moscow, December 13, 1895

[. . .] As far as my playwriting is concerned, it strikes me that I was not cut out to be a playwright. I have no luck. But I am not down-hearted, for I don't stop writing stories—I feel at home in this field, but while writing plays I feel ill at ease, as if something were weighing on my neck.

To A. S. Suvorin, Moscow, December 17, 1895

[. . .] My play [*The Seagull*] is a failure even without being produced If in fact it looks like I've depicted Potapenko[5] in it, of course, it's impossible to stage it or publish it.

To I. N. Potapenko, Melikhovo, August 11, 1896

DEAR IGNATIUS, the play has been despatched. The censor has blue-penciled the passages that he disliked because her brother and her son are indifferent to the actress's love affair with the novelist. On page four I cut the sentence "lives openly with this novelist," and page five "can love only the young." If the changes, which I have made on slips, are accepted, then paste them securely on those passages—and mayest thou be blest for ever and ever and mayest thou behold the sons of thy sons! If these changes are rejected, however,

---

4. Yelena Mikhailovna Shavrova-Yust (1874–1937), a writer influenced by Chekhov.
5. Ignaty Nikolaevich Potapenko (1856–1928), novelist and playwright. Suvorin believed that the character Trigorin was based on Potapenko, and that, in his relations with Nina, Chekhov had portrayed Potapenko's love affair with Liza Mizinova. Certain members of their circle, such as the writer Tatyana Schepkina-Kupernik, did spot the resemblance.

then spit on the play, I don't want to fuss over it anymore, and advise you not to.

On page five in Sorin's lines: "By the way, please tell me what kind of a person is her novelist"—substitute "the" for "her." Instead of the words (same place), "There's no understanding him. He never says anything," it can read, "You know, I don't like him" or whatever you please, even a text from the Talmud.*

That the son disapproves of the love affair is obvious from the tone he takes. On disgraced page 37, he says to his mother, "Why, why has this man come between you and me?" On the same page 37, you may cross out these words of Arkadina: "Of course, our intimacy cannot please you, but . . ." That's all. Check the underlined passages in the blue copy. [. . .]

* or the words "At her age! Oh, oh, isn't it a shame."

To A. S. Suvorin, September 23, 1896

[. . .] After reading your last letter, I settled on the following cast: Treplyov—Apollonsky, Sorin—Pisaryov,[6] Zarechnaya—Savina, the overseer—Varlamov, Masha—Chitau,[7] the novelist Trigorin—Sazonov, the Doctor—Davydov. And who will play the Actress? Dyuzhikova[8] I don't know, never in my born days have I seen her; if you think that the role will suit her, then let her play the Actress, if she chooses. If they listen to Potapenko and hand this role to Levkeeva,[9] then, for heaven's sake, the audience will start to expect this role to be something funny and will be disappointed. After all, Levkeeva enjoys a reputation as a wonderful comic actress, and that reputation can crush the role. But the role of the schoolteacher would benefit from being given to some naturalistic little actor with comic flair. [. . .]

To Ye. P. Karpov, September 29, 1896

If, as you write, Davydov has chosen the role of Sorin, he's got the script in hand. Delighted, let him have Sorin. But who, who will play the doctor? After all, it's the doctor who ends my play! Who will play the actress? The teacher? I am ill-acquainted with the acting troupe

6. Modest Ivanovich Pisaryov (1844–1905), an excellent realistic actor who created the role of Dorn. Many found him more impressive in the role than Vishnevsky, who later played it at the Moscow Art Theater.
7. Maria Mikhailovna Chitau (1860–1935), an actress proficient at comedy, noted for overacting to make an impression.
8. Antonina Mikhailovna Dyuzhikova (1853–1942) began as an ingenue and ended up a *grande dame*, impressive but rhetorical.
9. Yelizaveta Ivanovna Levkeeva (1851–1904), a much-beloved, fat, and mostachioed comic actress. *The Seagull* was staged on her benefit night, so the audience did come expecting something funny.

of the Alexandra Theater and, on my own, without your advice don't know how to cast the play. [. . .]

To Ye. P. Karpov, October 4, 1896

I approve your casting. Give the doctor to Pisaryov. I don't know either Panchin or Petrov:[1] in regard to both I rely on your good judgment and won't put up an argument. As to Masha, the overseer's daughter, I am still wavering. Aleksey Sergeevich has advised me to give this role to Chitau. I saw Chitau a couple of times and I've got nothing against her; but even the thought that Aleksandra Pavlovna[2] might act in my play makes me beam with happiness—and I am already strongly inclined to be unfaithful to Chitau. [. . .]

To M. P. Chekhova,[3] Petersburg, October 12, 1896

[. . .] Meanwhile, *The Seagull* is not very interesting. It's boring in Petersburg, the season doesn't start until November. People are ill-natured, picky, phony. The performance will come off without acclaim, with a dull thud. In general, my mood is so-so. I'll send you money for your trip today or tomorrow, but I advise you not to come. [. . .]

To M. P. Chekhov, Petersburg, October 15, 1896

[. . .] My *Seagull* opens on the seventeenth of October. Kommissarzhevskaya[4] acts amazingly. [. . .]

To A. S. Suvorin, Petersburg, October 18, 1896

[. . .] Stop the printing of my plays. I shall never forget last night, but still I slept well, and am setting off in a very tolerable good humor.

[. . .] I am not going to produce the play in Moscow. I shall *never again* write plays or have them staged.

To M. P. Chekhov, Petersburg, October 18, 1896

The play has fallen flat, and was a resounding flop. In the theater there was an oppressively tense feeling of bewilderment and ignominy. The actors played vilely, stupidly.

1. Aleksandr Semyonovich Panchin (1858–1906), actor specializing in dunces, and Vasily Ivanovich Petrov, a second-string actor at the Alexandra Theater.
2. Aleksandra Pavlovna Nikitina (b.1874), who played comic roles of lower-class young women; she did not appear in *The Seagull*.
3. Mariya Pavlovna Chekhova (1863–1957), the dramatist's sister, who ran his household and, after his death, collected his letters for publication.
4. Vera Fyodorovna Komissarzhevskaya (1864–1910), the greatest actress of pre-Revolutionary Russia.

The moral of it is: one ought not to write plays.

Nevertheless and all the same, I am alive, well, and abide in a state of eupepsia. [. . .]

To A. S. Suvorin, Melikhovo, October 22, 1896

In your last letter (of October 18) you thrice call me an old woman and say that I acted like a coward. Why such defamation of character? After the performance, I had supper at Romanov's,[5] all well and good, then went to bed, slept soundly, and the next day went home, without uttering a single murmur of complaint. If I had acted like a coward, I would have run around to the pressrooms, to the actors, anxiously craved their indulgence, anxiously inserted useless revisions and would have lived in Petersburg another two or three weeks, going to my *Seagull*, getting excited, dripping with cold sweat, complaining . . . When you were with me the night after the performance, didn't you say yourself that the best thing was for me to leave? And the next morning I got a letter from you in which you took your leave of me. What's cowardly about that? I behaved just as rationally and calmly as a man who has made a proposal, been turned down, and who has nothing left to do but leave. Yes, my vanity was wounded, and I was already prepared for that, for I had predicted it in all sincerity.

Once I got home, I took castor oil, washed in cold water—and now I could write a new play. I no longer feel weary and irritated and am not afraid that Davydov and Jean [Shcheglov] will come and talk about the play. I agree with your revisions—and thank you a thousand times. Only, please, don't regret that you weren't at the rehearsals. In fact, there was actually only one rehearsal, at which it was impossible to understand anything; the play was completely obscured by the revolting acting.

I got a telegram from Potapenko: a colossal success. I got a letter from someone I don't know named Veselitskaya (Mikulich), who expresses her commisseration in a tone as if a member of my family had died—it's quite inappropriate. And yet, this is all trivial. [. . .]

To N. I. Korobov,[6] Melikhovo, November 1, 1896

[. . .] My play made a very great noise—in the sense that some say that it's senseless and scold me to beat the band, still others assert that it is a "marvelous" play. I can't figure it out, but I shot out of Petersburg like a bombshell, and I am now receiving a multitude of letters and even telegrams; the mailboxes are stuffed. [. . .]

5. An inn on Obvodny Canal.
6. Nikolay Ivanovich Korobov (1860–1919), a doctor, formerly a fellow medical student who boarded with the Chekhov family.

To V. V. Bilibin, Melikhovo, November 1, 1896

Thanks for the letter. Of course, I'm glad, but all the same the success of the second or third performance cannot eradicate from my mind the impression of the first performance. I did not see all of it, but what I did see was depressing and strange to an extraordinary degree. They didn't know their lines, they acted woodenly, hesitantly, everyone lost heart; even Kommissarzhevskaya, whose acting wasn't too bad, lost heart. And the theater was as hot as hell. It seemed as if all the elements were against the play. But all the same and nevertheless, I can serve as an example for the young: after the performance I had supper at Romanov's, slept out the night soundly, didn't read the reviews the next morning (the newspapers had a villainous look), and at noon scampered off to Moscow. [. . .]

To Ye. M. Shavrova-Yust, Melikhovo, November 1, 1896

If, O honored "One of the Audience," you are writing about the first performance, then allow—oh, allow me! to doubt your sincerity. You hasten to pour healing balm on the author's wounds, supposing that, under the circumstances, that is better and more necessary than sincerity; you are kind, dear Mask, very kind, and it does credit to your heart. At the first performance I did not see it all, but what I did see was dingy, gray, dismal, wooden. I did not cast the play, I was not given new scenery, there were only two rehearsals, the actors did not know their lines—and the result was a general panic, utter loss of heart; even Kommissarzhevskaya's acting was not up to much, although at one of the rehearsals she acted so marvelously that people sitting in the stalls wept, pulled long faces. [. . .]

To Ye. M. Shavrova-Yust, Melikhovo, November 7, 1896

Beautiful Mask, I don't have the right to give permission or not, because I turned over my author's power of attorney to the Society for Dramatic Writers. Let amateurs stage *The Seagull*—but, first of all, far, far, far away from Serpukhov. In that town I would like to be a gentleman of the jury, a chairman of the rural board—a resident, but not a playwright. If *The Seagull* is staged in Serpukhov, I will lose any shred of prestige in the district. Besides, the audience in Serpukhov is such a gray, frumpy, crude, and tasteless sort of thing! It doesn't want a *Seagull* (even the word is unknown to it)—but a jackdaw.[7] [. . .]

---

7. A play on words: seagull is *chaika*; jackdaw is *galka*, but also stands for *Halka,* an opera by Stanisław Moniuszko (1848); Chekhov may have seen announcements of a major revival scheduled for Moscow and St. Peterburg in 1897 with the great tenor Leonid Sobinov.

To A. F. Koni,[8] *Melikhovo, November 11, 1896*

You cannot imagine how your letter cheered me up. I saw only the first two acts of my play from the front, and then I sat backstage and felt the whole time that *The Seagull* was a failure. After the performance, that night and next day, I was assured that I had hatched out nothing but idiots, that my play was clumsy from the theatrical point of view, that it was unintelligent, unintelligible, even senseless, and so on and so forth. You can imagine my position—it was a flop beyond my wildest dreams! I felt ashamed, vexed, and I went away from Petersburg full of all sorts of doubts. I thought that if I had written and staged a play so obviously brimming over with monstrous defects, I had lost all my intuition and that meant that my machinery must have broken down for good. When I got home, they wrote to me from Petersburg that the second and third performances were a success; several letters, some signed, some anonymous, came, praising the play and abusing the critics; I read them with pleasure, but still I felt ashamed and vexed, and the idea came into my head that if kindhearted people thought it was necessary to comfort me, it meant that I was in a bad way. But your letter has acted upon me in a most positive way. I've known you a long time, I deeply respect you, and I believe in you more than in all the critics put together— you felt that when you wrote your letter, and that is why it is so fine and persuasive. I am serene now, and I can recall the play and the performance without loathing.

Kommissarzhevskaya is a wonderful actress. At one of the rehearsals, many people wept as they watched her, and said that she is the best actress in Russia today; but at the first performance she was affected by the general attitude of hostility to my *Seagull*, and was, as it were, intimidated by it and lost her voice. Our press treats her coldly, not as she deserves, and I am sorry for her. [. . .]

To Vl. I. Nemirovich-Danchenko, Melikhovo, November 20, 1896

[. . .] Yes, my *Seagull* was, at the first performance in Petersburg, a colossal failure. The theater breathed malice, the air condensed with hatred, and I—obedient to the laws of physics—shot out of Petersburg like a bombshell. For all this you and Sumbatov are to blame, because it was you who egged me on to write a play. [. . .]

To A. S. Suvorin, Melikhovo, December 2, 1896

[. . .] They're being incredibly slow in printing my plays. They send me the proofs in such tiny doses that there's nothing left but to

8. Anatoly Fyodorovich Koni (1844–1927), distinguished criminologist and lawyer.

accuse the post office. So far I've proofread only *Ivanov* and the vaudevilles; two full-length plays remain to be set up in type: *The Seagull*, which you know, and *Uncle Vanya*, which no one on earth knows. [. . .]

To A. S. Suvorin, Melikhovo, December 7, 1896

Let *Uncle Vanya* be set up first. Can't it be set up in its entirety? When I can read it straight through, it'll be easier to make corrections and then to decide whether it's worth refashioning it into a short story. Oh, why did I write plays and not stories? I've wasted my plots, squandered them quite scandalously and needlessly [. . .]

To A. S. Suvorin, Melikhovo, December 14, 1896

I received your two letters about *Uncle Vanya*—one in Moscow, and the other at home. Not long ago I received another letter from Koni, who saw *The Seagull*. You and Koni gave me in your letters more than one happy moment, but still, my spirits are quite ironclad; I feel nothing but aversion for my plays, and read the proofs only by force of will. You will say again that this is not intelligent, stupid, that it's vanity, pride, etc., etc. I know, but what am I to do? I would gladly free myself of this stupid feeling, but I cannot, cannot. What's wrong is not that my play failed; most of my plays failed in the past, and each time it was like so much water off a duck's back. On October 17 it was not my play that failed, but I myself. [. . .]

To A. S. Suvorin, Melikhovo, January 4, 1897

[. . .] I didn't forget that I promised Anna Ivanovna [Suvorina] to dedicate *The Seagull* to her, but I've refrained from dedicating it on purpose. For me that play is bound up with some of the most unpleasant memories; it disgusts me, and to dedicate it makes no sense and strikes me simply as tactless.

To M. P. Chekhov, Melikhovo, February 4, 1897

[. . .] Of course, the doctor [Astrov] has to be played suavely, nobly, in tune with the words of Sonya, who in Act Two calls him beautiful and refined. [. . .]

To A. S. Suvorin, Nice, March 13(25), 1898

[. . .] You have become attached to the theater, while I am drifting away from it, apparently, further and further—and I am sorry, for the theater once gave me much that was good (also my earnings from it aren't bad at all; this winter my plays were more successful in the

provinces than ever, even *Uncle Vanya*). Formerly, there was no
greater pleasure for me than to sit in the theater; now I am there
with the feeling that someone in the gallery is about to shout "Fire!"
And I do not like actors. My work as a dramatic author spoiled it all
for me. [. . .]

To Vl. I. Nemirovich-Danchenko, Melikhov, May 16, 1898

[. . .] You write, "I'll come before rehearsals start to discuss things
with you." So, do come, please! Come, do me a favor! You can't
imagine how much I want to see you, and for the pleasure of meeting
and talking to you I'm ready to give you all my plays. [. . .]

To I. M. Serikov,[9] Melikhovo, August 13, 1898

[. . .] You may stage *Uncle Vanya* in Serpukhov without my special
permission. As to whether it will be succesful—I really don't know;
I suppose it won't be, because the characters are for the most part
alien and of little interest to the Serpukhov public. In Petersburg
and Kharkov it was successful; maybe you'll do good box office in
Serpukhov too. [. . .]

To P. F. Iordanov, Yalta,[1] September 21, 1898

[. . .] If you happen to be in Moscow, drop by the Hermitage, where
Stanislavsky and Vl. Nemirovich-Danchenko put on plays. The mise-
en-scène is wonderful, unprecedented in Russia. By the way, they're
going to stage my ill-fated *Seagull*. [. . .][2]

To L. S. Mizinova,[3] Yalta, September 21, 1898

[. . .] Nemirovich and Stanislavsky have a very interesting theater
company. Beautiful little actresses. Had I stayed a bit longer, I would
have fallen for them. The older I grow, the more frequently and more
fully the pulse of life beats within me. Make a note of that. [. . .]

To Vl. I. Nemirovich-Danchenko, Yalta, October 21, 1898

[. . .] Write me the how and the what, how the actors responded to
the success of their first performances [of *Tsar Fyodor*], how *The
Seagull*'s getting on, what changes have been made in the casting,
and so on and so forth. Judging by the papers, the opening was bril-

9. Ivan Mitrofanovich Serikov (1867–1939), secretary of the Serpukhov county council.
1. Definitively diagnosed with tuberculosis in 1897, Chekhov had to move to the milder
climate of Yalta, where he lived out the rest of his life, with occasional travel to European
spas.
2. Chekhov attended rehearsals for *The Seagull* in Moscow on September 9 and 11.
3. Lidiya Stakhievna Mizinova (1870–1937), a close friend of Chekhov.

liant—and I'm very, very glad, so glad you can't imagine. This success is yet another extra proof that the audience and the actors need an intellectual theater. [. . .]

To M. P. Chekhov, Yalta, October 26, 1898

[. . .] My *Uncle Vanya* is being performed throughout the provinces[4] and is a success everywhere. So you see, you never know where you'll make it and where you won't. I never put any stock in that play at all. [. . .]

To Vl. I. Nemirovich-Danchenko, November 12, 1898

[. . .] Is Luzhsky[5] really not to play Sorin? You write that you still have not decided about Sorin and Dorn, but it seems to me that Sorin was all right. Vishnevsky[6] would play Dorn wonderfully. [. . .]

To N. M. Yezhov, Yalta, November 21, 1898

[. . .] You ask how I liked *The Seagull* at Nemirovich's. I was at two rehearsals, I liked them. Roksanova[7] isn't at all bad. [. . .]

To A. M. Peshkov (Maksim Gorky),[8] Yalta, December 3, 1898

Your last letter gave me great pleasure.[9] Thank you with all my soul. *Uncle Vanya* was written long ago; I never saw it on the stage. In recent years it has been often produced on the provincial stage—perhaps because I put out a volume of my plays. My attitude toward my plays is, in general, cold; for a long time I have kept away from the theater and I no longer feel like writing for the theater. [. . .]

To M. P. Chekhova, Yalta, December 17, 1898

[. . .] *Uncle Vanya* is being played all over Russia. I think by summer the Society for Dramatic Writers will have collected a thousand

4. It was performed in late 1898 in Pavlovsk, Nizhny Novgorod, Odessa, Saratov, and Kazan.
5. Vasily Vasilyevich Luzhsky (Kaluzhsky, 1869–1931), actor and founding member of the Moscow Art Theater; in Chekhov's plays there he created the roles of Sorin, Professor Serebryakov, Lebedev, and later played Gaev, Simeonov-Pishchik, and Firs.
6. Aleksandr Leonidovich Vishnevsky (Vishnevetsky, 1861–1943), former schoolmate of Chekhov, actor, and founding member of the Moscow Art Theater, where he created the roles of Dorn, Voinitsky, and Kulygin.
7. Mariya Lyudomirovna Roksanova (Petrovskaya, d.1958), briefly with the Moscow Art Theatre, which she left in 1902 to act in the provinces. Her Nina was judged to lack ingenuousness and charm.
8. Aleksey Mikhailovich Peshkov (1868–1936), who became famous as a writer under the name Maksim Gorky.
9. Gorky had written in late November 1898 that he had seen *Uncle Vanya* in Nizhny-Novgorod and "wept like a silly female."

rubles. As I write these lines, *The Seagull* is on in Moscow. How did it go? It's unfortunate that you weren't at the opening performance. [. . .]

To Ye. Z. Konovitser,[1] Yalta, December 26, 1898

[. . .] So my play isn't on?[2] I am unlucky in the theater, terribly unlucky, mortally so, and if I were to marry an actress, we'd probably give birth to an orangutan—such is my luck! [. . .]

To Ye. M. Shavrova-Yust, Yalta, December 26, 1898

[. . .] From Moscow they write and pound the drums to beat the band that *The Seagull* is a success. But because for the most part I am unlucky in the theater, mortally unlucky, one of the actresses fell ill after the first performance—and my *Seagull* isn't on.

I'm so unlucky in the theater, so unlucky, that if I were to marry an actress, we'd probably give birth to an orangutan or a porcupine. [. . .]

To M. P. Chekhova, Yalta, January 18, 1899

[. . .] I've read that the seventh performance of *The Seagull* was played to a packed house. Yelena Mikh[ailovna] Yust wrote that she very much liked Roksanova as the Seagull.

To V. F. Kommissarzhevskaya, Yalta, January 19, 1899

[. . .] My *Seagull* is being repeated for the eighth time in Moscow; the theater is packed every night. They say that the play has been staged unusually well and that the actors know their lines thoroughly. When M. I. Pisaryov came to the end of the play, he'd said a "bottle" had burst in the next room—and the audience laughed; the Moscow actor said that a vial of ether burst—and there was no laughter, it came off properly. Be that as it may, I no longer want to write plays. The Petersburg theater cured me. [. . .]

To I. Ya. Pavlovsky, Yalta, January 21, 1899.[3]

[. . .] *The Seagull* plays in Moscow to full houses. The theater is packed, it's hard to get tickets. This means: virtue is triumphant. [. . .]

1. Yefim Zinovyevich Konovitser, lawyer and publisher of the newspaper *The Courier*, had married Chekhov's former "fiancée" Yevgeniya Éfros.
2. The second performance of *The Seagull* at the Moscow Art Theater was postponed because cast members had influenza. Konovitser had written that the staging was splendid, but the acting unsatisfactory.
3. Ivan Yakovlevich Pavlovsky (1852–1924), journalist for *New Times*, stationed in Paris.

To M. P. Chekhova, Yalta, January 23, 1899

[. . .] Why do they put on *The Seagull* only once a week? After all, it won't be on fifteen times before Lent.[4] [. . .]

To Vl. I. Nemirovich-Danchenko, Yalta, January 29, 1899

[. . .] This is what Yust writes: "*The Seagull* goes even more smoothly and better than at the second performance; although Stanislavsky as Trigorin acts much too limp a literary man both physically and morally, and the Seagull herself (*j'en conviens*)[5] could have been a touch more beautiful in the last act. But on the other hand Arkadina, Treplyov, Masha, Sorin, the schoolteacher (his small-town two-piece suit alone is worth the price of admission!) and the overseer are splendid, really living people . . ." That's a little sample of the reviews I've been receiving. [. . .]

If everyone taking part in *The Seagull* would have their picture taken in makeup and costume, it would be really kind of them! [. . .]

To M. P. Chekhova, Yalta, February 4, 1899

[. . .] I read in *The Courier* that Stanislavsky plays Trigorin as a wet rag. What kind of idiocy is this? After all, Trigorin is charming, attractive; in short, he's interesting, and only an untalented actor devoid of imagination could play him as limp and flabby. [. . .]

To Vl. I. Nemirovich-Danchenko, Yalta, February 8, 1899

[. . .] I write nothing about *Uncle Vanya*, because I don't know what to write. I verbally promised it to the Maly Theater, and now it's rather awkward for me. It would seem as if I were doing an end run around the Maly Theater. Kindly inquire as to whether the Maly Theater is inclined to stage *Uncle Vanya* next season. If not, then, of course, I will announce this play is *porto franco*;[6] if it is, then I'll write another play for the Art Theater. Don't be offended: discussions about *Uncle Vanya* have been going on with the Maly Theater folks for a long time; and this year I got a letter from A. I. Urusov,[7] who informs me that he had talked it over with A. I. Yuzhin and so on and so on. [. . .]

4. Russian theaters were legally compelled to close during Lent.
5. French, I agree.
6. Italian, an open port; figuratively, available to anyone.
7. Prince Aleksandr Nikolaevich Urusov (1848–1900), lawyer and literary critic, a zealous enthusiast for Chekhov's plays.

To M. P. Chekhova, Yalta, February 19, 1899

[. . .] I've just received a letter from Kondratyev of the Maly Theater they're asking for *Uncle Vanya*. Of course, I'll reply favorably. As to Nemirovich, if he takes offense, I'll write a another play for him, and that'll be that. [. . .]

To M. P. Chekhova, Yalta, March 29, 1899

[. . .] As to *Uncle Vanya*, I will write nothing or telegraph; because, first, I don't know where to telegraph to: the committee's address is unknown to me; second, they don't answer my letters—I've written to Nemirovich a thousand times; and third, it's all made me horribly sick and tired, to the point of stupefaction. In general, I repeat, I'm fed up with it all; I will no longer stage plays anywhere for anyone. And I won't write to anybody.

To K. M. Ilovaiskaya,[8] Moscow, April 27, 1899

[. . .] I have not seen my play, nor will I see it, but on the other hand every day I'm visited by the actors who perform it (the "Sea-gullians") and I've even had a group photo taken with them. [. . .]

To A. M. Peshkov (Maksim Gorky), Melikhovo, May 9, 1899

[. . .] I saw *Seagull* without any scenery; I can't judge the play in cold blood, because the Seagull performed so abominably, she blub-bered loudly, and Trigorin (the novelist) walked around the stage and talked like a paralytic; he has no "will of his own," and the actor interpreted this in a way that nauseated me to behold.[9] But on the whole it wasn't bad, quite gripping. There were moments when I found it hard to believe I had written it. [. . .]

To I. M. Kondratyev, Melikhovo, May 9, 1899

Be so kind as to arrange to send me the royalties for my play to this address: Lopasnya, Moscow gub. Incidentally, let me inform you that I've given my *Uncle Vanya* to Vl. Iv. Nemirovich-Danchenko for the Art and Accessible Theater[1] (1899–1900 season). [. . .]

---

8. Kapitolina Mikhailovna Ilovaiskaya, a landowner who had met Chekhov in Yalta.
9. Nina was played by Mariya Roksanova and Trigorin by Stanislavsky.
1. The original name of the Moscow Art Theater. "Accessible" (at popular prices, open to the lower classes) had to be dropped when the city refused to give the theater a subvention or the necessary license.

To P. F. Iordanov,[2] Melikhovo, May 15, 1899

[. . .] They performed my *Seagull* for me at the Moscow Art Theater. The production is marvelous. If you like, I will insist that the Art Theater visit Taganrog next spring, when it tours to the south in toto, with full company, scenery, and so on and so on. The Maly Theater has turned pale, and when it comes to mise en scène and staging, even the Meiningers[3] don't come up to the Art Theater, who are performing meanwhile in a wretched building. By the way, Vishnevsky is acting in *The Seagull*, our Taganrog Vishnevetsky, who drives me to distraction with his continual remembrances of Kramsakov, Osvyannikov[4] and so on. All the participants in *The Seagull* had their picture taken with me; an interesting group resulted.

To P. I. Kurkin,[5] Moscow, May 24, 1899

The Art Theater is putting on my *Uncle Vanya;* in the third act they need a survey map. Be so kind as to pick out a suitable one and lend it or promise to donate a suitable one, when you find one among those you don't need. [. . .]

To G. M. Chekhov,[6] Melikhovo, June 2, 1899

[. . .] In winter, the Art Theater will put on *Uncle Vanya*. I've seen two acts in rehearsal; it's going wonderfully [. . .]

To Vl. I. Nemirovich-Danchenko, Melikhovo, June 16, 1899

[. . .] My plays are not on sale, not a single copy, but we shall soon print and issue them, probably around August. I met with Marks.[7] My proposal is to print the plays and in general to publish them with the Art Theater mise en scène—he evidently was delighted, as if he'd been waiting a long time for that. He said that he will publish the plays with the scenery, makeup, complete mise en scène and so on and so on, and will sell them cheaply. I planned to meet with Alekseev[8] in Tarasovka twice: at the end of May—then the cold didn't let

2. Pavel Fyodorovich Iordanov (1858–1920), municipal sanitary inspector in Taganrog, with whom Chekhov helped organize a town library.
3. The acting troupe of the Duke of Saxe-Meiningen, which had visited Russia in 1885 and 1890; it was famous for its carefully drilled crowd scenes and picturesque groupings. Stanislavsky took notes on their special effects.
4. Ivan Fyodorovich Kramsakov, Chekhov's math and geography teacher in Taganrog. Yegor Andreevich Ovsyannikov, Chekhov's writing and drawing master.
5. Pyotr Ivanovich Kurkin (1858–1934), a physician. See *Uncle Vanya*, note 5, page 221.
6. Georgy Mitrofanovich Chekhov (1870–1943), the dramatist's cousin, who lived in Taganrog.
7. Adolf Fyodorovich Marks (1838–1934), a publisher who specialized in collected editions of popular authors; in 1902, he bought the rights to all of Chekhov's works.
8. Konstantin Sergeevich Alekseev, known as Stanislavsky (1863–1938), a wealthy industrialist and amateur actor-director, who, with Nemirovich-Danchenko, founded the Moscow Art Theater in 1898, where he directed the first Moscow revival of *The Seagull*.

up, and around June 10, but the rain didn't let up. And now Alekseev has probably already left. If I knew exactly where he is, I would write to him. If you find the needful, write to him about publishing the plays; let him devise a format. It seems to me that it wouldn't hurt to speed up this process. [. . .][9]

To Ye. P. Karpov, Yalta, September 22, 1899

I am sending you *Uncle Vanya* by registered mail. I am very, very sorry that, because of the great distance, I cannot meet with you and talk, and I cannot attend even a single rehearsal. I should like Sonya to be taken by V. F. Kommissarzhevskaya, Astrov by Samoilov,[1] if he is working for you. They say that in the provinces Samoilov has played Astrov. If he is not with you, then give this role to Mr. Ge.[2] Voinitsky, that is, Uncle Vanya, Gorev[3] will play beautifully, the Professor—N. F. Sazonov, Telegin—V. N. Davydov. [. . .]

To O. L. Knipper,[4] Yalta, September 30, 1899

At your command, I hasten to answer your letter in which you ask me about Astrov's last scene with Yelena. You write that Astrov addresses Yelena in that scene like the most passionate lover, "clutches at his feeling like a drowning man at a straw." But that's not right, not right at all! Astrov likes Yelena, she captivates him by her beauty; but in the last act he already knows that nothing will come of it, that Yelena is vanishing from him forever—and he talks to her in that scene in the same tone as about the heat in Africa, and kisses her quite casually, with nothing better to do. If Astrov carries on that scene tempestuously, the whole mood of the fourth act—quiet and despondent—will be lost [. . .]

To Ye. P. Karpov, Yalta, October 4, 1899

If Davydov takes the role of Uncle Vanya, I shall be delighted. He will give a beautiful performance. Sazonov's playing Astrov I accede to enthusiastically. But whom will you give the Professor to? Gorev? Lensky? The roles of Yelena Andreevna and Mariya Vasilyevna give to whomever you like; I only ask that Yelena Andreevna be younger

9. This project foundered on the need to pay Marks for the reproduction of photographs.
1. Pavel Vasilyevich Samoilov (1866–1931), an important provincial actor, later played Astrov and Treplyov.
2. Grigory Grigorevich Ge (1867–1942), an actor at the Alexandra Theater, specialized in playing villains in tragedies and melodramas.
3. Fyodor Ivanovich Gorev (1850–1910), a highly temperamental actor, tried to stage *Uncle Vanya* at the Alexandra Theater for his benefit but was prevented by Chekhov.
4. Olga Leonardovna Knipper (1870–1959), an actress at the Moscow Art Theater, played Arkadina, Yelena, Masha, Ranevskaya, and Sarra there; she met Chekhov in 1898 and married him in 1901.

and warmer; I would prefer Pototskaya to play her, rather than Michurina.[5] Savina won't take it, because it's a minor role. [. . .]

To A. L. Vishnevsky, Yalta, October 8, 1899

[. . .] The play we talked about at Malaya Dmitrovska still doesn't exist and probably won't be written any time soon. I set to work on it twice and gave it up because it didn't come out as it should. Explain to Glikeriya Nikolaevna [Fedotova] that if a year or, at least, half a year ago I had known that she needed a play for her benefit, that play would by now be ready; good or bad—I don't know, but it would be ready. You know how deeply I respect Glikeriya Nikolaevna; I would have considered her participation in my play a great honor, and my author's vanity would have been fully satisfied. So, no play, but the future lies before us, and the only thing left to do is put our trust in the future. [. . .]

How annoying and bitter it is for me that I cannot be with all of you, that both rehearsals and performances pass me by for no good reason, and I am acquainted with them only by hearsay, while all I need is to attend rehearsals in order to be cheered up, gain experience and sit down to work on a new play.

[. . .] Roksanova is playing the Seagull? You wrote nothing about how The Seagull went, how Trigorin was, etc. [. . .]

To P. I. Kurkin, Yalta, November 2, 1899

[. . .] I got letters from Moscow from the actors of Uncle Vanya. They are in despair that they got overexcited, overacted, got nervous. They expected a furor and wound up with an average success—and this upsets young actors. I've worked now for twenty-one years and I know that an average success is the most beneficial success for a writer and a performer. After a big success there always comes a reaction, expressed in heightened expectations and then in certain disappointment and cooling off—a reaction, easy to explain physiologically. [. . .]

To Vl. I. Nemirovich-Danchenko, Yalta, November 24, 1899

[. . .] I am not writing a play. I have a plot for Three Sisters, but I shall not set to work on the play until I have finished the stories I have long had on my mind. Next season, I will have to go on with my play—this is already decided.

5. Mariya Aleksandrovna Pototskaya (1869–1938), an actress at Korsh's theater, who played both Kommissarzhevskya's roles and light comedy. Vera Arkadyevna Micherina-Samoilova (1860–1948), an actress at the Alexandra Theater, was noted for her subtle style but lack of lyricism and freshness.

[. . .] The Art Theater forms the best pages of that book which someday will be written about the contemporary Russian theater. That Theater is your pride and joy, and it is the only theater that I love, although I have not yet set foot in it. Had I lived in Moscow, I would have tried to become a part of your management, if only in the capacity of a watchman, in order to be of even some little help, and, if possible, to prevent you from cooling towards this beloved institution. [. . .]

To Ye. P. Karpov, Yalta, November 27, 1899

I have a big favor to ask of you. Is it possible to postpone *Uncle Vanya* until next season, when, in all probability, I'll be in Petersburg? There's no reason to rush, the thing isn't a bear, and the forest isn't going away. [. . .]

To Vl. I. Nemirovich-Danchenko, Yalta, December 3, 1899

[. . .] An answer arrived from Karpov. He agrees to postpone the production of *U.V.* to next year (or, more accurately, next season). Now it remains for you to act on "legal" grounds, as good lawyers put it. The play belongs to you; you will get on with it, and I will pretend that I am powerless to struggle with you because I have already given you the play . . .

[. . .] You want a play for next season without fail. But what if it doesn't get written? Of course I'll try, but I can't guarantee it and will make you no promise. However, let's talk about it after Easter, when, if Vishnevsky and the papers are to be believed, your theater will be in Yalta. Then we'll talk it over.

[. . .] Yes, you're right, for Petersburg you have to refashion Alekseev's Trigorin at least a little bit. Inject some sperm in him or something. In Petersburg, where most of our novelists live, Alekseev's playing Trigorin as a hopeless impotent will provoke general bewilderment. My memories of Alekseev's acting are so depressing that I cannot separate them from him; I cannot believe that Alekseev is good in *Uncle Vanya*, although everyone unanimously writes that he is in fact good, even very good. [. . .]

To Vl. I. Nemirovich-Danchenko, Yalta, March 10, 1900

I got a letter from Gorev: he wants to put on *Uncle Vanya* for his farewell benefit. I wrote him that I'd be delighted, but the play belongs to the Moscow Art Theater, and that if this theater doesn't give up its intention to perform it in Petersburg now or next season, it cannot be put on on the State stage.

[. . .] Am I writing a new play? It's pecking its way out from the shell, but I haven't started to write it, I don't feel like it, and besides we should wait until the weather is warm. [. . .]

To Ye. P. Karpov, Yalta, April 20, 1900

[. . .] I talked to Vl. I. Nemirovich-Danchenko about *Uncle Vanya* and he asserts that I gave him this play over two years ago, not only for Moscow alone, but in general. If the Art Theater is to be in Petersburg at some time, I do not know, but if it is, my play will be put on no more than a couple of times—and afterwards, peace and quiet will prevail. As you see, I have no luck with my plays; in the last analysis it behooves me to acknowledge this and submit. Having turned over my plays to the Art Theater, I in no case presupposed that it would be in Petersburg at some time; it never came into my head. Be that as it may, I ask forgiveness, dear Yevtikhy Pavlovich, and leniency towards my involuntary errors, perhaps, for the reason that I have been living at a distance from the capitals and the people with whom I work for three years now.

I wish you all the best. If Nemirovich-Danchenko changes his plans, I shall immediately inform you.

To O. L. Knipper, Yalta, August 14, 1900

[. . .] I am writing not a play but some kind of maze. Lots of characters—it may be that I shall lose my way and give up writing. [. . .]

To O. L. Knipper, Yalta, August 20, 1900

[. . .] The play has begun well, it seems, but I have cooled to that beginning, it struck me as vulgar—and now I don't know what to do. After all, you have to write a play without stopping, without stopping to take a breath, but this morning—this is the first morning I've been alone, when I haven't been interrupted. Well, it doesn't matter, anyhow. [. . .]

To O. L. Knipper, Yalta, August 23, 1900

[. . .] I'm writing the play, but I'm afraid that it will turn out to be boring. I'll go on writing and, if I don't like it, I'll put it aside, hide it away 'til next year or such time as I'm in the mood to write again. One season will pass without a play of mine—that's no disaster. [. . .]

To O. L. Knipper, Yalta, August 30, 1900

[. . .] I'm not writing to you, because wait, I'm writing the play. Although it's turning out to be rather boring, but, it seems, not so bad, intelligent. I am writing slowly—it's beyond expectation. If the play doesn't come off as it should, then I'll put it aside 'til next year. But all the same, one way or another, I'll finish it now [. . .]

To A. L. Vishnevsky, Yalta, September 5, 1900

[. . .] I am writing a play; I've already written a good deal of it, but until I am in Moscow, I cannot judge it. Perhaps it won't turn out to be a play at all, but boring Crimean rubbish. It is called *Three Sisters* (as you already know); I am preparing the part of the high-school inspector, husband of one of the sisters, for you. You will wear a uniform frockcoat with a medal 'round your neck.

If the play doesn't go into production this season, I'll refashion it for the next. [. . .]

To O. L. Knipper, Yalta, September 5, 1900

[. . .] The whole time I was sitting on the play, thinking more than writing, but all the same I feel as I'm occupied with something and haven't time for letters now. I am writing the play but I am not hurrying, and it is very possible that I shall leave for Moscow without having finished it; there are a great many characters, it is crowded, I'm afraid it will turn out obscure or pallid, so I think it may be better to put it off 'til next season. By the way, *Ivanov* was the only one I allowed to be produced at Korsh's immediately after it was written; all the other plays I kept by me for a long time, waiting for Vladimir Ivanovich, and that way I had a chance to insert all kinds of corrections. [. . .]

To M. P. Chekhova, Yalta, September 9, 1900

[. . .] *Three Sisters* is very difficult to write, more difficult than the earlier plays. Oh well, it doesn't matter; perhaps something will come of it, next season if not this. It's very hard to write in Yalta, by the way; I am interrupted, and it always seems as if I were writing to no purpose, and what I wrote yesterday I don't like today. [. . .]

To Yu. O. Gryunberg,[6] September 13, 1900

My play, about which you write, *Three Sisters*, is barely begun; when it will be finished I cannot say precisely. Be that as it may, I will publish it only after a series of emendations, i.e., after it has appeared on stage, and that will probably be no earlier than Christmas.

6. Yuly Osipovich Gryunberg (1853–1900), chief comptroller of the publisher A. F. Marks and the journal *Cornfields*.

Besides, before it goes into an anthology, it will be published in a magazine, to which I've promised it. [. . .]

To O. L. Knipper, Yalta, September 15, 1900

[. . .] As for my play, it'll be done sooner or later, in September, or October, or even November, but whether I decide to have it staged this season—I'm not sure, my wee lassie. I can't decide because, first, perhaps the play isn't ready yet—let it lie on my desk for a while; and, second, it's absolutely necessary that I attend the rehearsals, absolutely! I can't leave four major female roles, four educated young women, up to Alekseev, for all my respect for his talent and insight. I have to keep at least one eye on the rehearsals. [. . .]

To O. L. Knipper, Yalta, September 28, 1900

[. . .] I'm of the opinion that your theater should stage nothing but modern plays, nothing but! You have to deal with modern life, the same one that's lived by cultivated people and that has had no treatment in other theaters, because of their complete lack of culture and, to some degree, lack of talent. [. . .]

Ah, what a role you have in *Three Sisters*! What a role! If you give me ten rubles, you'll get the role, otherwise we'll give it to another actress. We won't put on *Three Sisters* this season, let the play lie about a bit, stew in its own juice, or, as merchant's wives say about pies, when they put them on the table—let it breathe . . . [. . .]

To A. P. Peshkov (Maksim Gorky), Yalta, October 16, 1900

[. . .] Can you imagine? I have written a play. But because it won't open right now, but only next season, I have not made a fair copy of it yet. Let it lie as it is. It was awfully difficult to write *Three Sisters*. After all, three heroines: each has to be her own type, and all three daughters of a general! The action takes place in a provincial town, somewhere like Perm, the milieu is military, artillery. [. . .]

To V. F. Kommissarzhevskaya, Moscow, November 13, 1900

[. . .] The *Three Sisters* are already completed, but their future, at least their immmediate one, is veiled from me by the obscurity of ignorance.[7] The play turned out boring, slow-paced, awkward; I say awkward because, for instance, it has four female leads and its atmosphere, as they call it, is gloomier than gloom.

Your actors would very, very much dislike it, if I were to send it to

---

7. A jokey quotation from some literary source, which Chekhov later puts in the mouth of Lopakhin in *The Cherry Orchard*.

them at the Alexandra Theater. All the same, I guess I'll send it to you. Read it and decide whether it's worth taking it on tour this summer. It is now being read at the Art Theater (there is only one copy—no more), later I'll take it and make a fair copy again, and only then shall we print a few copies, one of which I shall hasten to send you. [. . .]

To O. L. Knipper, Nice, 15 December (28), 1900

[. . .] I am copying out my play and am filled with wonder that I could write this joke, What did I write it for? [. . .]

[. . .] [T]hen, when I get home, I'll start to make a fair copy—and tomorrow I'll send Nemirovich Act Three, and the day after Four—or both together. In Act Three, I changed something, added something, but very little. [. . .]

To O. L. Knipper, Nice, December 17 (30), 1900

[. . .] Yesterday sent Act Three of the play to Moscow, and tomorrow will send Four. In Three, I changed only a little here and there, but in Four I went in for drastic changes. I added lots of lines for you. [. . .]

To Vl. I. Nemirovich-Danchenko, Nice, December 18 (31), 1900

[. . .] In Act Three the last words uttered by Solyony are: (*Looking at* TUSENBACH.) "Cheep, cheep, cheep . . ."

It's to be added, please. [. . .]

To O. L. Knipper, Nice, December 21, 1900 (January 3, 1901)

[. . .] The play is finished now and sent off. For you, especially in Act Four, I added a great deal. You see, I spare nothing on your behalf, but keep on striving. [. . .]

To O. L. Knipper, Nice, December 28, 1900 (January 10, 1901)

[. . .] And I was in such a hurry with the last act, I thought you needed it. It appears that you will not start rehearsing it before Nemirovich's return from abroad. And if I'd had this act on hand for a few more days, it would probably have turned out juicier. [. . .]

To O. L. Knipper, Nice, December 30, 1900 (January 12, 1901)

[. . .] Have you already left the house and gone to rehearsals? Are you familiar with those rewrites I put into Acts Three and Four? Are you familiar with Act Two? Do you have fair copies of your roles? Or are you reading from the old scripts? Vishnevsky wrote that Solyony is to be played by Sanin, and Vershinin by Kachalov.[8] The latter won't be bad, and if Sanin doesn't overdo the rudeness, he'll be right on target. [. . .]

To K. S. Alekseev (Stanislavsky), Nice, January 2 (15), 1901

[. . .] As for that old play Three Sisters, it is not to be read at the countess's soiree under any circumstances or in any form.[9] I implore, for the sake of the author, don't read it in any way, shape or form; otherwise, you will cause me no little chagrin.

I sent off Act Four long ago, before Christmas, addressed to Vladimir Ivanovich. I've inserted many changes. You write that in Act Three, Natasha, making the rounds of the house at night, puts out the lights and looks under the furniture for burglars. But, it seems to me, it would be better to have her walk across the stage in a straight line, without a glance at anyone or anything, à la Lady Macbeth, with a candle—something a bit tighter and more frightening. [. . .]

To O. L. Knipper, Nice, January 2 (15), 1901

[. . .] Do describe at least one rehearsal of Three Sisters. Does anything need to be put in or taken out? Are you acting well, my darling? Uh-oh, be careful! Don't pull a sorrowful face in any of the acts. Angry, yes, but not sorrowful. People who go about with inner sorrow a long time and are used to it only whistle and often grow pensive. So you may every so often grow pensive on the stage in the course of the dialogue. Do you understand?

Of course you understand, because you are clever. [. . .]

To A. A. Vishnevsky, Nice, January 6 (18), 1901

[. . .] You wear the tailcoat only in Act One; as to the bandolier (a polished black strap) you are quite right. At least until Act Four you should wear the uniform such as it was before 1900 [. . .]

To O. L. Knipper, Nice, January 14 (27), 1901

[. . .] Dear actress, I'm worried. First, you wrote that you're sick, and, second, I've read in the Russian News that Uncle Vanya has

8. Aleksandr Akimovich Sanin (Shenberg, 1869–1955), an Art Theater actor, rehearsed the role of Solyony but never played it. Vasily Ivanovich Kachalov (Shverubovich, 1875–1948) joined the Art Theater in 1900 and rapidly became its leading man; in Chekhov's plays, he created the role of Trofimov and played Tusenbach and Ivanov, later taking on Vershinin.
9. Stanislavsky had asked Chekhov to veto a proposal to have Three Sisters read at a charity soiree at Countess Sofiya Tolstoya's.

been taken off. Why, why do you act if you are actually sick? [. . .] Why don't you write anything about *Three Sisters*? How is the play going? You only wrote about Sanin and Meyerhold,[1] but you've nothing at all about the play in general, and I suspect that my play is already a failure. And when I met with Nemirovich-Danchenko here and talked with him, I became very bored and it seemed that the play was bound to fail and that I will write nothing more for the Art Theater. [. . .]

To I. A. Tikhomirov,[2] Nice, January 14 (27), 1901

[. . .] Here are the answers to your questions: 1. Irina does not know that Tusenbach is off to fight a duel, but she surmises that something untoward happened the day before, which might have serious and therefore evil consequences. And whenever a woman surmises, she says, "I knew it, I knew it."

2. Chebutykin sings only the words, "A fig for you and tell me how you like it . . ." They're the words from an operetta that was once put on at the Hermitage. I don't remember the name; you could find out, if you wanted, from the architect Shekhtel. [. . .] Chebutykin shouldn't sing any more than that, otherwise his exit will take too long.

3. Actually, Solyony does think that he looks like Lermontov; but of course he doesn't—it's ridiculous just to think of . . . He should be made up to look like Lermontov. The resemblance to Lermontov is enormous, but only in Solyony's mind. [. . .]

To K. S. Alekseev (Stanislavsky), Nice, January 15 (28), 1901

[. . .] Of course, you're a thousand times right, Tusenbach's body should certainly not be shown; I felt that myself when I was wrote and told you about it, if you recall. That the ending is reminiscent of *Uncle Vanya* is a minor problem. After all, *Uncle Vanya* is a play of mine, not somebody else's, and when your work is reminiscent of yourself, people say that's the way it ought to be. The line "take this fig and tell me how you like it" should be sung, not spoken, by Chebutykin. It's from an operetta, but which one I can't remember, even if you were to kill me [. . .]

---

1. Vsevolod Yemilyevich Meyerhold (1874–1940), actor and director, a charter member of the Art Theater. He created the roles of Treplyov and Tusenbach there. He and Chekhov admired one another and shared a distrust of the Art Theater's approach.
2. Iosafat Aleksandrovich Tikhomirov (1872–1908), actor and director at the Art Theater; in Chekhov's plays, he played Medvedenko and Ferapont.

To A. L. Vishnevsky, Nice, January 17 (30), 1901

[. . .] In Act Three, of course, you can appear in a double-breasted uniform tunic, that's right; but why in Act Two should you come into the drawing room in a fur coat? Why? However, maybe, it will work that way. You know best [. . .]

To O. L. Knipper, Nice, January 17 (30), 1901

[. . .] Of course, the third act has to be played quietly onstage, so that one can feel that the people are exhausted, they're dropping with sleep [. . .] What's all this about noise? It should be coming from backstage, where the bells are ringing.

To O. L. Knipper, Nice, January 20 (February 2), 1901

[. . .] Well, how is *Three Sisters* going? Judging by your letters, you are all engaging in stuff and nonsense. In Act Three there's noise? . . . Why noise? The noise is only in the distance, backstage, a muffled noise, faint, but here onstage everyone is worn out, almost asleep . . . If you ruin Act Three, the play will flop, and I will be hissed in my old age. Alekseev in his letters praises you highly and Vishnevsky as well. Although I haven't seen it, I'll praise you too. Vershinin pronounces "trom-tom-tom" in the form of a question, and you in the form of an answer, and this strikes you as such an original joke that you pronounce this "trom-trom" with a grin . . . She *would* utter "trom-trom"—and begin to laugh, but not loudly, just barely. You mustn't create the same kind of character as in *Uncle Vanya* at this point, but someone younger and livelier. Remember that you're easily amused, angered. Well, I put my trust in you, my darling, you're a good actress.

I said even back then that it would be inconvenient to carry Tusenbach's body across your stage, but Alekseev insisted that he couldn't do without a corpse. I wrote to him that they are not to carry the corpse, I don't know whether he got my letter [. . .]

To O. L. Knipper, Nice, January 21 (February 3), 1901

Masha's confession in Act Three is not exactly a confession, but only a frank statement. Behave nervously but not despondently, no shouting, even smiling now and then and for the most part behave so that one can feel the weariness of the night. And so that one can feel that you are more intelligent than your sisters, you think yourself more intelligent, at least. As to "trom-tom-tom," do it your own way. You are smarter than I am [. . .]

To O. L. Knipper, Nice, January 24 (February 6), 1901

[. . .] I got your news that in Act Three, you lead Irina by the arm
. . . Why is that? Does this really suit your mood? You shouldn't
abandon the sofa. And can't Irina get there by herself ? What sort of
news is this? What's the news? The colonel[3] sent me a long letter,
complaining about Fedotik, Rodé, and Solyony; he complains about
Vershinin, about his immorality; goodness gracious, he's seduced
another man's wife! I think, however, that this colonel has done what
I asked him to, i.e., the military men will be dressed like military
men. He greatly praises the three sisters and Natasha, by the way.
He even praises Tusenbach. [. . .]

To O. L. Knipper, Yalta, March 1, 1901

[. . .] Personally, I am giving up the theater altogether; I will never
write for the theatre again. One can write for the theater in Germany,
in Sweden, even in Spain, but not in Russia, where dramatists get
no respect, are kicked by hooves, and forgiven neither success nor
failure. You are abused now for the first time in your life, that is why
you take it so hard; yet you will get over it in time, you will get used
to it. [. . .]

To M. P. Chekhov, Yalta, March 5, 1901

What my Ivanov says to Doctor Lvov is said by a worn-out, haggard
man: on the contrary, a man must constantly if not crawl out, then
peep out of his shell, and he must grapple with ideas all his life,
otherwise it's not a life, but an existence [. . .]

To O. L. Knipper, Yalta, March 7, 1901

[. . .] I got a letter from Petersburg from Kondakov,[4] the academi-
cian. He was at *Three Sisters*—and his enthusiasm is indescribable.
[. . .] Today I had a long telegram from Solovtsov in Kiev about a
performance of *Three Sisters*, an enormous, frantic success, and so
on. The next play I write will definitely be funny, very funny, at least
in concept. [. . .]

To G. M. Chekhov, Yalta, March 8, 1901

[. . .] *Three Sisters* is having an enormous success, but only because
there are three good, young actresses, and actors who know how to
wear military uniforms. I didn't write the play for the provinces.

---

3. Chekhov had asked V. A. Petrov to tutor the actors in military deportment, but he went
   beyond the call of duty to comment on the acting and staging in general.
4. Nikodim Pavlovich Kondakov (1844–1925), a scholar of Byzantine art who lived in Yalta.

To O. L. Knipper, Yalta, April 22, 1901

[. . .] Today I was sent a review of *Three Sisters* from the *Revue Blanche*. [. . .]

At moments, the most powerful feeling comes over me to write a four-act vaudeville or a comedy for the Art Theater. And I will write it, if nothing prevents me; only we won't hand it over to the theater until the end of 1903.

To L. V. Sredin,[5] Moscow, September 24, 1901

[. . .] *The Wild Duck*[6] on the stage of the Art Theater is not up to snuff, it seems. Flabby, uninteresting, and weak. On the other hand, *Three Sisters* is going splendidly, brilliantly, much better than the play text. I took a slight hand in the directing, made a few author's suggestions,[7] and the play, they say, now goes better than last season. [. . .]

To O. L. Knipper, Yalta, November 9, 1901

[. . .] Roksanova has acted in *The Seagull* again? Wasn't the play removed from the repertory until they got a new actress? And now suddenly it's Roksanova again! What a revolting way to behave! In the repertory schedule they sent I read that they are rehearsing *Ivanov*. In my opinion, this is wasted labor, unnecessary labor. The play will flop with your lot, because it will turn out uninteresting, given the wishy-washy mood of the spectators. [. . .]

To O. L. Knipper, Yalta, December 18, 1901

[. . .] I keep dreaming of writing a comic play, in which all hell will break loose. I don't know whether anything will come of it. Here in Yalta, it's so loathsome; I'm so fed up with the view from my big window that it seems as if none of my writing will come to pass. Well, we shall see.

To O. L. Knipper, Yalta, November 19, 1901

[. . .] Today I was visited by an actor-manager who is staging *Three Sisters* in Yalta; he came to invite me to take part, but, to his great astonishment and displeasure, I started to ask him not to stage *T.S.* He's putting on the play only to cause a sensation. He stayed with me for over an hour. I was tortured to death. [. . .]

---

5. Leonid Vitalyevich Sredin (1860–1909), a physician living in Yalta.
6. Henrik Ibsen's play was staged by Stanislavsky and Sanin.
7. These suggestions concerned the fire, Andrey being more indignant in Act four, and Vershinin saluting more like a colonel.

To O. L. Knipper, Yalta, November 24, 1901

[. . .] Here in Yalta they put on *Three Sisters*—disgusting! The officers were wearing police gunbelts, Masha talked in a hoarse voice.
A full house, but the audience swore at the play desperately. [. . .]

To O. L. Knipper, Yalta, December 24, 1901

[. . .] I received your holiday repertory schedule. In my plays, Samarova[8] isn't acting once, in *Three Sisters* Stanislavsky not once, Lilina[9]
not once. In general, the plays are in a certain state of neglect. I can't
stand Munt,[1] and she's in every performance of *Three Sisters*. [. . .]

To O. L. Knipper, Yalta, January 7, 1902

[. . .] [H]owever, if on January 11 in *Uncle Vanya* the Nanny won't
be played by Samarova, but by somebody else, I will fall out with the
theater forever. It's bad enough that Munt, the most dreadful actress
going, is still acting.

To O. L. Knipper, Yalta, January 21, 1902

[. . .] Gorky has set about writing a new play, as I already reported
to you, but Chekhov has not. [. . .]

To O. L. Knipper, Yalta, March 16, 1902

[. . .] I am not writing a play, and don't feel like writing one, because
there are plenty of play-carpenters nowadays and this activity is
becoming tedium-tum-tum, humdrum. [. . .]

To P. P. Gnedich,[2] Yalta, August 19, 1902

[. . .] You can have *The Celebration* and *The Wedding*; send me the
contracts to be signed. Only one thing: for the sake of its creator, do
not stage *The Seagull*! I read in the papers that the Alexandra Theater
was preparing to rehearse *Seagull*, and this rumor, despite the likelihood that it's apocryphal, troubled my spirit . . . Please write me
that this play will not be put on, and reassure me. [. . .]

---

8. Mariya Aleksandrovna Samarova (1852–1919), charter member of the Art Theater, plump
   and bold, whose Chekhov roles included Marina, Anfisa, and Zyuzyushka.
9. Mariya Petrovna Lilina (1866–1943), actress at the Moscow Art Theater and wife of K. S.
   Stanislavsky; she created the role of Masha in *Seagull* there, as well as Sonya, Natasha,
   and Anya, and in the 1920s took on Nina and Olga on tour.
1. Yekaterina Mikhailovna Munt (1875–1954), who doubled Lilina in the role of Natasha.
2. Pyotr Petrovich Gnedich (1855–1927), playwright; when he became manager of the Russian troupe of the Petersburg imperial theaters, he tried to get Chekhov's plays back onto
   the Alexandra stage.

To Vl. I. Nemirovich-Danchenko, Yalta, August 23, 1902

[. . .] Today I got a telegram from Prince Baryatinsky[3] asking permission to stage *Seagull* in Petersburg. I answered this way: *The Seagull* belongs to the Art Theater. The night before I wrote to Gnedich, asked him not to stage *The Seagull* at the Alexandra Theater. Kindly write or wire Pr. Baryatinsky, if he contacts you about *The Seagull*, that this play belongs to the Art Theater. [. . .]

To O. L. Knipper, Yalta, August 27, 1902

[. . .] I won't write a play this year, my heart isn't in it, but if I write anything at all play-like, it will be a vaudeville in one act. [. . .]

Did I write you about *The Seagull*? I wrote a tear-drenched letter to Gnedich in Petersburg begging him not to stage *The Seagull*. Today I received his reply: its performance cannot be avoided, for new scenery has been painted, etc., etc. Which means, there'll be more abuse. [. . .]

To O. L. Knipper, September 6, 1902

[. . .] I had a visit from an admirer of Nemirovich—one Fomin, who gives public lectures on the theme of *Three Sisters* and *The Trio* (Chekhov and Gorky), honest and pure, but, evidently, not a very bright little gent. I talked to him some rather ponderous stuff, said that I did not consider myself a playwright, that there is only one playwright in Russia now—Naidyonov,[4] that *In Dreams*[5] (a play he is very fond of) is a philistine work etc., etc. And he left. [. . .]

To O. L. Knipper, Yalta, September 22, 1902

[. . .] I read an article by August Scholz[6] about the Art Theater. What rubbish! Sheer laudatory German balderdash, in which more than half of the information offered by the author to the public is, among other things, a pack of lies; for instance, the failure of my plays on the stage of the Moscow Imperial theaters. Only one item is right: you are called the most talented Russian actress. [. . .]

3. Prince Vladimir Vladimirovich Baryatinsky (b. 1874), married to the actress Lidiya Yavor-skaya, created the so-called New Theater in Petersburg, for which he solicited Chekhov's plays.
4. Sergey Aleksandrovich Naidyonov (1869–1922), dramatist, whose play about generational conflict, *Vanyushin's Children*, was the hit of 1901.
5. A play by Nemirovich-Danchenko, staged at the Art Theater in 1901 by Stanislavsky and Sanin.
6. August Karl Scholz (1857–1923), German translator; the article was entitled "Neurussis-che Bühnenkunst" ("The New Russian Art of the Stage").

To L. A. Sulerzhitsky,[7] Moscow, November, 5 1902

The new playhouse[8] is very good: spacious, fresh, no cheap ostentation that knocks your eye out. They play in the old way, i.e., well, no new plays, and the only one there met with little success.[9] The absence of Meyerhold[1] goes unnoticed; in *Three Sisters*, he is replaced by Kachalov, who acts wonderfully well [. . .] They perform *Uncle Vanya* wonderfully.

To O. L. Knipper, Yalta, December 17, 1902

[. . .] I read in the *Perm Regional News* a review of *Uncle Vanya*; it says that Astrov is very drunk; he probably staggered through all four acts. [. . .]

To O. L. Knipper, Yalta, December 21, 1902

[. . .] I received news from Gnedich that for *The Seagull* I shall get not 8, but 10%, that *Seagull* has good houses, etc., etc.

To P. P. Gnedich, Yalta, December 22, 1902

I've already signed and returned the three papers I received from your office. *The Wedding* should do all right and turn out not too boring, but as to *The Celebration*, allow me to have my doubts. Anyway thank you. [. . .]

To O. L. Knipper, Yalta, December 22, 1902

[. . .] I have a dreadful craving to write a vaudeville, but there's never the time, I can't sit down to it. I have a sort of hunch that vaudevilles will come back into fashion. [. . .]

To A. S. Suvorin, Yalta, December 22, 1902

[. . .] I rarely go to the Art Theater, but it seems to me that you exaggerate Stanislavsky's role as director. It's the most ordinary theater, and the work goes on in a very ordinary way, same as everywhere else, only the actors are educated, very decent people; true, they aren't brilliant talents, but they are painstaking, they love their work and learn their lines. If a great deal fails, this is because the play isn't suitable or else because the actors haven't enough temperament.

7. Leopold Antonovich Sulerzhitsky (1872–1916), former sailor and Tolstoyan, exiled for political activities; he eventually joined the Moscow Art Theater and became Stanislavsky's closest assistant.
8. The Art Theater had moved to a new building on Kammerherr Lane in Moscow.
9. Gorky's *The Petty Bourgeoisie*.
1. Meyerhold quit the theater in disgruntlement when he was not made a shareholder.

Really, Stanislavsky is not to blame. You write that he will chase all the talented people from the stage, but actually during the whole five years this theater has been in existence, not a single person with the slightest trace of talent has left. [. . .]

To O. L. Knipper, Yalta, December 24, 1902

[. . .] My *Cherry Orchard* will be in three acts. So it seems, and yet I haven't made a final decision. [. . .]

To S. P. Dyagilev,[2] Yalta, December 30, 1902

I received *The World of Art* containing the article about *The Seagull*.[3] I have read the article—many thanks to you. When I finished it, I was desirous of writing a play once more, which I shall probably do after January. [. . .]

To O. L. Knipper, Yalta December 28, 1902

[. . .] Dyagilev sent me a letter and Number 11 of *The World of Art*, with a long review of *The Seagull* and myself in general. Read it, you'll turn up in it. [. . .]

Sweetie, when I start the play, I'll write you. The long-legged crane (as you dub your huband in your letter) will hand over the play, but who is to act the old lady is a mystery. I read that Azagarova[4] has been invited to some provincial theater, and besides she'd hardly suit this role.

To O. L. Knipper, Yalta, January 3, 1903

[. . .] I wanted to do *The Cherry Orchard* in three long acts, but I can also do it in four; it's all the same to me, whether it's three or four acts—the play will be the same either way [. . .]

To O. L. Knipper, Yalta, January 20, 1903

[. . .] Savina is putting on my ancient vaudeville *The Celebration* at her benefit. Again they will say that this is a new play and badmouth it. [. . .]

2. Sergey Pavlovich Dyagilev [Diaghilev] (1872–1929), aesthete, editor of the journal *World of Art* (*Mir Iskusstva*) and *The Annual of the Imperial Theaters*, later impresario of the Ballets Russes.
3. By M. Filosofov. *The Seagull* was published in this magazine, which was edited by Dyagilev.
4. Anna Yakovlevna Azagarova (d. 1935), worked in the Petersburg and provincial theaters from 1886, and at Korsh's Theater from 1896. Chekhov considered the central role in *The Cherry Orchard* to be that of an "old lady," and believed that the MAT had no actress capable of playing it.

To V. V. Kommissarzhevskaya, Yalta, January 27, 1903

[. . .] As to the play I will say this: 1. The play is already conceived, it is true, and the title chosen (*The Cherry Orchard*—but this is still a secret), and I shall set to writing it no later than the end of February, providing, of course, I am well; 2. In this play, the central character is an old woman!—to the great regret of the author; and 3. If I turn it over to the Art Theater, then according to the prevailing rules and regulations of this theater, the Art Theater has exclusive rights to this play for both Moscow and Petersburg—and there's nothing I can do about it. If the Art Theater does not tour to Petersburg in 1904 (which is altogether possible; it isn't touring this year), there can be no objection, if the play suits your theater, I shall give it to you with pleasure. Or, here is something else: why shouldn't I write a play *just for you*? Not for this or that theater, but for you. This has been a long-cherished desire of mine. Oh well, God's will be done. If I had my former health, I wouldn't talk about it, but simply sit down and write the play this minute. [. . .]

To K. S. Alekseev (Stanislavsky), Yalta, February 5, 1903

[. . .] All the same, after February 20 I count on sitting down to work on the play and finishing it by March 20. It's all completed in my head. It is called *The Cherry Orchard*, four acts; in the first act, flowering cherry trees can be seen through the window, an entirely white orchard. And ladies in white dresses. In short, Vishnevsky will have lots to laugh at—and, of course, no one will know why. [. . .]

To M. F. Pobedimskaya,[5] Yalta, February 5, 1903

Your opinion about Yelena Andreevna is entirely correct. [. . .] Perhaps Yelena Andreevna may seem incapable of thinking or even loving, but when I wrote *Uncle Vanya*, I had something entirely different in mind. [. . .]

To O. L. Knipper, Yalta, February 11, 1903

[. . .] I shall start to write the play on February 21. You will play a sweet little idiot. But who will play the old woman, the mother? Who? We may have to ask M. F.[6] [. . .]

---

5. Marianna Fyodorovna Podebimskaya, wife of a rural physician.
6. Mariya Fydorovna Andreeva (Zhelyabuzhskaya, 1868–1953), Art Theater actress of lyrical power and Gorky's mistress. She played Irina and Varya, and replaced Roksanova as Nina. She left the Art Theater to work for the Bolshevik cause. This reference is Chekhov's joke, since Andreeva usually played attractive young women.

To O. L. Knipper, Yalta, February 22, 1903

[. . .] Your role is a downright fool. Would you like to play a fool?
A kindhearted fool. [. . .]

To O. L. Knipper, Yalta, March 5–6, 1903

[. . .] In *Cherry Orchard*, you will be Varvara Yegorovna, or Varya,
an adopted child, twenty-two. Only don't be angry, please. [. . .]

[. . .] If my play doesn't come out the way I've thought it up, then
hammer at my forehead with your fists. Stanislavsky has a comic
role; so do you.

To O. L. Knipper, Yalta, March 18, 1903

[. . .] The play, by the way, isn't coming along very successfully.
One of the main characters hasn't been sufficiently thought out and
is slowing me down; but before Easter, I think, this person will come
clear and I shall be out of my difficulties. [. . .]

To O. L. Knipper, Yalta, March 21, 1903

[. . .] *The Cherry Orchard* will be, I'll try to make it so that there
are the fewest possible characters; something more intimate [. . .]

To O. L. Knipper, Yalta, April 11, 1903

[. . .] Does your lot have an actress for the role of the elderly lady
in *Cherry Orchard*? If not, there won't be any play, I will not write
it. [. . .]

To O. L. Knipper, Yalta, April 15, 1903

[. . .] I don't feel much like writing for your theater—chiefly for the
reason that you have no old ladies. They will try to foist the old
woman's role on you, despite the fact that there is another role for
you, and you've already played the old lady in *The Seagull*.

To O. L. Knipper, Yalta, April 17, 1903

[. . .] I got P. Veinberg's review; the same one wrote the same thing
about *The Seagull* too, but meanwhile *The Seagull* keeps creaking
along even now. These old-timers of ours nurse their hatreds, it isn't
good. [. . .][7]

7. Veinberg had published an interview with Stanislavsky about *The Lower Depths*. Apparently Veinberg, a literary conservative, had been annoyed by *The Seagull*'s novelty.

The play is pecking its way out of the shell little by little, but I'm afraid my style has, in general, grown out of date. [. . .]

To K. S. Alekseev (Stanislavsky), Yalta, July 28, 1903

My play is not ready, it progresses by fits and starts, which I explain by laziness, and wonderful weather, and the intricacy of the plot. When the play is ready or even before it's ready, I'll write to you or better wire you. Your role, I think, won't be too bad, though I can't undertake to judge, for I generally understand plays very badly when I read them. [. . .]

To Vl. I. Nemirovich-Danchenko, Yalta, August 22, 1903

[. . .] Well, sir, as to my own play, *The Cherry Orchard*, so far I am making good progress. I work on it little by little. If I am a bit late, it's no great problem; I've reduced the design element of the play to a minimum; so no special scenery will be required and you won't have to concoct any gunpowder. [. . .]

In the second act of my play, I replaced the river with an old chapel and a well. Rather more peaceful. But in the second act you are to give me a real green field and a road, and an expanse wider than usual for the stage. [. . .]

To Vl. I. Nemirovich-Danchenko, Yalta, September 2, 1903

[. . .] My play (if I continue to work as I have been working up to today) will be completed soon, don't worry. It was hard, very hard to write the second act, but it seems no problems arose. I shall call the play a comedy. [. . .] Olga will take the role of the mother in my play, but who is to act the daughter of seventeen or eighteen, a young slender lass, I will not attempt to decide. Well, we shall see what we shall see. [. . .]

To M. P. Lilina, Yalta, September 15, 1903

Don't believe anybody, no living soul has read my play yet; I have written for you not a "bigoted hypocrite," but a very nice young lady, with whom you will, I hope, be satisfied. I have almost finished the play, but eight or ten days ago I was taken ill, started coughing, got weak, in short last year's business all over again. Now, i.e., today— it is warmer and I feel better, but still I cannot write, as my head is aching. Olga will not bring the play; I will send the four acts together as soon as it is possible for me to set to work for a whole day. It has turned out not a drama, but a comedy, in places even a farce, and I am afraid I shall catch it from Vladimir Ivanych. Konstantin Sergeevich has a big role. Generally speaking, there are not many roles.

[. . .] As a writer, it is necessary for me to observe women, to study them, so, I regret to say, I cannot be a faithful husband. As I observe women chiefly for the sake of my plays, in my opinion the Art Theater ought to increase my wife's salary or give her a pension!

[. . .] When you see Vishnevsky, tell him that he should try to lose weight—this is necessary for my play.[8] [. . .]

To O. L. Knipper, Yalta, September 21, 1903

[. . .] The last act will be merry, in fact the whole play is merry, frivolous; Sanin won't like it, he'll say I've become shallow.

[. . .] I'll send the play addressed to you, and you deliver it to the management. Only when you read it and find it awful, don't lose heart. [. . .]

To O. L. Knipper, Yalta, September 23, 1903

[. . .] The fourth act of my play, as compared with the other acts, will be skimpy in content yet effective. The way your part ends does not seem bad to me. In any event, don't lose heart, everything is going well. [. . .]

Regards to Vishnevsky and tell him to start laying up blandness and refinement for a role in my play. [. . .]

To O. L. Knipper, Yalta, September 25, 1903

[. . .] This letter will probably arrive after you've already received the telegram about the completion of the play. The fourth act writes itself easily, almost smoothly, and, if I didn't finish it sooner, it's because I still ache all over on and off. [. . .]

It seems to me that in my play, however boring it may be, there is something new. In the whole play there is not a single gunshot, by the way. Kachalov's role is a good one. Look and see who's going to play the seventeen-year-old girl, and write me. [. . .]

To O. L. Knipper, Yalta, September 27, 1903

I already sent you a telegram that the play is finished, that all four acts are written. I am already making a fair copy. The people in my play came out living, it's true, but how alive the whole play is, I don't know. I'm sending it, you'll read it and figure it out. [. . .]

To O. L. Knipper, Yalta, September 29, 1903

[. . .] The play is already finished, but I'm copying it out slowly, because there happen to be things to refashion, rethink, a couple of

8. Chekhov envisaged Vishnevsky in the role of Gaev.

passages I'll send in an unfinished state; I'll put them off to later—
you'll excuse me [. . .]

[. . .] Ah, if only you would play the governess in my play. It's the
best role, I don't like the rest. [. . .]

To O. L. Knipper, Yalta, October 3, 1903

[. . .] Don't be angry about the play, sweetie; I am copying it out
slowly because I cannot write faster. Some passages I don't like; I
write them over and copy them out again. But soon, soon, my little
horsie, I shall finish and send it. As soon as I send it, I'll let you know
by telegram. After all, I'm not such a miser as you, my rich actress
[. . .]

Sweetie, forgive me for the play! Forgive me! Word of honor, I'll
finish it and copy it out. [. . .]

To O. L. Knipper, Yalta, October 7, 1903

[. . .] [M]eanwhile I still haven't made a fair copy of my play; I barely
dragged it to the middle of Act Three . . . I drag it out and drag it out
and drag it out, and because I drag it out, it seems to me that my
play is immeasurably huge, enormous; I get terrified and lose all
appetite for it. Today, all the same, I am copying it out, don't worry.
[. . .]

To O. L. Knipper, Yalta, October 8, 1903

[. . .] My play is coming along; today I finish copying out Act Three,
and take on Act Four. Act Three itself is the least boring, but the
second act is boring and montonous as a spider's web.

[. . .] Who, who is going to play my governess? [. . .]

To O. L. Knipper, Yalta, October 9, 1903

[. . .] My mood is excellent. I copy out the play, I'll be done soon,
dovie, I swear it. [. . .] I assure you, every extra day is one to the
good, for my play becomes better and better all the time and the
characters are already clear. Only I'm afraid that there are passages
which the censor might blue-pencil, that would be horrible [. . .]

To O. L. Knipper, Yalta, October 10, 1903

[. . .] For Luzhsky, I wrote a fitting role. The role is very short, but
the most genuine one [. . .] Kostya was here today; he spent a lot
of time in the restaurant and wrote out the billiards terms for my
play. [. . .]

To O. L. Knipper, Yalta, October 12, 1903

[. . .] The play is now finished, finally finished, and tomorrow night or, at the latest, the morning of the fourteenth it will be sent to Moscow. Along with it I shall send you some notes. If revisions are necessary, I think they will be very small ones. The worst thing about the play is that I wrote it not in one go, but over a long, very long period, so that a certain leisurely quality can be felt in it. Well, we shall see. [. . .]

Tell Vishnevsky [. . .] I wrote a role for him, but I'm afraid that after Antony[9] this role, contrived by Anton, will seem to him unsophisticated, angular. However, he will be playing an aristocrat. Your role is planned out only in Acts Three and One, in the rest it is only daubed in. But never mind, I don't lose heart. [. . .]

To O. L. Knipper, Yalta, October 14, 1903

[. . .] 1. You are to play Lyubov Andreevna, for there is no one else. She is dressed not luxuriously, but with great taste. Intelligent, very kindhearted, absent-minded; she acts affectionately to everyone, always a smile on her lips.

2. Anya must be played without fail by a very young actress.

3. Varya—maybe Mariya Petrovna [Lilina] will take this role.

4. Gaev is for Vishnevsky. Ask Vishnevsky to listen in on people playing billiards and jot down as many billiard terms as he can. I don't play billiards, or did once, but now I've forgotten it all, and stick them in my play any old way. Later on, Vishnevsky and I will talk it over, and I'll write in what's needed.

5. Lopakhin—Stanislavsky.

6. The student Trofimov—Kachalov.

7. Simeonov-Pishchik—Gribunin.[1]

8. Charlotta is a question mark. In the fourth act I'm still coming up with her lines: yesterday I had a stomach-ache when I was copying out Act Four, and I couldn't write in anything new. In Act Four Charlotta does tricks with Trofimov's galoshes. Raevskaya[2] is not to play her. What's needed is an actress with humor.

9. Yepikhodov—maybe, Luzhsky wouldn't turn it down?

10. Firs—Artyom.[3]

9. Vishnevsky was playing Mark Antony in Shakespeare's *Antony and Cleopatra*.

1. Vladimir Fyodorovich Gribunin (1873–1933), charter member of the Moscow Art Theater, a comic actor whose other Chekhov roles included Ferapont, Kosykh, Telegin, and the orderly in *The Clinic*.

2. Yevgeniya Mikhailovna Raevskaya (Ierusalimskaya, 1854–1932), charter member of the Moscow Art Theater, was relegated to old women characters; her Chekhovian roles included Polina Andreevna, Mariya Vasilyevna, Anfisa, and Zinaida Savishna.

3. Aleksandr Rodionovich Artyom (Artyomiev, 1842–1914), a former writing-master and charter member of the Moscow Art Theater, played old men; his Chekhovian roles included Shamraev, Waffles, Chebutykin, and Firs.

11. Yasha—Moskvin.[4]

If the play goes on, then tell them that I will come up with all the rewrites that are demanded by stage practice. I've got the time, although I confess I'm awfully fed up with the play. If there's anything unclear in the play, write to me.

It's an old manor house: once the life in it was very opulent, and this must be felt in the furnishings. Opulent and comfortable.

Varya is rather rude and rather stupid, but very kindhearted.

To O. L. Knipper, Yalta, October 15, 1903

[. . .] I have no particular expectations for my play, I'm fed up with it, therefore I don't like it. [. . .]

To O. L. Knipper, Yalta, October 17, 1903

[. . .] A few things in the play have to be redone and done 'til done, I think fifteen minutes should be enough for that. Act Four isn't finished and some things need to be moved around in Two, yes, most likely, a few words at the end of Act Three, otherwise, most likely, it'll resemble the end of *Uncle Vanya*.

If the play won't do, don't lose heart, little horsie, don't whimper; in a month's time I shall refashion it so that you won't recognize it. After all, I wrote it over a tedious long period, with an upset stomach and fits of coughing. [. . .]

To O. L. Knipper, Yalta, October 19, 1903

[. . .] [E]arly this morning I got a hundred-eighty-word telegram from Vladimir Ivanovich. A big thank you. I was so queasy, afraid. The things that worried me most were the second act's lack of action and a certain sketchy quality in Trofimov, the student. After all, time and again Trofimov is being sent into exile, time and again he is being expelled from the university, but how can you express stuff like that? [. . .]

Write me likewise who is to play Charlotta. Can it possibly be Raevskaya? In that case she wouldn't be Charlotta, but an unfunny, pretentious Eudoxia. [. . .]

To O. L. Knipper, Yalta, October 21, 1903

[. . .] Today I got a telegram from Alekseev, in which he calls my play a work of genius, which is to overpraise the play and remove from it a good half of the success that, under happier circumstances,

---

4. Ivan Mikhailovich Moskvin (1874–1946), charter member of the Moscow Art Theater, was one of Chekhov's favorite actors, a brilliant comic talent who created the roles of Rodé and Yepikhodov.

it might enjoy. Nemirovich has still not sent me the list of actors taking part in the play, but all the same I'm worried. He's already wired me that Anya is like Irina; obviously, he wants Mariya Fyodo-rovna [Andreeva] to play Anya. But Anya is as like Irina as I am like Burdzhalov.[5] Anya is first of all a child, cheerful to the last, who does not know life and doesn't cry once, except at the end of Act Two, in which she only has tears in her eyes. M. F. is bound to moan and groan through the whole role; besides, she's too old. Who is to play Charlotta? [. . .]

Aleksandr Pleshcheev[6] is going to publish a theater magazine in Petersburg like *Theater and Art*. [. . .] In January, I'll send him a vaudeville; he can publish it. For a long time now I've been wanting to write the silliest possible vaudeville.

When do rehearsals of my play begin? Write me, sweetie, don't torture me. [. . .]

To O. L. Knipper, Yalta, October 23, 1903

[. . .] You write that Vishnevsky can't play Gaev. Well, who can? Stanislavsky? Then who'll play Lopakhin? Lopakhin is not to be given to Luzhsky on any pretext; he'll either make him very bland or clown it up. He is to play Yepikhodov. No, please don't hurt Vishnevsky's feelings. [. . .]

Nemirovich writes that my play has a lot of tears and some coarse-ness. Write to me, darling, what you think isn't right and what they say; I'll correct it. After all, it's not too late; I could still rework an entire act.

So the actors like Pishchik? Delighted. I think Gribunin will play him splendidly. [. . .]

To Vl. I. Nemirovich-Danchenko, Yalta, October 23, 1903

When I gave your theater *Three Sisters* and a notice appeared in *News of the Day* that *both of us*, i.e., you and I, were at odds, I spoke to Éfros,[7] and he gave me his word that it wouldn't happen again. Suddenly I now read that Ranevskaya is living abroad with Anya, is living with a Frenchman, that Act Three takes place in a hotel, that Lopak-hin is a moneygrubbing sonofabitch, etc., etc. What was I to think? Could I suspect your involvement? In my telegram I had in mind only Éfros and accused Éfros alone, and it was very strange for me, I couldn't believe my eyes, when I read your telegram, in which you

5. Georgy Sergeevich Burdzhalov (1869–1926), an actor and director at the Art Theatre, noted for his diminutive size.
6. Aleksandr Alekseevich Pleshcheev (1858–1944), journalist, playwright, and dramatic critic.
7. Nikolay Efimovich Éfros (1867–1923), theater critic and journalist, one of the MAT's main boosters.

took all the blame on yourself. It's a sad thing that that's how you think of me, even sadder that such a misunderstanding arose. Tell Éfros that I don't want to know him any more, and then forgive me if I went too far in my telegram—and *basta*![8]

[. . .] I would very much like to attend rehearsals and keep an eye on things. I am afraid that Anya will take on a lachrymose tone (for some reason you think she's like Irina); I'm afraid that she will be played by an actress who is not young. The Anya in my play doesn't cry once, nowhere speaks in a lachrymose tone; in the second act, she has tears in her eyes, but the tone is cheerful, lively. Why in your telegram do you tell me that there are lots of weepy people in my play? Where are they? Only Varya, but that's because Varya is a crybaby by nature, and her tears must not stir up in the spectator a feeling of depression. In my plays you often come across "through tears," but this shows only the characters' state of mind, not the tears. In the second act there is no cemetery. [. . .]

To O. L. Knipper, Yalta, October 24, 1903

What's the point of translating my play into French? It's crazy, isn't it? The French won't understand a thing about Yermolay, the sale of the estate, and they'll just be bored. It's totally unnecessary, darling. [. . .]

If, as you wrote, Vishnevsky is not to act Gaev, what will he act in my play? [. . .]

To O. L. Knipper, Yalta, October 25, 1903

[. . .] No, I never wanted to suggest that Ranevskaya is chastened. The only thing that can chasten a woman like that is death. But maybe I don't understand what you mean. It isn't hard to play Ranevskaya; you only need from the beginning to take the right tone; you need to come up with a smile and a way of laughing, you have to know how to dress. Well, you know all this; she should be enthusiastic, she should be healthy [. . .]

To O. L. Knipper, Yalta, October 28, 1903

[. . .] Gribunin should play Pishchik. God forbid they give this role to Vishnevsky. Firs—Artyom, Yasha—Moskvin or Gromov,[9] who would make the most original Yasha. But of course Moskvin is better.

---

8. Italian, enough.
9. Mikhail Apollinaryevich Gromov (d. 1918), an Art Theater actor, was cast as the Vagrant; his other Chekhov roles were Solyony and Denis Grigoryev in a dramatization of the story "The Schemer."

But if Mariya Petrovna [Lilina] would agree to play Charlotta, that would be best of all! I thought about it, but don't dare say it. That she's dainty, short isn't a problem. For Anya, she's too old. But the main thing is that Vishnevsky not play Pishchik, God forbid. I don't know Leonidov.[1] Only Konstantin Sergeevich should play the merchant. After all, he's not a merchant in the vulgar sense of the word, that has to be understood. [. . .]

To O. L. Knipper, Yalta, October 30, 1903

[. . .] Stanislavsky will be a very good and original Gaev, but who then will play Lopakhin? After all, the role of Lopakhin is the central one. If it doesn't succeed, it means the whole play will flop. Lopakhin must not be played as a loudmouth, that isn't the invariable sign of a merchant. He's a suave man. Gribunin won't do, he should play Pishchik. God forfend you should give Pishchik to Vishnevsky. If he won't play Gaev, then there isn't another role for him in my play, so say so. Or here's what: would he like to try for Lopakhin? I shall write to Konstantin Sergeevich, I got a letter from him yesterday.

[. . .] If Moskvin wants to play Yepikhodov, I'm delighted. Then what is there for Luzhsky? [. . .]

To K. S. Alekseev (Stanislavsky), Yalta, October 30, 1903

[. . .] When I was writing Lopakhin, I thought of him as your role. If for any reason he doesn't appeal to you, take Gaev. Lopakhin is a merchant, true, but a very decent person in every respect; he must behave with perfect decorum, like an educated man, with no petty ways or tricks; and it seemed to me this part, the central one of the play, would come out brilliantly in your hands. If you take Gaev, give Lopakhin to Vishnevsky. He won't be an artistic Lopakhin, but he won't be a petty one either. Luzhsky would make an unfeeling foreigner of the role. Leonidov would turn it into a little moneygrubber. In casting an actor for the part, you must remember that Varya, a serious and religious young girl, is in love with Lopakhin; she wouldn't be in love with some little moneygrubber. [. . .]

To O. L. Knipper, Yalta, November 1, 1903

[. . .] It's utterly impossible for Vishnevsky to play Pishchik, that's Gribunin's role. I don't know why Mariya Petrovna wants to play Anya; after all, it's a bobtailed, uninteresting role. Varya, to my mind,

1. Leonid Mironovich Leonidov (1873–1914), a provincial actor who joined the Art Theater in 1903; of a highly emotional temperament, he was indeed cast as Lopakhin, and later played Borkin, Solyony, and even Vershinin in 1910 to 1911.

is much more suitable for her. Nemirovich writes that he's afraid of the resemblance between Varya and Sonya in *Uncle Vanya*. What resemblance? Varya is a little nun, a little silly [. . .]

To Vl. I. Nemirovich-Danchenko, Yalta, November 2, 1903

[. . .] Now about the play.

1. Anya can be played by anybody you like, even by an altogether unknown actress, only she must be young and look like a little girl, and talk in a young, ringing voice. This is not one of the major roles.[2]

2. Varya is a more important part, if Marya Petrovna were to take it. Without M. P., this role will turn out rather flat and crude; I'll have to refashion it, soften it. M. P. will not be repeating herself, first, because she is talented, and second, because Varya does not resemble Sonya and Natasha; she is a figure in a black dress, a little nun, a little silly, a crybaby, etc., etc.[3]

3. Gaev and Lophakin—let Konst. Serg. try them on and make his choice of these roles. If he were to take Lopakhin and succeed in the role, then the play would be a success. After all, if Lopakhin is bland, played by a bland actor, both the role and the play will fail.[4]

4. Pishchik—Gribunin. God forbid you give Vishnevsky this role.

5. Charlotta is a major role. It is impossible to give it to Pomyalova; of course, Muratova[5] will perhaps be good, but not funny. This role is for Miss Knipper.

6. Yepikhodov—if Moskvin wants it, let him have it. He will make an excellent Yepikhodov. I supposed that Luzhsky was to play it.

7. Firs—Artyom.

8. Dunyasha—Khalyutina.[6]

9. Yasha. If Aleksandrov, of whom you write, is the same one who is your assistant manager, let him have Yasha. Moskvin would make the most wonderful Yasha. And I have nothing against Leonidov.

10. The Vagrant—Gromov.

11. The Stationmaster, who reads "The Sinful Woman" in Act Three,[7]—an actor who has a bass voice.

Charlotta speaks correct, not broken, Russian; but occasionally she pronounces the soft ending of a word hard, and she confuses

2. The role went to Stanislavsky's wife, the thirty-seven-year-old Mariya Lilina.
3. Despite her protests, Mariya Fyodorovna Andreeva played Varya for a while; later, the part was taken over by Mariya Lilina, as Chekhov had hoped.
4. Stanislavsky, who came from a peasant and merchant background, chose not to emphasize his origins in Lopakhin, and the role went to Leonid Leonidov after all.
5. Aleksandra Ivanovna Pomyalova (d.1909), who at the Art Theater played folksy old women such as Marina in *Uncle Vanya*. Yelena Pavlovna Muratova (1874–1921), an Art Theater actress with a comic tinge, was cast as Charlotta; her other Chekhov roles were Avdotya Nazarovna, Mariya Vasilyevna, and Marina.
6. Sofiya Vasilyevna Khalyutina (1875–1960), charter member of the Moscow Art Theater, did take the role, but Chekhov disliked her performance; in 1908 she moved into the part of Charlotta.
7. See *The Cherry Orchard*, note, page 357.

the masculine and feminine genders of adjectives. Pishchik is a real Russian, an old man, debilitated by gout, old age, and over-indulgence, stout, dressed in a tight, long-waisted frockcoat (à la Simov[8]), boots without heels. Lopakhin—a white waistcoat and yellow shoes; walks swinging his arms, a broad stride, thinks while walking, walks a straight line. Hair not short, and therefore often tosses back his head; while in thought he combs his beard, back to front, i.e., from his neck toward his mouth. Trofimov, I think, is clear. Varya—black dress, wide belt.

For three years I planned to write *The Cherry Orchard,* and for three years I have been telling you to engage an actress for the role of Lyubov Andreevna.[9] There, now, go ahead and deal your game of solitaire, which simply won't come out right.

[. . .] There's no point in your saying that it's you doing the work while nevertheless the Theater is the Theater of Stanislavsky. It's only you they talk about, it's you they write about, and meanwhile they only revile Stanislavsky for his Brutus.[1] If you walk out, well, I too will walk out. [. . .] By the way, theaters for the people, along with literature for the people, is folly, all caramels for the people. The need is not to bring Gogol down to the level of the people but to bring the people up to the level of Gogol.

[. . .] Why is Mariya Petrovna [Lilina] so determined to play Anya? And why does Mariya Fyodorovna [Andreeva] think she's too aristocratic for Varya? After all, she plays in *Lower Depths,* doesn't she?[2] Well, God be with them. [. . .]

To K. S. Alekseev (Stanislavsky), Yalta, November 5, 1903

The house in the play has two stories, is big. After all, in Act Three, there's talk about "down the stairs." Nevertheless, the third act worries me . . . N. has it that the third act takes place in "some kind of hotel"; evidently I made an error in the play. The action does not take place in "some kind of hotel," but in a *drawing room.* If I mention a hotel in the play, which I cannot now doubt, after Vl. Iv's letter, please wire me. We must correct it; we cannot put it out this way, with grave errors distorting its meaning.[3]

8. Viktor Andreevich Simov (1858–1935), painter and designer who created set designs for the Moscow Art Theater from 1898 to 1912, including those for their Chekhov productions.
9. Chekhov had envisaged the role as that of an old woman, and asked the Art Theater to invite the elderly character actress Olga Sadovskaya from the Maly Theater to play it. Olga Knipper's performance in the part established a tradition of Ranevskaya as a much younger woman.
1. Stanislavsky had not wanted to play Brutus in Nemirovich-Danchenko's production of *Julius Caesar;* in particular, he regretted having to shave off his moustache.
2. In Gorky's drama of down-and-outers, *The Lower Depths,* Andreeva played the role of Natasha.
3. Nemirovich-Danchenko had misread *gostinaya,* drawing-room, as *gostinitsa,* hotel.

The house should be big, solid; of wood (like Aksakov's, which, I
think, S. T. Morozov[4] has seen) or stone, it doesn't matter which. It
is very old and grand, summer people don't rent such houses; usually,
such houses are torn down and the timber is used for building cottages. The furniture is old-fashioned, stylish, solid; the deterioration
and debts should not be reflected in the interior decoration.

When people buy such a house, they figure it's cheaper and easier
to build a new one than to renovate this old one.

Your shepherd played well. That is most essential.[5] [. . .]

To O. L. Knipper, Yalta, November 7, 1903

[. . .] I got letters from both Nemirovich and Alekseev, who are
evidently at a loss; you told them that I didn't like my play, that I
was worried about it. But can I have written so incomprehensibly?
So far I've been worried about only one thing, that Simov has begun
to paint a hotel for Act Three. The mistake has to be corrected . . .
I've been writing about this for a whole month now, and in reply they
only shrug their shoulders; evidently, they like the hotel.

Nemirovich sent an urgent telegram with reply requested by
urgent telegram—who is to play Charlotta, Anya, and Varya. Three
names were written next to Varya—two unknowns and Andreeva. I
had to pick Andreeva. That was shrewdly set up. [. . .]

To O. L. Knipper, November 8, 1903

[. . .] Muratova, in everyday life, is occasionally funny; tell her to
be funny as Charlotta, that's the main thing. But Lilina will hardly
make an Anya—she'll be an old-fashioned damsel with a screechy
voice and nothing more.

To K. S. Alekseev (Stanislavsky), Yalta, November 10, 1903

Of course, the scenery for Acts III and IV can be the same, with the
hall and the staircase. Please don't feel inhibited on account of the
scenery; I leave it entirely to you, I am amazed and generally sit with
my mouth wide open at your theatre. There can be no question about
it, whatever you do will be beautiful, a hundred times better than
anything I could come up with.

Dunya and Yepikhodov stand in Lopakhin's presence, they do not
sit. Lopakhin after all deports himself freely, like a lord, uses the
second person singular in speaking to the housemaid, whereas she
uses the second person plural to him [. . .]

4. Savva Timofeevich Morozov (1862–1905), self-made millionaire, patron of the arts, and
   major stockholder in the Moscow Art Theater.
5. Stanislavsky had sent Chekhov a recording he had made of a shepherd playing his pipe,
   for possible use as a sound effect in the play.

To O. L. Knipper, Yalta, November 10, 1903

[. . .] In his letter, Konst. Sergeev. says that for Acts Three and Four there will be a single set. And I am glad, glad not that there will be a single set, but because Act Three will evidently not be portrayed as a hotel, which for some reason Nemirovich and Éfros wanted. [. . .]

To O. L. Knipper, Yalta, November 20, 1903

[. . .] I got the groundplan for Act I. The house will have two stories; probably even the room ⌐ORCHARD⌐ has two stories; but after all in the little courtyard which is depicted by this room, there's very little sunlight, cherries couldn't grow there [. . .]

To O. L. Knipper, Yalta, November 23, 1903

[. . .] Konst. Serg. wants to let a train into Act Two, but I think I'll have to prevent him from doing it. He also wants frogs and corn-crakes. [. . .]

To K. S. Alekseev (Stanislavsky), Yalta, November 23, 1903

Haymowing is usually from the 20–22 of June; by that time the corn-crakes have stopped cawing, I believe, and the frogs have fallen still as well. Only the oriole cries. There is no graveyard; that was very long ago. Two or three slabs lying helter skelter—that's all that's left. A bridge—that's very good. If the train can be presented without noise, without any sound at all, then go ahead. I am not against Acts Three and Four having the same set; except that it would be con-venient to have exits and entrances in Act Four. [. . .]

To V. F. Kommissarzhevskaya, Moscow, January 6, 1904

[. . .] I haven't seen Savina nor been in correspondence with her, and it never occurred to me to give Cherry Orchard to the Alexandra Theater. The play belongs to the Art Theater. I let Nemirovich-Danchenko have it for both Moscow and Petersburg. This year it doesn't seem as if the Art Theater is going to Petersburg, but even so there would be no point in talking to the management about the play.

I write you this with a light heart, because of my deep conviction that The Cherry Orchard wouldn't suit you at all. The central role in this play—the female one—is an old woman, wholly of the past, with nothing in the present; the other roles, at least the female ones, are trivial and rather crude, of no interest to you. My play will soon be published in the anthology *Knowledge*, and if you read it, you'll be convinced that there is nothing in the play to interest you, no matter how indulgent you feel toward it. [. . .]

To I. L. Leontyev (Shcheglov), Moscow, January 18, 1904

[. . .] My play opened yesterday, so my mood is none too good. [. . .]

To F. D. Batyushkov,[6] Moscow, January 19, 1904

[. . .] At the opening of *The Cherry Orchard* on the 17th of January, they honored me so lavishly, affectionately, and really so unexpectedly, that I can't get over it even now.[7]

It would be as well if you came by Shrovetide. I think that only by Shrovetide will our actors have recovered and play *The Cherry Orchard* not so distractedly and shapelessly as they do now. [. . .]

To O. L. Knipper, Yalta, February 23, 1904

[. . .] Marya Fyodor[ovna Andreeva] is leaving? Well, that's a pity, for whatever reason. True, she is an ordinary actress, but it only means giving her role to Litovtseva,[8] which seems far too extreme a change. I think she will come back to the Art Theater. [. . .]

To O. L. Knipper, Yalta, February 24, 1904

[. . .] Tell Vishnevsky that Ilnarskaya[9] is touring throughout Russia in *Cherry Orchard* and printing on the posters SPECIAL AUTHORIZATION TO RIGHTS OF PRODUCTION GIVEN BY THE AUTHOR TO V. N. ILNARSKAYA. I never gave her any authorizations at all.

To O. L. Knipper, Yalta, February 27, 1904

[. . .] Meanwhile, *The Cherry Orchard* is having three or four performances in every city; it's a success, just imagine. I've just been reading about Rostov-on-Don, where it is having its third performance. Oh, if only it were not Muratova and Leonidov and Artyom

6. Fyodor Dmitrievich Batyushkov (1857–1920), a literary historian and critic, associated with the politically liberal Cadet party.
7. The opening night, January 17, 1904, coincided with Chekhov's name day and the twenty-fifth anniversary of his literary activity; gravely ill, he did not show up until the second act and was made to stay through Act Three, after which the ceremony took place.
8. Nina Nikolaevna Litovtseva (1881–1956); after Chekhov's death, she played in Art Theater revivals of his plays: Sarra in *Ivanov* and Mariya Vasilyevna in *Uncle Vanya*.
9. Vera Nikolaevna Ilnarskaya (Ilyinskaya, 1877–late 1920s), who, after a time at Korsh's in Moscow, toured the provinces.

in Moscow! Artyom is giving a really vile performance, but I just keep my mouth shut. [. . .]

To O. L. Knipper, Yalta, March 4, 1904

Write to Budkevich[1] that *The Seagull* and *Three Sisters* were long ago translated into German (and I didn't get a single penny from it), and *The Cherry Orchard* is already being translated for Berlin and Vienna, and will have no success there, because there they have no billiards or Lopakhins or students à la Trofimov. [. . .]

To O. L. Knipper, Yalta, March 18, 1904

[. . .] Tell Nemirovich that the sound in Act Two and Four of *Cherry Orchard* must be shorter, much shorter, and be felt as coming from a long way off. Trivial though this is, they can't even manage a trifle, a sound, although it's described so clearly in the play [. . .]

To O. L. Knipper, Yalta, March 20, 1904

[. . .] Tell Moskvin that he can insert the new lines, and I will put them in myself when I read the corrected proofs. I give him the most complete carte blanche.[2]

To O. L. Knipper, Yalta, March 24, 1904

[. . .] How glad I am that Khalyutina is pregnant, and what a pity that it can't happen to the other performers, for instance Aleksandrov or Leonidov. And what a pity that Muratova isn't married!
   [. . .] Tell the actress playing the parlor maid Dunyasha to read *The Cherry Orchard* as published in *Knowledge* and in the corrected proofs; there she will see where she is to powder her nose and so on and so on. Let her read it without fail; in your scripts everything is all mixed up and smeared over.

To O. L. Knipper, Yalta, March 29, 1904

[. . .] Lulu and K. L.[3] were at *The Cherry Orchard* in March; they both say that Stanislavsky in Act Four acts abominably, that he drags it out excruciatingly. How ghastly! An act, which ought to run twelve minutes *maximum*, with your lot lasts forty minutes. One thing I can say: Stanislavsky has butchered the play for me. Well, never mind.

---

1. Natalya Antonovna Budkevich (d. 1928), provincial actress and translator.
2. See *Cherry Orchard*, note 8, page 365.
3. K.L. was Olga Knipper's brother; Lulu was K.L.'s wife.

[. . .] I got a long letter from some student in Kazan; he entreats me for something, swears that in Kazan *The Cherry Orchard* went splendidly—and thanks me.

To O. L. Knipper, Yalta, April 10, 1904

[. . .] Why on posters and in newspaper advertisements is my play so persistently called a drama? Nemirovich and Alekseev insist on seeing something in my play which is not what I wrote, and I am ready to swear by anything you like that neither of them even once read my play through attentively. Forgive me, but I insist. I'm thinking not only of the scenery for the second act, so dreadful, and not only Khalyutina, who has been replaced by Adurskaya,[4] who does the very same things and absolutely none of what I wrote. [. . .]

[. . .] *The Cherry Orchard* is being staged here in Yalta by some touring trash.[5]

To O. L. Knipper, Yalta, April 13, 1904

[. . .] Yesterday, I got a letter and a review from the sympathetic Mr. Arabazhin.[6] He asks me to write him my opinion whether what he writes is true, that Lopakhin is in love with Ranevskaya. [. . .] Yesterday, *Cherry Orchard* was put on in Yalta—it's on a stage two paces wide.

To K. S. Alekseev (Stanislavsky), Yalta, April 14, 1904

[. . .] By the way, someone sent me from Berlin a German review, and in it I have read that Lopakhin bought "the cherry orchard for ninety thousand" and that "Mariya goes into a convent"—that's the limit. [. . .]

To O. L. Knipper, Yalta, April 15, 1904

[. . .] The day before yesterday in the local theater (which has no wings or dressing rooms), they presented *The Cherry Orchard*, copying the mise-en-scène of the Art Theater, some ham actors headed by Daryalova[7] (a reworking of the actress's name, Daryal), and today there are reviews, and tomorrow reviews, and the day after tomorrow; I am called to the telephone, acquaintances sigh, and I, an invalid, so to speak, who happens to be here for treatment, have to dream

4. Antonina Fedorovna Adurskaya (Durasevich, 1870–1948) played a few roles at the Art Theater from 1901 to 1904, including Natasha in *Three Sisters*.
5. The Sevastopol Municipal Theater Company.
6. Konstantin Ivanovich Arabazhin (b. 1866), literary historian and coeditor of the liberal newspaper *Northern Courier*, published by Prince Baryatinsky.
7. Vera Konstantinovna Daryalova, a provincial actress who in the summer of 1904 ran the acting company at the Simferopol Theater.

up some means of making a getaway. [. . .] Comical as this may sound, I must confess that provincial actors behave just like scoundrels. [. . .]

What is your box office like these days? Standing room only? I can imagine how worn out you all are. [. . .]

CRITICISM

CRITICISM

The Plays in General

GEORGE CALDERON

George Calderon (1868–1915), English author, spent 1895 through 1897 in Russia learning the language and absorbing the culture, supporting himself by writing articles and giving English lessons. His plays were produced by the Independent Stage Society in London between 1909 and 1912. His translations of *The Seagull* and *The Cherry Orchard* were used for the first productions of those plays in English, by the Glasgow Repertory Theatre (1909) and the Stage Society (1912) respectively. His introduction to their publication, despite the old-fashioned transliteration of Chekhov's name, is a very astute interpretation by a contemporary.

An Introduction To 'Tchekhof'†

I

APOLOGETIC

Tchekhof wrote five important plays—*Ivánof, Uncle Ványa, The Seagull, The Three Sisters,* and *The Cherry Orchard.* The rest are one-act farces. I have chosen *The Seagull* and *The Cherry Orchard* for this volume as representing him at two extremes. *The Seagull* is easy, *entraînant,*[1] not much unlike a Western play; *The Cherry Orchard* is difficult, *rébarbatif*[2] and very Russian.

While our new Drama is still in its plastic age, still capable of new impressions (for in spite of many obstacles a new Drama seems to be growing obscurely up in England), it is good for all who cherish it, playwrights, critics, and spectators, to keep the best foreign models before their eyes.

It is of course to Life itself that playwrights, like all other artists, must go, both for their matter and for their form. But Life is a very complicated affair. To different nations, to different generations, to

---

† G. Calderon, "Tchekhof," in *Two Plays by Tchekhof*, trans. by George Calderon (London: Grant Richards, 1912), 7–22.
1. French, fast-paced. [*Editor's note.*]
2. French, surly, stern, forbidding. [*Editor's note.*]

different individuals, different views of it seem important. We sit studying one aspect with all our might, till some day we discover that we have been neglecting a hundred others; and off we career to pitch our campstools under another tree, whereon learned arboriculturists then hasten to hang a neat label with its proper name, Romanticism, Realism, Post-Impressionism or the like. We peer and pry about, eager to know if anyone has found a new clue to the elusive secret. We do not want to pinch his particular recipe, but we do want to know all possible methods, to see the lie of the whole country, like carrier-pigeons that fly round in circles before they choose their own way.

With French and German one may do a great deal; there is Hervieu, Donnay, Capus, Maeterlinck, Hauptmann, Hofmannsthal, Schnitzler,[3] and a few translated Norsemen and Hollanders, all men with different philosophies of Art and Life, good to be inquired into. But the contribution of the Russians, though less accessible, is not less important. Sologúb, Górky, Brúsov, Blok, Yushkévitch, Tchekhof,[4] have studied aspects to which it is right that we should make ourselves sensitive.

It is in fact my Preface, not my Translation, that calls for apology. For, on the face of it, it is the business of a work of art to explain its own intentions. Still, the perfect work of art requires the perfect spectator; and it is in order to help the reader to become one, that I offer him the fruit of my meditations on Tchekhof; I want to clear his eyes, to make his vision "normal," like the unassuming Irishman's. For we Britons, perhaps more than any other nation, come to the contemplation of exotic art with a certain want of ease, a certain doubt where to focus our attention, a bewilderment as to what is foreignness in the matter and what is originality in its presentation.

And I do not think the queer performance of *The Cherry Orchard* (in another version) given before the Stage Society[5] will have done anything to dispel that bewilderment or forestalled me in elucidating the secrets of Tchekhof's genius.

3. Paul Hervieu (1857–1915), French author of powerful plays of modern life; Maurice Donnay (1859–1945), French comic playwright and wit; Alfred Capus (1858–1922), French playwright of Parisian bourgeois society; Maurice Maeterlinck (1862–1949), Belgian playwright, popular for his mystical and symbolist dramas; Gerhard Hauptmann (1862–1946), German playwright, who began as a naturalist but experimented with neo-romantic genres; Hugo von Hoffmannsthal (1874–1929), Austrian poet and playwright, decadent and neo-romantic in tone; Arthur Schnitzler (1863–1931), Austrian playwright, satirist of contemporary Viennese life. [*Editor's note.*]
4. The Russian dramatic avant-garde of the period: Fyodor Sologub (Fyodor Kuzmich Teternikov, 1863–1927), decadent poet and novelist, whose plays rarefy folklore and legend; Maksim Gorky (Aleksey Maksimovich Peshkov, 1868–1936), humanitarian and realistic playwright; Valery Yakovlevich Bryusov (1873–1924), symbolist poet who wrote "cosmic dramas" and argued against realism; Aleksandr Aleksandrovich Blok (1880–1921), symbolist and romantic poet, whose plays are satiric elegies; Semyon Solomonvich Yushevich (1868–1927), who wrote mystico-realistic plays about the huddled masses. [*Editor's note.*]
5. May 28, 1911. [The Stage Society, Incorporated, London, founded in 1899 to produce independent plays without the interference of the Lord Chamberlain's Office.]

II

THE CENTRIFUGAL METHOD

A competent professional critic would easily stick a label on Tchek-hof and push him without more ado into his proper pigeonhole; but, as a fumbling amateur, I must ask for the readers indulgence while I go the long way round, retail all the differentiæ which I see in him as systematically as I can, and leave it to some experter person to condense them afterwards into the appropriate but undiscoverable word.

The most general idea under which I can sum up the essential characteristics of his plays is this: That the interest of them is, so to speak, "centrifugal" instead of self-centred; that they seek, not so much to draw our minds inwards to the consideration of the events they represent, as to cast them outwards to the larger process of the world which those events illuminate; that the sentiments to be aroused by the doings and sufferings of the personages on his stage are not so much hope and fear for their individual fortunes as pity and amusement at the importance which they set on them, and con-solation for their particular tragedies in the spectacle of the general comedy of Life in which they are all merged; that Tchekhof's dra-matic philosophy resembles in fact that modern theory of Physics which, instead of seeking in Matter itself for the final explanation of its nature, regards its constituent atoms as so many gaps or spaces in the primary substance, and turns the imagination outwards to contemplation of the Ether of which they break the majestic continuity.

III

GROUP EMOTIONS

In real life there is nothing of which we are more urgently, though less expressly, conscious, than the presence of other life humming about us, than the fact that our experiences and our impulses are very little private to ourselves, almost always shared with a group of other people. The private life of feelings and opinions is lived far down beneath the surface, in the innermost recesses of the soul. The chief springs of human conduct are group emotions; and the groups with which we share those emotions vary in magnitude from a man and his companion to a nation, a continent, or a world.

For many reasons this truth, however well ascertained, has hardly found its way as yet on to the stage. Tchekhof is a pioneer.

He shows us his little group of personages (there are never many parts in his plays) all subjected to the same influence or generating the same impulse at the same time. In most plays the action is continuous; there are episodes, or byways, but all lead into the same main road. In Tchekhof's plays many things are said and done which have no bearing on the action, but are directed only to creating the atmosphere. The players have to show, by difference of tone and gesture, when they are speaking to the action, which concerns them as individuals, and when they are speaking to the atmosphere, which concerns them as members of a group. The spectators have to distinguish what is painted in low tones and what stands sharply out, in order to grasp the central design.

Sometimes the alternation of action-lines and atmosphere-lines is very rapid, as in *The Cherry Orchard,* in which the author has carried his method so far, that the surface seems as rough as that of a French "vibrationist" picture seen close at hand, but, when looked at aright, falls into a simple unity, and from that very roughness gets qualities of life and light not otherwise attainable.

In *The Seagull* action and atmosphere are broken into masses large enough to be easily distinguished. In the first two acts, for instance the author shows, by material symbols, the general tranquillity from which the commotions of individual life emerge.

We are in a garden at night; before us, a mile away, lies the seagull-haunted lake, shining in the light of the moon; about us hangs the enchantment of rustic quietude; and in our midst, only half divined, a storm is gathering that ultimately shatters the poetry of two young lives. In the dim moonlight of this scene the personages lose their individuality; they become shadows against the landscape, drinking in its beauty together, or setting off its grandeur by the banality of their conversation. When this was performed at Glasgow[6] all the characters but Nina, Trigórin and Madame Arcádina were gathered in a leisurely semicircle up-stage, facing the lake, some standing, some lounging in garden chairs; from time to time one sauntered across or stretched his arms, or lighted a cigarette. There was an air of idly trickling colloquy among them, and when Shamráyef told how the famous Silva once took the low C in the opera-house at Moscow, his discreet crescendo emerged only as a higher ripple of the unemphatic irony in the background.

In the second act, where a squall of nerves is brewing, the conversation and behaviour of the personages have nothing to do with the action of the piece, but are directed to convey the atmosphere of tedium and heat in which such squalls are possible. Here we had yawns and fannings and moppings of the brow. With the entrance of the boorish land agent the passive group-emotion becomes suddenly active. Everyone abandons his listless attitude, alert with the sense of impending perturbation. "There are no horses to be had."

6. Where Mr. Wareing, the manager bravely allowed me to do the producing. [Herbert Wareing, English composer, 1857–1918.]

A gust of anger goes through all the company; each breaks out in turn, according to the difference of his interest and disposition.

IV

ENGLISH ACTING

The English method of acting is evidently ill-suited to Tchekhof's work. The "centrifugal" Drama requires above all things "centripetal" acting, acting designed to restore the unity of impression. The French and English pieces on which our players have been brought up are so toughly made, their interest converges so powerfully on a central theme, that, so far from troubling their heads with restoring the unity, they have always been able to indulge their natural propensity to make the parts they play "stand out," like the choir-boy whose voice "was heard above the rest."

In the general struggle for conspicuity a sportsmanlike code has been established to give everyone a fair chance. As each actor opens his mouth to speak, the rest fall petrified into an uncanny stillness, like the courtiers about the Sleeping Beauty, or those pathetic clusters that one sees about a golf-tee, while one of the players is flourishing at his ball in preparation for a blow. But it is the very opposite of this cataleptic method that is required for the acting of Tchekhof. His disjunctive manner is defeated of its purpose unless the whole company keep continuously alive; and each line is so unmistakably coloured with the character of its speaker that there is no need for the rest to hold their breath and "point" that we may know who utters it.

In *The Cherry Orchard,* as the action of the play turns about the sale of the estate, all the means that the stage-manager has at his command for the differentiation of emphasis—as position, movement, change of pace in the delivery of the speeches—should be used to mark the superior importance of whatever concerns that transaction. And above all, the principal parts should be given to players of such imposing personality as to outweigh the rest of the company and throw them, without effort, into the second place.

V

CONTRAST OF MOODS

It is an old trick of novelists and playwrights to make surrounding Nature adapt herself to the moods of their personages; to make the dismal things happen in dismal weather, and the cheerful things in sunshine. In real life people as often as not make love on a foggy November morning and break it off on a moonlight night in June. The artificiality of the old method may be excused by the unity of effect which it produces in the mind of the spectator; but there is a far finer effect in disharmony, in contrasting instead of attuning the personages and their environment.

In his "Letters on the French Stage," Heine[7] retails an excellent scene from a comedy called *Mariez-vous donc!* where a man, driven by the extravagance of his faithless wife to fiddle for his bread in a low dancing-ken, relates his misfortunes to a friend, fiddling all the while, and breaking off now and again to skip out among the dancers with a "Chassez!" or "En avant deux!" The discord between his narrative and his occupation sets before us in a very poignant fashion the indifference of Life at large to the individual destiny.

Tchekhof has made a system of such contrasts; you find them in all his plays. One of the chief scenes in *The Cherry Orchard* recalls the episode described by Heine. In Act Three, we see Madame Ranévsky waiting to learn the result of the auction. She sits in the midst, a tragic figure, bewailing the imminent destruction of the orchard that is haunted by so many memories of her childhood and her ancestry. But everyone about her is indifferent; they have got in a band of Jewish fiddlers; a medley of ignoble guests and intrusive underlings dances to its silly jigging, "a tedious latter-day dance, with no life, no grace, no vigour in it, not even any desire of the flesh; and they do not realise that the very ground on which they are dancing is passing away from under their feet."[8] And for a climax of grotesqueness the half-crazy German governess dresses herself in a marionette costume, check trousers and tall hat, and dances a *pas seul* somewhere in the background amid the applause of the company.

The last act of *The Seagull*, where they sit down to play lotto ("a tedious game, but all right when you're used to it"; it takes the place of the dance music in *The Cherry Orchard*) while Sorin, fast hurrying to his grave, dozes in a corner, and Constantine, the deserted lover, wanders restless and melancholy about the house, is a whole symphony of contrasted moods.

VI

THE ILLUSION OF THE EGO

Subdued to the life about him, each pursues his own separate thoughts and lives his own solitary life. This individual disjunction is a sort of contrapuntal rejoinder to the group-scheme and leads to the most penetratingly ironical discords and solutions.

7. Heinrich Heine (1797–1856), German poet and essayist. [*Editor's note.*]
8. See Meyerhold's masterly analysis of the scene at p. 143 of the Sbornik "Teatr," issued by "Szipòvnik" in 1908. ["Naturalistic Theater and the Theater of Mood," in *Teatr. Kniga o novom teatra* (St. Petersburg: Shipovnik, 1908), 136–50. [This essay is reprinted on p. 598.]

At the card-table Trigórin and the doctor talk quite independently of Constantine's fortunes as an author; Madame Arcádina chatters to unheeding ears about her triumph at Khárkof and the bouquets that the students gave her, while Masha, attending strictly to the business of the game, cuts across them all with her incisive crying of the lotto-numbers.

So in Act Two, when Madame Arcádina explains how she keeps so young, nobody cares; the dingy Masha laments her own decay, and the Doctor, rather bored, turns back to the novel he was reading them.

In Act One, Constantine is all eagerness when the Doctor praises his play and bids him persevere; but his attention wanders as soon as Dorn begins to explain why, and his next question is, "Excuse me, where is Nina?" to which Dorn replies by developing his critical theory, and Constantine loses his temper.

There is a fine instance of this sort of counterpoint in *Ivánof*. Kosýkh, a gambler, dashes into the house of his friends to borrow money, breaks up their conversation, buttonholes each in turn to recount the *débâcle* of a hand that looked like a grand slam:

> KOSÝKH   I had ace and queen of clubs and four others; ace, ten and a little one in spades . . .
>
> LEBEDEF (*Stopping his ears.*)   Spare me, spare me, for the love of Christ!
>
> KOSÝKH (*To* SHABÉLSKY.)   You see? Ace, queen and four other clubs; ace, ten and a little one in spades . . .
>
> SHABÉLSKY (*Pushing him away.*)   Go away! I don't want to hear!
>
> KOSÝKH   We had the most infernal luck; my ace of spades was ruffled first round . . .
>
> SHABÉLSKY (*Picking up a revolver.*)   Go away, or I'll fire.
>
> KOSÝKH (*With a gesture of despair.*)   Good God! There's not a soul to talk to anywhere! One might as well be in Australia; no solidarity, no common interests; each lives his own life. . . . However, I must be off.

VII

TRAGEDY AND COMEDY

Life is never pure comedy or pure tragedy. Old age is always pathetic, and usually ridiculous. The Universe does not stand still in awe of our private success or misfortunes.

Tchekhof had that fine comedic spirit which relishes the incongruity between the actual disorder of the world and the underlying order. Seeking as he did to throw our eyes outwards from the individual destiny, to discover its relation to surrounding Life, he habitually mingled tragedy (which is Life seen close at hand) with comedy (which is Life seen from a distance). His plays are tragedies with the texture of comedy.

Some of his characters he endows with his own insight. They see their misfortunes, without malice, from the remote comedic point of view. Old Sorin in *The Seagull*, who is carrying to his grave a keen regret for an unadventurous life, lived without passion, without intensity, without achievement, spends his time in laughing. He sees the fun of the solemn practical joke that Nature has played with him. Masha, who is hopelessly and painfully in love with Constantine Tréplef,[9] when she hears him playing a melancholy waltz to solace his passion for someone else, instead of underlining the pathos, pirouettes slowly to the music, humming, with outstretched arms, before she comments on the situation.

As he developed his method Tchekhof sought more and more after the particular quality of life to be derived from the admixture of comedy with pathos. In his last play, *The Cherry Orchard* (his last work indeed, produced only a month or two before his death), the admixture seems at first sight excessive. Some of his personages— Yásha, Dunyásha, Ephikhódof, perhaps Charlotte and Gáyef too— would not be out of place in a knockabout farce. Even the sage, Trophímof, is made shabby and ridiculous, and sent tumbling downstairs at a tragic moment. It is true that real life is just as unceremonious with philosophers; but for the moment one is shocked. Let it be noted however that these folk are not random laughing-stocks; they are all sub-varieties of the species "nedotëpa" or "job-lot," and are expressly designed to carry out the central motive of the play. And are they indeed more farcical than actual people? Perhaps the respectable uniformity that we attribute to our fellow-men is all a convention, an illusion; they are in reality misshapen, gnomish and grotesque; we need a magician to open our eyes that we may see them as they are. I remember having that feeling very strongly in the street, on coming away from an exhibition of Mr. Max Beerbohm's[1] caricatures.

But one should not begin with *The Cherry Orchard*. Art that is too near to Nature always seems strange and unnatural. One should approach gradually, by way of something more conventional, like *The Seagull*.

9. By what strange mistake that eminent Tchekhovian critic, the Russian Eichenwald, convinced himself that Masha was in love with Trigórin, I cannot imagine; but he is very circumstantial about it. See. V. I. Pokrovsky, ed., *Anton Pavlovich Chekhov. Ego zhizn i sochineniya: sbornik istoriko-literaturnykh statey* [Chekhov: His Life and Works: A Collection of Historico-literary Articles] (Moscow: V. Spiridonov and A. Mikhailov, 1907), 856–57.

1. Max Beerbohm (1872–1956), the English writer and caricaturist, immortalized his contemporaries in gauzy drawings. [*Editor's note.*]

VIII

GOOD AND EVIL

Tchekhof's endeavour to establish the true relation of Man to the surrounding universe did not end in a system of artistic formulæ; it was not a mere literary artifice; it embraced a profound philosophy. He endeavoured to establish Man's relation to his environment because it is only by reference to his environment that Man's nature, his doings and his sufferings, can rightly be interpreted.

To sever the individual, to abstract him in thought and try to determine the forces that sway him without reference to the rest of humanity, is as if a philosopher living at the sea's edge, by a gully in the rocks, should watch the water rise and fall in his gully, should observe the fishes and floating weeds and bits of wreckage that pass through it, and endeavour to explain their appearance and disappearance without taking into account the wide sea beyond, with its ebb and flow and changing incidents. He would not be merely limited in the scope of his conclusions; he would be positively wrong. And so, since ever we began to think in Europe, we have been wrong about Man.

To skip and rest and come to morals, we have been wrong, most irreligiously wrong, about Good and Evil. Where suffering is due to human agency we have sought in the individual, not merely for those last movements which make the suffering actual, but for the very fount and origin of Evil itself. We have attributed it to human malevolence, to corrupt and wicked will. (For the Devil was always half a clown and wholly irresponsible; saving the perversity of individual men and women he could at any time have been shut altogether out from human life.)

But the Zeitgeist is slowly bringing a new doctrine to light in our generation—revealing it to divers at one time in different places—that Evil in the world does not arise from Evil in men, but is a constant element in life, flowing not *out* of men's souls, but *through* them; that if we examine the causes of suffering, say, in London or St. Petersburg at any given moment, we shall find that almost all is caused without evil intention, that it is the result of conditions over which no single person has any control, or of individual action prompted by motives of quite average innocence; that there are in fact no villains, or if there are, the amount of unhappiness they cause is so small that it may be neglected in a general estimate.

The old doctrine, that the man who did the thing was in himself the cause of his doing it, served well enough as a doctrine of the criminal law, for the criminal law rests, like magic, not on a theory of causation, but on the desire to express an emotion. But something better is needed in the arts, for they go behind common life to search out the hidden sequences.

I am afraid that this new doctrine of irresponsibility looks rather like another of those paradoxes which the writers of this generation, as is well known, now that all the true things have been said so often, are driven to utter in order to get themselves any reputation of originality. It has an air of inconvenience about it. It will never have a chance outside literature. It can have no hope of recognition among those stout upholders of exploded superstitions, the leaders of the Social Revolution. For with the legend of the Criminal Poor the fable of the Wicked Rich must also go overboard; and without that particular myth in their shot-garlands, they might as well haul down the red flag and put into port again.

Those two great platforms, the tub and the stage, both offer the same temptation to those who discourse from them: to choose the short way, not the right way, of convincing their auditors. When you have only minutes or hours to expound what requires weeks or years, it is no use trying to get new or right ideas into people's heads; the only thing to do is to execute variations on the old wrong ones they have there already. And the doctrine that individual man is the source of evil is such a handy one for the theatre; villains afford such a convenient machinery for developing our old favourite dramatic action, the struggle of opposing wills. Our sympathies need to be enlisted on this side or on that in the contest, by the assurance that the one is right and the other wrong, or a play is likely to be as dull as a cock-fight or a boxing-match where nobody cares which of the combatants wins.

Still, there is a growing disposition among the *sept cents honnêtes gens*,[2] who are pregnant with the public opinion of the next generation, to demand the Truth at any price, (after all, Mankind will always adjust itself to the Truth, if only the authorities will allow it); and this new dogma of irresponsibility is at last beginning to grope its way on to the boards. A certain semblance of it is to be found in Mr. Galsworthy's plays;[3] but only a semblance; for there is always a hobgoblin there, a phantom of Society, with an uncommon resemblance to the old bogle of the Wicked Rich, getting unmercifully thwacked in the background. Mr. Galsworthy, with his benevolent air, is a great hater, essentially a thwacker. But Tchekhof was like Dostoyévsky; he hated nothing and no one. He would not have said, "Woe unto you!" even to the Pharisees, but would have written short stories to explain their attitude.

For him the channels of Evil are innocent and lovable. Trigórin, who desolates two happy young lives, wakens affection and compassion in the audience. Tchekhof made him the express image of him-

---

2. French, the seven hundred respectable men. [*Editor's note.*]
3. John Galsworthy (1867–1933), English novelist and dramatist, whose plays dealt with contemporary moral issues and social conditions. [*Editor's note.*]

self, as who should say, "We are all capable of this." Trigórin seemed to himself to have recaptured the lost poetry of his youth; it was the instinct for beauty that set him on the adventure; it was by the irony of Life, not by the badness of his will, that his desire for a beautiful thing destroyed it. He was a simple-minded man with no vanities and no ambitions, with shy, kindly manners, a man who took a harmless delight, like Tchekhof himself, in sitting by a pond and fishing for chub with a worm and a float. Everybody liked him.

It is all very perverse, but it is the perversity of real life.

IX

VILLAINS AND HEROES

Having no villains, it goes without saying that Tchekhof has no heroes. His drama is not a drama of conflicting wills. He does not invite you to stake your sympathies on this side or on that. All his characters are ranged together against the common enemy, Life, whether they are drawn up in one battalion or in two.

It is idle therefore to discuss where the author's sympathies lie in *The Cherry Orchard*, whether with Lopákhin or with Madame Ranévsky and her brother Gáyef. And yet, thanks to the tradition of the theatre, such a discussion is sure to arise every time that *The Cherry Orchard* is seen on the stage. And the players will already have prejudged it by the reading they have taken of their parts.

On the whole, after the Stage Society performance, the general opinion was that the owners of the Cherry Orchard were meant to be delightful people and Lopákhin a brute. And well-informed Russians over here who had seen the piece in Moscow said that this opinion was undoubtedly right, and that was the way it was played at the Artistic Theatre, to the author's own satisfaction.

Nevertheless, for a hundred reasons, of which I will give only two or three, this opinion is undoubtedly wrong. In the conflict of classes, of traditions and ideals that shook his time, Tchekhof took no part. "I am neither a liberal, nor a conservative, nor a moderate, nor a monk, nor an indifferentist," he wrote to Pleshtchéyef.[4] "I want to be a free artist and nothing more." (What we call the "fine" arts are more finely called the "free" arts in Russia.) "You ought to describe everyday love and family life without villains or angels," he wrote to Leikin.[5] "Be objective," he wrote to Shtcheglóf,[6] "look at everything with your customary kind eyes; sit down and write us a story or play

4. A. P. Chekhov, *Sobranie pisem* [Collection of Chekhov's Letters], ed. Vladimir Brender (Moscow: Sovremennoe tvorchestvo, 1910), I. [For Pleshcheev, see note 1, page 391.]

5. *Nikolay Aleksandrovich Leikin i ego vospominaniya i perepiska* [Leikin's Reminiscences and Correspondence] [St. Petersburg: R. Golike, A. Vilborg, 1907). (For Leikin note 1, page 382.]

6. Chekhov's letters, *op. cit.* [For Shcheglov, see note 2, page 389.]

of Russian life, not a criticism of Russian life, but the joyful song of a goldfinch (*shicheglá*) about Russian life and human life in general, life which is given us but once and which it is foolish to waste on exposing the wickedness of" so and so.

To me he seems to have been most scrupulously fair in sharing out the virtues and vices evenly to all his characters alike. Gáyef and his sister are warm-hearted, generous and picturesque, but then how frivolous, how unpractical, how impossible! They are still the noblesse, but all the faculties of the noblesse for cleaving to their property have evaporated out of them. I think he must have chosen the name Gáyef for the faint flavour that it has of *gáyer*, a mountebank. Lopákhin is illiterate and material; his name suggests shovels and gobbling (*lopáty* and *lópat*); but then how efficient he is, how useful to his generation! He is like St. Nicholas, the ploughman-hero in the old ballad, whistling gaily to his team as he drives a furrow from the Dnieper to the Ural. He is tender-hearted and generous; he is an idealist, an artist in his way; he has "thin delicate artist-fingers," he has a "delicate artist-soul." A great part of him indeed is Tchekhof himself. Tchekhof's grandfather was a serf and his father kept a grocer's shop in Taganrog. "Peasant blood flows in my veins," he writes to Suvórin: "and you cannot astonish me with the virtues of the peasantry. I have always believed in Progress from my childhood up, and could not help believing in it, for the difference between the time when I used to get thrashed and the time when I stopped getting thrashed was something tremendous." It might be Lopákhin speaking.

No; Lopákhin is neither the villain nor the hero of *The Cherry Orchard*. There is no villain and no hero. Tchekhof is merely singing a song of Russian life and human life in general; not indeed the "joyful song of a goldfinch," but rather the plaintive elegy of a ringdove, contemplating our troubled world, a "free artist," from the solitude of the woods.[7]

X

REALISM

Mr. Maurice Baring[8] our principal expounder of modern Russian literature, says the great thing about it is that it represents ordinary

7. By no means all well-informed Russians maintain that Lopákhin is the villain of the piece. Górky, Kárpof and G. Petróff (see a deeply-felt article by him "In Defence of Lopakhin" in "The Tchekhof Jubilee Sbornik" [*A. P. Chekhov: sbornik statey* (Moscow: Obrazovanie, 1910)] look on him as the hero; indeed, Merezhkóvsky says, "All the Russian Intelligenz applauded this triumph of the new life." [D. Merezhkovsky, *Chekhov i Gorky* (St. Petersburg: M. V. Pirozhkov, 1906.]

8. Maurice Baring (1874–1946), English diplomat and writer, whose time in Russia made him an ardent apostle of Russian literature. [*Editor's note.*]

life; he says that the Russian goes to the theatre to see what he sees every day outside the theatre: that Tchekhof chooses for the action of his plays "moments which appear at first sight to be trivial."[9]

What a tedious and unnecessary literature it would be if that were true! What, however, are Tolstoy's themes? Seduction and adultery, battle, murder and sudden death. Dostoyévsky's? An innocent gentleman in a felon's prison, a student assassin hunted by the police, a girl who sold her virtue to feed her family. Tchekhof's? There is only one of his plays that does not end with a pistol-shot; they contain two suicides, a duel and an attempted murder. Surely Mr. Baring must have been very unfortunate if he thinks that this is everyday Russian life!

Is it not plain that, Russians and English, we all go to the theatre to see what we do *not* see in everyday life? For in everyday life we see, with undiscerning eyes, only the little corner penetrated by our own routine. Playwrights show us men and women in extraordinary circumstances; for it is only extraordinary circumstances that reveal the secrets of their nature and illuminate the whole path of their existence.

The differentia of Tchekhof is that the extraordinary moments which explode in pistol-shots are never the result of sudden causes, but are brought about by the cumulative tragedy of daily life; not ordinary daily life, in the sense of everyone's daily life, but the life of men tragically situated, like Tréplef, or Ivánof, or Uncle Ványa.

If the Russians are realists, it is not because they go to real life for their matter. Every artist goes to real life for his matter, and from its chaos brings us an idea. Even the least realistic artists are concerned with life to that extent; and the tragedies of Corneille and Racine are just as much extracts of life as the comedies of Ibsen or Mr. Granville Barker.[1]

The specific difference of the realist is that, having extracted his idea, instead of further distilling the extract (as the Classicist does) or disguising it with mysterious essences (as the Romantic does), he endeavours to restore to it the flavour of reality. He endeavours to manifest the very texture and illusion of Life itself. Having unravelled a thread, he shows it us with a new artful tangle of his own, cheating us by its resemblance to the tangle of the skein from which he drew it.[2]

---

9. *Landmarks in Russian Literature* (London: Methuen, 1910), p. 21. Baring's book was one of the first to introduce Chekhov to an English-speaking public. [*Editor's note.*]

1. Harley Granville Barker (1877–1946), British director, playwright and critic, advocate of the "new drama," an uncommercial form of intellectual play. [*Editor's note.*]

2. It is, in the same way, by their method, not by their subject matter, that Classicism and Romanticism are to be distinguished. "The expressions Classical and Romantic refer only to the spirit of the treatment. The treatment is classical when the form of the representation is identical with the idea represented; the treatment is romantic when the form does not reveal the idea through identity, but lets us divine it by an allegory" (Heine,

The Realist does not copy Life (the result would be meaningless); he explains it (that is the business of Art) and gives his explanation the air of a copy. His intention is to take in simple-minded people. What a triumph to have taken in Mr. Baring!

XI

SOLILOQUIES

There is one commandment in the decalogue of Realism that Tchekhof habitually breaks, and that is the commandment forbidding soliloquies. This is a law which no playwright must disregard if he would pass for modern. Indeed, one is often puzzled and embarrassed by the sudden silence which descends on a talkative stage-personage, when, by the exit of the others, he happens to be left by himself for a moment on the scene. If he says "Pshaw," or sighs, or clears his throat, it is the most you can expect of him. Usually he lights a cigarette.

But Tchekhof's plays are full of soliloquies; and I venture to protest that Tchekhof is right and the rest are wrong. Certainly the old-fashioned "aside," by which the comedian treated his audience as a confidential friend, winked and grinned, poked it, as it were, in the ribs and invited it to laugh with him at the rest of the company— that was a stupid thing, a mere trick, like cheeking the bandmaster in a pantomime. But to banish that other kind of solitary speaking, by which a man conveys to the audience what is passing in his mind when they could have no other means of learning it, is altogether a mistake. For what, after all, is the subject-matter of a play? It is not mere outward action; it is also thought and will culminating in action, and this latter element is, to the judicious spectator, "much the noblest" part of Drama, and indeed, with Tchekhof, the greater part; for his plays, rightly understood, are more than half soliloquy; the characters seem to converse, but in reality sit side by side and think aloud.[3]

"Our inner life moves in monologues from morning to night, and even our dreams are still monologues of the soul. They are not spoken aloud, that is all; that is the outward difference over which our petty little modern code of aesthetics makes so much ado," says an excellent critic of latter-day drama.[4]

It is true that a man does not talk aloud when he is left alone in

---

Deutschland: ein Wintermärchen, Book I [*Germany: A Winter's Tale*] [1844; innumerable eds.]

3. See Eichenwald in "Pokrovsky," *op.cit.*, p. 891.
4. Rudolf von Gottschall, *Zur Kritik des modernen Dramas: vergleichendes Studien* (Berlin: Allgemeiner Verein fur deutsche Literatur, 1900), p. 117.

a room; but then, to be consistent, we should also drop the curtain, for when a man is alone no one sees him.

XII

SYMBOLISM

Tchekhof did not often use symbols in the old-fashioned sense, material objects adumbrating immaterial meanings, designed to catch attention by their superficial irrelevance, like the lambs and lilies of pictured saints. Certainly the eponymous seagull that flew about the lake, and then was shot and stuffed and fixed on a wooden stand, is a symbol of that kind, in itself neither better nor worse than the sort of symbols that Ibsen was fond of using; only Tchekhof used his symbol beautifully and pathetically, while in Ibsen's use of symbols, such as that tower from which the Master-builder fell, while his sweetheart hopped about and waved a flag, or that wild duck which the old gentleman kept in the attic, there is always a touch of ugliness and insanity.

Except the seagull I can recall no other example in Tchekhof's plays of a symbol of the artless kind that can be stored in the property-room. But there is a more beautiful and recondite Symbolism, one that harmonises better with the realistic method, and that is the Symbolism by which the events of the Drama are not merely represented for their own sake but stand also as emblems and generalisations about life at large. The relation of the characters to each other in *The Seagull,* for instance, evidently symbolises the universal frustration of desire (and how intensely the author carries this idea through all the play!): Medvédenko is in love with Masha, Masha is in love with Constantine, Constantine is in love with Nina, Nina is in love with Trigórin, Pauline is in love with Dorn, and Dorn is in love with himself. Each yearns to change his lot, to go back or to go forward. Trigórin wants youth, Nina and Tréplef want glory; Trigórin has it but has never noticed it; he can only suppose that it "produces no sensation."

Perhaps at bottom all plays are symbolical. Perhaps Life itself is symbolical, and the pursuit of women's love is, as Maupassant[5] divined, only an allegory and image of the pursuit of that "beauté mystique, entrevue et insaisissable"[6] towards which some Protean instinct of our nature urges us.

The Russian critics are sure that there is a message of substantial hope in Tchekhof's plays, just as the shepherds in Tchekhof's story,

5. Guy de Maupassant (1850–1893), sardonic French author whose work makes an appearance in *The Seagull*. [*Editor's note.*]
6. French, "mystical, barely glimpsed and ungraspable beauty." [*Editor's note.*]

"Happiness," are sure that there is gold hidden in the old Tartar barrows on the steppe. Again and again his characters aver that this age of folly and wrong is drawing to an end, that in two or three hundred years (the date is always given) we may confidently look for the Millennium. And this, they say, is not dramatic and irresponsible; it represents his own view. In private life he more than once declared his faith in Progress. "How beautiful life will be in another three hundred years!" "Once upon a time this place was a wilderness covered with stones and thistles," he said to Kúprin in the garden of his Yalta villa;[7] "but I came and cultivated it and made it beautiful"; then, with an earnest face and in tones of the deepest conviction, "In two or three hundred years all the earth will become a garden full of flowers." Almost the very words used by Trophímof and repeated by the trustful Anya in *The Cherry Orchard*.[8]

Well, if anyone finds comfort in believing that Tchekhof's plays support this doctrine of shallow optimism, let him believe it! To me it seems the dolefullest renunciation of all hope. If Tchekhof, who saw so clearly that in real life all tales end badly, had to console himself by supposing that some day they would all begin to end well, it is enough to strike panic into one. Is Life then really so bad that strong earnest men must needs become timid and frivolous rather than face the conclusions to which reason leads them?

I fancy the Russian critics are mistaken. Tchekhof probably said many foolish things in private life, as other great men have done; but I doubt if he repeated them in the same good faith when the wisdom of the artist descended on him. The satirist, like every other writer, goes to himself for much of his material; pen in hand he sees his own foibles with the sobriety of inspiration. Do not believe that Tchekhof the dramatist was gulled by the enthusiasms of that Tchekhof who walked in the garden at Yalta! It is all his sad fun. Into whose mouth does he put the hopefullest sentiments in *The Cherry Orchard*? Into the mouth of Trophímof, the "mouldy gentleman," "the perpetual student"; a fine guarantor for the Millennium! Is not the whole play strown with the shattered illusions of the Trophímofs of the generation before, the men who thought that in Emancipation and Education they had found the talisman? And that constant reference to the date of its advent, the precision of the "two or three hundred years," did Tchekhof not relish the irony of that?

7. See *Pamyati A. P. Chekhova* [To Chekhov's Memory] (Moscow: Ob-vo lyubiteli ross. slovesnosti, 1906), p. 104.
8. In a letter which he wrote in 1902, Tchekhof changed the date to "tens of thousands of years" ahead (Chekhov's letters, *op.cit.*, 262). De Vogüé in a refreshing article, full of cold water, describes his attitude as "un découragement absolu quant au présent, corrigé par un vague millénarisme, par une foi tremblotante au progrès indéfini." [absolute discouragement in regard to the present, amended by a vague belief in the millennium and a wavering faith in an ill-defined progress.] [E. M. de Vogüé, "Anton Tchekhof," *Revue des Deux Mondes*, 7 [January 1, 1902]: 201–16.]

Surely it is another piece of Symbolism. Each generation believes that it stands on the boundary line between an old bad epoch and a good new one. And still the world grows no better; rather worse; hungrier, less various, less beautiful. That is true; but there is consolation in the assurance that whatever becomes of this husk of a planet, the meaning we put into it, hope itself, God, man's ideal, continually progresses and develops. If that is not what Tchekhof meant, it seems at any rate the best interpretation of what he wrote.

G. CALDERSON.
HAMPSTEAD, 1911.

P.S.—I ought to have mentioned that Tchekhof was born in 1860, studied medicine at Moscow, and died in 1904.

NAUM BERKOVSKY

Naum Yakovlevich Berkovsky (1901–1972), a graduate of Leningrad University, was a theater scholar who specialized in Western European and Russian drama. His books, many published posthumously, include *Literature and Theater* (1969), *Romanticism in Germany* (1973), and *The Universal Significance of Russian Literature* (1975).

Chekhov, Story Writer and Dramatist†

* * *

Chekhov's drama is an extension of his prose, a rich variation on his tales and short stories. Because Chekhov's best plays were written at the time of his fullest artistic maturity, they may be the fullest expression of the Chekhovian world and the Chekhovian style. Moreover, both Chekhov's world and style stand out in greater relief in his plays than in his narrative prose. Critics dismissive of Chekhov's theater have said that Chekhov's plays are short stories performed on stage. A better way of putting it might be to say not short stories in general, but Chekhov's own short stories. Concepts of Chekhov were still associated with the narrative form. A short story in which "the stream of life" is reconstructed was still close to what is taken to be the epic. "The stream of life" is the basis for the epic—if you like, the epic in its pure form. But to present this element in drama involves breaking the rules of dramatic performance in their basic principles; it involves putting special emphasis on its new view of

† From "Chekhov, povestvovatel i dramaturg," *Teatr* 1 (1960): 87–99. Trans. by Laurence Senelick.

things. Drama and theater in their usual form were for Chekhov the
least propitious of realms. That is precisely why Chekhov was constantly contending with them. He regarded the stage, which was so
unyielding to his dramatic works, with distrust or else with hostility,
yet he continued to write for it. The stage was opposed to Chekhov
and his style, but, by winning over the stage, Chekhov's style
achieved the most supreme power of expression, possible only for
him.

* * *

Something unprecedented in drama is already happening in Chekhov's earliest work, sometimes entitled *Platonov*. Here the dialogue
is very curious and audacious. Uninfluenced by Ibsen, whom he
could not possibly have known at this time, Chekhov carries on the
split-level dialogue familiar to the spectator of Ibsen. The characters
are shown onstage in certain everyday activities—for instance, a
game of chess in Act One—and their activities, this quotidian stream
with its accidental variations, are reflected in the dialogue. Beyond
the chess dialogue, people free associate as they will. In the first case,
people seem to be fettered to their environment, their workaday life,
things; in the other, they enjoy greater independence. The dialogue,
written on two levels, idiosyncratically discloses the presence of two
Chekhovian plots in the play: one originates in the initiative of the
characters themselves, and this is their personal plot; the other is
non-individual and presents the objective progress of the event, as
the "stream of life" flows and meanders. Chekhovian dialogue, which
is already present in *Platonov*, predetermines a great deal of the
nature and style of his later plays.

Like Chekhov's stories, his plays depict everyday life destroying
people in such a way that everyday life is itself destroyed. In both
Chekhov's stories and drama, the victor is always doomed. People
live in a society which has its own structure and laws. People suffer
from the laws that are in force. Individual attempts to dislodge or
change something in them, the individual "personal plot," come to
naught. At the same time it is obvious that these laws are not eternal,
that their power is faltering and may be swept away with their last
victims. We may deduce from Chekhov's plays a certain principle
common to them all: the action seems to be taking place in a con-
quered city, a hostile power is in control that sends good people to
prison, they lose their heads, but even this power will itself be condemned one of these days, when the forces of light enter the town.

In *The Seagull*, Konstantin Treplyov says, "the modern theater is
trite, riddled with clichés. When the curtain goes up on an artificially
lighted room with three walls, these great talents, acolytes of the
religion of art, act out how people eat, drink, make love, walk, wear

their jackets . . ." We don't have to believe that Chekhov is berating his own plays through Treplyov's words. They have people wearing jackets who walk through ordinary rooms, drink, eat, and love; they also constantly confront the spectator with the most trivial everyday life, and even so Kostya Treplyov's attacks are not addressed to them. Kostya Treplyov has in mind the kitchen-sink plays of the repertoire of his time, in which everyday life was depicted in its pristine form, with crude naiveté, with full belief in it, in its subject matter, in its unconditionally eternal power over people. And in Chekhov's plays, the action is that everyday life, in all its manifestations, swallows up everyone and everything. In this play, Kostya Treplyov shoots himself twice—unsuccessfully sometime between acts two and three, and mortally in the last, fourth act. Chekhov ran the risk of prolonging the suicide attempt on stage, of making the romanticism of gunshots prosaic. Suicide is Kostya's personal plot, the action which he considers to be self-liberating. But two shots instead of one—this is the style of everyday life, its amorphousness, its dilatory quality, its risky duplication in a reality that human beings regard as familiar and their own. In this way, everyday life subjugates even the means of deliverance from everyday life. On the other hand, in Chekhov's plays the very obtrusiveness of everyday episodes and details is a token that the structure of life, regulated for centuries, has suddenly begun to wobble. To take the example of the story "Calm and Collected," the excessive attention paid to the way people do the most ordinary things—who came in, who went out, who takes snuff or refrains from snuff, who catches a fish or who doesn't—this excessive attention to details becomes a symptom that a crisis has come to pass in the great and paramount things. Details ought to distract us from the crisis, but instead they are precisely what announces that the crisis is upon us. Chekhov resembles the playwrights of everyday life only in his form, in his meaning Chekhov is opposed to them.

In *The Seagull*, Chekhov uses devices of a very obsolete theater, investing them with a very modern meaning. On the model of the obsolete theater Chekhov introduces a myriad of parallel thematic lines, multiplying the main theme; more accurately, it is this multiplicity that enables us to realize which theme is the main one. There are five tales of unrequited love in this play: Kostya Treplyov's for Nina Zarechnaya, Nina Zarechnaya's for Trigorin, Masha Shamraeva's for Kostya, Masha's mother Polina Andreevna's for Dr. Dorn, and the schoolteacher Medvedenko's for Masha. There are nuances in these unrequited affairs: Medvedenko wins Masha's hand, for a short time Zarechnaya benefits from Trigorin's favors, Polina Andreevna has been in love with Dorn for a long time and cannot get him to make a formal declaration or become more intimate. Only Treplyov is unhappy to the end. But for all these differences, these five stories replicate one another; everywhere there is dissension, misprision, unfounded feelings, directed to the wrong address; if there is happiness, then it's not for long, with post-happiness grievances that cannot be suppressed. The only contented ones, though with lapses, are Arkadina and Trigorin. They evidently appreciate the mutual comfort of a shaky relationship and thus protect themselves. Other failures of a general character are also depicted in the play. Treplyov is unhappy not only in love, he is also unsure of himself as a writer, although he has been successful with the public. Pyotr Nikolaevich Sorin, a man of sixty, has made a career but has missed out on life.

In the short story *The Steppe*,[1] there are pages in which Panteley tells tales of highway robbers. People listen to Panteley at night around the campfire: "After grub they all fell silent and only thought about what they had heard. Life is terrible and wonderful, whatever horror story is told in Rus; however they embellish it with thieves' dens, long knives and miracles, it always resonates in the heart of the listener as a legend . . ." Therefore, according to Chekhov, what is important is not the material of the stories about highway robbers and knives. The truth of these stories lies not in the figures, not in the events, not in the details, but in the general emotion they evoke. "Life is terrible and wonderful," therefore the emotion of fear is infectious for the listener, although the plot and all its twists and turns may be strange to him—besides, Panteley's stories are not over-endowed with verisimilitude. Chekhov's play *The Seagull* is also powerful in the truth of general emotion. It need not be understood as a love drama, as simply stringing together stories of unhappy lovers. These very stories portray only the transition to another, more generalized meaning. These romantic failures, one after another, side by side, express a certain general failure of human existence: a failure of an epochal, dismal universal situation; a crisis the modern world is in. A time has come when success is not an option.

In *The Seagull* there are two generations. One is living out its life, while the other wants to and cannot achieve a real life. Trigorin and Arkadina are aging; Kostya Treplyov wants to be an innovator and only knows how to be a decadent. Nina Zarechnaya is seeking her hero; one of them, Trigorin, as a writer and as a character is still true to tradition, but it is no longer the classical tradition, but a different tradition instead. Kostya Treplyov has already entered something new, but has not grasped what makes it new. Treplyov's problem is that Trigorin, for all his frailties, is, for the time being, stronger than Treplyov, and holds sway over people while Treplyov only dreams about it. The crisis of life is depicted in this play of Chekhov's in its

1. A long narrative (1888) about a nine-year-old boy's experiences travelling across the steppe. [*Editor's note.*]

congealed forms, with its still intolerable resolutions, and this lends a special anguish to what goes on onstage.

Already in *The Seagull*, Chekhov has sufficiently developed his characteristic device of freezing the characters; the life of the characters seems to stop short, they disappear into themselves, and in the outer world they are manifested by a few gestures, lines, which are all similar, sometimes literally repeated. Shamraev constantly recalls actors and keeps retelling anecdotes of the theater, Medvedenko keeps affirming the hard lot of the village schoolmaster; Sorin asks for a cure for old age; Dr. Dorn hums. Later, especially in *Three Sisters*, these leitmotifs for individual characters are remarkably developed; characters will stick to the same phrases, quotations, grace notes, sayings, catch phrases. The characters appear to have escaped in this way from outside influences, creating a zone of personal inattentiveness and neutrality around themselves and cutting themselves off from the general fate. But their immobility, their attempts at isolation in Chekhov's plays only emphasize the most intimate bond each shares with the rest, with everyone, with collective involvement, and with the general course of events. Their immobility is of a concerted character and in quite another relation—it is each individual's manifestation of that frozen crisis, which has stricken all the characters together.

* * *

The Seagull is allied to the subsequent plays through individual plot motifs as well. Kostya Treplyov, Sorin, Shamraev, Masha, Medvedenko, and Dorn are regular inhabitants of the country, while Trigorin and Arkadina are guests. Treplyov and Sorin do not like the country, but are used to staying there. In his later plays, Chekhov preserves this division of the characters into the settled and the arrivals, the voluntary and involuntary in relation to everyday life. In *Uncle Vanya*, the Serebryakovs come to the country, while the Voinitskys and Astrov work there and will stay there forever. In *Three Sisters*, the military has come to town and will leave town, while there is no progress for the sisters: they will never get to the Moscow for which they yearn.

Repetitions and coincidences in Chekhov's plays bear witness to the fact that a certain general theme moves through these plays; while the motifs of the subject matter are its support, and since the support is a convenient one, Chekhov will use it more than once. In Chekhov's plays, it is immaterial that some of the characters are easily enthused, possessing freedom of maneuver. The mobility and buoyancy of these persons set off the confinement, the eternal doom of one's own footing, the stasis of the others, and namely the situation of these others. Treplyov, the Voinitskys, and the three sisters are all immobile, some on an estate, some in town. Motionless, they must face their personal fate; it beats them, they accept its blows. An exception to this stasis is *The Cherry Orchard*, in which, at the final curtain, the stage is empty. Everyone has abandoned Ranevskaya's estate, both hosts and guests, and beneath the blow of fate— beneath the blow of Lopakhin's axe—trees, not people, are felled; only old Firs remains on stage, but for a long time now he has not been so different from the estate's furnishings, from the cherry orchard itself.

Characters even move in Chekhov from play to play, although they change names and complexion in each. Chekhov sets store not in the personal idiosyncrasies of a character, but rather in the character's significance amidst the others in working out the general meaning of the play. The senior civil servant Sorin in *The Seagull* is replaced in *Three Sisters* by the army doctor Chebutykin. Both are old bachelors, both sigh that life cannot be lived over again from the beginning. Chekhov needs both to juxtapose them with the young, to fill out the young. The young are given what the old are refused: the young actually are beginning their own life before our eyes, but it is easily surmised that it will be as vacuous and fruitless as Sorin's and Chebutykin's. The young stand at the starting point, the old men at the finish line; but in Chekhov's plays, it is obvious that start and finish coincide and are identical to one another. The cycle of the generations, of birth and death, will resolve nothing, unless the way the lives of each and every one is organized is changed.

The main theme of *Uncle Vanya* is the disillusionment of the characters. It lies within the bounds of general human themes. The Voinitsky family, headed by Uncle Vanya, have worked all their life for Professor Serebryakov, have sacrificed themselves to him, and suddenly Uncle Vanya has seen how insignificant Serebryakov is in his field of learning, how Serebryakov fails to deserve coddling and admiration. In Chekhov's stories and plays, the modern world as a whole becomes disillusioned, loses its meaning; Serebryakov is only one of many modern tin gods whose twilights have arrived. The most painful thing of all is that Uncle Vanya, already aware that his life has lost all its former meaning, will go on living the way he used to live. The god is dethroned, but Uncle Vanya will go on sweeping the dust from his altar. He is reconciled with the professor and the Serebryakovs leave, while Uncle Vanya and Sonya again undertake to make money for the Serebryakovs. The old tune is resumed in the epilogue to the play. Uncle Vanya and Sonya are managing the estate again. Uncle Vanya's room is also the room for Professor Serebryakov's dealings, and is one of the tokens of the slavery into which Uncle Vanya has been sold. Prior to the epilogue, as Uncle Vanya and Sonya tote up accounts in Uncle Vanya's room, he notes aloud: "February second vegetable oil twenty pounds . . . February sixteenth another twenty pounds vegetable oil . . . buckwheat groats . . ." Once upon a time, these accountant's figures were the music to a religion, but the Serebryakov religion is overthrown while the notes are intoned as of old.

Two words about Uncle Vanya's wonderful neckties—Chekhov made special mention of them to actors. For Uncle Vanya, as we shall see, they were an unavailing attempt to uproot himself from the humdrum. The attempt is marked by this humble and minor detail, because it is weak and hopeless. The humdrum is extremely powerful. In the late 1880s, Chekhov wrote a vaudeville *The Proposal*. The comedy here is that the proposal has not even been made, yet already the couple-to-be are having conjugal arguments and spats. The temporal order is disrupted; the future tries to get ahead of the present. The prosaic and the humdrum are impatient and use such prerogatives to avoid making way for a celebration, even if its legitimate turn has come. The prosaic and the humdrum do not respect the laws of time and temporality, nor even the laws of locality; other vaudevilles of Chekhov, *The Wedding* and *The Celebration*, are constructed on this blueprint.

In the plot of *Uncle Vanya*, property relations are broached. Serebryakov wants to sell the estate that fed both him and Uncle Vanya; in future, let it feed only Serebryakov. After Uncle Vanya's gunshot, everything remains as before: the estate is not sold and Uncle Vanya will live out his life, a drudge running Serebryakov's farm.

In *Three Sisters* and *Cherry Orchard* in particular, the material circumstances are even more prominent. In these plays, Chekhov is reworking in his own way the "Balzacian" themes of property and acquisition. Chekhov's last plays are especially characteristic in their social coloration—these are dramas of middle-class interests, acted out in idiosyncratic conditions and milieux.

The three sisters Irina, Olga, and Masha aspire to Moscow, but Moscow keeps moving farther away from them in each act of the play. The sisters lose ground in their own town through Acts One, Two, and Three—and they are no longer mistresses in their own home, their brother Andrey has mortgaged the house to the bank, and Natasha, Andrey's wife, has grabbed all the money. An antagonist of the three sisters, Natasha is a petty bourgeoise; avaricious, a shameless interloper in the Prozorov family circle, impudent, unbridled in pursuit of her own ends. She is so repulsive that the spectator transfers his negative feelings for her to her little son and daughter, who are not at fault in anything, and it is not the spectator but Natasha who is responsible for these feelings. In Act One she is only a fiancée, in Act Two she has given birth to Bobik, and in Act Three to Sophiekins. Natasha expands corporeally; through Bobik and

Sophiekins she constricts everyone else who lives on earth, who lives in the Prozorov home. At first she confiscates Irina's room for Bobik, then Andrey's room for Sophiekins. Olga moves out, Irina moves out, the house is in Natasha's hands. The conquest progresses from scene to scene, from act to act. Evil moves at a deliberate pace, sure of its own capabilities.

The characteristic quality of Chekhov's play is that Natasha meets with no opposition. Natasha completes her intervention, while the sisters retreat farther and farther away. V. V. Yermilov[2] writes of *Three Sisters*: "The play contains a classic dramatic dilemma, which confronts the characters with the need to put up a fight, but the major characters . . . shrink from this need. The play contains an *attack*, but no *defense* or counterattack—in other words: no *struggle*. One side attacks, the other . . . goes away. One side forces them out, and the other . . . is forced out, without so much as an attempt to defend and retrench its positions."

Chekhov's play makes it clear why the sisters refrain from fighting—out of extreme fastidiousness, out of distaste at getting involved in this kind of fight. The dominant interests of life—property interests—are raging in Natasha. They are so unattractive, so vile in Natasha that they aid her. The sisters will not get engaged in property litigation with her—this would put the sisters on her level, and that would be a disgrace for them. The sisters' inaction is its own reward. It excludes every form of behavior except the uniquely individual. From the sisters' viewpoint, it is shameful and awkward to protect their property, to establish their right of ownership of the house, the land. After the sisters, the only thing left is to fight for the abolition of private property as such. When there is no need for one's own home, no need for one's own ground, then there will, incidentally, be no Natashas, whose instincts developed along with private property. The sisters are incapable of a fight that would have such consequences and such scale. But their abstention from the petty, egoistic struggle, which relies on the rights and laws of the old world, morally prepares society for this other struggle, whose goals are great and radically fundamental. The sisters' example teaches us that it is improper for a virtuous person to seek protection in ugly, compromising rights and laws, even if he or she is able to count on that protection.

There are very keen ethical issues in *Three Sisters*. Natasha's behavior—Natasha's *offensive*—raises ethical questions: Natasha and middle-class private property on one hand, ethics on the other. A very curious role is played by Protopopov, the chairman of the

2. V. V. Yermilov (1904–1965), leading Soviet critic, who published several monographs on Chekhov's plays (1946–48) before issuing his major work, *A. P. Chekhov* (1950). His standpoint was firmly Marxist and took the plays to be socialist realism. [*Editor's note.*]

rural board, Natasha's lover. All four acts are played out, the final curtain has fallen, and Protopopov is still behind the scenes. He's been making advances to Natasha for a long time, but lets Andrey marry her—the plot of "Big Volodya and Little Volodya."[3] We hear sleighbells—Protopopov has driven up in a three-horse sleigh to take Natasha for a ride. We are told that Protopopov is sitting in the drawing room of the Prozorov home. He has never once appeared before us onstage, and yet we see him clearly. We think this must be the result of his ethical portrayal. We are familiar with this ethical topos—it rubs elbows with Natasha, that is, it's on the wrong side of ethical values. In this play with so urgent an ethical theme a character's ethical nature is enough to make him visible.

Three Sisters reveals the secret of all of Chekhov's plays, indeed, everything he wrote. This play teaches us in the most graphic manner what constitutes the common disease of the Chekhovian world. It is not the people who are diseased, but the interests people represent. Middle-class interests are compromised, and hence people's spineless behavior, their mood swings, their wishy-washiness. Like the three sisters, they do not want to protect themselves, so little do they respect their own interests and goals, which need to be protected. The Chekhovian world is falling to pieces because the realm of reflection has turned into motives, spontaneously moving through human actions. This is the source of the originality of Chekhov's playwriting. Chekhov's plays pose no problem, let alone achieve a set goal. The goal and the struggle to achieve goals have themselves become problematic in Chekhov. There is only one play in world literature in which things work in exactly the same way—Shakespeare's *Hamlet*. Chekhov's continual interest in Hamlet is hardly coincidental. In other drama, reflection over motives and goals is an unusual phenomenon. Despite this, the essence of drama is in the struggle of interests, at their highest state of tension, in their greatest exposure. Classical heroes in classical dramas are naively and wholly devoted to interests which they try to vindicate; interests and heroes merge into one simple force. In Chekhov, it's quite different. The characters in Chekhov are both themselves and the interests. For a long time the characters are not sure that their goals and motives are correct, indisputable, and this uncertainty is where everyone begins; it is the whole depth of the crisis that befalls the Chekhovian world. In a play, the feebleness of interests and goals and people's loss of enthusiasm has to be displayed with graphic, sharply defined qualities, inaccessible to narrative. This was an abrupt renunciation of what was admissible in drama; it was an illegitimate genre, and Chekhov could calculate that this illegitimacy heightened artistic

3. A story of Chekhov's, published in 1893. [*Editor's note.*]

xpressiveness. Chekhov turned to drama not to obey its laws, but
o break them. And by breaking them he became one of the most
original and audacious dramatists in the world.

As to *Three Sisters*, a note about the character's personality traits:
many of them are fragmented, not whole people; but one side, the
human side, is entirely elaborated. Tusenbach is sweet and intelligent but painfully homely. Irina cannot come to terms with her own
dislike of him. Solyony, as his name implies,[4] pretends sarcasm and
cutting wit. His jokes have an element of wit but Solyony will never
produce real wit. One element of wit is surprise. This Solyony knows
but he does not know the rest. Solyony suddenly exclaims: "He
scarcely had time to gasp, When the bear had him in its grasp."
Solyony has taken it out of context—this is one of the conditions of
wit, but Solyony stops there. Solyony is not wholly witty, but only a
half-wit. When they hear Solyony, everyone is dumbfounded, and
no one laughs. He is a loser, as is usual with Chekhov's people, but
Solyony takes revenge for his losing on someone else who is also a
loser. In *Three Sisters*, we are shown humanity incomplete, as if left
unfinished by nature. So the feeling and the thought arise in the
spectator that we need a new era, when this work of perfecting
humanity will be consummated, completed.

The Cherry Orchard, the Chekhovian work chronologically closest
to the revolution of 1905, is invested with the greatest power of
foresight. There is no other work in which Chekhov's sense of the
obsolescence of the aristocratic and middle-class world is so developed. Time drags on slowly in this play. Maybe this is where one can
learn the meaning of Chekhovian pauses. They are inserted instead
of dialogue: instead of dialogue there is time—determined, empty,
barren time. It is not captured in this play by the action of some or
the reaction of others. A. P. Skaftymov[5] writes: "*The Cherry Orchard*
contains neither the hostilely aggressive merchant nor the resistant
landowner, fighting for his own proprietary interests." This is the
chief distinction between *The Cherry Orchard* and *Three Sisters*. In
Chekhov's last play, the breakdown of material interests is generalized: not only is it not on the side of those under attack, as in *Three
Sisters*, here it is even on the side of the attackers. Ranevskaya and
Gaev, landowners of long standing, put up a very poor fight for their
cherry orchard. But even the merchant Lopakhin is in no great hurry
to swing his axe; he tries to persuade Ranevskaya and Gaev, gives
them advice on how to defend themselves, and at the auction is not

4. The name means salty or briny. [*Editor's note.*]
5. A. P. Skaftymov (b. 1890), Russian literary theorist, an expert on poetics and folklore. His
   essay "On the Question of the Principles Underlying the Construction of Chekhov's Plays"
   (1958) became a classic. [*Editor's note.*]

the first to make the bid that defeats Gaev's fifty thousand. Lopakhin buys the orchard not so much out of commercial considerations as to prevent the annihilation of his childhood memories—he had been a peasant's child, pitiful in the eyes of the masters of the cherry orchard, but now the cherry orchard is passing under the sway of Lopakhin himself. This is a social topic, but even it is an insufficient theme, even if it touched interests of genuine commerce. In Chekhov's last play the middle-class triumphs over the aristocracy—its victory is tardy, it is itself partly phlegmatic in achieving its own victory. Lopakhin is "calm and collected" in matters of business, like the goods consignor in the early story of that name. Trofimov and Anya talk about new times and a new life, which will include neither aristocratic landowning or Lopakhinish warehouses and business offices. A breath of the future has touched the merchant Lopakhin as it touched the "middle-class" characters of Chekhov's stories "A Woman's Kingdom," "An Incident on the Jetty." Lopakhin is middle-class, already insecure in his middle-class status, like the rich heiresses described in those stories. In *The Cherry Orchard*, the impression of an obsolete life is more apparent than anywhere else; it is maintained by laws, the laws themselves are subject to a scrutiny very dangerous for them.

In this play of financial interests, where an auction is the main event, there are constant intimations that money itself has already lost its power, although it remains in circulation. In Act Two, Ranevskaya suddenly gives the vagrant a goldpiece. Simeonov-Pishchik pleads for a loan with such persistance that he doesn't take his own requests seriously. One might think that the action is taking place, as in Pushkin's *Rusalka*, in a half fairy-tale realm, where the little water-nymph granddaughter can't tell the difference between shells from the river bottom and the money her grandfather the miller asks her for.[6] However, as a matter of fact, a fairy tale does come true for Simeonov-Pishchik; Englishmen find white clay on his land, sign a contract with him, and this perpetual cadger of loans suddenly gets rich. The most businesslike character in the play is Lopakhin and at the auction he obeys his own passion more than is proper for calculation.

The old debate over Chekhov: is he an optimist or a pessimist? Severe in such matters, Thomas Mann[7] considered Chekhov to be an optimist. The most precise answer is probably that when it comes to the past Chekhov is a pessimist, and an optimist when it comes

6. *Rusalka*. See *Seagull*, note 9, page 174. [*Editor's note.*]
7. Thomas Mann (1875–1955), great German writer, whose much reprinted "Inquiry into Chekhov" (1954) argued that his writing insisted on carrying on work even when there are no answers to the ultimate questions. [*Editor's note.*]

to the future—an optimist about the more important thing. Chekhov has not a word of comfort for old Russia. But for Chekhov, his heavy dramas were in a certain sense optimistic comedies. He rises to face the future and then the most sinister collisions lose their tragic meaning. The future abrogates both of the competing factions; the very competition is also abrogated, and therefore a tragic spectacle is suddenly permeated with gaiety and humor. If you observe from above, if you observe from the future, then the defeats and victories of the present day are worthless; in this sense, defeats and victories cancel each other out. In Swift, Gulliver is in great fear and anguish in his cage as an eagle grasps it by the ring on top and flies off with it. From the eagle's vantage point, Gulliver's fear and anguish are insignificant.[8] The future gazes down on the present from on high. The old romantics called such a climb up the staircase of time, such a view of the steps below uttered from above, "irony." It is present in Act Three of *The Cherry Orchard*. This is the day of reckoning: the cherry orchard will be sold or is already sold, while musicians play, guests waltz, and Charlotta does tricks. Of course, there is everyday motivation: frivolity and slovenliness in the house of Ranevskaya. More important still is the general distant meaning: if one can overcome the present day, why shouldn't there be merrymaking at the sale of the cherry orchard? Even Ranevskaya and Gaev themselves secretly accept this sale as a liberation. So, even in *Three Sisters* Fedotik the lieutenant went to a dance after the town fire: everything he had burned to a crisp, nothing was left to weigh him down. Trofimov and Anya have learned that one has to say good-bye to the cherry orchard and find a more important occupation. Today's tragedy is tomorrow's comedy. Light is breaking in *The Cherry Orchard* from the dawning day.

BORIS ZINGERMAN

Boris Isaakovich Zingerman (1928–2000) was a contributor to the magazine *Teatr* from 1955 to 1962, and then taught at the Institute for the History of Art in Moscow. He was an expert on Stanislavsky and Meyerhold and drama of the modernist period. His ideas, spread by his many publications on theater, painting, film, and drama, were highly influential and demonstrate how the socialist approach, required at the time, could be partnered with sophisticated analysis.

8. In *Gulliver's Travels* by Jonathan Swift (1667–1745), the seaman Gulliver is kept in a cage like a bird while in the land of the giant Brobdingnags. [*Editor's note.*]

Space in Chekhov's Plays†

* * *

The place of action in Chekhov's plays is a space doomed to disappear.

A foreboding of the imminent destruction of the nests of the gentry "in the Turgenev style" intensifies the elegiac note in Chekhov's plays, especially those written in the south, far from Moscow and central-Russian nature, when an ailing Chekhov, like the three sisters, felt nostalgia for his favorite locales. The estate landscape was historically on the verge of disappearing, and Chekhov's illness had torn him away from it. Banished by the doctors to the Crimea, to Nice, to Badenweiler, Chekhov, like the warriors in *The Lay of Igor's Armament*,[1] might cry out woefully, "O, Russian land, now art thou beyond the hills!" The heroine of Chekhov's last play parts from her beloved nest forever; she is evicted from the estate to Paris, where, except for a sick, unfaithful lover, nothing awaits her.

* * *

In *Ivanov*, the hero, a landowner of thirty, hurtles between his own home, where everything is hateful to him, and the home of his friend Lebedev, to which he rides every night to relax. At the Lebedevs', a new bourgeois ethos prevails—not landed estates but the savings and loan. Ivanov's home and Lebedev's home are on the stage, but the whole district in a central Russian region is made manifest: a forest; hunting fields; the ten miles that Borkin, Ivanov's overseer, covers, toting a shotgun; the river that Borkin proposes to dam in order to force the neighbors to play tolls; a certain Zarevsky's factory; a monastery; the house of Marfa Yegorovna Babakina, a young female landowner and daughter of a rich merchant, run on a lavish scale; a school—Lebedev, the chairman of the County Council goes to its consecration.

And in *The Seagull*, the place of the action is not only Sorin's neglected estate—a flowerbed, a croquet lawn, a bench under an old linden tree, the lake and the dilapidated noble manor houses along its shores—but also all the provincial towns where Arkadina tours, such as Kharkov, where she made a smash hit, where the students arranged an ovation for her, and the rich fans presented her with an expensive brooch.

† From B. Zingerman, *Teatr Chekhova i ego mirovoe znachenie* [Chekhov's plays and their Worldwide Significance], ed. A. A. Anikst (Moscow: Nauka, 1988). This excerpt of a chapter, trans. by Laurence Senelick, constitutes about a third of the whole essay, which, in an earlier section, draws interesting parallels between Chekhov's plays and the impressionistic landscape painting of his time. [*Editor's note.*]

1. The twelfth-century Russian poetic epic about Prince Igor's campaign against the Polovtsians. [*Editor's note.*]

In the course of the action, the scenic space widens, opening up to the spectator perspectives near and far:

The dismal eight miles that the schoolteacher Medvedenko walks back and forth every day from school to Sorin's, in order to see Masha, to sit in a comfortable, well-appointed house, and to philosophize about his poverty;

Genoa with its splendid Mediterranean crowd, an unusual town that Dr. Dorn gets to visit in his declining years, and that Treplyov will never get to see;

The eternal wandering of the provincial strolling player Arkadina, dragging Trigorin along with her: "train compartments, stations, lunch counters, fried food, smalltalk . . ."

The big apartment building in the capital, where Arkadina lived long ago when she was on the national stage; there was a fight in the yard and a washerwoman who lived there was beaten up, and the young actress Arkadina "would go and see her, take her medicine, bathe her children in the washtub," two religious ballerinas lived in the same building and would visit Arkadina and have coffee.

The Moscow hotel "Slav Bazaar," where Nina Zarechnaya, like Anna Sergeevna in "Lady with Lapdog,"[2] waits for her middle-aged lover;

The famous summer theater outside Moscow, in Malakovka, where Nina made her debut, the big provincial theaters where she began her artistic career so much on her own and so unsuccessfully;

The mercantile town Yelets, where Nina has an engagement for the whole summer and whither she will travel early in the morning in a third-class carriage, with peasants . . .

Onstage in *Uncle Vanya*, there is a cozy old estate belonging to Sonya's late mother; the rooms in the house, part of the garden beside the terrace. But this enclosed, secluded space is connected in a very definite way with the distant capital, where Serebryakov, a famous university professor, had lived with his young wife (from the capital to the estate there came the professor's books, magazines with his articles, read by Voinitsky and his mother, while for twenty-five years money that Uncle Vanya earned, working like a slave for a niggardly wage, was punctually sent from the estate to the capital), with nearby Kharkov, where the Serebryakov couple head so speedily, with the usual inhabited backwoods, which start right outside the gates. The district is the neighboring village, where a rude shopkeeper insulted Telegin as a freeloader; the rural hospital, where Astrov works along with a half-literate orderly, who never says "ride" but "rod"—a terrible crook; the hamlet of Rozhdestvennoe, where Astrov will stop in on the blacksmith to have his trace horse shod;

2. One of Chekhov's last short stories. [*Editor's note.*]

the factory, which suddenly sends for the doctor; a government forest preserve, where the forester is old and sick, and where Astrov takes on all the work.

In the first speeches of the play, in the dialogue of the doctor and the old nanny, a sharp contrast is established between the well-appointed, poetic place of the action, shown onstage—the garden, the terrace, a table set for tea along the path under an old poplar, a guitar on a bench, a swing close to the table—and the enormous, wild expanse beyond the bounds of the estate: "In Lent, third week, I went to Malitskoe to deal with an epidemic . . . Spotted typhus . . . In the huts the peasants were packed side by side . . . Mud, stench, smoke, bull-calves on the floor right next to the sick . . . Piglets too . . ." In Act Two, which takes place in the cozy manor house, the sinister contrast is emphasized again: "Mud up to his waist on the roads, frosts, blizzards, vast distances, coarse, savage people, all around poverty, disease . . ." And, as if feeling that words, even long monologues cannot express this, in Act Three, Astrov unrolls his diagram on a card table, its colors vividly presenting a picture of the gradual and irrevocable decline of district life and district nature. *Uncle Vanya* is the only Chekhov plays in which an enormous space, located behind the scenes—beyond the borders of the landed estate—is depicted not only verbally but graphically—on the diagram of the district which Astrov explicates in his monologue. The play, all of whose action takes place on a landowner's estate, is called by the author not "Scenes from Life on an Estate" but "Scenes from Country Life."

In the last, fourth act there appears yet another reference to geographical space, somewhere much more spacious than the area map of a Russian district, and somewhere much more remote from Voinitsky's estate than the village of Rozhdestvennoe: the map of Africa hanging on the wall in the room of a Russian landowner, and, almost at the final curtain, Astrov's surprising remarks about the heat in Africa. This is one of those glancing, enigmatic strokes Chekhov uses to puzzle his readers and actors, but which play a role in his plays. A person of some imagination might be inspired by this perfectly useless map of Africa with thoughts about Voinitsky's unrealized potential. Not only didn't he become a Dostoevsky or a Schopenhauer, but—for the sake of the lifelong debt of honor he has taken on, on behalf of a false idol—he has confined himself to rural desolation and has probably never been anywhere else, Paris or Italy or Africa, having had no time nor money for travel, worn out with endless farmwork, sending Serebryakov all the money obtained by the sale of crops while he himself receives a clerk's salary. The rural physician Astrov too has probably never gone on an alluring trip to faraway places. (Only Dorn in *Seagull* takes a short trip abroad in

his old age, somewhere in Genoa, and there he spends all his savings—some two thousand, earned by the endless practice of thirty
years, when he couldn't call his soul his own day or night.) Why not
suppose that there was a reason why, at some time many long years
ago, the map of Africa appeared in Uncle Vanya's room? As a young
man, he may have dreamed about travelling, about distant lands,
yearning in his desolation; later, the dreams turned to dust, he forgot
about them, but the useless map continues to hang on the wall.

Chekhov had a high regard for freedom of experience and was
convinced that human beings needed the whole world for happiness.
He dreamed of travelling and, among other things, expressed more
than once in his letters the desire to visit Africa and Egypt in the
near future. (Chekhov never got to visit exotic Egypt; he went to the
prison colony of Sakhalin instead.)

The enclosed, strictly bounded estate space of *Uncle Vanya*
expands to comprise the adjacent village where Waffles was insulted
and a cottage in Finland which Serebryakov intends to buy and the
city of Kharkov and the city of Moscow and, finally, far-off torrid
Africa.

In *Three Sisters*—Chekhov's most epic play—the extremely
cramped stage space expands again to the world, corresponding with
the way the spaces of past and present unfold in this play. Irina,
Masha, Olga, and Andrey live not on an estate, but in a town, but
their house and garden, the spruce-lined pathway leading to the
steep riverbank—this is a spacious landed estate, rising amidst ordinary dwellings and government institutions like an off-limits island
or a besieged fortress. (That subtle connoisseur of estate culture G.
Lukomsky notes that the organizers of private life in the eighteenth
and nineteenth centuries put up "quasi-manor houses" in cities and
palaces on "landed estates." They transferred a spirit of the rural
locality to town, and a spirit of courtly, big-city life to the estates.[3])

We can picture this provincial town at first from the individual
specimens of its indigenous population of a hundred thousand (the
Prozorov family and the military feel themselves to be an extraneous
element here)—from Natasha, Andrey's wife, and from Protopopov,
his superior at work and his wife's lover. Gradually, this whole northern town built of wood in a forested area arises in our mind's eye. In
Act Three, it is thrown in a panic by a fire, the alarum is sounded
offstage, and through the open door one can see a window red with
the blaze; in the fourth act, upstage one can discern the border where
the town ends and the woods begin—the distant spot across the river
where the duel in which Tusenbach is killed takes place. We can
picture Moscow: Old Basmanny street, where the Prozorov family

3. G. K. Lukomsky, *Starye gody* (*Old Times*) (Berlin, 1923), 78.

lived; the Red barracks, where Vershinin served; the gloomy bridge along the road to the barracks; Moscow University, where Andrey dreams of being a professor; Testov's tavern or the Big Moscow restaurant with enormous dining rooms where "you don't know anyone and no one knows you, and at the same time you don't feel like a stranger." At the end of the play, the image of Moscow melts and fades away, while, one after another, quite different, truly real places in the action, which await each of the characters, rise up: the brick factory, where the now retired Tusenbach intends to work and where Irina will start teaching school—a place even more dismal than the town where Prozorovs are currently living; the girl's school, which Olga runs and where she has moved to live with her dear old nanny; and finally, all Russia—the regiment, in which Vershinin serves, marching across its boundless reaches.

Apart from Gaev's estate, the places of action of *The Cherry Orchard* are Paris, which Ranevskaya and her footman Yasha come from and to which they return after the sale of the estate;

The smoky Parisian sixth-floor walk-up, where Ranevskaya lived after selling her villa in Menton, and where Anya ran into some French people—a few ladies, and a Catholic priest with a little book;

The ravaged estate of the landowner Simeonov-Pishchik next door, on whose land Englishmen found white clay, essential for industrial purposes;

The estate of certain Ragulins in Yashnevo, about fifty miles from Gaev's estate, where Varya will go into service as a housekeeper;

The neighboring village, from which the manservant Yasha's old mother has come;

Kharkov, where Lopakhin, bored in the country without anything to do, will spend the winter doing things;

Moscow, where the university student Petya Trofimov is going with Anya;

The railway station located not far from the estate, from which guests are invited to the ball;

A nearby town, whose outline can be discerned on the horizon in the second act—in this town, Gaev's estate is sold for debts and there he heads to take up a employee's post in a bank;

Mineshafts in the steppe;

A railroad, heading somewhere far away, leading to Yashnevo, Kharkov, Moscow, and Paris. . . .

Space in Chekhov's plays is, firstly, the place of the action, designated by the author's sparse stage directions, and secondly, the place of the action that the spectator does not see on the stage, but which is evoked more than once, every so often described by the characters: the village next door, the district, Moscow, Kharkov, and Paris. We may get the impression in the first case that the space before us is like an artistic image, and in the second like a theme, discussed by the play's characters. Of course, this impression is deceptive, superficial. The spectator of a Chekhov performance is confronted with an integral, unique verbal and visual image of a stage space, whose invisible portion, which does not fit on stage, is just as real as that created by the scene designer.

The offstage space, which the characters conjure up in their dialogue, is often described in more detail than what is designated by the stage directions and which will—in due time—be lit by the footlights. Old Basmanny street where the Prozorov sisters lived and the fully populated, brightly lit dining room of the Moscow restaurant Andrey dreams of are no less credible than the private dwelling in the provincial town where the play's action takes place. When we read *The Cherry Orchard*, the mansard in Paris where Ranevskaya lived is etched in our imagination just as clearly—if not more so—as the nursery on her beloved estate, to which she returns after an absence of five years. The muddy, miserable village Astrov visited during the cholera epidemic is delineated in his monologue with greater detail than the stage directions use to describe the garden on the estate where Astrov tells his tale.

In delineating the scenic space, Chekhov is even more laconic whenever it's a job for the scene designer. He firmly counts on his largely verbal descriptions being realized on stage by a three-dimensional image. Innokenty Annensky,[4] the creator of a purely literary poetic theater, noted this demand for theatrical resources and theatrical spectacle in Chekhov and characterized it with a bit of a sneer: "If literary resources are not enough, the property-man is at his beck and call."[5] Of course, the reason is not that Chekhov wasn't the master of literary resources; rather, he felt the living bond between the verbal and the three-dimensional imagery in his plays, and did not distinguish what is heard from what is seen.

The background of Chekhov's scenic space is the invisible, boundless locus of the action. In this regard, the concept "background," usually employed in a metaphoric, conventional sense, acquires an exact meaning—the space, located beyond the bounds of the estate, extending far into the distance. In *The Cherry Orchard*, the author risked showing on stage a certain portion of this background—the telegraph poles, a big town in the haze on the horizon. One can imagine a Chekhovian production in which the invisible background is visually displayed, if some uninhibited stage designer were to cre-

---

4. Innokenty Fyodorovich Annensky (1855–1909), Russian poet, critic and classical scholar, whose essay on *Three Sisters*, published in *A Book of Reflections* (1906), regarded the play as a record of everyday Russian life in all its absurdity. [*Editor's note.*]
5. In. Annensky, *Ukaz.soch.*, 323.

ate a simultaneous spectacle on the backdrop, showing a Russian village and the county town and Kharkov and Moscow and Paris . . .

The locus of the action not shown on stage is seen by the spectator of a Chekhov play, due to his imagination being stimulated by the dialogue of the characters. The novelization of drama, undertaken by turn-of-the-century innovators—the introduction of an epic element into drama—was, among other things, expressed by expanding the zones of a scenic space that are unseen but actually exist in the structure of the performance.

In Chekhov, the offstage space puts its stamp on the locus of the action, designated in the stage directions and confined in the playhouse to the stage. The unseen space is imperceptibly revealed within the visible proscenium arch. Chekhov's estate makes an impression of seclusion by itself (it is screened off from the surrounding offstage space and dominates it) and, with it, a certain desolate neglect equivalent to those unconfined distances that stretch beyond its borders. The characters are domiciled within the estate as if they can no longer—or do not want to—make their residence habitable, they find themselves out of place; they huddle in corners as if they do not feel at home.

Voinitsky's office serves as a bedroom as well; horse collars hang there along with the map of Africa, a writing desk, and a bed. Treplyov's study, where he does his writing, has been converted into someone else's drawing room. Ranevskaya, arriving home from abroad, turns up in the nursery. It's as if the windows and doors in the other rooms were already boarded up. The reader feels the study of the landowner Ivanov, a married man, shown in the third act, to be a messy, untidy bachelor's den, although it is not so described. "Desk, covered with an unruly sprawl of papers, books, official letters, knick-knacks, revolvers; alongside the papers, a lamp, a carafe of vodka, a plate of herring, pieces of bread and pickled gherkins. On the wall regional maps, pictures, shotguns, pistols, sickles, riding crops and so on."

Chekhov does not provide overly detailed descriptions of the places of action that might constrict the set designer's imagination. Similarly, in describing the characters' costumes, he limits himself to hints, details, behind which the whole may be surmised. Chekhov's plays can be staged in elaborate scenery, but also in a spare, stylized setting, which would present only the atmosphere of this enclosed yet wide open performance space, full of lyricism and drama.

The space of Chekhov's plays is opened by the participation of metatheatrical individuals who populate the "unseen territories,"[6]

6. A. Vislov, "Za zelënoy dveryu" ["Behind the Green Door"], Teatr 3 (1979): 86.

which begin offstage in the locales adjacent to the stage and expand as far as you like. In *The Cherry Orchard*, we are reminded of the kitchen, where Varya for thrift's sake feeds the old folks nothing but beans, and still more distant places, where people live whom we never once see on stage. Every one of them is connected in his way to the fate of the play's characters and has an effect on them: the Englishmen who discover white clay on Simeonov-Pishchik's land and save him from ruin, the great-aunt in Yaroslavl who is supposed to send money, Ranevskaya's lover who sends her telegram after telegram from Paris . . .

Space in Chekhov's plays is the expanding Universe.

Moreover, the space shown onstage—the estate of Gaev and Ranevskaya—is, we know, doomed to disappear. In *The Cherry Orchard*, the characters abandon the place of action, as in other plays of Chekhov, and before our eyes the locus of action ceases to exist. At the end, the thud of the axe on the trees in the cherry orchard is heard, while onstage there is a boarded-up manor house, with torn curtains and piled-up furniture, consigned to demolition.

The Cherry Orchard puts the stamp of a certain predestination on all the preceding plays of Chekhov, helping us to see what might elude our attention when reading each of them individually. In the first act of Chekhov's last play the owners of the estate, Gaev and Ranevskaya, recall that, if extreme measures are not taken, the estate will be sold to pay their debts, and in *Ivanov*, his earliest play, the curtain has barely risen when the hero, the owner of the estate, is reminded that in two days the interest has to be paid—Ivanov's estate is also mortgaged. In *The Seagull*, we are told that the country houses arranged around the lake have been vacated: when Sorin dies, his estate too will be vacated or pass to a new owner—even now, it has one foot in the grave. Pathetic, incompetently managed farming is eating up the whole pension of the senior civil servant Sorin. In *Uncle Vanya*, one character delivers a speech about selling the estate. In *Three Sisters*, Natasha becomes the mistress of the Prozorov home and plans to remodel it according to her taste. Where Ranevskaya's estate currently stands, cottages will be built. Very soon—not within two or three hundred years, but in a couple of years—these estates, this landscape, these people will no longer exist.

In characterizing the places of action, Chekhov's double vision lends a special complexity to his theatrical poetics. The estate is a world of longstanding bulwarks, fortresses defending their privileged residents from rough contact with the surrounding world, oases of culture, the hearths of a comfortable, well-appointed everyday existence; but these oases are just on the verge of being blown away; these hearths will soon flicker out; this world, shaken to its foundations, will sink into oblivion.

Conversely, the features of estate life, literally limited and historically ephemeral, are colored in Chekhov with features of the upwardly-mobile lifestyle of the intelligentsia and blend into them. In scene designs and productions of the 1920s, 1930s and 1940s that preserve traces of the old estate culture, what appear are not ethereal romantic visions, shrouded in the haze of memory, subject to the power of an unspoken, dreamy lyricism, as in the canvases of Borisov-Musatov,[7] for instance; nor the theatricalized, costumed characters of Somov or Benois,[8] intentionally sidelined from the present to the past; but Chekhov's contemporaries, Russian intellectuals of the 1880s and 1890s. In the estate landscape, Chekhov, unlike the artists of the World of Art,[9] did not emphasize the decorative accessories, which transport this landscape into the historic past and distance it from contemporaneity. The beauty and poetry of the estate space are taken by Chekhov to be the ideal motif of the Russian landscape in general—the flowering of Russian culture per se; it is not bounded by an ephmeral aristocratic way of life, not joined to it at the hip, nor does it need to vanish with it. In the interior of the manor house the features of the old aristocratic everyday life are imperceptibly and actually interwoven with features of the everyday life of the upwardly-mobile intelligentsia, as they were interwoven in, say, Lyov Tolstoy's house at Yasnaya Polyana—a particularity which Stanislavsky and Nemirovich-Danchenko instinctively grasped in their productions of Chekhov's plays, bringing the aristocratic way of life down a peg, transferring it to the level of the democratic everyday life of the intelligentsia. (Akhmatova,[1] who did not like Chekhov, reproved him specifically because Ranevskaya was not more like a high-born lady.)

Only in *The Cherry Orchard* is the estate's interior presented as inviolable, without extraneous intrusions, as it evolved in an earlier age, because here the masters feel themselves more as guests than as permanent, settled residents, just as if the house where they once lived were to appear on a stage. This place, where they spent their childhood, where their parents died, is where they come to say good-bye to the past, to indulge in memories—and to depart.

* * *

7. Viktor Élpidiforovich Borisov-Musatov (1870–1905), influential painter known for the melancholy lyricism of his paintings, wrought in a realistic mode. [*Editor's note.*]
8. Konstantin Andreevich Somov (1862–1969) and Aleksandr Nikolaevich Benois (Benua, 1870–1960), painters, were members of the World of Art movement; they produced highly decorative designs. [*Editor's note.*]
9. The World of Art (*Mir Iskusstva*) movement was prominent in St. Petersburg from 1898 to 1904; it argued for a Western-looking Russian art, unconcerned with social matters. The editor of its journal, Sergey Dyagilev, asked Chekhov in 1903 to join him, but Chekhov declined the invitation. [*Editor's note.*]
1. Anna Andreevna Akhmatova (Gorenko, 1889–1966), the greatest female poet of twentieth-century Russia. [*Editor's note.*]

JOVAN HRISTIĆ

Jovan Hristić (b.1933) is a Rumanian academic and drama critic for the Belgrade monthly *Literature*. His works include *Poetry and Poetic Criticism* (1957), *Poetry and Philosophy* (1964), and *The Forms of Modern Literature* (1968), as well as two volumes of collected theater reviews. His important work *The Theater of Chekhov* was published in French in 1984.

Time in Chekhov: The Inexorable and the Ironic†

It is immediately evident that time is one of the most important, if not the most important, features of Chekhov's dramatic technique. The events which we witness in his plays more often than not do not have that compactness with which events succeed each other in classical drama: they are, so to speak, dissolved in time and we are aware not only of their casual interrelationship (which always tends to compress events closer to each other), but also of their separation in time. So, for example, the second act of *Ivanov* ends with the stormy scene in which Anna Petrovna surprises Sasha in her husband's arms; in the third act Sasha comes to Ivanov's house, but before she arrives we see Shabelsky, Lebedev, and Borkin having lunch in Ivanov's study, and their miniature banquet, placed between the two dramatic happenings, gives us more tangible evidence than any interval between the two acts—even before we find out that two weeks have passed since Sasha's birthday—that time has passed and that, after the momentary storm, things have resumed their more or less peaceful course.

In *The Seagull*, several of the most important things in the play do not even happen on stage, but off stage and between the acts: Treplyev attempts to commit suicide between the first and second, and the liaison between Nina and Trigorin begins and ends between the third and fourth acts. To Chekhov's reasons for not situating these events on stage which have already been noticed should be added another: it is by this means that the time which passes between the acts is rendered far more noticeable than in classical drama, in which only preparations for what is to be seen on stage are made.

In *Uncle Vanya*, too, the acts are separated by time, as is made clear by the change of season from summer to autumn, while at the beginning of the fourth act Telegin says to his old nurse: "Marya

---

† "Time in Chekhov: The Inexorable and the Ironic," *New Theatre Quarterly* 1.3 (Aug. 1985): 271–82. Translated by Bernard Johnson from *Le Théâtre de Tchékhov* (Paris: L'Age d'homme, 1984), 101–21.

Timofeyevna, I was walking through the village this morning, and the storekeeper shouted after me—Hey, you parasite. It was hard for me to have to hear that." This simple narration and the still simpler event—which, bearing in mind peasant coarseness, something that Chekhov had good reason to know all about, must have happened many times before—suddenly reveals to us the life which has continued to go on in between the shown action of the play.

In *Three Sisters*, time is measured by the birth of Natasha's children between the first and second, and between the second and third acts: each of these new lives in the Prozorov household shows us that time has passed and that the people we find on stage are no longer the same as those we left in the previous act.

As distinct, therefore, from classical dramatists, who bridged the temporal distance between events by linking them firmly and dramatically together, creating the impression that they follow immediately upon each other, Chekhov tries continually to make us aware that we are *not* taking up where he left off in the previous act—that many other things which we do not see must have occurred in his protagonists' lives, and that time in our own lives is an elemental force whose effect on us we cannot circumvent. For this reason it is necessary to examine all the ways in which he deals with time in his plays.

First and foremost, all Chekhov's characters *speak* of time: each and every one remarks on the fact that it has passed, is passing, will pass. At the very moment when Sasha tells Ivanov that she loves him, his first thought is of time—or rather, more precisely, he thinks about the possibility of life for him beginning anew from the beginning, of forgetting about everything he has missed and of making up for everything that has passed him by: "So, shall I live? Yes? Work again?" asks Ivanov, fired by the possibility that time which has passed irretrievably and which has brought him age and weariness, can, in one single instant, become unreal, can start afresh from the very point where everything had taken a wrong turning.

In *The Seagull*, our awareness of time's presence is achieved primarily by the emphasis on the generation gap between the play's main characters: Arkadina's son says of her, 'When I'm not there, she's thirty-two, but when I'm at her side she's forty-three" . . . Then there is Dorn, who defends himself from Paulina Andreyevna's excessive attentions with the pretext of his advanced years—he is actually fifty-five, but in the nineteenth century people became old earlier than nowadays, or at least began to feel older earlier—and Sorin, who at the age of sixty has achieved nothing that he wanted in life.

In contrast, we have Treplyev, Nina, and Masha, all in their twenties (although Masha looks much older), which we find out only at the beginning of the second act. And they all keep on talking about time, about the past, and about the future—with the sole exception of the thirty-year-old Trigorin who talks only of his work, since nothing else exists for him.

In *Uncle Vanya*, Voynitsky goes on interminably about his forty-seven years. Astrov is much younger, but for him time is mainly in the past. The old nurse Marina says to him at the very beginning of the play: "You were young then, handsome, but now you've grown old. And you're not so handsome any more. And another thing—you drink vodka." "Yes," answers Astrov, "In ten years I've become a completely different person." In *Three Sisters* it is almost superfluous to mention how time passes and how everyone continually speaks of time, of the past which has gone and of the future which refuses to come; and in *The Cherry Orchard* we feel an almost physical presence of time, which is carrying away with it the whole of a society, its values, and its way of life.

Time in the Early Plays

Of course, the fact that people talk about time, begin to feel their age, that plays such as *Ivanov* or *Uncle Vanya* take place at a time when their heroes are beginning to approach or are passing through the mid-life crisis of the forties, is not the only way in which Chekhov makes the presence of time tangible on stage. We have to take account also of the way that he sets out in time a series of events which are not actually seen in the play but which are of exceptional importance to it.

In *Ivanov*, the first and second acts take place the same evening, the third two weeks later, and the fourth a whole year after the third. It might be said that from the point of view of the events in the play this is the most natural order of things and, from the dramatist's point of view, the most conventional. At the end of the second act, Anna Petrovna finds Sasha in Ivanov's arms and it is quite natural that a certain time has to elapse after such an important event before everything can return to a more or less normal framework. Anna Petrovna dies some time after the end of the third act and a year after her death Ivanov intends to marry Sasha. And it is the lapse of time which is conventional and conditioned by the respect for the usual social customs rather than illustrative of the life and fate of the play's protagonists.

All in all, the plot in *Ivanov* develops quite naturally and time exists in order for the plot to develop in time—it cannot aspire to perfect neoclassical compactness without disrupting a number of psychological truths and perspectives—in the way in which such perspectives *are* disrupted by Corneille in *Le Cid*[1] in order for the drama to be kept within the limit of twenty-four hours.

But whereas *Ivanov* in many respects is still a relatively conventional play, *The Seagull* presents a rather more complex picture. The play begins on a summer evening; we are not informed of the amount of time which passes between the first and second acts, and this is of no great importance; and between the second and third acts a week goes by, although even this interval of time has no particular dramatic significance: whether or not the days are actually counted, we know that they must have passed because the development of the plot requires such a passage of time—not the condensed time of neoclassical drama but the extended time of the novel.

Nevertheless, time in the play is still not the active factor which, as Lukacs[2] says, "possesses the creative power of change." Even so, two years pass between the third and fourth acts, and during those two years a great deal has happened. Nina has run away to Moscow, lived with Trigorin, borne him a child, the child has died, and she has become an actress. Treplyev has begun to publish his stories in fashionable journals and has even achieved a certain *succès d' estime*. Masha has married Medvedenko and has a child. Sorin has aged enormously and can no longer move about. . . .

In short, life has radically changed for everyone, and when the curtain rises we cannot help but notice that the people before us are very different: the old and quite incapacitated Sorin is there is to remind us that the others, too, have grown older and weaker. It is in this time interval between the third and fourth acts of *The Seagull* that time finally becomes a fundamental part of Chekhov's dramatic repertoire and plays an active and creative role in it. We see it, in a rather crude manner, in the process of fashioning people's lives: it is no longer only a medium in which events happen simply because they cannot happen outside time, but an elemental force which shapes our very existence.

The time which passes between the third and fourth acts of *The Seagull* is that same time we are accustomed to encountering in the novel. It is for this reason that the last act of Chekhov's play produces an impression similar to that of the last chapter of a novel, where for the last time we eavesdrop on the group of characters whose lives we have shared closely for several hundred pages. But it would not be true to say that all that Chekhov achieved was to transpose the time-sense of the novel into the theatre. For time does not belong

1. In *Le Cid* (1636), a five-act play by Pierre Corneille (1606–1684), the author observes the rule of keeping the action within twenty-four hours, but at great cost to probability. [*Editor's note.*]

2. György Lukács (1885–1971), Hungarian literary critic and leading ideologue of Socialist art. [*Editor's note.*]

to any abstract definition or idea of the novel: it is rather that the novel coincidentally in its creation was able to express the experience of time as a basic element in which we live and an elemental force which shapes our life.

Before he died, Chekhov had time to write only three more plays, but each of them in its own way is concerned with the problem of time. And the one thing they have in common is that in all of them time has finally become dramatic space in which everything that happens arrives at its true meaning and the most profound significance of human existence is revealed.

Clearly, *Three Sisters* strikes one immediately as a play "about time," but this is no less true of *Uncle Vanya* and *The Cherry Orchard*. Each of these plays treats time in a different way, and it is exactly in these different way, and it is exactly in these different ways that Chekhov is able to expose to us the most important truths about the lives of his heroes. For Chekhov time is one of the most delicately refined instruments for the illumination of human destiny.

Uncle Vanya

Uncle Vanya begins on a sultry summer afternoon; the second act takes place during a stormy night late in summer; the third on a September day in autumn; and the fourth several hours after the third. Summer has come and gone, accumulated passions calm down slowly, and life gets on with its preparations for the gentle rhythm of a long peaceful winter and its everyday tasks.

This is a time with which we are already familiar, but it is not the only dramatically important time in *Uncle Vanya*. There is another time in the play, in which the temporal sequence of events on stage, from the moment the curtain rises on the first act till it falls at the end of the fourth, is only a part, a segment. At the very beginning of the first act, Astrov is with his old nurse, Marina, whose role in the drama is that of a living symbol of time that has passed—as is that of Anfisa in *Three Sisters*, Firs in *The Cherry Orchard*, Sorin in *The Seagull*, and Count Shabelsky in *Ivanov*—a left-over from the distant past whose events have floated up to the surface of the action.

> ASTROV   Nanny, how long is it that we have known each other?
> MARINA   How long? Lord help us. . . . You came here, to this region . . . when was it? . . . Sonya's mother, Vera Petrovna was still alive. While she was still with us you came for two winters. So that must mean eleven years have passed. (*Reflects*) Perhaps even more . . .

But this does not satisfy Astrov, who wants everything cut and dried and asks the dangerous question: "Have I changed a lot since then?"

And Marina gives the answer I have already quoted: "Oh yes, a great deal. You were young then, handsome, but now you've grown old. And you're not so handsome anymore. And another thing—you drink vodka."

The whole of this dialogue, which continues with Astrov's monologue about his own life, in which weariness and old age have come upon him prematurely, is of enormous importance to Chekhov's play. It is not just a mechanical exchange of opinions between people—the nurse already in her dotage and the doctor too soon on the verge of old age—or another of the Chekhovian "moods" which we refer to so readily: rather, it is a device used to give us a view of the time before the beginning of the play, in the same way that Sonya's final monologue makes us aware that everything does not come to an end with the lowering of the curtain.

The beginning and the end of *Uncle Vanya* are thus nothing more than two more or less conveniently chosen points in time—the former one from which the relation of events can begin, the latter one with which it can end—and life has gone on before and will continue to go on afterwards. For the real beginning of the play is not afternoon tea on a hot summer's day—nor even the arrival of the professor with his young wife at their estate, the arrival from which everything starts to go wrong (any more than their departure is the play's real ending). The real beginning of the play is somewhere back in the distant past—perhaps the moment when Voynitsky gives up his share of his inheritance so that his sister's dowry may be more substantial, or perhaps even before that, as far back as the nurse Marina's memory, which is a living mirror of the whole family, can go.

Similarly, the real ending is somewhere far into the future, when, as Sonya says in her fine monologue, she and Uncle Vanya will at last find rest. In that large timespan—which would need several hundred pages of a novel for the relation of all its important episodes—what we see on stage is only a small fragment; and we are tempted to say that the distant past from which the events before us are dredged up, and the distant future into which they will disappear, are more important than the fragment itself.

Aristotle said: "A beginning is that which is not necessarily after anything else," while "an end is that which is naturally after something itself and with nothing else after it." *Uncle Vanya* has neither a classical beginning nor a classical end. There is no king who suddenly decides to divide up his kingdom between his daughters, and so practically begins the play *ex nihilo*, and there is no full-blooded massacre at the end to finish it off conveniently, for the classical drama likes nothing better than an absolute ending, and what could be more absolute than death?

Instead, Chekhov provides us with an endless stream of time which flows by, and here and there we are allowed to see a segment of it. Chekhov's play emerges out of time and is again lost in it, and the past does not appear on the stage solely at moments of crisis in order to accentuate or evoke what has previously happened, as is the case with Ibsen, but is part of a great natural continuum towards which our gaze has been directed from the very beginning of the play as an element which contains everything that exists.

It is within this extended timespan that the events of *Uncle Vanya* acquire their real meaning and real measure: they are played out over a single summer, but what is briefer or more quickly forgotten than a summer? Chekhov knows very well that great dramas and great passions never take up excessive time in life, and so in *Uncle Vanya* he directs our attention to the past and to the future to show us how tiny is the fragment of time actually occupied by everything that we have seen on stage.

Three Sisters

Chekhov's method with regard to time in *Three Sisters* is completely different. Of all the plays, it is in this that we see most directly how time shapes people's lives: the heroes of the play change before our eyes as time passes, sinking deeper and deeper into the tedium of provincial life which progressively destroys their personality. The events in the play begin on May 5 of one year, Irina's name day, and end four years later, in autumn. In the first act Irina is twenty and Andrey is not yet married; in the third and fourth acts he already has two children and Irina is twenty-four. But Chekhov is not concerned with the physical appearance of ageing and neglect; as a dramatist he is very well aware of the fact that external signs of the passage of time are likely to seem no more than artificial on stage.

One of the indications of Andrey's complete immersion in provincial life and acceptance of its values could have been his tendency to put on weight, but he is already fat in the first act when he is still dreaming of a university career in the capital. It is certainly an ominous sign of the way things will go for him, but the process has begun before the curtain rises and in this way the actor is not obliged to appear artificially stouter and stouter as each act goes by, which in any case would verge on the farcical. On the contrary, from one act to the next Andrey becomes more and more ponderous as he becomes spiritually more and more sluggish.

In the third act Natasha says: "And they say that I'm putting on weight." But Chekhov, who had a more than acute eye for such real-life details, knows that a woman needs far less reason to feel she appears overweight: and, in any case, as with Andrey, it is not a question of whether Natasha really has become fatter or not, it is the fact that she feels herself to be so—that this single, perhaps insignificant physical degeneration has come about as a result of her much greater spiritual degeneration.

The characters in *Three Sisters* are not caricatures with padded shoulders, vast stomachs, and false moustaches. We take note of their physical deterioration as a sign of their gradual spiritual deterioration, and to achieve that end the pointers are quite sufficient. Andrey has not got all that much heavier, but he is much more sluggish; and Natasha is probably very little rounder at all, but she is very much more greedy when it comes to the Prozorovs' house, which room by room she is grasping for herself.

It is because *Three Sisters* is a play about the passing of time—which before our eyes gnaws away at and undermines people's lives—that reference is made to time in each and every act. The first sentence of the play is: 'It's exactly a year ago today since father died' ..., and there follows Olga's monologue which informs us of the working of time, which, as Baudelaire says, "mange la vie" [eats up life]. But this monologue of Olga's does not take us back, as does Marina and Astrov's dialogue at the beginning of *Uncle Vanya*, into the distant past from which have proceeded the events which we shall see in the play—it simply makes us aware of the time that has elapsed and passed beyond recall, and, consequently, that so too will the time which is presented to us, the present, inevitably pass beyond reach.

At the beginning of each new act, we are aware that what has happened in the previous one has disappeared into the darkness of the past, and that time has carried off a little more of the lives of Chekhov's heroes. For *Three Sisters* is a play about how time slips away from us and how the battle with it is always lost. In the second act, the name day which was celebrated in the first is spoken of as if in the distant past which has slowly sunk into oblivion, and only the pathetic cry, "To Moscow! To Moscow!" remains: but we know that that cornerstone, too, is slowly slipping away with the sands of time, that the sisters' wish to return to Moscow as soon as possible is no more than a desperate attempt to hold back time and to halt its treacherous workings, and that, in fact, Irina's cry is only a sign that the battle with time is slowly being lost, if it has not been lost already.

So when Vershinin appears on stage and the sisters remember the past in Moscow, Masha with tears in her eyes says to him: "Oh, how old you have grown! How old you have grown!" and we know that here is someone else who has lost the battle with time, whom the wind will blow away through the wilderness of provincial garrisons so that at the end of the play we do not even know where it is that he and his brigade have been sent.

From act to act, all the characters of *Three Sisters* make longer or shorter excursions into the past, continually keeping us aware that time does not stand still but flows on, carrying us along with it, and that this is an irresistible process. And what happens on stage is not, as in *Uncle Vanya*, a small segment of endless time which passes by before and after the drama, but time itself. From the continual use of the expression "long since," and from the tone of the references to time passing, we have the impression that more time has passed than is actually the case.

Thus, in Act Three Olga says of Chebutikin: "He hasn't drunk for two whole years and now all of a sudden he goes and gets drunk." And, speaking of Masha, who has given up playing the piano, Irina says: "She hasn't played for three years . . . or is it four?" Of the celebration of Irina's name day in the first act, Tuzenbach in the third says: "Once, a long time ago," and Andrey in the third act, speaking of how he stopped playing cards, says: "I gave that up a long time ago," whereas during the whole of the second act he has gone on about his card-playing debts.

Chekhov nowhere mentions—though elsewhere he knows very well how to do so—how much time has actually passed between the acts of his play, and we can only deduce this from the children who are born and grow up, so that in *Three Sisters* time is important as a quality rather than as a quantity. More exactly, for Chekhov it is more important how the characters in his play experience the passage of time than the actual number of years that have passed.

And for his characters time passes quicker than in actual reality; we know that his "long since" is somewhat exaggerated, that for events from which we are separated by a year or just a little more, we do not say "long since," but for Chekhov's heroes twelve or thirteen months ago are "long since" because with those months have departed the very best part of their lives, and because what has been irreversibly taken away is always further away in time than what continues to be lived and which we ourselves continue.

For this reason, the events in *Three Sisters* are relatively equally disposed in time, and the temporal intervals between the acts are in the main equal. With uniform punctuality Natasha gives birth to two children during the course of the play and in this way we are made aware of the sluggish rhythm of provincial life in whose monotony and sterility Chekhov's heroes are gradually submerged. Only between the third and fourth acts is this interval smaller: in the third we find out that the brigade has been posted, in the fourth it leaves, a speeding up of the action which shows us that events have begun to rush forward towards catastrophe.

And indeed, in the fourth act the attitude towards time changes radically. No one speaks of the past any more, but everyone begins to talk of the future which seems to be within everyone's reach. Chebutikin describes how he will retire and return to his small provincial town; Irina speaks of her future life with the Baron and their work together; Kuligin of how everything will be back as it was before as soon as the brigade leaves. Almost everyone is day-dreaming about the future, even if it will not be a very happy one, and for a moment it seems as if *Three Sisters*, just like *Uncle Vanya*, will be plunged into an endlessly long, grey future, and that the presence of the brigade was only a small, half-happy, half-sad disturbance of the uniformly monotonous current of provincial life.

But that is not so. In the fourth act of *Three Sisters* everyone speaks of the future, because in fact there is no more future for them. Olga's cry at the end, "If only we could know, if only we could know!" is actually the absolute end—of the play, of the story, of the lives of the people we have seen in it. Everything that could have happened has happened: only the emptiness of continuing time is left. Nothing of what the three sisters and their brother dreamed has come to pass—on the contrary, what has happened is what they most of all feared. They cannot sink any lower. There is no future because their life has been irretrievably expended.

For that reason Chekhov's play does not continue in time after the curtain comes down, but is lost in it. Just as Prometheus disappears for ever into the abyss of Hades at the end of Aeschylus' *Prometheus Bound*,[3] so too the Prozorovs disappear for ever into oblivion when it finally becomes clear that even their most minimal projects for their future lives will, like Irina's marriage to Tuzenbach, not be turned into reality. The presence of the brigade somehow kept everything together, gave a certain false vitality to their lives, and when it leaves everything falls apart: in Act Four in the garden, the sisters are together for the last time, along with their brother. When the curtain falls they will all disappear, each one into the darkness of her own unhappiness.

The Cherry Orchard

And so in *Three Sisters* the most important time is that which we see as it passes before us, and which from act to act changes before our eyes and consumes the heroes of the play. In *The Cherry Orchard*, Chekhov's last play, it is quite different. The sale at auction and the events connected with it are only the last episode in the life of an estate on which generations of the owners' family have followed one another. It is the estate which is the main "character" of the play and in it is embodied a lengthy passage of time which precedes the

3. The *Prometheus Bound* of the Greek tragic poet Aeschylus (ca. 525–ca. 456 B.C.) is considered to be his perfect play. [*Editor's note.*]

events played out in the drama. Its sale opens up a new possibility for the lives of the play's participants. More specifically: the future, however paradoxical this at first sight may appear, begins to be possible only after the orchard has been sold.

Whatever that future may be, *The Cherry Orchard* is first and foremost a play about two times: the past which proceeds up to the sale of the estate, and the future which begins with that sale. And therefore it is not only the internal time in the play which is important and relevant so much as the external time—the past before its beginning and the future after its end—whereas the present which we see on stage is no more than a moment of crisis between the past which no longer exists and the future which does not yet exist. And since the present is only that moment of crisis between past and future, the play itself is a point in time in which the past, the future, and the present are all brought together before separating once more and for ever.

These three times are presented, as J. L. Styan[4] has noted, "socially." That is: the distant past, which no one else remembers, is the manservant Firs; the past, which is living out its last days, is the landowning Lyubov Andreyevna and Gayev; the present is the rich merchant Lopakhin; the future is Anya and the eternal student Trofimov. Servant, landowners, a rich merchant whose father was once a peasant on the estate, and the eternal student: these are the three times of *The Cherry Orchard* which meet up in the play.

They are all held together by the orchard itself, and when it is sold each one of them goes their own way: Lyubov Andreyevna goes back to her lover in Paris; Gayev goes to work in a bank, where in all probability because of his laziness he will not stay long; Lopakhin goes off about his own affairs; Varya leaves to become the manager of some distant estate; Anya and Petya go off to start a new life, the idea of which delights them both, but which, from what we know of the lives of eternal students and schoolgirls who leave school before finishing their course, is unlikely to be very cheerful.

To tell the truth, the future which opens up after the sale of the cherry orchard will not be very cheerful for anyone: although he is proud to be the new owner, Lopakhin will remain alone with his business affairs; Lyubov Andreyevna will spend the last remains of the money she has taken and probably disappear into poverty; and Chekhov gives us some hint of the future which awaits Gayev in the person of the wandering beggar who appears in the second act, a beggar who evidently once belonged to the same upper class of Russian society. It is only for old Firs that everything is finished with the sale of the orchard: he remains shut-in and chained to the house, to

---

4. J.L. Styan, Anglo-American critic, author of *The Elements of Drama* (1960) and *Chekhov in Performance: A Commentary on the Major Plays* (1971). [*Editor's note.*]

die together with the estate where generations of his family have been servants, just as generations of the Ranyevsky and Gayev families have been its owners.

But, despite everything, the future exists. *The Cherry Orchard* does not sink into monotonous interminable tedium as does *Uncle Vanya*, nor disappear into oblivion as does *Three Sisters*: it is a play concerning a pitiless, stern, and not very cheerful future which begins with the destruction of an orchard that has long since ceased to bear fruit, but which has nevertheless preserved its fragile, sterile beauty. In the time which is to come, there will be no more beauty.

The Cycle of Organic Life

As far as the importance of time outside the drama is concerned—and in view of the fact that the events in the play are only one short crisis-moment in the history of the family estate and its owners—we might expect that *The Cherry Orchard* would be played quickly with an almost neoclassical unity of time. But that is not the case. The events in the play begin in May and end in October: they go on, therefore, for part of the spring, the whole of the summer, and part of the autumn.

It is not the first time that Chekhov stretches out his play over several seasons. *The Seagull* also begins one summer evening and ends on an autumn night two years later; *Uncle Vanya* begins on a summer afternoon and ends on an autumn evening; *Three Sisters* begins on a spring morning and ends on an autumn morning several years later. What did Chekhov wish to achieve by this? To give his plays a melancholy autumn ending with falling leaves and the noise of the first autumnal rains?

Nemirovich-Danchenko wrote of Chekhov's seasons: "His first act, a name day, spring, is happy, birds sing, the sun shines. . . . The fourth act: autumn, disappointed hopes, a triumph of triviality." Nevertheless, it is probably not only that. A lesser writer would have been content with the simple emotive echoes which the seasons of the year evoke in us, but Chekhov is a much greater writer than (at least in these remarks) Nemirovich-Danchenko perceived.

First and foremost, with the alternation of the seasons of the year, time in Chekhov's plays becomes unavoidably present and almost tangible to the very end. For the transition of spring into summer and summer into autumn is not simply an empty and rather abstract passage of time which we cannot notice and to which the dramatist has continually to draw our attention, but an act of nature which is just as present and real in the play as are the actions of its characters.

But in the same way, by this alternation of the seasons time in Chekhov's plays takes on a new quality. They do not represent human destiny simply because they pass by and will not stop for anything but because their passage has a very definite rhythm. It is the rhythm of the great cycle of birth and death, the renewal of life in nature, and when Chekhov places the events in the life of his characters in that cycle they cease to be simply private happinesses and unhappinesses and begin to take on that cosmic dimension which the events in a classical play, by its nature and the status of its heroes, naturally and directly possessed.

In Greek tragedy the actions of the heroes (or their ancestors) aroused the anger of the gods; in Shakespeare nature itself is roused when some unnatural deed is done or is being prepared; but the heroes of bourgeois drama—and Chekhov's with them—do nothing against which the gods or nature would have any reason to be roused. Quite the contrary: all the actions are of a kind which leaves gods and nature completely indifferent. No storm breaks out because a young girl has fallen in love with a second-rate writer, the lover of a well-known actress, and for him left the young man who loved her, or because four general's children do not manage to make anything of their lives, or because a family estate has to be sold at auction because of debts.

But, as with all great writers, Chekhov is not content with showing us living pictures of what happened one spring, summer, and autumn on some country estate, lost in the midst of the Russian plain, or in some no less forgotten small provincial town. He has to reveal in them something which will make them worthy of real, great drama. And since these events in their triviality and their inconsequentiality are not capable by themselves of moving the forces of nature and arousing them against themselves—since they are not capable of interfering with nature in order to become elemental in the same way that nature is elemental—nature interferes with them. It takes them, as it were, under its wing, making them no longer fortuitous and randomly chosen incidents from a monotonous, uninteresting and unimportant life, but part of a great natural cycle of the whole organic world.

This does not mean that Chekhov wants at any price to give cosmic meaning to something which does not and cannot merit such a meaning, but it does mean that in this way the events in his plays acquire a certain organic inevitability, a certain (however slight) inexorability which neutralizes the most serious and most incurable deficiency of every realistic play: that the events could have been played out in a different way, that they do not reveal to us the functioning of the elemental forces of life and nature but only human whims, hatreds, and stupidities.

In one extreme case, Ibsen was obliged to have recourse to illness in order to show that what occurs in a bourgeois drawing-room can have the same inexorability as the events of a Greek tragedy; but Chekhov knew only too well that the inexorability of tragedy in the drama of life cannot be achieved exclusively by an internal link between events, even when it is exaggerated to the extent of hereditary syphilis, but only by the setting of these events in an external framework in which they begin to be shown to us in a new light.

If we have nothing else, that framework can be the alternation of the seasons of the year which we usually consider as a simple emotive atmosphere surrounding the action. Chekhov has Treplyev kill himself on a wet autumn day; on a similar day Sonya and Voynitsky find themselves left alone somehow to carry on with their empty lives; it is under an autumn sky that the three sisters ask themselves what point there is in living and suffering; and on a cold autumn day everyone leaves the auctioned estate. And these are not just instances of Chekhov's use of a lyrical and melancholy atmosphere, but a significant question which man asks of nature—a question of the same order as the medical enigma as to why the greatest number of children are born between midnight and morning, between the setting of the moon and the rising of the sun.

The Ironic Perspective

The great cycle of organic life is not the only temporal framework in which Chekhov places the action of his plays. In them reference is often made to a distant future, in which the present which we see on stage will be no more than the distant and most probably long-forgotten past. Treplyev's clumsy symbolist play in the first act of *The Seagull* is a vision of that future in which organic life on earth has disappeared; in *Uncle Vanya* Astrov on several occasions speaks of what will happen in one or two hundred years time; Vershinin in *Three Sisters* philosophizes on the same theme—at such great length that it cannot help seeming amusing to us—as does Petya Trofimov in *The Cherry Orchard*.

It is by no means impossible that such fantasizing about the future was one of the most absorbing themes of Russian intellectual conversation in the 'eighties and 'nineties of the last century, when everyone had expectations of a future which would be better than the rather dismal present. Probably the monologues of Chekhov's heroes found a ready response amongst an audience desirous of social change, which everyone knew must eventually come about.

Nevertheless, Chekhov, as we have already had occasion to see, knows of a truth which is much more profound than the social one: it is that there is no better life: that we can better social conditions as much as we like, but there will always be people whose hopes are betrayed, whose ambitions will remain unrealized, men who fall desperately in love with women who do not love them, who will not know how to make use of the opportunity which is offered them, who will love useless beauty more than advantage and profit; people who, in a word, will be unhappy for reasons that no society is in a position to remedy because they are not social but existential reasons. No, it is quite certain that fantasies about the future, however bright his heroes imagine it, are not used by Chekhov to raise his audience's hopes that there will come a time when everything in the world will be better and more happily ordered. Chekhov is too intelligent and too great a writer for that.

What is it, then, that he is trying to achieve when he opens up before us in his plays the perspective of a distant future in which will live happily people who will most probably consider present-day perplexities and misfortunes amusing and trivial, if indeed they know anything at all about them? These flights into the future are used by Chekhov to broaden the "scene" on which the events are played out—not in space, as in the case of Greek tragedies where the interpolations of the chorus open up ever wider spatial perspectives in which our actions take on their final and complete significance, but in time, which has become that space where is revealed the sense of everything we do, because time for us, as Heidegger[5] says, "is the horizon for the understanding of being."

The widening of the time-perspective in which we observe them makes Chekhov's characters slightly ridiculous: from that future of which everyone speaks so much, everything that happens to them, all the misfortunes which they live through and survive, cannot help but appear to us like a storm in a teacup. 'I sit down, close my eyes like this, and think: those who live a hundred, two hundred years after us for whom we are now clearing a path, will they have even a single good word to say for any of us?" asks Astrov in the first act of *Uncle Vanya*: and it is as if he is placing in our hands a tool by means of which we shall convert everything which at first sight seems to us misfortune, not to say tragedy, into comedy.

For we see before us characters who are certainly not going to become part of the lasting memory of the human species. Neither do they imply fundamental possibilities of existence which will accompany us our whole lives long and which we cannot afford to overlook. They are ordinary people, preoccupied with their own ordinary troubles, troubles in which from time to time we are able to recognize some of our own. In the eyes of those whom they concern, such problems—which we are on the verge of calling banal—take on the proportions of earth-shattering crises.

But Chekhov knows very well what the true dimensions of these

5. Martin Heidegger (1889–1976), German philosopher, who explored the predicament of human existence and its search for "authenticity." [*Editor's note.*]

emotional worries are, and it is as if he gives them a certain natural, even physiological inevitability by placing them in the context of the cycle of organic life. By so doing he gives them their true dimension, placing them in a wide temporal context in which they become what they really are—not the great, fateful eruptions of passion which shake up the whole of human existence, but the short-lived explosions of a single emotional firework which uniquely for those who are part of them seem like a volcano.

So with the aid of time Chekhov widens the perspective from which we observe what happens in his plays in two directions. In one, the events we see on stage take on the organic, physiological inexorability and seriousness which everything that goes on in nature possesses; in the other, what seems to the participants to be a great and all-pervasive crisis appears to us as no more than a shudder of microscopic proportions which will be forgotten and disappear in the vast darkness of time. A less intelligent and lesser writer would ask, 'Where is the truth?' But Chekhov knows that truth depends on the angle from which things are observed, and, as an incorrigible ironist, he looks at things from two different angles at the same time. Which of them is the right one we cannot ever know.

Specific Plays

Z. PAPERNY

Zinovy Samoilovich Paperny, prolific Russian literary scholar, published an overview of Chekhov (1960), a study of his work habits (1974), and Chekhov's notebooks (1976). He also contributed to the annotation of the latest edition of the complete works of Chekhov. His most important Chekhovian monographs are *Against All the Rules: Chekhov's Plays and Vaudevilles* (1982) and *Chekhov and World Literature* (1997).

The Vaudevilles†

In a letter to A. S. Suvorin[1] dated December 23, 1888, Chekhov says, "When I'm all written out, I'll start to write vaudevilles and live off them. I think I could write a hundred a year. Vaudeville plots gush up in me like oil in the wells of Baku."

By this time, Chekhov had already written *On the Harmfulness of Tobacco* (first version), *The Bear*, and *The Proposal*. He was dreaming up new vaudevilles. In the same letter, he communicates a concept for *Thunder and Lightning*.

The late 1880s and early 1890s is a period, to use Chekhov's expression, of "forced march," marked by intensive work on plays (*Ivanov* and *The Wood Goblin*) and vaudevilles. However, the remarks about "a hundred a year" and "oil in the wells of Baku" contradict another remark of Chekhov's. Replying to I. L. Leontyev (Shcheglov),[2] he exclaims: "Am I turning into a popular writer of vaudevilles? Goodness gracious, the way they clamor for them! If in my lifetime I just manage to scribble a dozen airy trifles for the stage, I'll be thankful for it. I have no love for the stage. I'll write *The Power of Hypnosis* during the summer—I don't feel like it right now. This season I'll write one little vaudeville and then rest until summer.

† From Z. Paperny, " '*Vopreki vsem pravilam . . .* ' *Pyesy i vodevili Chekhova*" ("Against all the Rules: Chekhov's Plays and Vaudevilles") (Moscow: Iskusstvo, 1982), 236–46. Trans. by Laurence Senelick.
1. See Letters, note 9, page 381. [*Editor's note.*]
2. See Letters, note 2, page 389. [*Editor's note.*]

Can you call this labor? Can you call this passion?" (November 2, 1888).

So, on the one hand, "a hundred a year"; on the other, "If in my lifetime I just manage to scribble a dozen airy trifles for the stage . . ."

Both remarks are made with conviction. In reality, things turned out more in line with the latter than the former remark: *On the Harmfulness of Tobacco, The Celebration, The Bear, The Proposal, The Wedding, A Tragedian in Spite of Himself* . . . The total barely comes to ten.

Obviously, when we talk about Chekhov the vaudeville writer, we have to take into account both these tendencies: the writer's enormous fondness for vaudeville, and an opposing force.

The vaudeville is an inalienable part of the creative work of Chekhov the dramatist, not separate and apart. But in every case it seems as if something is preventing the vaudeville principle from being spontaneously carried out.

In a letter to Ya. P. Polonsky[3] dated February 22, 1888: "Ah, if they find out at *The Northern Herald* that I write vaudevilles they will excommunicate me! What am I to do, if my hands get to itching and want to commit something ooh-la-la? All my efforts to be serious come to nothing, and my earnestness invariably alternates with vulgarity. I suppose it is my horoscope."

And this is what I. L. Leontyev (Shcheglov) writes in his memoirs:

> When, a few years later, at one of our Moscow get-togethers, I reproached Chekhov for not working on our collaborative vaudeville (*The Power of Hypnosis*), Chekhov remarked pensively, as if to himself:
> "Nothing will come of it . . . the necessary mood is lacking! For a vaudeville, you understand, you need a very special state of mind . . . you have to love life, the way a freshly-baked junior officer does; and how will you manage that, blast it, in our nasty times? . . . "[4]

Therefore, the Chekhovian vaudeville is something that comes from the very depths of his creativity and at the same time requires a special state of mind, for which "our nasty times" are not propitious.

Some scholars have segregated Chekhov's plays from the vaudevilles. S. D. Balukhaty[5] wrote: ". . . the poetics of the Chekhov in

---

3. See Letters, note 6, page 387. [*Editor's note.*]

4. I. L. Leontyev (Shcheglov), "Remembrances of Anton Chekhov," in *Chekhov v vospominaniyakh sovremennikov* (*Chekhov Remembered by His Contemporaries*) 2d ed. (Moscow: Goslitizdat, 1954), 151.

5. Sergey D. Balukhaty (1893–1945), Russian literary theorist, whose *Problems of Dramatic Analysis: Chekhov* (1926) is an early structuralist approach; he later published Stanislavsky's directorial notes for *The Seagull* (1952). [*Editor's note.*]

vaudeville, original and theatrically expressive though they be, bear no relation to Chekhov's innovative concepts in drama."[6]

It must be said that even Chekhov's contemporaries scolded him for damaging his reputation as a serious dramatist by dissipating his talents on vaudeville trivia. The actor P. M. Svobodin,[7] a good friend of the writer, told him in a letter of May 2, 1889: "*The Proposal* is already printed. I just now read it and had to laugh. A prank of pranks, but there's still a lot of Chekhov in it, i.e., talent, although in your place I wouldn't publish such things: it diminishes your dignity. You ought to hammer things home, and sometimes you're just tinkering with thumbtacks . . ."[8]

However, what struck some scholars and contemporaries as distinct—"the hammer" and "the thumbtacks"—were in fact closely and mutually connected.

S. Balukhaty, having made a distinction between the vaudeville and "Chekhov's innovative concepts in drama," suggested that the latter made their very first appearance in the play *Ivanov*. But, curiously, that very drama gives rise to a tragi-farcical situation, akin to that of a vaudeville, particularly the situation depicted in *The Proposal*.

At the end of *Ivanov*:

> IVANOV   There will be no wedding!
> SASHA   There will! Papa, tell him there will be a wedding!
> LEBEDEV   Hold on, hold on! . . . Why don't you want there to be a wedding?

Compare this with the end of the vaudeville *The Proposal*, where Chubukov shouts to the suitor, "You'll get married right away and—and the hell with you! She's said yes! [. . .] She's said yes and all the rest."

I remember how during the production of *Ivanov* at the Art Theater (with I. M. Smoktunovsky[9] in the title role), when Sasha and Lebedev were almost dragging the hero to the altar, at the most dramatic moment the audience burst into laughter. And this is no coincidence—vaudeville themes permeate the structure of Chekhov's plays.

Another example: the sketch *Swan Song* (*Calchas*) begins with the comedian Svetlovidov falling asleep in his dressing room after a ben-

---

6. S. Balukhaty, *Problemy dramaturgicheskogo analiza*, 32

7. See Letters, note 4, page 392. [*Editor's note.*]

8. *Zapiski otdela rukopisey GBL* (*Notes from the Manuscript Department of the State Lenin Library*) (Moscow: 1954), Number 16, 195.

9. Innokenty Mikhailovich Smoktunovsky (1925–1994), outstanding Russian actor who played an aristocratic and sensitive Ivanov at the Moscow Art Theater in 1976. [*Editor's note.*]

efit performance. Everyone has left and forgotten him: "Everyone was in raptures, and now there's not a soul to rouse a drunken old man and take him home . . ."

In the manuscript variant of the fourth act of *The Wood Goblin*, the action ends with all the characters, reconciled with one another, leaving, and Dyadin, left alone, exclaiming, "They've all forgotten about me! This is delicious! This is delicious!"[1]

At the end of Act Four of *Three Sisters*, Fedotik and Rodé make their exit after saying good-byes all around, and Chebutykin says: "And they forgot to say good-bye to me."

And, finally, *The Cherry Orchard* with Firs, forgotten by everyone, at the final curtain.

One could adduce many more examples of the ways in which themes originate in the vaudevilles and are refracted, each in its own way, in the plays.

B. Zingerman,[2] author of one of the best articles on Chekhov's vaudevilles, tracks the way in which, in the playwright's minor and major forms, the very same theme is revealed—the festivities that "get under way but never take place, because humdrum life intervenes; somehow the festivities never manage to break through humdrum life." The article concludes, "The vaudevilles give us the key to Chekhov's dialectic, and through them to all his playwriting."[3]

The statement about the running theme in Chekhov—the festivities that get underway, but never take place because humdrum life intervenes—has to be refined and amplified. The subject of *The Bear*, one of Chekhov's earliest vaudevilles (1888), doesn't fit this definition. True, one may say that the ritual of mourning doesn't take place: the heroine Yelena Ivanovna, "a little widow with dimples in her cheeks," says "today is exactly seven months since my husband died."

But instead of the intended day of mourning in the end there's a "prolonged kiss." The plot develops from a grief-stricken memorial for a husband to a quarrel and duel with an uninvited guest, and then to a concluding kiss; everything is made emphatic by a certain expressive detail that frames the one-act "joke."

At the beginning, Yelena Ivanovna says to her late husband's old manservant, "He was so fond of Toby! He always rode him over to

1. E. Polotskaya draws attention to this echo in her book *A. P. Chekhov. Dvizhenie khudozhestvennoy mysli* (*Chekhov: The Progress of Artistic Thought*), 125.
2. Boris Isaakovich Zingerman (1928–2000), Russian critic, a contributor to the magazine *Teatr* 1955–62, and teacher at the Institute for the History of Art. [*Editor's note.*]
3. B. Zingerman, "Chekhov's Vaudevilles," in *Voprosy teatra 72. Sbornik statey i materialy* (*Theatrical Matters 72: Collection of Articles and Documents*) (Moscow: VTO, 1973), 211, 299. Also see his book *Ocherki istorii dramy 20 veka* (*Notes on the History of Twentieth-Century Drama*), 67, 83.

the Korchagins and the Vlasovs. He sat a horse so wonderfully well! [. . .] Remember? Toby, Toby! Tell them to give him an extra portion of oats."

And at the end, in the embrace of her guest, the landowner Smirnov, she tells the servant, "with downcast eyes", "Luka, tell the stableboys that Toby gets no oats today."

The Bear is the only vaudeville of Chekhov's that has a happy ending.

In the later vaudevilles the action develops this way: the characters want to come to terms, create family ties, unite in throwing a party, but it never works out.

* * *

[*The Wedding*] has elements of both vaudeville and drama. The comic and the tragic are inextricably interwoven in it.

B. E. Zakhava[4] remembered: when in 1920 Yevgeny Vakhtangov staged Chekhov's *Wedding,* after the performance, the actor M. A. Chekhov said to him, "What you've done is terrifying."[5]

R. N. Simonov[6] wrote about this production, "Vakhtangov wanted to stage Chekhov's *The Wedding* and Pushkin's *A Feast in Plaguetime* in the same evening.[7] Why? What for? Simonov answered, that the director's main goal was to contrast "the tragedy of everyday life with the tragedy of the heroic."[8] [. . .]

In *The Wedding*, the idea of the impossibility of human mutual understanding defines the whole shape of the work.

At the beginning of the one-act play, there is a dialogue between the bridegroom Aplombov and the bride's mother.

He: ". . . in addition to some indispensable domestic articles, you promised to give me, along with your daughter, two lottery tickets. Where are they?"

The question is asked very bluntly. But the answer can hardly be called an answer:

She: "I've got such a splitting headache . . . It must be this awful weather . . . we're in for a thaw!"

4. Boris Yevgenyevich Zakhava (1896–1976), Russian actor and director, who began working in Moscow with Evgeny Vakhtangov, playing Evgeny in *The Lanin Estate*, the doctor in *The Miracle of St. Anthony*, and Timur in *Princess Turandot* (for which he was co-scenarist). He played Aplombov in *The Wedding*. [*Editor's note.*]
5. B. Ye. Zakhava, "Vakhtangov and Chekhov," *Sov. Iskusstvo* (January 29, 1935). [Yevgeny Bagrationovich Vakhtangov (1883–1922) staged a brilliantly grotesque version of *The Wedding* at his Moscow studio in 1920. Mikhail Aleksandrovich Chekhov (1891–1955), the playwright's nephew, was one of the best actors of his generation and a close friend of Vakhtangov. (*Editor's note.*)]
6. Ruben Nikolaevich Simonov (1899–1968), a student of Vakhtangov, was artistic director of the Vakhtangov Theater in Moscow, from 1924 to 1939; he had played Dymba in *The Wedding*. [*Editor's note.*]
7. One of the "Little Tragedies" of Aleksandr Pushkin, *A Feast in Plaguetime* takes place during the Great Plague of London in the seventeenth century. [*Editor's note.*]
8. R. Simonov, *S Vakhtangovym* (*With Vakhtangov*) (Moscow: Iskusstvo, 1959), 44–45.

Aplombov asserts that he doesn't need the lottery tickets—any more than the characters of *The Proposal* needed Bullock Meadow. "I'm not complaining out of selfishness—I don't need your lottery tickets, but it's the principle of the thing . . ."

The disjunctive function of the speeches, when the characters deliberately speak beside the point, is underlined even more by the fact that the speech constantly drops out of the stream of logic and becomes nonsensical.

That same Aplombov proudly pronounces, "I'm no Spinoza to spin around with my legs bent into a pretzel." Or ". . . I'll make your daughter's life a living hell. On my honor as a gentleman!"

In the same spirit, the luckless telegraph clerk Yat makes the declaration, "You're accustomed, pardon the expression, to aristocratical society." Or he reminds the bridegroom, "As you like, I'll go . . . Only first pay me back the five rubles you borrowed last year for a quilted, pardon the expression, waistcoat."

The same Yat philosophizes, "Don't you realize what human tears are? A sign of feeble-minded psychiatrics, that's all!"

The characters of *The Wedding* do not exchange words, but rather use them to fence themselves off from one another.

The theme of lack of human contact is expressed with exceptional clarity in the final episode with retired Captain Revunov-Karaulov. Everything he says hangs in the air, receives no answer, no response, evokes nothing but misunderstanding.

But even the responsive speeches of the guests saying that his stories are uninteresting lead nowhere.

The bride's mother pleads with him: "you'd better talk about something that's more use . . .", to which he, not catching her drift, replies: "I've already eaten, thanks." And when, boiling over, she exclaims: "You ought to be ashamed at your time of life! It's unreal, stop!", the answer comes, "A veal chop? No, I haven't had one . . . Thanks."

Some works about Chekhov have stated that *The Wedding* is all about how philistine vulgarians unwarrantedly insult an old sailor, a worthy man.

This theme really does resound; nevertheless, the main point lies somewhere else. The people do not understand each other, nor can they understand. No speech connects with what came before, but is derailed, translated to another level.

Zmeyukina longs for "atmosphere." The telegraph clerk Yat is in love with her. "Tell me, please, why do I feel so smothered?", she asks him, pursuing her theme—"give me atmosphere!" He simplemindedly answers, "It's because you're sweating, ma'am . . ."

So it seems that at no time can a character communicate with his neighbor.

Yet it becomes even more evident that the participants are bound by a single purpose—to celebrate a wedding. They all seem to want the same thing, but time and again their unity turns out to be ephemeral; it breaks apart.

And there's no point to the best man saying at the end of the play, "trying to make himself heard," "My good friends! On this day of days, so to speak . . ."—just as Chubukov in *The Proposal*, also "trying to make himself heard," exclaims, "Champagne! Champagne!"

We have come to one of the most characteristic peculiarities of Chekhov's vaudevilles. His plot is based not on an unfolding action, but, on the contrary, on an action, for whose sake the characters gather and for which they prepare, but which cannot come to pass.

It was not like that in *The Bear*: there, Smirnov abruptly burst in on the widow, roughly demanded money, a skirmish ensued, in the course of which a mutual passion flared up, and the action irrepressibly, precipitously hurtled towards a happy ending.

*　*　*

In quite a different way the action in *The Wedding* comes unraveled. Instead of a celebration, there is a dispute between bridegroom and mother-in-law over lottery tickets, a quarrel of bridegroom and the luckless telegraph clerk Yat, who unwittingly insults somebody with every word he utters, finally, the episode with Revunov-Karaulov, totally disrupting the course of the wedding party. And the one-act play ends with what should have begun it: the best man unsuccessfully trying to make a congratulatory speech.

This principle of unconsummated action, which constantly runs up against the "anti-action" of characters who are disconnected and incapable of contact, is expressed with special clarity in *The Celebration* (1891).

The bank manager Shipuchin has pompous dreams of celebrating the fifteenth anniversary of institution he heads. He has apparently foreseen everything: the bookkeeper Khirin is writing him a speech with the impressive title "Our bank present and future." Shipuchin has personally devised the congratulatory address, which is to be read by his co-workers, and bought a silver loving cup, which they are to present to him. He has thought of everything, down to the last detail.

But the vaudeville begins with everything prepared by the celebrant failing to come to pass. At such a solemn moment the bookkeeper Khirin is "wearing felt boots, that muffler . . . some jacket of an uncivilized color . . ." Shipuchin heatedly rebukes him: "You're spoiling the effect of the ensemble!"

The plot of *The Celebration* is built of interruptions, which spoil the ensemble even more violently. Out of breath, Shipuchin's wife Tatyana Alekseevna rushes in—she has "so much to tell you about, so much." Her arrival is extremely untimely. "We're having the celebration today, my dearest, at any moment a deputation of the bank's shareholders might show up, and you're not dressed," Shipuchin tells her. Tatyana Alekseevna relates how she spent her time in the company of young men, but Khirin does not listen to her, clicking the beads on his abacus (he is preparing the speech for Shipuchin), nor does Shipuchin, waiting for "the deputation." At the moment when none of the three is listening to the others, Merchutkina shows up, the wife of a local secretary, with business that is totally "none of our affair" and bears no relation to Shipuchin's bank.

Thus the quartet warms up, a quartet in which no one listens to, understands anyone else, or can provide an answer to anyone else. Tatyana Alekseevna overwhelms Khirin with a story about her sister Katya and a certain Grendilevsky, Merchutkina demands that Shipuchin pay her the money deducted from her husband's salary. Shipuchin and Khirin in turn try to din into her that she has come to the wrong address, and they all reach an apogee of excitement and despair. Shipuchin, tormented by Merchutkina, weeps and pleads with Khirin to throw her out, Khirin mistakenly persecutes not her, but Shipuchin's wife . . . The ever so decorously concocted celebration turns into total pandemonium. And at the moment when everything reaches its climax—when Khirin is stamping his feet; Merchutkina has fainted, falling into Shipuchin's arms, and he, half-unconscious, is repeating, "Deputation . . . reputation . . . occupation"—at the very moment of the triumph of unreason, cross-purposes, misunderstanding, scandalous outbursts and curses—at that very moment, *there* appears the deputation, all in formal dress, carrying the address devised by Shipuchin and the loving cup he bought.

On seeing that Shipuchin is beside himself, and the ladies are moaning, a member of the bank, who has begun the congratulatory speech, says, in embarrassment, "We'd better come back later . . ." And the whole deputation withdraws.

So ends *The Celebration*—with the celebration not taking place.

The Proposal, The Wedding, and The Celebration are three vaudevilles in which the event advertised in the title cannot come to pass.

It is impossible not to feel the resonances between the way the plot is constructed in Chekhov's vaudevilles and in his plays. Generally, it lies in the drama being achieved not through the action itself, but through its expectation, if one may say so—through the lack of dramatic development.

However, it is impossible not to see basic differences as well. Uncle Vanya rebels against Serebryakov, and his rebellions end in nothing. The three sisters dream of going to Moscow, and never get there.

However, in the very striving of the characters there is profound meaning: the desire to break away from life as it is, with its established order, structure, routine.

The characters in the vaudevilles find themselves on a completely different, comic plane. Instead of aspirations they have pitiful pretensions, vain efforts, and absurd concerns.

In *The Proposal* [. . .] the hero finds a mass of arguments for getting married; all except one—love.

* * *

This relates in many ways to *The Wedding*. ". . . if you don't hand over those tickets today," the bridegroom threatens his mother-in-law, "I'll make your daughter's life a living hell. On my honor as a gentleman!"

Again we see: uncompleted action, "concerns" that are nothing other than profanation.

Sending A. I. Sumbatov-Yuzhin[9] *The Wedding* (an offer had been made that it serve as an afterpiece to *Macbeth* at the Maly Theater), Chekhov wrote, "Yesterday I got it from the censor, read it over, and now I find that after *Macbeth*, when the audience is keyed up to the Shakespearean pitch, this play will risk seeming outrageous. Truly, after splendid Shakespearean villains, watching the petty, shoddy riffraff that I depict is quite unappetizing" (December 14, 1889).

In *The Bear*, the heroine was mannered and pretentious, the hero crude and uncouth. And all the same something human came through them, and when all was said and done they seemed able to attract one another.[1]

The Proposal, *The Wedding*, and *The Celebration* are full of "shoddy" people. The more respectable they try to look, the more keenly their spiritual cheapness and insignificance comes to the fore. In all three vaudevilles the characters conceive of matters that cannot "envelope," unite, bind them into one.

Before us are three different attempts of characters to act so that everything will be "the normal way." And every time everything ends up not the normal way.

With all their might the characters "push the plot forward," but it cannot be realized.

* * *

9. See Letters, note 7, page 393. [*Editor's note.*]
1. This was beautifully shown in the movie of *The Bear*, where the roles of Yelena Ivanovna and Smirnov were splendidly performed by Olga Androvskaya and Mikhail Zharov. Incidentally, this is one of the few successful film adaptations of Chekhov.

LYOV SHESTOV

Lyov Shestov, the pseudonym of Lyov Isaakovich Shvartsmann (1866–1938), was a convert from Judaism to Russian Orthodoxy and a forerunner of existentialist philosophy. Shestov, in beautifully wrought prose, carried on Dostoevsky's attack on modern rationalism and defended free will. Shestov's criticism was devoted to the masters of Russian literature, and his essay on Chekhov, "Creation from the Void" (1905), is an influential portrait of Chekhov as pessimist, "the poet of hopelessness." These excerpts represent only about a fourth of the essay.

Creation from the Void: *Ivanov*†

Résigue-toi, mon cœur, dors ton sommeil de brute.[1]

CHARLES BAUDELAIRE

I

Tchekhov is dead; therefore we may now speak freely of him. For to speak of an artist means to disentangle and reveal the "tendency" hidden in his works, an operation not always permissible when the subject is still living. Certainly he had a reason for hiding himself, and of course the reason was serious and important. I believe many felt it, and that it was partly on this account that we have as yet had no proper appreciation of Tchekhov. Hitherto in analysing his works the critics have confined themselves to commonplace and *cliché*. Of course they knew they were wrong; but anything is better than to extort the truth from a living person.

* * *

I must remind my reader, though it is a matter of general knowledge, that in his earlier work Tchekhov is most unlike the Tchekhov to whom we became accustomed in late years. The young Tchekhov is gay and careless, perhaps even like a flying bird. He published his work in the comic papers. But in 1888 and 1889, when he was only twenty-seven and twenty-eight years old, there appeared *The Tedious Story* and the drama *Ivanov*, two pieces of work which laid the foundations of a new creation. Obviously a sharp and sudden change had taken place in him, which was completely reflected in his works.

† "Chekhov: Creation from the Void" was first published in the periodical *Voprosy zhizni* (Questions of Life) in 1905, and was reprinted in *Nachala i kontsy* (Beginnings and Endings) in St. Petersburg in 1908. In 1916, the book appeared in this anonymous English translation in London as *Anton Tchekhov and Other Essays* and in New York as *Penultimate Words*.

1. Give in, my heart, sleep thy brutish slumber.

There is no detailed biography of Tchekhov, and probably will never be, because there is no such thing as a full biography—I, at all events, cannot name one. Generally biographies tell us everything except what it is important to know. Perhaps in the future it will be revealed to us with the fullest details who was Tchekhov's tailor; but we shall never know what happened to Tchekhov in the time which elapsed between the completion of his story *The Steppe* and the appearance of his first drama. If we would know, we must rely upon his works and our own insight.

Ivanov and *The Tedious Story* seem to me the most autobiographical of all his works. In them almost every line is a sob; and it is hard to suppose that a man could sob so, looking only at another's grief. And it is plain that his grief is a new one, unexpected as though it had fallen from the sky. Here it is, it will endure for ever, and he does not know how to fight against it.

In *Ivanov* the hero compares himself to an overstrained labourer. I do not believe we shall be mistaken if we apply this comparison to the author of the drama as well. There can be practically no doubt that Tchekhov had overstrained himself. And the overstrain came not from hard and heavy labour; no mighty overpowering exploit broke him: he stumbled and fell, he slipped. There comes this nonsensical, stupid, all but invisible accident, and the old Tchekhov of gaiety and mirth is no more. No more stories for *The Alarm Clock*. Instead, a morose and overshadowed man, a "criminal" whose words frighten even the experienced and the omniscient.

If you desire it, you can easily be rid of Tchekhov and his work as well. Our language contains two magic words: "pathological," and its brother "abnormal." Once Tchekhov had overstrained himself, you have a perfectly legal right, sanctified by science and every tradition, to leave him out of all account, particularly seeing that he is already dead, and therefore cannot be hurt by your neglect. That is if you desire to be rid of Tchekhov. But if the desire is for some reason absent, the words "pathological" and "abnormal" will have no effect upon you. Perhaps you will go further and attempt to find in Tchekhov's experiences a criterion of the most irrefragable truths and axioms of this consciousness of our. There is no third way: you must either renounce Tchekhov, or become his accomplice.

The hero of *The Tedious Story* is an old professor; the hero of *Ivanov* a young landlord. But the theme of both works is the same. The professor had overstrained himself, and thereby cut himself off from his past life and from the possibility of taking an active part in human affairs. Ivanov also had overstrained himself and become a superfluous, useless person. Had life been so arranged that death should supervene simultaneously with the loss of health, strength and capacity, then the old professor and young Ivanov could not have

lived for one single hour. Even a blind man could see that they are
both broken and are unfit for life. But for reasons unknown to us,
wise nature has rejected coincidence of this kind. A man very often
goes on living after he has completely lost the capacity of taking from
life that wherein we are wont to see its essence and meaning. More
striking still, a broken man is generally deprived of everything except
the ability to acknowledge and feel his position. Nay, for the most
part in such cases the intellectual abilities are refined and sharpened
and increased to colossal proportions. It frequently happens that an
average man, banal and mediocre, is changed beyond all recognition
when he falls into the exceptional situation of Ivanov or the old professor. In him appear signs of a gift, a talent, even of genius.

* * *

Tchekhov himself, a writer and an educated man, refused in advance
every possible consolation, material or metaphysical. Not even in
Tolstoi, who set no great store by philosophical systems, will you find
such keenly expressed disgust for every kind of conceptions and ideas
as in Tchekhov. He is well aware that conceptions ought to be
esteemed and respected, and he reckons his inability to bend the
knee before that which educated people consider holy as a defect
against which he must struggle with all his strength. And he does
struggle with all his strength against this defect. But not only is the
struggle unavailing; the longer Tchekhov lives, the weaker grows the
power of lofty words over him, in spite of his own reason and his
conscious will. Finally, he frees himself entirely from ideas of every
kind, and loses even the notion of connection between the happenings of life. Herein lies the most important and original characteristic
of his creation. Anticipating a little, I would here point to his comedy,
The Sea-Gull, where, in defiance of all literary principles, the basis
of action appears to be not the logical development of passions, or
the inevitable connection between cause and effect, but naked accident, ostentatiously nude. As one reads the play, it seems at times
that one has before one a copy of a newspaper with an endless series
of news paragraphs, heaped upon one another, without order and
without previous plan. Sovereign accident reigns everywhere and in
everything, this time boldly throwing the gauntlet to all conceptions.
In this, I repeat, is Tchekhov's greatest originality, and this, strangely
enough, is the source of his most bitter experiences. He did not want
to be original; he made superhuman efforts to be like everybody else:
but there is no escaping one's destiny. How many men, above all
among writers, wear their fingers to the bone in the effort to be
unlike others, and yet they cannot shake themselves free of *cliché*—
yet Tchekhov was original against his will! Evidently originality does
not depend upon the readiness to proclaim revolutionary opinions

at all costs. The newest and boldest idea may and often does appear tedious and vulgar. In order to become original, instead of inventing an idea, one must achieve a difficult and painful labour; and, since men avoid labour and suffering, the really new is for the most part born in man against his will.

* * *

In *The Tedious Story* the idea still judges the man and tortures him with the mercilessness peculiar to all things inanimate. Exactly like a splinter stuck into a living body, the idea, alien and hostile, mercilessly performs its high mission, until at length the man firmly resolves to draw the splinter out of his flesh, however painful that difficult operation may be. In *Ivanov* the rôle of the idea is already changed. There not the idea persecutes Tchekhov, but Tchekhov the idea, and with the subtlest division and contempt. The voice of the living nature rises above the artificial habits of civilisation. True, the struggle still continues, if you will, with alternating fortunes. But the old humility is no more. More and more Tchekhov emancipates himself from old prejudices and goes—he himself could hardly say whither, were he asked. But he prefers to remain without an answer, rather than to accept any of the traditional answers. "I know quite well I have no more than six months to live; and it would seem that now I ought to be mainly occupied with questions of the darkness beyond the grave, and the visions which will visit my sleep in the earth. But somehow my soul is not curious of these questions, though my mind grants every atom of their importance." In contrast to the habits of the past, reason is once more pushed out of the door with all due respect, while its rights are handed over to the 'soul,' to the dark, vague aspiration which Tchekhov by instinct trusts more than the bright, clear consciousness which beforehand determines the beyond, now that he stands before the fatal pale which divides man from the eternal mystery. Is scientific philosophy indignant? Is Tchekhov undermining its surest foundations? But he is an overstrained, abnormal man. Certainly you are not bound to listen to him; but once you have decided to do so then you must be prepared for anything. A normal person, even though he be a metaphysician of the extremest ethereal brand, always adjusts his theories to the requirements of the moment; he destroys only to build up from the old material once more. This is the reason why material never fails him. Obedient to the fundamental law of human nature, long since noted and formulated by the wise, he is content to confine himself to the modest part of a seeker after forms. Out of iron, which he finds in nature ready to his hand, he forges a sword or a plough, a lance or a sickle. The idea of creating out of a void hardly even enters his mind. But Tchekhov's heroes, persons abnormal *par excellence*, are faced with this abnormal and dreadful necessity. Before them always lies hopelessness, helplessness, the utter impossibility of any action whatsoever. And yet they live on, they do not die.

A strange question, and one of extraordinary moment, here suggests itself. I said that it was foreign to human nature to create out of a void. Yet nature often deprives man of ready material, while at the same time she demands imperatively that he should create. Does this mean that nature contradicts herself, or that she perverts her creatures? Is it not more correct to admit that the conception of perversion is of purely human origin. Perhaps nature is much more economical and wise than our wisdom, and maybe we should discover much more if instead of dividing people into necessary and superfluous, useful and noxious, good and bad, we suppressed the tendency to subjective valuation in ourselves and endeavoured with greater confidence to accept her creations? Otherwise you come immediately—to "the evil gleam," "treasure-digging," sorcery and black magic—and a wall is raised between men which neither logical argument nor even a battery of artillery can break down. I hardly dare hope that this consideration will appear convincing to those who are used to maintaining the norm; and it is probably unnecessary that the notion of the great opposition of good and bad which is alive among men should die away, just as it is unnecessary that children should be born with the experience of men, or that red cheeks and curly hair should vanish from the earth. At any rate it is impossible. The world has many centuries to its reckoning, many nations have lived and died upon the earth, yet as far as we know from the books and traditions that have survived to us, the dispute between good and evil was never hushed. And it always so happened that good was not afraid of the light of day, and good men lived a united, social life; while evil hid itself in darkness, and the wicked always stood alone. Nor could it have been otherwise.

All Tchekhov's heroes fear the light. They are lonely. They are ashamed of their hopelessness, and they know that men cannot help them. They go somewhere, perhaps even forward, but they call to no one to follow. All things are taken from them: they must create everything anew. Thence most probably is derived the unconcealed contempt with which they behave to the most precious products of common human creativeness. On whatever subject you begin to talk with a Tchekhov hero he has one reply to everything: *Nobody can teach me anything.* You offer him a new conception of the world: already in your very first words he feels that they all reduce to an attempt to lay the old bricks and stones over again, and he turns from you with impatience, and often with rudeness. Tchekhov is an extremely cautious writer. He fears and takes into account public opinion. Yet how unconcealed is the aversion he displays to accepted ideas and conceptions of the world. In *The Tedious Story*, he at any rate preserves the tone and attitude of outward obedience. Later he throws aside all precautions, and instead of reproaching himself for his inability to submit to the general idea, openly rebels against it and jeers at it. In *Ivanov* it already is sufficiently expressed; there was reason for the outburst of indignation which this play provoked in its day. Ivanov, I have already said, is a dead man. The only thing the artist can do with him is to bury him decently, that is, to praise his past, pity his present, and then, in order to mitigate the cheerless impression produced by death, to invite the general idea to the funeral. He might recall the universal problems of humanity in any one of the many stereotyped forms, and thus the difficult case which seemed insoluble would be removed. Together with Ivanov's death he should portray a bright young life, full of promise, and the impression of death and destruction would lose all its sting and bitterness. Tchekhov does just the opposite. Instead of endowing youth and ideals with power over destruction and death, as all philosophical systems and many works of art had done, he ostentatiously makes the good-for-nothing wreck Ivanov the centre of all events. Side by side with Ivanov there are young lives, and the idea is also given her representatives. But the young Sasha, a wonderful and charming girl, who falls utterly in love with the broken hero, not only does not save her lover, but herself perishes under the burden of the impossible task. And the idea? It is enough to recall the figure of Doctor Lvov alone, whom Tchekhov entrusted with the responsible rôle of a representative of the all-powerful idea, and you will at once perceive that he considers himself not as subject and vassal, but as the bitterest enemy of the idea. The moment Doctor Lvov opens his mouth, all the characters, as though acting on a previous agreement, vie with each other in their haste to interrupt him in the most insulting way, by jests, threats, and almost by smacks in the face. But the doctor fulfils his duties as a representative of the great power with no less skill and conscientiousness than his predecessors—Starodum[2] and the other reputable heroes of the old drama. He champions the wronged, seeks to restore rights that have been trodden underfoot, sets himself dead against injustice. Has he stepped beyond the limits of his plenipotentiary powers? Of course not; but where Ivanovs and hopelessness reign there is not and cannot be room for the idea.

They cannot possibly live together. And the eyes of the reader, who is accustomed to think that every kingdom may fall and perish, yet the kingdom of the idea stands firm *in saecula saeculorum*, behold a spectacle unheard of: the idea dethroned by a helpless, broken, good-for-nothing man! What is there that Ivanov does not say? In

---

2. The prosy *raisonneur* of Denis Fonvizin's comedy *The Minor* (1782), a "positive" type always uttering tendentious maxims. [*Editor's note.*]

the very first act he fires off a tremendous tirade, not at a chance corner, but at the incarnate idea—Starodum-Lvov.

> I have the right to give you advice. Don't you marry a Jewess, or an abnormal, or a blue-stocking. Choose something ordinary, greyish, without any bright colours or superfluous shades. Make it a principle to build your life of *clichés*. The more grey and monotonous the background, the better. My dear man, don't fight thousands single-handed, don't tilt at windmills, don't run your head against the wall. God save you from all kinds of Back-to-the-Landers' advanced doctrines, passionate speeches. . . . Shut yourself tight in your own shell, and do the tiny little work set you by God. . . . It's cosier, honester, and healthier.

Doctor Lvov, the representative of the all-powerful, sovereign idea, feels that his sovereign's majesty is injured, that to suffer such an offence really means to abdicate the throne. Surely Ivanov was a vassal, and so he must remain. How dare he let his tongue advise, how dare he raise his voice when it is his part to listen reverently, and to obey in silent resignation? This is rank rebellion! Lvov attempts to draw himself up to his full height and answer the arrogant rebel with dignity. Nothing comes of it. In a weak, trembling voice he mutters the accustomed words, which but lately had invincible power. But they do not produce their customary effect. Their virtue is departed. Whither? Lvov dares not own it even to himself. But it is no longer a secret to any one. Whatever mean and ugly things Ivanov may have done—Tchekhov is not close-fisted in this matter: in his hero's conduct-book are written all manner of offences; almost to the deliberate murder of a woman devoted to him—it is to him and not to Lvov that public opinion bows. Ivanov is the spirit of destruction, rude, violent, pitiless, sticking at nothing: yet the word 'scoundrel,' which the doctor tears out of himself with a painful effort and hurls at him, does not stick to him. He is somehow right, with his own peculiar right, to others inconceivable, yet still, if we may believe Tchekhov, incontestable. Sasha, a creature of youth and insight and talent, passes by the honest Starodum-Lvov unheeding, on her way to render worship to him. The whole play is based on that. It is true, Ivanov in the end shoots himself, and that may, if you like, give you a formal ground for believing that the final victory remained with Lvov. And Tchekhov did well to end the drama in this way—it could not be spun out to infinity. It would have been no easy matter to tell the whole of Ivanov's history. Tchekhov went on writing for fifteen years after, all the time telling the unfinished story, yet even then he had to break it off without reaching the end. . . .

It would show small understanding of Tchekhov to take it into one's head to interpret Ivanov's words to Lvov as meaning that Tche-khov, like the Tolstoi of the *War and Peace* period, saw his ideal in the everyday arrangement of life. Tchekhov was only fighting against the idea, and he said to it the most abusive thing that entered his head. For what can be more insulting to the idea than to be forced to listen to the praise of everyday life? But when the opportunity came his way, Tchekhov could describe everyday life with equal venom. The story, *The Teacher of Literature*, may serve as an example. The teacher lives entirely by Ivanov's prescription. He has his job, and his wife—neither Jewess nor abnormal, nor blue-stocking—and a home that fits like a shell . . . ; but all this does not prevent Tchekhov from driving the poor teacher by slow degrees into the usual trap, and bringing him to a condition wherein it is left to him only 'to fall down and weep, and beat his head against the floor.' Tchekhov had no 'ideal,' not even the ideal of 'everyday life' which Tolstoi glorified with such inimitable and incomparable mastery in his early works. An ideal presupposes submission, the voluntary denial of one's own right to independence, freedom and power; and demands of this kind, even a hint of such demands, roused in Tchekhov all that force of dis-gust and repulsion of which he alone was capable.

Thus the real, the only hero of Tchekhov, is the hopeless man. He has absolutely no *action* left for him in life, save to beat his head against the stones. It is not surprising that such a man should be intolerable to his neighbours. Everywhere he brings death and destruction with him. He himself is aware of it, but he has not the power to go apart from men. With all his soul he endeavours to tear himself out of his horrible condition. Above all he is attracted to fresh, young, untouched beings; with their help he hopes to recover his right to life which he has lost. The hope is vain. The beginning of decay always appears, all-conquering, and at the end Tchekhov's hero is left to himself alone. He has nothing, he must create every-thing for himself. And this "creation out of the void," or more truly the possibility of this creation, is the only problem which can occupy and inspire Tchekhov. When he has stripped his hero of the last shred, when nothing is left for him but to beat his head against the wall, Tchekhov begins to feel something like satisfaction, a strange fire lights in his burnt-out eyes, a fire which Mihailovsky[3] did not call "evil" in vain.

Creation out of the void! Is not this task beyond the limit of human powers, of human *rights*? Mihailovsky obviously had one straight answer to the question. . . . As for Tchekhov himself, if the question

3. Nikolay Konstantinovich Mikhailovsky (1842–1904), Russian socialist theorist and critic, published a number of perceptive studies of Chekhov's prose in the author's lifetime and popularized the idea that Chekhov's main theme is banality. [*Editor's note*.]

were put to him in such a deliberately definite form, he would probably be unable to answer, although he was continually engaged in
the activity, or more properly, because he was continually so
engaged. Without fear of mistake, one may say that the people who
answer the question without hesitation in either sense have never
come near to it, or to any of the so-called ultimate questions of life.
Hesitation is a necessary and integral element in the judgment of
those men whom Fate has brought near to false problems.

* * *

The only philosophy which Tchekhov took seriously, and therefore
seriously fought, was positivist materialism—just the positivist materialism, the limited materialism which does not pretend to theoretical
completeness. With all his soul Tchekhov felt the awful dependence
of a living being upon the invisible but invincible and ostentatiously
soulless laws of nature. And materialism, above all scientific materialism, which is reserved and does not hasten in pursuit of the final
word, and eschews logical completeness, wholly reduces to the definition of the external conditions of our existence. The experience of
every day, every hour, every minute, convinces us that lonely and weak
man brought to face with the laws of nature, must always adapt himself and give way, give way, give way. The old professor could not
regain his youth; the overstrained Ivanov could not recover his
strength; Layevsky[4] could not wash away the filth with which he was
covered—interminable series of implacable, purely materialistic *non
possumus*[5] against which human genius can set nothing but submission or forgetfulness. *Résigne-toi, mon cœur, dors ton sommeil de
brute*—we shall find no other words before the pictures which are
unfolded in Tchekhov's books. The submission is but an outward
show; under it lies concealed a hard, malignant hatred of the unknown
enemy. Sleep and oblivion are only seeming. Does a man sleep, does
he forget, when he calls his sleep, *sommeil de brute*? But how can he
change? The tempestuous protests with which *The Tedious Story* is
filled, the need to pour forth the pent-up indignation, soon begin to
appear useless, and even insulting to human dignity. Tchekhov's last
rebellious work is *Uncle Vanya*. Like the old professor and like Ivanov,
Uncle Vanya raises the alarm and makes an incredible pother about
his ruined life. He, too, in a voice not his own, fills the stage with his
cries: "Life is over, life is over,"—as though indeed any of these about
him, any one in the whole world, could be responsible for his misfortune. But wailing and lamentation is not sufficient for him. He covers
his own mother with insults. Aimlessly, like a lunatic, without need
or purpose, he begins shooting at his imaginary enemy, Sonya's piti-

4. A character in Chekhov's novella *The Duel* (1891). [*Editor's note.*]
5. Latin: refusal to act or move. [*Editor's note.*]

able and unhappy father. His voice is not enough, he turns to the revolver. He is ready to fire all the cannon on earth, to beat every drum, to ring every bell. To him it seems that the whole of mankind, the whole of the universe, is sleeping, that the neighbours must be awakened. He is prepared for any extravagance, having no rational way of escape; for to confess at once that there is no escape is beyond the capacity of any man. Then begins a Tchekhov history: "He cannot reconcile himself, neither can he refuse so to reconcile himself. He can only weep and beat his head against the wall." Uncle Vanya does it openly, before men's eyes; but how painful to him is the memory of this frank unreserve! When every one has departed after a stupid and painful scene, Uncle Vanya realises that he should have kept silence, that it is no use to confess certain things to any one, not even to one's nearest friend. A stranger's eye cannot endure the sight of hopelessness. "Your life is over—you have yourself to thank for it: you are a human being no more, all human things are alien to you. Your neighbours are no more neighbours to you, but strangers. You have no right either to help others or to expect help from them. Your destiny is—absolute loneliness." Little by little Tchekhov becomes convinced of this truth: *Uncle Vanya* is the last trial of loud public protest, of a vigorous "declaration of rights." And even in this drama Uncle Vanya is the only one to rage, although there are among the characters Doctor Astrov and poor Sonya, who might also avail themselves of their right to rage, and even to fire the cannon. But they are silent. They even repeat certain comfortable and angelic words concerning the happy future of mankind; which is to say that their silence is doubly deep, seeing that 'comfortable words' upon the lips of such people are the evidence of their final severance from life: they have left the whole world, and now they admit no one to their presence. They have fenced themselves with comfortable words, as with the Great Wall of China, from the curiosity and attention of their neighbours. Outwardly they resemble all men, therefore no man dares to touch their inward life.

* * *

The Sea-Gull must be considered one of the most characteristic, and therefore one of the most remarkable of Tchekhov's works. Therein the artist's true attitude to life received its most complete expression. Here all the characters are either blind, and afraid to move from their seats in case they lose the way home, or half-mad, struggling and tossing about to no end nor purpose. Arkadina the famous actress clings with her teeth to her seventy thousand roubles, her fame, and her last lover. Trigorin the famous writer writes day in, day out; he writes and writes, knowing neither end nor aim. People read his works and praise them, but he is not his own master; like Marko, the ferryman in the tale, he labours on without taking his hand from the oar, carrying passengers from one bank to the other. The boat, the passengers, and the river too, bore him to death. But how can he get rid of them? He might give the oars over to the first-comer: the solution is simple, but after it, as in the tale, he must go to heaven. Not Trigorin alone, but all the people in Tchekhov's books who are no longer young remind one of Marko the ferryman. It is plain that they dislike their work, but, exactly as though they were hypnotised, they cannot break away from the influence of the alien power. The monotonous, even dismal, rhythm of life has lulled their consciousness and will to sleep. Everywhere Tchekhov underlines this strange and mysterious trait of human life. His people always speak, always think, always do one and the same thing. One builds houses according to a plan made once for all (*My Life*); another goes on his round of visits from morn to night, collecting roubles (*Yon-itch*); a third is always buying up houses (*Three Years*). Even the language of his characters is deliberately monotonous. They are all monotonous, to the point of stupidity, and they are all afraid to break the monotony, as though it were the source of extraordinary joys. Read Trigorin's monologue:

> . . . Let us talk. . . . Let us talk of my beautiful life. . . . What shall I begin with? [Musing a little.] . . . There are such things as fixed ideas, when a person thinks day and night, for instance, of the moon, always of the moon. I too have my moon. Day and night I am at the mercy of one besetting idea: "I must write, I must write, I must." I have hardly finished one story than, for some reason or other, I must write a second, then a third, and after the third, a fourth. I write incessantly, post-haste. I cannot do otherwise. Where then, I ask you, is beauty and serenity? What a monstrous life it is! I am sitting with you now, I am excited, but meanwhile every second I remember that an unfin-ished story is waiting for me. I see a cloud, like a grand piano. It smells of heliotrope. I say to myself: a sickly smell, a half-mourning colour. . . . I must not forget to use these words when describing a summer evening. I catch up myself and you on every phrase, on every word, and hurry to lock all these words and phrases into my literary storehouse. Perhaps they will be useful. When I finish work I run to the theatre, or go off fishing: at last I shall rest, forget myself. But no! a heavy ball of iron is dragging on my fetters—a new subject, which draws me to the desk, and I must make haste to write and write again. And so on for ever, for ever. I have no rest from myself, and I feel that I am eating away my own life. I feel that the honey which I give to others has been made of the pollen of my most precious flow-

ers, that I have plucked the flowers themselves and trampled them down to the roots. Surely, I am mad. Do my neighbours and friends treat me as a sane person? "What are you writing? What have you got ready for us?" The same thing, the same thing eternally, and it seems to me that the attention, the praise, the enthusiasm of my friends is all a fraud. I am being robbed like a sick man, and sometimes I am afraid that they will creep up to me and seize me, and put me away in an asylum.

But why these torments? Throw up the oars and begin a new life. *Impossible*. While no answer comes down from heaven, Trigorin will not throw up the oars, will not begin a new life. In Tchekhov's work, only young, very young and inexperienced people speak of a new life. They are always dreaming of happiness, regeneration, light, joy. They fly headlong into the flame, and are burned like silly butterflies. In *The Sea-Gull*, Nina Zarechnaya and Treplov, in other works other heroes, men and women alike—all are seeking for something, yearning for something, but not one of them does that which he desires. Each one lives in isolation; each is wholly absorbed in his life, and is indifferent to the lives of others. And the strange fate of Tchekhov's heroes is that they strain to the last limit of their inward powers, but there are no visible results at all. They are all pitiable. The woman takes snuff, dresses slovenly, wears her hair loose, is uninteresting. The man is irritable, grumbling, takes to drink, bores every one about him. They act, they speak—always out of season. They cannot, I would even say they do not want to adapt the outer world to themselves. Matter and energy unite according to their own laws—people live according to their own, as though matter and energy had no existence at all. In this Tchekhov's intellectuals do not differ from illiterate peasants and the half-educated bourgeois. Life in the manor is the same as in the valley farm, the same as in the village. Not one believes that by changing his outward conditions he would change his fate as well. Everywhere reigns an unconscious but deep and ineradicable conviction that our will must be directed towards ends which have nothing in common with the organised life of mankind. Worse still, the organisation appears to be the enemy of the will of man. One must spoil, devour, destroy, ruin. To think out things quietly, to anticipate the future—that is impossible. One must beat one's head, beat one's head eternally against the wall. And to what purpose? Is there any purpose at all? Is it a beginning or an end? Is it possible to see in it the warrant of a new and inhuman creation, a creation out of the void? "I do not know" was the old professor's answer to Katy. "I do not know" was Tchekhov's answer to the sobs of those tormented unto death. With these words, and only these, can an essay upon Tchekhov end. *Résigne-toi, mon cœur, dors ton sommeil de brute*.

PATRICE PAVIS

Patrice Pavis (b. 1947), French literary critic, is recognized as one of the world's most influential theorists of drama. His major works include *Voix et images de la scène* (1985), *Dictionnaire du théâtre* (1987), and *Le Théâtre aux croisements des cultures* (1990). Between 1985 and 1991 he edited and annotated a series of French translations of Chekhov's major plays for the Livre de Poche series.

The Originality of *The Seagull* and Its Context†

* * *

The Seagull was far from being nurtured in the compost of an experimental theatre. Rather, it was born in a cultural desert, for in those days nothing was performed in Russia except melodramas, musical comedies, and farces, adapted or imitated from the French stage, in an over-emphatic style, without the least attention to staging. What Treplyov thinks about the contemporary theater—"trite, riddled with clichés"—describes the Russian stage of this period (notably the Maly Theater). Such was the very mediocre situation Chekhov inherited before confiding his plays to Stanislavsky's Art Theater, which created brilliant misinterpretations of its own. When it first opened in October 1896, *The Seagull* had been played as a boulevard drama, centered on the love interest of a trio (the girl, the famous actress, and the celebrated writer). It is no surprise that the premiere at the Alexandra Theater was a resounding flop: neither the actors nor the audience were ready for this new kind of playwriting, so they rejected it completely. If the subsequent performances had an unexpected success, it was only with the revival directed by Stanislavsky at the Moscow Art Theater that the play was truly discovered. And there, the same phenomenon of surprise and enthusiasm was repeated, but this time in the course of the same night.

Chekhov was located at this favorable moment in the history of the theater when directing had just been invented and its importance to the construction of meaning in a script was understood. As author, Chekhov was fully aware of the importance of staging, even if he feared more than anyone else the director's "treason." ("The stage is the scaffold on which playwrights are executed.") Nor did he consider a play suitable for publication, he confided to Pleshcheev (November 27, 1889) until it had been revised during rehearsals. He composed his text while dreaming of the stage effects and its even-

† From Antoine Tchékhov, *La Mouette*. French trans. by Antoine Vitez. Preface by Antoine Vitez. Commentary and notes by Patrice Pavis. Paris: Actes Sud, 1985. 99–103. Trans. by Laurence Senelick.

tual performers. The abundance of instructions and concrete proposals for staging were meant to serve as suggestive restraints on the director. "I do not truly believe that a play can be staged, even by the most talented director, without the advice and instructions of the author. There are varying interpretations, but the author has the right to demand that his play be performed entirely according to his own interpretation . . . It is absolutely important that the particular atmosphere desired by the author be created."[1] The playwright becomes, in this concept, the collaborator or stand-in of the director. Hence every detail—the color of a necktie or the condition of a shoe—has its importance, both in the text and on the stage. Every element in the text, or every bit of byplay on stage possesses a function, for, according to his own famous (and variously interpreted) formula, "You don't put a loaded gun on stage unless someone is going to use it." Never does a character utter the slightest banality without a precise dramatic reason. Despite this saturation of the textual meaning, Stanislavsky felt the need, as a good practitioner of naturalism, to stuff the performance with objects, noises, or "atmospheric" variations, which exasperated Chekhov and persuaded him that no director had been able to serve his plays as he intended. Despite Stanislavsky's obsessional tendency to write a score that duplicated the text and created uniquely naturalist effects in opposition to Chekhov's very economical choice of certain details that are more symbolic than naturalistic, Stanislavsky's staging *revealed* to its author the text that he had just written. By slowing down its delivery, by swelling the flow of stage metaphors, Stanislavsky exhibited the unsuspected depth of the text, linking for the first time two elements which, in France at the same period, continued to be opposed: symbolism and naturalism, manifested theatrically—in the detailed sequences of signs—"the complex interior action" (*My Life in Art*).

Misgivings regarding the Stanislavskian interpretation, despite exceptional actors (Meyerhold as Treplyov, Olga Knipper as Arkadina, Lilina as Masha) explain the laboriousness of *The Seagull*'s takeoff. Not to mention the extreme difficulty of finding the proper tone for the characters, of motivating the silences, of treating the melodramatic elements with a humorous distance and a bland irony (which would not, however, raise a liberating laugh), of situating the play in terra incognita, at the boundaries of comedy and tragedy, of "continually depicting the prose of everyday life" and "Humanity with a capital H" (*My Life in Art*).

1. *Teatr i Iskusstvo* 28 (1904), 522.

Themes and Characters

The play is made up of four acts, or rather four tableaux, which take place in different locations on Sorin's estate. The act is not sub-divided into scenes in order to mark the shifts of situations and characters. However, certain major movements can be distin-guished, which correspond to the major thematic trends of the dia-logue: seven in the first, third and fourth, six in the second acts. The first and last acts are clearly the longest, owing to a detailed expo-sition in One and a duplication of reversals in Four. Chekhov is therefore not entirely faithful to his own poetic credo about dra-matic action: "The first act should last about an hour, but the others should last no longer than half an hour" (To his brother Aleksandr, May 9, 1889). If the climactic point of the plot (Nina's love for Tri-gorin, her decision to go on the stage and follow him to Moscow) is indeed located at the end of Act Three, the tragedy culminates in the last act, in the obligatory scene of Nina's return and the sugges-tion of Treplyov's suicide. The action possesses two powerful moments: the failure of the play (One), the failure of Treplyov and Nina, the suicide (Four). The story is still built according to the classic pattern (progression and rise of the action centered on a conflict), but each act—and this is something new—tends to auton-omy. *The Seagull* is a seminal play for the rest of Chekhov's drama; each act prefigures the principal theme of the other three plays. Act One: failure of the ideal, as in *Uncle Vanya* and especially in *The Wood Goblin*; Act Two: the estate as badly managed, as in *The Cherry Orchard*; Act Three: suffering, vacillation, departure as in *Uncle Vanya*; Act Four: boredom and gunshots as in *Three Sisters* and *Uncle Vanya*.

* * *

Meyerhold, the famous director who played Treplyov in the Art The-ater's production, remarked quite correctly that in Chekhov one always finds "a group of characters devoid of a center." In the absence of one or several heroes or leading individuals, there is, in fact, a constellation of characters, whose importance lies in their complementarity. More than family or clan—the tragic grouping par excellence—it is the household, the place where people rub elbows without seeing too much of one another, where these talkative per-sons gather. Their relatively high number (ten, thirteen with the ser-vants) allows all domestic, social or romantic possibilities to be depicted. They are all there, drawn by the spellbinding lake, like gulls, assembled by a gregarious instinct, bound to one another by habit, prisoners of a perpetually inhibited communication, where no one tries to persuade anyone else, where people are content to talk to themselves while addressing their neighbor: "Nobody lifts a finger, everybody philosophizes" (Act Two).

One of the basic and repetitive figures of this constellation is the triangle of unreciprocated love:

Nina—Treplyov—Trigorin (and even Sorin)
Arkadina—Nina—Trigorin
Arkadina—Treplyov—Trigorin
Masha—Treplyov—Medvedenko
Polina—Dorn—Shamraev

The parallelism of these triangular situations adequately expresses the imprisonment of each one, his role both as gull and hunter. The conflict of generations, of literary styles, of ideas about living, systematically places all the characters in opposition. What better way than by these parallel networks of love and indifference to configure the crisis of the couple and the family, the rending of the social fabric, the uniformity of the human condition?

At first sight, the characters seem characterized in a naturalistic way, very precisely delineated in their psychological outline and social identity. In reality, they come into existence only through enunciation and are defined only by certain signifying and recurrent indications: a recurrent action (Masha's taking snuff), a linguistic tic (Sorin's "when all's said and done," Masha's "don't be silly"), an obsessional theme (Sorin's old age, Trigorin's note-taking). A limited choice of repetitive speech both in their subject matter and in the formulas they use is enough to create a powerful sense of reality. Each character is, as it were, programmed to keep on repeating the same phrase or give utterance to the same fixed idea. "I'm a gull . . . No, that's wrong," Nina endlessly repeats in her great monologue. Everyone would be able to affirm the same thing, as if he were pursuing both a desire to speak and a desire for silence. Impossible to contrast these characters by means of a theme or a conflict: they are neither right nor wrong, neither good nor evil. Everyone has his own luck. Chekhov refuses to judge them or take sides, much less to use any one of them as his spokesman. It is in what results from their talk, the dialogue of their obsessions, the divergence of their reactions to the same question that one can, although always with difficulty, take the side of things.

The characters in *The Seagull*—except for Nina—do not change, they draw no lesson from their experiences, fail to communicate except through incessantly recalling their memories or their dreams, by quoting another without seeming to, by humming (Dorn) or whistling (Sorin). In this discordant concert of isolated voices given over to monologue or solipsism, the important thing is not so much what the character says as the moment when he says it, the instant when speech is granted to him and then withdrawn. Everyone in the play covers the distance, follows a trajectory that makes material, in Chekhov more than in any other playwright, the "topographic passages of the unconscious on the stage" (Antoine Vitez, *L'Ane*, no. 5).[2]

* * *

Dialogue

Not being bound in essence to a conflict, the dialogue tends to free itself from action and character. It is located, to use the fine analysis by Peter Szöndi,[3] under the sign of difficulty, renunciation, indeed incommunicability. Frequently the characters give up trying to convince or even address another person: Masha with Medvedenko, Treplyov with his audience (Act One), Trigorin with Arkadina (Act Three), Masha with her mother (Act Four). Thus liberated, the word constantly eludes its speakers: it is no longer incarnated by a given character; it is at most relayed and transmitted by him, uttered with the conviction of a speaking automaton. It is carried on by a psychological subtext, implicit and all the more pregnant with meaning. The dialogue alone is established between silence, the spoken and the unspoken, the word and the stage. Very often, verbal dialogue is broken off at the very moment when the characters may be just about to say something. The strangeness and teasing power of Chekhov's text originates in a sort of sadism which consists in never explaining, never giving the key to the quotations or to the characters, replacing any reference to the world by an infinite series of recurrences and allusions.

Echo and Absent Connection

The repetition of the same idea or an identical phrase is not simply the sign of the protagonists' boredom or the mark of a morbid "compulsion for repetition": it structures the text by reducing it to a limited series of themes, incessantly resumed or varied. Every theme is the anticipation of an ulterior theme or the resumption of something already said. Certain words, repeated six or seven times, characterize an individual; others crystalize an obsession or a general neurosis: the word *know* (*znat'*) and its derivatives (*uznat'*, etc.). The insistence on the term and the action reveal a crucial problem: the general

2. Antoine Vitez (1930–1990), French director who staged highly intellectual productions of Chekhov in his own translations. [*Editor's note.*]
3. Peter Szöndi (1929–1971), Rumanian literary critic, whose *Theory of the Modern Drama* (1956), articulated an "epic" view of Chekhov, emphasizing the loneliness of his characters. He stated that "the history of art is determined not by ideas, but by the form in which they are incarnated." [*Editor's note.*]

desire to be recognized by others as a loving person and, for Treplyov, Arkadina, Trigorin, and Nina, as an artist.

Echo is one of the playwright's favorite procedures. It suggests to the spectator, placed in the position of omniscient auditor, that an action, a situation, an expression has already been put in evidence and the repetition makes some sense. There is thus an echo effect between different characters who were not on stage at the same time and who come to the same conclusions:

> TREPLYOV (*concerning Trigorin*):   Charming, talented . . . but . . . compared to Tolstoy or Zola, a little Trigorin goes a long way. (Act One)
>
> TRIGORIN (*concerning himself*):   Charming, but a far cry from Tolstoy. (Act Two).

Often it's the same scornful word ("silly," "nonsense") which studs the speech of Masha, Sorin, and Dorn. Echo is also a more or less masked citation of some one else's remark: "It gets you going in circles!" (Act One) declares Medvedenko to Masha about his miserable salary, and Dorn swiftly picks it up, when the schoolteacher starts complaining again about the price of flour: "It gets you going in circles!" (Act Two). Metaphors form a network of repetitive terms, whether it concerns the *lake* or the *roots* of love which must be torn out of one's heart. The stage actions are also conceived according to the echoic principle: Treplyov plucks a daisy (Act One), Polina tramples on the flowers offered by Nina (Act Two). These echoes may seem involuntary—they are no less revealing of unconscious symbolic actions and they crystallize around apparently anodyne objects: Trigorin, after having been preached at and overpowered by Arkadina, despite his attraction to Nina, suddenly notices that he has forgot his cane (Act Three). Back onstage, he seems by chance to run into Nina and the forbidden object of his desire. Medvedenko, while still a young wooer, has no desire for the snuff offered him by Masha (Act One).

Echo also indicates the direction of the dialogue, the implicit ending towards which it tends. It reveals the distended connection between apparently unrelated words. Hence this involuntary exchange between Nina and Polina (Act One):

> NINA (*to* TREPLYOV)   And a play, I think, definitely ought to have love interest . . .
>
> POLINA (*to* DORN)   It's starting to get damp. Go back and put on your galoshes.

Love, the implicit linkage between the two lines, also means thinking about the other person's health. Of course, it's always up to the spectator what to make of such rapprochements, at the risk of extrapolation or going off on a tangent. "Hooking together" the fragments disseminated throughout, perceiving faint echoes give the text its meaning and make it eloquent. "In this critique of logocentrism, everything speaks: words no longer assume the chief importance; blanks, objects, bodies prevail over words, non-verbal signs prolif-erate."[4] How is one to know, then, if what is spoken has too much meaning or not enough! Everything is in the association and hier-archy between odd scraps of speech reduced to crumbs.

The same type of connection governs the countless quotations, authentic or disguised, from other literary works (Shakespeare, Tur-genev, Maupassant, Ibsen and his *Wild Duck*). This quotation epi-demic suggests to the reader parallels with classical texts, authorizing short cuts thanks to texts known to everyone, also marking them off from their problem. *The Seagull* is not afraid to attack *Hamlet* and *Oedipus*, establish an affiliation which is fixed on Treplyov's Oedipal conflict and the question of influence. It confirms the idea that every text—as Trigorin knows well (Act Two) and Treplyov is wrong to worry about (Act Four)—is a rewriting of earlier texts or notes, an echoic revival of a limited number of elements, an ironic or enigmatic deviation related to a model repeated or parodied.

This systematic theft of another person's speech is daily accom-plished by every character by parodying, more or less voluntarily, a way of speaking that is not his own: Shamraev drones on like a the-atrical gossip column; Arkadina speaks a Russian riddled with French expressions; Trigorin, the prosaic landscape artist, in love with the romantic Nina, launches into emphatic declarations (Act Three); Nina turns her own head by evoking the fame of writers (Act Three), often adopts Arkadina's actress lingo. It is an ironically inter-mingled Babel . . .

For irony is one of the organizing principles of the narrative of this *Seagull*. It often consists here in "leaving things unsaid," in opposing characters or ideas without determining who is right. By means of Treplyov, the immature "doomed poet," and Trigorin, the obsessive angler, Chekhov makes fun of literary men of his time, prophets of a new life or apocalypse in literature, but also the shrewd veterans of the pen. The tragic irony of the narrative (as the character himself points out in Act Three) is that Treplyov wanted to play the misun-derstood genius to seduce his mother and his girlfriend, while in the end it is Trigorin who, in a rather offhand way, seduces both women.

Irony runs the tortuous story of this *Seagull* off the road: the writer Trigorin is busy drafting a symbolic tale about a gull killed for no good reason (Act Two). As for Treplyov, he sees the cycle of deso-lation prophesied in his play (Act One) realized in his own private

4. Daniel Bougnoux, "Sourire entre les larmes," *Silex*, 16 (1980): 17–23.

life, a desolation confirmed by Nina, who returns to recite once more the passage in question (Act Four). And even good old Sorin actually writes with his unfulfilled life the story he had planned: "L'homme qui a voulu" (Act Two).

Each of the main protagonists (Treplyov, Nina, Trigorin) is in the situation of Oedipus: even though he knows the prophecy (the gull will be killed), he inexorably carries it out, despite all the warnings and allusions to the riddle of the Sphinx (Act Three). A tragic irony which has its outlet in no catharsis, since the heroes, in contrast with *Oedipus* or *Hamlet*, suffer or die unaware of what they did wrong—like Trigorin (Act Four)—or with the perspective to regain their freedom by sacrificing their life (Treplyov).

Anyway, not all of them has the honor of rewriting *Oedipus* or *Hamlet*. Ordinary mortals are content to whistle fashionable tunes or mix up Latin proverbs (Act One). The paradoxical responses to the noble leitmotiv of the "spell-binding lake" (Act One) are the overseer's anecdotes, the eternal prescriptions of valerian drops (Acts One and Two), Masha's "don't be silly" and the "linguistic tics" of each character. The subtlety of quotations, the ironic allusions, the rewritings are equalled only by the fragility of this text, so dependent on the associative power of the spectator, his musical memory, his taste for provocative associations. The "words of warning" of this ironic speech are very discreet and reserved for the most grotesque characters and situations. Most often, irony, denigratory and ungraspable, is conveyed by an "allusive" humor that is careful not to foreclose the text. Despite his reputation as a naturalist, due to Stanislavsky's productions—which were violently criticized by Chekhov himself—this drama does not seek to imitate real-life speakers, it does not recreate a totality. It is founded on a very sure knowledge of the mechanisms of rewriting, according to a refined technique of global composition in space-time.

Space

Such a composition of dialogue is possible only because space plays a role which is both realistic (the park, the lake, the house, etc.) and symbolic (interior and exterior, progressive enclosure, spatial disposition of dialogue). The first two acts unfold outside, the last two inside Sorin's house, the very last in Treplyov's study. After this process of reduction and interiorization of space, everything ends situated in the stifling confines of the household, the family, and in Treplyov's confused mind. In the face of this progressive enclosure, Treplyov has no way out except to make an exit to blow out his brains. As to his attempt, in the first act, to make the space of nature (lake, park) coincide with that of art (a theatrical setting), it is doomed to failure from the outset. In a romantically tragic manner confusing art and life, stage and lake, Treplyov is incapable of distinguished the imaginary from the real, of transposing nature and society into his art and of resolving his psychological problems through artistic creativity. The space of the other characters is hardly more propitious to individual expansion. The family space is exploded and degraded: no one feels comfortable in a private conversation (Act One, Three) and yet it continues to attract summer visitors and artists until Treplyov's departure and the desperate attempt to "take Irina Nikolaevna somewhere away from here" (Act Four). "Perhaps," writes Georges Banu, "the ultimate metaphor for this depleted space is Medvedenko pushing not a baby carriage, but a dying man's wheelchair."[5] Only Nina Zarechnaya ("she who comes from the other side of the river") is capable of leaving the enchanted precincts of the lake. The lake's idyllic space belongs either to childhood or dream, or to utopia, the unsatisfied and impulsive ideal. In this vast symbolic layout, it is only a shiny lure for catching birds.

* * *

MARIA DEPPERMANN

Maria Deppermann, a German expert in Russian and comparative literature, teaches at the University of Innsbruck. She has published studies of the symbolist poet Andrey Bely (1982) and the Norwegian dramatist Henrik Ibsen (1997), as well as essays on Chekhov's plays.

Uncle Vanya†

Poetics of the Everyday—Drama of the Inner Man

When, following the premiere of his play *Uncle Vanya* on October 26, 1899, at the newly founded Moscow Art Theater, Anton Chekhov celebrated his second success in that theatre after *The Seagull*, few could imagine that a new type of drama had been created: the drama of everyday life, apparently the "most undramatic play in the world"[1] about the "great little man."[2] Chekhov the physician turns his diagnostic acumen to an emergency of his time, which is still

5. Georges Banu, "Ruptures dans l'espace de *La Mouette*," *Le Texte et la Scène* (1978), 76.
† From "*Onkel Wanja*," in *Interpretationen: Tschechows Dramen*, ed. Bodo Zelinsky (Stuttgart: Reclam, 2003), 47–75. Trans. by Laurence Senelick and Maria Deppermann. Reprinted by permission of the author.
1. D. S. Mirsky, *A History of Russian Literature*, ed. Francis J. Whitfield (New York: Alfred A. Knopf, 1965), 365.
2. V. Yermilov, *A. P. Chekhov* (Moscow, 1959), 435.

relevant today: "Any idiot can face a crisis, but day-to-day living is what wears us out."[3]

As the grandson of a serf and the son of a bankrupt small trades-man from South Russian Taganrog, Chekhov had to deal with all the harshness of everyday life from an early age. As contributor of short stories to humor and amusement magazines, with which the medical student kept the family's head above water, and as a prac-ticing physician in Moscow and the provinces, he had for years thor-oughly studied the living world of a wide cross-section of the Russia of his time, the urban petty bourgeoisie and the new intelligentsia, but also the peasants, the landed gentry and its servants on estates, both well and badly managed. To bring "reality and humanity"[4] not only onto paper, but also onto the stage, was an artistic task which engaged Chekhov the short-story writer very early on. His "Platonov project,"[5] named after the title character of his first major play, was supposed to make an "encyclopedia of Russian provincial life" the subject matter of a new form of drama. Chekhov's goal was, however, not the naturalistic reflection of milieu and characters in a thrilling plot, but the condensation of everyday experiences into a poetic con-centrate, a "quintessence of life"[6] on the stage.

As reasonable as this may sound today, in his time criticism aimed at Chekhov was harsh. Old Tolstoy, at that time a foremost authority for Russian literature and the public, was ruthless in his opinions. Despite his high regard for Chekhov's narrative art, he said of his plays:

> Shakespeare's plays are dreadful, but yours are even worse . . . Where do your heroes take us? From the sofa to the pantry and from the pantry back to the sofa.[7]

Tolstoy was not alone in rebuking the experimental dramatist. Like Pushkin, Chekhov was scolded by the most various factions of "national literary criticism": he lacked impassioned ideas and an eth-ically and socially responsible moral program. Radicals and conser-vatives were surprisingly united in this criticism, and liberals complained of his lack of belief in social progress and especially the "positive."[8]

3. J. L. Styan, *Chekhov in Performance: A Commentary on the Major Plays* (Cambridge, 1971), 143.
4. On Chekhov's "Theater of Display," related to the painterly method of Cézanne, see Ilya Ehrenburg, *À la rencontre de Tchékhov* (Paris, 1962).
5. Siegfried Melchinger, *Anton Tschechow* (Velber bei Hannover, 1968), 33, 59, and 74.
6. E. A. Polotskaya, "Chekhov i Meierkhold" (Chekhov and Meyerhold), in *Chekhov*, ed. V. V. Vinogradov et al. (Moscow, 1960), 419.
7. N. N. Gusev, *Letopis zhizni i tvorchestva Lva Nikolaevica Tolstogo 1891–1910* (Chronicle of the Life and Work of Leo Tolstoy, 1891–191. (Moscow, 1960), 419.
8. H. Urbanski, *Chekhov as Viewed by His Russian Literary Contemporaries* (Wrocław, 1979), 9ff. Despite his aversions, Tolstoy wrote his play *The Living Corpse* under the influence of Chekhov's *Uncle Vanya*.

Among fellow authors, Chekhov was understood by Korolenko,[9] the influential story writer of the "populist" movement, and Gorky, who immediately and with painful clarity recognized the built-in "trigger effect"[1] in Chekhov's drama of muted colors and sounds. Gorky let himself be captivated by the filigree of atmosphere spun out of nuances and suggestive details, but also sensed the covert dramatic force with which Chekhov packed everyday life. They triggered a cathartic shock in him. When, in November 1898, before the Moscow premiere, he saw *Uncle Vanya* on a provincial stage in Nizhny Novgorod, Gorky wrote to Chekhov:

> A couple of days ago I saw *Uncle Vanya* and wept like a silly female [. . .] as if I were being sawn in half by a dull saw. [. . .] Your *Uncle Vanya* is an entirely new form of dramatic art, a hammer you use to pound on the public's empty pate.[. . .] In the last act of *Vanya* when the doctor—after a long pause—refers to the heat in Africa, I started to tremble in admiration of your talent, and in fear of the people, of our colorless, scurvy life.[2]

Gorky also recognized the defining feature of Chekhov's poetics of the trivial, that excess of naturalism which ensures the new poetics its timeless quality:

> [. . .] a new kind of dramatic art, in which realism is made spiritual and raised to the level of a thoroughly thought-out symbol. [. . .] I gave thought to a life which has been sacrificed to an idol, about the intrusion of beauty into the people's scurvy lives [. . .] Other plays do not lead a man from reality to philosophical speculation—yours do.[3]

Uncle Vanya represents a watershed in Chekhov's development as dramatist. In the first of his three pre-1890 "greatest" plays[4] one can recognize the young author's ambition to imbed sociological observations in Russian variations on the archetypes of world literature: Don Juan in *Platonov* and Hamlet in *Ivanov*.[5] In *The Wood Goblin*, Chekhov referred to the Slavic nature spirit, the *Leshy*. In the two

9. Vladimir Galaktionovich Korolenko (1853–1921), Russian novelist, conservative in technique but progressive in subject matter. (*Editor's note*.)
1. Eric Bentley, "Craftsmanship in *Uncle Vanya*," in *Chekhov: New Perspectives*, ed. R. and N. Wellek (New York, 1984), 139. "The 'trigger-effect' is as dramatic in its way as the 'buried-secret' pattern of Sophocles and Ibsen."
2. Chekhov, *Polnoe sobranie sochineny* (Complete Collected Works) (Moscow: Nauka, 1974–83), XIII: 404, 408ff (Hereafter referred to as *PSS*.)
3. Gorky to Chekhov, December 1898. *PSS*, XIII: 409.
4. In addition, Chekhov wrote popular vaudevilles or "farces" such as *The Bear*, *The Proposal*, and *The Wedding*, conventionally constructed plays of potent irony. They were immediate stage successes and even abroad have run as repertory pieces up to today.
5. See Thomas Winner, "Chekhov's *Seagull* and Shakespeare's *Hamlet*," in *Chekhov, New Perspectives*, ed. R. and N. Wellek (New York, 1984), 107–17, and Richard Peace, *Chekhov: A Study of the Four Major Plays* (New Haven / London, 1983), 50–74.

plays from his second period, 1895–1897, *The Seagull* and *Uncle Vanya*, the theme of the artist and the ruin of the idealistic intelligentsia after the emancipation of the serfs makes up the background. In the post-1900 plays, *Three Sisters* and *The Cherry Orchard*, there is no longer a central hero. What counts in these last two plays is the "Chekhov group" put in a precarious situation. *The Cherry Orchard* concerns the parting of a kindly but incompetent aristocracy from a way of life they can neither abandon nor change. In *Three Sisters*, three young women, orphaned daughters of an officer, recognize the need to make a bid for independence. Nevertheless, they run aground.

The physician and writer Chekhov made his socio-psychological diagnosis of the wide-ranging faith in progress prior to 1914, in a backward agrarian state, while Western Europe was prospering but the realm of the Tsar was also being violently modernized. He concentrated on the single individual; for he diagnosed the disease of his age to be a suspicious lack of selfhood. On one hand, there rages a reckless demand for respect, whatever the cost to others. On the other, people either timorously huddle in the shadow of the strong, mindful of their own security, not risking their own independence, inclined to admire themselves for their own weakness; or else they let themselves all too willingly lie down before the chariot of the utopia-addled activist, who sheds a glimmer of his ideals on their own spiritual impoverishment. Chekhov shows two varieties of the power and powerlessness of this psycho-social epidemic of hypertrophied egoists or stunted altruists: the dominant type of the "strong"—the "iron man," as Gorky would say—and the contrary type of the "weak," who, devoid of aim and will, contemplates his own navel or devotes himself to idols and is satisfied with the borrowed refulgence that spares him the effort of shaping an individuality of his own.

Chekhov's sympathies—although not manifested directly—in the "psychopathology of everyday life" are with those who fight for independence, but who want to preserve their humanity as well. But since Chekhov knew every stage of such a fight, he also turns his attention to the strong: he admires their strength and does them justice; however, he does not idealize them and thoroughly registers the damage they cause and suffer in their own souls.[6] With brilliant perspicuity and sympathy he records, however the mental strain of those who, despite the power of the banal, preserve their impulse towards a humane and rewarding purpose in life, and who enter the fray, even if they cannot summon up the energy necessary to effect

---

6. See Donald Rayfield, *Chekhov: The Evolution of His Art* (New York, 1975), 7.

a change. There are no winners in Chekhov, only losers.[7] Even the ostensibly strong do not leave the arena of everyday life unscathed. Neither the peasant entrepreneur in *The Cherry Orchard*, nor the prominent artists in *The Seagull*, nor the celebrated Professor in *Uncle Vanya* is happy in his "position of strength." They too have to pay the price: with isolation and anxiety, with loss of authority and love in a tormented, joyless old age.

The search for independence and personal happiness drives all the characters in *Uncle Vanya*—except for the contrasting pair of the totally dependent nanny Marina and sponger Telegin—all summer long. It culminates in the gunshot in the drawing room and proceeds to the awareness that the happiness they each desire is not attainable: a new life under his own control for Vanya, a loving husband for Sonya and Yelena, a beautiful wife for Astrov and a cottage in Finland for the professor.

Chekhov's central theme in *Uncle Vanya* is the disillusionment of the "idealists." After the "crisis," the idealists face the everyday question of survival.[8] How does one get over losses and disappointments that exhaust one's substance? How does one save oneself from self-destruction? To do this, the play's characters and their author, who has been unfairly called the "bard of frustration,"[9] need a formidable reserve of courage. Indeed, more than any other playwright, Chekhov brought to the stage the ambivalence and suffering within the magnetic field of frustration. However, this alleged distinction ignores the aura that surrounds frustration in his works: just as incorruptible as his analysis that palpates and X-rays the symptoms of everyday life, so steadfast remains his faith in humanity. It encourages a utopian horizon, his "principle of hope," which, undogmatic and tempered by irony, is present in every play.

Chekhov's theater of the seemingly "trivial" is therefore not only a "drama of everyday life," but simultaneously and especially a "drama of the inner man,"[1] as the progressive director Vsevolod Meyerhold, the student and antipode of Stanislavsky, recognized. In addition, Chekhov triggered the demand for an "intimate theater," which the Swede August Strindberg in the period of theatrical reform around 1890 located in a modernist drama.[2] This was supposed to evolve as a literary genre equivalent to the great European novel,

7. Harvey Pitcher, *The Chekhov Play: A New Interpretation*. 2d ed. (Los Angeles–London, 1984), 12.
8. Pitcher, *op.cit.*, 16.
9. J.-P. Barricelli, ed., *Chekhov's Great Plays* (New York–London, 1981), ixff.
1. Pitcher, *op.cit.*, 85.
2. See "Author's Preface to *Miss Julie*" (1888) in *Seven Plays by August Strindberg*, trans. Arvid Paulson (New York: Bantam Books, 1969), 62–75; also J. L. Styan, *Chekhov in Performance: A Commentary on the Major Plays* (Cambridge, 1971), 3.

which had already reached a high level. Edmond de Goncourt[3] wrote in resignation at the time, "The end of the theater has come; for it is impossible to present as complicated a psychology on the stage as can be done in the modern novel." Chekhov made the impossible possible. Thus he became a stumbling block in a double sense: one stumbles over the man who gave the most fruitful shock to the theater of the twentieth century. For the Chekhov play is a "problem of dramatic form."[4]

* * *

Story and plot

Uncle Vanya takes place in the late 1880s on the estate of the Voinitsky-Serebryakov family. The external conflict is the result of the management, the use, and the planned sale of this property. We are therefore dealing with a socio-critical play of its period with pointed discussions about work and earnings, money and ownership, respect and career, renunciation and sacrifice. Chekhov transcends the social element, however. He dovetails the problem of material existence and personal worth with the intellectual crisis of how to live, with doubts about the meaning of life at moments of personal crisis, such as midlife crisis, the experience of aging, and fleeting youth in frustrated love affairs. At such critical moments, feelings, ideals and illusions are put to the test and intensify external conflicts. This interweaving of the material of social and psychological conflicts against the background of a prominent "ecological idea" begets a multi-layered network of intellectual and emotional content, as great works of drama have always done. But with this major difference: Chekhov's dramatis personae are not exceptional figures. Their testing ground lies not in being extraordinary, but in the concrete everyday life of the family.

The action extends over the course of a summer. It begins in June during hay-making after the arrival of guests from the city and ends with partings in early autumn. This pattern of arrival and departure, along with the contrast of "residents" and "outsiders," bringing a latent crisis to the breaking point—that is, an exceptional situation (for instance, a visit) as a segment from an encompassing life process—is a structural constant in Chekhov's plays.[5] This applies as well to the four-act play as basic format. The situation takes three acts to unfold before the typical Chekhovian "anticlimax," and then

3. Edmond de Goncourt (1822–1896), French novelist and proponent of Naturalism, who emphasized the influence of environment and habit on human character. (*Editor's note.*)
4. A. P. Chudakov, *Poétika Chekhova* (Moscow, 1971), 279ff.
5. Bentley, *op.cit.*, 121; Pitcher, *op.cit.*, 14.

discharges into the fourth, which, at first sight, resembles the beginning.

The frame of the action is a family of landed gentry with a shared prehistory of over twenty-five years. This long period of time is what enables us to understand what happens in this "Indian summer." In the prehistory, work appears to be the primary occupation of everyday life: imposed or self-selected in service of a common cause, an ideal or an idol.[6] Onstage, there are certainly no scenes of the practice of rural medicine or university life or the actual agrarian management of the estate. We experience the world of work merely from what the characters say. What is shown onstage is that sphere of their everyday life in which they do not work, but talk to one another: conversation over tea, during a sleepless night, about Astrov's diagrams, and at a family council in the drawing room. Only after an argument, reconciliation, and farewell do the scenes at the very end of Act Four flow back into the interrupted average workday. Now we see the little office on the estate where Uncle Vanya and Sonya do the accounts and where he will soon have to deal with the peasants again, where he lives and sleeps, away from the labyrinth of the main house's twenty-six rooms, through which the guests wander and never find one another.

The plot[7] of the play provides a suspension of everyday work, in which the mosaic of the prehistory is gradually pieced together in the dialogue. The prehistory therefore appears in a subjective light, especially with Uncle Vanya, who is far too overwrought in his excitement, but who nevertheless brings the truth to light. The reader or spectator must—in life as well—pay close attention in the dialogue's polyphony to contradictions, overlaps, or confirmations. So it is noteworthy that the skeptical Doctor immediately sees through Uncle Vanya's envy of the Professor, that the latter's "devotee," Vanya's doting mother, unfeelingly condemns her protesting son, that Sonya, however, because she alone grasps the whole measure of Vanya's despair, for all his grotesque overstatements, stands by him in his righteous opposition to her own father.

In order to reconstruct the story, one has to arrange the prehistory within the plot. Important for the interpretation, therefore, are the sequence of episodes and the structural equivalences in the plot, especially the composition of the elements of the story over the course of the four acts. The opening episode and the "coda" strike the fundamental chord of the drama. Thus, with inner logic Dr.

6. On Chekhov's views on work, see G. Selge, *Anton Čechovs Menschenbild. Materialen zu einer poetischen Anthropologie* (Munich, 1970), 94ff; Pitcher, *op.cit.*, 109; Beverly Hahn, *Chekhov: A Study of the Major Plays and Stories* (Cambridge, 1977), 8.
7. In contrast to theoretical definitions of narrative, *story* here is understood to be the underlying, chronological story, whereas *plot* is the artistic organization of the episodes within the composition.

Astrov is first shown in dialogue with the nanny Marina. Both have almost no part in the external conflict over the estate. The physician, however, conveys the play's idea that is directed at the future: the responsibility of a thoroughly "beautiful human being" for the future of the earth, which goes far beyond the actual argument of the antagonists. And he intones the countervailing, all-pervasive theme of the apparently senseless wear and tear of everyday life. Chekhov's nanny is no irrelevant servant figure. She is most unchangeably associated with the routine of everyday life; but in rituals of care she has preserved, along with blunt honesty, her—albeit simple—beliefs and active sympathy. The emotional temperature of the drama is grounded in her. Astrov's complaint about the hardships of his way of life in his opening monologue and the comforting words of Marina, whom the rough G.P. kisses gratefully, correspond to Sonya's famous final speech. On the verge of despair herself, Sonya finds the inner strength to comfort her Uncle Vanya in his pain. Thereby she redeems, if only partially, Astrov's ideal, which, ironically, the doctor cannot love in her person, as a physically unattractive woman.

The impulse to the dramatic event is given by the arrival of the badly matched couple: the emeritus professor of art history, Aleksandr Vladimirovich Serebryakov (Silverling), and his thirty-year younger, beautiful second wife Yelena (Helen). Serebryakov, the son of a sexton, has worked his way up in society. He is the paragon of an upwardly mobile Russian social climber in the years following the period of reform and boosterism. In addition, he has married into the family of the upper-class state councilor Voinitsky. We are also dealing with a man who is admired and envied. Yelena, blinded by his brilliance, has given up her training as a pianist at the Petersburg Conservatory, but soon finds herself unhappy and bored at the side of a querulous hypochondriac. Courted by Astrov and Vanya, the young woman is torn between inhibited fidelity and fascination for the doctor's *élan-vital*.[8] Her only escape from this discord is departure. Neither she nor her husband can put up with the country for long; both are used to a conventional life in the civilized realm of the big city. But they lack the money for it. Hence, Serebryakov comes up with the idea of selling the estate, which his first wife, Vanya's sister, Vera Petrovna Voinitskaya, brought him in marriage and which after her death passed to their daughter Sonya. Vanya has managed the estate for twenty-five years and with hard work has made it debt-free and profitable. For ten years Sonya has been helping him. Both are satisfied with a skimpy salary, in order to send the greater part of the proceeds of their savings to support the Professor's

---

8. French, "vital spark," philosopher Henri Bergson's term for what George Bernard Shaw called the "life force." [*Editor's note.*]

way of life in the capital. Serebryakov is honored in this provincial
estate as an indisputable authority and the pride of the family. Vanya
and Sonya willingly sacrifice their labor to him. Occupied all day
long with farming, at night they copy out his manuscripts. This
arrangement has functioned for twenty-five years. It constitutes the
prehistory, the story, which Chekhov in this "Indian summer" drama
pulls together into a plot of a deep-seated crisis of property and relationships.

Complementary Men: Vanya and Astrov

How can it reach a crisis? Ideological differences and social grievances are not sufficient grounds. They are secondary. Vanya's protest
has a "psychological wrinkle." Specifically, following a psychic shock,
Vanya recants his given role in the voluntary "division of labor" for
the common cause. This shock plunges the farm manager into a
mental crisis and triggers the conflict in the daily confrontation with
the old Professor and his young wife on the estate. This is how Vanya
becomes the central figure.

The long functioning arrangement appears to Vanya in a new light
when the Professor marries a second time; Vanya unconsciously
experiences this move as a posthumous breach of faith with his
beloved sister.[9] Since then he also feels betrayed. The first key scene
between Vanya and Sonya in Act Two maintains their subtext
throughout:

> VOINITSKY What tears? Nothing of the sort . . . don't be silly
> . . . Just now the way you looked like your poor mother. My
> precious . . . (*Avidly kisses her hands and face.*) My dear sister
> . . . my darling sister . . . Where is she now? If only she knew!
> Ah, if only she knew!
> SONYA What? Uncle, knew what?
> VOINITSKY Oppressive, wrong . . . Never mind . . . Later . . .
> Never mind . . . I'm going . . . (*Goes.*)

Chekhov's ellipses and emphases as well the stage directions hint at
the unconscious process which Vanya cannot put into clear words.
Somewhat later his "eyes are opened." The scholarly achievements
of the learned man now strike him as mediocre, Serebryakov himself
as senile and his claims as hollow. Disappointed, Vanya calls his

---

9. The analysis of Vanya's relation to his sister is more convincing in J. Vitins, "Uncle Vanya's
Predicament," in Barricelli, *op. cit.*, 35ff., than in Maurice Valency, *The Breaking String:
The Plays of Anton Chekhov* (New York, 1966), 193ff., which sees a schematic construc-
tion of depression and masochism as the key to Vanya's character. For a literary-
psychological interpretation, see M. Depperman, "Zarte Anspielungen auf ziemlich starke
Stücke. Psychologische Motivierung und dramentechnische Innovation in Čechovs 'Onkel
Vanja,' " in W. Mauser, U. Renner-Henke, and W. Schönau, eds., *Phantasie und Deutung.
Psychologisches Verstehen von Literatur und Film. Frederick Wyatt zum 75. Geburtstag*
(Würzburg, 1986), 100ff.

former idol "an old fossil" and "a learned guppy." His respect turns into hatred and envy, above all because he realizes that he has wasted his own life in serving a discredited authority. But he does not seek the causes for it in himself. He does not realize that he viewed the adored one with the eyes of his deceased sister. Instead, he turns Serebryakov into his antagonist, the scapegoat for his wasted life. Thus he "forgets" that he had all too willingly subjected himself—for it is easier to see oneself in the role of victim than of fool.[1]

Vanya cannot live without illusions, and he immediately creates a new one in Yelena. He would like to unyoke her from the Professor and make her the subject of his "new life." In his wishful dreams, he first sees her full of hope as a sisterly confidante, whom he as a brother will protect, then—when she rejects him—as a "water-nymph" who, if not with him, then with "some water sprite . . ." could leap "head over heels into the whirlpool" and cheat the senile cheater. So he desires Yelena partly in anger and partly in hopeless adoration, blind to the fact that she cannot love him and that he is starting to come off as a comic relief—the eternal uncle—who misses the mark. Because of his identification with his sister, he has failed to mature from an adolescent to a man. All that is left to him are the roles of brother and uncle. Vanya is shown to us not in his element as a tough and efficient worker over the long years, a faithful, careful manager, but only from the seamy side of his emotions: an aging adolescent whose work has become questionable and who, shaken by the convulsions of a "midlife crisis," groans, "I haven't lived!" Vanya is a believer in illusions who let himself be harnessed for others. However, he is the only one who clearly recognizes the Professor's mediocrity and poses an obstacle to it.

Vanya and the doctor are presented as complementary figures. Dr. Mikhail Lvovich Astrov has ideals and stands up for his ideals: medical practice and the forests. Anyone in Russia at that time who was a country doctor and who also went in for land surveying or communal forestry had to be an idealist from the elite ranks of the *zemstvo* intelligentsia, the liberal movement for creating a local self-government, which—like the necessary infrastructure as well—was almost entirely lacking throughout Russia. The *zemstvo* intelligentsia earned scant respect for their efforts from society and did not find much support from the government, but were regarded with distrust and had to maintain themselves by hard labor in isolated outposts. Dr. Astrov belongs to this race of men. His self-portrait lies somewhere between trailblazer and crank. He has not given up defending

---

1. For Chekhov's views on work, see G. Selge, *Anton Čechovs Menschenbild. Materialien zu einer poetischen Anthropologie* (Munich, 1970), 94ff; Pitcher, op.cit, 109; Hahn, *op.cit.*, 8.

his ideals, but in the daily grind he has lost an inner belief in himself, his capacity for love and intimacy, as he reveals in Act Two:

> I work—as you know—harder than anyone else in the district, fate never stops hitting me in the face, at times I suffer unbearably, but in the distance there's no light glimmering for me. I've stopped expecting anything for myself, I don't love people . . . For a long time now I've loved no one.

Astrov feels himself to be really "vulgar, like everybody else," but he is no extinct volcano. He has preserved his conscience and feeling for beauty: "What still gets through to me is beauty. . . . In Lent a patient of mine died under the chloroform."

Astrov is clever and sensitive, noble but coarse, tough-minded, bold in action, and hard on himself. Without recompense, he tends to the district forest preserve and manages a model estate with a tree nursery. Once a month he gets drunk in order to reassure himself of his resilience; he feels threatened by wear and tear. Once a month, at the nadir of exhaustion, he comes to the estate to draw his diagrams while Sonya and Vanya do their bookkeeping: a camaraderie of work in cozy seclusion—nothing more. He cannot reciprocate Sonya's love. He can love only where he is physically attracted. Inner beauty, as incarnated by Sonya, leaves him cold. But Yelena's surface beauty and elegance awake his desire, although her languid idleness repels him and she contradicts his humane ideals. "Everything about a human being ought to be beautiful: face, dress, soul, ideas" (Act Two).

Astrov's ecological ideas and his ideal picture of a human being fit together: the woods are not only an adornment of the earth, they also "teach" people "to understand beauty" (Act One). Tempering the climate, they further the development of beautiful human beings in every way. Yelena is far from being only a languid beauty. Despite her fascination with the boldly thinking doctor's *élan vital*, she immediately spots the weak point in his large-scale idea of the environment: this idea is a surrogate and cannot conceal Astrov's incapacity for love, uniting love and lust. The "demon of destruction" is more deeply ensconced. It not only threatens nature, but has long attacked its protectors as well. Thus Chekhov invests the symbol of the forest with surprisingly disruptive force.[2] As the first to express the ecological idea in world literature, he simultaneously becomes its keenest critic.

ASTROV Russian forests are toppling beneath the axe, the habitats of birds and beasts are dwindling, tens of thousands

2. G. Bateson, *Ökologie des Geistes* (Frankfurt am Main, 1895), 220ff (Critique of instrumental thought).

of trees are perishing, rivers are running shallow and drying up, gorgeous natural scenery is disappearing irretrievably . . . Human beings are endowed with reason and creative faculties in order to enhance what is given to them but so far they have not created but destroyed . . . every day the earth grows more impoverished and ugly.

YELENA ANDREEVNA   . . . you all recklessly chop down forests, and soon nothing will be left on earth. The very same way you recklessly destroy a human being, and soon, thanks to you, there won't be any loyalty or purity or capacity for self-sacrifice left on earth. Why can't you look at a woman with indifference if she isn't yours? Because—that doctor's right—inside all of you there lurks a demon of destruction. You have no pity for forests or birds or women or one another . . . (Act One)

Complementary Women: Sonya and Yelena

The two women are also complementary figures. They do not embody contrasts, but instead two psychological types of the feminine. Their very names indicate the Greek prototypes of Holy Sophia (wisdom and goodness, full of the inner beauty of the soul) and the ancient Helen (incarnation of external beauty, who enchants and disarms men, but who herself becomes a doomed victim). In addition, Sonya and Yelena embody both aspects of Astrov's ideal of humanity, apportioned as the wishful image of perfect womanhood. This is why the doctor is allowed to express his criticism of the destructive thoughts of possession from a feminine perspective, which insists on the protection not only of nature, but of humanity as well.

Homely Sonya and captivating Yelena discover in their jealous reserve a reciprocal candor: the beautiful woman admits to the unhappiness of her marriage, and the unbeautiful girl to the happiness of her love for Astrov, for whom she still longs. Sonya, however, because of her inferiority complex, is incapable of persuading the man she loves that she exists as a woman. So she allows the other woman to "interrogate" him. Too late she learns of Yelena's double-cross. In love with Astrov herself, Yelena feels guilty towards Sonya.

The love affairs in this drama turn out so that everyone blindly falls into a self-made trap: Sonya allows the interrogation and learns the bitter truth; Vanya, with his talk about Yelena's "phony fidelity," pours oil on the fire that will consume him; Astrov desires a beauty, who, because he cannot love her, will destroy him; Yelena nurses a desire that, were she to achieve it, would throw her into a crisis of resolve and conscience, to which she as a "walk-on part" would not be equal. Vanya becomes the central character as a result of both the external conflicts and the inner events. For involuntarily, through his untimely entrance with autumn roses, "superb, mournful roses" (Act Three), which he brings as a token of reconciliation, he conclusively prevents a general human fiasco. He interrupts a destructive tangle of feelings and accelerates the departure of the baleful guests.

The Double "Anticlimax" and the Blundering Hero

The disruptive couple is doubly the trigger of the dramatic conflict. The professor triggers the external conflict through his discredited authority and his plan for the estate. Yelena's beauty becomes a catalyst for the internal events. The inner line of the plot culminates in the autumn roses scene: in a mere fifteen minutes all the love relationships are wrecked. The external plot lines culminate in the missed shot scene in the drawing-room: within the next quarter hour the infamous plan of sale provokes Vanya, who had just shown up with the roses of reconciliation, to such an extent that in blind rage he fires at the Professor twice—once offstage, once on stage, both times without hitting his adversary. Nevertheless, Vanya's misfires did make a hit, luckily without fatal consequences. They may not have hit the Professor, but they knocked his plan off the table: Vanya has saved the estate and its inhabitants from the impudent clutches of a parasite. No one regards his attempted murder as a crime. No one questions his right to resist. But Vanya doubts his own sanity and is ashamed of his rage at the Professor and his lamentable defeat in the eyes of Astrov and Yelena.

Vanya remains the country uncle, who missed his mark—twice. But he also remains the one who, by his "intervention," saves what is to be saved. Uncle Vanya is neither a hero nor a loser. He is a man who has his limitations: he can manage and increase what is before him. Nevertheless, he has preserved his living feelings and is capable of preventing destruction. To conceive something new and unique, to win a wife for himself or change matters, however, is not within his power. As a true uncle he is left to depend on work and illusion, comfort and sisterly aid. That is the only way he can survive.

Stagnation or Change?

After the double anti-climax of the autumn roses and the misfired shot scene—after the reconciliation and the resumption of the financial arrangements—things would seem to be the way the Nanny says: "Once again we'll live as we used to, the old way . . . It's a long time, bless my soul, since I've had noodles" (Act Four). But here opinions differ. The unchanged ones, who let the disruption pass over them like a violent storm, breathe easily; and the Professor falls back on his phrase-making: "Let the dead past bury the dead . . . one must take action, my friends!" The irony cannot be missed. The changed ones, however, who have gone through a trial by fire, have to swallow the bitter knowledge that nothing is the way it was before, and in particular, that nothing is the way it might have been.

How can they go on living, though? Uncle Vanya threatens to crack under this insight. Alone he would be lost. Only through shared exertion do Sonya and Astrov, her kindness and his determination, manage to get the morphine away from Vanya. She and the doctor do not come together in the play. Sonya remains alone with the whole burden of her unhappy love. But the subtle equivalences of the playwriting give hints that not all chances of a future may be foreclosed for this couple. As the secret "united couple," they are contrasted with the official "troubled couple." They preserve Vanya and themselves from destruction. In an "echo scene" Sonya accompanies the doctor, as before, to the door, while she lights him with the "light" that in his late-night talk in the second act he claimed he could no longer glimpse in his life. And as Astrov tells us, it does not draw him away either. Just as his farewell to Yelena was bitter and curt—"And so, wherever you and your husband set foot, destruction follows in your wake . . . *Finita la commedia*!"—so his parting from Sonya and Vanya is reluctant. "The pens scratch, the cricket chirps. Warm, cozy . . . I don't feel like leaving here." The leavetaking is protracted; the desultory change of subject makes the break painfully felt. All his doubt serves as a lightning rod to lead Astrov, a man eloquent but taciturn, to that laconic remark about the map of Africa located in a tiny office on an estate: "I suppose there must be a heatwave over in Africa right now—something awful!" The function of the wholly innovative and enigmatic detail of the map of Africa was immediately noted by Maksim Gorky. Along with its lethal climate, the torrid zone of desire, it stands for the Doctor's emotional intensity and accentuates in its spaciousness the "closed box" in which Vanya and Sonya resignedly go back to work, with the starling in its cage and the doormat for peasants.[3]

While the ensemble of the everyday hustle and bustle resounds— THE WATCHMAN *taps.* TELEGIN *quietly goes on playing;* MARIYA VASI- LYEVNA *writes in the margin of a pamphlet;* MARINA *knits a stocking.*— Sonya kneels beside her uncle, whose suffering breaks her heart. She lays her head in his hands and "in a weary voice" recites her final monologue. Taken out of context, as many commentators do, the monologue is hardly convincing. But as the finale of this drama

3. M. Valency, *op.cit.*, 186; V. Yermilov, "*Uncle Vanya*: The Play's Movement," in *Chekhov: A Collection of Critical Essays*, ed. R. L. Jackson (Englewood Cliffs, N.J., 1967), 118f; Chudakov, *op. cit.*, 154ff., 217ff.; Pitcher, *op.cit.*, 111; Peace, *loc. cit.*; E. S. Dobin, *Iskusstvo detali* (Leningrad, 1975), 99ff.; L. Lütkehaus, ed., "*Dieses wahre innere Afrika.*" *Texte zur Entdeckung des Unbewussten vor Freud* (Frankfurt am Main, 1989), Introduction, Colonial Metaphor.

of bitter awareness, which does not spill over into absurdity, but is instead courageously dissolved in the acid test of everyday life, Sonya's speech of consolation achieves rare human greatness and artistic validity.

The Chekhov Effect

With the double anticlimax, Uncle Vanya's two botched entrances, Chekhov subverts an age-old dogma of the theater: the climax of the plot is a decisive deed. His dramatic high point is a blunder. Vanya's greatness lies in preventing, not in creating. He misses his mark, but expels the "baleful ones."

Both plot lines, the outer and the inner events, have equal value in Chekhov in principle. That is new. The internal conflict and its psychological motivation are no longer merely ingredients in a dominant action. The primacy of the action, apparently a natural law of the genre, is casually demoted by Chekhov. In contrast, a corresponding process returns value to theatrical techniques beyond the word. The dialogue no longer drives the action; instead, it uncovers step by step the multifarious aspects of the situation. The non-verbal techniques of a theatrical sign language recover their long-lost prerogative: noises such as the sound of a snapped string, the thud of an axe, and the monotonous clack of knitting needles; music such as Telegin's soothing guitar and the concertina in the distance, but also the internal music of the soul in the rhythm of Astrov or Sonya talking; the change from day to night as in the contrast of the afternoon tea ceremony and the late-night conversation while a storm is brewing; the significant detail, such as Vanya's fancy necktie, which hints at his *cherchez la femme*,[4] the swing on which Yelena sits, the map of Africa and the floormat for peasants in Vanya's office. All these elements, similar to the colors of the Fauvists[5] or the half and quarter-tones of serial music, promote a completely new "semiotics of the theater" from an ancillary role to independent, indispensable elements of the theatrical on the stage. Even silence plays a part in the drama: the pause can determine the effect of a scene.[6] The mature Chekhov knew what he was doing when he took a special interest in Maeterlinck.[7]

Chekhov's drama of everyday life and the inner human being is a

4. French, "look for the woman," i.e., passion as motivation. [Editor's note.]
5. *Fauvisme* was a Parisian movement in painting associated with Henri Matisse, and known for its vivid use of color. Serial music involves compositions which start from an arrangement of the twelve tones of the chromatic scale, and is best characterized by the compositions of Arnold Schönberg and Anton Webern. [Editor's note.]
6. Pitcher, *op. cit.* 18ff.
7. Maurice Maeterlinck (1862–1949), Belgian dramatist, whose symbolist plays were very popular on the European stage at the end of the nineteenth century. Chekhov admired him greatly. [Editor's note.]

theater of the palimpsest: beneath the obvious levels a "subtext" is to be found. Hence the artful equivalences of the composition: out of the appropriate elements, Chekhov composes the symbolic sphere of the drama, which constitutes its timelessness. Notwithstanding, he never abandons the commonly understood sphere of the everyday. He includes knitting, lotto, and guitar playing, some people talk, while others sleep; people speak simultaneously about different things, and people speak in flowery phrases or repetitions. For their everyday communication, which proves to be far more than a symptom of alienation but brings a hitherto unknown intimacy to the stage, does not exhaust the event. It is surpassed by an equally burning question that had already animated all great Russian novels. "How are we to live authentic lives?" But nowhere, except in *The Wood Goblin*, does this question congeal into a didactic form. It always remains directed to the concrete; for it is implanted as a compass in Chekhov's "inner man."

* * *

JURIJ STRIEDTER

Jurij Striedter (b. 1926), a German philologist of Russian parentage, has taught Russian literature at the Free University Berlin, the University of Konstanz, and Harvard University. An expert on Russian formalism and Czech structuralism, he has published a monograph on the picaresque novel in Russia (1961).

Drama as a Game of Reflected Expectations: Chekhov's *Three Sisters*†

* * *

Three Sisters begins with a remark of the eldest sister, Olga, which characteristically functions both as a reflection on and a recollection of the past: "Father died just a year ago, this very day, the fifth of May, your saint's day, Irina." It is equally noteworthy that this memory includes an expectation of that time: "I never thought I'd live through it . . ." And for those who see Chekhov's dramas as the exposure of false hopes, let us add that this very first remembered expec-

† Excerpts from "Drama als Spiel reflektierter Erwartungen: Čechovs *Drei Schwestern*," in *Dramatische und theatralische Kommunikation. Beiträge zur Geschichte und Theorie des Dramas und Theaters im 20. Jahrhundert*, ed. Herta Schmid and Jurij Striedter (Tübingen: Gunter Narr Verlag, 1992), 192–223. Trans. by Karolina Wróbel and Laurence Senelick. This translation is of only three quarters of the original essay. Reprinted by permission of the author.

tation will turn out to quite the opposite of pessimistic. Olga goes on: "But a year's gone by now, and we don't mind thinking about it, you're back to wearing white, your face is beaming." Irina's reply, the first in the play, chimes in: "Why remember?"

She prompts Olga to turn to her present state, which Olga, as an unmarried, working woman, perceives as a burden. Yet Olga cherishes happier expectations of the future, the most important being the hope to return to a bygone happiness, a return to Moscow, which the family left eleven years before when their father was transferred to the provinces. "To Moscow!"—this central theme of *Three Sisters* is well known. However, the way it is introduced deserves attention. Even before she finishes, Olga is interrupted by Irina.

> OLGA   While that same old dream keeps growing bigger and
> stronger . . .
> IRINA   To go to Moscow. To sell the house, wind up everything
> here and—go to Moscow . . .
> OLGA   Yes! Quick as you can to Moscow.

The whole play's dominant theme is therefore introduced neither as *one* person's characteristic theme nor as a purely thematic, major theme unrelated to a character, but instead as a theme that binds the sisters together: a fundamental theme shared by two voices, sounded three times, at the onset of the dialogue.

This harmony, however, is repeatedly interrupted by the remarks of the three officers conversing in the next room. Olga's yearning for the old "home" is followed by Chebutykin's "To hell with both of you!" and Tusenbach's "You're right, it's ridiculous." The sisters' triple "To Moscow" is followed by the stage direction "CHEBUTYKIN *and* TUSENBACH *laugh.*" And Olga's later statements on how she would like to quit her job and get married are cut short by Tusenbach's remark, "You talk such rubbish, a person gets sick and tired just listening to you."

Of course, none of the three comments responds to the sisters' speeches; rather, they are fragments of a conversation among the men. Not coincidentally, however, the author points out that the men appear "behind the columns." Neither the subject of their remarks nor to whom they are addressed is clear. Only the last comment bears the explanatory direction: "TUSENBACH (*To* SOLYONY.)" And precisely because the communicative context of the officers' talk remains unclear, because there is no direct link between their comments and the sisters' conversation, it provokes expectation in the reader / spectator that the dramatic dialogue is bound to convey a meaningful context. *We* connect the men's general comments to the women's emotional speeches; perceiving them as contrast and interruption and assuming that that is the author's intention. Hence,

communication does not occur between the two groups of characters, but rather between the spectator and the author as composer of
the text—even though the author keeps strictly within the framework
of realistic drama and apparently leaves the dialogue entirely up to
the characters. The construction of the dialogue and the scenic
arrangement signals an additional level—that of the author's conception of the text as a script for the stage—which thus comes into play.

Once brought to our attention, however, it becomes evident that
the author's intentions show through more than just the characters'
speeches. The striking of the clock in the middle of Olga's first line
may be conventional symbolism ("How time flies!"); but it simultaneously introduces a non-verbal acoustic signal, an important material layer in Chekhov's plays. Its opposite is quiet, just as silence is
the opposite of speech. And the interplay of these factors imprints
the rhythm and the tone of the whole. Accordingly, Olga's first
speech is interrupted three times by the author with an explicit note
"*Pause*"—an occurrence whose meaning in Chekhov's plays has
already been discussed.[1]

Yet in noting the role of silence, we notice that throughout the
whole opening dialogue of the two sisters, the third sister Masha is
also present, but *silently* ("*reading a book*"). Her first utterance is
acoustically not verbal, but non-verbal: she "*quietly whistles a tune*"
and repeats it subsequently When she does begin to speak later on,
she does so in a fragmented quotation, the second line of which is
also repeated:

> "On the curved seashore a green oak stands,
> a golden chain wound 'round that oak . . .
> A golden chain wound 'round that oak . . ."
> (*Rises and hums quietly.*)

The literary origin and the intertextual function of this quotation is
discussed later. The point here is that it is has nothing to do with
the sisters' talk and the officers' conversation. Thus, the viewer might
question its relevance—for Masha, for us, for the play now or later.
Or is it supposed to make no "sense"—is it "nonsense"? Even nonsense has an important function as material in Chekhov's plays. In
Three Sisters, for example, Chebutykin, with his absurd remarks and
his interpolated "Ta-ra-ra-boomdeay," and Solyony, with his inapt
quotations and his annoying "Cheep, cheep, cheep," are indefatigable producers and repeaters of such nonsense. The frequency of
nonsense elements and repetitions in Chekhov's plays has been
repeatedly acknowledged and discussed by critics and scholars. My

1. For the function of the pause in the dialogue, see Adolf Stender-Petersen, "Zur Technik
der Pause bei Čechov" in Thomas Eekman, ed., *Anton Čechov, 1860–1960: Some Essays*
(Leiden: E. J. Brill, 1962), 187–206.

main concern here is specifically the *co-operation* of both elements. The repetition of nonsense ties it to other, equally emphasized repetitions, so that what seems to be nonsense takes on a significant poetic function.

Various kinds of repetition on differently correlated levels are a constitutive sign of poetry, whose structural principle was defined by Roman Jakobson[2] as the "recurrence of equivalences," a repetition or return of comparable elements. As such, repetition—for example, of verses, meter, and sound combinations such as rhyme—presupposes, on one hand, reversion and reminiscence, while on the other, raising the expectation of a renewed return of the same unity or the same principle. To that extent, it is always a game of reflected expectations. The poetic function of this principle appears most blatantly in elements that convey no clear meaning on the purely semantic level, such as repetitions of sound and meter, repeatedly tagged "pauses," or the repetition of seemingly or actually meaningless remarks. Conversely, the stressed and artful repetition of such elements rivets the attention to corresponding semantically meaningful remarks, motifs, themes, or clusters. As recurrent equivalents, they enter into new, significant relationships, realizing new, connotative meanings and thus acquiring an additional poetic function. This is precisely why poetry can be "nonsense poetry"—as is, for example, the provocative, alogical, and ungrammatical *Zaum* poetry of the Russian Futurists,[3] furthermore, this is why the repetition of apparently meaningless remarks within the overarching context of a play can have a poetic effect—as in Chekhov.

Chekhov's contemporaries already appreciated the "poetic," "lyrical," or "musical" qualities of his plays. This mode of writing, evoking a "mood," led to the description "mood plays" or "theater of mood"[4] (though it should be noted that the Russian word *nastroenie* means both "mood" and "tuning"). The concept, however, was frequently used vaguely and misused as justification for a purely "mood inducing," unreflective experience. In reality, finer tuning results when the recipient pays more attention to the nuance-rich game, entering into it but also consciously reflecting upon it.

Most observations concerning Chekhov's "musicality" haved proved to be equally vague or have focused solely on the direct application of music and related, acoustic elements. Only more recent study has worked out more clearly the musicality of the plays, espe-

2. Roman Osipovich Jakobson (1896–1982), Russian linguist and philologist, founder of the Prague school of semiotics. [*Editor's note.*]
3. *Zaum* or "transmental" poetry, originated by the Russian cubo-futurists, was an experimental language organized by phonetic analogy and rhythm, with the word valued for its poetic sake. [*Editor's note.*]
4. See Meyerhold's "Naturalistic Theater and the Theater of Mood", in this volume (pages 598–607). [*Editor's note.*]

cially *Three Sisters*, in regard to their "thematic, auditory, and structural" aspects and their "interaction."[5] Of course, these musical, mood-inducing, and poetic factors can be properly grasped, realized onstage, and technically described only in their "polyphonic" orchestration. And in this regard, specific attention to and correlation of the different levels are indispensable—the level of singular verbal and scenic signs with their own configurations; the level of the characters with their speeches and their behavior, and the all-embracing themes and structural principles of the whole composition that encompass all the characters.

Labelling Chekhov's plays as dramas of *mood* came as a response to the realization that they did not seem to be dramas of *action*. This should not, however, be understood as Chekhov's total disregard for the element of action, because even on that level expectations are evoked and reflected. In this respect, a contrast can be drawn between long-term expectations, concerning the totality of the action or the bulk of its progress, and short-term expectations, which concern immediately subsequent acts. The introductory, repetitive "To Moscow!" of the sisters already evokes one of the action-based expectations—if not *the* expectation—of the long-term kind. It is immediately supplemented by an additional long-term expectation of the future, concerning their brother: "Our brother is meant to be a professor." As the progress of the action reveals, neither the return to Moscow nor Andrey's hoped-for academic career comes to pass. But what fails to come to pass becomes an even greater expectation, of the characters as well as of the spectators. Right from the start, an expectation that is to determine the future is introduced and constantly repeated, postponed, and reflected upon, until it must eventually be accepted as an illusion and renounced.

In addition, short-term expectations of action are immediately presented. Thus, Tusenbach, one of the three entering officers, exclaims in his very first remark to the sisters, "Today our new battery commander Vershinin will pay you a visit." And, he adds, Vershinin is about forty and "not stupid," but he talks a lot and will certainly talk even here about his wife and his two daughters, and he will not divorce his wife, although she is deranged and plagues him with suicide attempts. This is a great deal of advance information, which evokes certain expectations on the part of the sisters and the spectators. They are immediately met. Vershinin turns up on his visit in the same act; he actually does talk a lot, and not stupidly, and

5. Harai Golomb, "Music as theme and as structural model in Chekhov's *Three Sisters*," in H. Schmid and A. van Kesteren, eds., *Semiotics of Drama and Theater* (Amsterdam / Philadelphia, 1984), 177. Golomb deals with all three aspects, reserving a more detailed analysis for his book which has, unfortunately, not yet appeared.

promptly tells of his wretched domestic situation. The only piece of advance information that Vershinin does not mention is that he will not leave his insufferable wife in the lurch; this topic remains open and is therefore a continuous foreshadowing of the love affair between Vershinin and Masha that, at this very point, begins "to chime in."

Characteristically, this love affair, so important for the future development of the dramatic action, starts with a reflection on the past and on past expectations of the future. Vershinin once frequented the Prozorovs' house in Moscow and was then, as Masha suddenly remembers, jokingly nicknamed "the lovesick major." Because he was de facto only a lieutenant and later became a lieutenant-colonel and a battery commander, the joke implies that one career expectation was more than fulfilled. In contrast, the attribute of "lovesick major" has since turned into its opposite, which does not prevent the disappointed Vershinin from becoming a lovesick lieutenant colonel (over Masha).

Yet even before that happens, the combination of being in love and career expectation, introduced through Vershinin, is expanded beyond that single character. Andrey Prozorov is introduced by his sisters to the erstwhile "lovesick major" as the "lovesick professor" or even "lovesick violinist." The academic training as well as the musical activities correspond to the cultural ideal in which the siblings have been brought up by their father. As the course of the action reveals, Andrey will not do justice to either expectation—in contrast to the over-fulfillment of the career expectations of the "lovesick major." The attribute of "being in love," on the other hand, does seem to suggest an immediate fulfilment; he proposes to Natasha before the end of Act One and she accepts. However, this parallel between the "lovesick professor" Andrey and the once lovesick, now unhappily married "lovesick major" Vershinin opens the possibility that Andrey could also end up in an unhappy marriage with an obtuse woman.

This possibility is strengthened by the way in which Natasha is introduced. As with Vershinin, her first appearance is prepared for by advance information from others. And in her case, too, the imposed expectations—she will probably come for dinner, Andrey is in love with her, and she is a tasteless provincial—are immediately confirmed. Despite this technically similar setup, the information connected to Natasha is constructed differently. She is introduced not by one person (Tusenbach), but, as the subject of controversy, by numerous persons. Irina and Olga declare that Andrey is in love with her; Masha contradicts that vigorously, because an educated man such as her brother could not fall in love with such an unrefined woman. Also, it is rumored that Natasha is to marry Protopopov, the chairman of the county council. Consequently, an open and self-contradictory spectrum of expectations opens up before the characters and is shared by the spectators. In reality, however, the spectator has an additional source of information available: the cast of characters. The cast of characters belongs to the so-called authorial text, which, unlike the dialogue, is absent in the staging. Yet the cast of characters has a specifically different status from that of the author's stage directions, because it is traditionally distributed in the theater beforehand—as a brief but necessary piece of advance information—and is usually read. In the cast of characters of *Three Sisters*, Natasha is clearly described as "Andrey's fiancée, later his wife." Here (and only in this one case), Chekhov's authorial text preempts the play's action. The reader / spectator, thus informed in advance, possesses an informational advantage over all the dramatis personae, and enjoys the same privileged level of information as the author.

In the light of Chekhov's skepticism, however, this advantage proves to be disappointing or at least covertly ambivalent, whereby the author spurs the recipient to reflect critically upon the seeming advantage of knowing. The positions and predictions do not easily split into right and wrong. Hence, Masha's vigorous declaration that not her brother but Protopopov will marry Natasha proves to be wrong later on or even right away, if one scans the cast of characters. Nevertheless, this faulty assumption contains an important and obliquely "correct" piece of advance information for the momentarily better-informed reader, in that it predicts the relationship of Natasha and Protopopov *after* her marriage to Andrey, so relevant to the play's action. Nor does the author offer the reader / spectator any other advance information about Protopopov at the start, even in the cast of the characters, where he is not listed because he never appears in the play. Even so, he indirectly becomes one of the play's main characters, insofar as his absence from the stage makes his increasing presence in the Prozorov house all the more conspicuously oppressive, until at the end he and Natasha have practically ejected the siblings from the house.

But while Masha's faulty assumption provides accurate advance information, Masha is also generally wrong when she assumes that culture and taste can protect against puppy love and unhappy marriage. After all, she herself, the intelligent and cultivated "daughter of a good home," once admired and married the apparently highly educated Latin teacher whose triviality she now soberly observes and suffers from. And the cultured, refined Masha, just like the trivial, provincial, unrefined Natasha, launches into an affair that is obvious to her husband. This turns reflection (by the characters as well as by the spectators) towards two themes, decisive for both the course of action and the character clusters: marriage and culture.

Matrimony and the institutionalization of marriage through matrimony are definitely connected with expectations. These could be directly perceived as institutionalized expectations, which, even if the expectations prove to be disappointments or self-deception, still frequently slog along as an institution. Chekhov's friend Tolstoy, in his famous opening sentence to *Anna Karenina*, said of families (and in that respect marriages as well), "All happy families are alike, each unhappy family is unhappy in its own way." None of Chekhov's famous plays portrays an even slightly happy marriage. The marriage of the elder Prozorovs in *Three Sisters* may or may not have been a happy one, yet the three marriages celebrated before or during the time depicted—Masha's, Vershinin's, and Andrey's—are all unhappy, each "unhappy in its own way," even though all three involve one of the spouses having an extramarital affair that is common knowledge but entails no divorce or even consideration of divorce. A decisive factor in the variations, besides the family's status (childless or with children of distinctly different ages) and the different characters and their standing in society—pertinent to the enclosed time structure of generic drama—is the shifting of timelines. Vershinin's marriage has long been in ruins and is portrayed merely though his reflections. The Kulygins' marriage has been a disappointment for Masha for some time, but is revealed as such only one step at a time (while her husband insists on being "happy" up to the very end). And the development of the Andrey / Natasha relationship is presented in its entirety from the marriage proposal to the resignation of the cuckolded husband, who, in the last act, pushes the baby carriage in circles outside the house. Hence, these shifts in time concern only the dates of the actual weddings, while the results are alike in all three cases and the love affairs run concurrently. And along with time the fourth variant of the theme of matrimony, more specifically marriage, runs through Tusenbach's (and Solyony's) wooing of Irina—this variant brings the timeline only up to the wedding, because Tusenbach is shot by Solyony in a duel.

Looking at all four variants in their shifting and overlapping timelines, the extent to which the different expectations reflect, influence, and hinder one another interchangeably becomes evident, to both the character concerned and the audience. The audience too is its own cast of characters, watching those in the play, projecting on them their own expectations, and reflecting and commenting on their expectations and disappointments. Thus, it becomes clear that considerable experience of expectation and reflection does not prevent the repetition of illusory expectations in oneself or in relation to others. Masha's example has already been mentioned. It is similarly valid for Olga, for example, who, despite her experience of Masha's and Andrey's disastrous marriages, never tires of talking her youngest sister Irina into marriage with Tusenbach as the only sound solution to her problems.

The fourth variation on the matrimony theme, the coupling of Irina and Tusenbach, is also a variation on the relation between expectation and reflection. Unlike Masha and Andrey, Irina's critical reflection on the willingness to marry occurs *beforehand* (and *without* Irina being in love with Tusenbach). Married one shall be, whether one is blindly in love or riddled with doubts, whether one has critically reflected on the problem of marriage before or after. The result depends more on external circumstances (like the pointless duel, fatal for Tusenbach, which prevents the marriage) than on personal emotions and reflections.

Generally, for most of Chekhov's characters, reflections accompany rather than determine the action. They either remove personal motivation to act or at least fail to alter the course of events to which they are linked. Tusenbach says as much in his picturesque metaphor of the philosophic cranes:

> Birds of passage, cranes, for instance, fly on and on, and whatever thoughts, sublime or trivial, may drift through their heads, they'll keep on flying and never know what for or where to. They fly and will keep on flying, whatever philosopher they may hatch; and let them philosophize to their heart's content, so long as they keep on flying . . .

"Philosophizing" is not ruled out. On the contrary, increasingly new expectations and reflections abound over "what for or where to." And every expectation, exposed by real life to be an illusion, is replaced by a new one, in hopes of a more reliable answer to the question of meaning. For the Irina / Tusenbach couple, the theme of work joins the theme of marriage in accompanying the constantly reflected on, discussed, and attempted expectations of life's meaning. While the eldest sister Olga, despite being a successful teacher, would rather marry than deal with the detested work, young Irina, so far unemployed, insists that only "hard work" can give her life meaning. Only after her obviously disappointing experience of work at the telegraph office is she willing to marry the equally resigned yet work-driven Baron Tusenbach, who has just given up his commission. When this expectation fails as well, Irina promptly returns to her refrain of "work, work."

* * *

For *Three Sisters,* and for the development of expectations and reflection in this play, the theme of culture and education is even more crucial.

Culture, as a goal and result of education, is a process deeply imprinted with expectations and reflections on expectations: the reflections and expectations of the teacher about the future of the pupil; expectations of the pupil and the educated about themselves and their present or future environment; and reflections of all the participants on the successes and failures of these processes and the meaning of culture. It may seem trivial to point this out, but it is precisely in this "trivial" perspective that the author of *Three Sisters* introduces the topic of culture: as a recollection of an earlier expectation of education and a reflection on their current questioning. The sisters tell Vershinin that their brother was brought up according to "Papa's will," with an "academic career" in mind. And the play shows the suffocating (for Andrey) consequences of these expectations. But the sisters were also raised by their father for a future life in an "cultivated" society, in which the knowledge of foreign languages, the ability to play a musical instrument, and good taste are assumed to be indispensable norms and values. Yet, after the move to the provinces, these expectations prove to be illusions and their cultured accompishments "irrelevant." As Masha observes, "In this town knowing three languages is a superfluous luxury. Not even a luxury, but a kind of superfluous appendage, a bit like a sixth finger." Masha's double use of "superfluous" is itself a "token of culture." In nineteenth-century Russian literary and social discussions, the type of man most frequently presented and debated was the so-called superfluous man, that is, a member of the declining aristocracy or intelligentsia, a more or less educated, critically-thinking individual, who, because of the given sociopolitical norms or due to his own weakness can neither realize his far-reaching expectations nor find a meaningful, practical vocation, and therefore lives, in his own and in others' view, "superfluously." This cultural background, evoked by Masha's remark, provides the context for the following dialogue about culture, including the plea for culture. Consequently, three types of justification are indicated.

The first, most obviously shaped by expectations, could be called the utopian, anticipated progress of culture. The present provincial life of the educated three sisters may be depressing, as Vershinin assures Masha; but later on six, twelve, indeed, most people will be educated; and "in two hundred, three hundred years" most of humanity. The second type can—with Schiller[6]—be called "the aes-

6. Johann Christoph Friedrich von Schiller (1759–1805), German dramatist and poet, whose

thetic education of mankind." It shares with the first the belief in a
future *beautiful* world, but stresses even more how much cultured
taste can beautify the life of today—just as the beautiful sisters in
their beautiful house with its beautiful flowers do here and now. In
fact, the sisters themselves value culture primarily as a culture of
taste, in which, according to their idealistic cultural tradition, the
cultivation of taste and the cultivation of the heart go together naturally. (The negative opposite, the "coarse" Natasha, lacks both taste
and heart.) The third aspect, most forcefully influenced by reflection,
concerns culture as the ability to think. While purely academic
knowledge—such as that of the Latin teacher Kulygin—is worthless,
thinking matters throughout, though almost exclusively as that "philosophizing" in endless conversations, which for good reason is
referred to as "typically Russian" and finds its most impressive quintessence in the image of the "philosophizing cranes."

For example, Masha's question of "What's the point?" to the flight
and philosophizing of the cranes, whether we should ask "why you
live or else it's all senseless, gobbledygook" (Act Two), is not
answered by her interlocutors. And as to the word picture of the
philosophizing birds of passage, it is enough that even the thoughtful
ones among them "can fly." The reality of daily life (that is, the fictional everyday world of the characters), however, poses the very
concrete question of who is the *better* flyer: Who can better assert
himself in life—the "philosophizing," aesthetically sensitive, cultured individual, or the tasteless and uncultured individual who
thoughtlessly follows his instincts. This conflict determines the relationship between the Prozorov sisters and Natasha and is therefore
decisive for the whole action of the play. And it is quite unambiguously answered over the course of the play, in which, by the end, the
tasteless and primitive Natasha has expelled the sensitive and cultured sisters from the house.

However, the final conclusions are left to be drawn by the reader
or spectator from this development. As such, the question of whether
culture is indispensable or "superfluous," whether it help or hinders,
transcends the level of the characters to the level of the recipients,
since the recipient, whether a reader or a playgoer, is cultured, or at
least educated. The question can also be asked of him, whether *his*
culture is pertinent to the understanding of this play, whether it
helps or hinders. Since literature plays an important role in the cultural canon of such a reader or spectator—and for *Three Sisters*—
and since the frequent literary quotations have been systematically
researched, they are particularly productive examples.

---

essay "The Theater Considered as a Moral Institution" (1802) advanced art as a major
tool of education. [*Editor's note.*]

The very first quotation, Masha's "On the curved seashore a green oak stands, a golden chain wound 'round that oak" and its relevance to the poetic function of "nonsense" has already been mentioned. Yet whether it is identified as a quotation and how it is interpreted depends solely on the cultural status of the reader or spectator. Consequently, a spectator unfamiliar with Russian literature will blithely be content to regard it as a more or less random verse that Masha has picked up in her cursory reading (the stage direction in the opening scene specifies that "she is reading a book") or that is simply running through her mind. In case such a spectator does heed the content of this quotation, which seems meaningless in the context of the dialogue, he could possibly relate it to the speaker's state of mind, either as an expression of her momentary distraction or, more generally, as a tendency to drift into a poetic fantasy world. In contrast, every educated Russian and everyone familiar with Russian poetry knows immediately that it is the opening couplet of Pushkin's famous poem *Ruslan and Lyudmila*. Between the two kinds of spectators there thus exists an information gap, revealed in the aesthetic reception. The cultivated connoisseur has the additional pleasure of recognition; he feels reaffirmed in his culture; he is able to derive additional possibilities for interpretation from identifying the quotation; and in that respect, he has an advantage over the "uncultivated" individual.

But is this really so *unambiguous*? Quotations within a literary text that refer to other literary texts—known in today's academic terminology as "intertextuality"—do indeed open far-reaching potentials of meaning, but can also easily lead to arbitrary speculations and misreadings. Is one confined to the fragment quoted or is what is quoted to be considered in the context of the whole original? What is meant by "the context of the original whole": only the immediate textual placement of the quotation, the entire work being quoted, or wherever possible even the life and works of the author concerned, the tradition of the genre concerned, the relevant cultural codes, and so on? And to what extent is the new context in which it is quoted pertinent to its meaning? And furthermore, is it pertinent only in the immediate textual or rather theatrical situtation of what is being quoted or in its totality as context (differing widely in scope)?

Masha's quotation from Pushkin vividly illustrates this set of problems. Since it has nothing to do with the dialogue of the others present, since Masha's one verbal utterance remains provisional and offers almost no clue to an unambiguous reading of the content, it is left up to the connoisseur to relate it to *Ruslan and Lyudmila* as a whole. But what this poem is "as a whole" generically is itself problematic. Pushkin himself refers to it in his subtitle as an "epic poem" (Russian, *poéma*) and even in later editions of his works it usually

appears along with other romantic "epic poems," and not under the
rubric "Fairy Tales" (Russian, *skazki*). The classification as a romantic epic of fantastical love adventures is just as admissible as a verse
fairy tale or a poetic fairy tale. If the first genre classification is
accepted and connected with Masha the quoter, then this quotation
can be interpreted as an expression of her emotional state or, in a
wider context, a foreshadowing of her love affair with Vershinin,
whereby it emphasizes and eventually overemphasizes the passionately romantic aspect of this affair. From the content of the quotation, the association of the genre "poetic fairy tale" is more strongly
suggested and is more commonly found in academic studies.

So, for instance, according to one of the experts, Chekhov
intended this quotation to elevate Masha's "truly poetic nature" and
wanted right at the outset of the play to create "an atmosphere full
of wonders and expectations."[7] It has, however, been properly
objected that a closer inspection of the quotation's context—particularly, Olga's direct reply to Masha's quotation: "You're in a funny
mood today, Masha"—could just as easily or even more so express
"Masha's longing recollections of the past" and as such "the worries,
sorrows, and bitterness of the present." This is also suggested by the
couplet of Pushkin's poem directly following the quotation: "And
night and day a learned cat / Walks 'round and 'round upon that
chain."[8] Justifiable as this emendation and nuance may be, especially
when one retrospects to the sequential development of the play (in
which Masha repeats the quotation), this quoted, playfully fantastical and ironically resonant poem of Pushkin's offers scant reason
to highlight the aspects of "sorrow" and "bitterness." Furthermore,
the quoted verses have nothing to do with the love theme of the poem
and the content of the actual fairy tale, but are taken from the so-
called narrative prologue (Russian, *priskazka*). This is, in turn, a specific type of Russian folk tale, appropriated by Pushkin and other
tellers of tales, which introduces the actual tale through a "prelude,"
by mixing grotesque themes, word and sound play, in order to show
off the storyteller's imagination and artistry as well as to elevate the
"true" fairy play above intentional nonsense.

But Masha's quotation, which she repeats and mangles several
times, also functions as "nonsense" in the aforementioned sense
(including the "poeticizing" repetition), leading her to reflect on this
repeated nonsense at the end:

> On the curved seashore a green oak stands, a golden chain
> wound around that oak . . . A golden chain wound around that

7. David Magarshack, *Chekhov the Dramatist* (New York: Hill and Wang, 1960), 262.
8. Witold Kośny, "Bedeutung und Funktion der literarischen Zitate in A. P. Čechovs '*Tri
sestry*,'" *Die Welt der Slaven* XVI, 2 (Wiesbaden 1971), 141.

oak ... A green cat stands ... A green oak stands ... I'm raving ... (*Drinks some water.*) Life's a failure ... I don't want anything now ... I'll be all right presently ... Doesn't matter ... What does that mean, on the curved seashore? Why is that phrase in my head? My thoughts are running wild.

How much it "doesn't matter" is affirmed by a glance at the extant variants of the play's text. In an earlier version, which Chekhov composed in auumn 1900 in Yalta and read to the Art Theater, and which was not rediscovered in the theater's archives until 1953, instead of Pushkin's verses, in all the corresponding places Masha quotes some doggerel war news she has picked up somewhere.

We took the town of Turtukay, And all of us were standing by, We beat the English, beat the Turks ... Damn it, I'm raving ... [9]

This substitution makes the point that it is the meaninglessness within the dialogic and scenic situation and its function as nonsense that matter here. Still, it cannot be denied that the replacement by the Pushkin quotations brings the poetic, as well as the fairy-tale, potential of this nonsense much more to the fore.

Even the spectator who cannot identify the quotation because of "lack of culture" can, however, perceive its function from the very outset. The effect of this passage is also fixed for non-Russian spectators. Simultaneously, however, the question arises whether or not the whole fund of culture expended is "superfluous"—should one be willing to regard the actualizing and problematizing of the existing culture, the teasing of the cultured individual away from his apparent advantage and sensitivity to fine points of language and the verbal work of art as superfluous?

If the connection of literary quotation and nonsense function is characteristic of Masha's quotation from Pushkin, the two can also be separated. Solyony is the most prominent example of this. He produces reams of nonsense with his pointless remarks and arguments, and his own interjected quotations might seem completely out of place in a given situation, but his recourse to Lermontov or to Pushkin's romantic poem *The Gypsies* is, in light of his characterization and his contribution to the play's action, unambiguously motivated and makes sense. For Solyony would like to be a romantic Byronic hero à la Lermontov, acts accordingly, and explicitly refers to this analogy, which the others notice as well.[1]

9. The Yalta version, Act Four. This earlier version was discovered in the archive along with corrections made in Moscow and Nice and published in 1960 in the series *Literaturnoe nasledstvo*, Volume 68.
1. Speaking with Tusenbach in Act Two, Solyony makes direct reference to Lermontov: "I don't have anything against you, Baron. But my temperament is like Lermontov's. (*Quietly.*) I even look a little like Lermontov ... so they say ..."

In this case, this explicit exposure puts even the spectator who is not familiar with the pertinent Russian literature in the picture. But only someone who knows that Lermontov and Pushkin were both killed in a duel, and that both writers in their famous novels—Pushkin in *Yevgeny Onegin*, Lermontov in *A Hero of Our Times*—describe duels with fatal consequences, will be alert from the start to Solyony's remarks, which point precisely in that direction. But even the well-informed spectator does not know whether Solyony is a loudmouth *poseur* who only wants to make a splash with his allusions and threats or whether he will turn them into actions. In addition, knowing more increases the alternatives (in this case, the foreshadowing of an eventual duel). For Lermontov's life ended with *his* death in a duel, and Solyony is copying *him*. Conversely, in Lermontov's novel it is the Byronic hero's *rival* who is killed by him, which would point to Solyony's rival, Tusenbach. Only in Lermontov's novel it is the rival who is a pronounced *poseur* and imitator of the Byronic hero—like Solyony himself. This proves once again that merely knowing more does not necessarily imply more reliable expectations.

This holds true not only for knowledge acquired through education, but also other forms of advantageous knowledge, both for the characters and the spectators. This becomes apparent in Andrey, the cuckold. At the end of the first act, still the "lovesick professor" who proposes to his sweetheart Natasha, Andrey is already a husband and father by the start of Act Two. And already by this point he confesses to the old government porter Ferapont that the expectation of becoming a professor is merely a dream that haunts him shamefully; that his wife does not understand him; and that he has to work as a functionary under Protopopov. When the nearly deaf Ferapont states that he cannot hear him well, Andrey replies that it's precisely because his deafness prevents Ferapont from understanding that Andrey told him those things; it allowed him the desired opportunity to "talk to somebody."

Here Chekhov combines two traditional dramatic devices: the old comic gimmick of misunderstood dialogue with a deaf man and a master's confession to a silent servant. The latter is one of the most common devices of the dramatist to inform the spectator about a character's private thoughts and feelings, while simultaneously keeping this information secret from the other characters. The organically conditioned impediment to communication (deafness), strengthened by the merging of the two devices, becomes a psychologically motivated strategy for avoiding communication, which nonetheless facilitates confession as self-deception. In this way, Chekhov deftly avoids the use of monologue, which does not come across as "lifelike" in realistic drama. He nevertheless informs his spectators, by means of the de facto monologue-like pseudo-confession, not only of the changed situation, but also of Andrey's critical self-assessment, which remains hidden from all the other characters, including Ferapont.

That is precisely the reason why, even in the third act, Chebutykin can state that only *he* knew about the Natasha / Protopopov affair. This is immediately objected to by Irina as an arrogant overstatement. Yet she herself later remarks, "The whole town's talking, laughing, and he's the only one who sees and knows nothing . . ." In this case, it is the spectator who sees through the other characters' assumptions, because he, unlike them, has overheard Andrey's confession in Act Two. But even the spectator is consequently confused anew by Chekhov, when, after the fire, towards the end of Act Three, Andrey exclaims to his sisters: "Let's clear this up right in the open, once and for all," but then insists that his wife is "a beautiful, honest person, forthright and upstanding" and that he is proud to serve on the County Council, which he finds "just as dedicated and exalted as service to scholarship." But just when the spectator is convinced that this weakling is unable to surrender his illusions despite his prior admissions, Andrey suddenly breaks off the conversation by saying, "My dear sisters, precious sisters, don't believe me, don't believe me . . ."

Contrary to Andrey, Masha's deceived husband Kulygin insists from start to finish that he is "happy" and loves his wife as she loves him. The seeming blindness of a Latin teacher, so proud of his academic learning, is highlighted and ridiculed in both stage productions and literary criticism. Yet, scrutinized more closely, this piercing repetition of his protest of happiness becomes increasingly suspect, as he himself appears to *see* what is going on between his wife and Vershinin, but *says* nothing about it. Chekhov signals this at the end by making Kulygin's insight graphic as the act of *seeing*. Kulygin, who waits with the others to say farewell to the departing soldiers, *sees* at a distance a tearful Masha kissing Vershinin goodbye. Only after this farewell does he console the weeping Masha, insisting "no matter what went on here," "I won't say a single word to you, no recriminations . . ."(Act Four).[2] Chekhov again leaves it

2. Chekhov leaves open whether Kulygin comes upon his wife parting from Vershinin. The old garden with the path of trees is the place of action, a number of not expressly named persons hang out in the background, such as Andrey, pushing the baby carriage back and forth. Kulygin is looking for Masha first in the garden (see the stage direction, *Kulygin crosses the stage, shouting "Yoo-hoo, Masha, yoo-hoo,"* before we are told *Kulygin enters* right after the farewell, whereupon he speaks comfort to the weeping Masha. Directors occasionally use this vagueness to leave him in the background beneath the trees during the farewell scene (like Andrey and—closer—Olga, of whom it is expressly said: OLGA *draws somewhat apart, not to intrude on their farewells*.

up to the spectator to respect or ridicule such behavior, but those with prior information can hardly feel more enlightened than the seemingly unaware and previously often ridiculous provincial school-master.

The trademark of most of Chekhov's characters is the inability to let go of illusionary expectations, with which they try to deceive themselves and others, but which sooner or later they recognize and acknowledge, at least to themselves, and in the play often to a trusted few (as the play's dialogue itself indicates). Act Three of *Three Sisters*, with its nocturnal fire and its subsequent sleeplessness and irritation, provides a particularly good basis for such avowals. It is almost a series of "open discussions" and "confessions," such as Andrey's to his sisters, the sisters to each other, and even the usually cynical Dr. Chebutykin, which prove to the spectator that these people do reflect upon their circumstances, expectations, disillusionments, and dis-appointments much more critically than may have been apparent at first.

What Eric Bentley so persuasively proposed concerning *Uncle Vanya* can be applied to all of Chekhov's great plays: they obey the old Aristotelian rule that drama has to portray "the change from ignorance to knowledge"; but whereas in Greek and French drama "recognition means the discovery of a secret which reveals that things are not what all these years they have seemed to be," Che-khov's characters arrive at the conclusion "that what all these years seemed to be so, though one hesitated to believe it, will remain so."[3] This, however, raises the question how this sobering realization affects the spectator as to the apparently unchangeable course of events and whether it leads to resignation and pessimism rather than to the desired Aristotelian catharsis. Yet before this problem can be explored, I would like to refer once more to the duel, since this par-ticular example clearly reveals Chekhov's dramatic construction, as well as the characters' behavior and the spectator's judgement of both.

We have already shown how the expectation of the duel was increasingly suggested by literary quotations and hints and through the behavior of Solyony, yet was left open for a long period of time. Chekhov presents neither the quarrel which leads directly to the duel nor the actual duel itself—the two events which could be considered the dramatic high points of the action—on stage. Both are drama-tized merely as expectations and reflections of the characters. We learn about them at the beginning of Act Four, first from the ques-

---

3. Eric Bentley, "Craftsmanship in *Uncle Vanya*," in *In Search of Theater* (New York, 1953), 353.

tions of a worried Irina and the others' evasive comments; then, in Irina's absence, from the talk of the others; and finally, from their reaction to the distant shot and the doctor's bringing the news of Tusenbach's death.

Thus, the spectator has just as much advance information about the approaching duel as the characters do—the only exception being Irina, who is specifically not told about the reason for or circumstances leading up to the duel. The other characters, along with the spectators, are more knowledgeable than she is. But Irina's fearful intuitions are strengthened, as are those of the spectators subsequently, precisely through the others' deliberate lying about the facts. When the news of Tusenbach's death in the duel is announced, it is precisely Irina who says, "I *knew* it, I *knew* it . . ." Judging by experience, many spectators react similarly at that moment—that is, they too are convinced: I knew it! And such a reaction is not improper, provided it is followed by critical self-reflection and the realization that even one's own expectation was not certain "knowledge" but merely an anticipated game of expected alternatives, the final one of which is declared to be the inevitable and predicted *post festum*.

If this reflection is triggered by Irina—who, in contrast to the spectator, had an informational disadvantage about the duel, so, contrariwise, the informational *advantage* of the other characters in relation to Irina can trigger the critical reflection—why did none of them try to prevent the imminent duel, even though they almost all disclaim it as dangerous and pointless? If this question is asked, then a socio-historical explanation may be offered. It might go like this:

These persons behave this way because in Russia at that time persons in this milieu in such situations were under such great pressure from society's expectations that they could not behave otherwise. The Russia of Chekhov and *Three Sisters* is no longer the Russia of Pushkin and Lermontov. Although at that time, despite official prohibition, a duel was almost unavoidable for officers and noblemen in cases of public insult, now, at the end of the century, it is no longer obligatory even in those circles. In addition, it so happens that Chekhov chooses to put the challenge to the duel right after Tusenbach's resignation from military service and his baron's life of idleness. It also coincides temporally with the departure of all the officers, including the challenger Solyony. And the comments of the "civilians" who stay behind are certainly negative. (Masha: "I say it's not right to let him do it. He might wound the baron or even kill him." Andrey: "In my opinion, even taking part in a duel, even being present at one, if only in the capacity of a medical man, is simply immoral.") The socio-historical motivation is thus insufficent in itself.

Yet it can be easily supported by psychology. Masha's protest is characteristic, in that she only *says* people shouldn't let him do it. She even accuses the others present: "So they waste the whole day here talking and talking . . . ," instead of possibly preventing the fatal duel. But she herself makes no attempt to prevent it. And this corresponds psychologically to her overall behavior, which has been accurately characterized:

> She makes no secret of her views, and would never do or say anything in order to please or to be liked. Her policy is to avoid any contact with falsehood and pretence, but not to challenge them, not to fight back, and certainly not to rally support.[4]

Correspondingly, Andrey's inactivity can be explained by his overall weakness, Chebutykin's indifference by his general cynicism. But despite the painstaking psychological motivation, the *fact* that none of those with advance information intervenes goes beyond individual psychological dispositions and results from an interaction of psychological and socio-historical factors.

The specific milieu, the socio-historical conditions in which these persons have grown up and been raised, and in which they now live (especially the living conditions in the Russian provinces) promote the type of the "superfluous man," who, in various psychological dispositions, dreams about illusionary expectations or reflects on their futility, but either denies their realization or denies himself their realization. And who immediately has ready-made excuses for this in "speeches," as in the beautiful image of the "philosophizing cranes," which implies one could not change anything in the predetermined "flight," the predestined course of things, although, as a *philosophizing* bird, one always has an intellectual advantage over one's fellow travellers who fly blindly to their destination.

* * *

4. Harai Golomb, *op. cit.*, 182.

ANDREY BELY

Andrey Bely was the pen name of Boris Nikolaevich Bugaev (1880–1934), Russian novelist, poet, and critic. Bely was one of the leading Symbolist thinkers before the Revolution and a leading formalist theorist after it. His experimental prose, particularly in his novel *St. Petersburg*, has much in common with the works of James Joyce.

The Cherry Orchard†

In reproducing reality, the realist artist starts by working on its most general details, and then turns into a photographer of reality. His vision dilates. He is no longer satisfied with the superficial delineation of phenomena. After the definite and the perdurable, he will linger at the indefinite and the fleeting, of which each type of definition and durability is compounded. He then reproduces the texture of an instant. The isolated moment becomes the aim of the reproduction. Depicted in such a way, life is subtle, almost transparent lacery. An instant of life taken by itself as it is deeply probed becomes a doorway to infinity. Like a loop of life's lace, it is nothing by itself, it outlines an opening into that which is behind it. Infinite is the intensification of inner experience. The lace of life, composed of discrete loops, becomes a series of doors in parallel corridors, leading to something else. The realist artist, still true to himself, involuntarily sketches, along with the surface of life's texture, also that which is revealed in the depths of the instants' labyrinths, parallel to one another. Everything remains the same in his depiction, but is permeated by *something different*. He himself does not suspect whereof he speaks. Tell such an artist that he has penetrated *the world beyond*, and he will not believe you. After all, he worked from without. He studied reality. He does not believe that the reality he depicts is no longer, in a certain sense, reality.

The mechanism of life diverts the channel of inner experiences into a direction other than the one toward which we strain, and surrenders us to the power of the machine. Our dependence begins with common causes unbeknownst to us and ends with trolley cars, telephones, elevators, railway timetables. In our midst the staccato mechanical cycle, from which it becomes increasingly difficult to break loose, evolves ever more and more. *A* kills himself for *B*, *B* for

---

† "Vishnevy sad," first published in the symbolist journal *Vesy* (*Balances*, no. 5, 1904), and reprinted in Bely's collection *Arabeski* (*Arabesques*, Moscow, 1911). This translation by Laurence Senelick first appeared in L. P. Senelick, ed. and trans., *Russian Dramatic Theory from Pushkin to the Symbolists* (Austin: University of Texas Press, 1981), 89–92. Reprinted by permission of the publisher.

C, but even C, to whom A and B devote themselves, remaining zeros instead of life organically cohesive through inner experiences, devotes himself to A and also turns into a zero. The machine is formed out of the aimless slaughter of souls.

The power of the instant is a natural protest against the mechanical organization of life. To free himself, man delves deep into the fortuitous moment of freedom, directing all the might of his soul toward it. Under such conditions man will learn more and more how to see into minutiae. The minutiae of life will appear ever more clearly to be the guides to Eternity. Thus, realism imperceptibly crosses over into symbolism.

Instants are pieces of stained glass. Through them we gaze at Eternity. We must stop at one pane of glass, or else we will never descry distinctly what lies beyond the fortuitous. Everything will get overly familiar, and we shall tire of looking at anything. But once we have experienced a particular instant intensively enough, we want a repeat performance. Repeating the experience, we will delve more deeply into it. Delving more deeply, we will pass various levels. A particular instant will become for us an unexpected outlet into mysticism: our inner path will be marked out and the wholeness of our psychic life restored. The mechanism of life will be controlled from within, discrete instants will no longer have any power. The lace of life, woven from discrete instants, will disappear when we discover the outlet to that which had earlier shown through behind it. By recounting what we see, we shall arbitrarily deal with the materials of reality.

Such is mystical symbolism, the reverse of realistic symbolism which presents the world beyond in terms of circumambient reality.

Chekhov is a realist artist. It must not be inferred from this that he uses no symbols. He cannot help but be a symbolist, if the conditions of reality in which we live have changed for modern man. Reality has become more transparent, owing to a refinement in the nervous system of the best of us. Without abandoning the world, we move toward what is beyond the world. This is the true path of realism.

Not so long ago we stood on a firm foundation. Now the earth itself has become transparent. We walk as if on slippery transparent glass; below the glass everlasting perdition dogs our footsteps. And lo, it seems to us that we walk on air. It is terrifying on this pathway of air. How can there be talk now of the limits of realism? Under such conditions can realism and symbolism be contrasted? Nowadays fugitives from life have reappeared in life, for life itself has changed. Nowadays the realists who depict reality are symbolists, at the very point where everything once ended, everything has now become transparent, pellucid.

Such is Chekhov. His heroes are outlined by external strokes, but we apprehend them from within. They walk, drink, talk rubbish, while we behold the spiritual poverty transpicuous within them. They talk like men confined in prison, but we have learnt something about them that they themselves have not noticed in themselves. In the minutiae by which they live, a certain secret cipher is revealed to us—and the minutiae cease to be minutiae. The banality of their life is in some way neutralized. Something grandiose is revealed throughout in its minutiae. Isn't this called seeing through banality? But seeing through anything means being a symbolist. *Seeing through*, I associate the object with what stands behind it. In such a relationship symbolism is inevitable.

The spirit of music is extremely diverse in its manifestations. It can penetrate all the characters of a given play equally. Each character is then a string in the general chord. Chekhov's *plays of mood* are musical. Their symbolism is a guarantee of this, for a symbol is always musical in an abstract sense. Chekhov's symbolism is distinguished from Maeterlinck's by its very essence. Maeterlinck makes the heroes of a drama vessels of his own mystical subject matter. His experience is revealed through them. To indicate the approach of death, he makes an old man say, "Is there not someone else amongst us?"[1] Too glaring a symbol. Isn't this allegory? Too abstract in its expression. Chekhov, attenuating reality, unexpectedly comes across symbols. He barely suspects them. He has put nothing in them with premeditation, for he has hardly undergone a mystical experience. His symbols therefore have unintentionally sprouted up in reality. Nowhere is the spider's web of the phenomenal torn. Thanks to this he manages more profoundly to reveal symbols reverberating on a background of minutiae.

Here sit these enervated people, trying to forget the terror of life, but a *vagrant walks by . . . Somewhere a bucket drops in a mine shaft.*[2] Everyone realizes that here is the terror. But mightn't it all be a dream? If we scrutinize *The Cherry Orchard* with a view to totality of artistic effect, we will not find the polish of *Three Sisters*. In this respect, *The Cherry Orchard* is not so successful. But it provides a more perfect presentation of the psychological depth of discrete instants. If our first glimpse was of the transparent lace texture viewed from afar, the author now seems to have drawn nearer to a few loops of that web, and to have seen more clearly what these loops outline. He skims over other loops. Hence perspective is violated and

1. In *Les Aveugles* [1890], Maeterlinck uses the old and blind, cut off from the turmoil of life, to sense death and other intimations from the beyond. [*Editor's Note.*]
2. In Act Two of *The Cherry Orchard*, as the characters are sitting beside the road, dreamily watching the sun go down, "suddenly a distant sound is heard, as if from the sky, the sound of a snapped string, dying away mournfully." The merchant Lopakhin offers the suggestion that a bucket dropped in a mine shaft, but the characters remain uneasy until a tramp enters and creates a welcome diversion by his begging. [*Editor's Note.*]

the play is rather uneven in tone. Relatively speaking, this is a step backward for Chekhov. Absolutely speaking—he has not stayed in one place, attenuating his technique. In some passages his realism is even more subtle, even more transparent with symbols.

How terrifying are the moments when fate soundlessly sneaks up on the weaklings. Everywhere there is the alarming leitmotiv of thunder, everywhere the impending storm-cloud of terror. And yet, it would seem there's good reason to be terrified, after all, there's talk of selling the estate. But terrible are the masks behind which the terror is concealed, eyes goggling in the apertures. How terrible is the governess cavorting around the ruined family, or the valet Yasha, carping about the champagne, or the oafish bookkeeper and the tramp from the forest!

In the third act there seems to be a crystallization of Chekhov's devices: in the foreground room a domestic drama is taking place, while at the back, candle-lit, the masks of terror are dancing rapturously: there's the postal clerk waltzing with some girl—or is he a scarecrow? Perhaps he is a mask fastened to a walking stick or a uniform hung on a clothes tree. What about the station master? Where are they from, what are they for? It is all an incarnation of fatal chaos. There they dance and simper as the domestic calamity comes to pass.

A detail is touched in with a certain brushstroke never seen before. Reality splits in twain: it is and it is not, it is the mask of another, and people are mannequins, phonographs are profundities—terrible, terrible . . .

Chekhov, remaining a realist, here draws back the folds of life, and what at a distance seemed to be shadowy folds turns out to be an aperture into Eternity.

DIRECTORS ON
CHEKHOV

KONSTANTIN STANISLAVSKY

Stanislavsky, the stage name of Konstantin Sergeevich Alekseev (1863–1938), Russian actor and director and co-founder of the Moscow Art Theater, is inextricably bound to the first productions of Chekhov's major plays. He staged the successful revival of *The Seagull* (1898), the first Moscow production of *Uncle Vanya* (1899), and the premieres of *Three Sisters* (1901) and *The Cherry Orchard* (1904), and played the roles of Trigorin, Astrov, Vershinin, and Gaev. As a director, he stressed subtext, ensemble playing, and the creation of atmosphere.

In January 1917, Stanislavsky proposed that *The Seagull*, which had received only sixty-three performances between its opening in 1898 and its excision from the repertory in 1905, be revived, employing many members of the original cast. He determined to concentrate on the "aesthetic realm" and to use art to educate "the people's sensibility, their souls." *The Seagull*, he now believed, was about devotion to art. Nostalgia for one of the Art Theater's great successes was overshadowed by his desire to create something fresh, youthful, and vigorous. His new vision of Chekhov and the play emphasized high spirits, activity, and courage. It was to be a therapeutic remedy for the woes he and his society were suffering. Hence the stress on youth and youthful feelings, and the repeated emphasis on moments of humor, joy, and faith.

Unfortunately, circumstances were not propitious. After five months of rehearsals, Mikhail Chekhov, who was to play Konstantin, fell ill, as did Alla Tarasova, who left for the Ukraine to avoid the famine in Moscow. The Art Theater would not restage *The Seagull* until Oleg Efremov completely rethought the play in 1980.

Of the rehearsals Stanislavsky held for the *Seagull* revival, only four sets of notes have survived. They were made by the assistant director Pyotr Sharov, who, later, as Peter Sharoff, would become a prominent Chekhov director in Italy and the Netherlands.

In applying his system in rehearsals, Stanislavsky used a vocabulary that is familiar to us now, but which at this time was newly minted. He has the actors break the play down into *kuski* (literally, pieces). Elizabeth Reynolds Hapgood's widely disseminated version of his writings renders this as "units," but I have chosen to translate it as *segments*. At times, he metaphorized small segments as *beads* (*busy*), which have to be strung together. He regularly refers to the *zadacha*, which I translate as *problem* (like a sum in mathematics), to be solved in each phase of the action. (Hapgood popularized the term *objective* in this regard; Jean Benedetti translates it more literally as *task*.) *Given circumstances* (*predlagaemye obstoyatelsta*) represent the situation in which the characters find themselves. *Through-action* (*skvoznoe deystvie*, what Hapgood calls the "through line of action") connects all the actions of a character and progresses towards the character's ultimate goal. He also makes a distinction between "activity" (*aktivnost*) and "action" (*deystvie*). At this point he is asking the actors to try to find the key (*klyuch*) to a segment, but later abandoned that term.

Second Thoughts on *The Seagull*†

September 10, 1917

Analysis of Act Three.

* * *

K. S. advises [Neronov][1] to forget about [Sorin's] illness. All this has to be pushed into the background. It interferes with the major, basic lines of the role. It's very detrimental to steer a characterization in the direction of infirmity.

K. S. talks about how Treplyov, though nervous, is not a neurotic. We have to show his courage, the strength of his convictions about his ideas. He is a fighter. His characterization is to be a man firm in his convictions.

The previous rehearsal achieved a great deal for Baksheev.[2] His role came closer.

K. S. asks them not to forget, to analyze the nature of their feelings. They must not forget the silent moments, when others are speaking, and they only listen.

Stakhovich[3] is somewhat embarrassed by his personal tendency to speak with a kind of sneer. Private rehearsals with V. L. Mchedelov[4] have been a great help in this regard.

Pavlova[5] continues to be perplexed and cannot find the essence of "sloppy sentimentality".

O. L. Knipper[6] is trying for a frivolous "actor's tone."
K. S. advises her [to base herself] on real-life observations of old performers, their way of speaking.

† From I. N. Vinogradskaya, ed., *Stanislavskii repetiruet. Zapisi i stenogrammy repetitsy* [Stanislavsky Rehearses: Rehearsal Notes and Transcripts], 2d ed. (Moscow: Moskovsky Khudozhestvenny teatr, 2002). Trans. by Laurence Senelick.
1. Vladimir Ivanovich Neronov (1867–1919), the new Sorin, had joined the Art Theater only in 1916 and was untested there.
2. Pyotr Alekseevich Baksheev (Barinov, 1886–1929), the new Shamraev, had been a useful character man in MAT productions since 1911 but was rarely entrusted with large roles.
3. Dr. Dorn was played by Aleksey Aleksandrovich Stakhovich (1856–1919), a former major-general and adjustant to the Governor General of Moscow, who had, after his retirement, become a stockholder and patron of the Art Theater.
4. Vakhtang Levanovich Mchedelov (Mchedlishvili, 1884–1924) was an assistant director on the production.
5. Vera Nikolaevna Pavlova (1875–1962), the new Polina Andreevna, had been a charter member of the Art Theater since 1898 but rarely played anything but small, nameless roles.
6. Of the original Art Theater cast, only Olga Knipper was enlisted into the new production. Now forty-nine, the widow of Anton Chekhov, and an established "star" of the Art Theater, she could be an anchor for the company.

They have begun to read the first act from the entrance of Treplyov and Sorin.

Sorin's first line is not right. He has to speak it as *usual*, and not as if for the first time. It follows that even Kostya must restrain [his uncle's] usual "maundering." Otherwise it will come across as the beginning of a scene. It has to be the continuation of a scene and not the beginning. Even here one has to pick the salient word to be stressed. "Somehow's *not the thing*?" You mustn't make automatic emphases.

With time you have to attain a high level of temperament in this role [Treplyov]. You must restrain your gestures. Especially [Mikhail] Chekhov's[7] tiny gestures, which appear to be his sole inadequacy for this role.

The more restrained the gestures, the more powerful the temperament.

"Underacting" simplicity always comes about when people don't appreciate the precious, salient words. That is the old Art Theater— to act simplicity is the worst, most appalling cliché.

Without kindliness there is no Sorin. He is not *calm*, but kindly, lively, interested in everything.

* * *

K. S. Stanislavsky's remarks.

[Mikhail] Chekhov's seriousness was evident, but his high spirits disappeared. There was no joy, no faith. They have begun to "act" [Anton] Chekhov. That's awful. They turned a performance into a funeral.

Shamraev has to be even more serious, authoritative. The stage of the old theatre is his "holy of holies." He has to talk with the "feelings" of a theater-buff, and not illustrate the words.

Neronov still doesn't have enough merriment and kindliness.

Pavlova has nothing but sloppy sentimentality. In her joys, her jealousies, everything—sloppy sentimentality.

Dorn is always inwardly cheerful, wise. His eyes are joyful. Without any strain. He even regards her affectionately, cheerfully.

Tarasova[8] has forgotten about [Treplyov's] play, the house has very much polluted her. Today this is a plus.

The first act went up to [the beginning of Treplyov's] play. Everyone is looking for the right direction, many new things happened and

7. Mikhail Aleksandrovich Chekhov (1891–1955), a nephew of the writer, had entered the Art Theater in 1912, and from the start Stanislavsky had tried to instill in him the principles of his system.
8. Alla Konstantinovna Tarasova (1998–1973), a plump, dark-eyed brunette, had caught Stanislavsky's eye in the Second Studio's *Green Ring*. In the Soviet period, she would become a leading actress of the MAT and a favorite of Stalin's, but at this point she was still a raw tyro.

earlier discoveries have been set aside; and this is very good. In the end everything will coalesce: all the "beads" will be strung.

They went on to the second act. They read as far as Nina's soliloquy. Then they began to analyze what's been read.

Arkadina is the only one who isn't depressed. She's all energy. Taken up with herself. Other people's attention still gets her worked up. Masha is struggling with what is dragging her down; she is suffering, but takes herself in hand. Dorn is living his own life. He hums—that's the nicest thing about the role.

Arkadina's energy is analogous to Savina's energy and liveliness. K. S. tells a story about a performance at his home at Red Gates. How everyone left [worn out and how Fedotova] was high-spirited and merry.[9] She's a firecracker.

Sorin has a joyful smile, and not the "routine" actor's smile, which does not admit seriousness. Sorin is very fond of Nina. He is happy when she's happy. Is he attracted to Nina? More accurately, it's a fondness for youth.

"I'm happy"—this line [of Nina's] contains both sadness and happiness. How quickly it has come, how soon it will pass. Youth is dust.

Is Arkadina jealous of Nina on account of Trigorin? Arkadina notices her outburst. She is jealous. Nina's arrival upsets her.

Her son interested her. [Arkadina] thinks about him seriously.

Masha warns Arkadina about Kostya: "He's very downhearted."

"Recite his poetry or something from his play"—this is connected with her torment over the last few days. She's all about Kostya, and all her lines connect to her love for Kostya. And then once more she "dons her toga."

"All that is so uninteresting"—it's a betrayal of Kostya. How can she do it? She, so young, so noble? She does it very delicately, gently: "Do I have to recite?" can be heard in [Nina's] refusal.

Here Masha is full of bravado. She wants to show that he [Treplyov] is a genius, a poet.

Why does she ask "timidly"? K. S. thinks that it is, rather, thoughtfulness, and, perhaps, the result of their strained relations. A bit of jealousy.

Shamraev arrives "to relax" among actors, at whom he immediately starts to yell. A kind of emotional outburst that can take place only in a heatwave.

Arkadina here reveals all that's worst in her actress's nature. Nina, affected by the scandal, the general agitation—gets excited herself

---

9. A charity performance of Nemirovich-Danchenko's *The Lucky Devil* with the participation of the Maly actors took place on March 27, 1892: Stanislavsky played the artist Bogucharov and the excellent actress Glikeriya Fedotova played his wife.

   Mariya Savina (1854–1915), imperious prima donna of the Alexandra Theater in St. Petersburg; no great admirer of Chekhov, she played Arkadina twice in 1902.

and is genuinely outraged by Shamraev. Sorin starts to shout at the
end of the scene because he's been frightened, like an "old biddy."

Nina goes into utter despair over what's happening in the house.
Polina's jealousy.

Nina alone. She is completely defeated. Her great naiveté. You
have to reveal her assumptions about life. Treplyov enters [with the
killed seagull].

They read the 3rd act.

Remarks.

Chekhovian moaning and groaning.

Arkadina's stinginess. She clutches at whatever's cheapest and
gradually refuses everything. The psychology of stinginess in Arkadina. One ruble for three servants. Sorin [talking to her about
money] is very candid, not chiding Arkadina. She joyously launches
into memories of her youth. In the quarrel with her son she hams it
up, and then immediately turns into a cook. An instant more—and
she is transformed into the kindest of women. It's all very sincere,
with an actor's temperament, it's all overblown, and therefore all the
feelings are exaggerated.

Trigorin? A bit of a coward. In Nina and Trigorin there's a reti-
cence and a hope that something will delay the departure. In the
whole scene there's great activity.

In the scene of Arkadina and Trigorin, some scene from a tragedy
is being played out, and with such effrontery, flattery, that it goes
right to Trigorin's head and he cannot struggle.

September 12, 1917

V. L. Mchedelov reports on the last rehearsal, specific concerns.

K. S. analyzes the third act, the scene between Treplyov and his
mother, and makes an analogy between Hamlet and Treplyov. Both
are at a time of life when they have nothing in their life except their
mothers. The dearer she is to them at this moment, the more they
want to reform her. The more they will restrain themselves. He
decided to commit suicide not because he didn't want to live; but
because he passionately wants to live, he grasps at everything that
offers a foothold in life, but everything collapses. For him, an aesthete, there is nothing in life that could hold him. His through-action
is *to live*, to live beautifully—to aspire to Moscow, to Moscow.[1]

Chekhov is always active. He is not a pessimist—life in the 1880s
was the way that Chekhov's characters created it. He himself loves
life, strives for a better life, as do all his characters.

1. The leitmotif of the heroines of *Three Sisters*. [*Editor's note*].

A question for Trigorin / Khokhlov.[2] In order to ascertain the correct problem, one must recall the correct state of mind. The better, the more smoothly the rehearsals proceed, the more profoundly one must consider and ascertain the problem "by means of the salient word."

A question for Arkadina / Knipper. The scene with Treplyov and Trigorin. All her psychology is very complicated.

About Tarasova.

Is there something getting in the way of the role?

Do you want to rehearse the first act?

What is there about it that frightens the actors?

This is a terrible thing to work with. One must come up with a serious attitude to circumstances, to a mother, to art.

You mustn't reinforce the role with "gimmicks." It's a natural habit for performers, which they have to break themselves of.

You have to get excited by the clash of passions. Forget about the external form, if you need something to hold on to, then for the time being you have to say that he is courageous, and how does this show itself now?

The main problem for the performer [Mikhail Chekhov] of the role has to be self-confidence.

With Sorin (Neronov), for some reason nothing new is developing.

With Shamraev (Baksheev),[3] things are doubtful. An agonizing period for Baksheev's talent—it's getting swallowed up by clichés. You have go back to your original condition (before *Wandering Minstrels*),[4] when there were no clichés.

With Dorn, the work is going in an interesting way, in the sense of finding the inner essence of the role. A. A. Stakhovich is gradually pulling away from his own personal characteristics, which interfere with the work.

Of Kryzhanovskaya.[5] You have to find a "pose," but not literally. Kryzhanovskaya objects, stating that [Masha] is always sincere, really likes taking snuff.

After short discussions we moved from the third act to the second act.

2. Trigorin, once Stanislavsky's part, was to be played by Konstantin Khokhlov, a character actor of some range, who had been seen as the moronic Greek Purikes in *Anathema*, the district prosecutor in *The Brothers Karamazov*, and Horatio in the Gordon Craig *Hamlet*.
3. Pyotr Alekseevich Baksheev (Barinov, 1886–1929), joined the company in 1911 and was entrusted mainly with minor character roles.
4. In the First Studio's production of *Wandering Minstrels* by V. M. Vol'kenshtein (1914), Baksheev played the boyar Yavolod.
5. Mariya Alekseevna Kryzhanovskaya (1891–1979) would later play Varya and Irina on the MAT tours.

Act Two

There's something of Astrov in Dorn. He somehow lives wholly within himself. Sees everything, understands everything. What is Dorn living off of in the second act? To create stage action, we have to find an activity. There's no way to live the "heat" of the second act. That's not an activity, only a mood.

Sorin has an activity in Act Two, "thirsting for life," which is why he's so happy around Nina.

For Baksheev: he [Shamraev] has come to make trouble either because he's cross, or an oppressive "life" is eating away at him, and he comes to talk about "art." . . .

They begin to read the second act.

After reading the act, K. S. poses them all a question: "Where who how did you feel?"

Baksheev could not control himself and got excited.

[Mikhail] Chekhov did not feel the truth.

Tarasova at the start of the act felt bad, but then it became easy, and by the end she was quite in control of herself.

Khokhlov felt comfortable.

K.S.   The basic problem of the act?

KHOKHLOV   To please Nina.

K.S.   Did you succeed?

[KHOKHLOV]   At moments. The joke, the talk about youth.

KRIZHANOVSKAYA—doesn't feel the role. She was reading lines.

K.S.   Aren't [we winding up with] two Ninas?

Masha [in contradistinction to Nina] doesn't reveal her feelings, her lyricism. Maybe, somewhere alone in the moonlight, she will open her heart to herself, but she immediately gets embarrassed. She is very homely, with a vast fund of feminine lyricism.

A hot summer's day. The residents sit around in a sour mood. In this stagnant society, [unexpectedly there appears] a sophisticated actress, "M. G. Savina." She makes merry, which is easy for her.

This is the picture you have to come to love, to delineate. No feminine image, the subtlety of competing with young people.

K. S. suggests they "shape" this scene.

Are they bored or not? They are bored. The eternal Chekhovian theme. People want to leave this boredom of life. In order to strive towards life, there has to be "boredom," which should make one pull away from this tedious, uninteresting life.

To express lyricism one must give [?] and use the whole range of the voice. A general fault of the theater is to express lyricism only by a certain lowering and raising of the voice. That's boring.

K. S. suggests they simply do an exercise; he wants to get them on stage. We have lost life. We all need to find it. Meanwhile this pressure, actor's temperament, but no artistic depiction.

Nina is a young girl whose excitement at meeting Trigorin is almost comic.

To create naiveté, one needs a naive frame of mind. For her, Trigorin is Shakespeare. Nina respects Trigorin the way A. K. Tarasova respects Shakespeare.

We should [along with Nina] smile at meeting Trigorin. It's all so naive, so overwrought.

It has to be clear to us that she is taking what glitters to be gold, and we should want to shout at her, "you're making a mistake! You are worth more than any of these celebrities!"

Her coming to this house of celebrities—it's Tyltyl and Mytyl coming to the "kingdom of unborn souls."[6]

Treplyov: does he have to go right out and shoot himself or not?

We have to create the picture: a happy young girl, and enter a suicide. Why did he come here? Why did he kill the seagull? This man has no reins to steer with; his soul has been emptied out. Nina instinctively feels something tragic in this dramatic figure, and when such individual artistic segments are created along the line of life, the result is tragedy.

We don't have to come up with the result of the whole scene.

We have to come up with a series of lifelike phases; otherwise, there will [only] be the result, it won't be interesting. In Chekhov, the words are the last thing—he's not Ostrovsky. We have to look for original feelings.

Heat. In exercises, we might find the true nature of feelings in a heatwave. At first, find what external adjustments there are.

K.S. himself plays an exercise without words: "Heat." We immediately know the results only too well.

Everyone comes onstage and plays the exercise, improvisations on "heat."

K.S. advises they seek the truth not with actor's devices: if you have to portray boredom, then the actor spends the whole scene "down in the mouth"; if the scene is high-spirited, the actor is bound to "jump up and down" and be constantly in motion. In fact, it could just as readily be the complete opposite.

From the exercises, they gradually move into rehearsing the second act. Getting as far as Shamraev's entrance, the rehearsal breaks off, and K.S. suggests he deal only with Tarasova, [Mikhail] Chekhov, and Khokhlov.

The whole rehearsal ends with an analysis of Nina's first line after

6. Reference to the scene "The Kingdom of the Future," in which the boy and girl Tyltyl and Mytyl in Maeterlinck's *Blue Bird* are guided by the Soul of the World into the realm of the unborn. [*Editor's note.*]

Trigorin's exit, when she is alone: "How strange this is, a famous writer . . ." etc.

September 14, 1917

Individual work with Tarasova, [Mikhail] Chekhov, and Trigorin [Khokhlov]. Act Two.

They start by going over the first act.

What is the best way to clarify Nina's attitude to Treplyov and Trigorin?

It has to be broken down into small segments.

Once the segments become clearly understood, one has to "model" segment by segment. And this will clarify the attitude. And to "model" a segment accurately, one has to know the precise problem in the segment.

Let's take the biggest segment in the first act—Treplyov's meeting with Nina. The closest through-action for Nina is to act onstage, to be a success, etc. Connected with this through-action, at the very beginning Nina wants to know the truth: is she late or not? Which means, there's a moment of inquiry; she is seeking, she wants to find out whether it's all over or not. You have to experience the "physical truth" of the inquiry. After: "of course, you're not late"—she is convinced. To reinforce this, you have to fit the keys to this scene: arriving, looking around, calming down—relaxing.

These keys may change over the course of the work. It's the internal modelling of the segment.

(Next segment.) Treplyov: "No, no!"

Which is more important for Treplyov at that moment—his play or Nina?

Nina, because he loves her. She has destroyed his mental equilibrium.

What is the nature of this feeling of love? "The key?" "You hear her footsteps?"—"Even the sound of her footsteps is pleasant!" The greater the love, the greater the attention. The greater the attention, the fewer smiles. Maybe, a smile may come, but a smile of strained attention, tension. He wants to share his attention with his uncle. To infect him, to persuade him of his feelings.

Keys [Treplyov]: 1. To listen to the footsteps, 2. To infect his uncle with his attention, to persuade him.

You have to find the salient word for this, to come to love it. This word cannot be found with the mind—it turns things cold, but you will find this word, and come to love it from frequent repetition.

She arrives. The nature of his feeling, *the key—to welcome her* (to express to her all his sensations, his joy).

Now the next phase.

When you want to tell someone something important, you don't begin by saying it, yet you don't calm down, you don't relax after fatigue. Which means, for Nina it's *preparation*, to say something important, to prepare the ground.

To depict one's inner feeling, one has to draw a whole series of little pictures, in order to achieve the overall big picture. What kind of feeling leads to "there are tears in your little eyes"? It's all offensive, annoying, inauthentic. Which means, the picture will be painted with a feeling of offense, annoyance, inauthenticity.

In an exercise, Tarasova tries out Nina's first entrance, using K.S.'s directions, his "keys." The experiment is a *wonderful* success.

At this point, Treplyov needs not a smile, but high spirits, great energy, activity. This is the sequence: activity, hence energy, high spirits, and high spirits may even lead to a smile.

In the next segment, the salient word to choose is "father"; "*father* knows nothing [about her leaving home]." This is not emphasis, but choice.

One must remember the "given circumstances": "What will happen to her if she doesn't get home in half an hour?" The circumstance is very important, and the colors must be laid on thick.

To convince people one needs calm, not electrical shocks, pressure.

One has to play psychological turning points the way Duse and Kommissarzhevskaya [did].

For Treplyov, "the given circumstances" are also important: they are: in order for the play to go on, it will be illustrated by a word: where is this salient word?

Hence Treplyov's great activity, his desire to act quickly.

Nina is confused.

The love scene does not occur by chance. At any other time, Nina would probably never say such a thing ["My heart is full of you"]. She is afraid of the feeling of love and [love for] the stage. Thanks to their activity, a love scene evolved. Love in Nina would come somewhat unconsciously.

You have to determine the exact way to solve all these problems in Nina: all joyously, all fearfully, all youthfully, which means, all expansively, rapidly. So you can weep as easily as you burst into laughter unconfined.

You have to lay a general color over all the problems.

"Father and stepmother won't allow me . . ." The key: she is *drawn* here. In the words, "my heart is full of you," she shows how she's drawn here. What she sees in him is art, Bohemia, but *not himself*.

The kiss is accidental, "stupid." He goes first. He is enthralled, absurd. People act foolishly at moments like this. They've lost their heads. Hence her question: "What kind of tree is that?" His "lecture" about how evening darkens all objects—that's also the result of awkwardness.

Their fright at Yakov's voice.

Would it be interesting, artistic, if all sincere, authentic feelings were *honestly* put onstage? *No.* You have [to add] a certain amount of acting, that is, a loving enjoyment of the role, of *acting the role*, but *acting the role* is not true stage art. All our psycho-physical work is necessary to mastering a role so that one can play the role and lovingly have fun with it.

Whenever the mind has gone through the psycho-physical process in a role, one can begin to enjoy the role, to play it.

Nina does not believe in (Trigorin) Treplyov as a writer. She doesn't understand him.

Again "they play the whole scene." K. S. says that [Treplyov] does not have to touch Nina. No physical intimacy. It's as if in the first scene [of Nina and Treplyov] there is no joyousness, merriment, hope, high spirits . . . They have to ascend to heaven, so that [Treplyov's] fall in the second act will be tragic. Her excitement, fear, worship of Trigorin make sense of the second act. One has to select salient words for this: "Trigorin," "a famous writer," "it's dreadful for Mama (Arkadina)," and it goes without saying it's all about Trigorin.

Then K. S. makes a few remarks about Treplyov and Trigorin.

September 17, 1917

Analysis of Act Three. The scene of Treplyov and his mother.

Grounds for reconciliation with his mother are found, and only Trigorin, their type of theater divides them again. And at the end of the quarrel he, Treplyov, immediately loses self-control, consciousness. The breaking point began with Trigorin; in the lines about theater Treplyov is defending all art. "Mr Avant-garde" is the complete break.

"Skinflint!" The end of the anger, the culminating point. After this scene, an enormous pause.

The nature of Arkadina's feelings here are all depicted through frivolity (with Sorin).

Arkadina is very stingy.

Sorin's request [that that she give] money for Kostya's trip abroad puts Arkadina in a panic.

You have to validate this feeling by an example from life: at first there will be a moment of intense attention, "probing" the heart of the person making the request. Self-defense. "My costumes alone . . ." is at first a way of protecting herself from the "trip abroad." And then, when she sees that the request is not especially insistent, she drops the costumes. The salient phrase in this scene is *"all the same."* When this phrase is to be played, you must find for yourself further on.

You mustn't confuse the problem with the way in which the problem will be resolved.

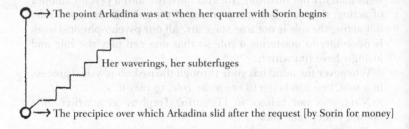

The point Arkadina was at when her quarrel with Sorin begins

Her waverings, her subterfuges

The precipice over which Arkadina slid after the request [by Sorin for money]

There is a great moment of entreaty in the scene. The stingier she is, the greater the entreaty. She turns pale with horror. Therefore, when Kostya asks on Sorin's behalf, without knowing that Sorin had already asked on his behalf, she falls into even greater horror, and Kostya's request for a bandage is a request to change the subject, and she does so joyfully, for her it's a bridge for crossing over to another theme.

"You won't do any more click-click?"—"No, mama, it won't happen again."

Here there is a certain fear of committing suicide. He is examining his feelings. To understand him properly, you must find the salient word, the key. "That was a *moment of insane despair*, when I could not get control of myself. It won't happen again." Analyzing himself, Kostya persuades himself not to do it again.

The key is auto-suggestion.

Pause. He kisses her hand. This connects with the auto-suggestion. That kiss connects him physically with life. It is a straw he grasps at. Hence the tenderness to his mother.

Kostya's memories of his mother's kindness are important in characterizing Arkadina. She does not remember her own kind deeds, but she does remember the ballerinas who drank coffee at her place. His memories provide him some foundation for a future life.

What's the reason he remembers: does he actually recall it or is he painting a picture of a blissful life? He is *painting,* because the pictures of a blissful life connect him with life, hence the salient words: *"golden hands," "you remember,"* "how can you *not remember,"* "these *last few* days, these days I love you as tenderly and uninhibitedly as in childhood." Pause. This line consolidates the relationship.

When he goes on to mention Trigorin he speaks very carefully, at first continuing to consolidate the relationship. If the whole previous dialogue was a mutual desire for peace and quiet, based on certain compromises, her line "I respect that man" will be very restrained, and the whole scene will be restrained. And the more restrained, the more powerful and tense it is, and if there's an outburst, it will be a real one.

The scene has to accumulate. Both of them plead not to destroy the relationship that's going so well. A compromise isn't found.

"Go back to your darling theater . . ."—he has exploded once and for all.

"I am more talented than the lot of you . . ." is very modest, but convinced.

If this whole little scene contains three huge psychological "phases," so that everything is exhausted, the pause will be huge.

Phases:

1. You have to calm yourself physically (he walks around, he calms down).
2. He understands, he appreciates what is happening.
3. Isolation.

This is only a hint. The actor's personal temperament can alter this logical division of a pause into phases.

So it is with Arkadina:

1. She calms down.
2. She justifies herself ("A nobody"), has understood.
3. Watches furtively, imperceptibly gropes for his situation.
4. Asks forgiveness; contrition.

"If you only knew: I've lost all hope."

Again a straw, but not because he loves her again; he's simply holding on to her physically. Here again he is in the despair of the second act. Activity, seeking a way out, for otherwise the actor will play despair.

Here: "Save me! Help!"

A scene of reconciliation. She pleads with all her blandishments for forgiveness, while he, burrowing into his soul, can hardly find a reason to embrace her again. He seeks support, he wants to be understood. And his embrace comes not from love, but from entreaty. She senses his condition and wants to help him.

The next segment: "We're reconciled now?"—"Yes, Mama."

K.S. suggests going on stage and physically verifying the truth. Knipper and [Mikhail] Chekhov play an exercise from the scene.

Clichés prevailed, especially in [Mikhail] Chekhov, where he wants to show his affection, love for his mother. Both make many automatic emphases.

It works best without words—finding the physical truth.

Moreover, one must live according to the ultimate problems (actions), and not by moving from problem to problem.

One must think not about *how* to do something, but *what* to do. Then something integral will result, physical truth will be freshly minted.

K. S. plays an exercise—the search for a lost pin.

In all the twists and turns of the acting, one must sense that one exists: *I am*.

*   *   *

VSEVOLOD MEYERHOLD

Vsevolod Yemelyevich Meyerhold (1874–1940), the highly experimental Russian director, actor, and theorist, created the roles of Treplyov and Tusenbach in the Moscow Art Theater productions of *The Seagull* and *Three Sisters;* however, he disagreed with Stanislavsky's interpretations and wrote his own views of how the plays were to be staged. As a young director of Chekhov, he copied the Art Theater stagings; but after the Revolution, he promoted a proletarian theater, with constructivist, functional scenery, acting based on biomechanics, and texts fragmented and rearranged. In 1935, he created *Thirty-Three Swoons,* an evening of *The Proposal, The Bear,* and *The Celebration.*

The Naturalistic Theatre and the Theatre of Mood†

*   *   *

The Moscow Art Theatre has two visages: the Naturalistic Theatre and the Theatre of Mood. The naturalism of the Moscow Art Theatre is a naturalism borrowed from the Meiningen players.[1] Accuracy in reproducing nature is its basic principle. On the stage everything has to be as real as possible—the ceilings, the stucco cornices, the stones, the wallpaper, the little stove doors, the ventilation holes, and so on.

---

†   From V. Ye. Meyerhold, "Naturalistichesky teatr i teatr nastroenii," in *Teatr. Kniga o novom teatre: sbornik statey* (Theater: A Book about the New Theater: A Collection of Articles) (St. Petersburg: Shipovnik, 1908), 136–50. Trans. by Nora Beeson. Reprinted by permission of *The Drama Review.*

1.   A court theatrical company organized and directed by Georg II, Duke of Saxe-Meiningen (1826–1914); his third wife, the actress Ellen Franz (1839–1923); and Ludwig Chronegk (1837–1891), an actor who was appointed stage director. Their annual tours, which began in 1874 and ended in 1890, and which included almost every major city in Europe, brought praise for their conception of the unified production of plays and for scenic investiture which featured pictorial realism. [*Editor's note.*]

On stage cascades a real waterfall and real rain falls. A little chapel is constructed of real wood, and a house is faced with fine plywood, its double frames stuffed with cotton. The windows covered with frost. All corners of the stage are clearly visible. The fireplaces, tables, and shelves are filled with a great quantity of small objects visible only with binoculars, which will engage the attention of the curious spectator for the entire act. The noise of the round moon creeping along its wire disturbs the audience. Through the window a real ship can be seen in a fiord. Not only rooms are built on stage, but even several stories with real staircases and oaken doors. The stage is cluttered and confusing. There are footlights and many borders. The canvas which represents the sky is hung in a semicircle. In plays calling for a country estate, the floor is covered with papier-mâché dirt.

* * *

When performing historical plays, the Naturalistic Theatre conforms to the rule that the stage must be transformed into an exhibit of authentic museum pieces, or at least of exact copies made after period paintings or from photographs. The stage director and designer try to reproduce as exactly as possible the year, month, and day of the play's action, and find it insufficient, for example, that the play takes place simply "in the age of powder." Elaborate hedges, fantastic fountains; overgrown meandering paths, rose gardens, clipped chestnut and myrtle trees, crinolines and capricious coiffures—all these do not satisfy the naturalistic directors. They find it necessary to reproduce exactly the kind of sleeves worn in Louis XV's times, or to speculate how the coiffures during the reign of Louis XVI differed from those worn under Louis XV. Such directors do not want to stylize a period, but rather follow a fashion journal of the year, month, and day on which the action occurs.

Thus, the Naturalistic Theatre devised the method of *copying a historical style*. Such a method, naturally, does not observe the rhythmic architectonics of a play such as *Julius Caesar*, for example, with its plastic conflict between two opposing powers. And not one of the directors realized that a synthesis of "caesarism" could never be achieved with a kaleidoscope of realistic scenes and an imitation of historical costumes.

The actors' make-up is *overly realistic*—real faces as we see them in real life, an exact copy. The Naturalistic Theatre considers the face the actor's main expressive tool and consequently overlooks all other means of expression. The Naturalistic Theatre does not know the advantages of plasticity and does not compel its actors to train their bodies. The schools connected with the Naturalistic Theatre do not realize that physical sport should be a basic training, especially for plays such as *Antigone* and *Julius Caesar*, plays which because of their music belong to *another* kind of theatre.

Many excellently made-up faces remain in one's mind, but no postures or rhythmic movements. During a performance of *Antigone* the director somehow unconsciously arranged his actors to resemble frescoes and vase paintings, but he was not able to *synthesize* or *stylize* what he had seen in actual relics; he could only photograph. On the stage before us we could see a series of groupings, like a row of hill tops, but realistic gestures and movements, like ravines, disturbed the internal rhythm of the reproduction.

The actor in the Naturalistic Theatre is extremely nimble at transforming himself, but his methods do not originate from *plastic* action but from make-up and an onomatopoeic imitation of various accents, dialects, and voices. Instead of developing his esthetic sense to exclude all coarseness, the actor's task is to lose his self-consciousness. A photographic sense of recording daily trivia is instilled in the actor.

According to Gogol, the character Khlestakov[2] "had nothing particularly distinctive," and yet Khlestakov is very clear-cut. *In the interpretation of images sharpness of outline is not at all necessary for clarity.*

* * *

The Naturalistic Theatre teaches the actor a crystal-clear, explicit mode of expression, never conscious underacting, or the play of allusions. And therefore, the Naturalistic Theatre smacks of *overacting*. Hints and insinuations are unknown in this kind of theatre. But even in this great period of naturalism some actors tried to bring moments of a new kind of acting to the stage as, for example, Vera Kommissarzhevskaia in her tarantella dance in A *Doll's House*.

The Naturalistic Theatre denies that the spectator has the ability to finish a painting in his imagination, or to dream as he does when listening to music. And yet the spectator possesses such an ability. In the first act of Yartsev's play *At the Monastery*[3] the interior of a monastery was shown and the curfew bells were heard. No window was shown on stage, but from the sound of the bells the playgoer imagined a courtyard covered, with piles of bluish snow, fir trees as in the paintings by Nesterov[4] little paths leading from cell to cell, and the golden cupolas of a church. One spectator imagined such a picture, the second another, and the third still another. Mystery had

2. Khlestakov is the main character in Gogol's *Inspector General* (1836), an airheaded nobody who is taken to be a V.I.P. [*Editor's note.*]
3. P. M. Yartsev (d. 1930), Russian theatrical critic, playwright, and stage director whose play *At the Monastery* was produced at the Moscow Art Theatre in 1904. (*Editor's note.*)
4. M. V. Nesterov (1862–1942), Russian painter who started his career as a member of the *peredvizhniki* (itinerants), established in 1870. [*Editor's note*].

taken hold of the playgoer, transporting him into the world of dreams. In the second act the director had a window showing the courtyard of the monastery but not those cells, those heaps of snow, nor the color of the cupolas. And the spectator was disenchanted and even enraged, for Mystery had disappeared and dreams were abused.

The Naturalistic Theatre consistently and consciously banished from the stage the power of Mystery. During the first performance of *The Sea Gull*[5] in the first act, one could not see how the actors made their exit from the stage. Running across some boards, they disappeared into a black cloth thicket, into *somewhere* (at that time the designer still worked without the collaboration of the carpenter); but when *The Sea Gull* was given again in a new version, all the stage was clearly visible: a little summerhouse with real cupolas and real columns, and a ravine into which the actors made their exit seen by all. During *The Sea Gull's* first performance, in the third act, a window was at the side of the stage, and no landscape could be seen; when the actors entered wearing galoshes, shaking their hats, shawls and kerchiefs, they conveyed the spirit of autumn, of freezing rain, puddles in the yard and boards squelching in the mud. When the play was restudied on a technically perfected stage, the window faced the audience and showed a landscape. Your imagination was lulled, and you did not imagine anything more than what the actors said about the weather outside. And the departure with horses and bells (the end of the third act in the first version) was only felt on the stage, yet was clearly pictured by the spectator's imagination; but according to the plan of the later performances, the audience had to see the horses with bells as well as the terrace from which the characters departed.

* * *

Somewhere Voltaire said: *"Le secret d'être ennuyeux, c'est tout dire."*[6]

When the spectator's imagination is not lulled to sleep but stimulated, then art becomes subtle. Why could the medieval plays be performed without any scenery? Because of the lively imagination of the audience.

The Naturalistic Theatre not only denies the playgoer the ability to dream, but even the ability to understand intelligent conversation on stage. All the scenes in Ibsen's plays are submitted to a tedious analysis which transforms the work of the Norwegian dramatist into something boring, dragging, and doctrinaire. Especially in the per-

5. Meyerhold, a member of the Moscow Art Theatre from 1898 to 1902, played the role of Treplyov in the 1898 production. [*Editors note.*]
6. "The secret of being a bore is to say everything." Francois Marie Arouet de Voltaire (1694–1778), French philosopher and writer. [*Editor's note.*]

formance of Ibsen plays the method of the naturalistic stage director is clearly demonstrated. The play is divided into a series of scenes, and each separate part is *minutely analyzed*. This painstaking analysis is applied to the tiniest scenes of the drama. From these various, thoroughly-digested parts the whole is glued together again. This piecing together of the whole from its parts is called the art of the director, but I think the analytical work of the naturalist-director, this pasting together of the poet's, the actor's, the musician's, the painter's, or even the director's work, will never result in a unified whole.

The famous critic of the eighteenth century, Alexander Pope, in his didactic *Essay on Criticism* (1711), enumerating the reasons which prevent critics from giving sound judgment, among other reasons points out their habit of examining parts of a work when the critics' first duty should be to look from the point of view of the author at work as a whole.

The same could be said for the stage director. The naturalistic director, profoundly analyzing each separate part of a work, does not see the picture as a whole and, fascinated by his filigree work—the trimming of some scenes which present excellent material for his creative imagination with some pearls of "characterization"—destroys the balance, the harmony of the whole.

Timing is very important on the stage. If some scene which the author wanted short is drawn out, then the weight of the next scene, which the author considered very important, is lessened. Having to look for a long time at something which should be forgotten, the spectator is already tired when the important scene opens. Such a distortion of the harmony of the whole appeared in the interpretation of the Art Theatre's director in the third act of *The Cherry Orchard*. The author makes Ranevskaya's premonition of the threatening storm (the sale of the cherry orchard) the leitmotiv of the act. All the others around her live stupidly—they are dancing to the monotonous rattle of a Jewish orchestra, and as in a nightmare, whirl around in a tedious dance without amusement, or fervor, or grace, or even lust, not knowing that the earth on which they are dancing will be sold from under their feet. Only Ranevskaya foresees Evil, expects it, and for a moment stops the turning wheel, that nightmarish dance of the puppets in their booth, as she lectures to the crowd on crime—how it is better not to be a "do gooder," for crimes may lead to holiness, whereas mediocrity leads nowhere. The act is divided into two parts: Ranevskaya's forebodings of the imminent Disaster (the fateful beginning of Chekhov's new mystic dramas), and the show booth of puppets (recently Chekhov had Charlotta dance among the "residents" in the favorite costume of the puppet theatre—the black dress coat and checkered trousers). Speaking in musical terms this act is like a movement of a symphony with a sorrowful melody vacillating from *piano* to *forte* (Ranevskayas's mood), and a dissonant accompaniment—the monotonous strumming of the provincial orchestra and the dance of the living corpses. And so the scene with the tricks is only another discord in the melody of the tedious dance. That is to say, this scene must fuse with the dance, only to separate a minute later, and again to join with the dancing which should continuously serve as a background.[7]

The director of the Art Theatre showed how the harmony of this act can be destroyed. He created a scene with many details which proceeded slowly and laboriously. For a long time the spectator concentrated his attention on this scene and lost the leitmotiv of the act. And when the act had finished, only the melody of the background remained and the leitmotiv had disappeared.

In Chekhov's *Cherry Orchard*, as in the plays of Maeterlinck; an unseen hero exists on stage whose presence is felt whenever the curtain drops. When the curtain closed on the Moscow Art Theatre's performance of *The Cherry Orchard* the presence of such a protagonist was not felt. Only types were remembered. To Chekhov the characters of *The Cherry Orchard* were a means to an end and not a reality. But in the Moscow Art Theatre the characters became real and the lyrical-mystic aspect of *The Cherry Orchard* was lost.

If in the Chekhov plays the particulars distracted the director from the *whole* because the impressionistically-drawn figures of Chekhov lent themselves well to precise characterization, so in the plays by Ibsen the director had to explain to the public what seemed incomprehensible to him.

The performances of Ibsen plays above all aimed to *enliven the "boring" dialogue* with something—with eating a meal, arranging a room, introducing scenes of packing, moving about furniture, and so forth. In *Hedda Gabler*, in the scene between Tesman and Aunt Julia they ate breakfast together. I remember well how awkwardly the actor playing Tesman ate, but I hardly heard the thesis of the play.

In the Ibsen plays, apart from showing definite "patterns" of Norwegian life, the director emphasized every passage of dialogue which he considered difficult. The essence of Ibsen's *Pillars of Society*, for example, was drowned in the analytical work spent on less important

---

7. Such passing, jarring notes which just but from the background the act's leitmotiv can be found in the stationmaster's reading poetry, in the scene of Yepikhodov's broken billiard cue, and Trofimov's fall on the stairs. And look how closely Chekhov interweaves the two melodies—the leitmotif and the accompanying background.

> ANYA (*Upset.*)   Just now in the kitchen some man was saying the cherry orchard's been sold already.
> LYUBOV ANDREEVNA   Sold to whom?
> ANYA   He didn't say. He left. (*Dances with* TROFIMOV; *they both go into the ballroom.*)

scenes. And the playgoer who knew the play well from reading, saw in this performance a new play which he did not understand. The director made many minor scenes as important as the major ones, *but the sum total of these secondary scenes did not convey the essence of the entire play*. The emphasis on one particular moment catches audience attention and the rest of the act is lost in *fog*.

The fear of not showing everything, the fear of Mystery, transforms the theatre into a mere illustration to an author's words. "I hear the dog barking again," says one of the actors, and immediately the dog's bark is heard. The spectator is made aware of a departure with the sound of bells and horses' hooves on a wooden bridge across a river. The falling of rain is heard on a tin roof, as well as birds, frogs, and crickets.

Let me relate a conversation between Chekhov and some actors. When A. P. Chekhov came for the second time to a rehearsal of *The Sea Gull* at the Moscow Art Theatre (September 11, 1898), one of the actors told him how frogs were going to croak, flies to buzz, and dogs to bark.

> "Why all this?" asked Chekhov in a dissatisfied tone of voice.
> "It's real," answered the actor.
> "It's real," repeated Chekhov laughing, and after a pause said:
> "The stage is art, Kramskoy has a genre painting with wonderfully painted faces. How would it be if the nose were cut out from one of the faces and a real nose inserted? The nose will be 'real' but the pointing is spoiled."

One of the actors told Chekhov proudly that at the end of the third act of *The Sea Gull* the director was planning to bring all the household servants onto the stage including a woman with a crying child. Anton Pavlovich said: "That's not necessary. It's the same as if you were playing the piano *pianissimo* and suddenly the lid of the piano were to fall down." "It often happens in life that a *pianissimo* is suddenly interrupted by a completely unexpected *forte*," one of the actors tried to object, "Yes," said A. P., "but the stage requires a certain convention: you have no fourth wall. Besides that, the stage is art, the stage reflects the quintessence of life and nothing superfluous should be introduced." It is clear from this conversation what Chekhov himself thought about the Naturalistic Theatre. This theatre wanted a fourth wall and only absurdities resulted. The Naturalistic Theatre resembled a factory: everything on stage had to be "as in life" and transformed into a shop of museum pieces.

Stanislavsky felt that the theatrical sky could be made real to the public, and the entire administration worried about how to raise the roof of the theatre. And no one noticed that instead of repairing the stage the foundation of the Naturalistic Theatre was being demolished. For no one believed that the wind blowing the garlands in the first scene of *Julius Caesar* was not the stagehand, especially as the costumes of the actors were not blowing. In the second act of *The Cherry Orchard* the actors walked in "real" ravines, over "real" bridges, near a "real" chapel, and in the sky hung two great lumps covered with blue cloth the likes of which had never been seen in any sky. The hills on a battlefield (in *Julius Caesar*) were built so as to diminish gradually toward the horizon, but why did the actors not diminish in size when moving in the same direction as the hills?

> The stage sets in use today show landscapes of great depth but do not show the human figure in perspective to these landscapes. And yet this theatre pretends to reproduce nature accurately. Actors moving ten or even twenty meters back from the footlights are just as large and distinct as when standing directly at the footlights. According to the laws of perspective in painting, the further an actor moves upstage, if he has to be shown in his true size with the surrounding trees, houses, mountains, the smaller he should become sometimes only a silhouette, sometimes even more indistinct.[8]

The trees used in the Naturalistic Theatre seem crude, unnatural, and much more artificial in their three dimensions than painted, two-dimensional trees. These are some of the absurd practices followed by the Naturalistic Theatre in its attempt to imitate nature. The fundamental aim of this theatre is to find rationality in any subject, to photograph, to illustrate with decorative painting the text of a dramatic work, and to copy a historical style.

Naturalism introduced a more complex staging technique in the Russian theatre, yet it is the Theatre of Chekhov, the second style of the Moscow Art Theatre, which demonstrated the power of *mood;* without this mood, or atmosphere, the theatre of the Meiningers would have perished long ago. But the development of the Naturalistic Theatre was not aided by this *new mood* originating from Chekhov's plays. The performance of *The Sea Gull* in the Alexandra Theatre did not dispel the author's mood, yet the secret was not to be found in the chirping of crickets, the barking of dogs, or in realistic doors. When *The Sea Gull* was performed in the Hermitage building of the Moscow Art Theatre, the *machinery* was not working perfectly, and *technique* did not yet extend its feelers into all corners of the theatre.

The secret of Chekhov's mood lies in the *rhythm* of his language. This rhythm was felt by the actors of the Art Theatre during the rehearsals of the first Chekhov play, was felt because of the actors' love for Chekhov.

8. George Fuchs, *Die Schaubühne der Zukunft* (The Stage of the Future), 28.

The Moscow Art Theatre would never have achieved its second style without the rhythmicality of Chekhov's words; the theatre of mood became its real character and was not a mask borrowed from the Meiningen players.

That the Art Theatre could under one roof shelter the Naturalistic Theatre and the Theatre of Mood was due, I am convinced, to A. P. Chekhov who personally attended the rehearsals of his plays and with the charm of his personality and with frequent conversations influenced the actors, their tastes, and their ideas about the problem of art.

This new kind of theatre was created chiefly by a group of actors known as "Chekhovian actors." They performed all the Chekhov plays and can be considered the originators of the Chekhovian rhythmic diction. Whenever I remember the active part taken by these actors in creating *The Sea Gull's* characters and mood, I understand why I believe so strongly that the actor is the most important element on a stage. Neither the sets, nor the crickets, nor the horses' hooves on the boards could create *mood*, but only the extraordinary musicality of the performers who understood the rhythm of Chekhov's poetry and could veil his work in lunar mist.

In the first two productions (*The Sea Gull* and *Uncle Vanya*) the actors were perfectly *free* and the harmony was not disrupted. But later, the naturalist-director made the ensembles more important and lost the key to a Chekhov performance. Once the ensembles became important, the work of the actors became passive; but instead of encouraging the lyricism of this *new key*, the naturalistic director created atmosphere with external devices such as darkness, sounds, accessories, and characters, and soon lost his sense of direction because he did not realize how Chekhov changed from subtle realism to mystic lyricism.

Once the Moscow Art Theatre had decided how to produce Chekhov plays, it applied the same pattern to other authors. Ibsen and Maeterlinck were performed "in the manner of Chekhov."

I have already written about Ibsen in the Moscow Art Theatre. Maeterlinck was not approached by way of Chekhov's lyricism, but rationally. The actors in *Les Aveugles*[9] were treated as characters, and Death appeared as a tulle cloud. Everything was very complicated, as was generally the case in the Naturalistic Theatre, and *not at all* symbolic, as was Maeterlinck.

The Art Theatre could have extricated itself from the impasse in which it found itself by using Chekhov's lyrical talent, but instead it used more and more elaborate tricks, and finally even lost the key to

9. *The Blind* (1891) was performed in an evening of three Maeterlinck one-acts produced by the Moscow Art Theater in 1904; in their repertoire, it came directly after *The Cherry Orchard*.

performing its very own author, just as the Germans had lost the key to performing Hauptmann who besides his realistic plays had written dramas (*Schluck und Jau* and *Und Pippa Tanzt*)[1] which demanded an entirely different approach.

OTOMAR KREJČA

Otomar Krejča (b. 1921), a Czech director, opposed both socialist realistic and optimistic interpretations of Chekhov. His productions at the Theater Beyond the Gates outside Prague and throughout Europe presented a cruel, unsentimental Chekhov in a non-realistic scenography by Josef Svoboda; these included *The Seagull* (1960, 1972), *Three Sisters* (1965, 1980), *Ivanov* (1970), *Platonov* (1974), and *The Cherry Orchard* (1976, 1991). He often created a collage of the variants of the text and kept the whole company onstage during the performance.

Chekhov's Plays†

Chekhov does not depict ordinary everyday life—nor can he if a theatrical form is to take shape. He seizes on high points, festive occasions, often moments that are almost tempestuous. His everyday life is concentrated; his everyday situations are seen in their oddity, their singularity, and their uniqueness.

* * *

Outwardly, nothing happens—and suddenly there is a violent explosion. As if each element might explode if it were touched in a certain way—that's how unstable, how easily combustible Chekhov's milieu is. We are alarmed by it—we weren't prepared for it. The fires flare up for no apparent reason; only a series of "accidents" of this kind come together unexpectedly in the logical flow of Chekhovian existence.

* * *

Chekhov never denied truth—never tricked it, reformed it, embellished it, or obscured it. Every hint of tendentiousness is alien to his art. Even the intention he refers to—being ironical about the self, which his interpreters attributed to him, which I too can't help adopting when I try to formulate my thoughts about him.

1. Meyerhold had rehearsed *Schluck and Jau* (1900), a comedy about the nature of truth and illusion, for the Moscow Art Theater Studio in 1905, but it never opened; *And Pippa Dances* (1906) is a mixture of realism, symbolism, and mysticism about a girl loved by three men. [*Editor's note*.]

† From Otomar Krejča, "Les pièces de Tchékhov," *Le Travail théâtral* 26 (1978). Trans. by Laurence Senelick.

Chekhov is rigorous, incorruptible—he wrote with a scalpel—which ought to clarify the actors' relationship to his characters. In our author, things are never sentimental, everything is always functional to the nth degree and ruthlessly objective—that is, faithful to his research and his views on life, people, and the world. Chekhov views everything with an aloof, scrutinizing, ironical gaze, and he always sees with acuity—beneath the skin of things and creatures. Even when dealing with the most serious, most sacred things, when dealing with human life, death, the spiritual climate of the age, etc. Read *Ward No. 6!*[1] . . .

Chekhov's world is not static and flattened by the intrusion of a superficial ideology, a sociological, social, or moral set of conventions. It is not viewed through the pious wishes of a weakling. Chekhov was incapable of playing so ruthless a dirty trick on the truth of life.

He believed neither in a predetermined purpose for art nor in the function of so-called great ideas, even when they were his constant preoccupation. He presents his "subtext" in a diversified way, but never sells it to the highest bidder. He doesn't raise a flag, he raises facts.

What respect did Chekhov have for the "progressive" phase of society? In his work, the greatest, most sacred "truths" are not uttered by exemplary beings—anyway, he never created or saw such a creature or such a truth. If I listen to the voices of Vershinin, Medvedenko, Trofimov, and, say, the Jew Solomon (in the short story *The Steppe*), I cannot avoid the impression that the only spokesmen for "revolutionary" truths are zealots, half-crazies and crazies, the overwrought and those on the margins of society, who are trying unsuccessfully to break into it. Chekhov lent scant credence to verbal "deeds of valor."

Since Chekhov's day, there has been plenty of misunderstanding when it comes to finding a place for him. O irony, the baggage car which transported his coffin was marked "Oysters"! Something of the sort is happening to him today.

In his work, we are used to connecting author and characters imperceptibly. The author does not intervene obviously; it's as if he left his characters to act freely. The deeds, desires, feelings, and imaginations of Chekhovian characters are complicated, coupled urgently both with true reality and fictional reality. Their outward behavior is in complex and indirect relation to their inner motivations. It's as if in his plays Chekhov imitated the boundless range of everyday human relationships, habits, and experiences. He himself remains in the background; his characters speak for him. And,

1. *Ward No. 6* (*Palata No. 6*, 1892) is a dark story in which Chekhov asks whether it is safe (and sane) to opt out of the world and view it from a distance.

although he is present in each of them, one cannot discover a definite attitude through so many partial points of view.

There are almost no dramatic conflicts, in the usual sense of the term. His plays are not built on clashes of opposed intentions stripped bare. All the heavier is the weight of individual conflicts, which crystallize in the characters' desires, unattained or unattainable.

The starting point for the dissatisfaction of all the characters is to be found most often in their desire for something better, higher. Hence the impatience of these people, their groping fears—out of which their inner activity, not the least important sort, explodes. It's precisely from that activity, from its abundant inner imagery, that the personalities of the characters are born: the actor cannot create them any other way, say by a heavy application of elements of external characterization.

The unattainable desires and false illusions of Chekhov's characters are so strong that they bind them and hold them firmly together in their attitude to the future. When the mental contortion becomes unbearable for the characters and they explode, they are often opened up to their core. After such a breakdown, when the frustrated soul seeks a refuge, when pain bursts without complexity, the actor has to give himself completely, to his very core. Chekhov's characters are not the puppets of their own boredom; they do not run themselves down or comment on themselves. They are energetic, coherent individuals. The moment of breakdown acts like a natural disaster; like a natural disaster, it is, so to speak, tranquil.

* * *

The characters must not be treated from the very start "in a Chekhovian manner," but as individuals who have been shipwrecked in life, individuals dedicated to illusions that have broken down, people with insoluble fates doomed to tragic feelings. Both at the beginning or the end, they believe that everything will be all right; they are not looking for despair, they do not rush towards suffering like moths to a flame, they force themselves to avoid it. So much so that in *The Seagull*, for example, no one believes in that gunshot they hear. The actors must carefully preserve this feeling of a vital, hopeful activity of their own.

Every character has at least one moment when he bursts into tears. These tears are something strange, terrible, like a tightly woven fabric accidentally ripped apart. It's not the same thing as the tears of women "who gush" to the tune of "wait, you'll see what I'm capable of"! Chekhov himself made interesting statements about the tears and the tearful tone of his characters.

Even the supreme inner exaltation, even the most overwhelming

events, are inserted into the grayness of life and act as if they were
an integral part of it. How immovable is the power of mundane life
for Chekhov's characters, how they arm themselves with it against
one another, how they hide behind it, how they find the necessary
comfort and solidarity in it! . . . And how powerless are the great
movements of the soul to modify the strongest desires, as the characters continue, despite it all, to do what they feel like doing! . . .
What self-control they demonstrate, how strong their will when it's
a matter of getting to the railway station on time! . . .

                              *   *   *

In Chekhov, there is an unknown, limitless reality beneath the text.
The text permits us only to glimpse its secrets. If an image of human
discourse is to be created onstage, we have to X-ray the text, both in
its relations with the real world and in the mystification in which the
characters take refuge. Every line is only a key to something else,
and this something else goes far beyond the characters even when
they are "merely" chatting. A single word or an exclamation repeated
can radiate to an immense range. Dialogue composed of pauses,
silences, interrupted sentences, and allusions also radiates. There
are often gaps, and often that is where the essential thing takes place.
The run-on monologue makes an effect of contrast in the script; it
pushes the character even further away from the reality he wants to
come in contact with; it brings him no relief or greater understanding
or the unity devoutly to be wished—rather, it creates an even more
profound rift. It also seems that dialogue is there because people
cannot understand one another. Then too, Chekhov's dialogue
sometimes sounds like a conversation of fluttering doves, like echo-
less cries in a desert landscape. Each character goes his merry way,
and during that energetic search for harmony an even more profound
desiccation occurs.

When they speak of themselves, Chekhov's characters are incapable of verbally formulating their desires to their own satisfaction,
although they go to great lengths to do so. When they speak of themselves, and they often do, they can barely enunciate a statement (nor
is it indirect information they impart to the spectator): most of the
time, the spectator encounters a character in a struggle with or a
polemic against himself, of a wish taken to be a reality. That is why
it is rarely worth the trouble to seek out the direct meaning of a
speech: the words habitually hide something more than or different
from what the characters say. If the characters have something on
their chest, they let it be known deviously; they expressly sit in such
a way that there is apparently no connection between their words
and what brought them up. The real stimulus of the words, their true
meaning, their true intentions, and the true desire of the character

do not enter directly into the dialogue, but only in various disguises. This is the "falsehood" of Chekhov's characters. This does not mean, however, that the true meaning disappears, that what the character really wants to communicate is lost, that in performance it is transformed into sheer untruth. On the contrary, the language of Chekhov's characters closely resembles its elementary veiled, manipulated stimuli, its true meaning, intentions, and wishes. That is probably what gives rise to that famous and so decried Chekhovian halftone. What we are dealing with is a frequent opening-up of language: an ambiguity, a double meaning. The intended sense does not enter directly into the expression; it does not enter immediately, without control. The manipulation of the real meaning renders the expression confused, irresolute, shaky, as if its color had been leached from it. Rather than color, we ought to say: its proper color.

A writer like Chekhov, so reserved and so true to life, constrains the director as well as the actors to be as farsighted as possible. What happened to Treplyov in *The Seagull* between his first confession and his suicide at the end of the play? And what, in *Three Sisters*, happened between Vershinin's "I love, I love" and his escape at the head of his regiment? Between Ivanov's "new beginning" and his suicide? Nothing "happened"—the characters have remained themselves, true to their wishes and desires. The innocent seeds have sprouted, only "something" has ripened.

The author has brought together so much truth that it defies any analysis. Can one make sense of a melodrama carved out of living bodies by a scalpel? Can one make sense of farcical episodes treated sadly, dubiously, and shamefully, or else a patchwork of dreary feelings? That would be a very dangerous approach for the actor in his work: the actor must grasp the whole of the material head on; he has no right to show the seamy side that reveals how the material is woven and sewn.

Chekhov gives his characters the responsibility—and the license— to lead a normal life. He does not bring them to life only through words, he charges them to live, even when they are silent. If an actor takes this marvelous opportunity for his character as a disagreeable task, it may be that the one line he says may destroy half an act.

Most of Chekhov's dialogue has an everyday, familiar character (it is not the "vehicle of action"). It testifies to the fact that every word (and every non-word) opens up gigantic spaces of inner life, that the acting cannot be conveyed by the word, that the characters really exist, must really be and possess their power of radiation through their sheer existence. This means that the actor is constantly being solicited, that he plays at once through the non-word and through the word, often even *more* through the non-word, more through his apparently indirect participation than through his avowed activity.

* * *

Tradition has made the pauses in Chekhov a reservoir of melancholy atmosphere, a sign (or rather a phantom) of the author's method; it has romanticized them, it has covered the characters with a thick layer of jam in which they drown as in a swamp: in the pause, the progress of the action slows down most of the time like a fly caught in flypaper. Ridiculous! . . . I am hardly exaggerating when I claim that the Chekhovian pause is instead a collision, an accident, a derangement—especially in the everyday activity of the characters, in their desires and their interests.

In Chekhov's plays, all the characters are equally important in their essence. The aggregate of their speeches and the number of situations in which they participate directly has nothing to do with the significance or "beauty" of the role. Behind each role lies the image of a complete human being that values none of the theatrical "hits" of conventional playing, but rather a humble and continuous liberation. Chekhov's characters do not yield to each incitement; they do not impose themselves on the actor's attention, nor let themselves be caught by any gimmick.

One must not "improve" Chekhov by embellishing his characters, deliberately or accidentally. The dramatist Chekhov knew how to write what he wanted, and what he had made up his mind to, and he could write it in a precise, natural, accessible manner. If we stage his plays, we should believe that that is the right way, even if it isn't that way "in reality." It is that way in *our* reality.

How rich and strange is the reality made by his demands! How firmly, how deeply the actors must anchor themselves in the characters and their world to be able to react naturally and fully! How tight and rigorous the acting of the ensemble must be!

* * *

GIORGIO STREHLER

Giorgio Strehler (1921–1997) was an Italian director, co-founder of the Piccolo Teatro di Milano (1947–68, 1972–82), and artistic director of the Theater of Europe, Paris (1982–89). A socially committed Brechtian, he found exquisite visual metaphors for Chekhov, Goldoni, Pirandello, and Shakespeare. His second production of *The Cherry Orchard* (1974) was one of the seminal reinterpretations of Chekhov on the twentieth-century stage and exercised immense influence throughout the world.

Notes on *The Cherry Orchard*†

* * *

The problem of the "cherry orchard" is fundamental. None of us has ever managed to render poetically, symbolically, and physically this orchard, which may represent too many things at once to be capable of "representation," at least by making visual a naturalism which has consequently become "poetic" realism.

The route chosen by Svoboda[1] and others, that is, symbolic abstraction, not only of the orchard but all the other locales in Chekhov in general, has led to results that are certainly interesting at times and even poetically rich. But the problem has been, so to speak, turned inside-out. Despite it all, when old Pitoëff[2] staged *The Cherry Orchard* in front of a gray velvet cyclorama with a few sticks of furniture and said that Chekhov was nothing more than an "atmosphere of words," he was performing the same operation with more ingenuity and less pretentiousness.

In reality, today we realize that we must stage Chekhov not in imitation of Stanislavsky (and it has been our task to conquer that dimension), but in another perspective instead. This perspective must be more universal and symbolic, more open to fantastic approaches, even if it runs the terrible risk of lapsing into a sort of one-size-fits-all abstraction. The risk is that one will leach all meaning from Chekhov's physical reality, that is, from things: the rooms, tables, chairs, windows—leach all meaning from things and also from history. For spectators "see" history as environment, as costumes, faces, hair, eyeglasses, detachable collars, etc. The rest is obviously necessary, that is, the history in the interior of things and characters. But to isolate an act of a Chekhov play in an "abstract setting," in a symbolic void, is to remove a physical "reality" from history. It comes down to saying that this act is unfolding today and forever. Now, the constant problem with Chekhov is what I call the "three Chinese boxes."

There are three boxes: one nested inside the other, the last contains the next to the last, the next to the last contains the first.

The first box is that of *Reality* (possible reality which, in the theater, is as far as reality can go), and the narrative is an interesting, human narrative. It is wrong to say, for instance, that *The Cherry*

† From Giorgio Strehler, *Per un teatro umano. Pensieri scritti, parlati ed attuati* (Milan: Giangiacomo Feltrinelli, 1974). Trans. by Laurence Senelick.

1. Josef Svoboda (1920–2003), Czech scenographer, whose Chekhov productions for Otomar Krejča discarded naturalistic scenery for a more symbolic approach. [*Editor's note.*]

2. Georges Pitoëff (Georgy Pitoev, 1884–1939), Tbilisi-born French director and actor, whose Parisian productions of Chekhov relied on draperies and minimal set pieces to create an atmosphere. [*Editor's note.*]

Orchard has no "entertaining" plot. On the contrary, it is full of theatrical moments: events, discoveries, atmospheres, characters who change. It is a very lovely human story, a moving human adventure. In this first box, therefore, we tell the story of the family of Gaev and Lyubov and the other characters. And it is a real story, certainly situated in history, in life in general, but its interest resides precisely in showing how and where the characters actually live. It is a "realistic" interpretative vision, similar to an excellent reconstruction, as one might handle it in an atmospheric film.

The second box is, on the other hand, the *History* box. Here, adventures of the family are seen entirely from a historical standpoint, one which was present in the first box, but only as a remote background, an almost invisible trace. Here history is more than "costumes" or "props"; it is the whole point of the narrative. What is most interesting here is the movement of social classes in their dialectical relationship; the modification of characters and things considered as transfers of property. The characters themselves are, certainly, "human beings," with precise, individual personalities, particular clothes or faces, but they represent—in the foreground—a part of history on the move: they are the bourgeois owners in the act of dying of apathy and resignation, the new capitalist class that is rising and taking possession of chattels, the whole young and inchoate revolution that is making itself heard, and so on. Here, the rooms, objects, things, clothes, gestures, while retaining their verisimilitudinous nature, are somewhat "displaced"; they are "distanced" in the discourse and perspective of history. Of course, the second box contains the first, but that is exactly why it is larger. The two boxes complete one another.

Finally, the third box is the box of *Life*: the big box of the human adventure; of man born, growing up, living, loving, not loving, winning, losing, understanding, misunderstanding, passing, and dying. It is an "eternal" parable (inasmuch as the brief passage of man on this earth can be eternal). And here the characters are still envisaged within the truth of a narrative, in the reality of a "political" history on the move, but also in a quasi-metaphysical dimension, in a sort of parable about human destiny. There are the old, the intermediate generations; the younger, the very young; there are masters, servants, half-masters; the circus girl, the animal, the comedian, and so on; a sort of picture of the ages of man and men. The house is "The House," the rooms are "The Rooms of Man," and history becomes a grand poetic paraphrase which excludes neither narrative nor history, but in which history is contained entirely within the great adventure of human beings as human beings, human flesh passing by.

This last box takes the production to the "symbolic and meta-

physico-allusive" slope—I can't find the exact word. It is largely puri-
fied of anecdote, raised to another level, flies very high.

Each of these boxes has its own aspect and its own danger. The
first represents the danger of pedantic minutiae, of the "taste" for
reconstruction (very Visconti),[3] of the narrative seen through the
"keyhole" and practically stopping there. The second is the danger
of isolating the characters as historical symbols, that is, freezing
them, petrifying them in a historic thematic (Marx, critic of Lassalle's
Sickingen,[4] et cetera; for example, "doing Schiller"), stripping the
genuine humanity from the characters to turn them into historic
symbols. The perennial student is no longer the perennial student
because he is one, but because history needs there to be a perennial
student who represents a part of oppressed society, old before his
time because he may have been in prison, representing the rising
new world with its uncertainties and its convulsions: he is the future,
there's something heroic and positive about him, much more than
negative. And Lyubov and Gaev are tender wastrels, but they are also
"vicious"; they are symbols of a "fallen" class. (In a Czechoslovakian
staging, Lyubov let the manservant Yasha knead her thighs beneath
her skirts. And Dunyasha—another example—in the last act
appeared manifestly pregnant. All this in homage perhaps to up-to-
date pan-eroticism, beyond which there is no modern theater!) The
setting is still the same as before, but already more transposed, more
emphatic now that it's taken to be a precarious milieu perhaps, old
and falling to pieces.

The third would risk being merely "abstract." Merely metaphysical.
Almost outside time. A neutral milieu. A stage hung with colored
cloth, with a few elements behind it. (Here we are back to Pitoëff,
perhaps with the clever techniques of Svoboda: it makes no difference.) The characters are dressed, but accurately "in period": they
try rather to become universal emblems, I'm not sure by what means
or methods. But the whole production becomes abstract, symbolic,
universal, almost losing its earthly gravity.

Now, Chekhov's *Cherry Orchard* is all three boxes in one, each in
the other. Together. Because every great poet for all time moves, if
he is truly a poet, on all three planes at once; and one can isolate
these three planes only in play or careful study, like the entomologist
who dissects a living being to study a few characteristics *in vitro*.[5]

* * *

3. Luchino Visconti (Count di Modrone, 1906–1975), Italian director, whose productions
of *Three Sisters* (1952, with Marcello Mastroianni), *Uncle Vanya* (1955) and *The Cherry
Orchard* (1965) were replete with period details and veristic settings. [*Editor's note.*]
4. *Franz von Sickingen* was the only play of the German socialist Ferdinand Lasalle (1825–
64); his colleague Karl Marx (1818–83) condemned it as "a work of no poetic value."
[*Editor's note.*]
5. Latin, "in the test tube." [*Editor's note.*]

A "correct" production should stage for us the three perspectives put together, sometimes giving us a closeup of a hand or a heart moving, sometimes letting history pass before our eyes, sometimes questioning us about the destiny of our humanity, which is born and must grow old and die no matter what anyone says, including Marx. A "correct" stage setting must be capable of flickering like a light, which oscillates to this triple stimulus . . .

*   *   *

It is the orchard properly speaking that is the locale of the crystallization of history, it is the hero of the play; and that is precisely why it is enormously difficult to interpret.

Not to show it, to let it be imagined, is a mistake. To show it, to make it tangible is another mistake. The orchard must exist, it must be something seen and almost felt (I'm coming around to the idea of an aroma or only an aroma, through acting!), but it cannot not be "a whole." Because the whole is concentrated in it.

*   *   *

Real time in *The Cherry Orchard* does not correspond to theatrical time.

Or else . . . it is one of those diabolically cryptic instructions of old Anton Pavlovich that drove Stanislavsky crazy.

The first act: it begins at two o'clock; by the end of the act, it is already "almost three o'clock." How long does the act last, performed at its proper rhythm? Forty minutes? That's too long. I don't believe it, despite the rhetoric of the pause in our interpretations of Chekhov. But now we are at the reverse rhetoric. The truth is that Chekhov has a rhythm of his own, an interior rhythm that is what it is. It has to be discovered beyond language, beyond habits, ways of speaking, our fantasies. Certainly, it is a more sustained rhythm than the one we used to use. It is more fluid, less emphatic, less "fatalistic."

But just because Chekhov said it is "almost a farce," one must not play it as a "sketch"! One must not be afraid of silence, if it is necessary. A forty-minute first act. We arrive there at real time and theatrical time combined.

The second act: real and theatrical time combined. Twilight, lasting thirty minutes?

The third: here too, real and theatrical time combined.

The fourth: it certainly must last twenty minutes or nineteen, as Chekhov says. And he expressly gives the direction: "In twenty minutes you've got to be in the carriage. The train leaves in forty-six minutes."

Remember that Chekhov writes that good old Konstantin made

the last act last about forty-five minutes and he clearly told him that it had to last nineteen. He leaves one minute for the departure of the carriages! "Can you imagine?" as Pishchik would say.

The time of *The Cherry Orchard* therefore corresponds mysteriously to real time. And as such, it must not be artificial. The rhythm of the last act seems rather steady, but it husbands its space in silence. One would have to ascertain the rhythm of Russian diction (at the linguistic level); and then that of the actors: it could not fail to be slow, due to habit. Hence, probably, the double indication "farce" meaning "not tearful," or "serious" or "slow in the Russian fashion." That's all. "Be lighter, more fluid, simpler, less fatalistic, less dramatic, also be more joyful, as in life. Life transposed, but life. As for my direction 'through tears,' I mean only that such was the inner state of mind of the character; I didn't mean he's crying. It's a conventional way of expressing oneself." Poor Chekhov! So many misunderstandings of this conventional way. Certainly, when Chekhov writes that he is in the act of writing a "completely comic" play, and then it turns out to be *The Cherry Orchard*, one may wonder what was going through his mind at the time. But one must reflect on the delicate Chekhovian irony, his indirect way of saying things, of addressing his critics: perhaps it all gets easier.

* * *

Time. Problems of time. In this vaudeville-tragedy-comedy-farce-drama, in this whole that seems always to grow greater, denser, more perfect in its limpidity, I would say, in its innocence. I am listening to Mozart, the quintet K 516, and I think about Mozart's limpidity . . . so true and so profound . . . The idea of time is fundamental.

I note today—for the first time, it seems—an obvious fact, but a fact on which I have perhaps never reflected enough: Lyubov has been away for five years. When she comes back, Lopakhin wonders, "Will she recognize me?" And then again, "Who knows what she'll be like now?" Then Dunyasha isn't recognized by Yasha. And Trofimov isn't recognized by Lyubov. And continually throughout the whole first act, the characters look around and say again and again that "the rooms have stayed the same, so has the orchard" and again and again how the characters have changed, entirely or almost. Even Firs: "How old he's grown!" Lyubov says, "Thank God, you're still alive!"

It is clear that things do not change, do not move—orchards, objects, walls, rooms, and furniture . . . (I think now of the superb opening of Comisso's *Gioventà che muore*,[6] with this woman who, in the snow, sun and blue sky, feels for the first time that these things

6. *Dying Youth*, a novel by Giovanni Comisso (1895–1969). [*Editor's note.*]

will stay this way forever while she will grow old and die: the ecstasy of static nature, while human beings are transient).

Then too, humans are transient in haste. Five years are enough to change them all. In this sense, the five years spent abroad represent a lifetime. They seem longer, subjectively and objectively. These five years represent not only five years, but *time passing and altering*. Hence this feeling of uncertainty between what has changed too much and what has not moved. This act so suspended, so hesitant, those footsteps backward in the past, while everyone is involved with the present and projecting into the future . . . that return to child-hood, in the sleepiness of dawn, in the inner and outer lassitude, in this exhaustion of nerves overstrained by too much life and cof-fee . . .

*   *   *

The second act of *The Cherry Orchard* takes place in the open air, the only act that does. It has the aspect of an "interlude," of a cantata for several voices in the four-act ensemble. In all the others, some-thing "happens": even lots of things happen. In the second act, there is a halting of real action, an ineluctable immobility of figures who "are there," sitting after a stroll, "waiting for the sun to go down," looking at the landscape, talking, and chatting.

And life is obviously going by, like Montale's little boats in a stream;[7] even if the characters remain physically motionless, the action continues on the inside; even if the plot is suspended, in a stupefied pause, a turning-back on itself, a lyrical meditation that requires only gestures, barely varied. (The example could be that of people who, smoking a cigarette, make the classic gestures of a smoker, but each one of these smokers repeats the gestures in his own way, according to his own rhythm, attentively or inattentively, with or without sensual pleasure, indifferently; but smoking is the unique gesture, identical to everyone.)

*   *   *

In the second act, for the first time we register the famous "sound" of the snapped string—a problem against which all stage directors have banged their heads. I do not believe that the demystifying solu-tion of certain directors nowadays—striking a little gong to change "the atmosphere"—is a good one. Better nothing, courageously. And why not? Why couldn't this sonic symbol be something the charac-ters hear in the twilight—"they" hear it, and we, the audience looking on, do not? I know that it may be a way of simplifying or avoiding the difficulty (or rather, it may seem that way), but one must not

7. A reference to a well-known poem by Eugenio Montale. [*Editor's note*.]

hear this sound clearly! It must remain indeterminate, described in the talk of the actor-characters. This is not an easy solution.

* * *

Each character will have jumped up, everyone will look around and lend an ear in different directions, sometimes opposing ones. One of them will come down to the footlights, perhaps step towards the audience, looking for the "sound" in the orchestra, questioning the orchestra with a look and a little gesture. But no one will manage to discover the "point" from which the "inner" sound has come. This sound is a quavering of history that the characters explain as banally as possible. Only Lyubov says, "I don't know why, but I don't like it." The quavering of history cannot be made symbolic or objective by a sound. Not even with the "genius" of Stanislavsky and Danchenko.

Today, until someone proves the contrary, I believe this famous sound to be a literary illusion, a sediment of writing to evoke a sonorous fact, which has the aspect of an objective theatricality. And that it surely does: it seems done on purpose to give a rhythmic bounce to the end of the last act, for example. But that is exactly where it is demystified as such; as one more expedient. I believe that no one can refuse the idea according to which the same sound heard in the second act, repeated in the last when the stage is empty, with Firs motionless, in his real and apparent death, is not necessary—is even superfluous. All the more so since with this sound there are the famous axe blows on the cherry trees. So much so that I do not believe in realizing it with a "sound," but instead with a "silent sound," more sonorous than a blade or a gunshot.

* * *

The scenery itself has come to define that white space imagined by Chekhov in his letter from Yalta of October 5. In this letter, there is an incredible concentration of "time": he speaks of a white summer garden, all white, totally white, with ladies dressed in white. A moment later he adds, "Outside, it is snowing." Extraordinary, this double image, summer-winter, combined in whiteness: eternal whiteness of this garden beneath the white flowers of springtime and the snow of winter. I am therefore sure that *The Cherry Orchard* was born in Chekhov's mind as a shooting flash of white, a whiteness "for all seasons."

* * *

This Chekhov—all Chekhov—is alive for me. He is not a poet of renunciation and despair. Nevertheless, he does know pain, the very pain of being alive and doing, to the end, what needs to be done.

Yes, *The Cherry Orchard* is a masterpiece, at every level. *The Cherry Orchard* is perhaps the greatest example of the best that bourgeois society has left us, in the theatrical sphere, in a self-awareness that other plays are incapable of achieving.

JEAN-LOUIS BARRAULT

Jean-Louis Barrault (1910–1994), a French mime, actor, and director, directed only one Chekhov play over the course of his long career: *The Cherry Orchard* (1954), in a translation by Georges Neveux. Barrault played Trofimov, with his wife, Madeleine Renaud, as Ranevskaya. The production was adapted to French tastes and managed to acclimatize the play to the Parisian stage.

Why *The Cherry Orchard*?†

I maintain that *The Cherry Orchard* is Chekhov's masterpiece. Of the four great plays he wrote for the theater, its generalizations are the most compelling and it comes closest to being universal.

While reflecting the Russian soul in a striking way, it spontaneously breaks away from it, and, thus projected into space, reverberates in the souls of all humanity.

At every level.

The Cherry Orchard is born first of SILENCE. It is a vast pantomime that unfolds over the course of two hours, adorned now and then with verbal devices, true poetry, much as a beautiful jewel is attached here and there to an ordinary necklace.

The rest? A discreet setting of short lines that highlight this rare silence.

The Cherry Orchard flows as slowly as life. It is a brook that babbles as delicately as a soul. Few other plays provide us this "physical" impression of time passing.

This is because, starting fundamentally from silence, it is exceptional in reproducing the PRESENT. Now, theater is the very art of the present.

This is what is *essential* to the theater.

In life, the present is the most difficult thing to grasp. No wonder that *The Cherry Orchard* is also difficult to grasp. The proper action of *The Cherry Orchard* takes place in silence, and the lines of the dialogue, beyond those isolated poetic speeches that gleam like jewels, are there, as in music, only to make the silence vibrate.

† J.-L. Barrault, "Pourquoi *La Cerisaie*?", in *Cahiers de la compagnie Madeleine Renaud-Jean-Louis Barrault* 6 (Julliard 1954), 87–97. Trans. by Laurence Senelick.

This silence at grips with time, that inflexible time that marches before us, beneath us, and behind us, immediately transforms this COMING FUTURE into MEMORY OF THE PAST.

We say that time passes. What does this mean? For it is all action. It passes life through a strainer [*passoire*]. With the aid of its magic strainer, it turns what happened to us, which exists only inchoately, into something finished that will henceforth exist only in memory. A purée of memory.

Coffee is a solid powder. It is "passed" through the coffee filter and becomes a liquid.

What is time doing? Hush! It is at work . . .

At what? It is "passing."

It is this mysterious, hard-to-grasp "passing" that forms our "present." Existence is manipulated by astonishing sleight of hand, performed by that surprising prestidigitator, time.

"Do you see this deck of cards?" someone says in *The Cherry Orchard*. And we assume the deck of cards to be life.

"Take one" (the moment you are about to live).

"Take a good look at it, put it back in the deck" (present action).

"*Ein, zwei, drei!* It is . . . in your pocket" (with your handkerchief on top of it, old boy! The present is past, it's over!)

So it is with *The Cherry Orchard*. It is a play about time passing. It doesn't matter whether the subject is Russian or Japanese. It is a universal masterpiece. On a par with certain works of Shakespeare or Molière, it is a masterpiece that ought to belong to our universal heritage.

But, just as British genius is the best at dealing with madness, just as French perspicacity is best found in the study of the heart's torments, the Russian temperament is the best prepared to apprehend present time. Does not the Russian temperament straddle the East and the West, just as the present straddles the future and the past? As international as *The Cherry Orchard* may be, we nevertheless pay homage to the Russian soul for opening the way into this intimate and infinitesimal perception of time passing.

Built on silence and living only in the present, the dramatic structure of this work is fundamentally *musical*. And the present is so elusive that once a theme is initiated, the author cannot develop it, still less complete it; he must pass to the next theme. Even if he could complete it, he wouldn't. A deadly fatality weighs on *The Cherry Orchard*; we barely skim its surface when we stop, then hide to avoid it. Thus it is that we pass from an everyday moment to an emotional moment, from that feeling to a general speculation, from this speculation to an outburst, from such clowning to social issues, and so on, without ever exhausting any of these moments, which are only evasions of a danger to which we constantly return. A succession of moments of inertia jolted by somersaults, as if to escape that magnetic attraction that draws us towards disaster . . . just as when we try to stay awake for fear we might die in our sleep.

This non-consummation of each moment leaves behind a silent residue of anguish that constitutes the real subject of play.

If a composer were to apply this subtle mode of theatrical composition to his art, it is likely that his music would be ultra-modern. Themes barely stated before they immediately vanish, as if consumed by fire; a seeming incoherence whose secret ramifications follow a profoundly thought-out technique.

The outcome of this dramatic composition, inspired by sophisticated music, is that the dramatic movement of the action is very tricky to handle; it is first and foremost a *slow* movement.

And that is something else I love about *The Cherry Orchard*. The dramatic rhythm of a stageplay does not correspond to the rapidity of events or the speed with which the characters are acted. It is a matter of density, not of velocity.

The dramatic rhythm of a work is effective when each moment is filled to capacity.

Nowadays it is customary to say that there is little action in Chekhov—the recent *Dictionary of Literary Works* even cites *The Cherry Orchard* in this regard!—This must be taken to mean that in Chekhov there are few contrived actions, few interwoven events, no complicated plots; but that does not mean that there is little action. Do not confuse Action and Plot. "Let what you do be always simple, and unified," says Horace. And Racine adds, "All invention consists in making something out of nothing."[1] In *The Cherry Orchard*, in fact, action is constant, taut and complete, for, once again, every moment is well filled. Every instant has its own density, but this density is not in the dialogue; it is in the silence, in life flowing by.

The subject of *Three Sisters* can be summed up this way:

We really want to go to the city.

Will we go to the city?

We shall not go to the city.

The only catalyst ("the objective" Stanislavsky used to talk about)[2] that exists in the play to effect the accomplishment of this unique and simple action is the military men.

In *The Cherry Orchard*, it is the catalyst itself which supplies the action: the estate of the cherry orchard.

1. Horace (Quintus Hortius Flaccus, Roman poet and satirist (65–8 B.C.), whose *Ars Poetica* became a code of laws for neoclassic writers. Jean Baptiste Racine (1639–1699), leading French tragic dramatist of the age of Louis XIV. [*Editor's note.*]
2. The "objective" is the usual translation of Stanislavsky's term *zadacha* (task, problem), which the actor must discover and solve at each moment of a play. [*Editor's note.*]

Act One: The cherry orchard is at risk of being sold.

Act Two: The cherry orchard is about to be sold.

Act Three: The cherry orchard is being sold.

Act Four: The cherry orchard has been sold.

As for the rest: life.

There is the house slumbering in the night—waiting—arrivals—coffee drinking—a telegram is torn up—going to bed—morning dawns—the birds awake.

A small group of persons sit in turn on the same bench, like flocks of swallows that gather on the same telegraph wire—Jewish musicians go by in the distance—the moon rises.

There is dancing—another telegram is torn up—a few glasses of kvas are handed around—card tricks are performed—two characters come back from town.

Now the cherry orchard has to be abandoned—trunks are packed—furniture is piled up—the harness bells on the horses jingle in the yard—the shutters are closed—the old walls are looked at one last time—it's over.

The house that, two hours earlier was awaiting life like a woman's womb ready to give birth is now a glacial tomb from which all life has fled.

This life made up of silence, these themes of transitory action mysteriously bound together, and this painful and anguished slowness in the unfolding of the action provide exciting problems for French actors.

To control his acting, the French actor is used to relying on the text, for in French drama the action is commonly enclosed in the text. But here, the acting takes place outside the text.

When the action is nestled in the text, and not outside the text, the action unfolds at a more rapid rate. The French actor is therefore essentially a rapid actor. The rhythm of *The Cherry Orchard* is slow, even for Russians. Now French slowness is not the same as Russian slowness.

Therefore *The Cherry Orchard, in French*, must unfold *for the French* with a French slowness and not with a Russian slowness that would make sense only to Russians.

But this slowness constitutes an excellent exercise for a French company—a true lesson in the *density of life*.

So, few plays involve actors as much as a play such as *The Cherry Orchard* does.

Rare is the actor who manages to lose himself in the play; but it does happen on occasion. When it does, the actor lives one of the best moments of his artistic life.

Rarer still is the company that manages to lose itself. *The Cherry*

Orchard is one of those very rare works in which an entire company can lose itself, ceasing to believe that it is in a theater, believing firmly that this *family* exists, that this *house* exists, and that this is *life*.

This unique metamorphosis is accomplished on a firm foundation; for the play belongs neither to naturalism, vintage 1904, nor even to realism. It belongs to truth; a truth that, with its two faces (truth always has two faces), is composed both of reality and poetry, the obvious and the hidden. It is, if you like, poetic realism—like Shakespeare.

At least, that is what we hope to present. For the rest, our love for *The Cherry Orchard* is so great that it permits us to "devour" it in our own way: love is more precious than respect.

But our love for *The Cherry Orchard* does not stop there.

The Cherry Orchard is comparable to nesting tables that fold into one another almost infinitely.

The intimate, familiar, common, everyday subject evolves irresistibly from the specific to the generic, like Japanese flowers that grow miraculously in a glass of water as soon as their mysteriously compressed packet has been thrown into it.

The Cherry Orchard has the value of a "parable." Starting from daily life it unfolds, imperceptibly, to the furthest limits of the metaphysical spheres.

Most remarkable of all, starting from the individual observed in his familiar and workaday universe, *The Cherry Orchard* rapidly reaches the vantage point of society in general. Nor does it stop there: it rises again to locate the individual, viewed this time from a broader, more philosophic, more universal angle. That is precisely what makes it a very great play.

Let us look at this evolution in detail.

At the play's center of gravity is a woman, full of charm, generous, unself-conscious to the point of amorality. She represents that enduring type of human being, weak, passionate, attractive in "that virtue prone to weakness," that is the stuff of real heroes. Her heart on her sleeve, a sinner filled with love, she scatters her money without counting it. Lyuba is the very symbol of humanity—the human being for all eternity. Around her, three men like the three angles of a triangle, who are the eternal representatives of social trends at odds with one another. Gaev personifies the older generation, the old civilization, and tradition—a whole social organization of a world which has had its day and has lost its vigor, an era that seems already to be fading away and inspires nostalgia even before it disappears, a way of life that is passing and can never return. Yet it is also a way of life that people loved, and there were good reasons to love it!

At the tip of the second angle is Lopakhin, the son of a serf, a peasant; a worker, a businessman, proud of his brand-new strength but somewhat ashamed of his persisting imperfections. He respects and still loves this world that is about to "pass away." He would like to save it, but social currents are stronger than he is one has to replace what is departing, what is irremediably disappearing. In spite of himself, Lopakhin is led to buy this cherry orchard, the symbol of a superannuated world. He has the idea of using it in a modern way, subdividing the estate into lots to build cottages. In a prophetic manner, he heralds the first revolution, which will break out a year later in 1905.

If Gaev represents the past, Lopakhin represents the present.

But everything in the present must, in turn, disappear; which is why Chekhov contrasts Lopakhin with another character, the third angle of our triangle: Trofimov, the perennial student. He, a prophet in embryo who will not come to fruition but who nevertheless heralds the imminent future, predicts to Lopakhin that these "tenants" of today, occupying his cottages, will become the landowners of tomorrow, and that everything will start all over again. Trofimov, a potential revolutionary rather than a true revolutionary—a *virtual* revolutionary, if you like—heralds the second revolution, that of 1917, and generally proclaims that every social revolution will be succeeded by another. Think of Trotsky's permanent revolution.[3]

Chekhov develops all these social positions, so crucial for our generation, with tact and moderation that compel the admiration of even the most finicky Frenchman. No heaviness: the touch is almost glancing. This social theme of *The Cherry Orchard* has the lightness of a feather. Its range is nonetheless effective, like pricks of acupuncture in Chinese medicine, it provokes formidable repercussions in the spectator that go beyond the "specific Russian case." They touch each of us, both in space (everyone in the world feels touched) and time (everyone feels that this is valid for every age). This is because the *social plane* has been transcended.

If a group of individuals becomes a case for sociology, sociology that attains the absolute becomes a science that concerns the *eternal Individual*.

In one of his speeches, Trofimov gives us the exact key to this new development that attains a universal plane: "It's so clear, isn't it, that before we start living in the present, we must first atone for our past, put an end to it, and we can atone for it only through suffering, only through extraordinary, unremitting labor." This sentence is obviously addressed to a whole generation, a whole society, even to the religious idea of redemption; but it can also be addressed plain and

---

3. Leon Trotsky (Lyov Davydovich Bronshtein, 1877–1940), a Russian revolutionary, advocated permanent world revolution, in opposition to Stalin's "revolution in a single country." [*Editor's note.*]

simply, throughout the ages, to every one of us, to the individual at his most general.

A human being, like societies and civilizations, is born, lives, dies, and is replaced. Isn't it said that three weeks are enough for all our animal cells to be replaced? Every three weeks, consequently, a human being becomes brand-new! Within him permanently there live the three types of man Chekhov puts on stage: Gaev, the being who is gradually disappearing; Lopakhin, the being who is due to replace him for the moment; Trofimov, who is already preparing the being who is to replace Lopakhin. One is the past, another is the present, the third is the future: the polarization of the eternal human being.

That is why *The Cherry Orchard* expresses the passing of life so well.

However adhesive our past may be, however attached to it we are and for legitimate reasons, we must win the right to welcome the future, to be admitted into the future; and to do that, at the cost of a terrifying and persistant effort, at the very cost of suffering, we must have the courage to tear ourselves away from that past. That is the purchase price of the right to live—the redemption, the ransom demanded by life.

"Good-bye, old life!"

"Hello, new life!" they shout towards the end. And while eyes are reddened by tears, teeth are already bared in a morning smile. That's life. That's the lesson of *The Cherry Orchard*. That's what is represented, on a plane superior to the social plane, by the three men with whom Chekhov surrounds Lyuba Ranevskaya, a moving symbol of eternal humanity . . . on the march.

The Cherry Orchard is not therefore a realistic play, nor it is a social play. Chekhov was too sophisticated to limit himself to the social plane; it is a play by a great poet who, with his profound heart and his exceptional antennae, goes beyond the social—which is granted its due importance—to the very sources of existence.

Another lesson from *The Cherry Orchard*: Chekhov, in dealing with his subject, shows us what an *artist* has to be. Hypocritical modesty generally prevents us from using the word *artist*. The artist is above all a *witness to his times*. The artist must therefore make a great effort to be first and foremost the servant of JUSTICE. How can one be a partisan and be just? Impossible. A pure artist cannot therefore be a partisan, except a partisan of justice. That is the one and only faction to which he can become committed; and since that is the only one, he must become all the more committed to it. For justice's sake . . . It is said that Chekhov was among the few writers who was respected by both camps.

In *The Cherry Orchard*, we love Gaev the way we still miss the good old days at the turn of the century. But we also love Lopakhin, and we want to help him, refine him, make him less timid, bring him the thing he knows he lacks and that makes him ashamed. And we cannot, at the same time, help but approve Trofimov's concerns; we're even sorry for our student's spinelessness, we would like him to be more realistic in his revolutionary prospects. In short, what *The Cherry Orchard* leaves behind, thanks to Chekhov, is a sense of *impartiality*. His art is an art of justice. Once again: great theater.

Chekhov is also an "artist" because he teaches us a lesson in tact, moderation; in sum, *modesty*. There is no great artist without modesty. Immodesty finds its excuse only in an excess of candor or naivety. Let us not confuse modesty with prudery. Finally he teaches us *economy*. One can delete absolutely nothing from *The Cherry Orchard*. Everything that could have been omitted has been. Chekhov has already done it. The excess has been pruned from it. And, studying this work, one is reminded of an observation Charlie Chaplin,[4] that incomparable artist, made about one of his films: "When a work seems finished, shake it, the way you shake a tree to keep only the fruit that clings firmly to the branches . . ." "Put nothing on the stage which is not wholly necessary, etc." said our master Racine.

So, in Chekhov, his stage directions should be examined with care and circumspection. As he says in one of his letters, "You often find in my plays the direction 'through tears,' but this implies the *state* of the characters and not the tears."

Finally, Chekhov is also an exemplary artist, because all of his characters, like those in Shakespeare, are ambiguous: Lopakhin the terrible is shy, indecisive, and a good man; Madam Ranevskaya, the fragile victim, is passionate; Gaev, upholder of the great tradition, is a sluggard; Trofimov, the revolutionary, is a slacker and a dreamer.

No conventional hero, only complex creatures; no robots, nothing but beating hearts.

And this will be the last point I want to make about why I love *The Cherry Orchard*: *The Cherry Orchard* is, definitively, "planted" in the *heart*. This heart, this super-flesh, which surpasses the mind and which contains, higgledy-piggledy, the ninety-five senses Trofimov refers to, the ones we don't know, and which far exceed in sensitivity the five poor senses that have been officially put at our disposal.

This heart puts us in this "state of tears" when we look back on the past, but which at the same time by its stubborn pulsation urges us towards the future and compels us to take pleasure in savoring all of the present.

This heart, which is all feeling, all willpower, is quite superior, it

4. Sir Charles Spencer Chaplin, English-born comedian and film director (1889–1977), was the creator of silent film's Little Tramp. [*Editor's note*.]

seems to me, to the mind, which produces only ideas, and to the senses, which produce only desire. It is above all revelation, perspicacity, and—why not say the word?—Love, that is, true knowledge.

PETER BROOK

Peter Brook (b. 1925) is an English director of Russian ancestry. After a distinguished career at the Royal Shakespeare Company, Covent Garden, and in the commercial theater, Brook began to explore the avantgarde, first with his Theater of Cruelty season, resulting in *Marat/Sade* (1964), then with *Orghast at Persepolis* (1971). In search of a universal language of theatre, he moved to Paris and, with an international company, has continued to experiment with the underlying myths of mankind. He directed *La Cerisaie* (*The Cherry Orchard*) in Paris (1981); the production subsequently toured to New York and Moscow.

The Cherry Orchard: An Immense Vitality†

People tell me that when they've attended rehearsals of *The Cherry Orchard* at the Bouffes du Nord,[1] they could not find the dark side that strikes them when they read Chekhov.

In a story, the author tells the tale from his point of view. The narrator is right there; he is telling the story. We read the story through him. Chekhov lived in Russia, where there was great misery; he suffered from what he saw and was an opponent of his time. As a doctor, he had developed a great sense of observation, as well as a lot of humor—often a very dark humor.

There are two important factors in Chekhov's life. The first is that he is a doomed man, death is hunting him down; the second is, in contrast to that—with the premonition of people who know they will die young—that he had an incredible amount of energy. Besides his activity as a doctor, he wrote so many short stories, articles, and he travelled much. For example, although he was ill, he made an unbelievable trip to the Devil's Island of Russia to visit the prisoners. They were living in absolutely horrible conditions; like Solzhenitsyn[2] in Siberia, Chekhov described it in a book. That sad and sensitive man, the man we know from the photos, that is the man we find in the short stories.

† Peter Brook, "La Cerisaie, une immense vitalité," ed. M.-H. Estienne, *Théâtre en Europe* (2 Avril 1984): 50–3. Trans. by Laurence Senelick.
1. A dilapidated, former operetta theater in the Paris suburbs, which is currently Brook's home playhouse. [*Editor's note.*]
2. Aleksandr Isaevich Solzhenitsyn (b. 1918), a dissident Russian author, whose massive work *The Gulag Archipelago 1918–56* details the history of Soviet prison camps. [*Editor's note.*]

When we turn to the theater, the fact that Chekhov's plays have a different tone than his short stories proves that this is not merely a good writer composing plays, but an absolutely exceptional talent. He understood that essential aspect of the theater (which only Shakespeare and a few others have also understood): that theater exists only when the necessarily personal viewpoint of the narrator is effaced by multiple viewpoints. That might seem impossible—it's like someone in India looking at the statues and thinking, Oh! Wouldn't it be wonderful to have twelve arms? It's one thing to make the statement, but another thing to achieve it.

It is no accident that there are very few great plays. For me, the greatest authors are Shakespeare and Chekhov. It is curious that two men with such different styles (one writes epic plays in verse, the other realistic plays in prose) should come together, so to speak, in this mutual viewpoint—a multiple viewpoint. In both cases, no judgment is made of the characters, each exists in a completely independent way; the actor can give as much solidity to one as to another and, at the same time, the spectator can get away from the usual Manichaeism: there are no "good guys" and no "bad guys."

Chekhov was very disappointed by Stanislavsky's staging of *The Cherry Orchard*. He thought he had written a comedy, but he was shown a tragedy. The director has to realize that the more he introduces his own viewpoint, the more he removes a crucial aspect of the play's vitality. An equivalent of the difference between short story and play is film and theater. In a film, the director shows his whole point of view; he is the narrator. In the theater, the director must seek this "multiple viewpoint" in his relation to the actors, in encouraging the actor's individuality to expand. If he doesn't, he will give one tone, his own, to the play. This must have been the case with Stanislavsky. Thinking of Chekhov of the short stories, Stanislavsky found the play tragic. He must have felt strongly about that; he once said to Chekhov: you're wrong, your play isn't a comedy, it's a tragedy.

Viewed as a comedy, life is necessarily much more objective than when it is viewed as a tragedy. If you look at it from a certain distance, you can see that every event, from birth to death, has a comic aspect. As a doctor, Chekhov could not help but see reality suffused with this comic tinge.

To come back to Stanislavsky, you mustn't forget the nineteenth-century middle class. This was the heyday of the bourgeois theater; people loved to go to the theater to shudder and weep. In Russia, France, and England, a crude picture of a Russia of depression, alcoholism and tears arose, an image that took root in people's hearts. For a long time, every comic aspect was inked out; it was replaced by a slow pace with long silences to show how monotonous life was.

We were shown de-energized but very beautiful people. This is a great mistake in treating reality, life as Chekhov saw it: it is clear that the conditions of frustration and boredom, instead of de-energizing the characters, gives them a desire to dramatize the least little thing, and this creates an immense vitality. It is both ridiculous and tragic. An immense vitality squandered on nothing . . .

In England—I don't know how it is in France—for some ten years now [i.e., 1974–1984], Chekhov was a sad and sentimental piece of music; suddenly, a reaction set in and actors started to play him as crude farce, often with regional accents. The best Chekhov I know is the film *Unfinished Piece for Player Piano*.[3] The characters in it act with immense delight in life, although there is no life or delight to be had. It's an explosion of vitality that goes nowhere.

This is the spirit in which we started to work, with the translator Lucia Laurova and Jean-Claude Carrière.[4] We compared different French and English versions; we noticed that the translators had invented a certain poetic vagueness that did not exist in the original at all. In Russian, the lines are often short. The style is very colloquial, very sinewy, and the poetry is not encumbered with grace notes. As in Beckett,[5] the poetry is often found in very ordinary phrases. Theater poetry is not literary poetry.

The version of Jean-Claude Carrière, which is very light and limpid, tries to reflect the Russian tone as faithfully as possible. If you give a tone to the play, you are also giving a tone to the actor. But if the text has no general tone, the actor is free to find a different tone for each moment; then too, he is encouraged to find what gives the characters the fullest solidity, the most heightened contrast. Characters start to exist only then and the play becomes something that can not only make you laugh and cry alternately, but especially make you laugh and cry simultaneously. And that is what gives rise to a real emotion, for you feel you are taking part in life.

Showing a character's versatility in this way does not mean that an author who shows all the viewpoints and effaces himself is less profound than in a short story; on the contrary, to achieve such a sure and subtle impresison, he has to put together a mosaic in which there is not a word or an incident too many. The greatest reproach Meyerhold made to Stanislavsky after *The Cherry Orchard* was to say that Stanislavsky did not know the fundamental rhythm of the play, and that, by acting it too slowly, he missed the essential movement.

3. *Neokonchennaya pyesa dlya mekhanicheskogo pianin* (1976), a loose adaptation of *Platonov*, directed by Nikita Mikhalkov. [*Editor's note.*]
4. Jean-Claude Carrière (b.1931), French screenwriter and dramaturge of Brook's theater. [*Editor's note.*]
5. Samuel Beckett (1906–1989), Irish writer whose plays present a darkly comic vision of the human plight. [*Editor's note.*]

PETER STEIN

Peter Stein (b. 1937), cofounder and artistic director of the Berlin Schaubühne am Halleschen Ufer, revolutionized the German stage with thorough critical analyses of each of his productions and direct address to the audience. His *Three Sisters* (1984) startled his public by using naturalistic techniques to go beyond naturalism. In his production, Stein claims that remembering is itself a political act. He later staged *The Cherry Orchard* (1992) and *Uncle Vanya*.

My Chekhov†

[. . .]Chekhov understood very well, I believe, that the role of a writer in society is not to answer the questions: What is to be done? How are we to live? These questions have no answers. He wrote and criticized his own statements as having no value. He went on writing more and more to try and correct himself, perfect himself, and he succeeded.

Through pitiless analysis with a scalpel, Chekhov established that life is devoid of meaning and, with an inexhaustible imagination, he reconstituted that life in all its aspects, which is typically Russian, affirming, perhaps often in a somewhat exaggerated way, that it is absurd to go on living if one does not seek a meaning in life, even if that meaning does not exist. Such is the original paradox he put forward.

* * *

His principal gift is to have announced or discovered the drama of the twentieth century, opening new paths to the theater. He transformed playwriting by suppressing the central hero, whom he replaced with a group of characters, and the observation of their mutual relations; that is, he "democratized" a play's cast. He also introduced to the theater the latest scientific discoveries—psychology, for instance—and invented a way of writing plays which fully corresponds to a twentieth-century person's perception of the world: he showed that if few grandiose events occur in ordinary life, the number of insignificant events which unfold there is also rather limited. Assassinations of rulers or actions of great scope or of national importance don't happen every day. So he went in search of a drama of daily life, found it and, to express it, he created a form of playwriting which develops without action, as such. And yet things do happen. The "drama of the spiral" that he invented rests on the rep-

† From Peter Stein, *Mon Tchekhov* (Paris: Actes Sud, 2002). Trans. by Laurence Senelick.

etition of the same events, without making notable progress or regression, but the passage from one of these events to another along a spiral creates a kind of progression.

Then Chekhov cut up the actions into a series of mini-actions, forming a chain of minuscule mini-scenes. This determined a form, a particular esthetic that other playwrights of the twentieth century would assimilate into their work later on.

Then he discovered a new structure: the play is not constructed on the development of the action. Rather, its structure is musical: words, themes, and speeches are repeated and come to notice like leitmotivs. At first sight, one has the impression of a lack of rational reflection, but that is only an appearance; in reality, Chekhov is much more complex and profound than he seems. By creating a new stage language, and especially a new dramatic text to be spoken onstage, he reformed the theater.

This actionless playwriting rests not on what is said but on the way of saying it. What changes are not the words, but instead the way or manner of saying them. This is the famous subtext, or "underground current," which you all know.

The actors of Chekhov's plays, thanks to the subtext, were given entirely new roles. Since what is important is no longer the content of the texts, but much more the manner of speaking it, the interpretation and acting took on such importance that the actor became a coauthor. Chekhov left so much space—so much freedom between speeches, the ends of speeches, and even between the words—that the actor can fill these voids with his psychological state, his self.

This is the greatest gift that Chekhov gave to actors. But this does not mean that it is easy to perform. Not at all. Who would dare take on the responsibility of being Chekhov's coauthor? Only a very few. It is very, very hard. So, this gift can be compared to the casks of the Danaides[1] or the original Trojan horse.

Chekhov's last gift, perhaps the most important (he actually gave us a great many), is the contact he established, towards the end of his life, with a living theater, created before his eyes. His marriage to an actress of this theater, Olga Knipper—opinions differ about this marriage—did not play a significant role in this intimacy. That is not what's important, but rather the happy occasion that meeting and collaborating with Stanislavsky and Nemirovich-Danchenko offers us: we have the possibility of realizing that a dramatist of very great talent can work in close and direct contact with a theatre and that this collaboration bears real fruit in practice.

Judging from the polemical discussions and confrontations Che-

---

1. In Greek mythology, the forty-nine daughters of Danaos, who murdered their husbands on their wedding nights were condemned in the underworld to gather water in casks perforated like sieves. [*Editor's note*.]

khov had with Stanislavsky, Nemirovich-Danchenko, and the actors of the Art Theater, we can understand what he wanted. That is why I always declare that it is impossible to understand Chekhov's plays without taking into account his personal relationship with the Art Theater. It is one of the necessary conditions for working on Chekhov. The second, no less necessary condition consists of a profound acquaintance with Russian theater in general and its acting traditions in particular, for I dare affirm that Chekhov conceived and wrote his plays to challenge these traditions of acting. If it is true that the actor can become Chekhov's coauthor, then he has to know above all what hopes Chekhov invested in his potential coauthor.

I read Chekhov's first play, *The Seagull*, when I was about twenty-three. For purely personal reasons, I didn't like it. Certain passages in that play, I still don't like. In Act One of *The Seagull* where there's talk of the theater, I have the impression that they are coming loose from reality. And I'm not even speaking of the difficulty of staging this first act, you'll agree with me that it rarely comes off[. . .]

My work on *The Cherry Orchard* leads me to make two remarks, connected to one another[. . .]

1. Its structure is radically different from that of all of Chekhov's other plays. Everything that is typical up through *Three Sisters* here seems to disappear, it's as if Chekhov were returning to his beginnings. He is composing a structure as a mosaic, whose tiny pieces, when brought together, will constitute a whole. Often, a simple speech represents a little piece of that whole, even when it has no direct connection with the phrases that come before or after. Yet the little tiles of this mosaic are united by the same elegiac touch. The playwright's technique resembles the one a composer uses to write a musical work.

I have spoken so far only of what is heard in the play, my reaction to the text. Now I will deal with the question of the motifs, which are taken up in different forms. These sonorous associations are emitted by both tragic and comic characters. Take the case of the phrase "tasty little pickle." Yasha is the first to utter it, to designate girls, specifically Dunyasha. Then Firs uses it when he mutters, "He swallowed half a bucket of pickles." Then the pickle actually *appears* in Act Two: Charlotta pulls it out of her pocket and munches on it. The same thing happens with other words and other notions . . . This is only a very small example of the way in which the play's structure is conceived, thought out.

2. What does the title *The Cherry Orchard* mean? That the play is centered not on the story of an individual or a group of people, but instead on a part of nature, an orchard, which the hands of man had made to grow. Man and nature, man and the universe—this is the main thing for Chekhov; for him, it seems to me, this is much

more important than the connections between people. Hence his habit of presenting the relations between the characters as unfinished, incomplete. They are always sketches, studies, devoid of logical completion. The characters all have a tendency, mind you, not to assemble but to disperse.

Thus, Chekhov at the start of the twentieth century grasped what characterizes the twentieth century: the incommunicability, the isolation of people. And you well know that the attempts, aided by ideology—communism, fascism, and any other "ism"—to escape from this incommunicability, to construct new relationships, were to no avail. Note that in *Three Sisters*, when it comes to losses, there is no doubt about the unity of the sisters. But in *The Cherry Orchard*? Brother and sister have not seen one another for a long time, and when they meet again, they are full of affection for one another; yet they spend their time casting darts at one another, then separate again. And the mother-daughter connections? Ranevskaya gives very little thought to Anya. Privileged relations may be formed between Varya and Lopakhin, and Anya and Petya, but they have no perspective, no future. The characters meet, love one another, but . . . a bit like tourists, in passing.

The Cherry Orchard for me is the most up-to-date of Chekhov's plays. He guessed what was going to happen. People spend their time travelling, moving around, they have become people without a country (while remaining attached to their country) . . . they show up at their own home as visitors.

No European play is built in so complex a manner as *The Cherry Orchard*. The hero is not a character or a group, but nature itself. However, these two elements are connected, for one cannot tell the story of relations between two characters, one can only tell of their relation to the orchard, to nature. And that is why the playwright invented a musical structure.

As a director, I am perhaps the first to have shown the attraction of Chekhov to the universal, but an attentive reader will no doubt have already noticed it. Have you paid any attention to Chekhov's stage directions? These are works of astonishing poetry and at the same time very ingenious theatre pieces. He suggests, for instance, that the upstage area be made almost transparent. At the very beginning of the act, the windows, if you follow his advice, must be closed. By this device, the spectator "sees" the leading character, the orchard. It's really brilliant! In the theater one cannot show real trees, one can only give a feeling of their beauty through the feelings of the characters. But Chekhov insists, "No, the audience has to see the orchard and believe that nothing is more beautiful!" It is hard to stage. He suggests in the middle of Act One that the curtains be drawn so that the orchard is visible to the spectators, then that the windows be opened. A precise and correct instruction . . .

In the last act, the orchard—which is no longer as beautiful, for the trees are bare—has a special role to play: it testifies that everything in this world is ephemeral. Note that the trees are being cut down not in springtime, when they are in bloom, but in autumn. The audience is invited to imagine what will happen next.

[. . .]In *Uncle Vanya*, as always in Chekhov, several themes crisscross. For me, the principal theme is the passing of time, which is represented onstage. Time passing is associated with the process of aging. It is a show about aging that sets in without our noticing it . . . Then about what follows when, suddenly, one does notice it.

I think that this play questions the aging process—its tragic, negative aspect, reversible or irreversible. . . . The play is centered on the obvious, the frightening process of aging in Uncle Vanya, on his situation, totally without a way out of this "rathole" where he is condemned to rub along for years, and where there is not even the slightest ray of hope at the end of the tunnel. Uncle Vanya, while accepting his fate and submitting to it, goes on believing that life has a meaning.

The characters in this play are far from ideal. Chekhov stresses that the inventors, the creators are not saints. They are riven by permanent doubts about what they're doing; they torture themselves with unending questions; they consider themselves insignificant and wasted. Only Dr. Astrov has accomplished something, and even he is tortured by doubts . . . At moments, his doubts and questioning turn to cynicism, irony, sarcasm, and even sometimes to an ostentatious indifference, which is both a weapon and a defense. In this regard, Chekhov's comment "Uncle Vanya weeps, Astrov whistles" is really first-rate. Stanislavsky must have understood at once what this meant. Chekhov was talking about the degree to which the temperaments of some converge with those of others. The slightest emotion, the slightest truth is made relative, placed in contrast, its meaning turned inside-out. If the actors start to sob, they immediately have to start laughing and, if they are sad, their sorrow immediately turns to sarcasm, it's always this way in Chekhov, let us remember Astrov's line, "Maybe all this is only crackpot talk." [Act One.] So Astrov's whistling is perhaps the only proper thing to do: it's a manifestation of a very great realism, a very great truth. . . .

All of Chekhov's comments are part of a strategy. He always has a horror of stagy sentimentality in all its aspects. All actors displease him because of their tendency to exaggerate, overact, yield to melodramatic excesses, gesticulate wildly, and play to the gallery. He tried everything possible to oppose stupid ideas, stupid arguments put forward by actors to justify their bad acting, their excesses and their exaggeration; to oppose the narcissistic and masturbatory manifestation of their feelings, which keeps them from projecting themselves into the next moment.

Chekhov's objective is to lure the spectator into the events, to give him a desire to hobnob with the characters in his plays, even if they are weird, somewhat stupid, idiotic, sometimes completely insignificant people, feebleminded and insane. They constantly make mistakes and yet one desires to be with them: what a tour de force Chekhov managed in that!

I have already mentioned the process of aging. There is also the matter of showing that, when tested by life, illusions die, pass, and that with time they become nothing more than illusions. The despair that succeeds them forces us to curse them, detest them, and renounce forging new ones. But it is impossible to live without illusions; one needs something which resembles them, a passionate spark or a regret. Faith is necessary! Even if faith, from the viewpoint of the natural sciences, is also a sort of illusion. One needs a more or less religious idea, I completely agree with that . . .

Let me refer to some episodes of my work on *Three Sisters*. The biggest problems were posed by the second act. I had the impression that it is a rerun of the first. The same words are repeated. Once again, a party takes place, something is going to happen, the characters forgathered in the same room. All right, true, this time it's winter. But still the same words, the same conversation about this and that, as in the first act! And to top it off, the party for which everyone is preparing does not take place. I kept thinking, "Lord! How do you stage that? It's simply impossible!" But, when you start to work, you notice that the same words repeated in different lighting and at a different season are received quite differently. The party which, in Act One, is interrupted by lowering the curtain at the climactic moment (but it's a little party, nothing special about it, a mere nameday like many others) is stopped short in Act Two right in full fling, just when they are still waiting, and nothing, so to speak, is an interruption, because nothing is happening; complete silence reigns over the empty stage. Then a couple comes to put out the candles, with the result that, finally, you can't see anything anymore. And that, right in the middle of the act. . . . These are important effects obtained by actions, minimal changes which ultimately draw attention to themselves.

The same thing happens in the second act of *The Cherry Orchard*. The motifs used at the beginning, inside the house, are taken up exactly identically in the second act, but this time in a natural context: sunset, moonlight, night . . . The perceptions, the sensations, as well as the minor events and the problems of the first act become in the second act purely decorative. Devoid of significance, intertwined with each other, they are a backdrop for cosmic phenomena. The absence of action is only apparent. This is the greatest discovery of the European theater of the twentieth century. Without Chekhov, we would never have had Beckett . . .

* * *

The essential thing about Chekhov's playwriting is the presence of contradictions in the least detail. Did these contradictions exist from the start? That raises the question about whether one is dealing with comedies or tragedies. You know that Chekhov was skeptical about the staging of *The Cherry Orchard* by Stanislavsky's theater. He always complained that the whole show was manifestly too sad, when he had quite simply written a comedy. He says, for instance, that the actors are constantly crying; that, yes, he did write "through tears," but that that doesn't mean they have to cry in reality; they are only in a state in which tears might be shed. There is an enormous number of such comments. In general, his commentaries on his plays are rather enigmatic, rather mysterious; I wouldn't say that he is being coy, but all the same they have a typically theatrical ambivalence. All these declarations express the refusal to be too univocal. He kept his emotions very close to his chest, but he detested emotion presented too explicitly in a production and seeking only its own confirmation, as it is slowly transformed into a lie. For Chekhov, reality would appear onstage when, at the same moment, a feeling of sadness is very closely allied to the desire to burst out laughing.

Chekhov's style is characterized by the fact that at the very moment when a line is spoken, as I always say, it is possible to spin the emotional top 360 degrees: from tears to laughter, then back to tears, and vice-versa—and all while saying the line, "Please hand me that fork!" It is impossible to give the illusion that any position is affirmed, even temporarily. In Chekhov's texts, that is absolutely ruled out, especially in his most consummate plays (one can already discern it in *Three Sisters*, but especially in *The Cherry Orchard*). Every production based on univocity—and, obviously, all theater people have a tendency towards univocity, something has to be "made"—veers away from Chekhov. This explains the enormous difficulties actors have with the text. They ask, "What should I act? Should I act being sad or should I act being cheerful?" The best answer for a director who tries to respect Chekhov's dramatic intention should be: "At that moment, you are profoundly sad and you express it by laughing, and at another such moment you are wild with joy and you burst into tears." There is the subtext and the supertext: both must be realized simultaneously. And to achieve an even greater distinction, one must, at the same time, most often realize three or four other subtexts, which is something an actor can do. Each actor knows that he is capable of it, even if expressing four or five different things at once in a single theatrical gesture requires great agility and a perfect mastery of dramatic interpretation. . . .

The director's task is first to create a space in which these multiple interventions of different voices can be deployed. There are several ways to approach this. My own tendency is to follow Chekhov's stage directions to the letter, as to the scenery, for instance. He fantasized a great deal abut his scenery; in fact, he cared a lot about it and also worked with the designer. The stagings of his plays he saw at the Moscow Art Theatre never satisfied him. He had a lot to say about this. His stage directions exist and some are minor prose master-pieces. Out of curiosity and by nature, I feel it a challenge to inte-grate them so far as can be done into my work. But it is not obligatory. It is however regrettable that some directors fail to intro-duce into their production the representation of certain essential natural phenomena. One finds them in all of Chekhov's plays, where they constitute a frame, a receptacle for the banal and everyday ele-ments with which one then acts onstage, as with ping-pong balls, until they get all mixed together. And I really feel this elimination as a great loss. I consider it necessary to supply this frame to the actors, to insist on heat and cold, summer and winter, springtime and autumn, morning and evening, on certain hours of the day as the different seasons color them. In each of the acts in his plays, this is regulated often with the greatest care. To reject it, to do without it, seems to me most regrettable. In my opinion, you lose thirty percent of the effectiveness before you even start.

That's why we contrived a vast stage setting for *Three Sisters*. At first, it wasn't at all clear in our minds. We weren't interested in having three benches next to the windows, six samovars, an armchair here and a flower there. After all, we are interested in the lives of the characters! However, if the actors don't have at their disposal the flowers and samovars they talk about and with which, at the same time, they juggle as with three different balls, you notice curiously that a strangely abstract space takes over, a purely symbolic verbal format. Finally, I believe that Chekhov does not easily lend himself to so-called modernization. It is only through the "presence" of actors that this can be achieved.

*   *   *

In *Three Sisters*, one is forced to keep in mind that, in each act, it is said that soon they will be moving upstairs or downstairs, from this room to another, that the house is in this or that state, that it's too cold in this room, that someone upstairs is rapping and he's going to come downstairs right away, or that he's rapping from downstairs and is going to go upstairs. One is endlessly confronted with such details, and one often finds them in the mouths of the characters. At the same time, the global theme is that they are taking leave of a house. Irina's second line is "To sell the house, finish up with everything here. And then go to Moscow!" The house in which they live is certainly the principal problem. On one hand it is beloved, and on the other it is hated like the plague. This theme will return next in *The Cherry Orchard*. In *Three Sisters*, the house is hated from the start and, at the end, its loss is regretted; in *The Cherry Orchard*, it's the other way around: the house and the cherry orchard are loved with a passion, and at the end the family is basically glad to get rid of it.

When you stage *The Cherry Orchard* as Peter Brook did, having it played on a carpet, then I have difficulty in imagining how the charm of the concrete in the actor's performance—which the play requires—can take effect, how the text offered onstage can function other than as a speech, which, as in Shakespeare's plays, demands that the spectator set his imagination in motion. Now that was not the author's intuition. He did not want the spectators to rely on their imagination to give shape to what the characters are saying, but instead he wanted them to show in a clear, distinct manner the absurdity in this object they speak of so passionately, which, a few moments earlier, others were considering the worst of white elephants. They make fun of the samovar, and then they repeat endlessly that they absolutely need samovars. At bottom, this quotidian incoherence, both concrete and funny as well, constitutes the true frontlines of human combat, to wit, the combat for control of everyday life, and not control of great crisis situations. These great catastrophes occur only occasionally. They too can lead to death, but, to tell the truth, daily life gets us there much more inevitably. That is exactly the level on which Chekhov's plays are played out, and what disturbed most of his contemporaries. But I believe we are learning more and more just how brilliant his contribution is.

ANATOLY ÉFROS

Anatoly Vasilyevich Éfros (1925–1987) was one of the leading Russian directors of his generation. Although he insisted on emotional truth, he eschewed paralyzing respect for tradition and invigorated the interpretation of the classics. From 1963 to 1967, he ran the Lenkom Theatre in Moscow, but he was thrown out for his controversial production of *The Seagull* (1966). A year later, his *Three Sisters* created a scandal and was withdrawn from the Malaya Bronnaya Theater. A talented teacher, Éfros could work with actors other than those in his troupe, as in *The Cherry Orchard* at the Taganka (1975), where he was named director in 1984.

Everything to Do with Chekhov†

Nowadays I regard Chekhov's *Three Sisters* quite differently than I did fifteen years ago.

At that time, I tried as hard as I could to find the tragic quality in the play. But now I think that this tragic quality has, on the contrary, to be concealed. The spectator should smile for a long time watching these dear people. They philosophize quite a lot, make good jokes, possess real charm and subtlety of feeling; they are artistic. Their breathing is easy. Even when we're still simply reading the play role by role, we keep laughing quietly. We laugh contentedly as we discern how ingeniously Chekhov constructs the dialogue, how the lines fit together. There's shrewdness and ingenuity throughout.

Compared with the first act, the second seems a bit somber. In the first act, they are merrily celebrating a name day, but in the second, even though it's evening and winter has set in, they still aren't grieving. They enjoy sitting with one another as they wait for tea and the arrival of the masqueraders. Everyone wants to laugh, dance, and have a drink. And, of course, it's nice to chat a bit, philosophize a bit. Even when Natasha throws everybody out, they don't leave depressed, but carry on laughing in the vestibule.

Masha and Vershinin are in love. Solyony has decided to declare his love to Irina. Tusenbach is off to a new, civilian life and insists that he is completely happy. Vershinin, true, raises an objection, says that happiness is not their lot, but he says this merrily, for he is philosophizing, and not because he's in a bad mood.

Fedotik and Rodé have arrived. They are quietly playing the guitar and singing. It's cozy, warm, and pleasant, because they're all together. Even that famous argument of Chebutykin and Solyony about the two universities should probably not be made too heated. I once tried to extract all the nervous tension I possibly could from this argument. I almost turned the scene into a fight. But now I think that that isn't necessary. And Solyony ought to be sincere in his reconciliation with Tusenbach, when the latter makes a peace offering, and sincere in drinking good fellowship with him. The drama is somewhere farther away, deeper down. Long ago the Moscow Art Theatre has good reason for coming up with such terms as "middle ground" and "subtext." Nowadays, we don't have a "middle ground"— we bring it to the front. And things come out flat. And when things are flat, it doesn't matter whether they are joyful or sorrowful. Flat is flat. But life has to flow as if there were nothing wrong, as if

† From *Prodolzhenie teatralnogo romana* (Sequel to the Theatrical Romance), 2d, enlarged ed. (Moscow: Panas, 1993), 29–56. Trans. by Laurence Senelick.

everything were in order; and if people in the background are very upset, after all, it's in the background.

We mustn't think that they are unhappy. We must think that they are good. We must admire them, ache for them, and dream along with them so that everything is good.

And so on until the end—so that drama in its pure form does not erupt. It is precisely this resistance to drama that is tragic.

To play drama in a properly light and elevated way is no easy thing nowadays. Watching a certain performance of Shakespeare, I was astounded at how a man killed another man and threw him into a horse stall. I was amazed, perhaps even delighted—in a purely artistic sense, of course. I was delighted by the outburst of realism. In those days, these outbursts illumined art. And sometimes one would like to invent something unsettling in Chekhov in order to break up the established style. But that is how we gradually lost the taste for beauty. When in some stage performance, say, a barrel was staved in with a crowbar, it seemed beautiful. (I'm not talking about a Chekhov performance, just in general.) And it really can be effective. But now, all the barrels are staved in, so to speak, and even the crowbar is bent out of shape. We shall rest. Later, perhaps, something else may come along to "break" things up. But not by us.

When the MAT folks rejected our *Three Sisters*,[1] my actors could not forgive them for it. When much later I began to work at the MAT, they started to despise me too. Why? For staging shows with people who had censured our beloved Chekhov production? Many years went by, and I staged *Three Sisters* again, at the Malaya Bronnaya.[2] Now almost all the actors involved in this performance were new. I did not want to repeat the old production. An entirely new treatment seemed possible. But the old-timers, the earlier ones, still regarded my project with mistrust up to the opening. A new treatment? Why? And with whom? With those little kids? The public welcomed our new production warmly enough, but not one of the earlier performers came backstage after the performance to share their reactions. Evidently, harshness to everything "alien" was a characteristic not only of the MAT actors. I saw in the eyes of my earlier actors the same misunderstanding and the same malice, yes, malice, which they had seen back then in those they had taken a dislike to on this very account. Evidently, it is very difficult to accept something that seemed *yours alone*, but that has become *not yours alone*.

There is a lot of talk in Chekhov about the need to work. I was once accused of sneering at these dreams about hard work. I scorned the

---

1. Éfros's controversial *Three Sisters* at the Lenkom Theater in 1966 provoked angry letters in the press from Moscow Art Theater actors, which led to the production being banned. [*Editor's note.*]
2. In 1982. [*Editor's note.*]

accusation. We had no intention of mocking what we ourselves believed in. But maybe an unconscious distrust of such words had surfaced, for, of course, we had forgotten how to work. A large amount of wasted energy is not work. Work is something remarkably expedient, precise, even in a certain sense narrow. But onstage we sometimes utter these words abstractly—at such times, they can even sound like parody.

But Chekhov instilled something else in this word—something genuine. The value of genuine work simply cannot be doubted. So much depends on people wanting and knowing how to work! . . . "You know, if only hard work were supplemented by education, and education by hard work," says Vershinin. Who is unwilling to subscribe to this dream of his?

In our work as actors and directors, we too are often vague and abstract, like those outside our profession whom we criticize. Is not a craftsman, who knows his business, beautiful? And is not a clumsy workman dreadful? There he is, say, screwing in a bolt, and I see how the screw-thread will immediately come loose. A hasty craftsman makes imprecise movements, and then he presses with all his might, hammers in the bolts, just to finish the job. No one will notice—and he'll have done his work. And if they do spot it, he'll do it over again with an ill will.

The first MAT *Three Sisters* (1901) was designed, as everyone knows, by Simov; the second one, in (1940), by Dmitriev.[3] The first design was more modest, more simple, "more provincial." None of those enormous, beautiful windows, as in Dmitriev's sets. None of those sparkling, glistening birch trees, arranged on stage with remarkable grace. In Simov's fourth act, next to the house, behind a humble little fence was a little stand of immature trees. In front of the fence some bricks were laid. And a simple little bench, the kind that always stands in front of a house in quiet provincial towns. A tiny little veranda shut off by two plain striped awnings.

But for some reason Simov did not follow Chekhov's stage directions and did not put a path bordered by fir trees onstage. The old MAT may have thought that a lane of fir trees was rather gloomy. This theater, for all its highly subtle psychology, always smartened up the world a bit. MAT realism was lyrical. I say this without a tinge of censure.

* * *

3. Viktor Andreevich Simov (1858–1935) was the chief designer for the Moscow Art Theater (1898–1912, 1925–1935), responsible for the scenery in its first productions of Chekhov. Vladimir Vladimirovich Dmitriev (1900–1948) worked at the MAT from 1928; although he began as a cubist expressionist, he became more realistic and decorative over time. [*Editor's note.*]

The early MAT folks were poets, not prose artists. And to join in the spirit of the Art Theater, one had to be a poet, and only later came the "system," the "method," and so on.

But let's go back to the path of fir trees. Perhaps Chekhov had in mind not some small town like Kaluga, but a more northern town, further away from Moscow, where, to quote Olga, it's cold and there are mosquitoes. On the road to Sakhalin, Chekhov probably stopped at such small towns. And in one such town, some fifteen miles from the station, he may have seen a well-educated Moscow family. God knows how they wound up there.

Judging by Dmitriev's scenery, the sisters live in the environs of an estate just outside Moscow. They live comfortably. But Chekhov may have envisaged something else.

A small, remote town full of Protopopovs, where, accidentally flung here by life, there live three young women from Moscow, who know foreign languages. Only why do they know them? These days in our work we often avoid being concrete. We seem to pluck our generalizations out of thin air. Or out of our *ideas*. And from that alone. That's why in *Three Sisters*, the dresses for the sisters are designed to be stunning, and Masha's hat is not only Muscovite-Petersburgian, but sheer Parisian. Let me state that I do not exclude the possibility of the most diverse interpretations—I'm only writing down those thoughts that arise in me, and today in particular. I think it may be worth returning, figuratively speaking, to the path of fir trees and to the homespun runners on the plank floor. I'll say in jest that these sisters ought to share the mood that Menshikov had in Berezov.[4] Maybe, incidentally, little windows as well? No, little windows aren't compulsory, they aren't needed on stage. It's not a matter of fir trees and little windows. It's a matter of organizing the material in our imaginations as something concrete.

That's why there is bound to be improvisation, but it will not issue from theatrical laws that you did not create. These remarkable windows of Dmitriev's and these birch trees have become a virtual law for *Three Sisters*, but it wasn't Chekhov who invented them, but Dmitriev, they were superb inventions of his, but so what?

So, these three young women live with a crackpot brother, who, you see, plays the violin and makes fretwork picture frames. And is in love with a woman who will hold him in a hedgehog's paws. There is something in Andrey sadly unadaptable to life, as there is, however, in the whole family. Although the sisters are strong-willed, they cannot cope with Natasha and never will. Because she is stronger than they are. But, perhaps, the guests in this home, military men, are

4. Aleksandr Danilovich Menshikov (1673–1729), favorite of Peter the Great; under Peter II, he was arrested and exiled to Berezov, where he died. [*Editor's note.*]

made of sterner stuff and are distinguished by the force and ability
to overcome the Protopopovs? Of course, not all military men are
like Vershinin or Tusenbach. But evidently they're the only kind that
come to this house. What kind is that? The naive, simpleminded,
childish, pure ones. Crackpots. They don't cheat at cards, they don't
drink as a great many others probably do, but they philosophize.
Military men in the sticks combat boredom and longing in different
ways. Chekhov selected for his military men those who are superior
to the best civilians in his town. What's the standing of Fedotik and
Rodé, with their cameras and gifts such as a little notebook with a
little pencil? This is a very peculiar regiment, wouldn't you say? And
so it comes to an end. Those flowers give off such a sweet smell, they
are far too delicate. Even Solyony, and it is optional that he be the
way Livanov[5] played him. Now, after Livanov, no actor can decide
to make radical changes in the way this role is interpreted, so
engraved in our consciousness is that swashbuckler and bully. And
yet, for some reason, Chekhov's Solyony is "hanging out" here,
amidst the three sisters, along with Tusenbach and Vershinin, and
not somewhere else with the other officers.

Nowadays they come up with all sorts of things—even Solyony's
being not averse to embracing Natasha secretly behind the door, if
Irina rejects him. You can come up with anything you please. You
can even come up with things that are dead wrong, but what's the
point? In Chekhov, Solyony is in love with Irina, precisely in love,
and precisely with Irina, with this very young, very radiant creature.
We don't know with what intonation Solyony says that his hands
smell like a corpse. What rings in our ears is only Livanov's intonations, precise, expressive intonations, but others are possible. And
sooner or later these intonations will be discovered. And perhaps
Solyony's unhappiness will be performed quite differently. Generally
speaking, all that's left for the artist is to stimulate his imagination
constantly. In winter one can sketch green leaves without end, but
in summer it's good to rush through the forest, to set these leaves in
motion again. Otherwise after winter you'll probably forget what
they're really like.

Should a classic be staged "aggressively" or "calmly"? I put both these
words in quotation marks, of course. Aggressively means not as a
museum piece, or an anthology piece, but so as to knock the corners
off it and shove your face in it. Aggressively means to splatter it with
your own up-to-date feelings.

Calmly has no meaning at all. As a specific case I have in mind
that calm that was in the first production of the MAT. The very first

5. Boris Nikolaevich Livanov (1904–1972) played Solyony in the 1940 MAT revival of *Three Sisters* as a swashbuckling bully, setting the style for the part for decades. [*Editor's note*.]

one. *Tsar Fyodor*.[6] Everything in it was true, and no one wanted to shock anyone. Except, perhaps, with the fact that everything was absolutely untheatrical, that is, not phony. But this was a novelty too—novel in its seeming calm. It was something in the nature of the calmness of the sea, a forest, a volcano. Not the volcano depicted in particularly awful colors, but a real volcano, calm for the time being until the moment of eruption arrives, and afterwards it calms down again. I used to subscribe to the former attitude of staging the classics, and now I incline to the latter. But I am not sure that I will forever.

Before me on the table are two highly interesting documents: Stanislavsky's directorial plan for *Three Sisters* in 1901 and an article that appeared a short while ago in a French periodical about Peter Brook's new production, of *The Cherry Orchard*. For his production Brook chose an old, abandoned theater somewhere on the outskirts of Paris.[7] It was once a popular commercial theater; now all you can see are traces of the gilding. The building is dilapidated; it looks ridiculous with its tiers and slender columns. One can only guess at its former splendor. Is this not a suitable location for *The Cherry Orchard*? asks the critic. The stage is denuded, and the eye is drawn to the scarred firewall with the red and green paint coming through. High window frames stand in front of the stone walls, without any glass in them. The stage space is covered with oriental carpets. Their beauty is also in the past, the colors have faded. On the big carpet are a bunch of smaller rugs which resemble hillocks and serve as seats for Ranevskaya, Gaev, and the others. That is all, except for a couple of chairs and a cupboard full of toys. In Act Four, the carpets have been rolled up—and everyone sees a repulsive, unattractive floor.

Gaev is played by a famous film actor; he is incredibly handsome, far from old.[8] A man who leads an idle life. Over the course of the play, Gaev physically breaks down. At the end, weeping, he embraces Ranevskaya, and they kiss; children grown old whom time has passed over and who now in despair ask where they are.

The Cherry Orchard has not been lost, writes the critic. The last performance was supposed to take place. Now in view of its enormous success, the production has been extended for another month.

* * *

6. *Tsar Fyodor Ioannovich* by Aleksey N. Tolstoy, a blank-verse tragedy about seventeenth-century Muscovy, was the opening production of the Moscow Art Theater in 1898. [*Editor's note.*]
7. Peter Brook (b. 1925), one of the world's leading stage directors, founded the International Center for Theater Research in Paris in 1962. He located his company in the Théâtre des Bouffes du Nord, a former operetta theatre. [*Editor's note.*]
8. Michel Piccoli (b. 1925), the French film actor, created Gaev in Brook's production, but Éfros may be referring to his replacement, the Swedish actor Erland Josephson (b. 1923). [*Editor's note.*]

Stanislavsky's directorial plan for *Three Sisters*. How extremely different the views of different artists of the same author can be. If you start only with the list of props for Act One of *Three Sisters*, which Stanislavsky drew up. This list alone bespeaks the most scrupulous approach to everyday life.

> Thirty pupils' lessonbooks. One blue, one red pencil for Olga. A necktie, a needle, thread for Irina. She is mending a necktie of Andrey's as she walks around. Chekhov didn't come up with this—Stanislavsky did.

> A portrait of the general in his youth, a big portrait of the general with his wife in old age, in a frame carved by Andrey.

> A (cuckoo) clock backstage sounding three or four times. A hanging clock in the drawing room, etc.

Stanislavsky has the most detailed workaday elaboration of the characters' behavior. Irina speaks her famous monologues in Act One while cleaning out a birdcage. She changes their water, shakes out the debris, as she hangs out the window . . .

Whereas in Brook, when the characters abandon the cherry orchard, the actors come down into the stalls, climb up to the balcony, and so on. Saying good-bye, they thrust themselves out of the empty window frames . . .

When Nemirovich staged his *Three Sisters* in 1940, he spoke of the need to renounce the naturalism of the past MAT production, in which he had taken part himself. It was a brilliant production. But Nemirovich considered that the time had come to do everything differently. The new performance had to be devoid of naturalistic, workaday verisimilitude. It was to be elevated, poetic, and philosophical. The people were to speak resonantly, heightening the poetic phrases. In addition they were all to be strikingly alive.

This new production was no less magnificent than the earlier one. It was perfect (in a literal sense). The young actors acted it, so to speak, about themselves or those like them. Something older was played by the actors in a new way, for they were no longer performing a contemporary play, but a *classic*.

Compared with what had come before, such an approach to Chekhov was absolutely new. Nemirovich called the earlier approach naturalistic. Now it was philosophic, poetical theater, but alive only in the MAT way. It came not from the mind, but from the heart.

Whereas Brook's approach to *The Cherry Orchard* could be called grotesque. In such a case something is particularly exaggerated, emphasized.

Eighty years have gone by, and Chekhov's plays have undergone the influence of at least three different approaches—the naturalistic, the poetic, and the grotesque. And it would seem that each approach has the possibility of making manifest Chekhov's feelings and ideas.

But there is, perhaps, a fourth approach. It is when each production contains naturalism and the grotesque and poetry. Not in mechanical proximity, of course, but indissolubly combined.

To some degree, the theater is a strange institution. One can study a play intensively, explain to oneself thoroughly that, say, Podkolyosin[9] is a slugabed, that he won't be parted from his pipe, that his room is cluttered and filthy. One can explain this to oneself as thoroughly as you please, but it won't result in a production.

Then suddenly you imagine that Podkolyosin is on his feet all the time, that he is far from being a dishrag, that he is constantly in motion, in a dream of activity, but that all this activity is hogwash, that it comes to no fruition. You imagine this—and suddenly a fantasy begins to take shape. And a production begins to evolve.

I have seen a great many fine versions of *Getting Married*, where a half-decrepit couch jostled a busted clock; where in the middle of the room, as Gogol prescribed, there stood an unpolished boot. But, creating my own production, for some reason I turned away from this, although I continued to regard many such settings as good. I thought at the time that it would be better to toss it all out—free myself of things, and draw only the outlines of the actor, without extraneous everyday life, without any sort of genre painting. And everyone later said that this was true Gogol, despite many lines of departure from him.

I bring this up because I once read an article about "beauty in Chekhov's plays." Everything it said about this beauty was very true and beautiful. Reading the article, I not only agreed with it, but I also got excited about Chekhov again. It said correctly that Chekhov's characters can be divided into two camps: those who have aesthetic feelings and those who do not. These were all familiar ideas, but successfully organized and formulated in the article. And Chekhov himself was satisfactorily evoked. And the fact that the action flows slowly in his works. And that in each of his plays immense significance is invested in nature and the weather and the time of day . . .

But I stopped reading this article as soon as I ran across a slight (luckily, only slight) irony concerning that strange institution, the theater, wherein so often one does not hear Chekhov as he is, but where they come up with something else, supposedly much worse. The words of Kozintsev[1] (true, a worker not in theater but in film)

9. Podkolyosin is the indecisive hero of Gogol's *Getting Married* (1841), who ultimately evades wedlock. [*Editor's note.*]
1. Georgy Mikhailovich Kozintsev (1905–1973) began as a theater director with the Factory of the Eccentric Actor in Petrograd, but later became an outstanding film director (*King Lear, Hamlet*). [*Editor's note.*]

were quoted, speaking of the need for a rapid and dynamic Chekhov. He also said that the staging of Chekhov's plays should be not too poetic, in the usual sense, and that such a change in the usual view of Chekhovian beauty may perhaps guarantee the success of future productions.

His remark struck me as crude. But Kozintsev was probably bothered by the fact that for a long time he had not seen good productions of Chekhov and was looking for a way out of the blind alley that had been created at that time.

There is a certain difference between research and creativity. One can be interested in nature and weather, devise a production with Chekhovian slowness, but nothing will come of it. On the other hand, one can, as it were, forget about the weather and the birdsong and the wind and the time of day and make a production as dynamic as if it were not Chekhovian, and it will seem truly Chekhovian and capable of *gripping* the audience.

I am only repeating what I have already said: the theater in a certain sense is a strange institution. A necessary part of it is an autonomous and independent way of seeing things.

In that article I am now recalling, it was also written that Bunin[2] did not accept *The Cherry Orchard*, because he was sure that such orchards did not in fact exist, and, needless to say, it was written in that article "no, nor will there be." With the appearance of Chekhov's play, this truth of Bunin's (and perhaps he was somehow right about it) stopped seeming to be true. Nowadays such orchards do exist in our consciousness, even if they don't literally exist.

It's just the same in theatrical matters. When a good production occurs, which is thoroughly unsuitable for Chekhov or Gogol or Shakespeare, but nevertheless reveals their essence and gives us some new, powerful representation of the world, then it is impossible to say that the play exists only in its text.

Both Shakespeare and Chekhov, thanks to many theaters, are not only such as they were—they are now such as they have been seen in the best productions.

When the theater lightly touches something old, it inevitably reveals itself and its own time. Of course, one mustn't forget about the author's times and himself, but you can't eliminate your own times from your mind.

Sometimes the times influence the production not only in a broad sense, but also in a narrower sense. The concrete, specifically up-to-date state of the theatrical situation, the given company and so on. So it was even with Stanislavsky.

2. Ivan Alekseevich Bunin (1870–1953), Russian writer whose book *On Chekhov*, written while he was an émigré in Paris, is full of strong and controversial opinions.

* * *

Once upon a time, Chekhov was staged polyphonically, then people got carried away by particular emphases. And, naturally, not because they had grown stupid. Times changed, and again the desire arose to see Chekhov in his entirety. And later on (and this is far from exclusive) someone will rejoice at a new powerful reversal, and again others will fight beside them for completeness.

In the article about Chekhovian beauty, the critic discusses Trigorin's spiritual insensitivity. Everyone is talking about the spell-binding lake, and Trigorin says that in this lake, there are probably lots of fish. But even Chekhov himself, to my mind, could have talked like that. He would more likely have talked about fish than about a spellbinding lake. In any case, this line doesn't mean that Trigorin is spiritually insensitive. The proof of his insensitivity is to be found not in this line, but in something else.

. . . Again in this article devoted to beauty in Chekhov's plays, it is said that the Vagrant in *Cherry Orchard* serves the same function as the cook and maidservant in *Seagull*, only in *Seagull* Chekhov needs to demonstrate Arkadina's penury by giving the cook a ruble to share among the three of them, and in *Cherry Orchard* he shows the prodigality and extravagance of Ranevskaya, who gives the Vagrant a gold piece.

But this is quite wrong. The critic simply has not listened to the emotional subtext of the second act. The Vagrant is also in his way the "sound of a breaking string." This is easy to demonstrate, but does it have to be demonstrated?

* * *

I would undertake to demonstrate that the appearance of the Vagrant in Chekhov is not at all the same thing as the entrance of the cook and the maidservant. I tried to demonstrate this in my production, but could demonstrate it theoretically as well, after tracking through the whole covert progress of the second act. The reader can do this too, if he doesn't have a head full of presuppositions that he is unwilling to abandon.

And all the same, the so-called question of spiritual beauty in Chekhov is essential. In our up-to-date creativity it often plays the role of litmus paper. In the production of these plays our inner lack of inspiration, even our lack of culture, looms large. No other author, it seems, is as capable as Chekhov in revealing our lack of theatrical subtlety and refinement.

We often love to say (I have said this repeatedly myself) that ours is an unrefined age and hence that our artistic thinking is harsher than Chekhov's. But such statements are half-bankrupt common-places, arising from a desire to justify our own imperfection. The art of any age must not be built on minor accomplishments, on acts of callousness, on the absence of inner artistic elitism.

Otherwise it will become amateurish in the worst sense of that word, and by its structure can only help cultural collapse.

In childhood we run around an alley, and not a garden; we have no tutor who teaches us languages. We are frequently left to our own devices in the street, and then we study in school in semi-oblivion—semi-oblivion because our ideas half remain in the street. At examinations, the kids say something about *War and Peace* and *Evgeny Onegin*, but in fact they haven't read them or have read them very inattentively. But, as Chebutykin says, everybody makes a face to show that he's read them.

We grow up on our own, at times caring little about the existence of world culture, but then imperceptibly the time comes when we ourselves begin, as it were, to take part in its movements. It so happens that we stage productions, write plays or act in them, but in fact we remain the same little kids playing in the alley. This is expressed in our intonations, in our unsubtle emphases, and in our superficial acceptance of the complicated atmosphere of producing things.

In short, I mean to say that our uncouthness, for all our desire and will, shows up in our productions, especially of Chekhov—a lack of refinement in the thinking, false simplicity, habits of the alley. Chebutykin, for instance, says that he hasn't had a drink in two years. The actor can speak this line to the audience, led only by disastrously modern associations of the "alley," wishing to evoke a far too familiar reaction, and the reaction is not slow in coming—but the result is so vulgar. Masha in reply to Vershinin's beautiful oration states that she will stay for lunch, and the actress can smile ambiguously and say: "I will stay . . .", and then, after a pause, add "for lunch." This sort of thing grates on me not because there is no pause between these words in Chekhov's sentence, but because at such moments the actor's intonation gleams with the same "alley quality."

The dramatic and the tragic, to which you often strive in art, should never be expressed in a coarsened form. And even when you want to present coarseness itself, it is not obligatory to present it by coarse means, that is, the means of a coarse artist.

These are the kinds of sorry thoughts that often come into my head.

Sometimes it seems to me that in *Three Sisters* everything depends on whether Olga succeeds in speaking the first line properly or not. If you can find out how this line is to be properly spoken, then the whole performance will go swimmingly—or so it seems. So what, specifically, is the problem? I am listening to a recording of an old transcription of the MAT production, in it Yelanskaya[3] is uttering these words resonantly, boldly, as if she had no idea of any hidden meaning or any problem. She boldly and simply says, "Father died just a year ago, this very day, the fifth of May, your saint's day, Irina. It was very cold, snowing in fact. I never thought I'd live through it, you had fainted dead away. But a year's gone by now, and we don't mind thinking about it, you're back to wearing white, your face is beaming."

These lines, in particular, and the whole short monologue—but for some reason I spend so much time wrestling with it and I don't know how to prompt my actors. It's as if in those days at the MAT they didn't wrestle with anything. It seems, everything was clear: today is May 5—Irina's saint's day. Today is merry, but a year ago it was sad . . .

Olga is correcting exam books and says aloud what she thinks. What need is there to be clever or to contrive something? You simply have to go and do it. But it doesn't work, it doesn't work, though you burst.

Possibly it was all in the blood of those old actors and they didn't have to think about anything special. But then you start to investigate, dismantle, sort out, and it all comes out somewhat one-sided. You keep wanting to emphasize, and to explain unnecessarily. It seems that otherwise, without special emphasis, it will come out hackneyed, trite. After all, how many times have we heard these lines. They have stopped sounding interesting to us. We've stopped paying attention to them. And then you think: well, maybe we'll have them dancing at the beginning and this is what prompts Olga to say that time has passed. It was gloomy, but it's gotten merrier. But then I stop short: no, we don't need any dancing. What's the point of a dance? Why have it? How this directing sometimes gets you fed up. But perhaps, it's an anxious reflection about the contradictions of life? There are so many contrasts, and these contrasts create anxiety, torment. In the first case you have imperceptibly slid into vulgar gaiety, in the second just as vulgar gloominess. And Chekhov is turning into something other than Chekhov. The old MAT folks were probably right. They put everything into a kind of totality, and in this totality was still a rare lack of turbidity, a simplicity and wisdom. Nothing sticking out, everything on the inside. And externally it was expressed simply, magnificently and resonantly: a year ago things were worse than they are now, although now it's not all good either. Clearly, simply, legitimately. Almost a readymade formula come of

3. Klavdiya Nikolaevna Yelanskaya (1898–1972), in addition to playing Olga in the 1940 MAT *Three Sisters*, spearheaded the letter-writing campaign to get Efros's *Three Sisters* banned. [*Editor's note.*]

long, long reflections and long, long experiences. But these reflections and experiences are so great that they gave birth to tranquility
and sublimity. *A tranquil sublimity of reflecting on a restless and dramatic life.*

Once we were rehearsing the fourth act of *Three Sisters* in a little
room. We were sitting, as the saying goes, on top of one another.
Usually I stop the actors at the second line, if I hear a false note,
but then I somehow could not force myself to get up even when I
heard an obvious clanger. And then the next clanger didn't jar against
my ear as badly. In short, instead of rehearsing, I began to listen and
look at what would would be the upshot of it all. The actors walked
around the little room where we were all sitting, recalling what I had
asked them to do last time, and with special anguish glancing at the
scripts, spoke the lines.

   "I shall watch it to the end and see where the biggest wrong note
is," I thought. "That's where I'll stop them." But little by little I was
somehow pulled into the Chekhovian plot and began to observe with
interest, without any critical discrimination. I even had the impression that everyone had been thrown together in this little space, and
that the actors did not pause, because they rejected the idea of acting
anything. They felt that it was necessary only to *run through* the
whole act, and they spoke quickly one after the other, emphasizing
nothing and lingering over nothing. Gradually in no time at all a
picture was created—perhaps the very one Chekhov had calculated.
Everything that happened that was serious, tragic, profound; it was
as if no one noticed. Everyone hurried, dispersed, gathered again.
One minor event tread upon another's heels, and inevitably everything skimmed along to somewhere. The Baron went to his duel;
Vershinin left forever; Chebutykin planned to take part as a second
in single combat; Olga, reproving Masha for her love for Vershinin,
now stood awaiting Masha's arrival so that Vershinin would have
time to say good-bye to her. It was as if some higher power were
running these people, and they submitted to this power. They submitted even when they spoke words of protest. Suddenly with special
force, as if for the first time, I grasped Olga's words about their garden, that it was like a double-exit courtyard through which people
came and went. It's not enough that Masha, Irina, Olga, Vershinin,
Chebutykin, Solyony, Rodé, Fedotik, Andrey, and musicians show
up here, but evidently total strangers drive and walk across it, soldiers
or relatives and friends. It's as if the whole town were moving out of
this place, as in a time of evacuation, and everyone was becoming
tragically disconnected, discordant. No one was in agreement with
anyone else. The things these people talk about. It seems, there
could nothing more disharmonious than these conversations. One is

on about one thing, others about something else. Often a conversation begins and suddenly ends quite abruptly. None of these people is in control of himself. Olga did not want to be a headmistress, but she became one, which means she won't live in Moscow. After dinner, Irina has to send her things to the brick factory, and tomorrow she will wed Tusenbach and go there with him. None of this will happen, because Solyony will kill Tusenbach. While Masha, beautiful Masha, on first hearing about this duel, starts to talk about it incoherently and only in passing remarks that this duel ought to be prevented. She does not run and does nothing decisive to keep it from happening, but merely makes a remark in passing. Not because she is so caught up in her own grief or is heartless, but because unfortunately this often happens in life, although people will angrily deny it. They don't want to confess to it. They start to say that it only happens with bad people. But from Chekhov's plays we know that this is not so. It happens not only with bad people. Chekhov loves Masha and Chebutykin and Andrey. But in many ways, life is a ridiculous sort of thing—so ridiculous that one can lose one's head if one looks at it a bit askance—to look that way in order to see just what it's like.

When Masha suddenly falls on Vershinin's chest, sobbing loudly, he does not run off to report that he won't be leaving with everybody else but will remain with Masha. On the contrary, he brusquely begins to distance Masha from himself because he has to go: the regiment is waiting. Kulygin, in order to get a laugh out of the weeping woman, puts on an absurd beard and moustache, which he confiscated from a boy at the school. Chebutykin, after reporting the Baron's death, immediately adds that he is tired. Sitting himself down at a distance, he begins to sing quietly to himself: "Ta-ra-ra-boom-deay . . ." You look at all this—and a chill runs down your spine, because it's all true. This is how people live. And yet they are remarkable, dear and, of course, better than Protopopov, because if they do evil, most likely it is unconsciously, whereas Protopopov may do it consciously. Although, who knows? But life for all that is bearing them all somewhere, and only a few succeed in extricating themselves from the current. Others only have time to ask, "Where? Why? If only we knew . . ." And very, very seldom does anybody stop, let alone reverse its course. But how expressive are the seconds of these stops. Masha suddenly looks up to the sky, from where the cry of the birds of passage reach her. And something is tenderly transmitted in the wake of these birds on the wing. Before his ultimate exit, Tusenbach also stops running in order to notice something beautiful. Up to now he was doing his utmost to leave unobserved, so that Irina would not find out about the duel. But Irina has long suspected something, though so far she has not inquired of anyone what happened, and when she tried to inquire, no one answered her. For she could perhaps run and stop Solyony, knock the pistol out his hand. Who knows what could happen? Kulygin, having begun to tell her about the duel, quickly broke off the theme and began to talk about something else, some nonsense. Yet in this run one more little halt occurred, when Solyony wanted to inform Chebutykin of the duel. He lingered, and Solyony suddenly said that he would wing Tusenbach like a woodcock.

That's the kind of play it is. What needs to be dramatized or turned into tragedy? One has only to recite it ever so quickly. Quickly and lightly. This fluency will immediately reveal the most terrible things.

I once saw a production where onstage they kept shouting, playing music, thunder roared, and suddenly one of the characters remarked, "Listen, what is that noise in the stove?" I mean, it is obvious that Chekhov intended silence so that that noise could be heard. In the general uproar this line sounded like irony. I thought then that the fear of silence onstage is also a kind of lack of artistic culture. It reminds me of someone who can't listen to his neighbor. His noisy chatter is tiresome.

And something else: Every play unfolds in space and in time. You can't spend three hours' running time examining a flower that is already dying. What is interesting in that time is to examine its appearance, maturation, death, and the kind of seeds this flower produced. But often we keep trying to present Chekhov's tragic quality in the very first moment, and by the twenty-first people have stopped paying attention to anybody's weeping, anybody's groans. There's something cruelly unnatural in this.

Stanislavsky on *Three Sisters*: "It seems they won't face their own grief, but, on the contrary, look for cheerfulness, laughter, boisterousness; they want to live, and not to vegetate."

. . . So there's a possible, or rather, even indispensable view of *Three Sisters*. To stage it *cheerfully, youthfully, brightly.*

Come what may.

Resistance to misfortune.

In the intermission of a new MAT *Seagull*, a theater critic shared his impressions with me. He liked Smoktunovsky[4] as Dorn, but not the rest.

A week later I read his review in the newspaper. In one line the

---

4. Innokenty Mikhailovich Smoktunovsky (1925–1994), a Russian actor of remarkable charisma and versatility. Successful both in tragedy and comedy, he was superb as Prince Myshkin (*The Idiot*), Tsar Fyodor, and, at the Moscow Art Theater, Ivanov (1976), Dr. Dorn in *The Seagull* (1980), and Astrov in *Uncle Vanya*, and Hamlet in Kozintsev's film (1964). [*Editor's note.*]

critic, true, made a favorable mention of Smoktunovsky, but only in a line or two, or perhaps three. All the rest of the article appeared to be an exposition of a complete theory, explaining why the production was well-received.

I am not denying that there were grounds for praising this production, only I understand that on the evening in question the critic did not like it, and for some reason this recollection distresses me.

Obviously, the next day he gave it a lot of thought and decided that all the same the production deserved to be liked and it was incumbent on him to write favorably about it. Better to bend one's mind a little than to "rock the boat."

The critic's idea that after many relatively bold experiments (and most often one-sided ones) Chekhov must be returned to Chekhov is probably a good idea. But what is Chekhov? And what is his *Seagull*? The love of a middle-aged actress for a novelist, along with a certain writer in love with a young actress, who in turn is in love with the novelist? Not enough for *The Seagull*. And the fact that all this takes place against the background of a spellbinding lake isn't enough either. Two writers, two actresses, a spellbinding lake, and all the rest . . .

After all, *The Seagull* is a very bold, disturbing play.

Once, our theatrical delegation saw a production of *Seagull* in England. After the performance ended, agitated, we rushed backstage, could not help but rush, this performance had had such an effect on us. It was about a young man trying to establish an oppositional, inchoate art, his own. But this man didn't even have a decent jacket. He was poor and dependent.

He evoked enormous sympathy, to the point of tears. And everyone rushed to tell this to the actor. Thanks to that kind of Treplyov, the performance got everyone excited.

That way or some other, *The Seagull* must be disturbing, that's what it was written for and not to show off some literary style. This play is about that kind of struggle and that kind of intransigence.

A general Chekhovian style is, of course, a good thing, but a style is not an idea. And every play of Chekhov's has, beside the general style, its own unique meaning.

The Cherry Orchard, *The Seagull*, *Three Sisters*—they have much in common, but can one understand anything about them if one doesn't expose exactly what distinguishes them? For me all the characters in *Seagull* on that evening at the MAT blended into a single entity. I only noticed that it really was a spellbinding lake, because everything was very somber and enigmatic and beautiful in its own way. Perhaps even at certain moments I experienced something like

a nostalgic feeling for a dying art, when everyone is acting equally
well and at the same level, when there is grand scenery and a tranquil, expansive mise-en-scène.

But they didn't get the meaning.

They say that the time for a cruel, unilinear Chekhov, shaped by the
experiments of the last few years, is over; that the time has come for
a gentle, spacious, lyrical Chekhov. Possibly. But why? That's what
I'd like to know. Maybe the times have changed to correspond with
the changes in life? And this requires a different Chekhov? But what
has changed in the times, and why is a Chekhov different from that
of past years required? Or is this demand for a gentle Chekhov made
by art itself?—Perhaps they're simply fed up with one-sided experiments and want a polyphonic production. Or perhaps a certain portion of the people, concerned with theory, has grown old and would
like lyrical serenity, while youth may now be dreaming of a bold
Chekhov. And perhaps nothing of the sort needs to be concocted,
because there will always be a demand for a cruel Chekhov and a
gentle one, so long as both are done with sense and talent.

But the best thing would be if he were simultaneously cruel and
gentle. I speculate and want to hear the speculations of others, but
when I am told without special proof that a time for a certain interpretation has gone and time has another has come, I take this to be
deliberate perversity or idle conceits.

One must love art, and not one's theories about it.

After Treplyov's suicide, the whole beautiful set of the new MAT
Seagull darkens, the stage dims out, becomes mournful, the
summer-house dark, gloomy. Nina, in a black dress, beneath the
curtain repeats her earlier monologue, which now sounds like a
funeral oration. This finale illumines the whole production with a
gloomy but powerful light. A requiem. A dying fall. A very powerful
finale. But all the same, *The Seagull* cannot support such a finale.
It takes far too much time to lead up to it, but mainly it is too remote
from how people live today. At times the blasphemous idea even
came into my mind that the play itself isn't very good. Old-fashioned
or something. "Pre-Chekhovian." A flimsy melodrama. Of course, it
isn't that, but *The Seagull*, perhaps, like any other play, demands a
very well-defined, rigorous treatment. One shouldn't build everything on a slow dying fall. This is life, and it is full of conflicts. When
Stanislavsky played Trigorin and Meyerhold played Treplyov that
very fact was probably eloquent in itself. It possessed in itself a great
sense of conflict. Such different types in art, such different paths.
True, all this would be expressed, revealed in the time to come. But
even then, I suppose, one could glimpse a bit of it. And in this new

production the difference between Treplyov and Trigorin was almost lost. After all, this is the very thing that art is supposed to reveal. Different worlds! Maybe that's what Chekhov's play is about. It mustn't be adjusted to fit a "general Chekhovian style."

* * *

MARK ROZOVSKY

Mark Grigoryevich Rozovsky (b. 1937) was one of the organizers of the cabaret-stage studio "Our House" (1958–69), and he staged an influential production of Tolstoy's *Story of a Horse* at the Leningrad Bolshoy Dramatic Theatre in 1978. In 1983, he became artistic director of his own theater-studio at Nikitsky Gates in Moscow, where he specializes in musical and modern works. He staged *Uncle Vanya* there in 1993.

Reading *Uncle Vanya*†

It has to be reemphasized that reading any play is a rather absurd activity, for the canonical text of a play is only the calm before the storm—preliminary to the performed version, when the singularity of the author's view will be transformed into a myriad of visions, each one bearing the name of the theatre where the characters of *Uncle Vanya* will be brought back to life. On one hand, the text exists apart from its potential treatment; on its own, as it were, in suspension, beyond any directorial concept, proudly, for it belongs to the ages. On the other hand, like a streetwalker, it beckons to its neighbors, lecherously craving intercourse with strangers—it waits impatiently for someone to take it in his grasp and start to maul it.

The theater is crude. In most cases, it USES the text, roughly hashes it up and gnaws the words . . .

That kind of theater turns my stomach.

I like Theater and Author to be in tandem.

If Chekhov turns out to be nothing but a bone in the fangs of a hungry wolf, then there will be productions like the one in which Astrov and Voinitsky are two pederasts, Sonya is a drug addict, and the nanny Marina is living with Telegin.

Nowadays, anybody feels free to violate Chekhov with special intensity, special sadism . . . "Help yourself!"

To tell the truth, the desire to stage my own *Uncle Vanya* at the

† From Mark Rozovsky, *Chtenie "Dyadi Vani"* (A Reading of *Uncle Vanya*) (New York: Slovo, 1996), 305–14. Trans. by Laurence Senelick.

Nikitsky Gates Theater arose a long time ago, when I saw a foreign performance of this play in a production by the Vilnius director Nek-rošius.[1]

What I saw there surprised me, to put it mildly. Right at the start of the performance, Doctor Astrov was applying cupping glasses to the "corpulent, imperturbable old woman," the nanny Marina; then in the night scene, Voinitsky himself crawled along the stage with a bare back, on which the prints of similar cupping-glasses were probably supposed to show that his chill, diagnosed by the director, was being treated in a steamroom, and, finally, at the end, the great Chekhovian text was accompanied by those same cupping glasses—Sonya, as she said "We shall see all heaven lit up with diamonds," vigorously thumped Uncle Vanya with the zeal of a therapeutic masseuse.

In addition, the workers in this production were turned into a dance trio of comedians, polishing the floors to cabaret music. One of the comedians is an unkempt old woman, symbolizing, evidently, all-Russian boorishness. In a room of the country house, I mean right in the middle of the stage, stood an enormous African palm tree—both as setting and free association with "the heat wave." Yelena examined Astrov's ecological charts through a lens the size of a television screen, not forgetting to stick her head into it. A drunken Astrov crawled along the floor on all fours in a bearskin, depicting the forest fauna and, at the same time, probably personifying savage Russia. And all this our critics enthusiastically pronounced this a new theatrical concept, and called it "avant-garde."

Honestly, at that time, although I did not consider myself enrolled among the zealous conservatives and orthodox of the theater, I simply howled at the provincial novelties of this uncouth production, which was not a version or treatment of Chekhov, but, rather, a conceited use of his text to show off its own genius and purely directorial self-assertion. Nekrošius is unquestionably great, but so great as to stage Chekhov in the idiom of Kostya Treplyov?—that is, refined taste ruined by vulgarity and stylization. And this is "avant-garde"?

Why do I bring this up?

Because in the theater the artist had, has, and will have the right to create independently, but not irresponsibly.

Chekhov is silent. He is patient.

And, by the way, when all is said and done, he seems to be indomitable.

---

1. Eimuntas Nekrošius (b. 1952), Lithuanian director, noted for his rock musicals at the State Youth Theatre in Vilnius; his highly controversial but imaginative *Uncle Vanya* (1986) toured throughout the world. [*Editor's note*.]

I saw a production of *Seagull* in Rumania, in which Kostya Treplyov practiced yoga and generally behaved like a Japanese samurai,
such as portrayed by Toshiro Mifune.[2]

In America, the same play was staged at machine-gun pace; the
whole text rattled along for exactly one hour and fifteen minutes.

All this is crap, barbarism, vulgarity, nothing more.

These theaters do not know how to stage Chekhov, thus they med-
dle with the brilliant text. A certain deliberate obfuscation of consciousness occurs as the critics once again display their total
pointlessness and mental aberration. Honestly, you really have to
hate Chekhov to stage him that way! . . . and to praise these productions and productions like them, persuading the world that this is
just a "new interpretation" of Anton Pavlovich. For pity's sake, what
"new interpretation"? The text has been written and does not need
any such interpretations, especially not "new ones."

A new one will be really new only when it bores into the textual
massif with an obligatory analysis of the author's language, style, and
worldview. The only theatrical creativity that can begin and exist as
a spiritual continuum in harmony with the author's work is one
whose prime motive is to carry out the intentions of the Author.

Presaging the "silver age," the example of Chekhov—himself a
writer without poses, without a literary mask—destroyed the art of
wilful affectation and tendentious irreality. Chekhov pronounced a
death sentence on everything that later was proclaimed to be "bal-
anced thinking" and "great incomprehensibility of significance." In
his notebooks, there is a decadence greater than that of all the decadents of the fin de siècle put together, but this is a decadence with
a difference—a Chekhovian difference. He is enwreathed not by the
cigarette smoke of the "Stray Dog,"[3] not by tortuous pseudo-
philosophical systems and mental aberration, but by refined feelings,
observations of what is most secret, most treasured in human beings.

So Chekhov compounds human interiority—no one can do it better. His characters are as tangible and interactive as billiard balls in
play. Sometimes their behavior is belatedly and characteristically
frivolous and their contact with one another is barely appreciable,
but sometimes the playing achieves a picture of headlong struggle,
in which the passion for intimacy and collision is defined by the
meticulous vision and accurate hand of the author.

Someone once calculated that in his works Chekhov described
nearly eight thousand different characters. Compare that with Bal-

2. Japanese film actor (b.1920) who played violent swordsmen in the films of Akira Kurosawa,
including *The Seven Samurai* and *Yojimbo*. [*Editor's note.*]
3. *Brodyachaya Sobaka*, a cabaret opened in a St. Petersburg wine cellar in 1911 and habit-
uated by Acmeist poetics, futurists, and all manner of avant-garde artists and writers; it
lasted until 1916. [*Editor's note.*]

zac in *The Human Comedy*,[4] three thousand "in all." Can you imagine a stadium in which every one of them is gathered together? Who wouldn't you see there? . . .

However, there is not a single mug or snout—only human faces.

For Chekhov, any character he created, even a caricatural one, always stayed within the bounds of that absolute, all-embracing, honest, ad nauseam realism, born of a vast artistic will and constructive imagination.

Even the colors of his grotesques are never fanciful, although at times extremely mordant. Reality hallucinates in Chekhov's characters, transformed into worlds where the norm of existence always preserves an amazing measure of taste—nothing extra, because anything extra is inessential. Hence the value of any human detail, any of his minutiae.

However, the most wonderful thing in Chekhov seems to be his relation to the human being as a work of art.

Korney Ivanovich Chukovsky[5] once made the extremely shrewd remark: "Gorky was weak-willed, easily gave in to outside influences. Chekhov had an iron character, an indomitable will. Isn't that why Gorky sang hymns to strong, wilful, competent people, while Chekhov did so to weak-willed, impotent ones?"

There's only one thing wrong in this.

Chekhov didn't sing hymns—never to anybody.

Chekhov is against "hymn singing."

Chekhov's theater teaches that humanism as a mental faculty is useless in struggle with a metaphysical enemy and a mysterious collective human existence of isolated individuals. Chekhov does not ask the questions of "Why am I here?" and "What's the point of what surrounds me?", but they hover eternally in the air of his plays, along with the answer, "Why not? There is no point." The people who crop up in these plays as concrete and real while the stage action is in the process of being dismantled inevitably evolve into mentally ill characters, whose languor and debility make them absurd and strange in the most familiar of domestic situations. Their lack of originality condenses to such a point that the character becomes original. The familiarity is so powerful that any idiocy and freakishness in Chekhov seems to be the most effectively expressive means of achieving Truth. Chekhov, of course, is a creator, but this means that he boldly *fabricates* life, whose movement is the main subject of his inquiries.

Everything ephemeral, everything secondary and semi-conscious, is necessary to Chekhov, and in the last analysis defines the harmony

---

4. *La Comédie humaine* is the collective title given to the series of novels by Honoré de Balzac, intended to depict all French society. [*Editor's note.*]

5. Pen name of Nikolay Vasilyevich Korneychukov (1882–1969), Russian children's writer and translator. [*Editor's note.*]

of his chords. Therefore, Chekhov's plays are like dreams. The real life in them looks evanescent, refracted in a world temporhythmically organized by the Atmosphere—in some productions the atmosphere is defined to such a point that the Author matters only insofar as he *serves* the director's clichés of that kind of theater—quiet, almost distraught speech; white costumes; autumn leaves falling onto the characters' heads; the chirping of crickets; the cawing of crows; and the rest of the phoniness and theatricality . . .

Thus, Chekhov is endangered from two directions: On the left, by avant-garde condiments that lead to the dispersal and misappropriation of the author's treasures, to doing away with the special values of the text. And on the right, by the staging of Chekhov in a boring, monotonous way, without a thorough examination of the text, prechewed and easily digestible, allegedly traditional, allegedly stylized, and allegedly "atmospheric."

Both ways are bad. Both tendencies end up with a flat, meaningless Chekhov.

Nowadays we need to move between or, if you prefer, beyond these two tendencies, to discover something of our own.

* * *

Chekhov is indulgent, he asks nothing of us. Artaud's[6] expression "the dictatorship of the Author" can in no way be applied to him; Chekhov *offers us possibilities*, while we stand aghast at the questions: do we know how to use these possibilities? Will we destroy the concept or will we be able to *grasp* what is offered to our grasp? For Chekhov's word blazes with ineffable meaning.

* * *

If you examine Chekhov's themes, you may come to the conclusion that most often there lies at their base a special case of nothing happening, the sort of workaday nonsense recounted in a story under the rubric "You'd never imagine in a million years . . ." Chekhov does imagine, but still his "special cases" are not taken to be intentional "in a million years." In life, extraordinary situations often have no turning points, endings, antepenultimate plot twists; a man is battered to death by uneventfulness as he bumps into stupid, coarse reality, the humdrum, as if into sharp-edged furniture, scattered at random. In every case, Chekhov extracts from this collision a little drama of innumerable conflicts; in his hands the annals of the everyday seem to expand, becoming refined in their construction, a finished work of art.

---

6. Antonin Artaud (1896–1948), French surrealist actor and director, noted for his theory of the Theater of Cruelty. [*Editor's note*.]

In his plays, Chekhov moves away from the "special case," the "anecdotal" (except for the one-acts, where this principle is observed), to the creation of dramatically sophisticated structures, not unlike integrated, multilayered labyrinths. *Uncle Vanya* is a play, a form, that outwardly flowing like time is compressed into drama, with its iron architectonics in plain sight. If we were to make a list, episode by episode, of all the changes in the characters over the course of the play as it is constructed, we would end up admiring the logic of the entrances and exits of the characters, the harmony of Chekhov's construction of the drama. This drama is extracted from trivial life, and therein lies its exclusive, purely Chekhovian singularity. The theater of Chekhov is a flow of trivial, real life, without the convulsions of extraneous events, but with cataclysms that grow out of the quiet music of the banal, ordinary, and humdrum.

* * *

Chekhov was not a "thinker" in the manner of Dostoevsky and Tolstoy, but that does not mean that he did not think or thought any the less. The wonder is that Chekhov thought principally in images. He avoided socio-political journalism and moralistic preaching; his method is to tell a story, a narrative of a private incident, of individual behavior. Private life is tea drinking and the road, fishing and toothaches, walks in Sokolniki and dandling the baby. The fragmentary quality of life is poeticized; an interest in "splinters," which inevitably reveal the whole and reflect the general, inspire Chekhov to the epical. Russian life, written down in one anecdote or another, constitutes an enormous mosaic picture in which the pen of a genius mythologizes every kind of absurdity and everyday trash much the way Biblical subjects are made legendary. Chekhov is convinced that the private life of some unsung deacon or cabman is just as tremendous as the lives of the gods, angels, heroes, and military leaders . . . Chekhov punctures every kind of bombast. His style of pathos is close to kitsch.

Hence his blatant split from those who promoted Russians as the chosen people, from the Russia that has its "own path." He is no patriot, still less a chauvinist, still less an anti-Semitic, ultra-nationalist monarchist.

But Chekhov is a supreme patriot, at least because he blended a love for the Russian people with a tragic knowledge of their strange, ridiculous life; he spoke a word of truth about them.

The four acts of *Uncle Vanya*, designated by the author in the subtitle as "Scenes from Country Life," connect what goes on onstage to the life of all Russia, which *could* make an effort to change its fate, but is *incapable* of any kind of action. For that very "Slavic apathy" (Chekhov's expression in a letter to Grigorovich[7]) leads to the fact that "If the Russian does not believe in God, it means that he believes in something else."

It is precisely this "something" that led Russia to Communist self-deception, but all this took place here in Russia only after Chekhov. In Chekhov's time, "Russian life offers a series of beliefs and enthusiasms but, if you must know, there still isn't a whiff of disbelief and skepticism."

Exactly! . . . We have now had a whiff. And in the twentieth century, the whiff got to the point that it seemed to replace belief with "beliefs"—not in God, but in idols! . . . "Skepticism" came to us as the most evil, hypocritical ideology, as a doctrine of atheistic destruction—in *Uncle Vanya* one can already see it in embryo, in its tragic historicism.

Hatred will triumph over love, and Russia will perish, "all heaven lit up with diamonds" will open to its martyrs and sufferers only at the point of death.

In his art Chekhov was guided not by ideas, but rather by the desire to diagnose the plague-ridden world of ordinary Russian life in all its impartiality, grubbiness, petty feelings, and conflicts.

In his own stoic obstinacy, he has no equal. What we call "psychological art" has one unconquered summit—Chekhov.

---

7. Dmitry Vasilyevich Grigorovich (1822–1899), Russian writer and critic who "discovered" Chekhov and persuaded him to take his writing more seriously. [*Editor's note.*]

Anton Chekhov: A Chronology

1860   Anton Pavlovich Chekhov, third son of the shopkeeper and choirmaster Pavel Yegorovich Chekhov and Yevgeniya Yakovlevna Morozova, is born in Taganrog, a port of the Sea of Azov on January 17 (Old Style) / 29. (New Style). Anton is the grandson of a serf who managed to purchase his liberation. Ostrovsky's play *Thunderstorm* wins an award from the Academy of Sciences.

1861   Tsar Alexander II abolishes serfdom, but without providing land for the emancipated serfs.

1862   Turgenev's *Fathers and Sons* is published. Academic freedom restored to Russian universities.

1863   Flogging with birch rods abolished by law. Stanislavsky is born, as Konstantin Alekseev, son of a wealthy textile manufacturer. Chernyshevsky writes *What Is To Be Done?*, the gospel of nihilism, in prison.

1864   *Zemstvos*, self-governing rural councils, are created.

1865   Tolstoy begins to publish *War and Peace*.

1866   An attempted assassination of the Tsar prompts a wave of political reaction, especially in education and the press. Chekhov, as a student, will suffer from the new emphasis on Greek, Latin and grammar. Dostoevsky's *Crime and Punishment* published.

1867–79 Chekhov's primary and secondary education in Taganrog in very rigorous schools. He gives lessons, frequents the theater, edits a student newspaper, and writes plays now lost.

1868   Dostoevsky's *The Idiot* is published serially.

1871   Dostoevsky's *The Devils* is published.

1872   Special court set up to try treason cases.

1873   Only two hundred and twenty-seven factories in all of Russia. Nekrasov begins to publish his populist poem *Who Can Be Happy in Russia?*

1874   Trade unions made illegal. All males over twenty-one, regardless of class, now liable for conscription into the armed forces.

1875	Chekhov writes comic journal *The Stutterer* to amuse his brothers in Moscow. Tolstoy begins to publish *Anna Karenina*.
1876	Chekhov's father goes bankrupt and moves the family to Moscow, leaving Anton in Taganrog.
1877	Chekhov visits Moscow, where he finds his family in penury. The Russians fight the Turks in the Balkans, ostensibly to free the Christian Slavs from Moslem oppression. An armistice, signed in 1878, greatly reduces the Turkish presence in the Balkans, but the Congress of Berlin humiliates Russia by reducing its spoils to part of Bessarabia.
1878	Public outcries against the government and acts of terrorism increase. Chekhov writes plays now lost: *Without Patrimony*, *Diamond Cut Diamond*, and *The Reason the Hen Clucked*.
1879	Chekhov finishes high school and in June moves to Moscow, where he enrolls in the medical school of the University of Moscow on a scholarship. Starts to write cartoon captions for the humor magazine *Alarm Clock*. Dostoevsky begins to publish *The Brothers Karamazov*.
1880	In March, Chekhov's first short story, "Letter of a Landowner to his Learned Neighbor Dr. Friedrich," is published in the comic journal *The Dragon-fly*.
1880–87	Chekhov writes for Moscow and St. Petersburg comic journals under pen names such as Antosha Chekhonte, Doctor Who's Lost His Patients, Man without a Spleen, and My Brother's Brother.
1881	Chekhov writes play later known as *Platonov* (not published until 1923). Tsar Alexander II is assassinated; his son, Alexander III, initiates a reign of political repression and social stagnation. Dostoevsky dies.
1882	*Platonov* is turned down by the Maly Theater. Chekhov publishes "Late-blooming Flowers." The Imperial monopoly on theater in Moscow and St. Petersburg is abolished. Several private theaters are opened. Troops are used to suppress student uprisings at the Universities of St. Petersburg and Kazan.
1883	Chekhov publishes "Fat and Lean," "At Sea," and "Christmas Eve."
1884	Chekhov finishes his medical studies and starts general practice in Chikino outside Moscow. Publishes his first collection of stories *Fairy Tales of Melpomene*, under the

name Antosha Chekhonte. His only attempt at a novel, *The Shooting Party*, is serialized in the *Daily News*. Writes one-act play, *Along the Highway*, forbidden by the censor and not published until 1914. In December, symptoms of Chekhov's tuberculosis are diagnosed.

1885   Chekhov's first trip to St Petersburg. Meets the publisher Aleksey Suvorin and the painter Isaak Levitan, and the three become close friends. Romances with Dunya Éfros and Nataliya Golden. Publishes "Sergeant Prishibeev" and "Grief."

1886   Chekhov begins writing for Suvorin's conservative newspaper *New Times*. Puts out a second collection of stories, *Motley Tales*, signed both An. P. Chekhov and Antosha Chekhonte. The dean of Russian writers, Grigorovich, encourages him to pursue his literary career in a more serious fashion. Publishes "The Witch," "The Chorus Girl," "On the Road," and the first version of the comic monologue *The Evils of Tobacco*.

1887   Chekhov publishes third collection of short stories, *In the Gloaming*, and fourth collection, *Innocent Conversations*, which includes "Enemies," "Typhus," "The Siren," and "Kashtanka." Also writes one-act *The Swan Song*. On November 19, *Ivanov*, a full-length play, is performed at Korsh's Theater, Moscow. It receives a mixed press.

1888   First serious long story, "The Steppe," published in St. Petersburg magazine *Northern Herald*, initiating a new care in his writing. One-act farces *The Bear* and *A Proposal* produced with acclaim. *In the Gloaming* wins the Pushkin Prize of the Academy of Sciences. Student uprisings at the universities of Moscow, Odessa, Kharkov, and Kazan are put down by the military. The government determines that all Jews must live within the Pale of Settlement in Poland and the western provinces. Tolstoy publishes his play of peasant life *The Power of Darkness*, but the censor will not allow it to be staged. Maksim Gorky is arrested for subversion and is henceforth under police surveillance.

1889   The Social Democratic Workman's party is founded. "A Dreary Story," one of the first of Chekhov's mature stories, is published in *Northern Herald*. On January 31, the revised *Ivanov* premieres at Alexandra Theater, St. Petersburg. In October, Chekhov's finishes his play *The Wood Goblin*. Played at Abramova's Theater in December. The play is poorly received by the critics; he is scolded for "blindly copying everyday life and paying no attention to the requirements of the stage."

1890   According to a letter to Dyagilev, Chekhov reworks *The Wood Goblin* into *Uncle Vanya*, which will not be published until 1897. Chekhov publishes the collection *Glum People,* which includes "Thieves" and "Gusev." Writes one-act comedies, *The Tragedian in Spite of Himself* and *The Wedding.* From April to October, to travels through Siberia to Sakhalin Island, where he visits prison camps and carries out a census. Sails in the Pacific and Indian Oceans.

1891   Six-week trip to Western Europe. Publication of the novella *The Duel.* Buys a small farmstead in Melikhovo.

1892   Chekhov settles in Melikhovo with his family. Work begins on the Trans-Siberian Railway, to be completed in 1905. Sergey Witte becomes Minister of Finance, and turns Russia into a modern industrial state, increasing industrialism, railways, and Western trade by 1899.

1892–93   Severe famines in the grain-growing provinces in the South and along the Volga. Chekhov acts as head of the district sanitary commission during the cholera epidemic, combating the famine and treating the poorest peasants for free. Publishes eleven stories, including "The Wife," "The Grasshopper," "Ward No. 6," "Peasant Women," "An Anonymous Story," and "Big Volodya and Little Volodya," as well as the one-act farce *The Celebration.*

1893   Dalliance with Lika Mizinova, whom he decides not to marry, but who sees herself as a prototype for Nina in *The Seagull. The Island of Sakhalin* published serially.

1894   Second trip to Italy and to Paris. Health worsens. Publishes "The Student," "Rothschild's Fiddle," "The Head Gardener's Story," "The Literature Teacher," "The Black Monk," and "At a Country House." Alexander III dies, and is succeeded by his son, the conservative and vacillating Nicholas II.

1895   Book issue of *The Island of Sakhalin.* Chekhov meets Lyov Tolstoy at his estate Yasnaya Polyana. Chekhov writes *The Seagull,* "Three Years," "Ariadna," "His Wife," "Whitebrow," "Murder," and "Anna Round the Neck."

1896   Chekhov sponsors the construction of a primary school in the village of Talezh. Serial publication of "My Life" and "The House with a Mansard." On October 17, *The Seagull* premieres at the Alexandra Theater in St. Petersburg and fails. Chekhov flees during the second act.

On October 21, the play is a relative success at its second performance.

1896–97 Strikes of factory workers lead to a law limiting adult work to eleven and a half hours a day.

1897 The first All-Russian Congress of Stage Workers meets in Moscow to argue questions of trade conditons and artistic principles. Stanislavsky and Nemirovich-Danchenko found the Moscow Art Theater. Chekhov sponsors the construction of a primary school in the village of Novosyolky. Participates in the All-Russian census of the population. Father dies. From March to April, Chekhov is hospitalized with his first acute attack of pulmonary tuberculosis. Reads Maeterlinck. In September, travels to France for medical treatment. *Uncle Vanya, Ivanov, The Seagull,* and one-act plays published, as well as stories. "Peasants," "The Savage," "At Home" and "In the Cart."

1898 Thirteen thousand students at Moscow University go on strike to protest repressive moves on the part of the authorities; orders are given to enlist them into the army. In May, Chekhov returns from abroad. Relations with Suvorin strained in connection with the Dreyfus trial. In September, Chekhov settles in Yalta after suffering a pulmonary hemorrhage. Publishes the stories "Calling on Friends," "Ionych," "Gooseberries," "About Love," "A Case History," and "Ionych." On December 17, *The Seagull,* staged by Stanislavsky, is revived with great success at the Moscow Art Theater.

1899 Theaters in Kiev, Kharkov, and Nizhny Novgorod play *Uncle Vanya.* Chekhov decides to turn it into a short novel, but does not. Offered to the Maly, *Uncle Vanya* is considered too offensive to professors and is turned down. Tolstoy's *Resurrection* and Gorky's *Foma Gordeev* published. Chekhov attends a performance of *The Seagull.* Sells all rights to his works to the publisher A. F. Marks for 75,000 rubles. Begins to edit his complete works. Awarded Order of St Stanislav, second class, for work in education. Publishes "On Official Business," "Lady with Lapdog," "The Darling," and "The New Villa." In June, sells his estate in Melikhovo. Has a house built in Yalta. On October 26, *Uncle Vanya* premieres at the Art Theater.

1900 In January, Chekhov is elected to honorary membership in the Literary division of the Academy of Sciences. Publishes "In the Ravine" and "At Christmas." In April, the Art Theater plays *Uncle Vanya* and *The Seagull* in Sevastopol, in the presence of the author. From August to December, Chekhov writes *Three Sisters*. Finishes the play in Nice.

1901   From January through February, Chekhov takes a trip to Italy. On January 31, *Three Sisters* premieres at the Moscow Art Theater to considerable success. On *May 25*, Chekhov marries the actress Olga Knipper, who plays Masha in *Three Sisters*. The Marxist journal *Life*, which publishes Gorky, is banned. Gorky is expelled from Nizhny-Novgorod.

1902   Chekhov publishes "The Bishop." Complete works published in eleven volumes. Awarded Griboedov Prize of Society of Dramatic Authors and Opera Composers for *Three Sisters*. Begins *The Cherry Orchard*. In August, resigns in protest from the Academy of Sciences when Gorky's election is nullified at the Tsar's behest. Gorky writes *The Lower Depths*.

1903   At a Congress in London, the Social Democratic Workers' Party is taken over by the radical Bolshevist wing, led by Vladimir Lenin. Second edition of Chekhov's complete works published in sixteen volumes. Publishes his last story "Betrothed"in the magazine *Everybody's*. In June, his plays are forbidden by the censor to be performed in people's theaters. In September, *The Cherry Orchard* is finished. Nemirovich-Danchenko and Stanislavsky are enthusiastic. Chekhov attends rehearsals. A particularly atrocious pogrom occurs in Kishinyov.

1904   Chekhov's health deteriorates. On January 14 or 15, attends a rehearsal of *The Cherry Orchard*. On January 17, the play premieres at the Art Theater, where a celebration in Chekhov's honor is held. In the spring, a new, grave attack of tuberculosis. On April 2, the first performance of *Orchard* in St. Petersburg a great success; greater than in Moscow, according to Nemirovich and Stanislavsky. On June 1, publication of the play in a separate edition by Marks. On June 3, departure for Germany with Olga Knipper. On July 2 (old style) / 15 (new), dies in Badenweiler. On July 9 / 22, buried in Novodevichy cemetery in Moscow. The Mensheviks drive the Bolsheviks from the Central Committee of the Social Democratic Workers' Party, but drop out the fol-

lowing year, leaving the field to the Bolsheviks. The
Russo-Japanese war breaks out.

1909   First performance of a Chekhov play in English: *The
Seagull*, translated by George Calderon, at the Glasgow
Repertory Theater.

Selected Bibliography

This bibliography concentrates on Chekhov as dramatist, not as short-story writer. For Russian-language works, it uses a more technical method of transliteration than does that of the text.

• indicates works included or excerpted in this Norton Critical Edition.

TEXTS AND EDITIONS OF CHEKHOV'S WRITINGS

English-Language

• Calderon, George, ed. and trans. *Two Plays by Tchekhof*. London: Grant Richards, 1912.
Friedlander, Louis S., ed. *Anton Chekhov: Letters on the Short Story, the Drama, and Other Literary Topics* (1924). Repr. New York: Dover, 1966.
Hingley, Ronald, ed. and trans. *The Oxford Chekhov*, Vols. 1–3. London: Oxford University Press, 1964–83.
Karlinsky, Simon, ed. *Anton's Chekhov's Life and Thought: Selected Letters and Commentary*. Trans. Michael Henry Heim and Simon Karlinsky. Berkeley: University of California Press, 1973.
Koteliansky, S. S., ed. and trans. *Anton Chekhov: Literary and Theatrical Reminiscences* (1927). Repr. New York: Benjamin Blom, 1965.
——— and Philip Tomlinson, ed. and trans. *The Life and Letters of Anton Tschekhov*. New York: George H., 1925.
——— and Leonard Woolf, trans. *Note-books of Anton Chekhov*. New York: B. W. Huebsch, 1921.
———. *The Personal Papers of Anton Chekhov*. New York: Lear, 1948.
Yarmolinsky, Avrahm, ed. and trans. *Letters of Anton Chekhov*. New York: Viking, 1973.

Russian-Language

Čexov, A. P. *Polnoe sobranie sočinenie v tridcati tomax* [Complete Collected Works in Thirty Volumes]. Ed. N. F. Bel'čikov et al. Moscow: Nauka, 1974–84.

Other Languages

Pavis, Patrice, ed. *La Cerisaie*. Trans. Elena Pavis-Zahradnikova and Patrice Pavis. Paris: Livre de Poche, 1988.
• ———. *La Mouette*. Trans. Antoine Vitez. Paris: Actes Sud, 1985.
———. *Oncle Vania*. Trans. Tonia Galievsky and Bruno Sermonne. Paris: Livre de Poche, 1986.
———. *Les trois soeurs*. Trans. Jean-Claude Huens, Karel Kraus, and Ludmilla Okuniéva, 1991.
Urban, Peter, ed. and trans. *Das dramatische Werk in 8 Bänden*. Zurich: Diogenes, 1974–80.

BIOGRAPHICAL STUDIES

English-Language

Bruford, W. H. *Chekhov and His Russia: A Sociological Study*. London, 1948.
Eeckman, T., ed. *Anton Čechov, 1860–1960: Some Essays*. Leiden: E. J. Brill, 1960.
Gorky, Maxim, et al. *Reminiscences of Anton Chekhov*. New York: B. W. Huebsch, 1921.
Hingley, Ronald. *A New Life of Anton Chekhov*. Oxford: Oxford UP, 1976.

671

Jackson, Robert Louis, ed. *Chekhov: A Collection of Critical Essays*. Englewood Cliffs, N.J.: Prentice-Hall, 1967.
Koteliansky, S. S. *Anton Tchekhov: Literary and Theatrical Reminiscences*. London: George Routledge and Sons, 1927.
McVay, Gordon. *Chekhov: A Life in Letters*. London: Folio Society, 1994.
Rayfield, Donald. *Anton Chekhov: A Life*. New York: HarperCollins, 1997.
Senelick, Laurence. *Anton Chekhov* (Macmillan Modern Dramatists Series). London: Macmillan; New York: Grove Press, 1985.
Simmons, Ernest J. *Chekhov: A Biography*. Boston: Atlantic Monthly Press, 1962.
Tourkov, Andrei, comp. *Anton Chekhov and His Times*. Trans. Cynthia Carlile and Sharon McKean. University of Arkansas Press, 1995.

Russian-Language

Aleksandrov, B. I. *A. P. Čexov, seminarij . . .* [A. P. Chekhov, Seminars . . .] Moscow: Prosveščenie, 1964.
Bunin, I. A. *O Čexove* [About Chekhov]. New York: Chekhov Publishing House, 1955.
Čexov, M. P. *Vokrug Čexova: Vstreči i vpečatlenija* [Around Chekhov: Encounters and Impressions]. Moscow: Moskovskij rabočij, 1980.
Gitovič, N. I. *A. P. Čexov v vospominanijax sovremennikov* [A. P. Chekhov in the Reminiscenes of his Contemporaries). Moskva: Xudožestvennaja literatura, 1986.
―――. *Letopis' žizni i tvorčestvo A. P. Čexova* [Annals of Chekhov's Life and Works]. Moscow: Goslitizdat, 1955.
Pokrovskij, V. I., ed. *Anton Pavlovič Čexov. Ego zhizn' i sočinenija* [Chekhov's Life and Works]. Moscow: Sklad v knizhnom magazina V. Spiridonova i A. Mikhailova, 1907.
Varencova, I and G. Ščeboleva, eds. *A. P. Čexov. Dokumenty, fotografii* [A. P. Chekhov. Documents, photographs]. Moskva: Sovetskaja Rossija, 1984.
Vinogradov, V. V. et al. *Literaturnoe nasledstvo: Chekhov* [Literary heritage: Chekhov]. Moscow: 1960.

Other Languages

Urban, Peter, ed. *Anton Čechov. Sein Leben in Bildern*. Zurich: Diogenes, 1987.

LITERARY CRITICAL STUDIES

English-Language

Barricelli, Jean-Pierre, ed. *Chekhov's Great Plays: A Critical Anthology*. New York: New York UP, 1981.
Brahms, Caryl. *Reflections in a Lake: A Study of Chekhov's Four Greatest Plays*. London: Weidenfeld and Nicholson, 1976.
Clyman, Toby, ed. *A Chekhov Companion*. Westport, Conn.: Greenwood Press, 1985.
Čudakov, A. P., ed. *Čexoviana. "Tri Sestry" 100 let*. Moscow: Nauka, 2002.
Emeljanow, Victor, ed. *Chekhov: The Critical Heritage*. London: Boston and Henley, 1981.
Gottlieb, Vera. *Chekhov and the Vaudeville: A Study of Chekhov's One-Act Plays*. Cambridge: Cambridge UP, 1982.
―――― and Paul Allain, eds. *The Cambridge Companion to Chekhov*. Cambridge: Cambridge UP, 2000.
Jackson, Robert Louis, ed. *Reading Chekhov's Text*. Evanston, Ill.: Northwestern UP, 1993.
Kataev, Vladimir. *If Only We Could Know! An Interpretation of Chekhov*. Trans. and ed. Harvey Pitcher. Chicago: Ivan R. Dee, 2002.
Magarshack, David. *Chekhov the Dramatist*. New York: Hill & Wang, 1960.
―――. *The Real Chekhov: An Introduction to Chekhov's Last Plays*. London: George Allen & Unwin, 1972.
Peace, Richard. *Chekhov: A Study of the Four Major Plays*. New Haven: Yale UP, 1983.
Pitcher, Harvey. *The Chekhov Play: A New Interpretation*. New York: Barnes & Noble, 1973.
Rayfield, Donald. *Chekhov: The Evolution of His Art*. New York: Barnes & Noble, 1975.
―――. *The Cherry Orchard. Catastrophe and Comedy*. New York: Twayne Publishers, 1994.
• Senelick, Laurence, ed. and trans. *Russian Dramatic Theory from Pushkin to the Symbolists*. Austin: University of Texas Press, 1981.
Styan, J. L. *Chekhov in Performance: A Commentary on the Major Plays*. Cambridge: Cambridge University Press, 1971.
Tulloch, John. *Chekhov: A Structuralist Study*. New York: Macmillan, 1980.

Valency, Maurice. *The Breaking String: The Plays of Anton Chekhov*. New York: Oxford University Press, 1966.
Wellek, René and Nonna D., eds. *Chekhov: New Perspectives*. Englewood Cliffs, N.J.: Prentice-Hall, 1984.
Winner, Thomas. "Chekhov's *Seagull* and Shakespeare's *Hamlet*: A Study of a Dramatic Device." In *American Slavic and East European Review* (Feb. 1956).
Young, Stark. "The Seagull." In *Immortal Shadows*. New York: 1948.

Russian-Language

Baluxatyj, S. D. *Problema dramatičeskogo analiza: Čexov* [Problems of Dramatic Analysis: Chekhov]. Leningrad: Academia, 1927; repr. Munich: Wilhelm Fink, 1969.
——— and N. V. Petrov. *Dramaturgija Čexova. K postanovke p'esy 'Višnëvy sad' v Xar'kovskom Teatre Russkoj Drame* [Chekhov's Drama: Toward the Production of *The Cherry Orchard* at the Kharkov Russian Drama Theater]. Kharkov: Izd. Xudozhestvennaya literatura, 1935.
Berdnikov, G. P. *Čexov-dramaturg: tradicii i novatorstvo v dramaturgii A. P. Čexov* [Chekhov the Dramatist: Tradition and Innovation in Chekhov's Playwriting]. 3rd ed. (enlarged and revised). Moscow: Iskusstvo, 1972.
Čudakov, A. P., ed, *Čexoviana. "Tri Sestry"-100 let*. Moscow: Nauka, 2002.
Ermilov, V. *'Čajka' materialy i issledovanija* [*The Seagull*: Materials and Research]. Moscow: Iskusstvo, 1946.
Gofman, Viktor. 'Yazyk i stil Čexova-dramaturga,' in *Yazyk literatury* [Language and style in Chekhov's plays]. In *The Language of Literature*. Leningrad: Xudožestvennaja literatura, 1936.
Grigor'ev, M. *Sceničeskaja komposicija čexovskix p'es* [The Theatrical Composition of Chekhov's Plays]. Moscow: Izd. KUBS'a i V.L.X.I., 1924.
Lenin Library, Moscow. *Čexovskie čtenija v Jalte. Čexov i teatr* [Chekhovian Readings in Yalta. Chekhov the Theater]. Moscow: Kniga, 1976.
———. *Čexovskie čtenija v Jalte. Čexov: Vzgljad iz 1980-x. Sbornik naučnik trudov* [Chekhovian Readings in Yalta. Chekhov: A View from the 1980s. Collection of Scholarly Labors]. Moskva: Ministerstvo Kul'tury SSSr, 1990.
Paperny, Z. S. *'Čajka' A. P. Čexova* [Chekhov's *The Seagull*]. Moscow: Xudožestvennaja literatura, 1980.
• ———. *Vopreki vsem pravilam: p'esy i vodevili Čexova* [Against All the Rules: Chekhov's Plays and Vaudevilles]. Moscow: Iskusstvo, 1982.
Polner, Tixon. *Simvoly 'Višnëvskogo sada.'* Moscow: 1906.
Polotskaja, E. A. "*Nedotyopa* i *vrazdrob'* (o trudnostjax perevoda p'esy)" ["*Nedotyopa* and *vrazdrob'* (On the Difficulties of Translating Plays)"]. In *Russkij jazyk* [Russian Language] 4 (364) (Jan. 23–31, 2003): 7–15.
Rossijskaja Akademija Nauk. *Čexoviana. Polet "Čajki"* [Chekhoviana. The Flight of *The Seagull*]. Moscow: Nauka, 2001.
• Rozovsky, Mark. *Chtenie "Dyadi Vani"* [A Reading of *Uncle Vanya*]. New York: Slovo, 1996.
• Zingerman, Boris. *Teatr Chekhova i ego mirovoe znachenie* [Chekhov's Plays and Their Worldwide Significance]. Ed. A. A. Anikst. Moscow: Nauka, 1988.
———. 'Vodevili A. P. Čexova' ['Chekhov's vaudevilles']. In *Voprosy teatra* 272 [Theatrical Questions 272]. Moscow: Vserossijskoe teatral'noe obščestvo, 1973.

Other Languages

• Hristić, Jovan. *Le Théâtre de Tchékhov*. Trans. Harita and Francis Wybrands. Lausanne: L'Age d'homme, 1982.
Schmid, Herta. *Strukturalische Dramentheorie: semantische Analyse von Čechovs 'Ivanov' and 'Der Kirschgarten.'* Kronberg: Scriptor Verlag, 1973.
• Schmid, Herta and Jurij Striedter, eds. *Dramatische und theatralische Kommunikation. Beiträge zur Geschichte und Theorie des Dramas und Theaters im 20. Jahrhundert.* Tübingen: Gunter Narr Verlag, 1992.
• Zelinsky, Bodo, ed. *Interpretationen: Tschechows Dramen*. Stuttgart: Reclam, 2003.

THEATER-HISTORICAL STUDIES

English-Language

Allen, Patrick. *Performing Chekhov*. London: Routledge, 1999.
Balukhaty, S. D. *Stanislavsky Produces "The Seagull."* London: Batsford, 1952.

Miles, Patrick, ed. and trans. *Chekhov on the British Stage*. Cambridge: Cambridge UP, 1993.

Nemirovich-Danchenko, Vladimir. *My Life in the Russian Theatre (1936)*. Trans. John Cournos. Repr. New York: Theatre Arts Books, 1968.

Senelick, Laurence. *The Chekhov Theatre: A Century of the Plays in Production*. Paperback ed. Cambridge: Cambridge UP, 1999.

Stanislavsky, Konstantin. *My Life in Art*. Trans. J. J. Robbins. Boston: D. Appleton, 1924.

Russian-Language

Čexov v mirovaja literatura. Literaturnoe nasledstvo 100 [Chekhov and World Literature: Literary Heritage]. 3 vols. Moscow: Nauka, 1997-(still in progress).

Čepurov, A. A. *Aleksandrinskaja 'Čajka'* [The Alexandrine *Seagull*]. St. Petersburg: Rossijskij gos. akademičeskij teatr dramy im. A. S. Puškina, 2002.

Éfros, Nikolaj. *'Tri sestry' i 'Višněvij sad' v postanovke Moskovkom Xudožestvennom teatra* [*Three Sisters* and *The Cherry Orchard* as produced by the Moscow Art Theater]. Petrograd: Svetozar, 1919.

• Meyerhold, Vsevolod. *Teatr. Kniga o novom teatre: sbornik statey* [Theater: A Book about the New Theater: A Collection of Articles]. St. Petersburg: Shipovnik, 1908.

Nemirovič-Dančenko, V. I. *Iz prošlogo* [Out of the Past]. Moscow: Academia, 1965.

Rudnickij, K. 'Čexov i režissery' [Chekhov and Directors]. In *Voprosy teatra 1* [Theatrical Questions 1]. Moscow, 1965.

Šax-Azizova, T. K. *Čexov i zapadno-evropejskaja drama ego vremeni* [Chekhov and Western European drama]. Moscow: Nauka, 1966.

Stanislavskij, K. S. *Sobranie sočinenij v tomax* (Collected Works). 12 vol. Moscow: Iskusstvo, 1988–99.

Stroeva, M. N. *Čexov i Xudožestvennyj teatr* [Chekhov and the Art Theater]. Moscow: Iskusstvo, 1955.

———, ed. *Nemirovič-Dančenko vedet repeticiju "Tri sestry" A. P. Čexova v postanovke MXAT 1940 goda: rabota Vl. I. Nemiroviča-Dančenko s aktёrom* [Nemirovich-Danchenko Runs Rehearsals of *Three Sisters* of A. P. Chekhov in the MAT Production of 1940]. Moskva: Iskusstvo, 1965.

Surkov, E. D., ed. *Čexov i teatr: pis'ma, fel'etony, sovremenniki o Čexove-dramaturge* [Chekhov and the Theater: Letters, Articles, and Contemporaries on Chekhov the Dramatist]. Moscow: Iskusstvo, 1961.

• Vinogradskaya, I. N., ed. *Stanislavskij repetiruet. Zapisi i stenogrammy repetitsy* [Stanislavsky Rehearses: Rehearsal Notes and Transcripts]. Second Edition. Moscow: Moskovsky Khudozhestvenny teatr, 2002.

Other Languages

• Barrault, Jean-Louis. *Cahiers de la compagnie Madeleine Renaud-Jean-Louis Barrault* 6. Julliard, 1954.

• Éfros, Anatolij. *Prodolzhenie teatralnogo romana* [Sequel to the Theatrical Romance]. Second Enlarged Edition. Moscow: Panas, 1993.

Silex 16 (1980). Chekhov issue.

• Stein, Peter. *Mon Chekhov*. Paris: Actes Sud, 2002.

• Strehler, Giorgio. *Per un teatro umano. Pensieri scritti, parlati ed attuati*. Milan: Giangiacomo Feltrinelli, 1974.

Théâtre en Europe 2 (Avril 1984). Chekhov issue. Paris: Beba, 1984.

Travail théâtral 26 (Winter 1977). Chekhov issue.